Business Finance

To Toby and Louise

Business Finance

Second edition

Chris Higson
London Business School

Butterworths
London, Dublin, Edinburgh
1995

United Kingdom	Butterworths, a Division of Reed Elsevier (UK) Ltd, Halsbury House, 35 Chancery Lane, LONDON WC2A 1EL and 4 Hill Street, EDINBURGH EH2 3JZ
Australia	Butterworths, a Division of Reed International Books Australia Pty Ltd, CHATSWOOD, New South Wales
Canada	Butterworths Canada Ltd, MARKHAM, Ontario
Hong Kong	Butterworths Asia (Hong Kong), HONG KONG
India	Butterworths India, NEW DELHI
Ireland	Butterworth (Ireland) Ltd, DUBLIN
Malaysia	Malayan Law Journal Sdn Bhd, KUALA LUMPUR
New Zealand	Butterworths of New Zealand Ltd, WELLINGTON
Singapore	Butterworths Asia, SINGAPORE
South Africa	Butterworths Publishers (Pty) Ltd, DURBAN
USA	Lexis Law Publishing, CHARLOTTESVILLE, Virginia

First Edition 1986
Reprinted 1990, February and October 1991, 1992, 1993, 1998 and 2000

A CIP Catalogue record for this book is available from the British Library.

ISBN 0 406 50339 7

Printed by Hobbs the Printers Ltd, Totton, Hampshire

Preface

In *Business Finance* we study the investment and financing decisions of firms. These decisions are often large in scale and uncertain in outcome, and this makes them amongst the most difficult but important that managers have to make, with far-reaching consequences for the welfare of the firm, and for society. Theory provides a powerful analytical framework to help managers think about these problems and in this book I show how this can be used to guide financial decisions in practice. But however elegant the theory, students are right to reject it unless clearly grounded in the world they recognise. So I try to show how the concepts of business finance can be applied under the constraints of the real world, how they link up with surrounding disciplines: accounting, economics, decision analysis, corporate policy and marketing, and how they relate to some of the wider issues that affect the firm.

The structure of the book reflects the building blocks of business finance: the nature of the firm and its tax environment, valuation and investment, the capital market, financing decisions and the cost of capital, company performance measurement, and some important applications: working capital management, merger and failure.

The book is intended for students in management, accounting and finance, and economics; but also it will be of interest to students of other disciplines, for example in science and engineering who increasingly need a knowledge of finance. Equally the book will be of value to practising managers who want a fresh perspective on what they are doing.

Many colleagues and students have helped in the development of this book, but I am particularly grateful to Maria Andruskiewitcz, Steven Connell, Jamie Elliot, Claire Farrow, Veronica Kalema, Ana Paula Serra and James Steel whose research efforts made the Second Edition possible.

Chris Higson
January 1995

Preface

Contents

Acknowledgments

Grateful acknowledgment is made to the following for their kind permission to reproduce various materials:

Bank of England Quarterly Bulletin, The Body Shop, Central Statistical Office, The Economist, The Financial Times, Harvard Business Review, Journal of Banking and Finance, International Economic Review, Lord Hesketh, Nottingham University Centre for MBO Research, Richard Pike, Unilever plc, The Wilson Committee.

Part I
Preliminaries

CHAPTER 1

Introduction

In this book we study the investment and financing decisions of firms – how firms should invest and how they should raise the money to pay for it. These are some of the most important, but also the most difficult of economic decisions.

Firms *invest* when they buy machines, build factories, pay the wages of the research and development department, mount advertising campaigns, build stocks of raw materials, or do anything which involves committing resources in the present to increase income in the future. Firms can *finance* this investment in various ways: by selling shares, by using cash generated from existing projects, by borrowing. Because resources in this world are scarce, investment involves choice and sacrifice. The firm must choose between rival projects; by choosing some it foregoes others. And the people who finance the firm must choose too. By financing firms they sacrifice present consumption, and by financing one firm they forego another. But in each case the choice criterion is the same and is surprisingly simple – the alternative which offers the best stream of returns in the future will be the most valuable. Since firms are owned by their shareholders, we expect firms to make decisions that give the best stream of returns to them, as signalled by their valuation of the firm, in other words to make the investment and financing decisions *that maximise the value of the firm.*

The central aim of this book is to study the effect of these decisions on the value of the firm so as to develop the analysis needed for making the best financial decisions. The characteristic of all decisions is that while their effects lie entirely in the future, the only thing about which we have information is the past. The future is by its very nature *uncertain*. This is what makes investment and financing decisions difficult in practice, since they often have effects stretching for many years ahead. In our study of financial decision making we have to come to terms with the fact that decision-makers have only limited information with which to form expectations about the future, and that there are *costs* to getting more information. So while it is easy to generate neat and well-qualified examples of decision making in textbooks, in practice quantification is often partial and decisions may be made subjectively and judgementally. This gap between theory and practice tends to make decision-makers impatient with theory and students overly critical of decision-makers. Both reactions are inappropriate so long as we bear in mind that the decision-rules we develop must be useful in a world where obtaining information is costly.

This book is about the financial decisions of firms in 'market' or 'capitalist' economic systems. In reality most economies in the world fall somewhere between the pure 'market' model and the 'centrally-planned' alternative. Many European countries, for example, have a significant public sector in which financial decisions are made by state and local government and by nationalised enterprises. Since the core of our analysis concerns the efficient allocation of resources, it would be relevant to any system, but the special problems of the public sector are outside our scope. However, we do examine public policy issues where they impinge on the firm. As well, we relate the analysis of financial decisions to other areas of study that are relevant – economics, accounting, decision analysis, corporate policy, marketing. It is not possible to get useful understanding of business finance in isolation from the world of which it forms a part.

Figure I is a simple picture of the investment and financing process. At the centre is the firm. The firm commits resources to projects, which are the basic building blocks of investment, using funds raised from investors or generated by existing projects.[1]

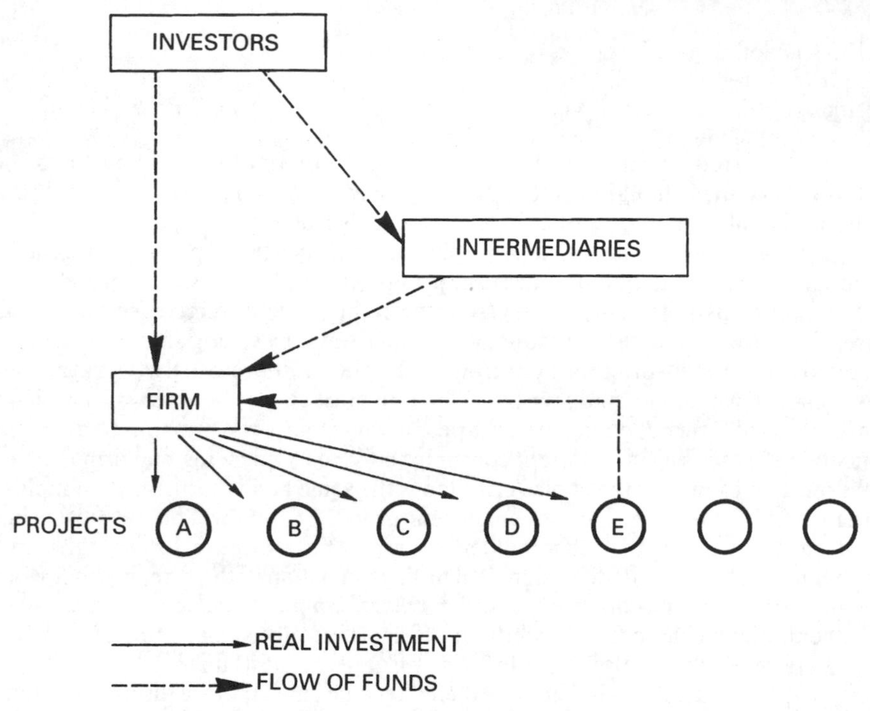

Figure I The investment and financing process

The firm is clearly the major force in modern market economies, active in seeking out investment opportunities and the resources to exploit them, bringing about technological change, and wielding immense economic power. But it is useful to look beyond this monolithic image and see the firm, or rather its managers, as agents investing resources on behalf of the owners. Chapter 2 examines the firm more closely. It considers the legal nature of the firm, and particularly the limited liabilities joint-stock company. It also raises some important questions: on the one hand – why do firms exist at all, and why is it necessary to have firms intermediating between investors and projects? On the other hand, do managers in fact try to maximise the value of the firm in a world in which managers and owners are separate people? Thinking about these questions sheds some useful light on

1 The terminology may confuse. The word 'investment' is commonly used to describe the actual commitment of resources to projects by firms, more accurately described as 'real investment', *and* for the original decision by individuals to forego consumption. The words 'funds' and 'finance' and sometimes 'capital' are all used synonymously to describe the claims on resources that individuals transfer to firms to enable them to undertake the real investment. To describe the whole area of study we use the words 'business finance' or 'finance and investment'.

the investment and financing process. Chapter 3 discusses one aspect of the firm's environment that has a major impact on financial decisions: taxation.

Valuation

Part II of the book develops the theory of investment decision-making, assuming for simplicity that the future is known with certainty. At this stage we also leave aside the financing decision, and assume that the firm is financed entirely by equity.

The building blocks of investment are *projects*. Table I gives an example of a simple project in which, over a period of time, funds are spent on researching and developing a new product, on laying in the necessary productive machinery and stocks of raw materials, on advertising and promotion and subsequently on production costs, which are then to be recovered in revenues.

Table I Project 'X' expected cash flows

Year		*Cash flows £m*
1993	Research and development	(200)
1994	Plant and equipment	(300)
	Stockbuilding	(50)
	Advertising and launching	(200)
1995–2000	Annual revenues	600
	Annual costs	(200)
	Annual overheads	(50)

To decide whether a project is worthwhile the firm should evaluate all the costs and benefits now and in the future and combine them into a single measure, the *value* of the project. Each project with a positive value that the firm undertakes should increase the value of the firm itself. Chapter 5 derives the arithmetic of discounted cash flow valuation for projects and firms, and Chapter 6 shows theoretically how the discounted cash flow decision-rules lead to value-maximising investment decisions. However, to find the value of a project the decision-maker has to confront several problems. He or she must identify the costs and benefits that are relevant to the decision and these fundamentals of decision analysis are discussed in Chapter 4, while the practicalities of project appraisal are examined in Chapter 7.

In reality of course the decision-maker needs methods of analysis that take into account the uncertain nature of future events, and Part III is devoted to developing these.

We can diversify some risk away by building portfolios of investments and it follows that, capital markets permitting, rational risk-averse investors will only be concerned with the undiversifiable risk in any investment. Chapter 8 explains how the 'capital asset pricing model' provides a simple rule for pricing this risk. Chapter 9 shows how the approach can be used in practice and also suggests other, of necessity cruder and less elegant, approaches when the perfect market assumptions of the capital asset pricing model do not hold. There are of course other methods of reducing the firm's exposure to risk by hedging using financial instruments, and Chapter 10 examines how risk may be managed in this way. The final chapter of this part of the book provides an appropriate point at which to review the evidence on how firms go about making investment decisions in practice.

Financing

All investment must be financed. Firms raise their finance in various ways, through issuing 'equity', by retaining earnings, by borrowing. These all represent different types of contract the firm can make with its suppliers of funds. In Part IV of the book we examine the main types of financing contract and analyse the firm's financing choice.

The firm raises its finance in the capital market and in Chapters 12 and 13 we address the rather important question of the structure of this market and its efficiency of operation. As in other markets demand and supply in the capital market are regulated by a market price, termed from the supplier's point of view his return and from the firm's point of view, the cost of capital. This market price has a central role in ensuring the efficient allocation of funds in the economy. Firms which have the most valuable projects can afford to bid higher for the necessary finance, so that if the market is working efficiently it should be the most valuable projects which are undertaken. In Chapters 14 and 15 we investigate in more detail the nature of equity, and debt, finance. We then consider how the firm can choose the best *mix* of financing – the financing policy that maximises the value of the firm. We analyse two key financing decisions, in Chapter 16 the capital structure decision – 'what is the right balance of equity and debt?' and in Chapter 17 the dividend decision, 'how much of the firm's earnings should it pay out as dividend, and how much should it invest?'

In Parts II and III of the book we study the investment decision under the convenient assumption the firm was financed entirely by equity – the cost of capital we used was the cost of equity. In the final chapter of Part IV we complete the circle by calculating the cost of capital when the firm is pursuing its optimal financing policy.

Performance measurement

When we measure the returns to a project or a firm the relevant data are the cash flows which they generate; similarly when we put a value on a firm or project it is their future cash flows we are valuing. In practice, though, heavy use is made of company accounting data in performance measurement, in risk assessment and in forming expectations about the future. Indeed for outsiders the firm's financial report will often be the prime source of information. In Part V, Chapter 19 examines the nature of accounting income and value while Chapter 20 describes how financial ratio analysis is undertaken. Because the world seems to pay more attention to financial reports than economic theory might predict, companies have developed a number of ways of structuring their activities in response. Chapter 21 discusses the possibilities for 'balance-sheet management'.

Topics in investment and disinvestment

Part VI examines some particular applications of investment decision making. Chapters 22 and 23 consider the process of investment and disinvestment at the level of the whole firm. So far we have talked about firms investing in single projects, but an alternative and very popular method of growing for firms is through merger and acquisition. Apart from particular issues of decision analysis, mergers raise the whole question of the growth of the firm and the rationale for combining many projects within single firms.

Inevitably projects and whole firms fail on occasion and it is appropriate to disinvest. In the case of the firm, it may be possible to reorganise so that part of the firm survives – otherwise the whole firm must be liquidated. We review the liquidation process and consider when firms ought to be liquidated, and why they are liquidated in practice, in Chapter 23. Chapter 24 considers how to determine the optimum balances of working capital for the firm.

CHAPTER 2

The firm

Business finance is concerned with the investment and financing decisions of firms, so in this chapter we consider 'the firm'. Section I examines the legal nature of the firm and particularly the 'limited liability joint-stock company'. In Section II we consider the firm's objective, value maximisation, as well as some 'managerial' alternatives to value maximisation. While Section III considers the effectiveness of the constraints on managers, Section IV considers whether value maximisation is an appropriate objective for other stakeholders, such as workers, consumers and society at large. The final sections of the chapter consider two applications of the 'contractual' approach to finance theory. One is Oliver Williamson's analysis of the question 'why do firms exist?' and the second is the application of 'principal and agent' theory to the capital structure of the firm.

I TYPES OF FIRM – THE LEGAL BACKGROUND

The first step in understanding the firm is to distinguish between incorporated and unincorporated firms. The word 'incorporate' comes from the Latin – *corpus* (a body) and if a firm is incorporated in law this means that legally the firm becomes 'a person', separate from its owners and with certain legal rights and duties a person would have, such as the right to incur debts and be sued on its own account. An incorporated firm is called a 'company' in the UK, and a 'corporation' in the US, though sometimes the US word is used in the UK for a particularly large company.[1]

An unincorporated firm is viewed by the law merely as a collection of owners, rather than as a separate legal person, and such a firm is known as a 'partnership' if there is more than one owner, and a 'sole-trader' if there is only one. To set up in business as a sole-trader or partnership requires no action at all in law. There are few special legal constraints on the internal and external behaviour of partnerships and the relevant statute remains the Partnership Act 1890 which laid down guidelines for resolving internal conflicts between partners.

All partners are personally liable to the extent of their personal wealth for the debts of the whole firm, and thus for debts arising from the negligence, incompetence and fraud of other partners. This argues in favour of choosing your partners carefully! It also raises the question of what constitutes a partner. This depends on the circumstances, but receiving a share of the profits tends to be evidence of partnership since it is the hallmark of an ownership or 'equity' interest.[2]

Most of the duties imposed on partnerships are duties individuals have in equity and

1 Very broadly the word 'firm' describes any unit undertaking economic activity for gain. The word 'business' is a similarly loose term covering the same ground. In this book the words 'firm' and 'company' will be used interchangeably.

2 However the 1890 Act also deems anyone a partner who 'holds-out' as a partner, that is, gives the impression of being a partner to the outside world.

common law. The law imposes few additional constraints, but it offers no concessions either. This is not the case with companies.

Companies

The company limited by shares and registered under the Companies Act has two important characteristics:[3]

Limited liability

Incorporation gives the firm the legal status of a person, able to incur debts and be sued, separate from its owners. But if the company has been incorporated with *limited liability*, the liability of the owners for a company's debts is limited to their investment in the firm.[4]

Joint-stock

In a company the ownership rights are divided into transferable shares or 'stock'. The company is managed on behalf of its owners by a board of *directors* whose duties towards the shareholders are defined by law and by the company's articles of association.

Private, public and quoted

Table 1 shows the numbers of public and private companies. It is important to distinguish between private, public and quoted companies. The vast majority of companies are *private*, even allowing for the fact that according to Inland Revenue figures, perhaps only half of the number registered are actually trading. The largest companies are usually also *quoted*. These are public companies which have decided to seek a wider market for their shares by having them quoted on The Stock Exchange. The number of public companies is declining. This may be due to the more stringent legislation contained in the Companies Act 1980, which diminished the advantages to being a public company.

Table I Companies in the UK

	1994	*1979*
private	1,075,483	710,602
public	13,746	16,015
public quoted (UK, all markets)	2,264	2,431

Source: DTI, The Stock Exchange

3 There are other legal forms a company can take, though these are less common. Companies can be incorporated by Act of Parliament rather than registered and can be limited by guarantee, or unlimited. Conversely, it is worth noting that not all partnerships have unlimited liability: it is possible, but very rare, to register a limited partnership. The requirement of a share capital excludes companies limited by guarantee formed on or after 22 December 1980, when the law was changed so that companies limited by guarantee could no longer have a share capital. Existing companies which were limited by guarantee and had a share capital at that date were not affected.

4 There is a minor exception to this – if the company has any partly-paid shares the owners can be asked to contribute the balance of the nominal value of these shares to meet the company's debts.

Only limited companies can become public companies, that is raise funds by offering shares for sale to the general public. In the UK public companies are identifiable by having *plc* (public limited company) after their name, while private companies have *Limited*.

Since the Companies Act 1985 a private company has been defined as any company which is not a public company. The advantages to being a private company have diminished over the years. Since 1967 private companies have had to file an annual report and accounts. The introduction of corporation tax removed many of the tax advantages which small closely-owned companies known as *close companies* used to have, and since the Companies Act 1980 public companies, like private ones, may have only two shareholders,[5] and it is no longer the case that private companies are limited to no more than fifty shareholders and are required to restrict share transfers. However, private companies do not have to issue a prospectus when raising new capital, and where public companies have a statutory minimum share capital of £50,000, 25% of which should be paid up in cash before they start trading, there is no minimum for private companies and a private company can in theory have just two shares of 1p each.

The key difference between private and public companies is that the public can subscribe freely for a public company's shares and debentures.

Quoted companies are public companies which have shares quoted on a stock market. Only public companies can join a stock market. A private company can become a public company (a process known as flotation) and vice versa.

Forming a limited company

To form a limited company a business must register at Companies House and issue several documents including the *memorandum* and *articles of association*. Capital duty and a registration fee are paid, and particulars such as the address of the registered office, and the names of the directors, are filed. Since only two shares in a private company need be issued initially, it is still possible to register a limited company in the UK for less than £100.

The memorandum of association describes the company's relationship with the outside world. It sets out the objectives of the company, the basis of liability, the initial authorised share capital and the nominal value of the shares. The authorised share capital puts an upper bound on the number of shares the company can issue. The borrowing powers of the company are often linked to this. Also, if the company is a public company, the founding shareholders' names are published, along with their initial holdings.

The articles of association deal with the internal administration of the company. They define the powers of the board of directors and their responsibilities to the shareholders. They describe procedure for meetings, the payment of dividends, and matters concerning different classes of shares, the transfer of shares, etc.

The pros and cons of incorporation

Limited liability looks like 'manna from heaven' for entrepreneurs. They receive the fruits of success yet are protected from suffering the losses beyond a certain level. But in an efficient market, there should be no 'free lunches'. The risk of loss is merely transferred to the creditors of the firm: trade creditors, employees, and other unsecured lenders. Why do they accept this risk? The answer is that in many cases they either do not accept it, or they seek compensation for it. New and unknown companies will find that suppliers insist on cash payment, and that banks require loans to be secured by personal guarantees from the

5 Once incorporated, private companies need only have one shareholder.

directors. Personal guarantees effectively circumvent limited liability. Further, in an efficient market we would expect those who lend to the company or trade with it and have not covered their risk another way to do so by charging a higher interest rate on their loans or a higher price for their goods and services.

Every year a certain number of firms do go bankrupt leaving creditors partly unpaid. Whether these creditors had 'insured' themselves against this risk in the ways we suggested would be very hard to establish. Few people would suggest that the market is fully efficient in this respect, and cases involving unscrupulous use of limited liability to swindle creditors are regularly reported. But the reader should recognise the existence of processes which reduce the value of limited liability. In one respect creditors may benefit from limited liability. One constraint imposed by the law in exchange for limited liability is the requirement to publish financial information, limited though this may be.

The vital characteristic of companies which provides a strong motive for incorporation is the *joint-stock* principle. Joint-stock permits the *separation of ownership and control*, and hence the separation of two quite distinct inputs to the firm – the provision of finance and the provision of management skills. There is no reason why these two should be possessed by the same people, and to require the same individuals to provide them can impose a real constraint. Anyhow, where managers do possess personal wealth they may prefer to spread their personal risk by investing in other firms.

A second advantage of the separation of ownership and control relates to the continuity of the enterprise. Continuity in management is a thing of value to the firm, continuity in ownership is not. In a joint-stock company free transfer of shares can take place without the running of the business being disturbed. Contrast this with a partnership, where the death or retirement of a partner may mean the repayment of his capital and can impose severe strain on the finances of the firm, or on the other hand where the partner finds a good deal of his personal wealth is tied-up in the firm and can only be released if he resigns. But company status does not solve all continuity problems. The plight of the family company, forced to sell part of the shareholding to outsiders to pay capital taxes is well known. This problem arises because continuity of management dictates a break in ownership, and the family is not prepared to accept a separation of ownership and control, or fears that the loss of ownership will sooner or later lead to a loss of control. Though incorporation permits the separation of ownership and control, in many firms, particularly smaller ones, they are not separate.

Another advantage of joint-stock is that larger investments can be financed this way. A wider ownership can be sought by pooling contributions from many individuals. Instead of their fortunes being entirely bound up in the success of one or two firms these individuals can spread their risk by buying shares in many firms. The real function of limited liability may be as a necessary condition for joint-stock. If shareholders had unlimited liability the purchase of even a small number of shares would render the owners liable to the full extent of their wealth. Of course, this is the case in a partnership. The difference is that in a partnership he or she can monitor and influence the conduct of the business, and control the admission of other partners. But in a joint-stock company they are less able to assess or control their risk.

The separation of ownership and control offers some advantages but it also raises a potential problem. If ownership and control are separate, how can owners *control* managers, and ensure they are pursuing the shareholders' objective? This is the issue we examine in the next section.

II OBJECTIVES OF THE FIRM

Value maximisation

In finance we assume that when managers make decisions they do so with the objective of *maximising the value of the firm*. Given the number of shares in issue, and if capital markets are working efficiently,[6] the objective can be restated as *maximise share price*. We assume this objective because we expect the firm to provide its owners with the best stream of returns through time and the shareholder's evaluation of a share will simply be the value he or she puts on this stream of returns.

If you asked the man in the street what the objective of the firm should be, he would most likely say 'profit'. How does profit relate to the value goal? They are closely related. The returns a shareholder gets from a firm come in the form of a stream of dividends through time. The investors' evaluation of the dividend stream will depend on their opinion of its 'quality' – its riskiness and the comparison with returns available on other investments. The dividend stream depends on the profit of the firm, period by period. However, as an objective, profit maximisation is inadequate in coping with the dimensions of time and risk. Profit is essentially a one-period measure of performance whereas the whole thrust of finance is to see the firm as a continuing entity and to see managers as making financing and investment decisions which have effects now and in the future.

Value maximisation is the cornerstone of finance theory but in reality it is not without problems. For one thing, once we recognise that different shareholders may have different tax positions, then there may be no single or unique financial policy which will be preferred by all of them. What is more, it may be very hard in practice for the financial manager to *know* what the value-effect of a particular financial policy will be – how the shareholders will evaluate it. But the issue that has been a major preoccupation of theorists concerns the motives of managers. Once ownership and control of the firm are separate how can we be sure managers will pursue the owners' objective? There are two questions – first, how will managers' objectives conflict with shareholders'; second, what sort of control do shareholders have over managerial behaviour?

Several arguments have been produced why, unconstrained, managers will pursue different objectives from shareholders.[7] The main ones concern *size*, *security* and *satisficing*.

Size of the firm

Managers may well be more interested in the size of the firm than its profits if their remuneration – pay, power, status and so forth – are associated with the size of the firm rather than its value. In practice this appears to be the case. Research suggests that the remuneration of managers is related to the size of the firm,[8] and it seems likely that the same goes for power and status. Size in this context is usually measured by *sales revenue*. It may not be immediately obvious why size and value are conflicting objectives since we usually expect bigger firms to be more valuable. However, a conflict will occur when in the pursuit of sales revenue managers undertake projects which have negative value, are

6 We develop the concept of market efficiency in Chapter 13.

7 An excellent discussion of these issues and the more general issues concerned with competition and the firm discussed in this book is contained in Auerbach (1989).

8 For example, Cosh (1975) found size to be the major explanatory variable in the remuneration of chief executives.

'unprofitable', so that the value of the whole firm is reduced. We demonstrate this possibility in Figure I which plots total sales, costs and profit for a firm. The profit-maximising output is Q_p but the sales maximising output is higher, at Q_s. Profit maximisation occurs where marginal revenue equals marginal cost. Units sold between Q_p and Q_s still have positive marginal revenue and so increase total sales revenue, though they decrease total profit since their marginal costs exceed their marginal revenue. Beyond Q_s the search for revenue can go no further since any further increase in sales volume will be more than offset by the price cutting needed to achieve it.

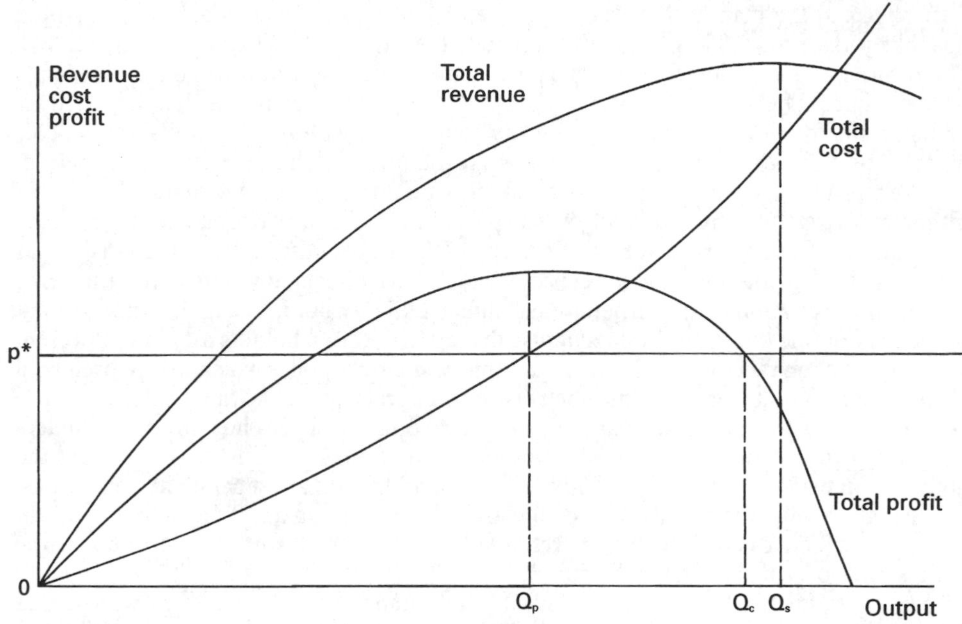

Figure I Sales maximisation

The virtue of this model is that it reminds us that there *may* be a point beyond which increased sales can only be bought at the expense of profit, or value. The model could be extended by allowing that managers have *some* interest in profit, to the extent of meeting a minimum profit requirement or constraint set by shareholders. For example the constraint p* in Figure I would restrict sales to Q_c.

A problem 'sales maximisation' shares with 'profit maximisation' is its neglect of the time dimension. In practice managers making sales strategy over multiple time-periods will be conscious of providing the organisational structure and productive capacity needed to accompany increase in size, and of the response of the shareholders if there were uneven growth: large gains in sales one year, and smaller gains another. Both of these argue in favour of *orderly growth*. For this reason firms often express their size objective in terms of a target annual growth rate.

Security and risk

By 'risk' in finance, we usually refer to the variability of a stream of returns. If managers and shareholders are both risk-averse they will both have an interest in reducing this variability and in particular in avoiding the liquidation of the firm which is a negative outcome with particularly heavy costs. But even where managers and owners are risk-averse a conflict of interest may arise if they value risk differently. Managers can reduce the risk of the firm in two ways: they can avoid single projects which are risky, and they can reduce the risk of single projects by *diversification* – pooling projects with different profiles of risk to form a 'portfolio'. In Chapter 8 we show that the risk associated with an investment decision is the effect of the decision on the risk of the overall portfolio. This provides one reason why owners and managers may disagree about a particular decision – they may be evaluating it in terms of different portfolios. Managers may treat the firm itself as the portfolio, while for owners, shares in the firm are probably just one asset in their portfolio. Consider the costs of the extreme outcome – liquidation – to the two parties. To managers there will be a loss of income and a good deal of disruption during the period of search for a new job, and there may be long-term lowering of income resulting from the damage to the manager's reputation. For the shareholder there may be a loss of wealth following the sale of the firm's assets at distress prices with associated selling costs.

For shareholders there are costs as well as benefits to diversifying the firm. In a diversified firm the owners of loss-making projects bear the whole loss by setting it off against other projects. However, had each project been independent, part of the loss might have been shifted to creditors, through limited liability. Suppose, to take a simple example, that we have two projects A, B, and two future 'states of the world' which may occur, I, II. A 'state of the world' is a set of external factors – level of demand, weather, etc – which affect the returns on a project. At present we attach equal probability, .5, to each state of the world. Table II shows the 'value' each project would have if either state I or II occurred.

Table II

States of the world and probability		*Project values* A	B	*Firm C's value* = A + B
I	.5	£4m	£3m	£7m
II	.5	£3m	(£1m)	£2m

If each project constituted the sole activity of a firm then the expected value of firm A would be .5 × £4m + .5 × £3m = £3.5m. But the expected value of B would be .5 × £3m + .5 × £0m = £1.5m. This is because the shareholders in B are protected from negative outcomes by limited liability, so the £1m loss would be borne by creditors. Hence, as independent firms, A and B have a total value of £3.5m + £1.5m = £5m. But if a firm C were formed to hold projects A and B then its expected value would only be .5 × £7m + .5 × £2m = £4.5m. The difference is that in the latter case the loss of £1m, with a probability of .5, and thus an expected value of £.5m, has been borne inside the firm rather than by outsiders. In practice, the value of limited liability, and thus the loss incurred by losing it, may be reduced by the ability of creditors to extract compensation for the increased risks that limited liability imposes on them. In general, though, liquidation can affect owners and managers in different ways, and they might well disagree on how much risk-avoidance the firm should do.

Satisficing

One important strand in the managerial literature is provided by writers such as Simon (1959) and Cyert and March (1963). These 'behaviourists' considered the possibility that so little precise information relevant to firm profitability was available to the firm that it might well now maximise anything. Simon introduced the notion of 'satisficing' to describe managers who aspire only to a 'satisfactory' rather than an optimal level of attainment of their goals, and for whom the motive to act is a response to a state of affairs that has become unsatisfactory. The characteristic of these writers is that they were looking within the firm to find explanations for its behaviour and not at the external constraints which the environment imposes upon the firm.

Decisions of the firm are in fact decisions of the management group which controls the firm. In practice this group comprises individuals with personal goals which may conflict. Cyert and March suggest that the compromises necessarily reached to resolve these conflicts impose upon the firm a set of unrationalised and conflicting objectives which reflect themselves in a form of inefficiency called 'organisational slack'. This approach has an affinity with the 'contractual' theories of the firm discussed below.

III CONTROL OF MANAGERIAL BEHAVIOUR

Legal controls on directors

A company's board of directors is elected by the general meeting of shareholders. A private company need only have one director, a public company must have at least two. Although there is no formal legal definition of what a director actually does, the board's powers, and those of individual directors, are set out in the company's articles of association. A director's duties can be summarised as follows:

> Directors must act bona fide in the interests of the company and must not exercise their powers for any collateral purpose . . . A director must not profit from his position, or place himself in a position where his duty to the company conflicts with his personal interests.

In addition he must:

> exercise reasonable care and such skill as might reasonably be expected of a person of his knowledge and experience.[9]

The assumption of the Companies Acts is that directors are the shareholders' representatives. However, their responsibility is to the company as a whole and not to individual shareholders. Once a year they produce a financial report on the performance of the firm which is independently audited and presented to shareholders at the *annual general meeting*. At the same time, some directors offer themselves for re-election, by rotation. So in theory directors' tenure is contingent on their performance; but there are several obstacles to this process. One is a lack of information. To judge someone's performance and objectives it is necessary to compare what they did with what they might have done. On the former, the information in the financial report is both limited and is an aggregate of all the firm's activities. On the latter, even managers may not have full information; rejected choices and possibilities are rarely quantified and often not even recognised by managers. Owners are forced to make judgements by comparison with other firms and other time periods, with all the associated problems of comparability.

Another problem is that the attendance of shareholders at AGMs is notoriously poor.

9 *Source*: Farrar (1991).

Shareholders receive the financial report by post before the meeting, and with it a proxy form in case they will not be attending. Under the proxy system a shareholder is free to nominate anyone to vote for him, but the proxy form usually proposes a director as proxy, thus reinforcing managerial control. As a result the number of shares needed for actual control can be surprisingly small.

Weak shareholder control is sometimes attributed to the inadequacies of individual shareholders. Individuals with small holdings may be too dispersed and isolated to form an effective coalition against the directors. And small shareholders are sometimes painted as financially illiterate, unable to understand the information they are given, and without the resources to analyse it.[10] In contrast, the trend in the UK towards ownership of shares by the 'institutions', pension funds, insurance companies, etc may be significant. By dint of close and continuous scrutiny, experts such as security analysts may be able to form a better view than other outsiders about the performance of managers. Often the investment decisions of individual shareholders are guided by analysts too, but the presumption is that institutions have much closer continuing access to the advice of experts.

But institutions usually claim to avoid interference in management if possible. They see their role as investors, so their more likely reaction if they are dissatisfied with the performance of managers is to sell the shares. However one fund manager we spoke to summed up his experience in dealing with companies in Exhibit I.

Exhibit I The view from the institutions

'Forget about the idea of the shareholder-wealth-maximising manager. On balance managers prefer to ignore their shareholders and they usually can get away with this and perpetrate their own existence indefinitely. What really excites managers is the game they are playing with the managements of rival companies. What really motivates them is the love of the game, and the charisma and self-esteem that can come with success.

But as institutional shareholders we do intervene when things go too far: probably more often than the public realises. Essentially it is a matter of power, we weigh up whether we have the muscle and the will to shift them, and they make the same calculation. If we have, they usually prefer it to be done quietly. If it's a matter of some directors resigning they will prefer to avoid publicity and leave their reputations intact. Very often once you have decided a manager is going you can find some technical infringement to lever him out – some breach of the articles of association, he may be over age, and so forth. Often, though, I think we intervene too late.

I think the institutions *are* getting more active in intervention. Perhaps this is why managements tend to be so lyrical nowadays about the need for small shareholders; all they get from small shareholders is adulation!'

When an institution does intervene it will often gather the support of other institutions through one of the organisation of institutional investors.

In practice, a board's role is more often supervisory rather than managerial, and extensive power tends to rest with a few individual directors and professional executive managers. An increasingly important distinction is that between *executive* and *non-executive* directors. Many companies' executive directors have extensive powers conferred on them

10 Lee and Tweedle (1977) researched the private shareholders' comprehension of accounting data and found it to be very weak.

by the articles of association and are responsible for the firm's day-to-day running. The full board concerns itself only with general policy and overall supervision.

As a company's articles will in most cases grant practically unlimited powers to the board of directors, there is legislation which is designed to regulate directors' conduct. The Insolvency Act 1985 aimed to curb the activities of directors who shelter behind the principle of limited liability. The Companies Act 1985 already provided for the disqualification of directors on certain grounds. These provisions were strengthened and extended in the Company Directors Disqualification Act 1986. The Insolvency Act 1986 supplemented the existing law on fraudulent trading by introducing provisions on wrongful trading. Now directors and, under some circumstances, their advisers ('shadow directors') may be liable in cases of business failure where they can be shown to have acted irresponsibly.[11]

Wrongful and fraudulent trading

Under the provisions of the Insolvency Act 1986, directors may be disqualified or find themselves personally liable to contribute to the assets of the company if it can be proved that they failed to take the necessary steps to minimise loss to the creditors once they realised or should have realised that the company was heading towards liquidation. It is hoped that this legislation will force directors to act responsibly, and to keep creditors informed when the company faces a financial crisis.

Before the 1986 Act directors were only liable if they had engaged in fraudulent trading. In the case of wrongful trading, directors can be held personally liable without requiring criminal standards of proof (they need merely to be unrealistic, not dishonest). A director of a company can be liable for not minimising the loss to creditors, given what a reasonable director should know, conclude, or do, given the general knowledge, skill and experience of that director.

Essentially this is a shift of emphasis. Where, in the event of company failure, a liquidator would have to prove a director guilty of fraudulent trading, a director, at the court's discretion, must prove that he is innocent of wrongful trading.

Produce Marketing Consortium

April 1989 saw the first case of company directors having to contribute personally to the assets of their failed business. The two directors of PMC were held (jointly and severally) liable to contribute £75,000 to the company's assets because they ignored the advice and warnings of their accountants, and continued to trade when they knew that insolvent liquidation was virtually inevitable.

The 5th EC Directive addresses the need for a Community-wide standard on the duties and liabilities of company directors. A general provision is proposed which will make directors personally liable for loss suffered by the company as a result of breaches of the law, of the corporate constitution, or other wrongful acts. Individual directors may be exonerated if they can prove that they personally are not at fault. The standard of care required by directors is not clearly defined, but it has been suggested that 'other wrongful acts' might include negligence and might go further than current UK law.

11 'Shadow directors' are people who direct or instruct the directors of a company (but not those who provide such instructions and directions in their professional capacity).

Market forces

How far are managers constrained to be value-maximisers by market forces? Consider the capital markets first. Suppose managers make a decision in which present and future profits are sacrificed for the sake of sales or security. The market value of the firm should fall to reflect this. What has happened is that managers have chosen to use the resources under their command in a way which yields a lower value than alternative strategies. In principle it is now possible for the firm to be bought at this value by investors deploying another management team, in order to reap a capital gain by implementing the higher-value alternative strategy. So *fear of take-over* may constrain managers to maximise value.

However there are some obstacles to the effectiveness of the threat. First, the potential acquirer faces the same information problems as existing shareholders in knowing which firms could be doing better. Second is the possibility that it may be 'too late' to transfer usefully the resources to new uses. Once committed, many of the costs associated with a project become sunk and the value of the assets in other cases may be significantly less. Finally, there are the transactions costs of the capital market itself, including the need to pay a premium over share-price to induce sufficient existing shareholders to sell. In practice these factors can allow some latitude for managerial objectives to be pursued.[12]

The nature of the product markets in which the firm trades will also determine the degree of freedom managers have to pursue their objectives. It only makes sense to discuss a trade-off between sales and value to the extent that managers are able to choose the markets, and the prices and quantities, at which they sell. The degree of control managers have over the firm's destiny will depend in part on the degree of market power the firm has in its product markets, and thus on the competitiveness structure of the market.

Final comments on managerialism

The idea that a conflict in objectives will follow the separation of ownership and control is not new. Discussing joint-stock companies in 1776 Adam Smith observed:

> The directors of such companies, however, being the managers rather of other people's money than of their own, it cannot well be expected, that they should watch over it with the same anxious vigilance with which the partners in a private co-partnery frequently watch over their own . . . Negligence and profusion, therefore, must always prevail, more or less, in the management of the affairs of such a company.

The first thing to note is that the debate on the separation of ownership and control essentially concerns larger firms. Small and medium-sized firms are for the most part 'closely-controlled', owned and managed by a small group, often including the founding family. In the larger firms the shareholding is often widely spread, but even in these firms there is not necessarily a divergence of objectives, since many company directors are also shareholders. Indeed the encouragement of share-ownership amongst managers and workers is an obvious ploy by owners concerned about divergent objectives. Prais (1976) found that the holdings by voting shares by directors of the hundred largest quoted manufacturing companies in the UK declined between 1968 and 1972 from a mean of 7.3 to 5.4%. But even this level of share-ownership might encourage a value-maximising orientation amongst managers.

How effective are the available controls and constraints on managers? In practice both the controls provided by company law and the threat of take-over can leave some leeway

12 For evidence on the characteristics of firms that get taken over see Chapter 22.

for managers, but researchers have failed to find compelling evidence that managers are consistently pursuing other objectives.

One reason why firms may not *appear* to pursue value maximisation is that it is not easy to operationalise, to convert into rules for guiding actual decisions. So to the extent that firms overtly set objectives at all they often set 'intermediate' goals derived from the main objective. These more manageable goals may be a certain level of profit, return on investment, sales growth, market share, or some mixture of these. So long as these goals generate the strategy that maximises value, the assumption of finance theory is not violated.

IV OTHER STAKEHOLDERS

The claims of certain other groups are sometimes advanced as relevant to the objectives of the firm, notably the claims of consumers, society as a whole and, of course, workers. At present the welfare of these groups tends to enter the decision making of firms as constraints to be satisfied in attaining the main objective.

The constraint may be a legal one or a behavioural one. Examples of the first are the costs to the firm of complying with consumer legislation such as the date stamping requirement on food retailers, or the costs of fitting anti-pollution equipment on cars destined for the American market. Examples of the second are the cost of meeting workers' demands under threat of strike, or of building a sports club which it is perceived should improve worker morale. In either case these constraints are merely additional costs of operation.

The interesting case arises when the welfare of one of these groups becomes the objective of the firm, the 'thing to be maximised', or to be jointly maximised along with the attainment of other goals. The consumer co-operative movement provides examples of firms designed to set objectives in terms of consumers' interests, and the nationalised industries could be seen as attempts to do the same for society as a whole. In practice public sector firms in the UK have tended to pursue financial objectives akin to those of the private sector, perhaps because of the difficulty in making an operational objective out of social welfare, and the same problem may afflict consumer co-operatives. But in either case the problem is not severe since society or the consumers own the firm. Value maximisation carries through as the objective – it can serve any master who owns the firm. The same applies when considering the group whose interests have been pressed most vigorously in recent history – workers.

The analysis of the labour-managed firm is examined in Ireland and Law (1982), and Vanek (1975) provides a useful sample of literature in the area. A long-run analysis of labour-managed firms is Furubotn (1976). A key assumption in Furubotn's analysis is that workers cannot sell their share of the future profits of the firm when they leave the co-operative, so investment decisions are biased towards projects yielding high returns in the short term. A common prediction of theory is that labour-managed firms may display a preference for *minimising* the size of the workforce, since new workers would acquire an equal share in the 'surplus value' of profitable projects belonging to existing workers. For our purposes it is sufficient to note that the analysis of the labour-managed firm is very similar to that of the conventional firm, with wages taking the place of dividends in combining the roles of payment for a factor of production and in the distribution of the surplus of the firm. The dilution of ownership of this 'surplus value' is equally a problem in conventional firms. It is got round by means of 'rights' issues' to existing owners which permit them to capture the benefits from a new issue and which give them a vested interest in the maximisation of firm value. Both models of the labour-managed firm have not adapted to the possibility of this sort of institutional device and in general those predictions which deviate from value maximisation can be attributed to the assumptions about the allocation of ownership and control rights possessed by labour groups, rather than to the firm being labour-managed per se.

V WHY DO FIRMS EXIST?

The firm is the centre piece in finance, taking funds from investors and investing them in projects. But why do firms exist? The question may seem odd, but there are closely related questions – What is the optimum size for the firm? Are big firms better than small firms? What is the best organisational structure for the firm? – which often arise. The seminal discussion of this topic was by Ronald Coase (1937). Coase said that the *firm* and the *market* were alternative modes of economic organisation and that *transaction costs* would determine whether a given set of transactions were *internalised* in a firm or left to the market. We can put this another way. Bearing in mind that market prices are bearers of economic information, the firm will be chosen as a method of economic organisation when it provides a less expensive way of exchanging information than the market. Williamson (1975) provides a highly influential development of this approach.

Williamson

Oliver Williamson depicts economic activity as a set of transactions in which productive inputs or resources are transferred and combined into outputs. These transactions either take place in markets, where individuals contract with each other to supply goods and services, or within *hierarchies*, eg firms, where goods and services are called forth and supplied through relationships of authority and direction between individuals in the firm. So firms have replaced or 'internalised' markets in certain areas, and the question is why this has happened.

As a simple example in which the market and the firm are alternative ways of doing something consider the choice that faces you when you build an extension to your house. You get an architect to draw up the plans, then you can either get a building firm to build it, or organise the building yourself by subcontracting various craftsmen, joiners, bricklayers, electricians, etc, to do the work, and arranging with builders' merchants to supply the materials. In the latter case the job is completed through a series of contracts with individuals, in the former case you contract with a firm and the firm directs the craftsmen it employs to do the job. Even in this simple case, where the nature of the tasks are relatively clear-cut and the time duration relatively short there are problems in the market mode of contracting. For example the exact task facing the bricklayer will not be clear until the foundations are dug, and this and the weather will determine when the joiner, the electrician and so forth will be needed. A contract with these craftsmen which allowed for all these possibilities would be *complex* and *contingent* on future events. The building firm, on the other hand, avoids these complexities by writing employment contracts. These are known as *incomplete contracts* since the nature of the tasks the employee will be expected to undertake is not fully specified at the outset.

It is clear that many of the contracts that would need to be written in the absence of firms would be exceedingly complex and time consuming to write; in other words they would be 'costly'. Hierarchical organisations such as firms replace markets in Williamson's view when it is less costly to use the internal than the external mode.

> The shift of transactions from autonomous market contracting to hierarchy is principally explained by transactional economies that attend such assignments.
> (*Williamson*, op cit, p 248)

It is not that relationships within the firm are not contractual, but rather that they involve different types of contracts that are often incomplete or informal. Some writers are more explicit about this.

> Most organisations are legal fictions which serve as a nexus for a set of contracting relationships among individuals.
> (*Jensen and Meckling* (1957) p 310)

Williamson identifies two sets of factors which will determine the costs of contracting through markets, and thus the likelihood of markets *failing* and being replaced by hierarchies. The first is the uncertainty of future states of the world combined with the 'bounded rationality' of humans. To define bounded rationality he quotes Herbert Simon:

> The capacity of the human mind for formulating and solving complex problems is very small compared with the size of the problems whose solution is required for objectively rational behaviour in the real world.

Uncertainty means that long-term contracts that covered every contingency in the future might need to be very complex. The limitations of the human mind mean that the costs of writing such contracts would be high. The virtue of a firm in this situation is that in a firm there may be less need to anticipate the future, the future can be allowed to unfold, and be dealt with in a sequential fashion.

The second set of factors concern the combination of 'opportunism' where 'opportunism refers to a lack of candour or honesty in transactions, to include self-interest seeking with guile', with 'small-members' of participants in a transaction. One reason why hierarchies might be preferred in a world where people behave self-interestedly is that in general 'the internal incentive and control machinery is much more extensive [in a firm] . . .' The relevance of 'small numbers' to this needs explaining. Basic economic theory shows that when the supply of some good or service is monopolised or controlled by a small number of individuals its price is likely to be higher than in a perfectly competitive market. Williamson points out that although contracting often starts as competitive the parties build up specialist knowledge about 'the business which, when subsequent contracts are written, gives them monopolistic powers which permit them to behave opportunistically'.

There are information *costs* associated with firms too. Larger hierarchies tend to have more levels of authority and an increased risk of loss of control as information is delayed and distorted on its way up and down the hierarchy and as top management are plied with more information than they can handle. And if the functional departments of the firm are handling a large range of heterogeneous projects it becomes difficult for top management to get accurate signals of the performance of these separate activities. The solution to this excess of hierarchy suggested by Williamson and practised by many firms since Dupont and General Motors in the early 1920s is to adopt a multidivisional, or '*M-form*' structure. In the M-form firm operations are broken up along product or geographical lines, into semi-autonomous divisions, quasi-firms. According to Williamson the main function of the parent company in the M-form enterprise is as a 'miniature capital market', monitoring divisional performance and allocating funds for investment.

The divisions of an M-form enterprise are only one step removed from separate firms interrelating through the market. Unless the hierarchical 'miniature capital market' is clearly superior to the capital market itself, there is no clear reason not to break the enterprise up into separate firms. In recent years this view has gained ground and in Chapter 22 we tell the story of just such an attempt on BAT, a large UK tobacco and financial services conglomerate.

VI THE COSTS OF AGENCY AND THE SEPARATION OF OWNERSHIP AND CONTROL

Business finance is particularly interested in one subset of the firm's contractual relationships – contracts for the supply of finance. Financial contracts have a time dimension: they give the supplier claims against the future assets of the firm. But this time dimension introduces uncertainty and means that the future assets of the firm, and thus the claims, are contingent on future states of the world that cannot yet be known with certainty. Moreover, financial contracts tend to be complex in that they cover many time-periods and potential states of the world. We saw in the previous section that the costs of writing contracts like this that were complete in that they fully specified claims in all possible states of the world, would be prohibitive. It would mean working out in advance every future action of the firm in every contingency! The contract between the supplier of finance and the firm is usually left 'incomplete', and managers are entrusted with running the firm and making decisions on behalf of the shareholders or creditors sequentially as a future unfolds. So the separation of ownership and control can be seen as a response to the costs of writing complete complex contingent claims contracts.

We can describe the relationship between the suppliers of finance and the managers as one of *agency*, where an agency relationship is

> . . . a contract under which one or more persons (the principle(s)) engage another person (the agent) to perform some service on their behalf which involves delegating some decision-making authority to the agent.
> (*Jensen and Meckling* (1976) p 308)

The application of the theory of agency to problems in finance is relatively recent and still developing, but the classic paper by Jensen and Meckling gives a taste of the contribution this particular form of 'contractual' approach can make.

Jensen and Meckling

Jensen and Meckling address two questions, whether the value of the firm will be maximised when there is a separation of ownership and control, and why firms choose the capital structures they do. As they freely acknowledge, their analysis is very restrictive. It assumes a simple world in which a manager who initially owns 100% of the equity sells 5% to outsiders, and where there are no taxes, outside equity has no vote, and no financing contracts more complex than debt and equity are possible.

Jensen and Meckling assume that managers make decisions which maximise their own utility, and that this involves not just the cash income, or 'value', of the firm but a whole range of non-cash perquisites,

> . . . the physical appointments of the office, the attractiveness of the secretarial staff, the level of employee discipline, the kind and amount of charitable contributions, personal relations ('love', 'respect', etc) with employees, a larger than optimal computer to play with, purchase of production inputs from friends, etc.
> (*Jensen and Meckling*, op cit, p 312)

And leisure, which conflicts with the single-minded quest for profitable projects, will have utility for managers as well. Once it is accepted that managers get utility from non-cash perquisites, it necessarily follows that a separation of ownership and control will reduce the value of the firm. Consider a firm in which the manager initially owns 100% of the equity, then subsequently sells 5% to outsiders. In the former case the manager will expand his consumption of perquisites until at the margin he is sacrificing £1 of cash to get £1 of utility from perquisites. But if 5% of the equity is held by outsiders, 5% of the sacrifice of cash is borne by them too, and the manager only bears 95p of the cost of the £1 worth of perquisites. It will be in the manager's interest to expand his consumption of perquisites further, and reduce the free cash flow, and thus the value of the firm.

The difference between the value of the firm when it is owner-controlled and when there is a separation of ownership and control is a cost of the agency relationship. The principal may incur costs to *monitor* the agent's behaviour and the agent may himself find it worthwhile to incur *bonding* costs to demonstrate that his behaviour is not harmful to the principal. The total cost associated with an agency relationship has thus three components: these monitoring and bonding costs, and the *residual loss* of value that remains after the optimal amount of monitoring and bonding has taken place.[13] Examples of monitoring and bonding costs include 'auditing, formal control systems, budget restrictions, and the establishment of incentive compensation systems' (p 323).

Jensen and Meckling apply their analysis to the question of the ownership structure of the firm: why it is that firms employ a mix of debt and equity and that the mix varies from firm to firm? The risk to debt-holders in a firm in which the manager holds a significant amount of equity is that after the terms of the debt have been agreed the manager will change his policy in favour of undertaking riskier projects, which offer potentially greater gains to equity but a greater risk of loss to debt. Hence there will be a value loss to debt-holders arising from the agency relationship between debt-holders and management, and as before it will be in the interests of managers that this should be mitigated through monitoring and bonding. So it is common to find clauses in debt agreements that limit the scope of managers to do things like paying dividends, issuing more debt or running down working capital.

The agency costs of inside equity, outside equity, and debt will differ between industries. So in industries such as the bar and restaurant trade where theft, shirking, and favouring of special customers are easy for managers little outside equity will be found, and inside finance will tend to be debt. But in, say, conglomerates where the riskiness of the earnings of the firm can be changed to the detriment of debt-holders by changing the mix of the firm's activities, then debt-financing will be less popular. Again, in highly regulated industries where the scope of managers to undertake risky projects is constrained, debt will be more prevalent.

VII SUMMARY

There are many legal forms a firm may take, but the significant one for the study of business finance is the 'limited liability joint-stock company'. With this structure there can be a separation of ownership and control, so that the management of the firm is entrusted to a continuing team of people with management skills, while ownership may be in the

13 The 'optimal' amount of these activities will occur where the marginal cost equals the marginal benefit. If the marginal costs are positive it will not be worthwhile to eliminate all of the value loss.

hands of a potentially large and changing group of individuals or institutions with savings available to finance the firm. However, the separation of ownership and control raises the potential problem of a conflict of interest between owners and managers.

We reviewed the arguments for a divergence of interests, and the constraints on managerial behaviour which might limit the divergence. Though the arguments have some appeal, and the constraints appear to leave scope, there is no strong empirical evidence that managers are consistently pursuing objectives other than value maximisation.

The final sections of the chapter reviewed the work by Williamson on the rationale for the existence of the firm, and by Jensen and Meckling applying agency theory to analyse problems arising from the separation of ownership and control. This work provides examples of the 'contractual' approach which underlies many current day theoretical developments in finance. Under this approach the framework for economic analysis is a world of rational individuals freely contracting with each other in the face of future events which are complex and uncertain.

REFERENCES AND BIBLIOGRAPHY

Auerbach, P R — *Competition* (1989) Basil Blackwell, Oxford.

Berle, A A and Means, G C — *The Modern Corporation and Private Property* (1932) Macmillan, New York.

Coase, R H — 'The Nature of the Firm', Economica, 1937.

Cosh, A — 'The Remuneration of Chief Executives in the United Kingdom', Economic Journal, March 1975, pp 75–94.

Fama, E F — 'Agency Problems and the Theory of the Firm', Journal of Political Economy, February–June 1980, p 289.

Farrar, J H, Furey, N E, Hannigan, B M and Wylie, O P — *Farrar's Company Law* (3rd edn, 1991) Butterworths.

Furubotn, E G — 'The Long-Run Analysis of the Labour-Managed Firm: An Alternative Interpretation', American Economic Review, 1976, pp 104–123.

Herman, E S — *Corporate Control, Corporate Power* (1981) Cambridge University Press.

Ireland, N J and Law, P J — *The Economics of Labour Managed Enterprises* (1982) Croom Helm, London.

Jensen, M C and Meckling, W H — 'Theory of the Firm: Managerial Behaviour, Agency Costs and Ownership Structure', Journal of Financial Economics, Oct 1976, pp 305–360.

Prais, S J — *The Evolution of Giant Firms in Britain* (1976) Cambridge University Press, Cambridge.

Smith, A — *An Inquiry into the Nature and Causes of the Wealth of Nations* (1776). Cannon, E (ed) (1961) Methuen University Paperbacks, London.

Vanek, J — *Self-Management* (1975) Penguin, Harmondsworth, England.

Williamson, O E — *Markets and Hierarchies* (1975) Macmillan, New York.

QUESTIONS

1 We tend to associate unincorporated firms with small scale, and limited liability with large scale enterprise. What is the reason for this?

2 In finance we assume managers seek to maximise the value of the firm. Why might this be a desirable objective? Why do managers not pursue alternative goals?

3 What constraints exist on managers pursuing their own interests?

4 What objectives should the managers of a public utility be asked to pursue?

5 Markets are usually considered an efficient way of organising economic activity. If this is so, how can we explain the existence of large hierarchical structures called 'firms'?

6 What are the problems of running large firms and how does 'M-form' help overcome them?

7 Explain how the problem of the separation of ownership and control can be described in terms of the principal-agent relationship.

CHAPTER 3

Taxation

This chapter outlines the UK tax system and examines some taxes that have an impact on financial decision making. The first section gives an overview of the tax system as a whole. In Section II we examine corporation tax, and in Section III some taxes borne by investors, personal income tax, capital gains tax and inheritance tax. Section IV compares corporate taxes across Europe. In Section V we examine value added tax to show how even taxes which appear to be borne by others can have an impact on the firm.

I THE UK TAX SYSTEM

Table I shows an outline of the UK tax system in terms of the main sources of tax revenue and the forecast contribution to total government tax revenues. Essentially government extracts three kinds of tax. *Income taxes* are taxes on incomes as they are earned. Companies pay corporation tax on their profits, and individuals including sole-traders and partnerships pay two forms of income tax, personal income tax and national insurance contributions.[1]

Table I The UK tax system – main sources of tax revenue, forecast

			1994/95 percentage of total revenue
Taxes on income			
(i) Companies		Corporation tax	7
(ii) Individuals		Personal income tax	26
		National insurance	17
Commodity taxes		Value added tax	17
		Tobacco, alcohol and betting	6
		Fuel duties	6
		Other duties	3
Capital taxes		Inheritance tax	0.5
		Capital gains tax	0.5
		Stamp duty	0.5
Other		Petrol revenue tax	0.5
		Business rates	5
		Council tax and community charge	3

Source: HMSO, *Financial Statement and Budget Report 1994–95*

1 Though easy to overlook, national insurance was second only to personal income tax as a source of revenue in 1992–93, yielding 15% of total revenues.

Commodity taxes are taxes on expenditure. The most widely felt are value added tax (VAT) and excise duties which are taxes on specific items, notably alcoholic drink, tobacco, gambling, and petroleum. *Capital taxes* are taxes on the disposal of assets. Capital gains tax (CGT) is charged on the proceeds of sale of certain types of asset, notably land, buildings and securities. In general, if it moves it is taxed! However, since there is no intellectual reason to restrict taxation to things that move, the proposal for a wealth tax is receiving consideration in certain quarters. Of course since most assets yield income even if it is only utility or 'psychic income' the difference between income tax and a tax on capital stock or wealth is smaller than at first appears, it is a difference of the 'tax base' government uses.

Taxation is and has always been an emotive issue. For one thing people do not like paying tax and tend to complain about it. More significantly the fiscal system provides government with major instruments of economic and social policy, and whichever the government, there are sure to be a lot of people who either disagree with its objectives, or with its means of achieving them.

A major problem is that tax policy often poses a conflict between *equity* and *efficiency*, between who gets the cake and how big the cake is. This problem was evident in the UK personal income tax system where until the early 1980s it was possible for certain individuals to pay a marginal rate of tax of 98% on some of their income. Many people felt that the redistributive (= equity) effects of this tax were outweighed by its disincentive and distortive (= efficiency) effects on economic behaviour. In fact the effect of personal income tax as a disincentive to the supply of effort and to risk-taking has been much researched, but with no strong conclusion emerging. The problem is that, in economic terms, there is a substitution effect, but also an income effect. Though high income tax makes work less attractive at the margin, it also means that more work is needed to achieve a given income. Which of these factors predominates is likely to depend on the income, the social group and the nature of the work of the individual. But one argument which tends to be influential in the low-growth UK is the international comparison. No other advanced country sported such a high marginal rate of personal income tax, and the top rate of personal income tax was reduced to 40% by the Thatcher administration. Since the removal of this 'anomaly' the UK sits fairly well in the middle of advanced economies both in terms of the overall tax burden and in the balance of taxes which it collects.[2]

Taxes and financial decisions – a look ahead

As a starting point in building the theory of financial decisions we will often assume a perfect capital market with no taxation. But in the real world the earnings of firms are liable to corporation tax, and the returns to investors are liable to personal income tax or capital gains tax. So in a taxed world the job of the financial manager is to choose the projects and to find the financing mix that give the best after-tax returns to investors. However the picture can get complicated because effective tax rates may differ between companies, and between investors. Companies can find themselves permanently or temporarily non-taxpaying with the result that they pay no corporation tax or pay at an effective rate which is below the full rate. More problematic is the fact that the investors' tax rates may differ too – some pay tax at higher rates, whereas others may be exempt from tax. The problem is that not only may managers not be sure about their investors' tax positions, it may be actually impossible to find a financing policy that suits them all. Take dividends as an example:

2 Some of the efficiency aspects of the tax system are referred to below where they relate to financial decisions, but for a comprehensive introduction and critique of the UK tax system which is easy to read, the reader is referred to Kay and King (1990).

tax-exempt investors may want high dividends, while high taxpayers may prefer to take capital gains.

Taxation complicates financial decisions and raises some questions that theory cannot completely answer. We will be returning to the issues raised by taxation throughout the book. Before we proceed, however, another caution on tax rates.

Traditionally, in the UK, changes to the structure of the tax system and to the rates of tax are made by the annual Finance Act and announced by the Chancellor of the Exchequer each March in his budget, though Chancellors sometimes present interim budgets at other times in the year. (Since 1993 there is a joint tax and expenditure statement in November.) So the details of the tax system in this chapter were correct in early 1994 but may soon change, though the general principles which they illustrate are less likely to change. And it ought to be remembered that these *are* only general principles; tax law in reality is a mass of special cases and exceptions which generate handsome incomes for lawyers and accountants. There are several regularly updated sources available for the reader who wishes to check the detail of tax law, for example *Simon's Taxes*.

II CORPORATION TAX

Companies pay corporation tax (CT) on their *taxable profit* at the prevailing rate for the financial year in which the profit is earned. Throughout this book we assume a corporation tax rate of 35%. The actual rate in 1994 was 33% in the UK. The rate is set for the fiscal year beginning each 1 April; so the fiscal year 1994 is the year beginning 1 April 1994. If the company's accounting year does not correspond to the fiscal year an average rate is used.

There is a special 'small companies' rate of 25%, which should more accurately be called a small profit rate since it applies when 'profits'[3] are below a given level. Companies paid this rate when profits were below £300,000 and an intermediate rate on profits between £300,000 and £1,500,000 after which the full rate applied. The small companies rate is usually set equal to the basic rate of personal tax so that, at least to this extent, the tax system is neutral between small incorporated and unincorporated businesses.

The profit on which the Revenue charges tax is based on the profit before tax reported in the accounts, but with some important changes. Certain expenses are not allowed for tax and have to be added back to profit. Some examples are expenses incurred in entertaining people, fines, general provisions for events that have not yet occurred, and costs of tax appeals! The general principle is that expenses must be *wholly and exclusively* incurred for the purposes of the business.

On the other hand some revenues are not taxable either. An example is dividends received from other UK companies which are not taxable since they are paid out of profits that are already taxed.

Capital allowances and investment grants

In order to encourage investment, governments allow firms to accelerate the depreciation they can charge in finding taxable profit, so conferring cash-flow benefits on them by postponing tax. The UK Revenue ignores the firm's depreciation charge and deducts instead *capital allowances*, in the form of *writing-down allowances*. Table II shows the current rates. Additionally, in the past, for some assets companies were able to claim a higher *first-year allowance* instead of the writing-down allowance in the year of purchase.

3 For this purpose only 'profits' is defined in a slightly different way to the usual 'taxable profit'.

For plant and machinery first-year allowances have been 100%, allowing the firm to write off the whole cost against tax immediately. This reflected the view that a slowness to invest in new machinery embodying more efficient technology had contributed to the low rate of growth of the UK. However the 1984 budget phased out first-year allowances.

Table II Writing-down allowances

Plant, machinery, ships, aircraft, vehicles, etc	25% per annum of the reducing balance
Qualifying industrial buildings, agricultural buildings and hotels	4% pa straight-line
Other assets	Nil

When a company disposes of an asset it may well sell it at a price which is above, or below, its tax written-down value. The tax treatment then depends on whether the asset is 'pooled' or not. If not the Revenue either reclaims the excess allowances by making a *balancing charge*, or allows the write-off of the remaining cost through a *balancing allowance*. However for plant and machinery and motor vehicles, with certain exceptions, the treatment is different. They are added to a *pool* of similar assets, and writing-down allowances are given on the value of the whole pool. When the asset is sold the sale proceeds are removed from the pool. The company still receives in effect balancing allowances and charges. However these are spread into the future as the surplus or deficit left in the pool is written down in future periods, and since writing-down allowances on plant, machinery and vehicles are 25% on a reducing-balance basis, assets are never fully expunged.

Typically, as a further incentive, investment in certain underdeveloped regions attracts cash grants from government. In Great Britain grants are treated as corporate income and taxed at the prevailing rate, while in Northern Ireland grants of up to 45% of costs are not taxed and grants of 50% are taxed on the incremental 5% at a very low rate. Whether all these incentives have a significant effect is hard to say. UK investment has remained low, but might have been lower without them. Governments, in their efforts, have changed the law so often that it is sometimes said that uncertainty about the tax system has itself provided a disincentive to invest.

The effects of inflation

The base for CT is accounting profit with adjustments. But as we will see in a later chapter when there is inflation, accounting profit, being based on historic cost, is likely to overstate profit and in particular understates the cost of stocks and fixed assets. This means that under-inflation companies are liable to be over-taxed. The reason is that by the time the historic costs are taken into account for tax they understate the cost of replacing the fixed assets and stocks. When UK inflation was particularly high the Revenue was forced to recognise this problem. The system of 100% first-year allowances on plant and machinery did this by allowing tax relief immediately the cost was incurred. In addition between 1974 and 1984 companies could claim STOCK RELIEF by deducting from taxable profits the purely inflationary part of their stock profits. However, in 1984 both these concessions were withdrawn, despite the fact that UK inflation, though lower, was still positive.

Inflation also has an effect through the lag in tax payments. There is a lag of nine months before companies need pay their mainstream corporation tax, and if there is inflation this reduces the real cost of the tax to the firm. On the other hand it reduces the value of the tax-saving associated with any expenses the firm incurs. This becomes more significant when the tax payment is postponed still further because the firm is carrying forward tax losses.

Tax losses

For various reasons, because the firm has large capital allowances, or perhaps because it was making an accounting loss anyway, it can make a TAX LOSS. Sadly, the Revenue does not start paying the firm 35% of its losses at this juncture, but losses *can* be used to reduce tax liability. The precise rules depend on how the loss arose, but in general losses can be carried forward to reduce taxable income of the 'same trade' in future periods, or they can be set off against the profits of the whole firm, or of other firms in the same group or consortium, in the present or previous year. So in the latter case it may be possible to reclaim money from the Revenue.

The problem with carrying forward tax losses is that the cash-flow benefit is postponed until they are offset. But strategies such as LEASING or MERGER can assist. Firms with excess capital allowances can make mutually beneficial arrangements with other firms which have excess taxable profits. The 'profitable' firm may buy the plant and machinery for the other firm and lease it to them. This way it can qualify for the capital allowances and postpone some of its own CT, and the benefits can be split with the other firm by charging advantageous rates for the lease. Occasionally tax benefits have been used to justify a permanent merger between a firm expecting chronic taxable profits and a firm expecting chronic tax losses, caused perhaps by heavy investment.

Accumulated past losses do not provide a motive for merger though, and there is no longer a market in firms with accumulated losses. The Revenue allows 'GROUP RELIEF' of *current* tax losses and of unrelieved ACT, but carry-forwards of losses are carefully monitored and are only allowed where there is a clear continuity of ownership and trade. 'Diagonal' off-set of losses, against future profits of other group members, are not allowed, though there can be some scope for transferring profits to group members with losses by judicious choice of transfer prices.

Deferred taxation

It is clear that because of the exclusions and allowances the Revenue makes in measuring taxable profit, few companies will have an accounting profit and a taxable profit which are the same. The differences between the Revenue's and the accountant's methods of measuring income are of two sorts, permanent differences and timing differences, PERMANENT differences relate to revenues and expenses recognised by the accountant, but not taxable or allowable under tax law, or vice versa. Examples are certain types of entertainment expenditure and dividend income. TIMING differences relate to items which are recognised by both but in different time periods, so that while in the long run the accounting and tax treatments are the same, in any given year they will differ. Examples are capital allowances and revaluation surpluses.

Shah & Co

Shah & Co buys a machine for £1,000 which it expects to use for 10 years to earn a profit each year before depreciation of £200. Assuming it depreciates the machine on a straight-line basis its accounting profit each year will be:

Profit before depreciation	200
Depreciation	(100)
Accounting profit	100

On the other hand Shah can claim writing-down allowances of 25% of the reducing balance. This will determine its taxable profit and thus the tax it pays each year. Assuming a CT rate of 35% the taxable profit and tax payable are shown below. Note that in the first year the firm's capital allowance exceeds its profit so the excess has to be carried – 50 is carried forward from year 1, 38 from year 2.

Year	*1*	*2*	*3*	*4*	*5*	*6*	*7*	*8*	*9*	*10*	*TOTAL*
Profit before depreciation	200	200	200	200	200	200	200	200	200	200	2,000
Cap allow's limited on	250 200	188 200	141 179	105	79	59	45	33	25	75	1,000
Taxable profit	–	–	21	95	121	141	155	167	175	125	1,000
Tax (35%)	–	–	7	33	42	49	54	59	62	44	350

Over the ten years the accounting profit and the taxable profit both add to £1,000. But they are distributed differently, and the relationship between the accounting profit and the tax charge is uneven. So in year 1 the firm makes £100 profit and pays no tax. In year 9 the firm makes £100 and pays £62 in tax.

This unevenness has led firms to adopt an accounting procedure called 'DEFERRED TAX accounting'. Under deferred tax accounting firms show in their published income statement a CT charge which is NOT what is actually payable in the year, but is calculated as though tax were charged on the basis of the accounting treatment of items with a timing difference.[4] So in the example, where there are no absolute differences between

Table III Corporation tax 1990 (£m)

Company	*Pre-tax profits*	*Corporation tax*	*%*
Allied Lyons	565	161	28
Argyll	276	68	25
Bass	535	144	27
Courtaulds	202	46	23
GEC	872	309	35
Marks & Spencer	604	215	36
Reed International	302	90	30
British Airways	345	100	29
British Telecom	2,302	767	33
Maxwell Communications	172	35	20
Next	(47)	(16)	(34)
Sainsbury	451	141	31

4 Under the present guidelines from the accountancy bodies, SSAP 15, companies need provide deferred tax only if the deferral is likely to reverse.

accounting and taxable profit the tax charge calculated this way would be £100 × 35% = £35 each year. The difference between tax calculated this way, and the actual tax charge is transferred to or from a reserve in the balance sheet. This reserve represents a liability to the Revenue for tax whose payment has temporarily been deferred. The rationale for deferred tax accounting is that of matching revenues with the expenses incurred in earning them, contingent or actual: cash flow is replaced by a measure of the change in the liability position of the firm. On the other hand deferred tax accounting may conceal a fact of real economic significance to firms – the deferment of tax liability. More tellingly much of deferred tax provisions may never be paid because of the continuous replacement policies of most firms and the continuing scaling-up of costs through inflation.

For various reasons, therefore, taxable profit and accounting profit can differ markedly, and even after deferred tax provisions a company's tax charge is rarely the statutory proportion of its pre-tax profit. Table III above shows the relationship of tax charge to pre-tax for twelve large UK firms in 1990 when the corporation tax rate was 35%.

The imputation system

There are various possible ways of taxing companies, but in the UK since 1973 CT has been collected under the IMPUTATION system. Under this system CT is normally paid in two parts,[5] advance corporation tax (ACT) and mainstream corporation tax (MCT).

When the firm pays a dividend it must remit to the Revenue fourteen days after the end of the quarter some ACT, an amount of tax equivalent to the basic rate of personal income tax which would have been deducted, as if the dividend were one paid net of income tax.

Atherton Ltd

Atherton Ltd pays a dividend of £500,000 in March 1992, and the basic rate of personal income tax is 25%. The firm must pay ACT of £166,667. Why? Because £166,667 is the tax that would have had to be paid if £500,000 were a payment net of basic rate income tax, since the gross amount would be:

	£500,000 + £166,667	=	£666,667
tax:	£666,667 × 25%	=	£166,667
net of tax:	£666,667 × 75%	=	£500,000

What we have done is to 'gross up' the £500,000 at 25%. The tax was found by multiplying the net amount by

$$\frac{\textit{tax rate}}{1\text{-}\textit{tax rate}}$$

So in this case,

$$\textit{tax} = £500{,}000 \times \frac{0.25}{1\text{–}0.25} = £500{,}000 \times \frac{25}{75} = £166{,}667$$

This procedure may seem rather complex at first sight. But it is aimed to reduce the bias in the tax system against paying dividends. The dividend the shareholder receives is

5 Or three, since if the company pays an interim as well as a final dividend it will need to pay two instalments of ACT.

deemed to have borne basic rate income tax already, personal income tax is 'imputed' to it, so he does not have to pay this again. The company on the other hand can set the tax off against its overall tax liability, hence it is 'advance' corporation tax. The balance of CT is referred to as MAINSTREAM corporation tax and a redeeming feature for UK companies is that there is a significant lag before mainstream tax need be paid. They do not have to pay their mainstream tax until nine months after the end of the accounting year.

So if Atherton's accounting year ends on 30 April 1992 it will pay MCT on these profits on 31 January 1993. The lag amounts to costless finance for the firm, provided by the Inland Revenue.

Developing the previous example, Atherton's dividend was paid on 31 March 1992,[6] out of taxable profits for the year ended 30.4.92 of £2 million, hence the ACT will be payable on 14 April 1992. Its overall tax position is as follows, with the position if it had paid no dividend shown as a comparison.

	Position if dividend is paid (£000s)	*Position if no dividend is paid* (£000s)
Taxable profits	2,000	2,000
CT (35%)	700	700
	1,300	1,300
Dividend (net)	500	
Retained profit	800	1,300
Position of shareholders		
Dividend received	500	—
Liability of Atherton to Inland Revenue		
ACT payable 14.4.92	166.7	—
Mainstream payable 31.1.93	533.3	700
	700	700

Classical versus imputation tax systems

A principle of taxation with great significance for finance is that though interest – the cost of servicing debt finance – is an allowable deduction in arriving at taxable profit, dividends – the cost of servicing equity finance – are not. With a rate of CT of 35% this significantly reduces the cost of debt finance and alters the optimal mix of finance in favour of debt. The rationale is that dividends are a distribution of the profits of the firm rather than an expense in earning them. But for most firms dividends are both a distribution and a necessary expense in obtaining equity finance. It could be argued that dividends have two components, the minimum return required by equity to induce them to invest in the firm given its risk and growth prospects, and a premium representing the distribution of

6 Note, for simplicity we have assumed that the dividend is paid in the accounting year to which it relates. In practice the final dividend is usually paid after the accounting year, and this causes allocation complications since ACT is set off against the CT of the period *in which*, not *for which*, the dividend is paid.

surplus profits. We might want to allow the first component as an expense and tax the second. However, the size of these two elements is not directly ascertainable. Part of the popularity of 'convertible loan-stock' as a method of financing is that it is debt to the Inland Revenue, but offers the appeal of equity to the investor. Strictly speaking, these comments aptly describe a *classical* tax system such as that which prevails in the US.

The main aim in introducing the imputation system was to remove the incentive to retain rather than pay dividends which the previous system provided. In the Atherton case, we can see the system is neutral. *If the shareholders are basic rate taxpayers*, they will have no further tax to pay on the £500,000 dividend and, viewed together, the company and its shareholders are in the same cash position whether or not a dividend is paid. Whether the imputation system *is* neutral in this sense is explored further in Chapter 17. In fact, a disincentive which remains in the system is one of timing of cash flow. In the example above, by paying a dividend, Atherton has also committed itself to paying £166,667 a year earlier than otherwise.

Close companies

Corporate status might provide opportunities for tax avoidance. Believing that abuse is most likely in firms that are owned and managed by a small, close group of people, the law has defined a *close company*. Roughly speaking this is a company which no more than five 'participators' control.

'Participator' is defined widely and individuals who tend to act as a unit, for example husband and wife, are defined as one participator. The close company law has been softened a great deal since its inception, but it remains the case that:

1 The Revenue has the right to treat certain profits as dividends above a certain level and if they are surplus to the requirements of the business; they may 'apportion' them and charge shareholders income tax on their share. The purpose of this is to discourage the conversion of income into capital gains which attract a lower rate of tax.
2 If the firm makes loans to shareholders they will have to remit ACT to the Revenue as though the loan had been a dividend. This restricts the advantage of hidden dividends being paid by making loans to shareholders, which are subsequently written off in the books or linger there forever.

Defined in this way, the vast majority of small and medium-sized firms are 'close', as are some large firms where control has stayed in the hands of a small number of families. However, an additional clause in the legislation allows that a company may not be 'close' if the 'public' own at least 35% of the voting power, so long as the company's five largest vote-holders do not between them hold more than 85% of the voting power. This perhaps explained the decision by some firms to 'go public' in the years when the penalties for close companies were more severe.

III PERSONAL INCOME TAX AND CAPITAL GAINS TAX

Since companies belong to their shareholders we start by examining taxes which shareholders bear.

Income tax

In the UK an individual is liable to pay tax on his or her taxable income which is basically all income from any source, at home or abroad, less certain 'allowances'. If the Chancellor has set the personal allowance at £3,000 for the year, then the first £3,000 of income would be tax free for all individuals. Another allowance that is significant for many individuals is the facility to deduct from taxable income the interest paid on loans of up to £30,000 for the purchase or improvement of their private residence.

As well as generally available allowances the law allows certain expenses associated with earning the income to be set off in calculating taxable income. This depends on the type of income, and there are several different sets of rules, or 'schedules', defining in each case how taxable income is calculated, what expenses are deductible, and when the tax is payable. Individuals who are employees usually have income tax deducted by the employer under the 'Pay-as-you-earn' (PAYE) system. Income from employment is dealt with under 'Schedule E', which offers very little scope for setting-off expenditure, or for postponing payment of tax. But self-employed people, sole-traders and partnerships, pay tax under 'Schedule D' which offers considerably more potential for individuals to arrange their affairs so as to reduce tax and postpone paying it. One key difference is that to be deductible under 'Schedule E', expenses have in general to be 'wholly, exclusively and *necessarily*' incurred in earning the income, whereas under 'Schedule D', they only have to be 'wholly and exclusively' incurred.

Personal income tax is progressive and in the UK there are currently four rates. On the first portion of income, to the extent of any allowances, the individual pays no tax. Then the first portion of taxable income is taxed at 20%, a wider band is taxed at the BASIC RATE of 25%, then the rest is taxed at the higher rate of 40%. However, institutions such as pension funds and charities are not liable to income tax. The upshot is that the marginal tax rate of a firm's investors can range from zero if they are institutions, to 40% if they are high income individuals.

Capital gains tax (CGT)

Gains made by selling assets may be taxed as *capital gains*. The rules for determining just what gains qualify in this respect are complex, but they need not concern us beyond noting that if buying and selling the particular type of asset effectively constitutes a trade then the gains will be taxed as income. Hence, for example, the law attempts to distinguish people who buy and sell shares short term for speculative gain from those who buy shares to hold as income producing assets. In the former case gains would be taxed as income, in the latter case as capital gains. The taxpayer can deduct from the gain inflation as measured by the change in the RPI during ownership of the asset. The rate of CGT is the same as the individual's top marginal income tax rate, though the first slice of gains in any year is tax free. Pension funds, charities etc do not pay CGT on any gains they make from 'dealing' in assets rather than holding them.

In practice the *effective* rate of CGT is much lower. CGT is not paid as gains accrue, but only when they are realised. The longer the asset is held the longer the tax payment is postponed. King (1977) found that in the UK in 1971 the average effective tax rate on capital gains was 14.9% whereas the mean income tax rate on all shareholders was 44.1%.

Inheritance tax

Inheritance tax is a tax on gifts of assets and transfers at death. Until 1986 it was known as capital transfer tax. The tax is assessed by adding all the liable transfers made by an individual during his lifetime and at death and charging tax on the total as follows:

Slice of cumulative chargeable transfers	*Cumulative total*	*% on slice*	*Cumulative total tax*
The first £150,000	£150,000	Nil	£Nil
Remainder	—	40	—

IV CORPORATE TAXES IN EUROPE

Europe does not yet have a harmonised corporate tax system. Table IV contrasts certain aspects of corporate taxation in some European countries, plus the US and Japan for additional comparison. The tax system and rates are as at early 1994.

Table IV Corporate taxes in Europe, Japan and the US

Country	*Corporate tax rate (%)*	*Type of tax system*	*Imputation rate(%)*
Belgium	39	Imputation	
Denmark	34	Imputation	20
France	33⅓	Imputation	33.3
Germany	30/45	Split/rate Imputation	36
Greece	46	Imputation	44
Ireland	40	Imputation	53
Italy	36	Imputation	36
Luxembourg	34	Classical	
Netherlands	35	Classical	
Portugal	35/47	Split rate	
Spain	35	Imputation	9.1
UK	33	Imputation	25
Japan	32/42	Split rate	
USA	35	Classical	

Source: Various

Imputation is now the dominant system of taxation in Europe, though there is variation in the corporation tax rate and the imputation rate. European corporation tax rates have tended to converge in the last few years to between 30 and 40%. By contrast the Netherlands and Luxembourg retain a classical system. The imputation system attempts to correct the double taxation of dividends found in a classical system. Another approach is to tax distributed and undistributed profits at different rates. Japan has a split rate system, and in Europe, West Germany and Portugal there is a similar system.

Additional dimensions of variation are provided by local taxes and small companies concessions. In some countries companies pay local taxes in addition to national corporate taxes, though in the case of Germany and Italy, local taxes are deductible at the national level. A number of countries offer reduced rates for smaller businesses.

Almost as important as the corporate tax rate, is *when* the tax has to be paid. Many European countries expect companies to pay most or all of their tax in instalments during the year in which the profit is being earned, following the US model. For instance France, Germany, Belgium, Italy and Portugal base instalments on the previous year's taxable profits. By contrast, in the UK, companies do not pay their corporation tax until nine months after the accounting year end, and in Denmark the lag may be over eighteen months, so the effective tax rate faced by these companies is much reduced.

V VAT AND THE SHIFTING AND INCIDENCE OF TAX

To give a full picture of the government's overall fiscal impact on the firm would be a large task. It would mean looking at the taxation and subsidies borne directly and indirectly by the firm, its investors, customers and suppliers; at the effect of government consumption and expenditure on the pattern of economic activity in the economy, and of the pricing and investment decisions of government controlled firms. These are all issues that the firm should be alive to, but they would be expensive to quantify on a regular basis though this might be justified in the context of a particular project.

So far we have examined some taxes that bear most directly on the firm. But to undermine the easy notion that the rest of the tax system is irrelevant to the firm we briefly examine the INCIDENCE of taxation as against its SCOPE. The incidence of a tax describes who actually bears the tax, the scope who nominally bears it. In practice most tax is 'shifted' at least partially onto firms or individuals other than those for whom it was planned. Take VAT as an example.

Value added tax (VAT)

VAT is a tax on consumption. It is currently charged at a rate of 17½% on the sale price of most goods and services. In principle the tax is merely collected by firms on behalf of the taxman (in this case the customs and excise authorities). The tax is charged even on sales from one firm to another, but most firms can set off the VAT they pay against the VAT they collect or get a refund if they have paid more than they have collected. This way VAT is intended to be passed on through the economy to final consumers who must bear the tax. Firms act as unpaid collectors of VAT. They have to remit quarterly to the Customs & Excise the excess of collections over payments and they have to be able to account in detail for all VAT-bearing transactions. This accounting imposes a cost on firms, and for some firms it meant the introduction of an accounting system where none previously existed, and thus perhaps a larger liability to tax than previously existed! However we are interested in another cost, relating to the fact that firms not only collect the tax, but may indirectly suffer the burden of it.

Figure I depicts some conventional upward and downward sloping supply (SS) and demand (DD) schedules for a product, say shoes. The present equilibrium price is £10 giving a sale volume of 50,000 units. According to the legislation VAT is a tax on consumption, collected by the producer. Suppose the government introduces 17½% VAT in the expectation of collecting £1.50 from each sale of shoes. It is immediately obvious things will not work out this way. The effect of the tax is a vertical shift in SS of 17½% to S′S′. There will be a new equilibrium at the intersection of DD and S′S′. Not only has the producer been left with lower sales of 45,000 but the new equilibrium price is only £11. This is the 'gross' price, of which the producer must remit 17.5/117.5 to the Customs & Excise. So the VAT is £1.64 leaving the producer £9.36. The firm has borne part of the consumption tax. The incidence of the tax clearly depends not so much on the intentions of the government as the elasticity of demand and supply in the market. Had the demand curve been infinitely inelastic (vertical) inspection of the diagram shows that the whole tax would have been borne by the consumer. Infinitely elastic (horizontal) demand would shift the whole tax to the producer.

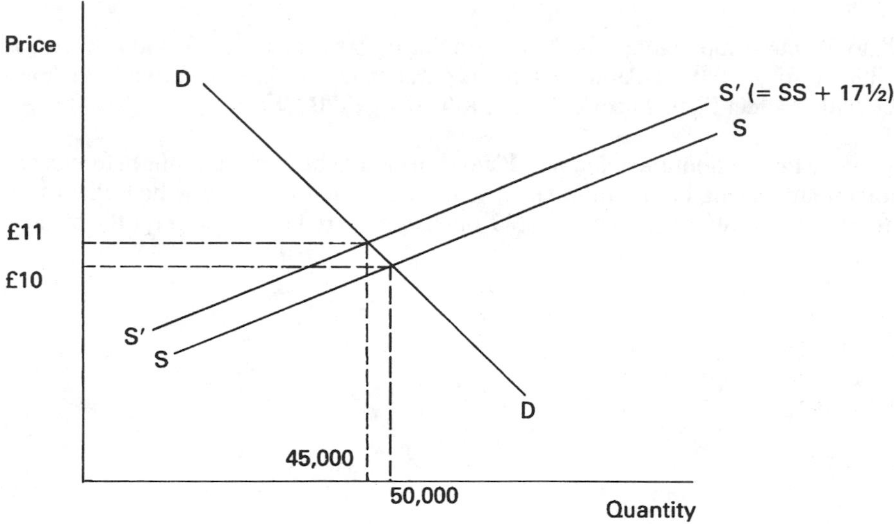

Figure I Shifting and incidence of VAT

The same arguments could be applied in the markets for labour and capital, and the recognition that the incidence of taxes can differ from their scope bedevils discussions of tax policy. One current controversy of this sort is whether the firm's social security contribution is a tax on the firm, or the employee concerned.

VI SUMMARY

This chapter has examined those taxes that are encountered most frequently in business finance; corporation tax, personal income tax, capital gains tax and inheritance tax. All of these taxes can have an impact on financial decision making. The aim has been to depict the general structure of the relevant taxes but in practice detail and minutiae are of the essence of the tax system, and the law and rates of tax are constantly changing, so the reader must be on the look out for this. We examined those taxes whose impact on the financial decisions of the firm is relatively direct, but many other taxes such as VAT affect the firm indirectly and their impact will be implicit in the analysis of project cash flows.

REFERENCES AND BIBLIOGRAPHY

Kay, J A and King, M A — *The British Tax System* (4th edn, 1990) Oxford.

James, S and Nobes, C — *The Economics of Taxation* (2nd edn, 1983) Philip Allen, Oxford.

Simon's Taxes — Yearly. Butterworths.

QUESTIONS

1 Fred Ltd pays an interim dividend to its shareholders on the 2 July 1986. How much ACT will Fred have to pay, and when? How will this affect Fred's overall corporation tax liability?

2 Plato plc buys an oil tanker for £3 million during tax year 1986/87, then sells it for £1 million during 1990/91. Assuming the corporation tax rate is 40% throughout, how will the tanker affect Plato's tax bill from 1986/87 to 1990/91?

3 Suppose that without the oil tanker Plato expected to be earning profit before tax of £3 million and paying corporation tax of £1 million, each year. Show how Plato's profit after tax will be affected each year if he opens a deferred tax account for the oil tanker.

Part II
Valuation

CHAPTER 4

Costs and contribution analysis

In practice the effects of investment decisions spread through time, and this affects the analysis in two ways. First, the money tied up in a project has a time-value, and second, the effects of the decision, the project costs and benefits, will be more risky and uncertain the further into the future they occur. These two issues are taken up in subsequent chapters. But it is convenient at this stage to abstract from the impact of time in order to develop some basic principles. The sort of decisions we are interested in in this chapter are ones in which these two effects are insignificant.

Section I considers what costs and benefits of a project are relevant in making a decision about undertaking it, and derives a decision-rule in terms of the 'contribution' of the project. This section is essentially concerned with how the effects of a project should be quantified. It is easy to generate neat and well-quantified examples of decisions in textbooks, but in practice quantification is often partial and decisions may be subjective and judgemental. A project can have a multitude of effects, direct and indirect, and the question also arises of how far the decision-maker should go in tracking down and quantifying the costs and benefits of a project. Section II discusses this question in terms of information costs. In Section III a commonly used approach in business decision-making, 'break-even analysis', is examined in the light of the concepts developed earlier, and Section IV applies the 'relevant cost' approach to the pricing decision of the firm.

I RELEVANCE AND CONTRIBUTION

For decision-making purposes, the costs and benefits of a project[1] are the *effects* of the projects, beneficial or costly, wherever and whenever they occur. In other words, the only aspects of an alternative that are *relevant* in deciding whether or not to choose it, are those aspects that depend on the decision. Only the *increment* in costs and benefits as a result of the decision are relevant; benefits we would receive irrespective, and costs which we would have had to incur are irrelevant. On the other hand, we should consider *all* the effects of the decision, however remote. The more relevant data we consider, the better the decision.

The only thing that can be changed by decision-making is the future – the past is immutable. It follows from this that past, historic data can *never* be 'relevant' for decisions. The phrase *sunk cost* has acquired a pejorative as well as a descriptive sense for just this reason. It describes costs which have been committed to a project in the past, and are therefore irretrievable. Of course there is a sense in which the past *is* relevant. By virtue of its immutability it is the only thing about which we can be certain, and upon which we can

1 The word 'project' is normally used in this book in the context of investment decisions, where the effects spread through time. But for convenience we are using it in this chapter to describe activities such as pricing and output decisions as well.

base our expectations of the future. It is the data from which we predict future costs and benefits, but should never be included as a cost or benefit itself.

Marvell Ltd

Some years ago Marvell Ltd acquired ten litres of technologically advanced metallic paint at a price of £100, the price reflecting the special nature of the paint. Unfortunately the product for which it was bought was never produced and it remains in the stock room, unused and now technologically superseded. The maintenance man has approached the manager. He has to paint the men's washroom and suggests using up the old metallic paint for the job. He will have to mix £5 worth of thinner with it, but will thereby avoid paying £20 for a new tin of industrial emulsion.

Should the manager accept the idea?

The answer must be yes. The *relevant* effects of using the paint are:

BENEFIT – saved on new paint	£20
COST – thinner	(£ 5)
	+£15

The fact that we once paid £100 for the paint is sad, but irrelevant.

But the determined reader might still persist: 'There may be a better use for this special paint which we will think of tomorrow, saving *more* than £20'. We reply that we know there will not be. Can we be certain? No. But in this chapter we assume certainty.

Opportunity cost

Unfortunately, when used for decision making the everyday concept of 'cost', which tends to be the accountant's historic cost – 'what was paid for it' turns out to be inadequate.

Suppose project G requires an input of 5 tons of material X. If undertaking project G means buying an extra 5 tons of X at £20 per ton, then the cost is truly what is paid for it, the *replacement cost*. This is consistent with the relevance principle which says it is the effect, or increment in cost as a result of undertaking project G that should be considered as the cost to the project.

The other possibility is that we have *already in stock* some or all of the material. This opens up new possibilities for costing, all of which are instructive. Assume the material cost £15 per ton when bought. The storekeeper has it in his records at £15 per ton. For his purpose – control – this may be appropriate. But for our purpose – decision making – the cost will not be £15 other than by chance. 'Cost' depends on context and purpose. To find the cost of material X in the current context, the effects of using it on project G have to be examined. This means looking at alternatives.

Suppose material X can be used on project K as well. In the normal course of events the firm will use the material now and replace 5 tons when it is needed for project K. So, again, the cost of X to project G will be £100, the replacement cost. But X may be well nigh irreplaceable at a reasonable price. The effect of using X on G is that K will be impossible: K will have to be sacrificed with the loss of its contribution to profits. So the cost of X in this case would be the loss of profit from K.

The alternative 'project' may be outside the firm. It may be possible to sell the material to outsiders, if only for scrap. In this case the *net realisable value*, the proceeds of selling the material after deducting any costs associated with selling, is the cost of using it on project G.

The final case to consider is the extreme, but important real-world case where a resource has no other uses either inside or outside the firm. (This was the case with the metallic paint in the example earlier.) The cost of such resources for decision making purposes is *zero*, because using them has no effects at all.

This variety may appear confusing, but the underlying principle is simple. In decision making only *effects* are relevant. To find the cost of a resource we simply examine the effects of using it; which means examining alternative uses inside and outside the firm. This type of cost is called *opportunity cost*, which is the *benefit foregone from the best alternative use*.

Opportunity benefits?

If opportunity costs are so important, why is more not heard of opportunity benefits? The criterion of relevance is equally important on the benefit side. Suppose another firm is considering a product P which will yield revenues of £1 million per annum, but partly at the expense of lost sales on the existing product R which will fall by £.2 million per annum. In deciding whether to launch P the real benefit to the firm is £1 million − £.2 million = £.8 million. We might call £.8 million the opportunity benefit, the benefit after allowing for foregone alternatives. In practice this would be accounted for in two parts, revenue would be held at £1 million, and the £.2 million entered as a cost to the project. There would otherwise be a serious risk of double-counting, given the similarity between opportunity costs and benefits.

A decision-rule in terms of relevant costs

In analysing decisions we can split the measurement of the overall worth of a project into two stages.

The opportunity cost of the resources used in the project is deducted from the incremental revenue of the project to find the *contribution*. From this is deducted the opportunity cost entailed by having to sacrifice other projects to undertake the project in question, in other words the contributions of those projects, to find the *net benefit*.

incremental revenue	xxx
opportunity cost of resources used	(xxx)
CONTRIBUTION	xx
opportunity cost of other projects	(xx)
NET BENEFIT	x

Assuming the objective of maximising the wealth of the owners we can define a decision-rule in terms of contribution, this is: choose all projects with a positive contribution. These are all projects which are 'covering their own costs' and making a contribution to the central burden of committed resources ('overheads') and to the profit of the organisation.[2]

It will be observed that it is only when the decision-maker is forced to *choose between* projects by limited resources or because of the nature of the service that she or he wishes to have provided, that the second stage will be relevant. And that only one project out of a

2 The reader who has studied some economics and wonders what all this has to do with it, should note that 'choose all projects with a positive contribution' is the same as 'set output where marginal cost equals marginal revenue', the short-run profit maximising rule in economics. The difference is merely one of terminology. Where economists think in terms of increasing output until the marginal revenue from the last unit just exceeds its marginal cost, we are talking of accepting projects up to those whose incremental revenue just exceeds their incremental cost.

group from which we may only choose one, which is known as a *mutually exclusive* group, will have a positive net benefit. This is because the opportunity cost of each project is the contribution of the best alternative.

Some projects are 'naturally' mutually exclusive. For example, the choice of a new photocopier for the office. Only one photocopier is wanted, it is a matter of choosing the best. But in practice decisions very often involve mutually exclusive projects for another reason, because of *constraints*.

Constrained decisions

The two-part decision-rule in the previous section provided a motive for choosing between mutually exclusive projects. When the choice is being forced by a 'constraint', we have a different way of expressing the same rule. We choose that project or projects which *maximise the contribution per unit of the constraint.*

Tanner

Tanner makes two products x and y with the following costs and revenues:

per unit	x	y
	£	£
Selling price	18	15
Labour	(10)	(6)
Materials	(5)	(6)
CONTRIBUTION	3	3

Which product should Tanner make?

Both products have incremental benefits greater than incremental costs, that is, a positive contribution. So it would be worth Tanner's while to make both x and y up to the limits of demand by the market at the ruling prices.

But suppose demand for the existing price exceeds the capacity of the firm to produce. In other words suppose the firm's resources are insufficient to meet the demand. Which produce should be produced? The answer is the product yielding the best contribution per unit of the constraint. So the production plan depends on which factor is limiting or constraining output. Suppose labour is the constraining factor, then:

	x	y
contribution/£ labour	£3/10 = 30p	£3/6 = 50p

The best plan would be to produce as many y as possible, and produce x only when demand for y is satisfied. But if materials are scarce then the following figures suggest the reverse strategy:

	x	y
contribution/£ materials	£3/5 = 60p	£3/6 = 50p

Another possibility is that the constraint may be one not costed in the contribution calculation – for example factory capacity. The decision-maker will have to get estimates of how much 'capacity' each product uses, perhaps in machine-hours, or plant square-footage, to quantify the demand on limited resources.

This example, though instructive, is excessively simple for most practical cases. It assumed only one constraint. But in practice there may be hundreds, and finding the best production plan needs a mathematical programming technique capable of processing this complexity.[3]

Managerial effort as a constraint

Managers regularly appear to choose a smaller set of projects than they might on the basis of our analysis so far. That is, they sometimes reject or, what is the same thing, fail to seek out projects with a positive contribution even where tangible resources, plant, materials, labour, could be obtained to service them. This behaviour appears more rational if we recall that managerial effort is a limited resource, though one which may be hard to quantify. Indeed we would expect rational managers to choose the set of projects which maximise contribution per unit of managerial time.

Constraints are factors which are limited in the short term (this is what 'short term' means in economics). But the longer term decision-makers should be seeking ways to remove the constraints, and thus increase contribution. The managerial effort constraint can be one of the hardest to remove. Skilled management may need to be trained over a long period of time, though good manpower planning should anticipate these needs.

II WHAT COSTS AND BENEFITS TO INCLUDE

Bundy

Bundy, an engineering company, is short of work to the extent that it is planning to make some of its skilled machinists redundant. An old customer rings up to ask if Bundy can complete special fabrication work at a price of £2,000. When the job is costed, the figures look like this:

		£
Revenue		2,000
Costs:	Materials (bought out)	(1,800)
	Labour (machinists)	(1,200)
	Fixed overhead* (pro rata on labour)	(600)

The job would permit Bundy to postpone sacking the machinists for three months. Should the job be accepted? (Ignore redundancy pay.)

In analysing this problem, the message of the previous pages is seek *relevant* costs and benefits. In this case, the 'fixed overhead' is clearly irrelevant, it has to be paid whether or not we take the job. So the relevant figures are:

	£
Revenue	2,000
Incremental costs 1,800 + 1,200	(3,000)
CONTRIBUTION	(1,000)

Bundy would be using other resources on the job, namely the factory, but as the factory would otherwise be idle, its opportunity cost is zero.[4] With a negative contribution of £1,000 should the job be accepted? In practice, few people would categorically say no, for the simple reason that so many considerations have been left out of the analysis, for example:

3 See Chapter 7.
4 In the short run the opportunity cost is zero. In the long run the factory could be sold.

(a) The revenue is poor, but the customer may withdraw his goodwill if Bundy does not accept, thereby losing future business.
(b) If Bundy sacks the machinists it may be costly or impossible to replace them if trade improves.
(c) Bundy may feel a moral duty to keep the machinists employed.
(d) On the other hand the prospects for Bundy's survival in the long term may be poor anyhow.

In fact, it is very uncommon for decisions to be so 'cut and dried' as at first appears. Decisions have a whole host of effects, direct and indirect. Moreover the effects are very often not quantified, they may be *qualitative*, and so even if discovered may be hard to incorporate into the calculation.

An INDIRECT effect is one whose impact is on another project or department of the firm. Effect (a) above is of this sort, rejecting the current project will have an effect on revenues from future projects. We encountered another effect of this sort when we talked about 'opportunity benefit' earlier. There, the launch of a new product involved taking sales away from an existing product of the firm, an effect which could not be ignored. These effects are at least in principle in quantitative form, though in practice their measurement causes considerable problems. But consider effect (c): Bundy may feel a moral duty to keep the machinists employed. This sort of consideration could be decisive in a decision to take on new work. How can it be incorporated in the decision? The first thing to note is that in principle this effect *could* be quantified just by asking the management of Bundy to put a price or value on it. The key question would be 'how much are you willing to pay to avoid sacking your workers?' This measures the cost of sacking them, the benefit of not doing. In practice this sort of measurement is rarely attempted.

Quantification versus judgement

We claimed above that the more information about the effects of a decision that can be incorporated into the decision the better. Information may be deficient in two ways:

1 the decision-maker may lack relevant information: *new information is needed.*
2 The decision-maker may have all the relevant information, but in judgemental not quantified form: *existing information is judgemental.*

In one respect these two are the same. Most information can be acquired in quantified form at some cost. But the guiding principle is that the decision-maker should acquire better information when the *benefits of better information exceed the costs of acquiring it.*

In practice information that is routinely collected in a firm's accounting system can be used at a low or zero cost. The cost and revenue information in the Bundy example is of this sort. Information for which collection techniques are well-established, but which is not routinely collected will have a greater cost. Items (a), (b) and (d) concerning the external environment of Bundy are of this sort, and could presumably be illuminated by consultants: market researchers, economists, financial analysts. Information that is rarely collected, such as (c), the ethical implications of laying off workers, might be expensive to quantify.

The cost and benefits of better information might be represented as in Figure I.

Figure I assumes that the cost of information is a linear function of the quantity, but that the marginal benefit from having it is reducing; in other words the benefits from extra information eventually become fairly small. The exact shape of the lines is not critical. What matters is the notion that there is some point, K, where the net benefit of extra information (the gap between the lines) is at a maximum.

The reader may accept that we can calculate the cost of getting more information; we know the cost of running the computer, the fees usually charged by market researchers and so forth. But how can we know what the benefits of better information will be before we know what the information will be? This is usually rather hard and decision-makers may make judgements about the value of information.

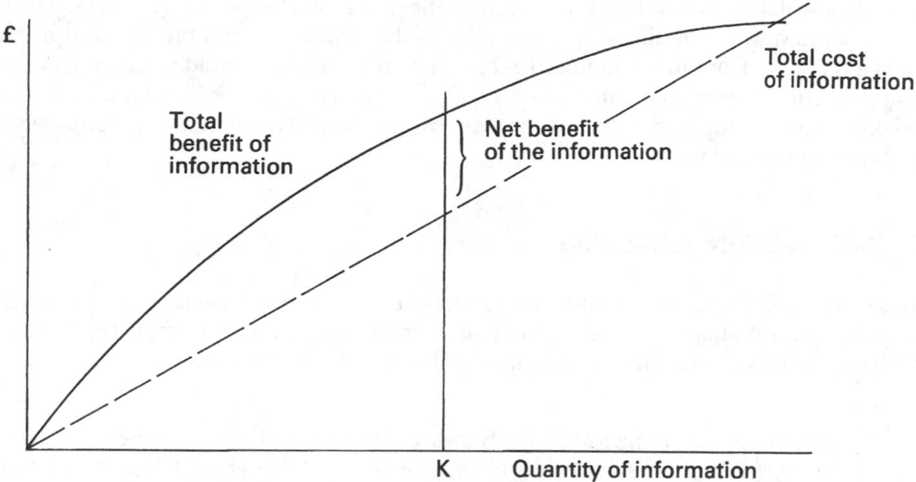

Figure I Information costs and benefits

A key issue in the study of financial decision making is the role of *quantified* information. In Bundy we encountered an example where the decision-maker was presented with certain quantitative information, but where some non-quantified information might be decisive. It should be possible, at some cost, to quantify these views and combine them in the quantitative presentation. Our previous rule suggests doing this if the benefits exceed the costs. When are there benefits in quantifying data which decision-makers already possess judgementally or in 'externalising' information which managers already possess 'internally', 'inside their heads?' The benefits of quantifying information are:

1 The information may be improved by quantification. Forcing decision-makers to externalise their views may force an ordering or reappraisal of the information, and perhaps reveal data with internal inconsistencies.
2 Quantification, and thus recording, of all the inputs into a decision may be necessary for *control* when decisions are decentralised to subordinates. This will occur in any organisation where some decisions are not taken by those ultimately responsible; in other words most organisations of any size.

Often the benefits of quantification will be exceeded by the costs. In these cases managers *may* be behaving rationally in apparently irrational decisions; such as choosing projects with a negative contribution, rejecting projects with a positive contribution, etc.

Externalities

One set of effects of a project can generally be ignored by the firm in making decisions about it: the *external* effects, the effects on outsiders. Sometimes firms do appear to take some account of externalities in their decisions. For example, a firm may voluntarily decide to install expensive pollution control equipment to reduce pollution to the surrounding countryside. This can come about for two reasons: the firm may fear a future reaction to the pollution, from government or consumers, and may be seeking to forestall this. In this case the pollution has indirect *internal* effects which the decision-maker should allow for. On the other hand the effects of the pollution may be purely external in the sense that no financial damage to the firm can be anticipated, now or in the future. But the decision-maker may still be influenced by the pollution effects. This could be because he has some view of the moral responsibility of the firm to the community, and he thus derives disutility from the pollution. In this sense the pollution could again be viewed as having internal effects on the firm. Governments tend not to rely on these indirect effects and often seek to 'internalise' the externalities by imposing taxes or quantity restrictions on the activity in question.

III 'BREAK-EVEN' ANALYSIS

Break-even analysis, or cost-volume profit analysis as it is also known, is an approach to analysing certain simple business problems. This section considers what the approach involves, what its limitations are, and how it fits in to the analysis of this chapter.

> *Vijay*
>
> Vijay is thinking of renting a stall at a Sunday market to sell cassette tapes. He can get the tapes for £1.50 each, sale or return, and hopes to sell them for £4. The rental on the stall is £80 per session. How many cassettes must he sell to break even?

This problem can be solved either by computation, or graphically by drawing a break-even chart.

Computation

To find the break even sales we start by noting that

Sales – Variable cost – Fixed cost ≡ Profit

So if Y = number sold

Y × Unit selling price – Y × Unit variable cost – Fixed cost ≡ Profit

If we define CONTRIBUTION MARGIN as unit selling price less unit variable cost, then Profit ≡ Y × Contribution margin – Fixed cost, and noting that at break-even profit is zero, we can solve for Y to find BREAK-EVEN SALES $= \dfrac{\text{Fixed cost}}{\text{Contribution margin}}$

In Vijay's case:

$$\text{CONTRIBUTION MARGIN} = £4 - £1.50 = £2.50$$

$$\text{BREAK-EVEN SALES} = \frac{£80}{£2.50} = 32 \text{ tapes}$$

Suppose more realistically that Vijay will only consider the stall if the operation will leave him £20 in his pocket. The desired profit is equivalent to an additional fixed cost. Now we have:

$$\text{BREAK-EVEN SALES} = \frac{£80 + £20}{£2.50} = 40 \text{ tapes}$$

Break-even chart

The same approach can be illustrated by constructing a chart. Figure II charts the initial break-even decision above.

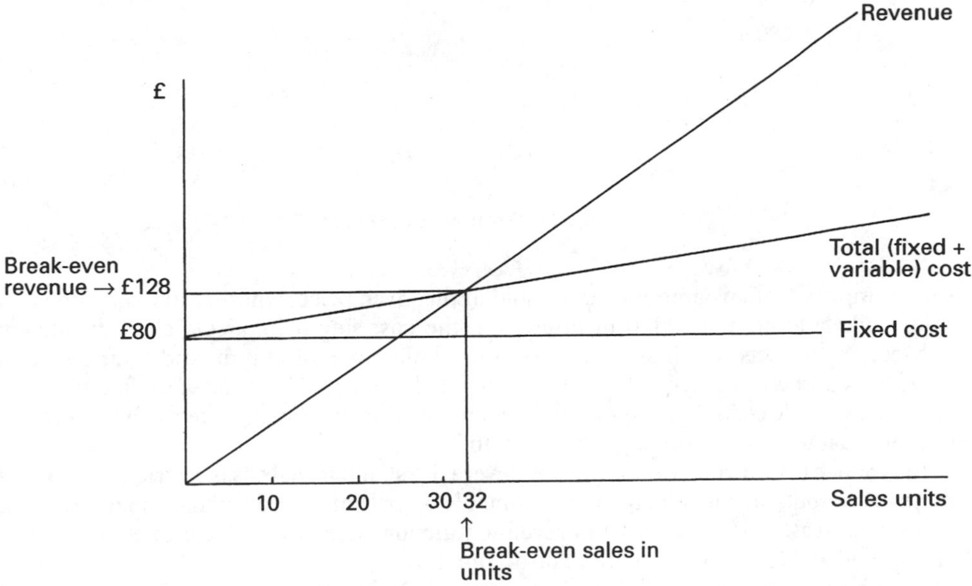

Figure II Break-even chart

The break-even chart displays the cost and revenue assumptions of break-even analysis. The break-even point is at sales of 32 units, with revenue of £128. The profit or loss at sales above or below this point is the vertical distance between the Revenue and Total cost lines, in Figure II. This information is sometimes plotted on to a 'profit-volume chart' which simply shows the profit or loss at each level of sales, as in Figure III on the next page.

An analysis of break-even analysis

The Vijay problem was as simple a business problem as could be imagined, but break-even analysis is applied to larger business decisions too, and the user needs to be aware of the limitations inherent in the approach.

(1) Shape of the curves The most obvious weakness of break-even analysis as it is usually presented is the assumption of linearity in the revenue and cost curves since linearity appears to conflict with our beliefs as to how costs and reserves behave. On the revenue

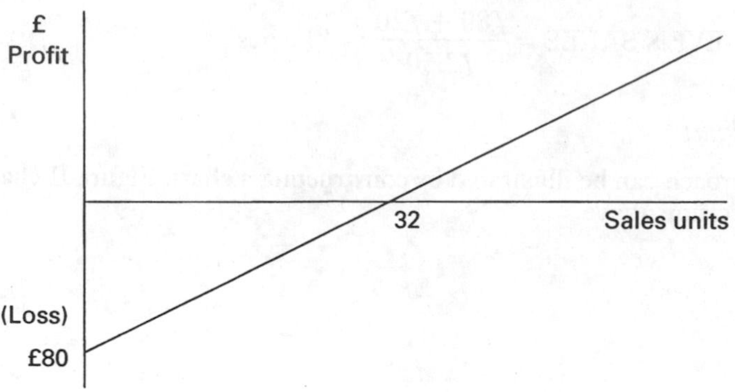

Figure III Profit-volume chart

side it implies that any amount can be sold at the given price, whereas in reality quantity sold is likely to be a function of price.[5] On the cost side it implies a clear distinction between some costs which are fixed over the whole range of output, and a variable cost which is constant per unit. This seems to preclude step-like fixed-cost functions, or marginal variable costs which increase or decrease because learning effects, imperfections to input markets, stockbuilding, and so forth.[6]

In practice these problems may not be severe. First, if the analysis is restricted to a small range of outputs linearity may be a reasonable approximation over that range. Second, there is no reason why the cost and revenue functions need to be linear on a break-even chart. The analysts can use more realistic functions if he wishes. But the computational approach to break-even analysis will cease to be simple once the assumption of constant contribution margin disappears.

(2) Concept of cost A more insidious weakness of break-even analysis is that it appears to embody the wrong concept of cost. We know that for decision-making purposes the appropriate measure of cost is opportunity cost. Consider fixed costs. In the Vijay example fixed cost was a misnomer since Vijay could have avoided them by not taking the stall, but fixed cost usually refers to the cost of overhead, of using productive capacity already owned. The cost of using capacity depends on what else is happening. If the enterprise is working at less than full capacity the opportunity cost of using capacity is zero. If the enterprise is at capacity, the cost is the contribution lost from the displaced alternative. The sensitivity of costs to other opportunities is rather hard to embody in a break-even chart.

5 To be precise, quantity sold will be a function of price other than in the limiting case of perfect, atomistic competition in which the firm 'takes' the ruling market price and optimises output by producing until marginal cost is equal to price. See a standard text, for example Scherer and Ross (1990), on the background microeconomic theory.

6 Each firm must find the shape of its own cost function. There have been many empirical cost studies testing the linearity assumption against the predictions of traditional economic theory. Although no consensus has emerged or is likely to, a significant number have revealed linearity over at least part of the range.

(3) Indirect effects An associated weakness of the break-even analysis is its failure to represent the indirect effects of decisions. For example in a multi-product firm there often exist relationships of substitution or complementarity between products, in other words, sales of one product may diminish or enhance sales of another. This would clearly be a relevant effect for decision-making, but is rather hard to incorporate in a break-even chart.

(4) Future effects Another dimension of complexity which tends to be overlooked in break-even analysis is time. In reality few decisions have effects which all occur within one time period, but unless this is the case the timing as well as the level of costs and revenues becomes important.

Why do people use break-even charts? Apart from indicating the break-even level of sales the strength of break-even charts is their ability to depict the rate at which sales generate profits and to show how the fixed charges of the business, the financial and operating leverage, increase the volatility of that profit. But the problem with traditional break-even charts is that they can suppress a lot of relevant information in the process. This is inevitable, since any attempt to depict a complex process in a two-dimensional graph involves a great deal of selectivity as to what is depicted. They may severely mislead the decision-maker in any but the most simple situations.

IV RELEVANT COSTS IN THE PRICING DECISION

Pricing decisions exemplify the importance of using the right cost concept, and also the limitations of costs in decisions. Earlier, a problem involving the decision whether to accept an order was examined. The pricing decision is the same problem viewed from the other end: the decision to charge £10 for a product y is the decision that orders for y will not be accepted at less than £10.

We will examine the pricing problem in two contexts: first, when the firm has spare capacity; second, when the firm is working at or near full capacity.

Spare capacity

It is well known that a firm which is short of work, has spare capacity, would be wise to accept any job or project which offers a positive contribution. The reason is that the incremental revenue from such a job will cover the incremental costs and contribute something, at least, to the overheads of the organisation (by 'overheads' is meant anything that does not change on this occasion, for example if it is not practicable to hire and fire labour at will, labour is an overhead). In pricing terms, this means that the firm would be wise to accept any price for a job, so long as it covers incremental costs.

The value of this perception is that it will prevent managers being misled by the standard output of cost accounting systems, which often includes overhead with labour, or with some other cost, on a pro rata basis. Overhead, by definition a cost which does not change if the job is accepted, is irrelevant for decisions. The opportunity cost of the resources it represents is zero, since there is spare capacity.

But this rule needs some qualification!

First, as we saw in the Bundy example, consideration of all the relevant effects might even condone a price yielding negative contribution.

Second, 'condition-pricing' suggests a minimum price. It would be pointless to charge this price if the market would accept a higher price for the same volume. Indeed it could be damaging to the firm to signal its problems by charging 'distress' prices.

Third, a firm which is not 'covering its overhead', and sees little prospect of doing so, would be advised to withdraw from the market as quickly as possible, albeit earning any contribution it can on the way.

Full capacity

We turn now to the 'normal' situation where firms are at or near full capacity.
In practice many pricing decisions by firms are based on *cost plus*. That is, prices are calculated thus:

incremental cost	xx
+ overhead (pro rata)	xx
+ required profit (% on cost)	x
COST-PLUS PRICE	xxx

Smythe

Smythe measures its annual activity level in terms of its labour cost. This year its budgeted activity level for labour is £500,000 and fixed overheads are expected to be £200,000.
Smythe expects to earn a pre-tax return on capital employed of 25%.
This year it is employing capital of £600,000.
Job No 73 is estimated to have the following direct costs:

labour	£6,000
materials	£2,000

A cost-plus price for this job could be calculated as follows:
First Smythe must re-set its profit objective in absolute terms:
25% of £600,000 = £150,000.

Assuming that labour is the appropriate measure of capacity usage of Smythe, the overhead recovery and profit requirement can be set in terms of labour:

Overhead	=200,000/500,000	=	40% of labour
Profit	=150,000/500,000	=	30% of labour

So the job can be fully costed or priced thus:

			£
Job No 73	Labour		6,000
	Materials		2,000
			8,000
	Overhead recovered	6000 × 40%	2,400
	Profit	6000 × 30%	1,800
	COST-PLUS PRICE		12,200

In practice this would be presented more simply as

Labour at 170%*	10,200
Materials	2,000
	12,200

*100% labour plus the two mark-ups.

Rationale for cost plus

Cost-plus pricing is often criticised. Critics suggest that by ignoring demand it can lead the firm to a sub-optimal position, assuming a firm is facing a downward sloping demand-curve DD for its product, and has a corresponding average cost curve CC (see Figure IV). The firm is a cost-plus pricer. It chooses its desired output or activity level q_1, it discovers the average cost c at this level, and applies a profit mark-up, the 'plus'.

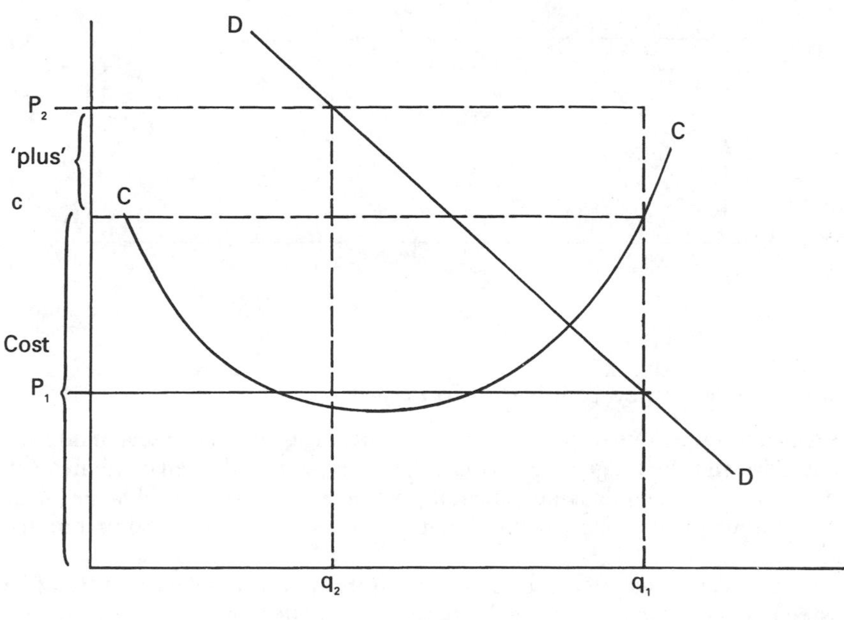

Figure IV

Suppose the firm chooses $q = q_1$ in Figure IV. This leads to a planned price and quantity combination, $p_2\ q_1$. But the market will not accept this, it is to the right of the demand curve. The firm will be forced to revise its plans. The actual outcome will depend very much on the speed with which the firm receives information back from the market, and the extent to which resources have been irrevocably committed to producing q_1. Two things are sure.

1 The actual outcome *must* be a price/quantity combination on or to the left of the demand curve.
2 The actual outcome will be sub-optimal, whether it sells planned q_1 at price p_2, or q_2 at planned price p_1, the firm will not make its planned profit.

Similar arguments apply if the firm aims too low and chooses p and q below the demand curve, say $q = q_3$, $p = p_3$ in Figure V. In this case the market would bear a higher price, and the firm could, for example, increase the price to p_4 to the pure benefit of profit.

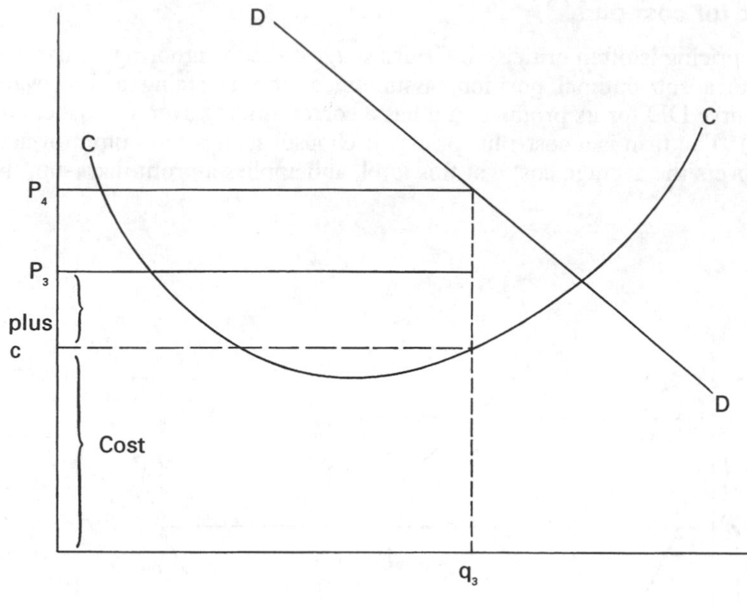

Figure V

Cost plus as a response to information costs

We described in a previous section how decision making involves two sets of information, the quantitative and the judgemental. Some data are quantified, then combined with the remaining non-quantified data judgementally by the decision-maker. The problem with the above critique of cost-plus pricing is that it ignores the judgemental part of decision making.

The reality of cost-plus pricing for most firms is that it provides a base figure which can be adjusted by decision-makers using their experience of demand, and competition, in the light of their marketing strategy. The profession of marketing attempts to provide techniques for ordering, analysing and quantifying this sort of information. But the acquisition of quantified market information is costly. The benefits are more likely to exceed the cost the more the product is homogeneous and of high volume, and the more homogeneous the market. This will be the case when soap powder or baked beans are the product. But for many products, and in many firms, these conditions do not pertain.

At the beginning of this chapter the importance of using relevant costs was emphasised. Are the costs in a full-cost price – overhead allocated on a pro rata basis, and a proportionate profit mark-up – relevant measures of the cost of using 'capacity'? When the firm has idle capacity it is appropriate to treat the cost of using overhead as zero. But when the firm is at or near full capacity projects or jobs compete for resources. The best position is found by choosing those projects that have the highest contribution per unit of limiting factor. Faced with the problem of applying this criterion in a multi-product firm of any size, where jobs may be heterogeneous, possibly made to order, and where pricing and order acceptance are decentralised to sales clerks, cost-plus pricing provides an excellent decision aid. If overhead and profit are allocated *pro rata to the constraining factor*, be it labour, machine-hours or whatever, the cost-plus price will indicate the contribution necessary for a job to be chosen. The firm should be happy that customers accept or reject individual jobs on the basis of such prices. If there is a preponderance of rejections then this is a signal that a downward revision of the profit mark-up is called for, and if excess demand an upward revision.

V SUMMARY

This chapter has explored decision making in the relatively simple cases where one can ignore the effects of time. We saw that in this case the firm should accept projects, fix output, set prices, or whatever, so as to maximise 'contribution'. If some factors are in limited supply this can be done by choosing the projects that maximise contribution per unit of limiting factor. 'Contribution' is the appropriate decision statistic and is measured as the surplus of the incremental revenue over the incremental cost resulting from the project, where these are measured at 'opportunity cost'. Only the effects of a project, the changes in cost and benefit associated with the decision to undertake it are relevant in analysing the decision. But often these effects can be indirect and it will only be rational to quantify them when the benefit of doing so exceeds the cost of getting the further information. The chapter concluded by applying these concepts to break-even analysis and to the pricing decision.

REFERENCES AND BIBLIOGRAPHY

Arnold, J, and Hope, T — *Accounting for Management Decisions* (1990) Prentice-Hall International, Englewood-Cliffs.

Coase, R N — 'The Nature of Costs', The Accountant, London, 1.10.1938–17.12.1938, reprinted in Solomons D (ed) *Studies in Cost Analysis* (2nd edn, 1968) Sweet & Maxwell, London.

Scherer, F M and Ross, D R — *Industrial Market Structure and Economic Performance* (1990) Houghton Mifflin, London.

QUESTIONS

1 Trubshaw makes two sorts of smoke detector, W and WPW. The company allocates overheads on the basis of direct labour hours. The budgeted costs, selling price and estimated annual sales and production are:

Per unit	*W*	*WPW*
	£	£
Direct labour (£2 per hour)	6	14
Direct material	13	10
Fixed overhead	9	21
	28	45
Selling price	32	44
Annual sales/production in units	20,000	4,000

As WPW is making a loss should this product be discontinued? (What will be the overall effect on profitability?) If the company could purchase WPW from another company at

£30 each would it be worthwhile doing so? What assumptions have you made in arriving at your answers?

2 Grimshaw makes two sorts of door-bell, type A and type B, with the following costs and selling price:

	A	*B*
	£	£
Selling price	10	11
Direct material (50p per lb)	2	1
Direct labour (£2 per hour)	4	6
Profit per unit	4	4

What production/sales programme should be chosen if:

(1) materials are limited to 1,000 lbs but labour is unlimited?
(2) only 4,000 direct labour hours are available but materials are unlimited?

3 Patel Engineering produces and sells for £250 a control device for which there is a heavy demand but which the company is prevented from satisfying because of a shortage of skilled labour. The direct material and labour costs of the machine are £118 and £45 respectively. The labour force is paid 150p per hour. All other costs may be regarded as fixed. The company has been invited by one of its customers to supply, for £20,000, a batch of machines of modified design which the customer wishes to incorporate into his own product.

Patel's estimator has calculated that to execute the order, 2,000 direct labour hours would be required and the cost of material would be £8,000 excluding the cost of special switches which could be bought in for £1,000 or, alternatively, made by the company for a material price of £550 and labour time of 100 hours.

Advise the Patel management of whether to accept the order. What factors other than those mentioned are likely to be relevant in practice?

4 (a) From the following profit and loss statement, construct a break-even chart and determine:

(i) the break-even point
(ii) the contribution margin
(iii) the sales necessary to obtain profit of £10,000

Profit and Loss Statement

		£	£
Sales			84,000
Costs	Materials	20,000	
	Labour	20,000	
	Sales commission	2,100	
	Direct overhead	13,900	
	Fixed overhead	14,000	
	General administration (apportioned)	10,000	80,000
	Profit		4,000

(b) What assumptions underly the traditional break-even chart? Evaluate break-even charts as a tool for managers.

CHAPTER 5

Valuation arithmetic

This chapter introduces the basic arithmetic of financial evaluation. Investments have returns which spread through time; these returns are cash flows, or streams of returns that can be expressed as cash flows. Usually people will not value equally a pound received in the future and a pound received today, so money has a 'time-value'. *Discounted cash flow* (DCF) is the technique which is used to quantify the time-value of the money. DCF can either be used to put a *value* on an asset, or to calculate the *yield* or *return* the asset is earning. Section I develops the logic of DCF while Section II contrasts the net present value (NPV) and internal rate of return of an investment project and shows the general relationship between value and return. DCF can be used to evaluate any asset; whether it is the firm evaluating capital expenditures, new projects, acquisitions, leases, or the firm's investors evaluating the shares or bonds (loans) they hold in the firm. Since shares and bonds usually have more regular profiles of cash flows than capital investments, or at least we treat them this way, some rather simplified DCF formulae are often used for valuing them. These are discussed in Sections III and IV. Appendix A to this chapter contains some mathematical proofs and Appendix B derives an expression from the limiting case of continuous compounding.

I THE LOGIC OF DISCOUNTED CASH FLOW

Investments have returns which spread through time in the form of a stream of cash flows positive and negative. Money has a time-value because it has an opportunity cost, which is the return, r, the investor can get from alternative investments. The purpose of the *discounted cash flow* (DCF) technique is to incorporate this *opportunity cost of funds* into the analysis. This explains, by the way, why it is cash flows, rather than, say, profit flows, that we are interested in. It is upon receipt and payment of cash that the financing charges clock starts to tick. The first step in developing the DCF analysis is to recall some elementary mathematics.

Compounding

If £100 is invested today (at time, t_0) at 10% per annum interest, then one year later (t_1) the investor will have £100 × (1 + .10) = £110.

If he leaves the capital and interest to earn interest for another year he will have by the end of the second year (at t_2)

$$\begin{aligned} &£110 \times (1 + .10) \\ &= £100 \times (1 + .10) \times (1 + .10) \\ &= £100 \times (1 + .10)^2 \\ &= £121 \end{aligned}$$

This process of reinvesting capital and interest to earn interest for another period is called *compounding*. We call the outcome of this process the *future value* of the initial amount, compounded at a certain rate of interest for a given number of time-periods. Symbolically if

FV = Future value
PV = Initial outlay
r = Periodic rate of interest (expressed as a decimal)
n = Number of periods for which the sum is invested

then
$$FV = PV\,(1 + r)^n \tag{1}$$

For simplicity we will assume that interest is paid annually, in other words we assume *annual compounding.* In practice examples are commonly found in semi-annual compounding (banks, building societies, may pay interest twice a year) right down to daily compounding. Formula (1) applies to all these cases provided r is the semi-annual, daily, or whatever rate of interest, and n is the number of half-years, days, etc. We consider the important case of continuous compounding in an Appendix.

Han

Your friend Mr Han approaches you and says

> My father is giving me £5,000 in two years' time. The trouble is I want to sail round the world now. If you'll just lend me the £5,000, I'll return it when I get back in two years.

Does this seem a good deal to you? Probably not. For one thing Mr Han might easily perish in the Magellan Straits. But ignoring this risk, by lending the money you are prevented from investing it at a real rate of interest elsewhere. The *opportunity cost* of the loan is the interest you could earn elsewhere.

You decide to calculate the amount you would need in two years to compensate for the loss of £5,000 now, the future value of the £5,000. You discover you could invest at 7%.

$$\begin{aligned} FV &= £5{,}000\,(1 + .07)^2 \\ &= £5{,}725 \end{aligned}$$

Clearly £5,725 in two years is equivalent in value to £5,000 now. If the going rate of interest is 7%, no one would accept less than £5,000 now for £5,725 in two years, and no one would offer more.

Discounting

Having established the link between a present sum and a future sum, the logic can be reversed to find the *present value* (PV) of a known future amount. For the situation we know FV, and wish to find its present value, PV we can arrange (1)

$$PV = \frac{FV}{(1 + r)^n} \tag{2}$$

Jamila

Jamila wants to have £1,000 in three years time. She can invest at 9%. How much does she need to invest now?

To solve this problem we merely have to find the PV of £1,000 received in three years' time,

$$\text{where PV} = \frac{1{,}000}{(1 + .09)^3}$$

$$= \frac{1{,}000}{1.295} = £772.20$$

You can confirm that £772.20, compounded at 9% for three years yields £1,000. The procedure we just adopted was unwieldy in one respect. £1,000 was multiplied by $\frac{1}{(1 + .09)^3}$, which is called the *discount factor*, and which had to be calculated. Tables of these factors have been calculated, and are reproduced at the end of the book. They are called *discount tables*, or *present value tables*, and they give the PV of £1 received after n years at interest rate r. To find the value of $\frac{1}{(1 + .09)^3}$ inspect the 9% column and three-year row of the table: the factor is .772.

Vladimir

Vladimir will inherit £20,000 in six years' time. He wants to sell the right to his inheritance to Estragon. What is it worth now, if the interest rate is 14%? The 14%, six-year discount factor is .456, so the present value of the inheritance is

PV = £2,000 × .456 = £9,120

Another piece of terminology: the % rate used for discounting, 14% in the previous example, is commonly called the *discount rate.*

Annuities

Suppose one wants to find the present value of an equal sum of £200 received *each year* for the next five years, discounting at 10%. This can be calculated as follows:

Year	*1*	*2*	*3*	*4*	*5*	Total
Cash (£)	200	200	200	200	200	
10% discount factors	.909	.826	.751	.683	.621	
present value	200 × .909	200 × .826	200 × .751	200 × .683	200 × .621	
	182	165	150	137	124	£758

This is correct, but it would have been quicker to sum the discount factors then multiply the total by £200, saving computations. Even better, tables exist which do this: they are reprinted at the end of the book. Using *annuity tables* to perform the above calculation we inspect the 10% column, five-year row: the annuity discount factor is 3.791. (You can check this, .909 + .826 + .751 + .683 + .621 = 3.790, there is a small rounding difference.)

So the present value of the annuity is £200 × 3.791 = £758.

If a discount factor is wanted for a run of equal cash flows, but starting some time in the future, this can be found by combining annuity factors. Suppose we wish to find the present value of an annual amount of £300 to be received in the 12th to the 16th years from now, with a 10% discount rate

16-year, 10% annuity factor	7.824
subtract the 11-year, 10% annuity factor	(6.495)
12 to 16-year factor	1.329
So the present value is £300 × 1.329	£ 399

II VALUING PROJECTS: NPV AND IRR

In project appraisal we want to find the present value of the whole bundle of cash flows, positive and negative, which result from undertaking the project. The term *net present value* (NPV) is used for this. If C_t is the cash flow (+ or −) in period t, and r is the required periodic return, then the logic of discounted cash flow suggests that:

$$NPV = \sum_{t=0}^{n} \frac{C_t}{(1+r)^t} \tag{3}$$

Discounting cash flows enables us to take account in project decisions of the fact that the cash tied up in projects has a time-related cost. It implies a decision rule: *accept all projects with a positive NPV.* NPV is the time-adjusted equivalent of 'contribution' – it is the contributions yielded by a project in different time-periods, discounted at the cost of capital and summed. By discounting we now also ensure that the capital tied up in the project is fully costed. Moreover the concept of cost remains 'opportunity cost': r is the investors' opportunity cost of capital, the return they could get on the best alternative investment. The NPV of a project measures the amount of cash the owners could immediately withdraw as a result of the project: the immediate increase in the owners' wealth associated with owning the project. In the next chapter we show the theoretical foundation of the NPV decision rule – why choosing projects with a positive NPV is the policy that maximises shareholders' wealth.

The internal rate of return

The internal rate of return (IRR) measures the yield of a set of cash flows in percentage terms and is the discount rate which makes the NPV of the cash flows equal zero. Mathematically it is R in the following formula, where C_t is cash flow in period t and n is the life of the project.

$$NPV = \sum_{t=0}^{n} \frac{C_t}{(1+R)^t} = 0 \tag{4}$$

Consider the project that comprises an initial outlay of £12,500 followed by four annual receipts of £4,000. We can find the IRR by repeated solving with different discount rates in order to find the discount rate that gives NPV = 0. Try 8% first.

	t = 0	1	2	3	4	Total
cash flows (£)	(12,500)	4,000	4,000	4,000	4,000	
8% discount factor	1		3.312			
present value	(12,500)		13,248			NPV = £748

Discounting at 8% yields a positive NPV of £748, so a higher rate is needed to reduce the impact of the future inflows. Try 10% and 12%.

We derive the following results:

Discount rate	*NPV*
8%	748
10%	180
12%	(352)

Hence the IRR is between 10% and 12%. We can estimate it with greater accuracy by *interpolating* between 10% and 12% thus:

$$\text{estimate rate} = 10\% + \underset{\substack{\uparrow \\ \text{interval between} \\ 10\% \text{ and } 12\%}}{2\%} \times \underset{\substack{\uparrow \\ \text{distance along the interval} \\ \text{which gives NPV} = 0}}{\frac{180}{180 + 352}}$$

$$= 10.7\%$$

This type of solution method is called an *iterative* process. It involves converging on a solution by informed trial and error. In fact, there is no other way of finding the IRR. Manual solution of IRR can be very time consuming, but the task is the sort that computers and calculators thrive on.

The relationship between the IRR and the NPV of a project is as follows:
NPV is the project's value using the cost of capital as the discount rate.
IRR is the discount rate which makes a project's NPV zero.

The general relationship between the cost of capital and value

With most commodities that are bought and sold the market price is easy to determine, the total payment is agreed by the parties when the transaction is made. But with finance the price – which is the return to the supplier, and the cost of capital to the user – usually needs some calculating. This is because a financing contract involves the right to *use* an amount of finance for a limited or unlimited period, so the return or cost is a *rate per unit of time*. The payment will consist of cash flows in different time-periods, and these may not be fully specified at the time the contract is made. In the case of equity the payment is an uncertain stream of dividends, with a final payment in the form of the proceeds from selling the shares or a liquidation dividend.

In general the relationship between the present outlay of finance, V_o, the subsequent inflows of cash, C_t, and the cost or return, r, when the financing contract lasts for n periods, is given by the present-value formula:

$$V_o = \sum_{t=0}^{n} \frac{C_t}{(1 + r)^t} \tag{5}$$

If we know the present value, V_o, and the future cash flows, C_t, we can find the actual return, r. Conversely if we know the C_t associated with a contract and if we know the *required* return, which is the cost of capital, r, we can value it. As always in finance the central problem is knowing the future, in this case, the future cash flows, C_t. Most of the formulae and rules of thumb we encounter below simply reflect different attempts to tackle this problem by making assumptions about the future values of C_t.

III VALUING SHARES

The dividend valuation model

The return to a shareholder from owning shares has two components: *dividends* and *capital gains*. Suppose I buy a share today for 100p with the expectation of getting a dividend of 10p in a year's time, and then selling it for 105p. I can find my equity return, r_e, from holding the share as follows:

$$100 = \frac{10 + 105}{(1 + r_e)}$$

$$1 + r_e = \frac{115}{100}$$

$$r_e = 15\%$$

In general, if S_o and S_1 are the values of the share at t_o and t_1 and DIV_1 is the dividend received at t_1

$$S_o = \frac{DIV_1 + S_1}{(1 + r_e)} \qquad (6)$$

rearranging, to find the return in terms of the dividend-yield and capital gain, we get:

$$r_e = \frac{DIV + S_1}{S_o} - 1$$

$$= \frac{DIV_1}{S_o} + \frac{S_1 - S_o}{S_o}$$

What determines the current share price, S_o? The share in the previous example gave a dividend yield of 10% and a capital gain of 5%, so r_e was 10% + 5% = 15%. But just suppose investors would have been happy with a 10% return – the return they could get on investments of similar risk elsewhere. In this case the share is under-valued and demand would bid up its price until it gave a return of 10% too. People who had the same expectations about its future value and dividends, and had the same required return of 10% would be prepared to pay 104.5p for a share like this, since $104.5p = \frac{10p + 105p}{1 + .10}$, so in an efficient market 100p would not be an equilibrium price.

This does not mean that all shares always yield the market's required return, *ex post*. An efficient market sets share prices to do this *ex ante*, but these prices reflect investors' best guesses about the future. As the future unfolds it often turns out in ways investors did not anticipate.

We have seen that the present value of a share held for a year depends on the investors' required return r_e, which is their opportunity cost of the capital invested in the share, i e

$$S_o = \frac{DIV_1 + S_1}{(1 + r_e)}$$

What determines S_1? Clearly the next person to buy the share is buying the right to future dividends and a subsequent capital gain too. Suppose she in turn receives a dividend after one year of DIV_2, then sells for S_2. The share's value to this investor at t_1 will be, similarly,

$$S_1 = \frac{DIV_2 + S_2}{(1 + r_e)} \tag{7}$$

Substituting (7) into (6) we get

$$S_o = \frac{DIV_1}{(1 + r_e)} + \frac{DIV_2}{(1 + r_e)^2} + \frac{S_2}{(1 + r_e)^2}$$

Pursuing this argument indefinitely we can see that the value of a share is the present value of its future dividend stream summed to infinity,

$$S_o = \sum_{t=o}^{\infty} \frac{DIV_t}{(1 + r_e)^t} \tag{8}$$

Expression (8) is the *dividend valuation model* which is our fundamental share valuation model. If the firm is liquidated at some point, rather than surviving indefinitely, we can still use the model – in this case there is a final liquidation dividend and subsequent dividends are zero.

It is useful to see that the valuation of the firm is simply an extension of the valuation of individual projects. This should be no great surprise; the firm is effectively a bundle of projects, and a project is simply a part, existing or potential, of a firm. Whereas in project appraisal we find the present value of the cash flows generated by a single project, the dividend valuation model is simply finding the present value of the firm as a whole. The big difference, however, is in the quality of the information being used. In project appraisal the valuation is done by insiders with best access to information for estimating likely cash flows. Share valuation is usually done with highly aggregated information, and often by outsiders.

Another problem with the dividend valuation model is the immense quantity of information apparently needed to service it. Rather than being limited to the life span of one project, it sums to infinity. To find S given r_e, or to find r_e given S, appears to require forecasts of the dividends on the share in *all* future time-periods. These will depend not only on the future internal performance of the firm, but on external factors such as future levels of demand, the behaviour of other firms, and the macroeconomic environment, all forecast into the distant future! We seem to need the future history of the world to value one share. We do not know the future of the world but we do need to value shares, so we have to make the best use of the information we have got. One way we might make life easier is by working to a *time-horizon*. The idea of a dividend stream to infinity is fairly daunting, but discounting means that more distant dividends become relatively insignificant. Table I shows what proportion of the value of a perpetuity, which is a constant amount received each year for ever, is accounted for by the earlier years under different discount rates. These proportions are easy to find using annuity tables. We can see that if we cut the calculation off at 7 years we would get 29% of the value when the discount rate is 5%, but 62% of it is 15%. Bearing in mind that we are allowing no growth in the cash flow so the discount rate is effectively a 'real' rate, then 5% may be the more realistic. Either way the earlier cash flows predominate in valuation.

In practice financial analysts tend to respond to the information problem by valuing shares using *dividend-yields* and *price-earnings ratios* (P/E). These express share price as a multiple of current dividends and earnings, and analysts develop a view on the right multiple from studying other firms and industry averages. As we show next, dividend-yield and P/E are closely-related to the dividend valuation model and can be derived from it by making simplifying assumptions about what dividends are going to be.

Table I Percentage of the value of a perpetuity contributed by different years			
Discount rate	*5%*	*10%*	*15%*
first 1 year(s)	5%	9%	13%
2	9%	17%	24%
3	4%	25%	34%
4	18%	32%	43%
5	22%	38%	50%
7	29%	49%	62%
10	39%	61%	75%

Perpetuities and constant growth models

If we *assume* that dividends will grow at a constant rate, g, indefinitely then the dividend valuation model can be re-expressed

$$S_o = \sum_{t=o}^{\infty} \frac{DIV_t}{(1+r_e)^t} = \sum_{t=o}^{\infty} \frac{DIV_o(1+g)^t}{(1+r_e)^t}$$

Now *so long as* $r_e > g$ the sum of this infinite series is[1]

$$S_o = \frac{DIV_1}{r_e - g} \tag{9}$$

Assuming a constant g, less than r_e, the value of the share is the first-year dividend capitalised using the 'dividend-yield', which is $r_e - g$, the required return less the growth rate in dividends. Rearranging (9) we get

$$r_e = \frac{DIV_1}{S_o} + g \tag{10}$$

So the cost of equity is the dividend yield plus the expected growth rate in dividends. This result is often known as the 'Gordon growth model' following an early statement of it in Gordon and Shapiro (1956).

Globule Ltd

Globule Ltd, is expected to pay a dividend of 20p per share this year. The market's required return from a firm of Globule's risk is 12%. We forecast that Globule will maintain an annual growth in dividend of 4%.

So DIV_1 = 20p, r_e = .12, g = .04, and the value of a Globule share, S_o, is

$$S_o = \frac{20p}{.12 - .04} = 250p$$

1 The proofs of this and the subsequent theorem are in Appendix A to this chapter.

Cum div and ex div values

We say a share is 'cum div' when its owner also gets the right to the latest declared dividend, and it goes 'ex div' when that right lapses. When we set up the dividend valuation model we assumed the first dividend would be received one year hence, and since it is derived from the dividend valuation model, the Gordon growth model makes the same assumption too. Hence, we are implicitly finding an 'ex div' share price. Suppose we want to value a share 'cum div'. Then we simply add the latest dividend, DIV_o, to the 'ex div' value:

$$\text{'cum div' value} = \frac{DIV_1}{r_{e-g}} + DIV_o$$

If we find the latest declared dividend on a Globule share was 18p then the 'cum div' value of Globule is 250p + 18p = 268p.

Price-earnings ratio

Another commonly-used relationship in share valuation is the price-earnings (P/E) ratio where

$$P/E = \frac{\text{share price}}{\text{earnings per share}} = \frac{S}{E}$$

The relationship of the P/E ratio to the dividend valuation model is not quite so direct as it was with dividend-yield. To examine it we will make two new assumptions. Instead of assuming a constant growth rate, g, in dividends *assume*

(a) the firm maintains a constant ratio of dividends to earnings, or 'payout ratio' which for convenience we will describe as (1 − b), where b is the ratio of retentions to earnings; and it is entirely financed by these retentions;
(b) the firm can invest retained earnings in projects within the firm which have an internal rate of return, R.

One useful result follows immediately – if we assume a constant payout ratio the growth rate in earnings is the same as the growth rate in dividends. This must be so, since DIV is a constant proportion, 1 − b, of E at all times. The new assumptions are rather powerful since they define the earnings of the firm in all future time-periods! Suppose the firm has earnings of E_1 in year 1. Earnings in the year 2, E_2, will be E_1 (since the firm continues to earn the same yield on existing capital) PLUS the return R on that part of E_1 that was reinvested, bE_1.

so $E_1 = E_1$

$E_2 = E_1 + bE_1R = E_1(1 + bR)$

similarly $E_3 = E_2 + bE_2R$

$= E_2(1 + bR) = E_1(1 + bR)^2$

$E_4 = \ldots\ldots\ldots = E_1(1 + bR)^3$, etc

Evidently the growth rate in E is a constant, bR. Since we saw that dividends and earnings growth rates are identical if there is a constant payout ratio, then

$$bR = g \qquad (11)$$

In other words an assumption about a constant payout ratio, and a given internal rate of return are sufficient to define a constant growth rate in dividends. We defined

$$DIV = (1 - b)E \qquad (12)$$

Substituting (11), (12) into the dividend-yield formula, $S_o = \dfrac{DIV_1}{r_e - g}$

we get
$$S_o = \frac{(1-b)E}{r_e - bR} \tag{13}$$

This defines the value of the firm in terms of current earnings, the payout ratio, the internal rate of return of the firm, and the required return from the firm. Next consider the special case where the firm's internal rate of return equals the required return from the firm. If $R = r_e$, (13) reduces to

$$S_o = \frac{(1-b)E}{(1-b)r_e} = \frac{E}{r_e}$$

Hence
$$r_e = \frac{E}{S_o} \tag{14}$$

The ratio of earnings to price, the reciprocal of the price-earnings ratio, measures the cost of equity.

To summarise, if we assume a constant payout ratio and a constant internal rate of return it follows that the earnings and dividend growth rates are identical and constant. In the special case where $R = r_e$, we can value the share by capitalising earnings at the cost of equity rate and $\dfrac{E}{S_0}$ is a good measure of r_e.

Fisher-Hirshleifer

This is a convenient place to anticipate a fundamental result in finance which we prove formally in the next chapter, the Fisher-Hirshleifer theorem that the all-equity firm should use the investor's required return as its discount rate for projects. Recall that there are only two things a firm can do with its earnings, pay a dividend or reinvest them.[2] If the firm is maximising shareholder wealth it will choose the policy which has the highest value to shareholders.

Suppose a firm is trying to decide whether to pay a dividend of DIV or reinvest the money, and assume we are in a simple Fisher-Hirshleifer world with no taxes. The value to the shareholder of the dividend, DIV, paid at time t_o is simply DIV since this is the value of the alternative investment that he can make with the money. The value of DIV reinvested in the firm is the present value of the infinite stream of future dividends generated by the extra investment. By the end of the first year the DIV investment will yield earnings of $R \times DIV$ of which the proportion $(1 - b)$ will be distributed, and b reinvested. By the end of the second year the earnings from the initial DIV investment will have grown to $R \times DIV\ (1 + bR)$ of which the proportion $(1 - b)$ will be distributed, and so forth. Hence, the reinvestment will generate a stream of dividends which will be valued thus:

$$\text{Value of reinvestment} = \frac{(1-b)RDIV}{1+r_e} + \frac{(1-b)RDIV(1+bR)}{(1+r_e)^2} + \frac{(1-b)RDIV(1+bR)^2}{(1+r_e)^3} \ldots \infty$$

As we show in Appendix A to this chapter this infinite series sums to

$$\frac{(1-b)\,R.DIV}{r_e - bR} \tag{15}$$

2 Funds held 'idle' in the firm are simply being reinvested at zero return.

The shareholders will prefer reinvestment when the value of reinvestment exceeds the value of the dividend i e

$$\frac{(1-b)\,R.DIV}{r_e - bR} > DIV$$

Dividing each side by DIV, and multiplying out the top line of the left-hand side the criterion becomes

$$\frac{R - bR}{r_e - bR} > 1$$

Clearly when $R = r_e$ the shareholder is indifferent between the two policies – he values them equally. He prefers reinvestment when $R > r_e$ and he prefers a dividend when $r_e > R$. Hence the firm will maximise the shareholders' wealth by using r_e as the cut-off rate for projects.

A closer look at growth

In deriving the dividend-yield and P/E ratio we saw that the question of valuing shares hinges on 'g' – the growth rate in dividends. This is no surprise since the growth rate is simply a compact way of describing the future time-profile of dividends, which is the great unknown in valuation. Let us take a closer look at growth.

'Growth' has a virile sound to it, but recall that $bR = g$. Any firm with $b > o$, and $R > o$ will have positive growth, even though it may be retaining hardly anything and the internal rate of return R may be very low. If this sounds surprising it is because we are forgetting that accounting earnings are net of depreciation. Hopefully any necessary amounts for replacement, to maintain the productive capacity of the firm, have been deducted in measuring earnings so that *any* reinvestment augments the firm's productive capacity.

In Table II we show the growth rate and value of a firm with current earnings, E, of 1,000 and a required return, r_e, of 10%, under various assumptions about internal rate of return and retention policy. The value of the firm in each case is calculated using expression (15) above.

Table II Growth rate and value when £ = 1,000, r_e = 10%

	1 *Internal rate of return* R	2 *Retention policy* b	3 *Growth rate* $g = bR$	4 *Value of the firm* $= \frac{(1-b)E}{r_e - bR}$
		.25	1.25%	8,571
	5%	.5	2.5%	6,667
		.75	3.75%	4,000
E = 1,000		.25	2.5%	10,000
	10%	.5	5.0%	10,000
r_e = 10%		.75	7.5%	10,000
		.25	3.75%	12,000
	15%	.5	7.5%	20,000
		.75	11.25%	∞

Several things are worth noting in Table II.

— If $R = r_e$ shareholders are indifferent between reinvestment and dividends, and the value of the firm is £10,000 in each case. This follows since when $R = r_e$ the value of the firm reduces to $\frac{E}{r_e}$ which is independent of b. In this case $\frac{E}{r_e} = \frac{1,000}{10\%} = 10,000$.

— If $R < r_e$ then the more the firm reinvests, the worse off the shareholder is. But if $R > r_e$, then the reverse holds and it is in the shareholders' interests that the firm reinvest as much as possible. In the first three rows of Table II the firm is achieving growth through reinvestment but it is 'bad' growth, since it is bought at the expense of shareholders.

— With .75 retention and 15% internal return, the value of the firm approaches infinity! This embarrassing result arises because the value is the sum of an infinite series which is growing faster (at 11.75%) than the rate at which we discount it (10%). In other words we have broken the condition of the 'dividend-yield model' – that $r_e > g$. Further on, we consider whether it is feasible that a firm could have $g > r_e$ indefinitely.

Final thoughts on growth rates

We have talked widely about using g in valuation. But the 'random-walk' literature has suggested that annual earnings cannot be forecast and that the time-series behaviour of earnings follows a random-walk-with-drift process where the 'drift' is a common growth factor across all firms.

We can reconcile this apparent paradox in two ways. First, even in a random-walk context it still makes sense to try and forecast the general 'drift' factor for all firms and a specific growth rate when we can. Second, empirical research in this area can only work with a narrow range of published data – viz the past earnings series of firms. In practice the analyst has a great deal more information available – detailed information about the firm gleaned from close scrutiny and close contact with the firm's management. Having said this, the random-walk results provide a valuable caution, a reminder that the future is inherently unknowable and the rather neat and shiny models described in textbooks do nothing to change that. At best they provide a framework for marshalling our thoughts.

We cannot use the dividend-yield model when $g > r_e$, since it yields infinite share values. In practice though, we regularly come across firms which achieve, over periods of years, very high annual growth at rates which must be above their cost of capital. This is often interpreted as a weakness in the Gordon model, though of course the dividend valuation model also yields an infinite solution where $r_e < g$. The problem is with the assumption of $g \geqslant r_e$ *indefinitely*.

We know that $g = bR$, and we expect that $0 \leqslant b \leqslant 1$. So we will get infinite solutions – the valuation models will 'diverge' rather than converge – when the firm can maintain internal returns, R, which are sufficiently above r that even the proportion bR is greater than r. Hence $R > r_e$ is not sufficient on its own for $g > r_e$. In Table I we saw that only when an R of 15% was combined with a retention of .75 did the value of the firm become infinite. With a b of .25 the firm would need to maintain a return of over 40% to yield $g > r_e$. But there are compelling reasons (apart from a desire to preserve the reputation of the valuation model!) why this cannot last.

First, as the firm gets relentlessly larger, it will need to find more and more projects yielding the high R to service its growth, yet because of what we might call diminishing marginal efficiency of investment, this cannot happen. Faced with a variety of potential projects the rational firm chooses first the ones that yield the highest return, and once the potential of these products and markets has been exhausted, it turns to others. For a firm to find a return of R wherever it turns there must be *constant* returns throughout the economy. But if there is a constant return throughout the economy it must be r_e!

We can make this argument from the other end, in terms of r_e. 'r_e' is the shareholders' required return from the firm, based on the returns available elsewhere in the market. But as our cuckoo-like firm relentlessly expanded, it would start to dominate the market and eventually swamp it. Under the influence of our firm's returns the market r_e will rise and tend towards R, preventing S from ever reaching ∞. In any case we expect that firms and projects yielding excess returns to attract competition, which drives returns to a 'normal' level.

In practice, what research exists on the topic suggests that some firms do maintain above-normal returns for long periods, yet they remain finite in size and do not swamp the economy. We must presume that they do this by containing their reinvestment rate in the long term so that $r_e > bR$.

If there are firms with $bR > r_e$ for a limited period we need to know how to value them. Consider a firm with 'super-growth' of g_s for three years which then reverts to a normal growth rate g. We know that from year 3 onward the firm will have constant growth, so we can find its value at $t = 3$ as $S_3 = \frac{DIV_4}{r_e - g}$. To find its value today we value this and the first three years' dividends.

$$S_o = \frac{DIV_1}{(1 + r_e)} + \frac{DIV_1\,(1 + g_s)}{(1 + r_e)^2} + \frac{DIV_1\,(1 + g_s)^2 + S_3}{(1 + r_e)^3}$$

Sparkler plc

For example, suppose Sparkler plc is expected to pay a dividend of 40p per share at the end of this year, and to increase this by 50% per annum for the next two years, after which it will settle back to 5% growth. The required return is 15%.

The dividends for the next four years will be

Yr	1	2	3	4
DIV	40p	60p	90p	94.5p

The share value at the end of year 3 will be

$$S_3 = \frac{94.5}{.15 - .5} = £9.45$$

Today's share value is

$$S_o = \frac{40p}{1.15} + \frac{60p}{(1.15)^2} + \frac{90p + £9.45}{(1.15)^3} = \underline{\underline{£7.60}}$$

Summary: A strategy for valuing shares

We can assemble what we know about the arithmetic of share valuation into a strategy:

1 If you can estimate it, use the dividend valuation model:

$$S_o = \sum_{t=o}^{\infty} \frac{DIV_t}{(1 + r_e)^t}$$

Note that we do not actually need to estimate dividends to infinitely. Later dividends will be discounted to insignificance, so we will not go too far wrong by working to a finite horizon.

2 If our best guess is that dividends will grow at a constant rate g, use the dividend-yield formula:

$$S_o = \frac{DIV_1}{r_e - g}$$

This will give the right answer so long as g is constant and maintainable. But we know that $g > r_e$ is *not* maintainable.

3 If the firm has a g_s which is only maintainable for n periods we can use the formula for a limited period of super-growth

$$S_o = \frac{DIV_1}{(1 + r_e)} + \frac{DIV_2}{(1 + r_e)^2} \cdots\cdots \frac{DIV_n}{(1 + r_e)^n} + \frac{DIV_{n+1}}{(r - g)(1 + r_e)^n}$$

4 A study of earnings is useful. If b and R are constant and maintainable we can use them to estimate g, since $g = bR$.

Also, compare the earnings price ratio $\frac{E}{S}$, to the dividend-yield estimate r_e. It will give a good estimate if $r_e = R$. If $\frac{E}{S}$ is significantly less than r_e we can expect $R > r_e$. This may signal a g that is not maintainable.

IV VALUING BONDS

The value of a share was the present value of the future stream of cash flows to the investor. We can use the same approach in valuing debt. In the simplest case where the firm raises a loan D and agrees to pay a constant annual *coupon* or interest charge, C, and to repay an amount P after n periods, then

$$D = \sum_{t=0}^{n} \frac{C}{(1 + r_d)^t} + \frac{P}{(1 + r_d)^n} \qquad (16)$$

As with equity we can use this expression either way round. The investor who knows her required return from debt, r_d, can value a debt contract using (16), and the firm which observes the value, D, of its debt can calculate its cost of capital using the formula.

The big problem in valuing shares was uncertainty about future dividends; but in valuing debt there should be less uncertainty. The cash flows are known, save for the risk of default which will guide the investor's choice of required return.

Othello plc

Suppose Othello plc has £1 million of loan-stock in issue, redeemable on 31.12.2005 at a premium of 10%. The loan-stock bears an 8% coupon and interest is payable at the end of each calendar year. How should the market evaluate the loan-stock on 1.1.1994 if the required return on comparable risk loan-stock is 12%?

Using equation (16) we can find the value of the loan-stock as

$$D = \sum_{t=0}^{11} \frac{80{,}000}{(1 + .12)^t} + \frac{1{,}100{,}000}{(1 + .12)^{11}}$$
$$= (80{,}000 \times 5.937) + (1{,}100{,}000 \times .287)$$
$$= £790{,}660$$

Loan-stocks are issued with a nominal value and the coupon interest rate will be expressed as a percentage of that value. But the nominal value will not necessarily be the sum raised or repaid at the end. Loan-stock is often issued at a *discount* and redeemed at a *premium*. Either way, the *value* of a debt contract once issued reflects current interest rates in the market. If market rates fall after issue, the value of the security and all other securities in the market, will rise, and vice versa.

The Othello example assumed a known and constant annual coupon, but there are other possibilities. Short-term finance such as bank overdrafts typically has a variable interest rate related to the bank's base lending rate. Long-term loans can be at a variable rate too, though these are not yet common – an example is in the 'index-bond' we discuss in the next section. Secondly, even when the schedule of interest payments is predetermined it may not be constant through the duration of the loan. It is common for institutional lenders to tailor repayment schedules to the tax and financing needs of the client. Sometimes payments may be stepped up or down, 'rolled-up' until the end or 'front-end loaded'. Thirdly, interest is more likely to be half-yearly, quarterly or monthly than annual. Equation (16) can be modified to accommodate this variety.

Coupon yields and redemption yields

In the case of a perpetual debt, $n = \infty$ and the loan is never repaid, so

$$D = \sum_{t=0}^{\infty} \frac{C}{(1 + r_d)^t}$$

which, summing the infinite series, gives $D = \frac{C}{r_d}$, so $r_d = \frac{C}{D}$

So in this case the so-called 'coupon yield', $\frac{C}{D}$, which would be our instinctive estimate of the cost of debt, does indeed tell us the cost. But otherwise the cost of debt has two components, as in expression (16), the cost of the annual interest payment, and the cost of eventually repaying or 'redeeming' the loan. We call the cost of redeemable debt calculated as in (16) and taking into account the final repayment of the loan, the 'redemption yield'. Clearly the redemption yield is the correct estimate of the cost of a debt contract of finite duration, and is different from the coupon yield, C/D. But the longer the duration of the loan and the further away is redemption the closer the redemption yield converges on the coupon yield, and the more faith we can put in the coupon rate as an approximation of r_d.

Taxation

A key difference between debt and equity is in the tax treatment of interest and dividends. The Revenue treats interest payments as an allowable expense against profit. If the corporation tax rate is 35% the effective cost of debt is only .65 of the nominal return received by the supplier of finance. If the firm pays £100 interest, its taxable profit is reduced by £100 and its CT bill by £35. So the effective cost of the interest is £65. But dividends paid to equity are treated as a *distribution* of profit rather than as a business *expense*, so dividends are not tax deductible.

If the firm is using the debt valuation formula to find its cost of debt capital when it has a marginal rate of corporation tax of T, we need to modify equation (16) thus:

$$D = \sum_{t=0}^{n} \frac{(1 - T)C}{(1 + r'_d)^t} + \frac{P}{(1 + r'_d)^n}$$

And in the case of a perpetuity we can rearrange to get

$$r'_d = \frac{(1-T)C}{D} = (1-T)\frac{C}{D} \tag{17}$$

Now r'_d is the after-tax cost of debt.

In fact (17) is rather inexact, since it ignores the lags in tax payments. Firms pay their corporation tax with a lag, L, so they suffer the same lag in capturing the benefits of any tax deductibility. Developing (17), the general model for the cost of debt with lags in tax payments is

$$D = \sum_{t=0}^{n} \frac{C_t}{(1+r'_d)^t} - \sum_{t=0}^{n} \frac{C_t.T}{(1+r'_d)^{t+L}} + \frac{P}{(1+r'_d)^n}$$

where the second term on the RHS reflects the lagged tax relief on the interest payment.

APPENDIX A SOME DERIVATIONS

1 The 'Gordon growth model'

Assuming a constant rate of growth in dividends, g, the dividend valuation model becomes

$$S_o = \sum_{t=0}^{\infty} \frac{DIV_0(1+g)^t}{(1+r_e)^t},$$

expanding, we get:

$$S_o = \frac{DIV_o(1+g)}{(1+r_e)} + \frac{DIV_o(1+g)^2}{(1+r_e)^2} + \ldots\ldots \frac{DIV_o(1+g)^\infty}{(1+r_e)} \tag{1}$$

Multiplying (1) by $\frac{1+r_e}{1+g}$ gives

$$S_o\frac{(1+r_e)}{(1+g)} = DIV_o + \frac{DIV_o(1+g)}{(r+r_e)} \ldots\ldots \frac{DIV_o(1+g)^\infty}{(1+r_e)\infty} \tag{2}$$

Subtracting (1) from (2) gives:

$$S_o\frac{(1+r_e)}{(1+g)} - S_o = DIV_o - DIV_o\frac{(1+g)^\infty}{(1+r_e)^\infty}$$

If we *assume* $r_e > g$, then $DIV_o\frac{(1+g)\infty}{(1+r_e)\infty} = 0$, so

$$S_o\frac{(1+r_e)}{(1+g)} - S_o = DIV_o$$

$$S_o\frac{(1+r_e)-(1+g)}{1+g} = DIV_o$$

$$S_o(r_e - g) = DIV_o(1+g)$$

and since $DIV_1 = DIV_o(1+g)$

$$S_o = \frac{DIV_1}{r_e - g}$$

2 Expression for the value of reinvestment

$$\text{Value of investment} = \frac{(1-b)RDIV}{1+r_e} + \frac{(1-b)RDIV(1+bR)}{(1+r_e)^2} + \frac{(1-b)RDIV(1+bR)^3}{(1+r_e)^3} + \ldots\ldots\ldots\ldots\infty$$

$$= \frac{(1-b)RDIV}{1+r_e}\left[1 + \frac{1+bR}{1+r_e} + \left(\frac{1+bR}{1+r_e}\right)^2 + \left(\frac{1+bR}{1+r_e}\right)^3 + \ldots\ldots\infty\right]$$

$$= \frac{(1-b)RDIV}{1+r_e}\left[\sum_{i=0}^{\infty} x^i\right] \text{ where } x = \frac{1+bR}{1+r_e}$$

Now for any $|x|<1$, $\left[\sum_{i=0}^{\infty} x^i\right] = \frac{1}{1-x}$, so assuming $bR<r_e$

$$= \frac{(1-b)RDIV}{1+r_e}\cdot\frac{1}{1-x}$$

$$= \frac{(1-b)RDIV}{1-r_e}\cdot\frac{1+r_e}{r_e-bR}$$

$$= \frac{(1-b)RDIV}{r_e-bR}$$

APPENDIX B CONTINUOUS COMPOUNDING

When FV is the future value of a sum, and PV the present value, r is the annual rate of interest and n the number of years for which the sum is invested, then

$$FV = PV\,(1+r)^n$$

However, if interest is paid twice a year:

$$FV = PV\left(1+\frac{r}{2}\right)^{2n}$$

If four times:

$$FV = PV\left(1+\frac{r}{4}\right)^{4n}$$

In general if interest is compounded m times per year:

$$FV = PV\left(1+\frac{r}{m}\right)^{mn}$$

One important case is the one where m tends to infinity, and thus interest is compounded continuously. To help to interpret this case we recall from mathematics that the value 'e' is defined as the limiting value of $\left(1+\frac{1}{m}\right)^m$ as m tends to infinity.

$$e = \lim_{m\to\infty}\left(1+\frac{1}{m}\right)^m = 2.718$$

substituting e in the previous expression gives

$$FV = PVe^{rn}$$

and conversely

$$PV = FVe^{-rn}$$

It should be clear that e^{rn} is the continuous compounding equivalent of $(1 + r)^n$. Continuous compounding is interesting in several ways. One great virtue is that value becomes a continuous function of time, so that value functions are differentiable with respect to time. For this purpose it is worth noting that

$$\frac{d}{dn}(e^{-rn}) = -re^{-rn}$$

Since e forms the basis of *natural logarithms*, future values are easy to evaluate using natural logs. The future value of £1 continuously compounded for n years at r% is

$$FV = e^{rn}$$

taking logs of each side

$$\begin{aligned} \ln FV &= rn. \ln e \\ &= rn \text{ since } \ln e = 1 \end{aligned}$$

If £100 is to be continuously compounded at 8% per annum for three years

$$\begin{aligned} \ln FV = rn &= .08 \times 3 \\ &= .24 \end{aligned}$$

If we look up natural log tables we find that the number with a natural log of .24 lies between 1.27, which has a natural log of .23902, and 1.28 which has a natural log of .24686. Interpolating we get $\frac{98}{98 + 686} = 0.125$, so the number we seek is 1.27125. Hence in three years at 8% £100 will compound to £127.13. Conversely the present value of £100 received in three years at 8% is $\frac{£100}{1.27125} = £78.66$.

In many situations it *is* more realistic to assume that cash is received continuously throughout the period, but even if this is not the case the shorter the periods, and the lower the interest rate, the less significant is the difference between continuous and periodic compounding. For example the following are the present values generated by various compounding periods of £100 invested at 8% per annum for three years:

compounding period	*present value (£)*
annual	79.38
six months	79.03
three months	78.85
continuous	78.66

In summary, the present value, PV, of a future sum, FV, received at time n, is given by $PV = \frac{FV}{(1 + r)^n}$ under discrete compounding and $PV = FVe^{-rn}$ under continuous compounding.

REFERENCES AND BIBLIOGRAPHY

Gordon, M J, and Shapiro, E — 'Capital Equipment Analysis: The Required Rate of Profit', Management Science, Oct 1956, pp 102–110.

Mueller, D C — 'The Persistence of Profits Above the Norm', Economica, Nov 1977, pp 369–380.

Sharpe, W F — *Investments* (1990) Prentice-Hall, Englewood-Cliffs, New Jersey.

QUESTIONS

1 I desire to have £5,000 in four years' time. The interest rate is 11%. How much money do I need to invest now? If interest rates are 13% how much do I need?

2 If interest rates are 12% how much would I expect to pay for an annuity of £2,500 per year for the next five years?

How would the answer be different if I want the annuity to start in five years for the subsequent five years?

3 A project has the following expected cash flows over its four-year life:

t =	0	1	2	3	4
Cash flows	(17,800)	8,000	4,000	6,000	6,000

Work out the project's NPV at the following discount rates:

0%, 6%, 9%, 12%, 15%, 18%,

and plot your results on a graph.

4 Wheel is expected to pay a dividend per share of 10p next year. The market requires a return of 18% from companies of Wheel's riskiness, and Wheel's dividends are expected to grow at a constant 10% indefinitely. Value a Wheel share.

5 Heel is in the same business as Wheel, but its dividends are only expected to grow at 5%. Value a Heel share.

6 At the same time as valuing Wheel, we need to value Snail. Snail anticipates 8% growth indefinitely, and investors require a return of 21½% from Snail. Value a share in Snail.

7 Slug is expected to have earnings per share of 20p at the end of the current year. Slug retains 50% of its earnings, and has an internal rate of return of 14%. From a share of Slug's risk, the market requires a return of 20%. Value a Slug share.

8 What is the expected share price of Lizard, today and in three years' time, if Lizard's dividend in a year's time is expected to be 30 pence per share and to grow at 40% for another two years, then 6% thereafter. The required return of Lizard's shareholders is 17%.

9 What is the required return of Snake's shareholders if Snake has a share price of £1.64, and has just paid a dividend of 10p, which is expected to grow indefinitely at 8%?

CHAPTER 6

The perfect market model

The last chapter showed how to find the *net present value* of a project, and said that the firm should invest in projects which have a positive NPV. We now look at the theory behind that assertion.

In Section I we present the model developed by Jack Hirshleifer from Irving Fisher's pioneering work. The Fisher-Hirshleifer model[1] provides a rigorous proof of why in a world of certainty accepting all projects with a positive NPV maximises the wealth of shareholders. In doing this the model illustrates the central relationships in finance, the relationship between projects, firms, investors and the capital market. Section II examines the assumptions of the model and assesses their realism.

I INVESTMENT DECISIONS IN A PERFECT CAPITAL MARKET

We asserted that the firm could maximise the wealth of its shareholders by accepting all projects with a positive NPV. This section explains why.

Consider a simple world with only two time-periods, this one and the next, which we can call t_0 and t_1. There is an investor with an amount of cash X, and with some production opportunities available to him, projects which require an investment of cash now, at t_0, but will yield a return of cash in one year's time at t_1. So the investor can split the X he holds between consumption at t_0, and investment, which will yield consumption at t_1. His objective is to get the best balance of consumption in the two periods, to get the mix which he values most highly or, as we usually term it, which *maximises his wealth*. There are going to be two sides to consider. On the one hand his decision will depend on how much t_1 consumption can be gained by sacrificing t_0 consumption – on the returns to investing in projects, in other words. On the other hand there is the investor's preference for a pound's worth of consumption next year as against a pound's worth this year – his rate of time preference.

The return to projects

Figure I plots the consumption the investor can obtain in each period if he invests in projects. We can call it the 'production opportunities curve'. Points X and Y are the two extremes.

If he invests nothing now he can consume all his X this period, but nothing next period, while by consuming nothing this period and investing the whole X he can obtain a maximum consumption of Y next period. Most likely he will move to an intermediate position such as A requiring investment of X–C in projects, and yielding consumption of C

1 The graphical analysis of Fisher (1930) was explored and extended with respect to capital market imperfections in Hirshleifer (1958). A more rigorous and full account of the theory of investment is found in several texts, notably Huang and Litzenberger (1988).

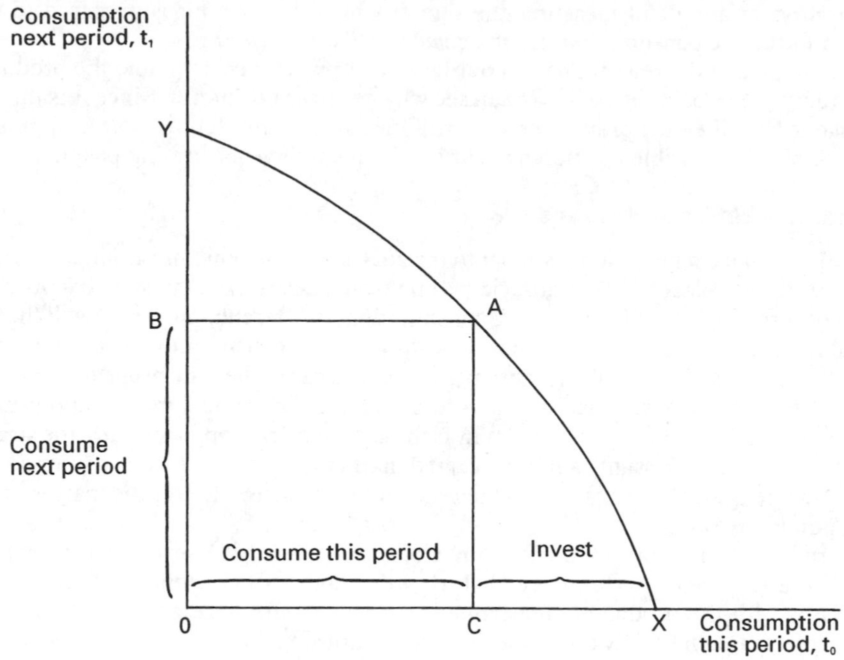

Figure I Production opportunities

this period and B next. But why is the curve the shape it is? The shape is determined purely by assumptions we are making. We assume projects are infinitely divisible and that projects are independent of one another so that accepting one does not affect the returns on another. This gives a smooth curve. We assume that not all projects yield the same return, so for example £1 invested in one project might yield £1.10 of consumption next period while in another it might yield £1.30. Since the rational investor will choose the best projects first, this gives a curve which is concave to the origin. The slope of the production opportunities curve at any point indicates the marginal return to investment at that point, the consumption at t_1 that can be got from sacrificing £1 of consumption at t_0. Towards Y the curve flattens out, indicating that as nearly all the £X is invested the marginal returns are low.

The investor's preferences

We can depict the investor's preferences about various mixes of consumption this period and next in terms of a set of indifference curves. Indifference curves are familiar from microeconomics. They join points of equal utility for the individual, and if the individual's preferences follow the basic axiom of rationality in that he prefers more to less then he will seek to be on the highest possible indifference curve.

As before we assume smooth curves, this time convex to the origin. This convexity reflects the assumption of diminishing marginal utility to consumption in either period, that is, the investor will require increasing amounts of consumption in one period to compensate for successive units of consumption sacrificed in the other period. The slope of the curve at any point measures the rate at which the investor is prepared to trade present for future consumption, his *marginal rate of time preference.*

Superimposing the relevant part of our investor's preference map onto the production opportunities curve, in Figure II, we can see why he chose position A. Since A is the point of tangency between the production opportunities and an indifference curve, it puts him onto the highest possible indifference curve; it is his utility-maximising position.

Capital market opportunities

We will now make a major innovation into the analysis by introducting a capital market. A *capital market* is a place where funds, claims on resources, are exchanged, and it provides a different sort of opportunity for mixing consumption in different time-periods. If there is a capital market and our investor wishes to postpone some consumption he can lend at the prevailing interest rate until the next period, alternatively he can bring forward some consumption by borrowing against his future income. The capital market opportunities are depicted in Figure III as line UV. Why is the capital market opportunities line straight? This is because if we assume a perfect capital market the rate at which consumption this period can be traded for consumption next period is the same all over the market and for every pound invested.

There is a common rate of interest or rate of return, r, so that V invested at t_0 returns U at t_1 where $U = V(1 + r)$. Hence $(1 + r)$ is the slope of the capital market line. The contrast is with the production opportunities curve, where there were good and not so good projects and the behaviour of the investor in choosing the good ones first gave a curve which was concave to the origin.

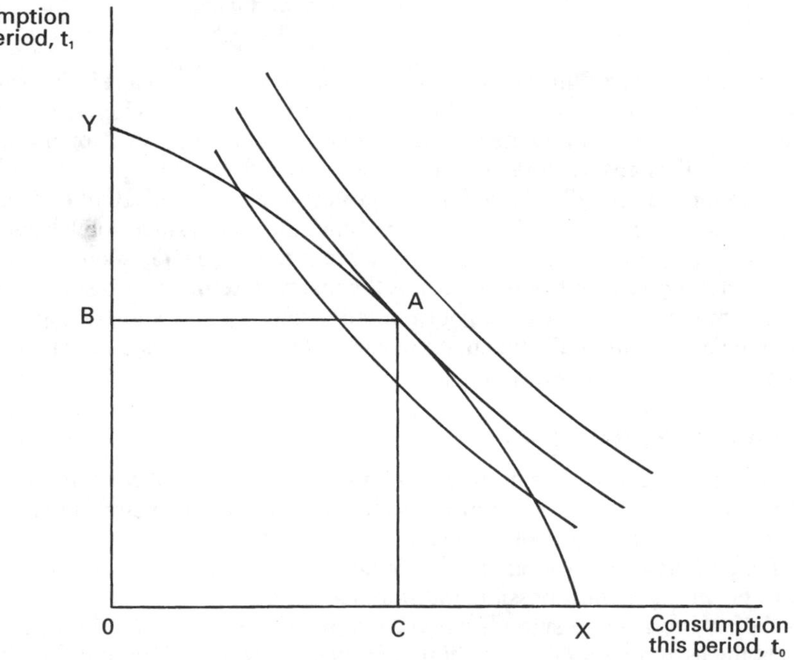

Figure II The investor's preferences

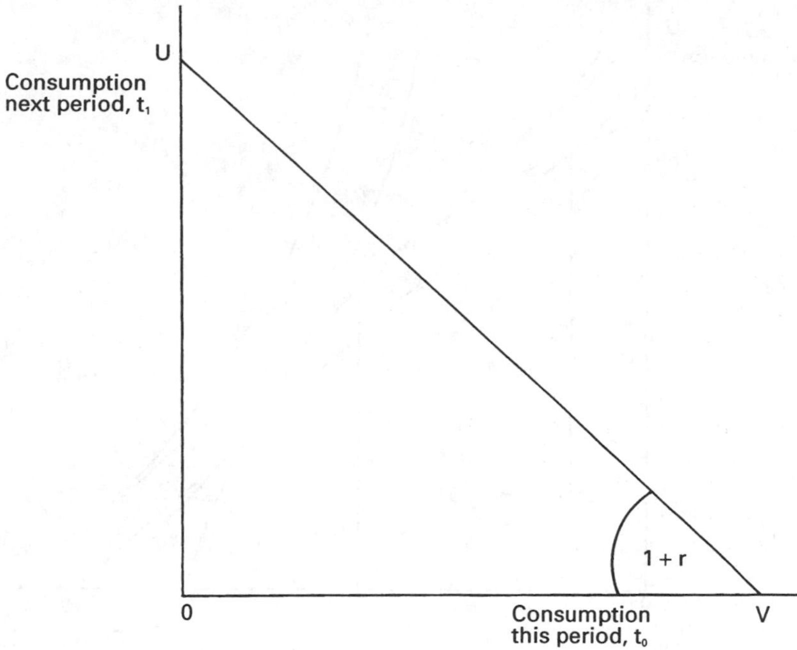

Figure III The capital market opportunities line

Figure IV combines capital market and production opportunities. Recall that the pre-capital market equilibrium was A. The introduction of a capital market permits a new equilibrium at E, which is a point of tangency to a higher indifference curve and so represents an increase in the investor's utility. The investor achieves this in two stages. He invests in projects, that part of the initial funds X which are needed to give the mix of present and future consumption represented by D. He chooses D because, at the tangency point, it permits him to get on to the highest capital market opportunities line. He then exchanges D for E on the capital market. He is free to do this since D and E are both on the same capital market opportunities line. In this case getting from D to E is a matter of selling some future consumption to receive more present consumption – 'borrowing'. To summarise, our investor finds that by undertaking some productive projects that yield relatively high consumption at t_1, then borrowing against those future returns to make up his t_0 consumption, he is better off overall.

The firm

We have talked about the investment decision of the individual investor, but the argument extends easily to firms. The only difference is that in a firm there will probably be more than one investor, with managers running the firm on their behalf. If there were more than one investor each with different tastes, *and no capital market*, managers could face a

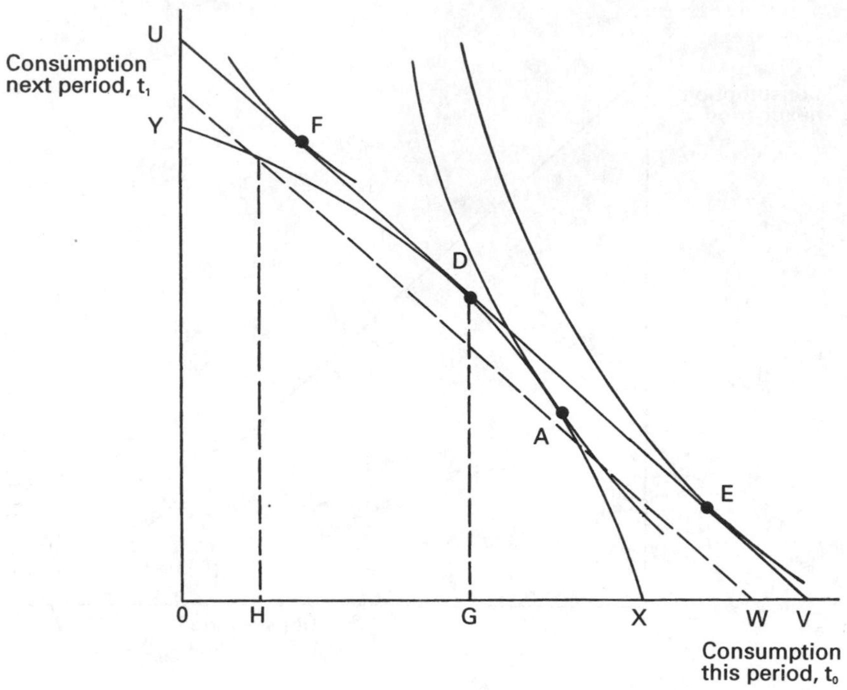

Figure IV Capital market and production opportunities

problem in finding an investment policy to suit everyone's tastes, since each investor might want the firm to choose a different point on the production opportunities curve. But once we introduce the capital market, each investor can choose their own mix of consumption and saving in response to the going rate of interest, *independent* of the behaviour of the others. Another investor with a relative preference for future consumption might find her point of tangency at F in Figure IV, compared to our initial investor's choice of E.

The firm has done its best by all its investors by investing up to point D.

At D the firm is investing GX and freeing OG for consumption, it is paying a *dividend* of OG and *retaining* GX. Our investor who preferred E is simply saying he wants a bigger dividend now and less in the future – and he achieves this by borrowing on the capital market against next year's dividend. On the other hand our F-person does not need all the t_0 dividend, so she lends some.

There are some profoundly important results lurking in Figure IV:

(1) The project investment decision and the capital market borrowing/lending decision were both made by reference to an objective external statistic, the market interest rate (= the slope of the capital market opportunities line). This means the decisions could be taken independently, it permits a *separation of ownership and control* without loss of efficiency. In Figure II the optimum would have to be found by evaluating all points on the production opportunities curve in terms of the investor's preferences. In practice this would be a time consuming task requiring first-hand knowledge of the investor's preferences. With the introduction of a capital market a more efficient arrangement

becomes feasible. Project decisions can be made by managers, who can undertake the utility-maximising level of investment for investors, without needing to consult them.
(2) Consider the manager's decision – his choice of point D – more closely. At D, a part OG of the initial funds X are consumed now or equivalently, if there is a separation between owners and managers, are distributed as dividend now. The remainder GX are invested. If all the proceeds of this investment were exchanged on the capital market for present consumption it would yield GV. So GV is the 'present value' of the investment and since GX is the cost of the investment, XV is its *net present value*. It is clear that the point of tangency D is the point of maximum net present value. Suppose the manager invested more and went to, say, H. Since H lies on a lower opportunities line the investment has a lower NPV of XW. The extra projects between D and H must have had a negative NPV. A decision rule is implied. The manager will maximise investors' wealth by maximising NPV; in other words managers should *choose all projects with a positive NPV*. This will maximise investors' utility. It also maximises the funds they can immediately consume, or, their wealth.
(3) The rule could be expressed another way. Since D is the point of tangency between the production possibility curve and the capital market line, their slopes, the marginal return to investment, more commonly called *internal rate of return*, and the rate of interest in the market, are equal at D. So the manager would arrive at D if he were to: *invest until the market rate of interest equals the IRR of the marginal project*. So in this case we can recommend managers to accept all projects whose IRR is greater than the cost of capital.

II THE ASSUMPTIONS OF THE MODEL

What about the assumptions of the model? Throughout the argument we made the following assumptions:

1 Rational shareholders
2 Certainty
3 Two time-periods
4 Perfect capital markets
5 Project divisibility and independence.

How does a model derived under such artificially simple assumptions stand up in the real world?

Rational shareholders and certainty

The assumption that future cash flows are known with certainty is of course utterly unrealistic. The assumption is relaxed in the next chapter. The assumption that shareholders are rational might sound questionable to some people too. But all we are assuming here is that shareholders prefer more dividends to less in all time-periods.

Two time-periods

It was convenient to assume investment decisions were being made over just two time-periods, so as to present the argument graphically. But this is not a critical assumption. The existence of a capital market permits firms to raise finance and investors to spread their consumption over many periods. The NPV rule is completely robust over multiple time-periods, but as we will see in the next section the IRR becomes difficult to interpret.

Perfect capital markets

We will be looking at the capital market is some detail in later chapters. In fact, though the market appears to be fairly efficient in its operation, it is not perfect. This is likely to have two effects on the analysis: borrowing and lending rates may diverge; and in some circumstances the firm may not be able to borrow at all.

Suppose the borrowing rate is higher than the lending rate. Then we get the outcome in Figure V.

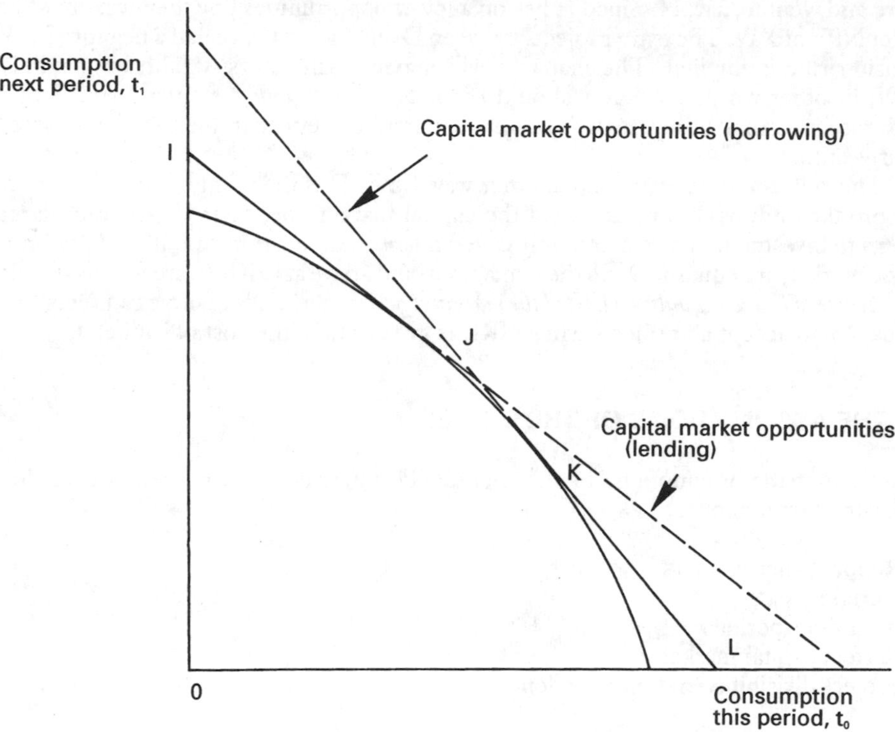

Figure V When borrowing and lending rates differ

Since the market rate of return determines the slope of the capital market opportunities line, differing borrowing and lending rates effectively mean different lines, as the opportunities facing a lender are different from those facing a borrower. So investors whose preferences place them between I and J will seek to *lend* from this period's income to increase next period's consumption and will prefer the manager to invest up to J. Similarly others will be *borrowers*, and prefer K, and others still will prefer an outcome 'in the middle', on the curve between J and K. Different borrowing and lending rates bring indeterminacy into the analysis: different groups of shareholders may have conflicting views on the firm's investment policy, and the best the firm can do may be to choose a policy and stick to it, knowing that the dissatisfied investor can always invest elsewhere.

If there are actually quantity limits on the finance the firm can raise, we say the firm is suffering *capital rationing*. In this case capital is a constraining factor and it is necessary to modify the NPV decision-rule so as to maximise NPV per unit of capital – we explore the practicalities of this in the next chapter.

Project divisibility and independence

We assumed that projects were infinitely divisible, giving a smooth and continuous production opportunities curve. Also we assumed that projects were independent in that the cash flows of one project were not affected by the acceptance or rejection of another. In practice neither of these may hold – projects can be 'lumpy' and highly interrelated. For example if you are a car manufacturer you may find that the design, testing and launch of a new model costs you hundreds of millions of pounds and there is no halfway house – the project has to be undertaken in full or not at all. In this sort of situation the lumpiness of projects means the marginal IRR may be either well above or well below the cost of capital. Similarly the value of one model is likely to be interrelated with the value of other models – the appeal of the company's cars may partly depend on its offering a credible range; there may be cost savings on common spare parts; on the other hand the new model may take sales from the company's existing models. This means the project analyst has to be particularly careful in defining the *relevant* cash flows of the project. As we saw in Chapter 4 all the project costs and benefits, direct and indirect, have to be taken into account. However, the NPV decision-rule is robust in the face of lumpy and interrelated projects so long as some care is taken in defining the relevant cash flows.

An extreme form of project interdependence occurs when projects are *mutually exclusive* – we can only undertake one of them. In this case we can use NPV successfully so long as we ensure we are making the right comparisons. We can see this in the case of the replacement decision in the next chapter.

REFERENCES AND BIBLIOGRAPHY

Fisher, I — *The Theory of Interest* (1930) Macmillan, New York.

Hirshleifer, J — 'On the Theory of Optimal Investment Decisions', Journal of Political Economy, 1958, pp 329–372.

Huang, C F, and Litzenberger, R H — *Foundations for Financial Economics*, North-Holland, 1988.

QUESTIONS

1 Explain why in a perfect capital market under certainty firms maximise shareholders' wealth by choosing projects with positive NPV, or with IRR greater than the cost of capital.

2 How robust are the Fisher-Hirshleifer results to more realistic assumptions?

CHAPTER 7

Valuing projects under certainty

We now consider the practicalities of project valuation. Section I describes how to value a typical investment project. In Section II we examine the effect of inflation on project appraisal. At the moment we are continuing to leave to one side the question of risk and we are abstracting from the financing decision by assuming firms are all-equity financed.

Section III considers a particular application of NPV analysis, the problem of finding the optimum replacement period for an asset. Section IV considers how the NPV rule needs to be modified in the face of a common market imperfection – capital rationing. In this case the firm has to choose between worthwhile projects. The complexities of choosing the best bundle out of a large set of possibly interrelated projects point to the use of mathematical techniques such as linear programming, so we explain how linear programming can be used in project choice, and how the results should be interpreted.

A seemingly equivalent measure of project worth to NPV emerges from the Fisher-Hirshleifer model in the form of 'internal rate of return' or 'IRR'. But though NPV stands up well when we relax some of the assumptions of the Fisher-Hirshleifer model, the IRR runs into problems. We discuss the IRR and its limitations in Section V.

Throughout this chapter we contrive, for convenience, to assume a world of certainty. The subsequent chapters address the issue of how risk and uncertainty should be handled in valuation.

I VALUING A TYPICAL INVESTMENT PROJECT

Finding the relevant cash flows

This section considers how to identify the cash flows associated with an investment project, and how to calculate its NPV.

Anglo-Precision

Anglo-Precision is considering buying a machine to make bearings. The machine costs £1.2 million and will last five years. Scrap value of these machines is currently £200,000. An investment of £150,000 in working capital will be needed initially. The accountant has prepared the following estimated annual trading account for the project:

	£
Bearing sales	1,400,000
Materials, labour	(800,000)
Depreciation	(200,000)
Fixed overhead allocated	(250,000)
ANNUAL PROFIT	150,000

A-P's discount rate is 10% per annum, and the company pays a marginal rate of tax of 35%. What is the NPV of this project?

Incremental costs and benefits

A general point – the principles established in Chapter 4 apply equally to this. The relevant effects for appraising a project are the incremental costs and benefits; and the cost of employing resources is their opportunity cost. Purely for convenience we assume all cash flows take place on the last day of the year. Specifically we also assume that the machine acquired at t_0, was actually bought on the last day of the previous year. In reality cash flows can arise on any day of the year, and computer packages to calculate NPV take account of this and discount for the appropriate number of days.

Asset cost

For NPV calculation the cost of the machine is the cash outlay, when it occurs. In the A-P example the anticipated scrap value means there will be a cash receipt in period 5.

t=		0	1	2	3	4	5
Cash flow of machine	(£)	(1,200,000)	–	–	–	–	200,000

Depreciation

Depreciation should be ignored in DCF, as it is a non-cash expense. Depreciation is an accounting contrivance designed to inject a measure of capital consumption into the measurement of annual performance. Since DCF considers all time-periods at once, including the periods when the cash flows occur, depreciation is unnecessary.

Interest

Interest payments should not be included as cash flows. The cost of capital is measured directly by the discount rate.

Overheads

Overheads, if they would be incurred anyway and are merely allocated to the project, should be ignored. This follows from the ruling principle that only increments in cost as a result of the project are *relevant*. So the trading proceeds of the project can be calculated:

	each year
Bearings sales	1,400,000
Materials, labour	(800,000)
Cash flow = Trading proceeds	£ 600,000

Working capital

Projects usually require an investment in additional working capital. But unlike fixed capital, working capital is not consumed by the project in which it is used. Rather it represents an advance payment, or 'stockpiling', of inputs that are already costed in the project. So the appropriate treatment is to charge the outlay as a cost when it is incurred, and add back the same amount at the end of the project. The rationale is that in the final year of the project cost savings can be achieved on materials by running down stocks. Thus the effective cost of the investment in working capital is the 'interest cost' during the period in which it is held. In the case of A-P this means:

t=		0	1	2	3	4	5
Capital	(£)	(150,000)	–	–	–	–	150,000

Taxation

The tax system was discussed in Chapter 3. For project appraisal the following aspects of the tax system are important:

(I) Costs and revenues are with some exceptions[1] tax-deductible and taxable, respectively, at the prevailing corporation tax rate. Assuming a tax rate of 35% then the Inland Revenue will take .35 of the revenues and, effectively, pay .35 of the costs (– the latter because tax-deductibility means allowing the firm to avoid paying tax it would otherwise have had to pay).

(II) Lags in assessment and collection of company tax mean that tax is not paid until nine months after the year in which the income arises.[2] For convenience we assume that tax effects are lagged by one year.

(III) Tax relief on the cost of the machine is given through capital allowances. In this case the machine qualifies for a writing-down allowance of 25% on the reducing balance. Hence annual capital allowances are:

	0	*1*	*2*	*3*	*4*	*5*	*6*	*TOTAL*
25% WDA (£)	300,000	225,000	168,750	126,563	94,922	84,765		1,000,000
Tax saved		105,000	78,750	59,063	44,297	33,223	29,667	350,000

Because we assume that the machine was bought on the last day of the previous year, the first WDA (of 1,200 × 25% = 300) is credited to that year, enabling tax relief of 105 (= 300 × .35) to be claimed at t_1. Subsequent WDAs are 25% of the reducing balance, which means that when the machine is finally scrapped for 200,000 the balancing allowance in the final period is 84,765.

Assembling these cash flows, and using 10% as the discount rate, we can now calculate the NPV of A-P's bearings project, as an Exhibit I. The project has an NPV of £749,162.

We have seen how to set up the cash flows for calculating NPV, but we have neglected some key issues. Where does the discount rate come from? How do we know how long the project will last, and for that matter, how do we know what the cash flows will be? How does inflation affect the analysis?

The discount rate

The discount rate should measure the cost of the capital used in the project – the investors' opportunity cost, the best return they could get elsewhere. In a perfect capital market where the future is known with certainty there will be just one cost of capital or discount rate, a uniform rate of interest prevailing throughout the market. This is what we assume in this chapter. Once the assumption of certainty is removed then we expect the cost of the capital invested in a project to reflect the riskiness of the project. Subsequent chapters discuss how the risky discount rate for a project can be found.

In this chapter we are also assuming that the firm is financed entirely by equity. However, in the world of certainty the distinction between equity and debt is meaningless.

1 Some expenses, for example entertaining UK businessmen, the Revenue will not in general allow for tax deduction at all. Other expenses, such as industrial buildings and company cars, are allowed only piecemeal.

2 In practice the simple timing structure we are presenting here may be considerably complicated. When the tax effects of a particular project are felt depends on the overall tax-paying position of the firm. For example, if the firm is making a loss overall, of a 'tax loss' created by heavy capital allowances, then the tax is in a tax-paying position, which could be some years hence. In general the decision-maker should seek professional guidance from the company's tax adviser as to the tax implications of the project in question.

Exhibit I DCF appraisal of bearings project

t =	0	1	2	3	4	5	6
Machine – cost	(1,200,000)					200,000	
– tax		105,000	78,750	59,063	44,297	33,223	29,667
Trading proceeds		600,000	600,000	600,000	600,000	600,000	
– tax			(210,000)	(210,000)	(210,000)	(210,000)	(210,000)
Working capital*	(150,000)					150,000	
ANNUAL CASH FLOWS	(1,350,000)	705,000	468,750	449,063	434,297	773,223	180,333
10% Discount factors	1	.909	.826	.751	.683	.621	.564
PRESENT VALUES	(1,350,000)	640,845	387,188	337,246	152,004	480,171	101,708

Total = NPV = £749,162

*Note the working capital cash flow has been assumed to have no tax effects

Later on we relax this assumption and consider the financing alternatives available to the firm. Again, we can show that in a perfect capital market the way in which the firm raised its finance would not affect its cost of capital and the investment and financing decisions of firms would be independent of one another. In reality though, financing decisions may affect the cost of capital.

In this chapter we just take the discount rate as 'given' but this does not mean its importance should be neglected. The study of business finance is all about the transfer of capital from investors to projects through firms. The cost of capital is the key statistic in that process since it is the market price of what is being transferred.

Economic life

Deciding on the life, or time-horizon of the project is difficult yet crucial. The NPV of the project may be significantly affected by the decision to add another year's cash flow to the appraisal, but the year in question is the remotest from now, the one about which we know least. The project life decision confronts us with the inadequacy of the 'certainty' assumption we are making in this chapter. The existence of uncertainty probably explains the popularity of the decision rule that concentrates on *payback period*. It also raises the possibility that the firm will have to make decisions about *abandoning* or *disinvesting* in projects when the future does not unfold as well as was expected. We discuss these issues in subsequent chapters.

But the assumption of certainty we are making at present is a convenient one for highlighting another feature of project life. In discussions of project appraisal, and in computer packages for calculating DCF, the 'life' of the project tends to be treated as a parameter, as part of the data of the project. It is important to see that on the contrary the life of a project should be calculated simultaneously with its NPV.

The *physical life* of, say, the machinery used on a project may be a datum. But this rarely constrains a project in practice since it is usually possible to buy or lease extra years of machine services, where it is economic to do so. Similarly, further investments of marketing or design expenditure can often bolster the sales of a flagging product.[3] Whether it is worth prolonging the life of a project another year depends on the effect of the costs and benefits of doing so on the NPV of the project. Hence we can define the *economic life* of a project as the life which *maximises NPV*. In practice we may need to explore different assumptions about termination and reinvestment to find the economic life.

II THE EFFECT OF INFLATION ON PROJECT VALUE

The impact of inflation on the value of projects could be signficant. We know that NPV = $\sum \frac{C_t}{(1+r)^t}$. Inflation is likely to affect both our estimates of the cash flows C_t, and the required return, r. There are two aspects of inflation that need to be separated. First, that it exists, and second, that it is uncertain. So if we are working out the cash flows associated with operating a machine for making widgets it will be important to know that while widgets sell for £2 each this year they will be selling for £5 in two years' time. That would be a case of 'certain' inflation. But in reality the rate of inflation is not known, so that in two years' time the best that could be predicted may be that widgets will be selling between

3 Marketing often talks about the *life cycle* of a product but recognises there are various ways the life cycle can be stretched. See, for example, Kotler (1991).

£3.50 and £5.50. The latter problem we will leave until later as part of the general problem of the uncertainty of future cash flows, and consider here what to do about inflation in a certain world.

At first sight the best thing to do about inflation might be to ignore it. Suppose there was a uniform expected rate of inflation across the economy, i. Then actual or 'nominal' future cash flows, C_t, would be related to their 'real' or 'current price' equivalents, C'_t, as follows:

$$C_t = C'_t\,(1 + i)^t \qquad (1)$$

and, as Fisher (1930) suggested, nominal interest rates, r, would be related to real rates, r′, as follows:

$$1 + r = (1 + r')\,(1 + i) \qquad (2)$$

This is the so called 'Fisher effect'. So long as the market is efficient, we can expect nominal interest rates to fully embody inflationary expections.

It follows from (1) and (2) that $NPV = \sum \frac{C_t}{(1 + r)^t} = \sum \frac{C'_t(1 + i)^t}{(1 + r')^t(1 + i)^t}$

and the i terms cancel, so $\sum \frac{C_t}{(1 + r)^t} = \sum \frac{C'_t}{(1 + r')^t}$

In the case of uniform inflation we get the same answer working in current prices with the real discount rate as with inflated prices and the nominal discount rate. In practice, though, ignoring inflation is both unsafe and more difficult than it might look. We can see this by looking at the cash flows and the discount rate again.

Cash flows

Inflation strikes unevenly. The decision-maker just cannot assume that the prices of the particular inputs and outputs that make up his cash flow will inflate uniformly and at the average or general expected rate the market builds into the nominal interest rate.

Taxation provides a good example of non-uniform inflation. Tax receipts and payments are fixed in terms of the expense or income to which they relate, but follow it with a lag of, we assume, 12 months. If my tax rate is 30% and I earn £100 today, I will have to pay £30 tax in a year's time, whether the rate of inflation to the intervening period is 20% or 200%. In this sense taxation is subject to zero inflation.

Discount rate

If we decide to use real rather than nominal cash flows we need the real cost of capital to discount them. Unfortunately we cannot directly observe the real rate. The costs of capital, r, that we observe in the market are nominal ones. They reflect the return required by providers of funds to give a real return, r′, **and** to compensate for the loss in the purchasing power of the capital due to inflation, i.

As we saw in (2)

$$1 + r = (1 + r')\,(1 + i)$$
$$r = r' + i + r'i$$

assuming the likely magnitudes of r′ and i make the r′i term insignificant,

$$r = r' + i$$

To find the real return r′, we need to deduct i from the market rate, r, where i is the market's expectation of future inflation. But we do not know what i is. After the event we know what inflation *was*, but not what people thought it was going to be; we know the 'ex post' but not the 'ex ante'. In fact the market rate is one of our main sources of information about the market's inflation expectations, so the process of estimating r is likely to be circular and conjectural. But if our knowledge of the composition of r is circular and conjectural, how can we know that r fully reflects future inflation? In general we may prefer to assume the market is correct on the pragmatic grounds that, before the event, we lack the evidence to assume otherwise.

In summary, our prescription for handling inflation in project appraisal is to forecast cash flows at nominal values, and discount them using the nominal cost of capital.

III REPLACEMENT DECISIONS

Very often when a piece of equipment wears out it is replaced by something else, reflecting new technology or the changing needs of the firm. But for some items like is replaced more or less by like – for example, company vehicles, lathes and workshop machinery, office furniture. Firms can anticipate a continuing need for items such as these, moreover they tend to share certain characteristics. First, their efficiency can be expected to decline over time as the quantity or quality of their output declines and the maintenance costs needed to maintain output increases. Second, steady technological improvement may be expected through time in the efficiency of the 'latest model'. It should be possible to estimate both of these factors. Third, there are well established second-hand markets in all these items, so the realisable value of equipment of any age can be ascertained from dealer's lists. These features make it feasible to calculate an *optimal replacement period* for the asset.

Antioch Manufacturing

Antioch Manufacturing is trying to establish a replacement policy for a lathe with the following characteristics:

Year	*0*	*1*	*2*	*3*	*4*
Machine values					
Purchase cost	5,000				
Second-hand value		4,000	3,600	3,000	2,000
Net cash flow during period		2,000	1,800	1,600	1,400

Incorporated into the cash flows is a 10% per annum expected decline in efficiency of the asset in use. We are ignoring taxation, inflation and technical improvements in the new machine, and assume a discount rate of 10%.

The firm is considering the alternatives of replacing the machines every one, two, three and four years. Denoting the NPV of a machine kept for one year as NPV_1, for two years as NPV_2 etc, then:

$$NPV_1 = (5{,}000) + \frac{2{,}000}{1.1} + \frac{4{,}000}{1.1} \qquad = 455$$

$$NPV_2 = (5{,}000) + \frac{2{,}000}{1.1} + \frac{1{,}800}{(1.1)^2} + \frac{3{,}600}{(1.1)^2} \qquad = 1{,}281$$

$$NPV_3 = (5{,}000) + \frac{2{,}000}{1.1} + \frac{1{,}800}{(1.1)^2} + \frac{1{,}600}{(1.1)^3} + \frac{3{,}000}{(1.1)^3} = 1{,}762$$

$$NPV_4 = (5{,}000) + \frac{2{,}000}{1.1} + \frac{1{,}800}{(1.1)^2} + \frac{1{,}600}{(1.1)^3} + \frac{1{,}400}{(1.1)^4} + \frac{2{,}000}{(1.1)^4} = 1{,}830$$

Effectively each replacement policy represents a rival project. As a set they are mutually exclusive. However, we cannot just compare these NPVs as they stand: since each project covers a different time-period we would not be comparing like with like. The different policies must be compared over equal time-horizons. The one-year policy involves a yearly cycle of purchase and replacement. To compare this with the two-year policy we must look at a two-year time-horizon, involving two runs of the one-year cycle. So the appropriate NPVs for comparison would be:

$$\text{NPV of 1-yr policy} = (5{,}000) + \frac{2{,}000}{1.1} + \frac{4{,}000}{1.1} + \frac{(5{,}000)}{1.1} + \frac{2{,}000}{(1.1)^2} + \frac{4{,}000}{(1.1)^2} = 868$$

$$\text{NPV of 2-yr policy} = \text{as originally} = 1{,}281$$

Now the NPVs are being calculated in comparable fashion. The calculation of the NPV of the one-year policy could have been simplified by noting that it is

$$NPV = NPV_1 + \frac{NPV_1}{1.1} = 455 + 413 = 868$$

To compare all four policies we must find a time-horizon which permits completed cycles of all the policies. This is the lowest common denominator of one, two, three and four years, which is 12 years. So we would compare 12 cycles of the yearly policy, six of the two-yearly and so forth. The calculations for this are clearly rather onerous. If we allow the possibility of a five-year policy, the appropriate time-horizon is 60 years!

Surprisingly, the solution is to take each policy to an *infinite* time-horizon since this permits us to use the formula for the sum of a geometric progression. The NPV of the one-year policy repeated each year to infinity is

$$NPV^{\infty}{}_1 = NPV_1 + \frac{NPV_1}{1.1} + \frac{NPV_1}{(1.1)^2} \ldots \infty = NPV_1 \sum_{t=0}^{\infty} \frac{1}{(1.1)^t}$$

Similarly the NPV of the two-year policy repeated to infinity is

$$NPV^{\infty}{}_2 = NPV_2 + \frac{NPV_2}{(1.1)^2} + \frac{NPV_2}{(1.1)^4} \ldots \infty = NPV_2 \sum_{t=0}^{\infty} \frac{1}{(1.1)^{2t}}$$

and so forth. Now, in general if k>0, where m is the replacement period,

$$\sum_{t=0}^{\infty} \frac{1}{(1+k)^{tm}} = \frac{1}{1 - \frac{1}{(1+k)^m}}$$

So the NPV of the one-year policy to infinity simplifies to

$$NPV^{\infty_1} = \frac{NPV_1}{1 - \frac{1}{(1+k)^m}} = \frac{455}{1 - \frac{1}{1.1}} = 5{,}005$$

similarly $NPV^{\infty}{}_{2} = \dfrac{1{,}281}{1 - \dfrac{1}{(1.1)^2}} = 7{,}381$

$NPV^{\infty}{}_{3} = \dfrac{1{,}762}{1 - \dfrac{1}{(1.1)^3}} = 7{,}085$

$NPV^{\infty}{}_{4} = \dfrac{1{,}830}{1 - \dfrac{1}{(1.1)^4}} = 5{,}773$

Inspection of the NPVs to infinity shows that the optimal replacement period is two years, Antioch should replace every two years.

IV CONSTRAINED INVESTMENT DECISIONS

In an ideal world decision-makers would accept all projects with a positive NPV. But in practice investment decisions may be constrained by scarcity of resources so that the firm has to *choose between* projects which have positive NPVs. In this section we will consider the case where just one resource is fixed: FINANCE. This restriction is imposed for two reasons, one virtuous, one not-so-virtuous. The not-so-virtuous reason is that as the reader will soon discover, making investment decisions with just one constraining factor is quite complicated enough. And anyway the analysis of one resource limited in several time-periods is effectively an analysis of several constraints. The other reason is that the assumption of investment funds as the one constraint is probably realistic in a great many cases. We start by explaining why this is so.

The notion of resource constraints is essentially a short-run one. In the longer run we prefer to think that managers can arrange the supply of all the inputs they require, albeit at a price. So in appraising capital investments, which are essentially longer-term projects, we do not expect to find serious shortages of labour, raw materials and plant. These can be hired or trained, bought, and built as appropriate. Why does the same not apply to investment funds? Extra funds should be available from the market at some rate of interest.

Capital rationing can come from inside or outside the firm. Earlier in the book we observed that firms may undertake less projects than would be worthwhile 'rationally' because of a hidden resource constraint, that of 'managerial effort'. We can expand this concept of the scarce resource of managerial effort to include not just limitations of managerial time, but also situations where the aims and objectives of managers about the growth rate of the firm imply a limit on the scale of investment to be undertaken. Managers may choose to restrict the growth rate of the firm because of uncertainty about the future, or because the absolute size of the firm, or its rate of growth may pose a threat to their ability to exercise control. Managers may prefer orderly, sustainable growth. One way managers can control the growth of the firm is through limiting the investment funds available during any period.

The previous comments related to the top, policy-making level of the firm where the power to raise new investment funds resides. Capital rationing can also be encountered lower down the firm, for if investment decisions are decentralised to divisions and an annual budgeting system is in operation which requires funds to be allocated to divisions prior to the decisions on how to use them, decision-makers find themselves confronted by a fixed ration of investment funds. The sort of capital rationing we have been describing, which the firm imposes upon itself, is usually called *soft* capital rationing.

But we cannot ignore the possibility that a firm may face externally imposed or *hard* capital rationing, when the supplier of funds, say a bank, will not provide finance at any price. This could arise if the bank itself were constrained, perhaps because the government had imposed lending limits on banks as part of its money supply policy. This would be a situation in which the suppliers of finance agreed that the firm had potential projects with a positive value but were unable to help. Alternatively, though, the constraint may arise because of a disagreement between the firm and the supplier of funds as to the value of the project, and particularly as to its risk. There is a real problem here since much of the relevant information about, for example, the skill of management and the realism of their expectations, is hard to quantify. It is often said that the capital market is too cautious in lending, particularly to small firms where the information problem is greatest.

Hard capital rationing implies imperfections in the capital market, beyond the control of the firm, while soft capital rationing is within the firm's control. But all capital rationing involves lost opportunities. The extent to which the firm imposes capital rationing on itself depends on the extent to which it is prepared to trade one objective, value, off against others such as orderly growth.

We start by analysing the situation where funds are limited in only one time-period, then introduce two-period and multiple-period constraints.

One-period capital rationing

If capital rationing only holds for one period we have a simple constrained maximisation problem of the sort we investigated in Chapter 4. The decision-rule is *choose the projects which yield the highest NPV per unit of the constraint.*

Harlequin plc

Harlequin plc has the following possible projects available:

Project	*Initial capital outlay*	*NPV*	*NPV per £1 capital*
	(1)	(2)	(2) ÷ (1)
1	£75,000	7,663	.1022
2	£30,000	7,906	.2635
3	£25,000	150	.0060
4	£160,000	25,814	.1613
5	£50,000	7,195	.1439
6	£10,000	1,011	.1011
7	£30,000	2,892	.0964
	£380,000		

Harlequin has a capital budget of £250,000 for the year. Which projects should it undertake?

The solution is to rank the projects in terms of NPV per unit of constraining factor which in this case is capital. The final column provides the necessary data.

The ranking is:

	Project	Cumulative capital requirement
	2	30,000
	4	190,000
	5	240,000
£250,000 cut-off point		
	1	315,000
	6	325,000
	7	355,000
	3	380,000

So the firm should accept projects 2, 4, 5 as they yield the best NPV per unit of capital. This uses £240,000 capital. The remaining £10,000 would best be used by undertaking a proportion $\frac{10,000}{75,000}$ of project 1. This will give a total NPV of (7,906 + 25,814 + 7,195) + $\left(\frac{10}{75} \times 7,663\right)$ = £41,937.

Project indivisibility

But is it realistic to assume we could undertake a fractional project, such as $\frac{10}{75}$ of project 1? If we can do that, the reader may counter, why not go to the other extreme, and undertake project 2, $\frac{25}{3}$ = 8⅓ times. If the firm could do it this would give the best solution of all, with an NPV of 7,906 × 8⅓ = £65,883. Commonly, though, projects will be *indivisible* and in this case our decision-rule will not always give the best solution.

In the present case, if project 1 is indivisible, inspection suggests that the best alternative will be project 6, which will just use up the £10,000 of capital budget left unused. Project 1 is better than 6 in terms of $\frac{\text{NPV}}{\text{capital}}$ but does not 'fit' so well. The lumpiness, or indivisibility, of projects has meant that some shuffling of projects is necessary to make the best use of the budget. Improvements like this are not always so easy to spot by eye and the task of shuffling to find the best set is better left to a computer. Implicitly we have had to relax our decision-rule. Now, when projects are indivisible, the rule is *choose those projects that maximise NPV subject to the constraint.*

If a firm expects capital rationing each period it would clearly be unwise to treat the problem as a one-period one. The danger is that when the second period arrives insufficient funds will be available to complete the committed investment projects. However, if management experience is that this danger is not real, and that residual financing requirements from previous years' projects never exceed subsequent years' capital rations treating capital rationing in this simple one-period way may be feasible. Each period's capital ration will simply be the uncommitted residue of new financing. But the treatment will never be optimal, it ignores too much information, it considers one period's cash flows and constraints, and ignores future periods.

Two-period capital rationing

The choice between capital investment projects under multiple constraints is best handled by using the linear programming (LP) technique. In this section we consider a simple two-project, two-period, investment problem, and in the next section how more complex problems could be handled.

Gerald & Co

Gerald & Co, builders, have two designs of factory to offer. They have just acquired a large green field on which they plan to build these factories. Unfortunately, the factories take two years to build, and Gerald have strictly limited investment funds in the next two years. The capital requirement during building, and estimated NPV of the two sorts of factory is:

Factory	*A*	*B*
Capital Year 1	3	8
Year 2	4	4
NPV	6	14

(figures are in £ millions)

The firm has £24 million to invest each year. How many of each factory should the firm build?

The constrained decision-rule is *choose those projects that maximise NPV subject to the constraints*. The question is how to choose.

The first step is to set the problem up in linear programming form:

Maximise: $NPV = 6x_A + 14x_B$

Subject to constraints: $3x_A + 8x_B \leqslant 24$

$4x_A + 4x_B \leqslant 24$

$x_A, x_B \geqslant 0$

where x_A = number of A factories built

x_B = number of B factories built

Again we face the indivisibility problem since this formulation permits the building of fractions of factories. The reader must bear with this problem, which is a limitation of the simple technique being used. Economic sense could be given to the idea of part-factories if it is possible to undertake a joint venture with someone else to complete the factory. The requirement of part-factories can be avoided by using more sophisticated techniques such as integer programming.

Because a simple two variable problem was chosen it can be solved graphically. Figure I graphs the two constraints. For example, in the first year the term could have $\frac{24}{3} = 8$ of A, or $\frac{24}{8} = 3$ of B, or some linear combination of these. There is a similar constraint in the second year.

A feasible solution must comply with all the constraints, including the requirement that only positive quantities of factories can be built. The shaded area in Figure I is the feasible set.

To find the best combination of factories from this feasible set, we superimpose on the diagram a set of equi-NPV lines. These lines link the various combinations of projects that yield a particular NPV in total, they are the dashed lines on Figure I. The best combination is the member of the feasible set which lies on the highest NPV line. By inspecting the graph we can see the optimal solution consists in building 4.8 of A and 1.2 of B.

The NPV of this solution will be: $(6 \times 4.8) + (14 \times 1.2) = £45.6$ m.

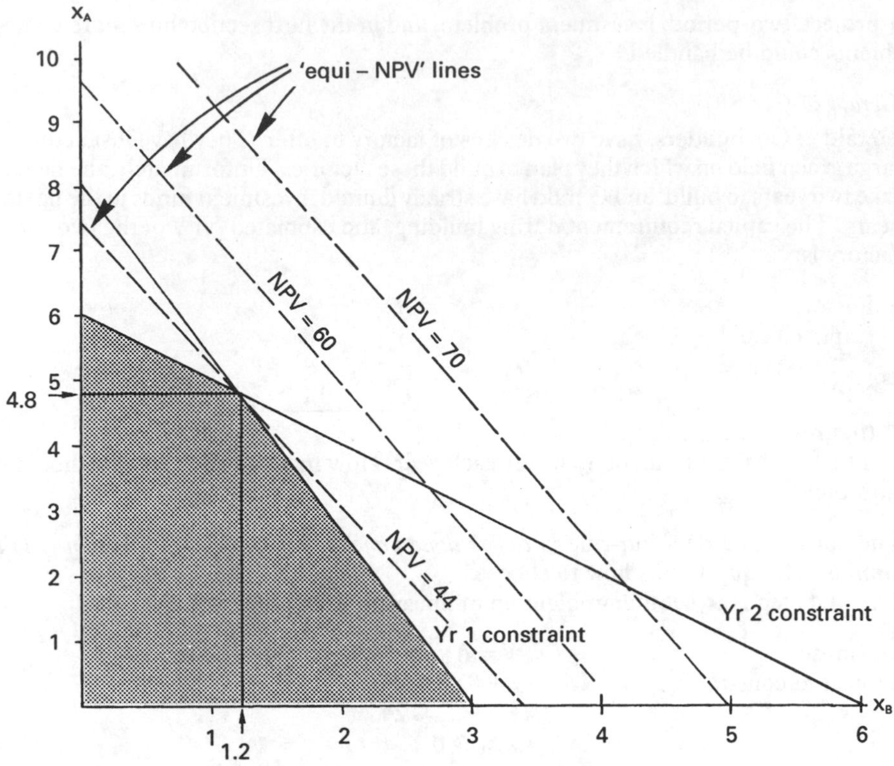

Figure I Two-period capital rationing

Multiple-period capital rationing[4]

The main virtue of the two-period, two-project case is that it permits the solution of the programming problem to be presented graphically. But real-world problems can be very complicated, and are best solved using a computer package. We now consider how a more complicated problem would be solved using a package. Suppose a firm is contemplating four projects extending over three years as follows:

Projects		*1*	*2*	*3*	*4*	Capital available
Capital required	Time 1	11	20	40	25	120
	2	40	40	80	50	80
	3	60	20	0	55	60
NPV		39	20	79	60	

(Figures are in £ millions)

4 For further reading on this topic the reader is referred to Lorie and Savage (1955), Weingartner (1974). Weingartner (1977), Bernhard (1969), Bhaskar (1976), Hughes and Lewellen (1974).

We can set the problem up in linear programming form as before:

$$
\begin{aligned}
\text{Maximise} \quad \text{NPV} &= 39x_1 + 20x_2 + 79x_3 + 60x_4 \\
\text{Subject to constraints:} \quad & 11x_1 + 20x_2 + 40x_3 + 25x_4 \leqslant 120 \quad (1) \\
& 40x_1 + 40x_2 + 80x_3 + 50x_4 \leqslant 80 \quad (2) \\
& 60x_1 + 20x_2 \qquad\qquad + 55x_4 \leqslant 60 \quad (3) \\
& x_1 \leqslant 1 \quad (4) \\
& x_2 \leqslant 1 \quad (5) \\
& x_3 \leqslant 1 \quad (6) \\
& x_4 \leqslant 1 \quad (7) \\
& x_i \geqslant 0 \; i = 1 \text{ to } 4 \quad (8)
\end{aligned}
$$

Constraint (8) says, as in the previous example, that the firm cannot undertake negative amounts of projects. But now we are also stipulating in (4) – (7) that the firm cannot undertake any project more than once. The constraints are all inequalities at present, but we can convert them to equalities by introducing 'slack' variables. Letting S_1, S_2, S_3 represent the capital unused at time points 1, 2, 3 respectively and S_4 to S_7 represent the unpurchased proportion of projects 1 to 4, the problem becomes:

$$
\begin{aligned}
\text{Maximise} \quad \text{NPV} &= 39x_1 + 20x_2 + 79x_3 + 60x_4 \\
\text{Subject to constraints:} \quad & 11x_1 + 20x_2 + 40x_3 + 25x_4 + S_1 = 120 \\
& 40x_1 + 40x_2 + 80x_3 + 50x_4 + S_2 = 80 \\
& 60x_1 + 20x_2 \qquad\qquad + 55x_4 + S_3 = 60 \\
& x_1 + S_4 = 1 \\
& x_2 + S_5 = 1 \\
& x_3 + S_6 = 1 \\
& x_4 + S_7 = 1 \\
& x_i \geqslant 0 \quad i = 1 \text{ to } 4
\end{aligned}
$$

This problem was processed using the LINDO package. A final solution was reached after two iterations as the printout below:

```
LP Optimum found at step 2
Objective function value: 89.625
VARIABLE      VALUE
X1            0.0
X2            0.0
X3            0.375
X4            1.0
  ROW         SLACK        DUAL PRICES
  (S1)        80.0           0.0
  (S2)        0.0            0.9875
  (S3)        5.0            0.0
  (S4)        1.0            0.0
  (S5)        1.0            0.0
  (S6)        0.625          0.0
  (S7)        0.0            10.625
```

The printout indicates that the optimum return in terms of NPV is £89.625 m. This is obtained by purchasing all of project 4 ($x_4 = 1$) and three-eights of project 3 ($x_3 = 0.375$). This investment leaves spare capital at time point 1 of £80 m ($S_1 = 80$) and £15 m at time point 3 ($S_3 = 5$). The project slack variables confirm what we know from the x values. In the optimum solution projects 1 and 2 are unused ($S_4 = 1$, $S_5 = 1$) and project 3 is only .375 used ($S_6 = .675$).

The computer package uses the so-called *simplex* method of solution and the *dual* or *shadow price* is a valuable piece of information generated by simplex solutions. It tells you how much the value of the objective function would have increased if a particular constraint had been relaxed by one unit. In other words it tells you the opportunity cost of the constraint. By definition, the dual is only positive when the corresponding slack is zero and vice versa: a constraint only has an opportunity cost when it is binding. Capital was a binding constraint in period 2($S_2 = 0$). The dual tells us that had another £1 m of capital been available at time point 2, the value of the objective function would have increased by £987,500. Similarly we can see that had we been able to undertake project 4 twice instead of once this would have added £10,625,000 to total NPV.

An assessment of LP

The LP approach is powerful but it has its limitations, some only apparent, some real:

Linearity

As the name implies, the objective function and the constraints must be linear. In practice this is not a severe restriction since it is usually possible to approximate a non-linear relationship with a series of linear relationships.

Divisibility

The assumption that projects are divisible is again not as severe as at first seems. If the assumption that projects can be scaled up or down and their NPVs scaled up or down proportionately, does too much violence to the facts, in other words if the projects use resources with significant indivisibilities, then integer programming models can be used.

Opportunity cost of capital

A more perplexing problem in capital rationing is what discount rate to use. In the example above the NPVs of the alternative projects were worked out using the opportunity cost of capital, which was taken to be known and constant for the duration of the projects. The trouble is that, on the face of it, capital rationing is exactly the situation when this cannot be assumed! The opportunity cost of capital in any period is the return on the marginal project in that period. But we do not know what the marginal project is until we have gone through the optimising process, and we cannot do that without the discount rate! However, the distinction between 'soft' and 'hard' capital rationing is important here. It is the investors' opportunity cost of capital that is significant, but this will vary with the composition of the firm's optimal bundle of projects only if the capital market has imperfections and there is 'hard' capital rationing. If the capital market rationing is 'soft', self-imposed by the firm, then it will not affect the investors' opportunity cost of capital and we are safe to go on using the firm's cost of capital as a discount rate.

Uncertainty

Perhaps the most telling limitation of LP is its requirement of certainty about cash flows from future projects, and about capital constraints. At present no very satisfactory way has been devised of incorporating uncertainty into the model. In reality, though, in an uncertain and changing world, opportunities and constraints are constantly changing and unfolding. But this limitation is common to all optimising techniques including DCF analysis itself. The answer is to recognise that optimising must be a continuous, rather than a 'once-for-all' process, with plans being constantly revised in the light of new information. But decisions still have to be made, and LP can be a valuable aid in project choice.

V THE INTERNAL RATE OF RETURN

We saw that our investment decision-rule could be specified in terms of a project's internal rate of return: accept all projects with an IRR greater than the cost of capital. In practice IRR is in widespread use in decision making. Unfortunately, though NPV is robust to relaxing most of the Fisher-Hirshleifer assumptions (see Chapter 6), IRR is less so. On closer inspection IRR betrays major weaknesses as the basis for a decision-rule.

For 'conventional' projects in which an initial outflow of cash is followed by a succession of inflows, the relationship between IRR and NPV is shown in Figure II. This would be the relationship under the Fisher-Hirshleifer assumptions. We can see that IRR and NPV give completely consistent signals – when IRR > r_1 NPV is positive, when IRR < r_2, NPV is negative. However if some of the Fisher-Hirshleifer assumptions are relaxed this may not be so.

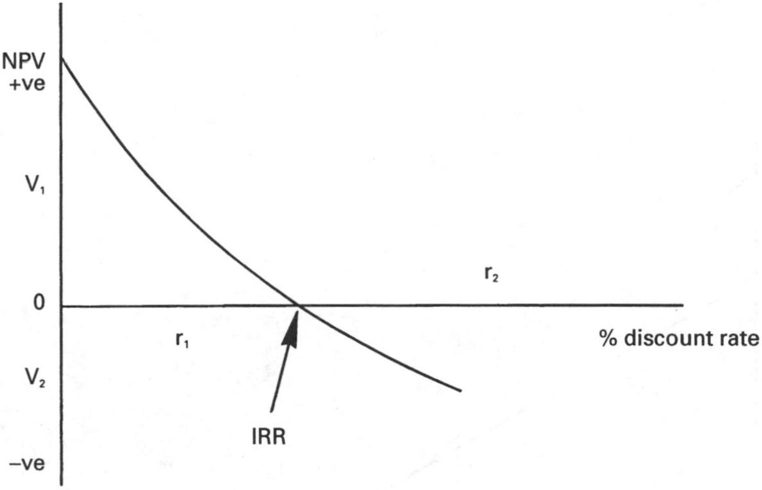

Figure II The relationship of the NPV and IRR of a project

Project interdependence

If projects are not independent IRR may fail. Suppose projects are *mutually exclusive* – the firm might be choosing a new computer and though there are many acceptable makes available it only wants one. In this case the decision-maker needs additional information to *rank* the computers in order of merit.

IRR cannot be relied upon to rank projects correctly. Consider the mutually exclusive projects J and K:

	Cash flows			
	Yr 0	Yr 1	IRR	NPV at 10%
Project J	(£100)	£150	50%	£36
Project K	(£300)	£400	33%	£64

On this basis of IRR we would choose J, on the basis of NPV, K. We can rely on the NPV signal – it tells us how much projects J and K would increase our wealth. The IRR is merely beguiling – project J does offer a higher percentage return per pound invested, but this is not the appropriate criterion for project choice. In the case of mutually exclusive projects the relative efficiency of the smaller project is *irrelevant*, it is the absolute level of NPV that counts. In this example the problem was caused by the fact that the competing projects were of different *scale*. But more generally the ranking problem can arise whenever two projects' NPV functions intersect in the positive quadrant. Figure III shows the nub of the problem. The NPV for two projects A and B is graphed at different discount rates. The IRR of B is higher than that of A, as its line cuts the X axis at a higher discount rate. But, because the A and B lines intersect, which project has the better NPV *depends on the choice of discount rate*. If the discount rate is x, A has the higher NPV. If it is y, then B is preferred. The discount rate is crucial. It provides the correct rate for reinvestment, and it reassures us that the capital which is used in the project is fully costed, and that a uniform measure of the cost of capital is being used for *every* project being pursued. On these grounds we have confidence in NPV as always giving an accurate ranking.

The problem of IRR with mutually exclusive projects can be solved however. The

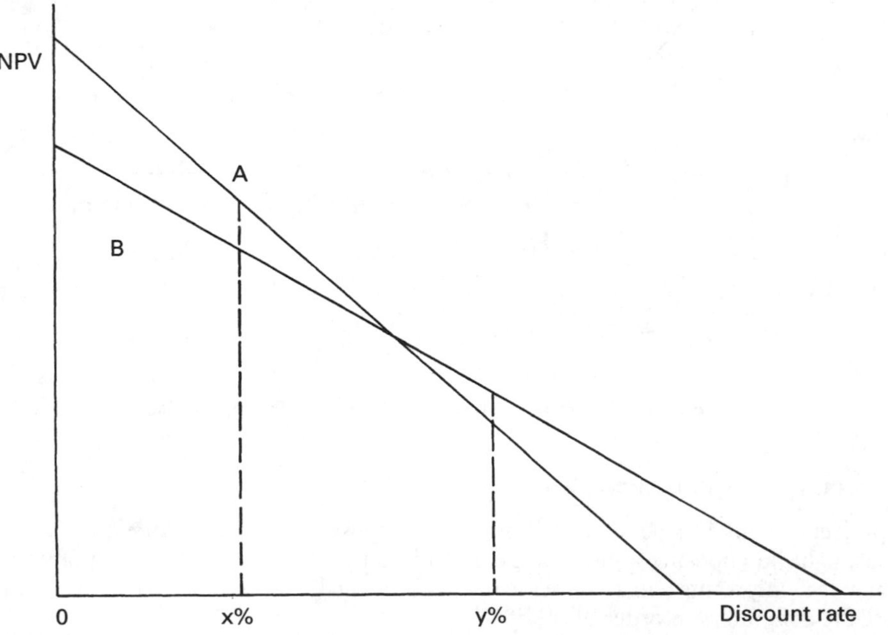

Figure III NPV for two projects

solution is to combine projects into one project for appraisal by taking one from the other and appraising the difference.

Consider the following cash flows of projects A, B and the difference A−B

	Cash flows		
	t_0	t_1	t_2
A	(500)	100	600
B	(500)	500	150
'A − B'	0	(400)	450

Calculating NPV for A and B at a 10% discount rate, and IRR, we get

	NPV	IRR
A	87	20%
B	79	29%

with IRR preversely favouring B. But if we are determined to use IRR we can find the IRR of 'A − B', which is 13%. Since the IRR of 'A − B' is greater than the cost of capital, A is preferred, and this is consistent with the NPV analysis.

Multiple time-periods

Once projects stretch beyond two time-periods in length (Assumption 3) it becomes possible they will not have a 'conventional' profile of cash flows, ie an initial outlay followed by positive inflows in all future periods. If the cash profile is any different it may have multiple solutions to its IRR, or even no IRR at all. Consider the following project:

Year	*0*	*1*	*2*	*3*
Cash flow	(25)	150	(275)	150
Sign of cash flow	−ve	+ve	−ve	+ve

This project has three IRRs: 0%, 100%, 200%! The decision-maker would be hard put to interpret this information.

The problem is that the IRR formula $NPV = \sum_{t=0}^{n} \frac{C_t}{(1+R)^t}$ is a polynomial with n roots of which the number of *real* roots, which are the IRR values, can be up to but not greater than the number of sign changes in the cash flows, C_t. In the case of the previous project there were three sign changes and three solutions.

In reality there are very many projects with unconventional cash flows. For example, processes which require re-equipping halfway through; projects with heavy contractual costs at the end for refurbishment; orders for which the customer makes a significant advance payment; and so forth. In terms of the NPV function all these projects share the characteristic of cutting the x-axis more than once, hence their multiple IRRs. Figure IV depicts this for the project mentioned above.

Varying costs of capital

Another problem where there are multiple time-periods is that IRR gives an average return over the life of the project. This may not matter too much if the cost of capital is constant through time, but forecasting a constant cost of capital is usually a simplifying

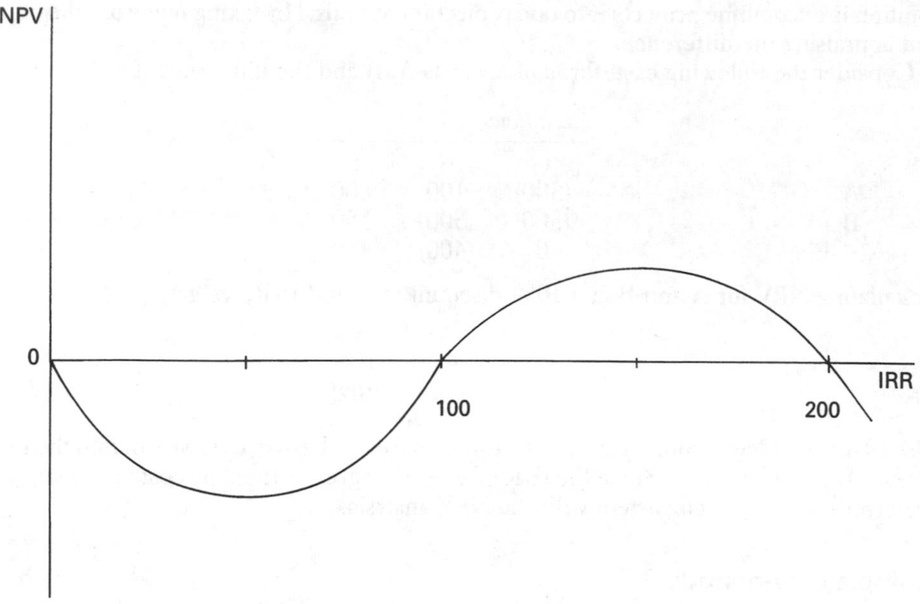

Figure IV The relationship of NPV and IRR for the project with unconventional cash flow

assumption forced by lack of better information. Suppose we have the following data about a five-year project.

Project IRR 12%

	Year	1	2	3	4	5
Forecast cost of capital:		8%	8%	10%	14%	14%

We could not ascertain the project's acceptability without further analysis – it would be simpler to calculate NPV at the outset.

The economic significance of IRR

The fundamental problem with IRR is rather simple. IRR tells us what the cost of capital *would need to be* to give NPV = 0. This is interesting, but only indirectly related to our real concern which is what NPV *is* at the ruling cost of capital. The problem is that to make the calculation we assume the cost of capital to be different from what it actually is: we assume that the firm can borrow needed cash and invest spare cash during the project at the project's IRR rate. This is the so-called *reinvestment* assumption. This is a safe assumption, one that does not yield confusing or downright misleading results, only in the Fisher-Hirshleifer world.

The appeal of IRR is that it is expressed as a rate of return, and these are the terms in which businessmen like to talk. Our objection is that it attracts attention to the wrong feature of projects, and this can be dangerous. The oddness of IRR as a decision-criterion becomes clearer if we recall that capital is just one input to a project. Labour and materials might be others, and we could just as well calculate what the cost of labour would need to be to give a zero NPV, or the cost of materials, and call these the internal return on labour, IRL, or the internal return on materials, IRM. As we see in the next chapter, firms do explore these issues as part of the analysis of the sensitivity of project NPVs to changes in assumptions. But the appropriate *overall* measure of project worth remains NPV. We encounter a similar problem when we look at some decision criteria such as *payback* in a later chapter. The payback criterion says *choose the project which recovers its initial outlay first*. Again, speed of payback is one component of a project's success, but by raising it to the status of a decision-rule problems arise.

In general we have two reasons for prefering NPV. First, NPV provides a robust decision-rule in situations where IRR fails. Second, NPV relates directly to the objective of value maximisation, it measures the amount by which a project adds to the value of the firm.

VI SUMMARY

In this chapter we have seen how to find the NPV of a typical investment project, and discussed the problem of inflation, and the concepts of the cost of capital and of the 'economic life' of the project. The Fisher-Hirshleifer model showed how by adopting the decision-rule – *choose all projects with a positive NPV* – the wealth of shareholders would be maximised. However, we saw in this chapter that the associated rule in terms of *internal rate of return* can run into significant difficulties of interpretation under fairly realistic assumptions about projects.

The NPV has to be modified when capital is rationed, either by outside suppliers of finance or internally as a policy decision. The solution is an application of the constrained-resource analysis of Chapter 4, we recommend the firm to choose the bundle of projects with the highest NPV. We pointed out that the more likely form of capital rationing encountered was internal, and that here the loss of value was often more apparent than real since the imposition of capital rationing might well be a method of accounting for risk and for indirect costs that are hard to quantify. The practical problem of choosing between positive valued projects can be handled by using linear programming, though the usefulness of a technique such as this is in practice limited by its inability to cope with the uncertainty of the real world.

REFERENCES AND BIBLIOGRAPHY

Fisher, I — *The Theory of Interest* (1930) Macmillan.

Keane, S M — 'The Internal Rate of Return and the Reinvestment Fallacy', Abacus, June 1979.

Kotler, P — *Marketing Management, Analysis, Planning and Control* (1991) Prentice-Hall, London.

Weingartner, H M — *Mathematical Programming and the Analysis of Capital Budgeting Problems* (1974) Kershaw, London.

Weingartner, H M — 'Capital Rationing: "n" Authors in Search of a Plot', Journal of Finance, Dec 1977, pp 1403–1432.

QUESTIONS

1 Sharpcrease plc is considering the possibility of opening a new factory to produce inlaid rosewood trouser-presses. The company expects to be able to sell each one for £2,000.

The factory will cost £700,000 to build and equip, and will have annual fixed costs of £40,000. The company purchased the site for the factory for £200,000 two years ago, and have already spent £20,000 on excavation of it. If they decide not to open the new factory, they will sell the site as it stands for £350,000.

The production costs per trouser-press will be as follows:

Materials	£400
Direct labour	£300
General administrative overhead	£200

Although the company can sell unlimited quantities for £2,000 each, the materials used in its production are so specialised and scarce that only enough can be purchased to produce 250 a year.

The market for the presses is expected to last for ten years, at which point ABC will sell the site complete for £400,000. The company's discount rate for appraising such project is 15%; and the company does not expect to pay tax for the foreseeable future.

How much better off will Sharpcrease be if it accepts the project?

What annual production level will be just sufficient to allow Sharpcrease to break even on this project?

What other information would you find useful in appraising this project?

2 How would your answer to Question 1 be affected if:
(a) all the project costs and revenues were expected to rise in line with the RPI over the life of the project, and the RPI itself is expected to rise at 5% per year,
(b) materials and labour costs will rise by 2% per annum more than the RPI?

3 Evaluate the following project. Your company's cut-off rate for investment projects is 12%.

Cost of machine	£40,000
Scrap value, after 5-year life	£2,000
Annual net revenues from machine	£14,000

Tax is payable one year in arrears. Assume the tax rate is 35% and the company will receive 25% per annum writing down allowance on the reducing balance.

4 Jack Ltd is considering two projects A and B with the following cash flows:

t =	0	1	2
Project A	£(8,000)	£6,000	£4,000
Project B	£(2,000)	£1,000	£2,000

Calculate the NPVs of projects A and B using a discount rate of 10% and 25%, and their IRRs.

Which project(s) should Jack choose if A and B are (i) mutually exclusive (ii) not mutually exclusive?

5 The Smith Company has a lathe of a sort for which an active new and second-hand market exists. The net revenues from using the lathe are £21,000 per year. The lathe could be retained for six years or replaced at any point at a replacement cost of £60,000.

The second-hand prices for such lathes are:

Years old	*Market value*
1	£50,000
2	£42,500
3	£37,500
4	£30,000
5	£16,000
6	£3,000

What is the optimal replacement policy assuming a 10% cost of capital? What will your answer be if the net revenues are £30,000 p a not £21,000?

Explain the apparent paradox that an optimum exists at all, assuming a perfect market for a second-hand asset, with national buyers.

6 A choice has to be made of some combination of six available projects in such a way as to maximise the net present value of the returns. The projects require investments during the next three years, and these together with the net present value of the returns are given below (in £000s).

		PROJECT					
		I	II	III	IV	V	VI
	YEAR 1	25	5	18	22	4	13
Investment	2	10	20	18	—	10	5
required	3	—	5	18	—	18	5
NPV of returns		48	40	65	40	36	32

Capital is rationed to 65 per year.

(i) Formulate (without solving) this as a linear programming problem assuming that it would be possible to purchase any proportion of each project.

(ii) Explain how you would interpret the solutions to the LP, including the shadow prices on the constraints.

Part III
Risk

CHAPTER 8

Risk aversion and portfolio building

We have seen how the firm would choose its projects if the future were known with certainty. But the future is far from certain and we need to be able to make investment decisions under conditions of risk.

This chapter examines the theory behind risk analysis. In Section I we consider what risk means. Section II introduces the fundamental assumption that investors are risk-averse, and Section III shows how investors can reduce their risk by building portfolios of assets. Section IV brings together these two elements, the preferences of investors and the asset portfolios they can build, to analyse risky investment decisions. The 'capital asset pricing model' which we describe in Section V gives an expression for the return we should expect to get on any risky asset, and in the next chapter we use this as the basis for a decision-rule for choosing risky projects.

I MEASURING RISK

Suppose we are not certain what return we are going to get from an investment decision. The variety of possible outcomes the decision can have can be described in terms of the value, r_i, of each outcome i, and the probability p_i, of it happening. The probability of a certain outcome is 1, and of an impossible outcome 0. The probabilities of all possible outcomes must sum to 1, that is $\sum_{i=1}^{n} p_i = 1$ where n is the number of possible outcomes.

Hardcastle Manufacturing Company

Hardcastle Manufacturing Company is wondering what return it will get from its umbrella division if it keeps the division going next year. The results of the last ten years were:

Umbrella Division

year	19*0	1	2	3	4	5	6	7	8	9
% return	9	14	14	8	15	17	17	10	14	22

Hardcastle believes the last ten years were representative, permitting us to make the vital step of assuming that the actual outcomes over the last ten years describe the distribution of probable outcomes in any individual subsequent year; and of reading the *proportion* of times a return was achieved in the last ten years as the *probability* it will be achieved subsequently. To describe a probability distribution like this we can use two statistics, the *expected value* and the *variance*.

The expected value is the mean of the outcomes, $\bar{r}$, where $\bar{r} = \sum_{i=1}^{n} r_i p_i$

The variance is a measure of the spread of the various possible outcomes around this mean. We measure the variance, σ^2, of a distribution as

$$\sigma^2 = \sum_{i=1}^{n} (r_i - \bar{r})^2 p_i$$

So the $\bar{r}$ and σ^2 for the Umbrella Division are

r_i	p_i	$r_i p_i$	$r_i - \bar{r}$	$(r_i - \bar{r})^2 p_i$
8	.1	.8	−6	3.6
9	.1	.9	−5	2.5
10	.1	1.0	−4	1.6
14	.3	4.2	0	0
15	.1	1.5	1	.1
17	.2	3.4	3	1.8
22	.1	2.2	8	6.4
expected value = $\bar{r}$ =		14.0	variance = σ^2 =	16.0

An alternative way of describing the spread which is sometimes more convenient is the *standard deviation*. The standard deviation, σ, is simply the square-root of the variance, so the Umbrella Division's σ is $\sqrt{16} = 4\%$. In one sense, σ may be easier to interpret than σ^2 since it provides a measure of spread which is of the same scale as the original data.

In finance we use variance and standard deviation to measure risk. The greater the variance of outcomes from a project, the more risky we will say the project is; the greater the variance in returns from a division, or from the firm as a whole, the more risky the division or firm. Measuring risk this way, we can proceed to build a theory of how individuals choose risky assets. But before we do that there are one or two important cautions to bear in mind.

The first is a technical point. Probability distributions can come in all shapes and sizes, and not all of them can be completely described in terms of mean and variance. Variables that follow the so-called 'normal distribution' *do* have this property – if you know the mean and the variance you can work out the whole distribution and the probability of each outcome. For example we know from mathematical tables that 95% of the area of a normal distribution lies within 1.96 standard deviations either side of the mean, and 99% is within 2.58 standard deviations. Applying this to the Umbrella Division, we know that the mean return $\bar{r}$, is 14%, and the standard deviation, σ, is 4%. So if the division's returns are normally distributed, there is a 95% probability that the returns in any year will be between 6% and 22% (= $14 \pm 1.96 \times 4$), and a 90% chance they will be between 4% and 24%.

Figure IA shows the symmetric, bell-shaped pattern of the normal distribution. A remarkable number of variables in nature follow this distribution, but do the returns to projects and firms? In the long run returns to firms are likely to be 'skewed' as in Figure IB. This is because while there is no upper limit to the returns a firm can earn, firms earning inadequate returns will sooner or later go out of business. Despite this it is convenient to assume 'normality' so long as it does not do too much violence to the facts.

The second thing we might question about variance is whether variance is really what people worry about when they consider risk. In calculating variance, positive and negative deviations from the mean get equal weight, but are people really indifferent between positive and negative? Surely the preoccupation of most decision-makers is with the so-called *downside risk*, and in particular the risk of failure, the shaded area in Figure IC? As we develop the story in this chapter it will become clearer why finance theory does not pay more attention to this. Finance theory envisages people holding bundles of assets, projects, or shares in firms, so that the risk of failure on one individual asset *is* balanced by the possibility of success on another, and it is overall risk and return that matters. In any case if returns are normally distributed standard deviation will be a perfect *proxy* for downside risk. We will assume that people choose assets on the basis of their mean and variance. But how far decision-makers actually think this way is another question and it may be that finance theory should pay more attention to downside risk.

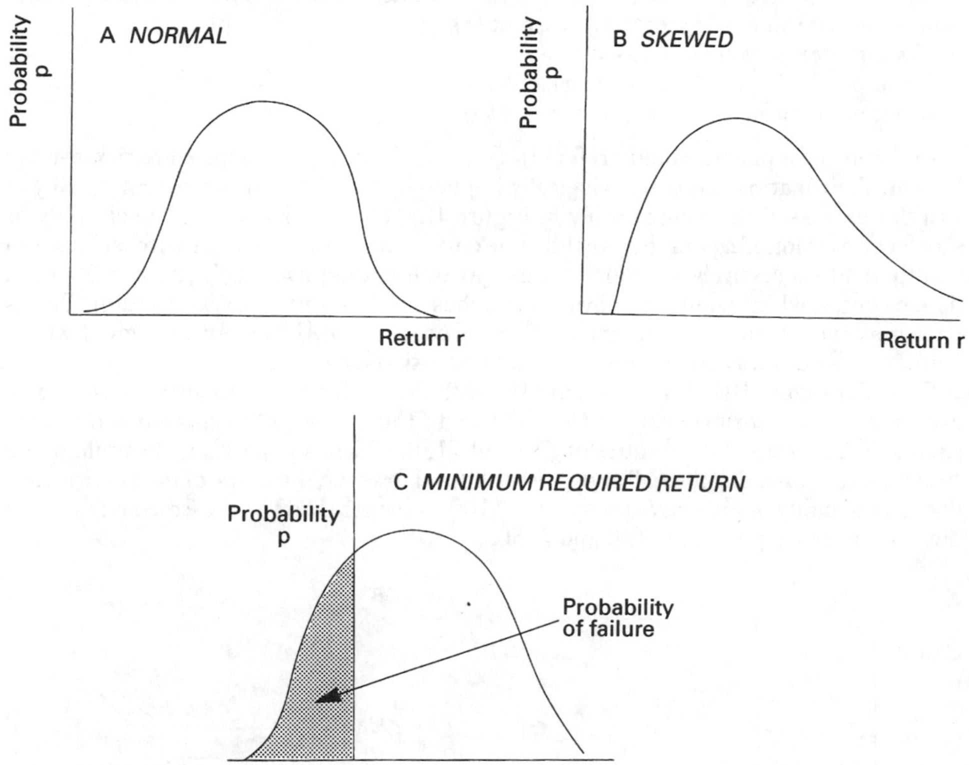

Figure I Some probability distributions

One final reservation before we proceed. We can talk about risk when we have sufficient information to estimate the mean and variance of the distribution of outcomes. But this still requires a relatively high level of information. At the other extreme we may find decision-makers operating under such *uncertainty* that they are unable to produce any clear views about future outcomes. This situation does not provide such attractive material for finance theorists but may describe the predicament of many decision-makers. The prevalence of uncertainty puts a limit on the usefulness of risk analysis and we return to this topic at the end of the next chapter.

II RISK AVERSION

In everyday usage of the word, 'risk' is clearly 'a bad thing', something to be avoided.

Example

You are offered the choice of two deals:
either (a) the certainty of £100
or (b) a .5 chance of £150 and a .5 chance of £50.
Which would you prefer? Don't forget that the 'expected value' of (b) is $.5 \times £150 + .5 \times £50 = £100$
Your answer will indicate if you are 'risk-averse' or not. The riskier alternative is clearly (b) – the expected values of (a) and (b) are the same, but the spread of actual outcomes around that value is higher in the case of (b).
If you prefer (a) you are RISK-AVERSE.
If you prefer (b) you are RISK-PREFERRING.
If you are indifferent you are RISK-NEUTRAL.

Probably most people would prefer (a). But why do we believe people are risk-averse? We can show that risk aversion is logically implied by the 'diminishing marginal utility of wealth', expressed diagrammatically in Figure IIA. Here an individual's total utility or satisfaction is plotted against her wealth. The curve is drawn so that successive increases in wealth yield successively smaller increases in utility, until eventually the curve almost flattens out, at which point the individual attaches hardly any value to extra wealth. This is known as the 'diminishing marginal utility of wealth' (DMUW). An individual whose attitude to wealth was one of this sort would be risk-averse.

Consider Figure IIB. which is Figure IIA with the earlier example superimposed. The expected return from an equal gamble of £50 and £150 is £100. The expected *utility* of the gamble is the mean of the utilities of £50 and £150, which is point U_b halfway along the straight line connecting the £50 and £150 utilities. However, the shape of the curve means that U_a the utility of the *certain* prospect of £100, is higher than U_b, the expected utility of the two uncertain prospects, £50 and £150.

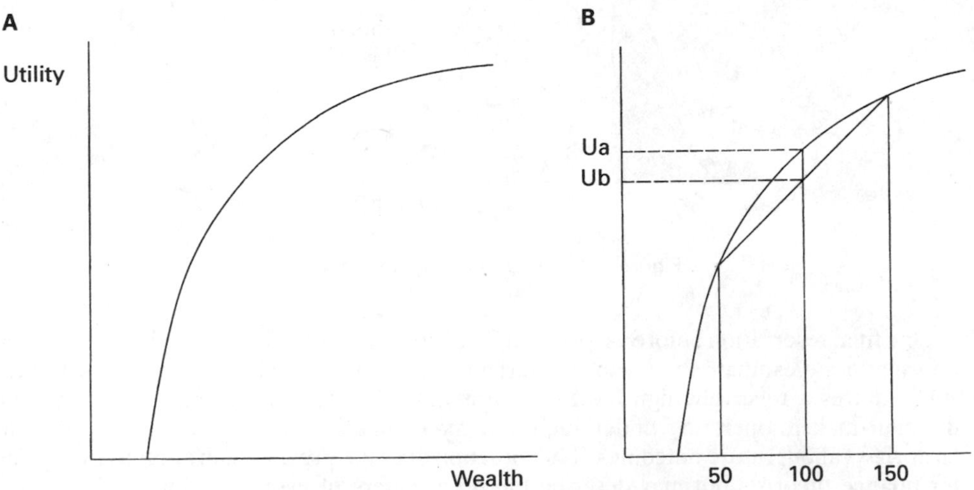

Figure II Diminishing marginal utility of wealth

Demonstrating risk aversion as a logical implication of DMUW is only helpful if DMUW can be validated some other way. The idea that the more wealth you have the less you value money is intuitively appealing – we have an image of the tycoon lighting his cigar with a $1,000 bill with the pauper agonising over the loss of a coin. But the idea needs some qualification. For example does MUW diminish over its whole range, or is it constant (linear) over part of the range? Constant marginal utility of income would imply risk-neutrality. Moreover, the concept of DMUW was developed to describe the individual consumer. Does it apply equally to the decision-maker in a firm? We can think of two reasons why managers may exhibit DMUW. One is the effect of the target-setting process. The other is the risk of bankruptcy.

Managers' performance is often appraised by comparing actual performance to a preordained target or budget, and the manager may prefer to be on target, rather than below *or* above it. He or she may prefer a certainty of achieving budgeted sales of say £100 to an equal change of achieving £50 sales and £150 sales. Under-performance may have damaging career implications, over-performance may involve the need to set targets next period which are hard to live up to. The lower the risk, the better the manager's control over his or her future.

For most managers bankruptcy is to be avoided at all costs, and outcomes which make bankruptcy possible have a particularly heavy 'disutility'.

But if neither of these factors is present: if there is no institutional risk aversion created by the appraisal system, and if there is no real risk of bankruptcy then the manager's MUW may be linear, and the manager may be risk-neutral. Henceforth though we will be assuming that decision-makers, be they investors or managers, are risk-averse and have diminishing MUW.

The risk return trade-off

The key problem posed by risk is that asset choice now has two dimensions, return and risk. If they only had one dimension, return, as they do under certainty, it would be easy to choose between them, and find a decision-rule which any 'rational' person would agree to. For example, if project A yields a return of 8% and project B 6%, A must be preferred on the most basic axiom of all, that more is preferred to less. One-dimensional choices are easy to make. But suppose A and B have the following:

	A	B
expected return	8%	6%
variance	11	9

So A has more return and more risk. Now it is unclear which is the better project, and no amount of studying the projects will make it clearer. To find which is the better project it is necessary to study the decision-maker, and the relative valuation he puts on risk and return, his *risk-return trade-off*. Any decision-rule needs to take account of subjective data, the preferences of the decision-maker. We depict these preferences between risk and return as a set of concave indifference curves as in Figure III.

The E–V rule

Underlying Figure III is a fundamental assumption: that people choose assets according to the EXPECTED RETURN-VARIANCE rule.[1] It says project A will be preferred to project B if

1 The E–V rule was first presented by Harry Markowitz (1952). The theory of choice under uncertainty shows that given certain fundamental axioms about their preferences, people will seek to maximise their expected utility of wealth. They can do this by choosing according to the E–V rule, but only if asset returns are normally distributed, or if the individuals have quadratic preferences. The theory behind Figure IV is described in more detail in, for example, Huang and Litzenberger (1988).

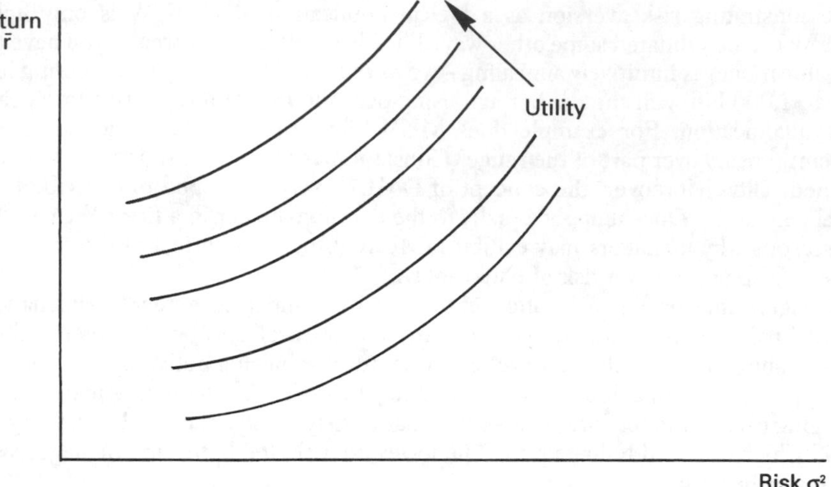

Figure III The individual's preferences

1 Expected return of A exceeds (or is equal to) the expected return of B and the variance of A is less than the variance of B, or
2 Expected return of A exceeds that of B and the variance of A is less than (or equal to) that of B.

The rule is easily understood in a graph.

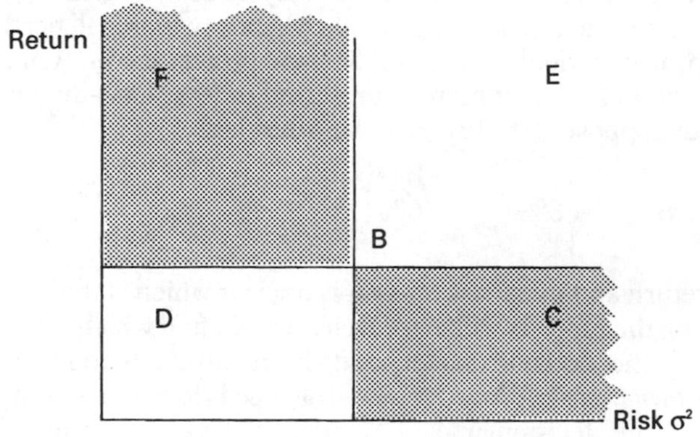

Figure IV The E–V rule

Any project in segment F will be preferred to project B. Similarly B will be preferred to any project in C.

As it stands, though, the E–V rule is not an operational rule for choosing projects. It correctly points out that in practice many 'two-dimensional' decisions are effectively 'one-dimensional' in the above sense since certain projects *dominate* other projects; are not worse than them on either dimension. But the E–V rule is silent on the important question how we should choose between B and projects in D and E, that is, between projects which are better in one respect and worse in another. We need a rule which will cover these cases but before we can develop it there is another factor to be taken into account, the effects of diversifying risk.

III PORTFOLIO BUILDING

Few firms have just one project, and few investors own shares in just one firm. People like to spread their risks, hold *portfolios* of assets. In everyday life the advice is 'don't put all your eggs in one basket'. We can get the idea behind this if we compare Hardcastle's Umbrella Division with another of its divisions, Deckchairs. Figure V plots the returns of the two divisions through time, and also the return of the two divisions together. If the two divisions are combined the expected return is summed, but not the variability. The return of the joint project fluctuates less than the individual projects because their fluctuations have cancelled each other out to some extent.

Before we can be more precise about portfolio risk and return, however, we need to understand the concept of covariance.

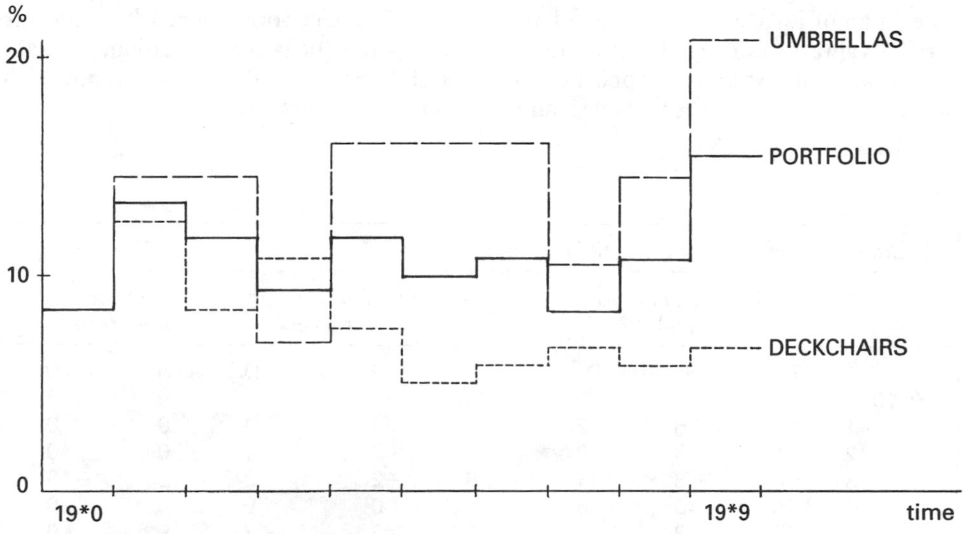

Figure V Hardcastle returns

Covariance and correlation

Closely linked to variance is another key concept, *covariance*. If we know the distribution of returns to an asset we can work out the expected value, and the variance will tell us how widely the actual outcomes are likely to be spread around this expected value.

But suppose we have *two* assets. It will be useful to know the extent to which the returns on these two assets vary together. Do high returns on one asset tend to occur when the other asset has high returns, or when it has low returns, or is there no relationship? Covariance measures this. The covariance between two assets j and k, σ_{jk}, is calculated as follows:

$$\sigma_{jk} = \sum_{i=1}^{n} (r_{ij} - \bar{r}_j)(r_{ik} - \bar{r}_k)p_i$$

The above formula is similar to the variance formula we met before except that now, instead of being squared, each deviation from the mean is matched with the corresponding deviation for the other asset. In fact variance is a special case of covariance. The variance of a series of numbers is simply its covariance with itself.

Hardcastle Manufacturing has a Raincoat and a Deckchair Division, as well as the Umbrella Division we met earlier. In Table I we chart the divisional results and work out the covariance between Raincoats and these two other divisions.

The covariance between Umbrella and Raincoats is 5.9. In absolute terms this does not mean much, but we can interpret it by relating it to the standard deviations of the two divisions to measure the *correlation* between them.

The *coefficient of correlation* between two variables j and k, R_{jk}, is measured by

$$R_{jk} = \frac{\sigma_{jk}}{\sigma_j \sigma_k}$$

The value of R_{jk} can range from +1 in the case of perfect correlation, where the two variables always move together, to −1 in the case of perfect negative correlation, when the two variables always move in opposite directions. If R_{jk} is around 0 then there is obviously no assocation between the variables, and we say they are *independent*.

Table I Hardcastle Manufacturing Co

	Divisional returns (%)			*Deviations from mean* $(r_i - \bar{r})$			*Product of deviations*	
	U	R	D	U	R	D	UxR	UxD
Yr 19*0	9	9	9	−5	−1	1	5	−5
1	14	6	12	0	−4	4	0	0
2	14	8	9	0	−2	1	0	0
3	8	8	11	−6	−2	3	12	−18
4	15	10	8	1	0	0	0	0
5	17	13	5	3	3	−3	9	−9
6	17	13	6	3	3	−2	9	−6
7	10	10	7	−4	0	−1	0	4
8	14	10	6	0	0	−2	0	0
9	22	13	7	8	3	−1	24	−8
	14%	10%	8%				59	−42

So, $\sigma_{UR} = 59 \div 10$ $\quad \sigma_{UD} = -42 \div 10$
So, $\sigma_{UR} = 5.9$ $\quad = -4.2$

In Hardcastle's case we know $\sigma_{UR} = 5.9\%$, and $\sigma_U = 4\%$. The reader can check that $\sigma_R = 2.28\%$, so $R_{UR} = \dfrac{5.9}{4 \times 2.28} = .65$

The returns are highly correlated, and this partly reflects the close relation between demand for umbrellas and raincoats. With deckchairs though it is a different story. There we have $\sigma_{UD} = -4.2\%$, $\sigma_U = 4\%$, and again the reader can confirm $\sigma_D = 2.15\%$, so $R_{UD} = \dfrac{-4.2}{4 \times 2.15} = -.49$. There is a fairly strong inverse correlation between the returns on umbrellas and deckchairs.

The risk and return of a two-asset portfolio

The expected return and variance of a two-asset portfolio are given by

$$\text{expected return } \bar{r} = p_j\bar{r}_j + p_k\bar{r}_k$$
$$\text{variance } \sigma^2 = p_j^2\sigma_j^2 + p_k^2\sigma_k^2 + 2p_jp_k\sigma_{jk}$$

where p_j, p_k, are the proportions of the two assets in the value of the portfolio.

The expected return is just the weighted average of the returns of the two assets. To understand the variance, though, it will be useful to substitute $\sigma_{jk} = R_{jk}\sigma_j\sigma_k$, to get

$$\sigma^2 = p_j^2\sigma_j^2 + p_k^2\sigma_k^2 + 2p_jp_k R_{jk}\sigma_j\sigma_k$$

Now suppose the two assets are perfectly correlated, so that $R_{jk} = 1$, this reduces to

$$\sigma^2 = (p_j\sigma_j + p_k\sigma_k)^2$$
and $\sigma = p_j\sigma_j + p_k\sigma_k$

At worst the standard deviation of a portfolio is the weighted average of the individual standard deviations, and there are no gains to diversification. This will happen when the asset returns are perfectly correlated. Anything less than perfect correlation means a reduction in standard deviation. So by building portfolios we can potentially reduce risk for no loss of return.

Recall what we know about Hardcastle and its divisions:

	$\bar{r}$	σ^2	σ	
Umbrellas	14%	16%	4%	
Raincoats	10%	5.2%	2.3%	$R_{UR} = .65$
Deckchairs	8%	4.6%	2.1%	$R_{UD} = -.49$

Suppose Hardcastle only owned the umbrella and raincoat operations, and had the same investment in each, so that $p_U = p_R = .5$. We can find Hardcastle's overall return and risk thus:

$$\text{expected return} = \bar{r} = (.5 \times 14) + (.5 \times 10) = 12\%$$
$$\text{variance} = \sigma^2$$
$$= (.5^2 \times 16) + (.5^2 \times 5.2) + (2 \times .5 \times .5 \times .65 \times 4 \times 2.3)$$
$$= 8.1\%$$

Now, suppose Hardcastle only invested in umbrellas and deckchairs but this time in the proportions 2:1. We choose this proportion so the return would be, as before,

$$\bar{r} = (2/3 \times 14) + (1/3 \times 8) = 12\%$$

but the risk would be

$$\sigma^2 = (2/3^2 \times 16) + (1/3^2 \times 4.6) - (2 \times 1/3 \times 2/3 \times .49 \times 4 \times 2.1)$$
$$= 5.8\%$$

Even though deckchairs look less attractive on their own than raincoats – they have a lower return and only marginally less risk – their negative covariance with umbrellas makes them ideal for *diversification*. In Figure VI we plot the standard deviation and return of the three divisions and different permutations. The dotted line shows what would have happened if deckchairs had *perfectly* negatively correlated with umbrellas. When R = −1 there is some investment proportion that will eliminate risk altogether. In this case it turns out to be $p_u = .344$, $p_D = .656$ as shown below.

When R = − 1, and $\sigma^2 = 0$, the variance formula becomes

$$0 = p_j^2\sigma_j^2 + p_k^2\sigma_k^2 - 2p_jp_k\sigma_j\sigma_k$$
$$= (p_j\sigma_j - p_k\sigma_k)^2$$
$$= p_j\sigma_j - p_k\sigma_k$$

so $\dfrac{p_j}{p_k} = \dfrac{\sigma_k}{\sigma_j}$

so in this case $\dfrac{p_U}{p_D} = \dfrac{\sigma_D}{\sigma_U} = \dfrac{2.1}{4}$, so $p_U = .344$, $p_D = .656$

With these proportions the portfolio has

$$\bar{r} = .344 \times 14 + .656 \times 8 = 10.1$$
$$\sigma^2 = .344^2 \times 16 + .656^2 \times 4.6 - 2 \times .344 \times .656 \times 4 \times 2.1 = 0$$

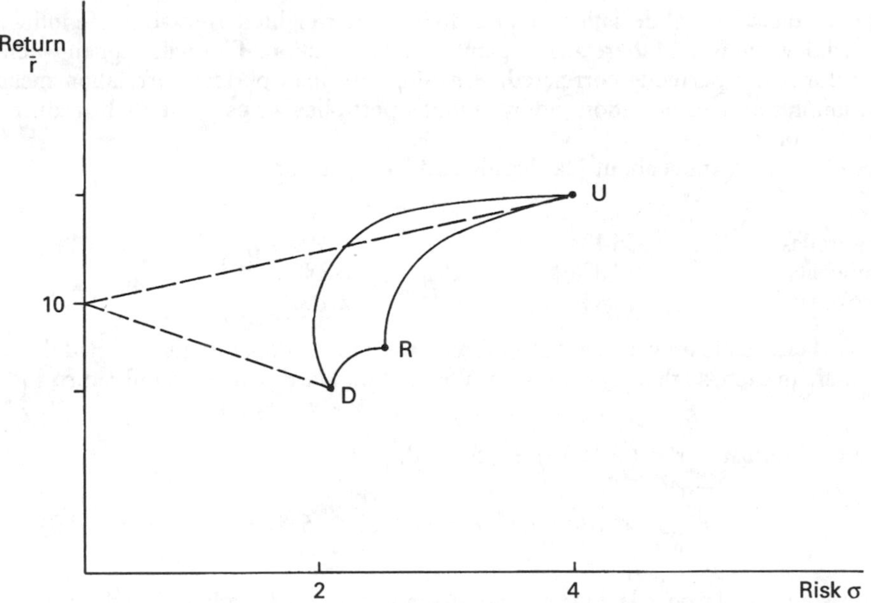

Figure VI Portfolio risk and return at Hardcastle

Portfolio risk with many assets

What happens to portfolio risk as we add more assets? The general formulae for the risk and return of an n-asset portfolio are:

$$\bar{r} = \sum_{j=1}^{n} \bar{r}_j p_j$$

$$\sigma^2 = \sum_{j=1}^{n} \sum_{k=1}^{n} p_j p_k \, \sigma_{jk}$$

The equation immediately above says that the variance of a portfolio is the sum of an n × n matrix of covariances, $p_j p_k \sigma_{jk}$, depicted in Figure VII.

When n was 2 (see variance expression on page 117), we find two variance terms, $p_j^2 \sigma_j^2$ and $p_k^2 \sigma_k^2$, and two covariance terms $2\ p_j p_k \sigma_{jk}$. In general with n assets we get n variance terms, and all the rest, n^2–n, are covariances between assets. So in a 20 asset portfolio, the variance would be an average of the 20 individual variances, and 380 ($=20^2-20$) covariances. As the portfolio grows the covariances between assets become the dominant factor in determining risk.

The diagonal terms in Figure VII give each asset's covariance with itself, i e its variance. We can see what this means in practice in Figure VIII. If we build an equally weighted portfolio of assets, chosen at random, then plot the variance of the portfolio against the number of assets, we find the portfolio variance drops sharply up to about 10 assets, then levels out rapidly. We can achieve the benefits of full-diversification with 10–20 assets.

asset	1	2	3	4	→ n
1	$p_1^2 \sigma_1^2$	$p_1 p_2 \sigma_{12}$	$p_1 p_3 \sigma_{13}$	$p_1 p_4 \sigma_{14}$	
2	$p_2 p_1 \sigma_{21}$	$p_2^2 \sigma_2^2$	$p_2 p_3 \sigma_{23}$		
3	$p_3 p_1 \sigma_{31}$	$p_3 p_2 \sigma_{32}$	$p_3^2 \sigma_3^2$		
4	$p_4 p_1 \sigma_{41}$				
↓ n					

Figure VII The variance of an n-asset portfolio

However as Figure VIII shows, risk can be minimised, but not eliminated entirely. To build a zero-variance portfolio we would need assets whose returns had perfectly negative correlation. In the real world these are hard to find. In reality returns *covary* to some extent. They rise and fall together in response to overall economy-wide influences. The risk that remains in a fully-diversified portfolio comes from these correlations between asset returns, the systematic movements in the market as a whole. Hence this residual risk is commonly called *undiversifiable, systematic* or *market* risk.

Suppose now we view the whole market as a portfolio, say all the 2,500 or so shares in

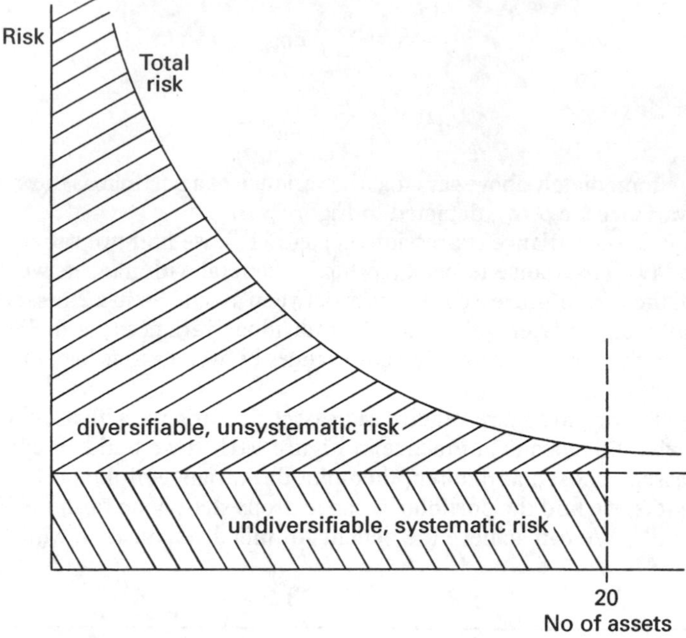

Figure VIII The effect of diversification on risk

the UK stock market. The *market portfolio* has a variance of σ_m, and the proportion of each share j in the market is $p_j = \dfrac{\text{value of shares in j}}{\text{value of all the shares in the market}}$. We can get an expression for the contribution of an individual asset to the overall risk of the market. If we take Figure VII as describing the risk of the market portfolio we can find the contribution of a particular asset by adding across a row. So for asset 1 we have:

$$\text{contribution of asset 1} = p_1 \sum_{j=1}^{n} p_j \sigma_{ij}$$

$$= p_1 \sigma_{1m}$$

If we added these together for all n assets in the market, that is added up all the rows in the matrix, we would of course get the variance of the market, σ_m^2. As a proportion of this market risk, asset 1 is contributing:

$$\text{proportionate contribution of asset 1} = p_1 \frac{\sigma_{1m}}{\sigma_m^2}$$

So the relative riskiness of an asset depends on $\dfrac{\sigma_{jm}}{\sigma_m^2}$, which we call the asset's *beta*. Beta tells us how risky an asset is compared to the market as a whole, and is a key statistic later on.

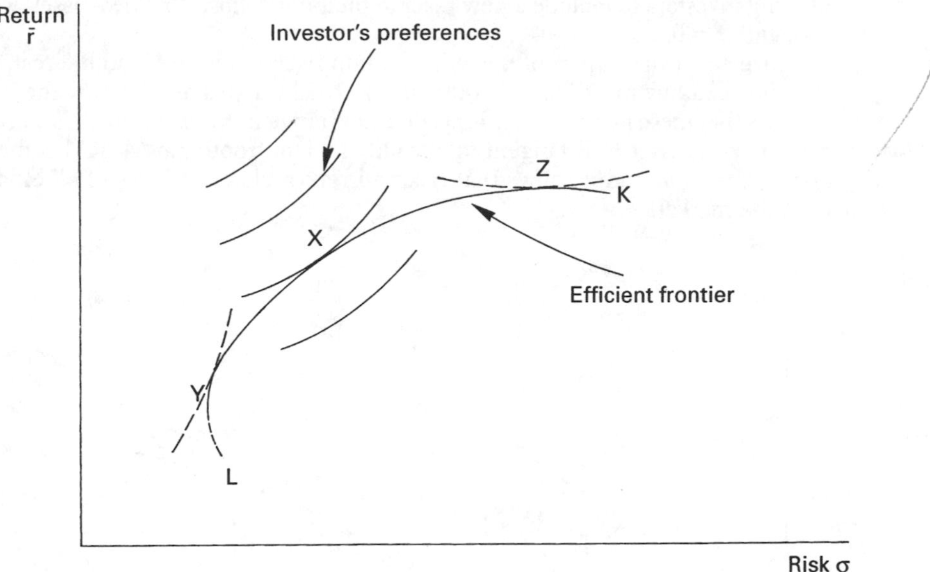

Figure IX Xavier's investment opportunities

IV THE OPTIMAL INVESTMENT DECISION UNDER RISK

Suppose Mr Xavier has £1,000 to invest. How will he make his investment decision? To start with, we will limit him to risky assets. There is any number of different portfolios he can hold out of all the risky assets on the market and these investment possibilities are the area in Figure IX bounded by the line LXK.

The efficient frontier

The first thing to note is that no rational investor, that is no investor choosing according to the E–V rule, would ever choose a portfolio on the interior of LXK. For every point within LXK there is a point on the frontier giving the same risk but a higher return. By the same token rational investors will only choose points on the solid part of the frontier. Points on the broken line below L, where the frontier bends back, are dominated by points on LXK. So we call LXK the *efficient frontier*.

To find out which portfolio on the efficient frontier Xavier will choose we introduce his preferences in the form of a set of indifference curves. He will choose the portfolio that gets him on to the highest indifference curve, which is X, the point of tangency with the efficient frontier. But different investors may have different points of tangency, for example Yolanthe is a more risk-averse individual and finds her optimum at Y, while Zoltan, a less risk-averse person, might prefer Z. Investors with different preferences over risk and return will choose different portfolios from the efficient frontier.

Borrowing and lending

However as we found in the Fisher-Hirshleifer model the analysis is transformed if we assume investors can borrow and lend at a rate of interest, r_i, and at no risk. In other words we are allowing investors to include a new asset in their portfolios, a 'riskless asset' with a return of r_i, and $\sigma = 0$.

Now our investors can put part of their £1,000 into risky assets and lend the rest, or if they prefer they can buy more than £1,000 worth of risky assets and borrow the extra. Figure X shows that these new possibilities yield a new efficient frontier, which is a *straight line* from the riskless asset as R tangent to our old efficient frontier at M. RM is the so-called *capital market line* and it shows that risk and return characteristics of all efficient portfolios in the market.

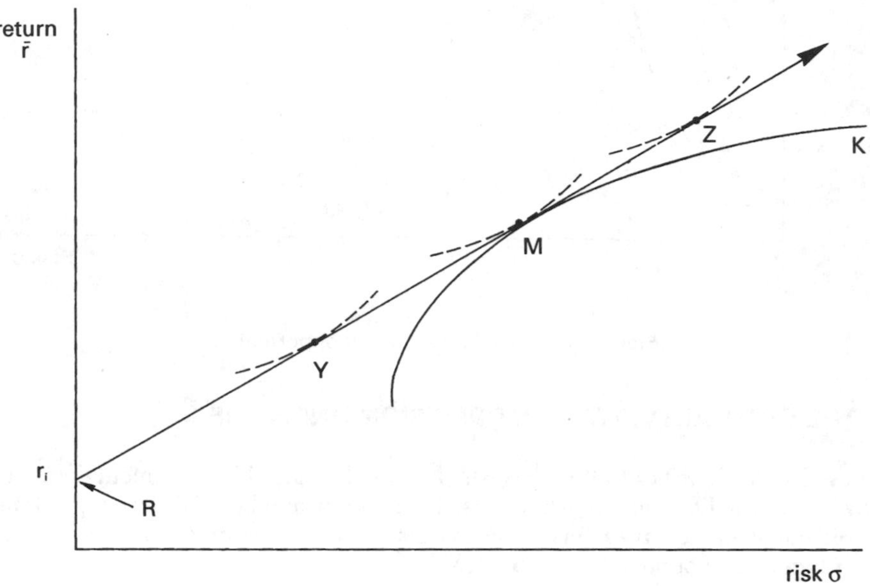

Figure X The capital market line

To see why the new frontier is a straight line we just need to recognise that the investor's new portfolio now contains two components, the riskless asset, R, and a composite of the risky assets, M. We know that the mean and variance of this two-asset portfolio are:

$$\text{mean} = \bar{r} = p_i r_i + p_M \bar{r}_M$$

$$\text{variance} = \sigma^2 = p_i^2 \sigma_i^2 + p_M^2 \sigma_M^2 + 2 p_i p_M \sigma_{iM}$$

But the variance of the riskless asset, σ_i^2, is by definition zero so the variance of this two-asset portfolio reduces to $\sigma^2 = p_M^2 \sigma_M^2$, and its standard deviation is $\sigma = p_M \sigma_M$. If we use standard deviation as the measure of risk, RM is a straight line.

There is any number of straight lines we could draw between R and the set of risky portfolios LMK, but the tangent RM gives the efficient frontier because, as before, it offers a higher return for the same variance than any interior point.

The reason borrowing and lending transforms the analysis is even clearer when we add back the investor's preferences from Figure XI. As before our investors have different preferences between risk and return and so have different points of tangency on RM. An investor with tangency at M invests 100% of the £1,000 in risky assets. In terms of proportions, $p_m = 1, p_i = 0$. If the tangency is at Y, investors hold some M and some R. But investors can borrow as well as lend, so there is nothing to stop then choosing Z if they prefer. Here he or she buys more than £1,000 worth of risky assets, and borrows the money to do it. Now, the portfolio proportions are $p_m > 1$, $p_i < 0$, with, as always, the proviso $p_m + p_i = 1$. This possibility explains why we can extend the efficient frontier out past M.

The thing that does not change is the tangency between RM and the set of risky portfolios. Investors all combine risky assets in the same relative proportions M, their only difference is in how much of M and R to hold. The composition of the optimal portfolio of risky assets is independent of the preferences of investors. This is the *separation theorem* and it is exactly equivalent to the separation result we got in the Fisher-Hirshleifer model. In both cases introducing borrowing and lending opportunities means that each investor can make his own investment choice independent of other investors, and independent of the determination of the optimal portfolio, in investment projects in the case of Fisher-Hirshleifer, and of risky assets in the present case.

V THE CAPITAL ASSET PRICING MODEL

Let us concentrate now on point M in Figure X, the optimum portfolio of risky assets chosen, in some proportion, by all investors. M must be the market portfolio. This follows because everyone, we assume, has the same view so if one person decides an assets return is too low no-one else will want it either, and its price will fall, and return rise, until it is include in the risky portfolio again. Of course this does not mean that all individuals have to have in their portfolios some of every asset in the market. What matters is that every asset earns a return relative to its risk, equivalent to that earned by all other assets in the market portfolio. If so, all assets will be perfect substitutes for one another. What is this relation between risk and return? During the 1960s the *capital asset pricing model* (CAPM) was developed to provide the answer to this question.[2] The CAPM shows that in equilibrium the return, r_j, on a risky asset j can be calculated as

$$r_j = r_i + \beta_j (r_m - r_i)$$

where as we saw earlier in this chapter $\beta_j = \frac{\sigma_{jm}}{\sigma_m^2}$, a measure of the volatility of assets j's return relative to the market. This equation is sometimes known as the *security market line*. The capital market line told us the relationship between the risk and return of efficient portfolios. The security market line tells us the relationship between risk and return of the individual assets in an efficient portfolio. It says that the return on any risky asset is the riskless interest rate plus a risk-premium which is a multiple β_j of the premium on the market as a whole. What the CAPM is saying is this: We know the return to risky assets on average, which is the return on the market portfolio, so the return to any assets will be in proportion to its risk compared to the average. This becomes clearer if we rearrange the equation slightly so that

$$(r_j - r_i) = \beta_j (r_m - r_i)$$

The risk-premium on j should be a proportion β_j of the risk-premium on the market as a whole. Figure XI shows this relationship for different betas.

2 The key articles in the development of the CAPM are Markowitz (1952), Sharpe (1964), Lintner (1965), Mossin (1966).

An asset whose return always rises and falls by the same percentage as the market so has a risk-premium of 5% when the market has a risk-premium of 5%, has a $\beta = 1$. The $\beta = 2$ line depicts a so-called 'aggressive' asset, whose return rises and falls by more than the market. A 'defensive' asset has $\beta < 1$. So with a β of .5 we would expect the return on an asset to rise by only 5% for a 10% increase in the market.

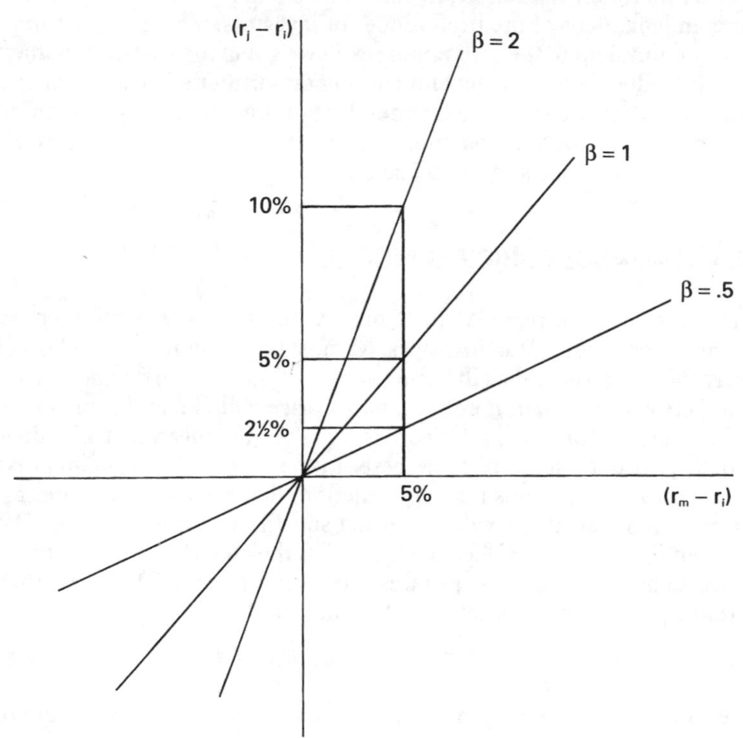

Figure XI The effect of different betas

VI SUMMARY

An investment decision is risky if it has more than one possible outcome. In this chapter we developed the theory behind the analysis of risk. We saw that investors are probably averse to risk, and that they can reduce their risk for no loss of return by holding portfolios of assets. Indeed in a perfect capital market everyone will hold full-diversified portfolios and the only risk investors will be unable to eliminate will be the 'specific' risk of each asset they hold. The CAPM shows us that this risk is measured by the asset's beta, and in such a world beta determines the price of risk.

The beauty of the CAPM is that it gives us a rule for quantifying risk in terms of return, and in the next chapter we will use it to find a discount rate for risky projects. The CAPM has found many applications in finance and is appealing for its simplicity and intuitive appeal. The problem with the CAPM is the rather restrictive assumptions under which the model holds. We will take a closer look at these in the next chapter.

REFERENCES AND BIBLIOGRAPHY

Friedman, M, and Savage, L J	'The Utility Analysis of Choices Involving Risk', Journal of Political Economy, Aug 1948, pp 279–304.
Huang, C F, and Litzenberger, R H	*Foundations for Financial Economics*, North-Holland, 1988.
Kondel, S, and Stanbough, R F	'On Correlations and Inferences about Mean–Variance Efficiency', Journal of Financial Economics 18, March 1987, pp 61–90.
Lintner, J	'The Valuation of Risk Assets and the Selection of Risky Investments in Stock Portfolios and Capital Budgets', Review of Economics and Statistics, Feb 1965, pp 13–37.
Markowitz, H	*Portfolio Selection* (1959) Yale University Press, New Haven.
Mossin, J	'Equilibrium in a Capital Asset Market', Econometrica, Oct 1966, pp 768–783.
Pratt, J W	'Risk Aversion in the Small and in the Large', Econometrica, Jan–April 1964, pp 122–136.
Sharpe, W F	'Capital Asset Prices: A Theory of Market Equilibrium under Conditions of Risk', Journal of Finance, Sept 1964, pp 425–442.

QUESTIONS

1 The Bouncy Beachball Company has experienced the following series of returns over five years:

1991	1992	1993	1994	1995
4%	−6%	13%	24%	18%

Find the mean and variance of this series.

2 Sam's Sailboard Company had the following returns:

1991	1992	1993	1994	1995
8%	2%	18%	25%	30%

Calculate the covariance and coefficient of correlation between Sam and Bouncy. Would Sam and Bouncy join well in a portfolio?

3 You are given the following choices:

a) a gift of £1,000, or
b) a 10% chance of getting £5,000, and a 90% chance of getting some other amount.

How much would the other amount have to be for you to be indifferent between the two alternatives if you were risk-neutral?

4 Why might the finance theorist be troubled if he found some people were taking out fire insurance on their houses and also filling in football pools?

5 Cedric is considering three projects with the following mean and variance of returns:

	mean	*variance*
project A	20	20
B	15	15
C	18	13

All we know about Cedric's preferences is that he is risk-averse. What can we say about his ranking of these projects?

6 The ordinary shares of Black Ltd and White Ltd have the following expected returns and standard deviations:

	Black	*White*
Expected return	8%	18%
Standard deviation	16%	20%

Calculate the expected return and variance for the following portfolios:

(i) 100% Black
(ii) 75% Black + 25% White
(iii) 50% Black + 50% White
(iv) 25% Black + 75% White
(v) 100% white

Assuming that the returns have a coefficient of correlation R = + .5 graph the resulting transformation curve.

7 Explain the difference between an efficient and an optimal portfolio, and show how the possibility of borrowing the lending at 5% affects the investors' opportunities in question (6). What are the relative proportions of Black and White in the optimal portfolio?

8 In a given economy, the standard deviation of the returns from a typical share is about 50% per year. The correlation coefficient between the returns of a typical pair of shares is .4. Calculate the variance and standard deviation of the returns on a portfolio that has equal investments in N shares. How many shares do you need to invest in to decrease the standard deviation of your portfolio to .332?

9 (i) Plot the following risky portfolios on a graph:

Portfolios	A	B	C	D	E	F
Expected returns (%)	10	13	15	16	17	17.5
Standard deviations (%)	25	20	22	21	27	30

(ii) Which of these portfolios are efficient and which are not? Which one would you choose to invest in?
(iii) Suppose you can lend and borrow at 12% which of the above portfolios is the best?

CHAPTER 9

Project investment under risk

In the last chapter we developed a theory of how investors will choose risky assets. The fruit of this was the capital asset pricing model, which yielded a very simple formula relating the return on any asset to its risk, measured by beta. Now we consider the firm's project investment decision under risk. Section I establishes the need for a simple and reliable method of adjusting the project discount rate for risk. Section II explains how the beta of a company can be found, and Section III shows how beta can provide a risk-premium for an individual project.

The beta technique is simple and intuitive but the underlying capital asset pricing model seems to rest on some fairly unrealistic assumptions. In Section IV we examine its assumptions and empirical support, and consider the usefulness of beta in practice. We then assess some alternative. In Section V we consider how risk can be handled when managers cannot use beta, and in Section VI we recognise that very often in practical situations managers will be working under extreme uncertainty and have nothing like the information needed to calculate beta or variance. So we present alternative techniques, of necessity cruder, which permit decision-makers to make efficient use of what information they have.

I A DECISION-RULE FOR RISKY PROJECTS

A good decision-rule will have the following properties. It should be *economical*, not requiring too much costly information. And what is much the same thing, it should be easy to *delegate* to subordinates. In large organisations it is essential to be able to delegate decisions, but it will only be feasible if checking and controlling subordinates is not too costly in terms of information. Making investment decisions under certainty we said 'choose all projects with a positive NPV' where

$$NPV = \sum_{t=0}^{n} \frac{C_t}{(1+r)^t}$$

How can we modify this rule for a world where the cash flows, C_t, are not known with certainty? Suppose there are two projects, one whose cash flows are known with certainty, the other whose cash flows have the same *expected* value, but whose actual outcomes are risky. Assuming the decision-maker is risk-averse, so that risk is a 'bad thing', it follows that the risky project should have a lower value than the certain one. Inspection of the NPV formula shows that we can give it a lower value in two ways, by reducing the cash flows (the numerator), or by increasing the discount rate (the denominator).

Certainty equivalence

The first approach handles risk by replacing the expected value of risky cash flows by the 'utility' to the decision-maker of those cash flows, that is, the *certain* sum of money the decision-maker values equally to the risky cash flows. We can find these amounts by using the decision-maker's utility of wealth schedule. Figure I recalls the information from Figure II of the last chapter where we were comparing the utility a decision-maker attached to a certainty of £100 as against a 50/50 chance of £50 and £150. If the cash flow of £100 we are using in our NPV formula is in fact the expected value, or mean, of a 50/50 chance of £50 and £150, then its *certainty equivalent*, the certain sum of money giving the same utility, can be found by inspecting the utility schedule at U_c. The certainty-equivalent is £80 in this case.

The certainty equivalent approach is conceptually sound: if we calculated NPVs using certainty equivalents instead of cash flows then 'choose all projects with a positive NPV' this will still lead to value-maximising choices, even in a world of risk. But it is rarely attempted in practice since it does not meet our requirement for a good decision-rule. Its heavy demand for information about the decision-maker's utility of each cash flow would make it uneconomical and difficult to decentralise.

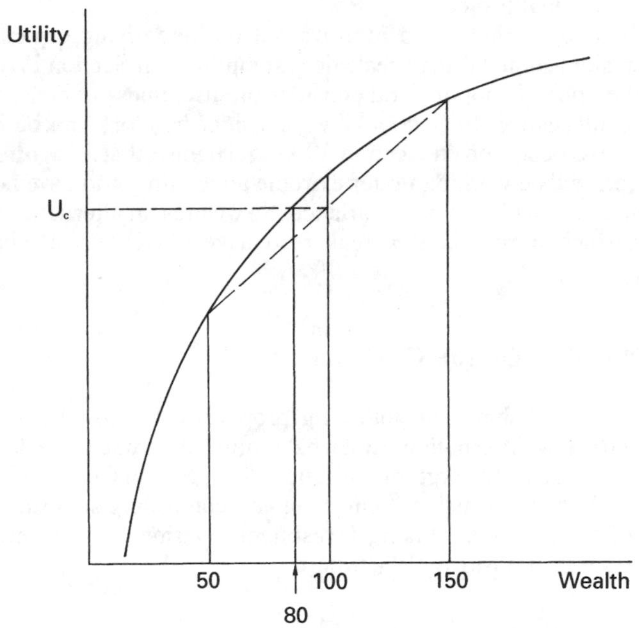

Figure I The utility of wealth

The risk-premium

A more common approach is to adjust the discount rate for risk. Since the higher the discount rate the less value we are attaching to future cash flows, this means adding a *risk-premium* to the discount rate we would use for risk-free cash flows.

We need $r_j = r_i + r_p$ where r_j = required return on risky asset j

$$r_i = \text{risk-free rate}$$
$$r_p = \text{risk-premium}$$

The practice of using a higher discount rate to value risk is widespread, but in the past readers of textbooks must often have been puzzled when they looked for instructions on how to calculate the risk-premium. The problem was that theorists had not worked out how to calculate a risk-premium that was theoretically sound, i e would lead firms to make value maximising investment decisions, but was economical to use and easy to delegate. There were two problems:

Portfolio effects We saw that what matters is the impact of a project on the risk of *the portfolio* in which it is included. So, on the face of it, before a project's risk can be appraised a study is needed of its interrelationship with all the other projects in the firm. This requires a lot of information; if the firm has 100 projects there are 100 variance, and 9,900 covariance terms in the calculation of its overall portfolio risk.

Subjectivity To use a risk-premium to evaluate risk is to put a price on risk in terms of return. But how risk averse are the investors? This is a subjective evaluation which requires knowledge of the decision-maker's preferences between risk and return. This sort of information is costly to obtain.

These information requirements seemed to undermine the idea of the risk-premium as a quick and efficient tool. But in the 1960s a model for the valuation of risky assets was developed which revolutionised finance theory: the *capital asset pricing model.* We described the CAPM result at the end of the last chapter. As we saw, if we make certain assumptions about investors, assets and the capital market the required return from an asset j, r_j, can be calculated as

$$r_j = r_i + \beta_j (r_m - r_i)$$

where r_i is the return on riskless borrowing and lending and r_m is the return on the market as a whole. Hence we have a *decision-rule* for risky projects *which makes no mention of other projects or the preferences of the decision-maker.* The rule is *accept projects with a return greater or equal to* $r_j = r_i + \beta_j (r_m - r_i)$.

In the next section we see how to find project betas in practice. There are some real practical problems here, and as we will see later there are some conceptual problems too, so it would be foolish to think beta gives any easy answers. But used carefully the CAPM can give useful insights into the problem of analysing risk in the real world.

II HOW TO FIND THE BETA OF A SHARE

The problem facing the project appraiser is what risk-premium to build into the discount rate for a risky project. The capital asset pricing model gives us a simple and intuitive formula for calculating risk-premiums on assets. It says: 'You know the *average* risk-premium on the market as a whole. The risk-premium on your project will be proportionate to this, and the proportion is easily found in terms of the covariance of the project with the market.' How is beta measured in practice? As a first step we will see how to find the beta of a share. There are two ways of getting the beta for a share; we can estimate it ourselves or we can use one of the published estimates that are available.

We want to estimate the beta of shares in South Pacific Tropical Packers plc. The beta of an asset j is defined as, $\beta_j = \frac{\sigma_{jm}}{\sigma^2_m}$ where m signifies to the market as a whole. So we need two things, the returns on South Pacific over a period of time and the returns on the market over the corresponding period. What exactly do we mean by 'return' in this context? The return on a share has two components, the dividend-yield and the capital gain,

$$\text{so return in period } t \rightarrow t+1 = \frac{DIV_{t+1} + (S_{t+1} - S_t)}{S_t}$$

where DIV_{t+1} = dividends received in period ended t+1
S_{t+1} = share price at t+1

In the case of 'the market' we can get the equivalent information by looking at the return on a market index such as the FT Actuaries, and the dividend-yield on the index. These are published weekly in the Financial Times.

Table I shows the returns data for South Pacific and the market over the last ten years.

Table I Returns on South Pacific and the market

Date	*South Pacific* Share price	Dividend	Return %	Index	*Market* Div yield %	Return %
1 Jan 19*0	46			530		
31 Dec 19*0	50	4	17	564	5	11
1	49	4	6	602	4	11
2	60	5	33	586	4	1
3	48	5	(12)	443	5	(19)
4	52	5	19	567	7	35
5	58	5	21	651	6	21
6	54	5	2	683	5	10
7	57	5	17	789	4	20
8	63	6	17	832	4	9
9	63	6	10	882	5	11

We found, for instance, the 19*0 return of South Pacific as $\frac{4 + (50 - 46)}{46} = 17\%$.

Since the dividend figures for the market are already in yield form, we got the market return by simply adding the percentage capital gain in the market index to the dividend yield, for 19*0 this gave $\frac{564 - 530}{530} + 5 = 11\%$. These points are plotted in Figure II.

To find the straight line that best describes the relationship between South Pacific returns and market returns the statistician would run simple linear regression of South Pacific on the market. The best line would be the 'least squares' line. This is found by measuring the distance of each of the ten actual observations from the line, squaring them and adding them up. The 'least-squares' line is the one which minimises this sum. We can express this line as

$$r_{jt} = \hat{a}_t + \hat{b}_t \, r_{mt} + \hat{e}_t$$

where a and b are the intercept and the slope, and e is the error. Readers who know some statistics will recall that the slope coefficient is found by $b = \frac{\sigma_{jm}}{\sigma_m^2}$. This is beta!

In other words we do not need the theoretical framework of the CAPM to give us beta, it is something anyone interested in the responsiveness of the return on a particular share to movements in the market as a whole might plot or calculate.

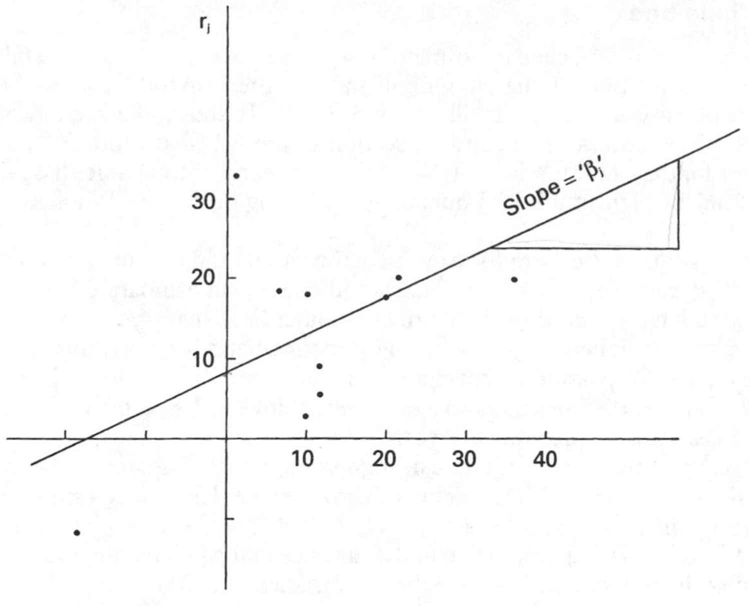

Figure II Returns on South Pacific and the market

Table II provides the data to calculate South Pacific's beta as follows:

$$\sigma_{jm} = \frac{813}{10}, \quad \sigma_m^2 = \frac{1762}{10}$$

so, $$\beta_j = \frac{813}{1762} = \underline{\underline{.46}}$$

Table II

Returns South Pacific	Market	*Deviations* South Pacific	Market	*Products of deviations* South Pacific × Market	Market^2
17	11	4	0	0	0
6	11	(7)	0	0	0
33	1	20	(10)	(200)	100
(12)	(19)	(25)	(30)	750	900
19	35	6	24	144	576
21	21	8	10	80	100
2	10	(11)	(1)	11	1
17	20	4	9	36	81
17	9	4	(2)	(8)	4
10	11	(3)	0	0	0
130	110	0	0	813	1,762
Mean 13.0	11.0				

Using a 'beta book'

In practice there is no real need to estimate beta yourself, since there are several sources of published betas for quoted shares. One of these is the London Business School Risk Measurement Service, and as an illustration Table III shows the section of the LBS 'beta book' which covers the electricals section of the All Share Index. Recall that the average beta for the whole market is 1. Six of the ten electrical companies have betas above a 1, with Delta the highest at 1.17. Four are below 1, ranging down to Wholesale Fittings at .52.

When we estimated the beta for South Pacific we did not say much about estimation problems. For example, how much data should you use in estimating beta? For quoted companies we have a record of daily prices running back many years. Statistically, it is usually best to use all the data you have. In estimating betas however, this may not be the case since there is the possibility that changes in the nature and activity of the firm over the years may make earlier observations unrepresentative. LBS estimate their betas on monthly prices over the previous five years.

Another important issue with linear regression is the *strength* of the relationship between the two variables. The figures following the LBS beta estimates are very informative on this. Take Scholes. Its beta of .86 has a standard error of .18 and an R^2 of 21%. The R^2 tells us what proportion of the variance in the independent variable a model is explaining. In this case, 21% of Scholes' variance is market risk. LBS give us the information to observe this in another way. Scholes' total 'variability' (= standard deviation) was 43%. The part *not* explained by beta was 38%, which is of course the 'specific risk' of Scholes.[1]

It may seem that beta does not explain very much. Does the low R^2 we often find with betas matter? The CAPM says NO. It tells us not to worry about specific risk, since in a fully diversified portfolio only market risk matters. But if we do not accept the CAPM beta may not be a reliable risk measure, since it explains only a small part of total risk in many cases.

III USING BETA TO MEASURE PROJECT RISK

Betas for quoted shares are fairly easy to find, we have a reliable and well-documented history of market values to work from. This is not the case with projects. Projects are not quoted on the stock market, and in any case the most difficult projects to value are the ones that are new and untried. Projects usually fall into one of the following categories:

1 expanding existing capacity
2 replacing and improving technology in existing capacity
3 moving into adjacent product areas
4 moving into new areas of activity.

In the case of 1 and 2 the project may have a history on which a beta could be calculated. But these investments tend to be fairly uncontroversial anyhow. The projects that worry managers most are types 3 and 4. These are the ones with no history and whose future is most uncertain. There are two strategies for finding a beta in this case. In theory the decision-maker could build a *simulation*, that is, model the returns to the project under

1 The two *do* reconcile. Scholes' variance was $43^2 = 1{,}849$, of which $38^2 = 1{,}444$ was unexplained, so 405 was explained. $\frac{405}{1{,}849} = 21\%$.

Table III Electrical industry betas

SEDOL number	*Company name*	*FT-A Industry classification*	*Market capit'n*	*Market-ability*	*Beta*	*Vari-ability*	*Specific risk*	*Std error*	*R-sq'rd*	*Qly ab return*	*Ann ab return*	*Ann act return*	*Gross yield*	*P/E ratio*	*Price 28.3.91*
	ELECTRICALS														
96162	BICC plc	ELECTRCL	1230	OTFa	1.10	31	19	.10	63	15	−4	8	5.8	11.1	446
195207	Chloride Group plc	ELECTRCL	36	O Aa	1.13	40	31	.15	40	−24	−69	−56	.0	27.8	15
261506	Delta plc	ELECTRCL	586	OTAa	1.17	33	20	.11	63	12	15	28	4.7	11.1	400
278807	Dowding & Mills	ELECTRCL	91	.4TAa	.66	30	25	.13	27	16	21	34	4.2	11.8	68
313496	Emess plc	ELECTRCL	43	.2TAa	1.00	45	39	.17	27	15	−61	−48	11.4	4.8	41
415314	Hawker Siddeley Group	ELECTRCL	1155	0TFa	1.12	30	16	.09	70	14	−11	1	5.7	14.3	583
665045	Oxford Instruments plc	ELECTRCL	129	0TAa	1.04	40	33	.16	34	−8	26	38	2.0	14.6	268
779690	Scholes Group plc	ELECTRCL	48	2TAa	.86	43	38	.18	21	0	−26	−13	5.1	10.6	126
939007	Volex Group	ELECTRCL	40	1TAa	.73	30	25	.13	31	5	−14	−1	8.7	8.2	260
964430	Wholesale Fittings	ELECTRCL	47	1TAa	.52	23	20	.11	25	5	3	16	6.7	11.7	329

Source: LBS Risk Measurement Service, April/June 1991

different scenarios about the future, then find the implied beta. In practice this would require a lot of information, so that even if they felt capable of it managers would only be interested in doing it for major projects.

An easier alternative is to find a share beta to proxy the project beta, or at least to serve as a starting point. If we are going to do this, however, we need a good grasp of what determines systematic risk, and what characteristics to look for in a proxy.

(1) The prime factor is LINE OF BUSINESS. We need to find a firm which is 'doing the same thing' as the project. We cannot expect to find a perfect match: details of markets, technology, and management style may differ, but these may not affect beta too much. A real problem, however, is diversification. Most firms have a variety of projects, and their share betas are an average of the betas of these different activities. Unless we are confident the proxy company we are looking at is predominantly engaged in the activity in question, it may be safer to use the *industry beta* in the hope that these extraneous factors cancel out in aggregate.

(2) Much of the variability in returns from a project or a company comes from its cost structure and in particular the relationship of fixed to variable cost, which we call GEARING. The lower the gearing, that is, the more its costs are variable, the better able the firm is to absorb increases or decreases in revenues by corresponding increases or decreases in costs. A particularly important source of gearing is *financial gearing*, the proportion of debt financing the firm uses, and this can differ between firms within the same industry. So far in this book we have assumed projects are all-equity financed and we continue this assumption now. But in a subsequent chapter we will show how betas can be adjusted for financial gearing.

Tuckwell Foods

Tuckwell Foods is planning to open a chain of freezer centres, where frozen foods are sold in bulk. Jack Berry, the corporate planner of Tuckwell wants to find a beta for this activity. He chooses Bejam plc as a quoted company in this line of business. LBS Risk Measurement Service shows Bejam's beta to be .81. Should Tuckwell use this for its project? Before it does, Berry needs to ask these questions:

— What else does Bejam do?
— What is Bejam's financial structure?
— Have we any other clues that might be relevant?

Bejam's annual report gives some answers to the first two questions. It shows that 75% of Bejam's business is in food sales, and the rest is mainly in hardware, freezers and ovens. This matches fairly well with Tuckwell's expected revenue mix. Berry also found that Bejam has little or no long-term debt, and is effectively all-equity, so he adopts .81 as a good proxy for the project beta.

We have seen how to find a project's beta, β_j. To calculate the discount rate for a project we also need estimates of the future values of the market return, r_m, and the riskless rate, r_i. All three of these need to be forecasts: we want values that will be appropriate over the future life of the project.

The riskless rate

How can we know what the risk-free interest rate will be during the future life of the project? Unless we feel we have special knowledge the best we can do is take the market's view embodied in the spot rate for the appropriate period. For a ten-year project this means the prevailing rate on ten-year loans at the start of the project, since this tells us the market's required return on a risk-free investment lasting ten years, including compensation for the inflation the market expects during that period. As a proxy for this we can use the yield on government bonds of the appropriate duration.

Market return

From one year to the next the return on the market can vary dramatically. But this is the *actual* return the market earns and it reflects unanticipated events that push up, and down, the present and expected future profits of companies. But what returns do investors *require* from the market? One way to estimate this is to take the average of achieved returns on the market over a long period. In Chapter 18 we show that the historic *after-tax* risk-premium on the UK market has been 8.75%. There are times, in wars, depressions and so forth, when the risk to business activity in general rises, and other times when it falls. If the decision-maker feels confident that the market will require a lower premium for equity risk in the future, he can adjust it accordingly. Otherwise we recommend using $r_m - r_i = 8.75\%$.

Jack Berry can now find a discount rate for Tuckwell Foods' freezer centre project. The project has a ten-year time-horizon. He finds the after-tax yield on ten-year government bonds to be 6%, and estimates the market risk-premium at 8.75%. A suitable beta for freezer centre projects was .81 so Berry calculates an equity required return of $r_j = 6\% + .81 \times 8.75\% = 13\%$.

IV HOW USEFUL IS BETA?

There is a forecasting worry with beta too, though when we described how to estimate a project beta we did not say much about it. Can we be sure that betas drawn from historic data will still be relevant over the life of a project lasting, say, ten years? In other words, are betas stable through time? The evidence suggests that share betas may not be too stable through time, though industry betas are more stable. This argues, again, for not using single share betas without keeping an eye on the rest of the industry.

It is clear that the step from a past share beta to a future-oriented project beta requires a good deal of judgement and the project-appraiser still needs to use all his or her instincts about the project in hand when he is measuring its beta. But like all the theory we encounter, the real role of beta is to aid the thinking of managers rather than substitute for it.

Apart from any practical problems in using bcta, there are some theoretical problems too. The capital asset pricing model that underlies it rests on some apparently unrealistic assumptions. Beta and the CAPM commonly encounter a lot of consumer resistance from practitioners unfamiliar with the concepts, who see them as too abstract for the real world. So how useful *is* beta?

The key to understanding beta is diversification: beta is the risk measure for fully diversified investors in a world where all investors are full diversified. We said there seemed to be two problems in finding a decision-rule for risky assets: the computational problem of working out the portfolio effect of each individual asset, and the apparent subjectivity of the risk-return trade-off. The assumptions of a CAPM world are designed to make these problems go away.

The effect on the investor's risk of acquiring another asset depends on the asset's covariance with the portfolio the investor is adding it to. But in a fully-diversified portfolio only market risk remains, and investors can ignore the interrelationship of an asset's risk with the other assets they hold. To find an appropriate risk premium they look outside to the market, where they will find the asset's risk premium as the market premium multiplied by the asset's beta. The assumptions of the CAPM describe a world in which investors *will* be fully diversified. They will want full diversification because they are risk-averse, and they will be able to fully diversify because in a perfect market there are no barriers to doing it.

The second problem was that we needed to know the decision-maker's preference about risk and return. Under the CAPM assumptions, though, all investors have the same trade-off between risk and return at the margin. The line of argument is a familiar one in microeconomics. Consider a world where bananas sell for 10p each, and oranges for 20p, in other words, where two bananas trade for one orange. Suppose an individual visits the market and observes this rate of exchange. He also reflects that as far as he is concerned oranges are worth more than that; he would trade three bananas for one orange given his tastes for bananas and oranges. His response is to buy less bananas and more oranges. However, as he does this his interest in oranges will diminish as his appetite for them is satisfied, yet the appeal of bananas will grow. The individual's consumption pattern will only be in equilibrium when his preferences between marginal increments in consumption are in line with market prices. For bananas and oranges read return and risk. The risk-premium on an asset is the market price of its risk in terms of return. An investor whose preferences do not accord with this market evaluation will adjust his consumption of risk and return until they do. He can adjust the proportions of risk and return he consumes by lending or borrowing at the risk-free rate.

The realism of the CAPM assumptions

The CAPM is derived on the following assumptions; the first four of which are our usual perfect market assumptions.

About the market:

1 There are no taxes, and no 'transactions costs' – costs to buying and selling.
2 Information is fully and freely available.
3 There are many buyers and sellers, so none can influence prices.

About investors:

4 Investors are rational, that is, risk-averse and wealth-maximising.
5 They have homogeneous expectations about the future.

About assets:

6 Assets are all marketable and infinitely divisible, and have normally distributed returns.
7 There is a riskless asset.

Some of these assumptions are innocuous, but other are less so. Let us consider some of the apparently unrealistic ones.

In reality asset returns are subject to taxation at rates which can differ between investors and between firms and so yield differing after-tax returns on the same asset. The effect of this is rather like investors having different expectations about the future.

There are other frictions in the market besides tax. Buying and selling shares incurs costs: the market-maker's turn, adviser's fees, and VAT, and these may inhibit investors from fully adjusting their portfolios. Transactions costs will also have the effect of driving a wedge between borrowing and lending rates. Put another way, the buying and selling prices of the riskless asset will differ.

Is there a *riskless asset* anyhow? In reality no asset has a future return which can be known with certainty. Three-month Treasury Bills are the closest thing we have to a riskless asset. The risk of default is, we hope, zero. But only the *nominal* return is certain. The future rate of inflation and so the *real* return on treasury bills, is unknown. However, Black (1972) showed that the conclusion of the CAPM can be derived without a riskless asset, but using instead a portfolio of zero-beta assets – assets whose records are uncorrelated with the market portfolio.

In developing the CAPM we assumed that the distributions of asset returns are *normal.* In reality returns tend to have infinite variance and to be skewed, since firms can make any amount of positive returns, while negative returns are restricted by limited liability.

It is fairly easy therefore to challenge the CAPM assumptions, and show that some of them are unrealistic. But does it matter? Is the theory completely invalidated or is the damage slight and the CAPM still a reasonable approximation to the way the market prices risk? This is the important question, and it can only be answered empirically, by seeing if the beta equation accurately describes how assets are priced in practice.

A large number of research studies have examined this,[2] with perhaps the best known early study by Fama and Macbeth (1973). The easiest way to understand their findings is to recall the beta equation and consider some of its properties. Expressed in terms of excess returns the CAPM says

$$r_j - r_i = \beta_j \, (r_m - r_i)$$

If the excess return on security j is plotted against its beta we get the solid line in Figure III. This is the *theoretical* market line and it has the following properties:

— It is straight, that is, the return on an asset is a linear function of its beta
— It slopes upward, that is, return is an increasing function of risk as measured by beta
— It goes through the origin, that is, no other factor influences return
— The slope on beta is $r_m - r_i$.

Typically, researchers have grouped shares into portfolios of shares with similar betas to avoid the measurement problems associated with individual securities, and regressed the excess returns and betas of these portfolios. The *empirical* market line estimated this way has usually looked like the dotted line in Figure III.

We can see some similarities and some differences between theory and practice. Excess returns are a linear and increasing function of beta. But the slope is less, and the intercept is above the origin. Hence it seems that in practice low beta securities earn a higher return

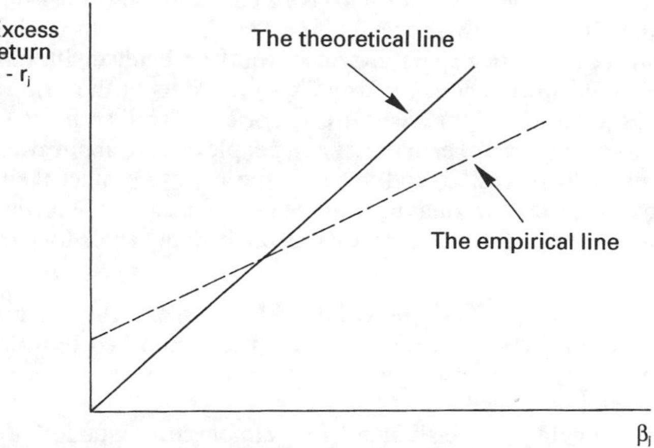

Figure III The empirical market line

2 We consider some of the more recent evidence on the CAPM when we discuss market efficiency in Chapter 13.

than the CAPM would predict, and high beta a lower return. Moreover researchers have found that beta is not the only factor that explains return, for example size appears to be a factor, with small firms earning higher returns than large.

However, Roll (1977) has raised serious doubts about the possibility of ever testing the CAPM. He points out that the CAPM is a theory of the pricing of assets: shares, but also land, human capital, oil paintings, and so forth. Any test of the CAPM is also a test of the efficiency of the whole market portfolio. But for reasons of data availability, empirical testing tends to be restricted to the securities markets, and this makes it difficult to interpret empirical results as decisively accepting or rejecting the CAPM.

Diversification by firms versus diversification by investors

The cornerstone of the CAPM is the notion of the fully-diversified investor. The CAPM world is one in which investors will want to be fully diversified, and the capital market will contain no obstacles to their achieving it. But how does diversification by the *firm* fit into this? Since we assume investors are risk-averse 'fully diversified' is something the rational *investor* will seek to be, but is diversification a strategy *firms* should pursue? In a perfect capital market the answer is NO, diversification by the firm would not be a thing of value. As the reader works through the book the argument for this will become familiar. In a perfect capital market there are no transactions costs, firms and individuals have the same information, face the same taxes and can borrow and lend at the same rate, and so forth. The upshot is that many financial strategies can be pursued just as well by individuals as by the firms they own. So, for example, in a perfect capital market it becomes *irrelevant* what capital structure the firm has and what dividend policy the firm adopts, because shareholders can recreate the policy themselves at no extra cost.

The same applies to portfolio building. In this ideal world there is no need for firms to diversify, since the owners of the firm can do it for themselves by buying shares in the potential subsidiaries. Investors will be fully diversified and will use beta; so managers, who are simply the agents of shareholders, should use beta when choosing projects for them. In practice, though, managers do not seem to behave like this. Rather than taking a shareholder view of risk, they often seem to take a company view. We explore the reasons for this in Chapter 10. First, if there are significant bankruptcy costs it might actually be in shareholders' interests for managers to protect the firm by diversification. In a perfect market no one would worry about bankruptcy – the assets of the firm would just slide smoothly and costlessly to their next best use at a price that fully reflected their economic value. In reality there *are* costs to bankruptcy and people do care about avoiding it. Second, managers may be self-interested, and diversify the firm to protect their jobs. In other words they may trade value maximisation off against managerial objectives.

However, diversifying a firm is not so easy as diversifying a portfolio of shares for the following reasons:

- Real projects are often large and indivisible while the size of the firm may be limited by externally imposed capital constraints, or internally imposed growth constraints. A possible remedy is to form joint ventures with other firms to own large projects, but this may be costly and unattractive.
- There may be 'benefits to specialisation', for example cost reductions with scale. These are 'return benefits' which can outweigh the 'risk benefits' of diversification.

In a world like this managers may be interested in the total risk of projects, and not just their systematic risk.

It is worth noting that we cannot always rely on shareholders being fully diversified either. If one firm forms a significant part of their asset holdings they may not be fully insured against fluctuations in its income. This can happen when for example a family has a significant involvement in the family firm. Why would investors do this, when portfolio theory tells us it is always rational to be fully diversified? Again, we have to question the assumption that assets are infinitely divisible. Owning most or all of a firm gives you *control*, and the returns, financial and psychological, to owning 5% of 20 firms may not equate with the returns to owning 100% of one.

Summary – the role of beta

In recent years the capital asset pricing model has assumed a central role in finance theory and in empirical research; amongst practitioners betas have found acceptance amongst fund managers, but less, though apparently growing, acceptance amongst project appraisers. It could be that acceptance of beta will grow slowly, as it has done with DCF. But before recommending beta wholeheartedly, we need a balanced view of the pros and cons of using it in practice.

The beta formula is based on an elegant theory of how people choose risky assets. But the theory uses some seemingly unrealistic assumptions, and the evidence suggests that in determining the return on risky assets beta is an important part of the story, but not the whole story. Researchers are now looking at multi-factor asset pricing models to get a better explanation of the return to risky assets. The Arbitrage Pricing Theory (APT) proposed by Steven Ross is the one which has received most attention.[3] Unfortunately a more complex model may not meet our requirement for a decision-rule which is simple and economical to use.

When we apply the CAPM to project appraisal we meet two problems. The first is a practical one; investment projects are often unique events for which estimating a beta may be far from straightforward. The second is more fundamental. Beta is the measure of risk for fully-diversified investors. Unless this is the context in which managers are working, they may want to look at the total risk of projects they are appraising.[4]

However, the fundamental appeal of beta is that it provides a method for getting risk-premiums which is simple and intuitive but theoretically based. In the next two sections we look at risk analysis in a world where we cannot assume the CAPM. This may be the world many managers inhabit. The problem is that, now, risk analysis involves a trade-off between simplicity and soundness.

V RISK IN A NON-CAPM WORLD

What do we do when the assumptions of the CAPM are so significantly breached by the facts of the case that beta cannot be used? Unfortunately there are no easy answers. In the rest of this section we will see what can be done when the decision-maker at least has enough information to estimate the distribution of future outcomes. In the final section we consider the all too common case of extreme uncertainty.

3 See Ross (1976) for the original description of the APT. Roll and Ross (1980) and Chen, Roll and Ross (1986) provide empirical tests of the theory.

4 Strictly, of course, the CAPM does not hold in a world where some investors are optimising and others are not. Unless it is appropriate for everyone, it will not be appropriate for anyone.

A total-risk approach

If the investor is less than fully diversified she or he will need to take account of total risk, that is, systematic *and* unsystematic risk. The following discussion is conceptual rather than practical since no simple technique is available.

Suppose Specialised plc is trying to choose some combination of three projects, I, II, III, to add to its existing investments. The problem facing the decision-maker who is using a 'total risk' approach is how to select the best portfolio out of the eight depicted in Figure IV. Each point in Figure IV represents the risk and expected value of the firm's return under the eight possible combinations of projects (I + II + III, I + II, I + III, . . . 0) added to the existing firm.

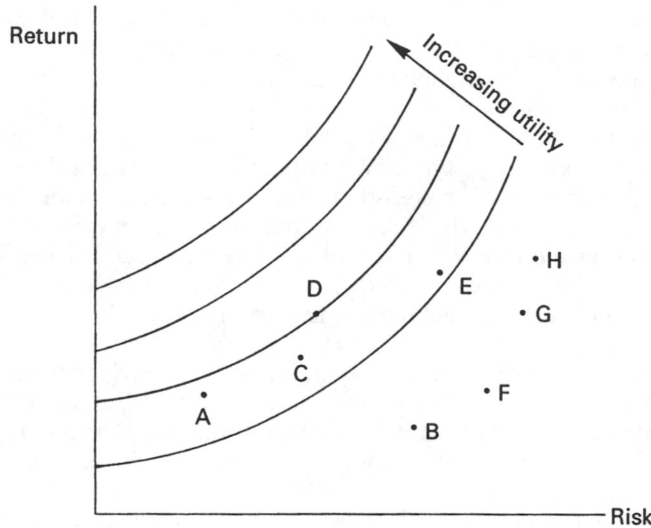

Figure IV Specialised's decision problem

Some combinations can be eliminated immediately using the expected return/variance rule. These portfolios are 'dominated' by one of the others: there exists a portfolio which is better in one respect and not worse in the other. Points B (A is better), C (D is better), F (E is better) and G (E is better) can be eliminated this way.

We have a portfolio choice problem similar to the one we encountered in the last chapter, except now we are leaving aside borrowing and lending, and we are assuming the projects are indivisible so we have discreet points instead of a continuous efficient frontier. As before, to find Specialised's choice we must introduce its preferences between risk and return in the form of risk-return indifference curves. D turns out to be the preferred combination.

This looks straightforward in a diagram, but how will it work in practice? These decisions have heavy information requirements. Once we reject the CAPM, we are back with calculating the impact of each project on the portfolio risk and return of the whole firm and with mapping the decision-makers' preferences over risk and return. The example we just took was a simple one. In general if there are n assets, there are 2^n different combinations of those assets (including zero). So a firm with 20 projects to choose from would have $2^{20} = 1{,}048{,}576$ portfolios to think about if it wanted to be *sure* of getting the right choice.

If we believe that the corporate view of the board of directors correctly embodies the organisation's preferences then we can perhaps avoid overtly measuring the organisational preference function by presenting them within data on alternative policy implications and expecting them to make the right decisions. But there will be no theoretically sound way of decentralising these decisions.

Single-project risk profiles

A step down in sophistication from the total-risk approach is to ignore portfolio effects and present the decision-maker with the risk profiles for single projects. So he or she might be presented with a probability distribution of net present values, to accompany the expected value information on each project being appraised. Consider the three profiles in Figure V.

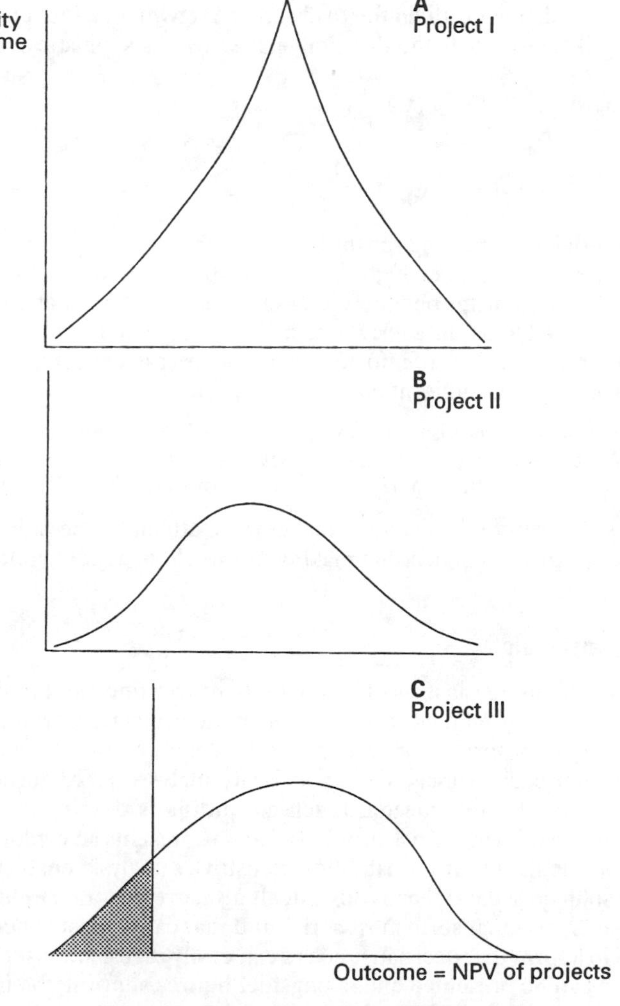

Figure V Examples of risk profiles

Project I is relatively riskless, project II is riskier, and project III has some risk of negative outcomes.

The risk-averse decision-maker who prefers to avoid variance, positive or negative, will prefer I. The decision-maker who may be less generally risk-averse but is averse to the risk of failure will prefer I and II but spurn III. The well-diversified decision-maker may find all three risk profiles, I, II and III, acceptable.

By presenting risk profiles we avoid having to quantify the decision-makers' preferences; they make their own judgements about projects in the context of their knowledge of the firm as a whole. In that respect it is like presenting the board of directors with the set of efficient portfolios to choose from under the total-risk approach, except that now we are relying on decision-makers to supply both the preferences *and* the intuition about portfolio effects. But the problem with single-project risk profiles is that they suppress useful information. Though we would require full information about the future distribution of the project's returns to calculate the variance of its NPV, we are not presenting this detailed information to the decision-maker. But to form a judgement about the fit of the project into the existing portfolio the decision-maker will need it. The single-project risk profile is not likely to satisfy the decision-maker who is sophisticated enough to understand it!

VI EXTREME UNCERTAINTY

The reality of decision-making for most firms is that their expectations about the future are nowhere near complete enough to estimate the distribution of future outcomes, and our guess is that most firms operate under extreme uncertainty about the future. But far from seeing this state as an aberration, most businessmen and some writers, such as Shackle (1970), see this lack of information as of the essence of business life in a world of competition, change and innovation.

> The whole spirit of business is to out-do one's rivals by inventing or adopting a new technique or a new product and exploiting its potential during some interval before it can be imitated . . . Secrecy and misguidance are as much a part of business as of war. (From Shackle (1970) p 94.)

But even in such a world the decision-maker must attempt to be rational. We are going to describe two approaches to decision making in a world of extreme uncertainty, 'sensitivity analysis' and 'payback'.

Sensitivity analysis

In sensitivity analysis key aspects of the project are identified and their values changed to see what effect this has on the expected value of the project as a whole. In other words we see how sensitive the project is to changes in assumptions. We recommend this very strongly as an approach to uncertainty. Sensitivity analysis is the equivalent of feeling one's way on a foggy road – by repeated touch an outline is developed of what is there. Its relationship to the drawing of risk profile is that it represents an exploration of possibilities rather than a calculation of probabilities. Sensitivity analysis enables the firm to use as much of the subjective data it has as possible. It disaggregates the problem and lets the firm identify those aspects that seem most at risk and that cause most concern. Also it provides information in a form that decision-makers can easily digest and use. The expected value of the project can be presented and, alongside, figures showing the impact of changes in the assumptions going into the main figure.

Perrin Popcorn plc

Perrin Popcorn plc is planning to launch Makropop, a new brand of mackerel-flavoured popcorn. Percy Perrin, the M-D expects the project to have the following annual cash flows:

Sales	£400,000	
Materials, labour	£150,000	
Net trading proceeds		£250,000

The initial machinery will cost £600,000, and Percy is working to a five-year horizon. The company does not pay tax and has a cost of capital of 10%.

We can easily work out the NPV of this project using annuity tables. The five-year annuity factor is 3.791. So the NPV of this project is:

$$250{,}000 \times 3.791 - 600{,}000 = \underline{\pounds 347{,}750}$$

Clearly there is no certainty things will turn out this way, and Percy thinks it might be instructive to consider the following scenarios;

1 a shortfall in sales of £200,000 per annum with an associated reduction in expenses of £50,000
2 an increase in wages and materials costs to £200,000
3 curtailment of the project in three years.

We calculate the effect of these alternative assumptions and present the results as follows:

Central assumptions	*(1) Sales short-fall*	*(2) Wages and materials up to £200,000*	*(3) 3-year life*
NPV £347,750	(£220,900)	£158,200	£21,750

Alternatively, decision-makers often like to know how far key parameters could fall before the project makes a loss, in other words to know their break-even values. In the present example it is easy to find these:

If X is the break-even level of trading proceeds, assuming a five-year life, then

$$3.791\text{X} - 600{,}000 = 0, \text{ so X} = \underline{\pounds 158{,}270}$$

So the project will have a positive NPV if it can clear more than £158,270 per year. Alternatively we can examine the time horizon. If X is the 10% annuity-factor which just breaks even assuming £250,000 annual trading proceeds, then

$$250{,}000\text{ X} - 600{,}000 = 0, \text{ so X} = 2.4$$

Exploring the annuity tables we find that this implies about two years of life.

With a more complicated series of cash flows we would have to do this sensitivity analysis by trial and error, or by using one of the many computer packages that permit sensitivity analysis.

Payback: a decentralisable decision-rule for an uncertain world

Is it possible to develop decentralisable decision-rules under extreme uncertainty? Payback – 'accept the project or projects with the shortest payback period' – is such a rule. It works by taking just one element, the length of time to the recovery of the initial investment, from the sensitivity analysis of a project, making it paramount and ignoring all the others. By ranking all projects on this one dimension it is decentralisable since no information about preferences is needed to make a one dimensional choice. Decision-makers who adopt this criterion are implicitly asserting that very low utility is attached to uncertain outcomes and that uncertainty increases with time, as it does with distance on a foggy road.

VII SUMMARY

In reality decisions give rise to a range of possible outcomes in the future, and this causes problems in the search for an economical and decentralisable decision-rule. Under the assumptions of the CAPM, we can derive a rule which is simple and economical to use. Otherwise sound decisions will need a good deal of information, both about the preferences of the decision-makers, and about the interrelationships between projects. Very often the situation of the decision-maker is one of extreme uncertainty about the future. In this case we recommend techniques such as sensivity analysis which help him or her to make the best of the information available, and to explore those aspects of projects that are of particular concern.

REFERENCES AND BIBLIOGRAPHY

Black, F Jensen, M C, and Scholes, M — 'The Capital Asset Pricing Model: Some Empirical Tests' in *Studies in the Theory of Capital Markets* ed Jensen, M C (1972) Praeger, New York, pp 79–124.

Chen, N F, Roll, R, and Ross, S A — 'Economic Forces and the Stock Market', Journal of Business, July 1986, pp 383–403.

Fama, E F — 'Risk, Return and Equilibrium', Journal of Political Economy, Jan/Feb 1971, pp 30–55.

Fama, E F, and Macbeth, J D — 'Risk, Return and Equilibrium: Empirical Tests', Journal of Political Economy, May/June 1973, pp 607–636.

Jensen, M C — 'Capital Markets: Theory and Evidence', Bell Journal of Economics and Management Science, Autumn, 1972, pp 327–398.

Roll, R — 'A Critique of the Asset Pricing Theory's Tests', Journal of Financial Economics, March 1977, pp 129–176.

Roll, R, and Ross, S A — 'An Empirical Investigation of the Arbitrage Pricing Theory', Journal of Finance, December 1983, pp 1393–1414.

Ross, S A — 'The Arbitrage Theory of Capital Asset Pricing', Journal of Economic Theory, Dec 1976, pp 343–362.

Ross, S A — 'The Current Status of the Capital Asset Pricing Model (CAPM)', Journal of Finance, June 1978, pp 585–601.

Rubinstein, H E — 'A Mean-Variance Synthesis of Corporate Financial Theory', Journal of Finance, March 1973, pp 167–182.

Shackle, G L S *Expectation, Enterprise and Profit* (1970) George Allen and Unwin, London.

QUESTIONS

1 Exotic Specialities is thinking of starting-up a tinned pilchard operation to supplement its product range. It wants to know what return one would require from such a project, and brings you in as a consultant. You find that Portuguese Pilchards, a single-product firm, had the following dividend and share price data, relative to the markets:

	Portuguese Pilchards		
	Share Price	*Dividend*	*Market return*
1994	300	20	20%
1993	240	20	30%
1992	195	20	(10%)
1991	240	10	10%
1990	200	10	(10%)
1989	240		

Find an appropriate beta for Exotic's pilchard operation and show how you would use it to derive a required return on equity for the project.

2 Orange-Blossom Cosmetics seek to determine a CAPM-based cost of capital, and identifies Musk Ox, a quoted firm, as being similar in its mix of activities.

Orange-Blossom ascertains the following data about Musk Ox and the market over the last ten years:

Standard deviation of Musk Ox equity returns	8%
Standard deviation of FT Actuaries index	12%
Correlation Musk Ox/FT Actuaries	+ .6
Average return on FT Actuaries	13%
Average return on three-month Treasury Bills	6%

Estimate a cost of capital for Orange-Blossom to use in evaluating future investment projects, noting any assumptions you are making.

3 What are the assumptions of the CAPM? Say whether they appear realistic, and how robust the conclusions of the CAPM would be to their not holding.

4 What considerations would guide a firm wondering whether to use the beta to measure risk in project appraisal? How would you recommend firms that cannot use CAPM to choose amongst risky assets?

5 What characteristics are likely to be possessed by a company with a high standard deviation of return and a low beta?

CHAPTER 10

Risk management

So far business risk has been a 'given' and the issue has been how investors will price the business risk of the firm, what return they require. In fact companies can do something about the riskiness of their cash flows. One strategy is to diversify the firm; but we argue strongly elsewhere that firms do not add value by doing what investors can perfectly well do for themselves. However, something firms are increasingly doing is using financial instruments to *hedge* risk. In this chapter we provide two examples of this. In Section I we describe the sources of exchange risk, and in Section II we show how currency risk can be hedged. In Section III we investigate options, and Section IV shows how options can be used to hedge equity risk.

I PRICES ACROSS EXCHANGES

Different countries have different currencies. In itself, that has no significance for financial decisions. Suppose Anglo-Moldavian is considering building a new factory in Moldavia and most of the costs and revenues of the project will be incurred in the local currency, dinars. Suppose the dinar–sterling exchange rate, the rate at which AM can convert one pound into dinars, is fixed at 8. Then it is of no importance whether AM figures out the NPV of its new project in pounds or dinars, the answer will be the same. In a world of fixed exchange rates investing and financing in another country will be no different from investing and financing in another region of the same country.

Fixed and floating exchange rates

In the years leading up to the First World War exchange rates were regulated through the 'gold standard'. Under the gold standard the pound sterling was deemed to contain 113 grains of gold, and the US dollar 23.22. This fixed the dollar–sterling exchange rate as $4.87 to £1. Demand and supply was balanced by movements of gold. If more Americans were demanding British goods than vice versa gold would flow into the UK to pay for them, and in principle, the increase in UK money supply would push up the prices and reduction in US supply would deflate US prices until the demand imbalance was eliminated. During the First World War the gold standard was suspended and never successfully re-established.

The appeal of stable currencies is strong so in 1944 the Bretton Woods agreement provided that only the US dollar was convertible into gold. Member countries were expected to try and maintain the value of their currencies within 1% of official level, but if this proved impossible up to a 10% devaluation could be made without reference to the International Monetary Fund, and devaluations of over 10% if approved by the IMF. This 'adjustable peg' system had some features of the gold standard with the US dollar proxying for gold. However, as the pre-eminence of the US waned, the 1960s became an era of perpetual balance of payments surpluses in West Germany and Japan and deficits in the

US. In 1973 the fixed rate system was abandoned and a period of freely floating rates ensued. Towards the end of the 1970s this crystallised into a mixed system or 'managed float'. Under this system some countries try to maintain a fixed parity between their currencies, while others float. Some smaller nations will maintain a fixed rate with their major trading partner; often this means the US dollar. Another fixed group were the members of the European Monetary System which was founded in 1979. The EMS was formed by the members of the European Community and acted like a local Bretton Woods. Again, this system suffered partial collapse in the early 1990s.

Though the desire for stable currencies is a powerful one, fixed rate systems have tended not to survive the constant pressure of market forces towards 'purchasing power parity'.

Purchasing power parity

Purchasing power parity requires that exchange rates must be such that they permit someone with a given amount of wealth to exchange it for the same bundle of goods and services in any country. If PPP does not hold arbitrage will be possible.

> *Doris*
>
> Doris has got £100 which she desperately wants to spend on brass door knobs. In England knobs cost £5 each, in Moldavia 40 dinars. Suppose the dinar–sterling exchange rate is 10. While Doris could get 20 knobs in England, by changing her money into dinars and buying in Moldavia she could get 25. Indeed it will pay Doris not only to spend her £100 but to borrow more and to buy large quantities of knobs in Moldavia and sell them in England. By the same token if the exchange rate were 6 the flow would be the other way, and Moldavians would be importing door knobs from England. As we have noted before in other contexts, 'arbitrage' will take place wherever the same commodity is selling for different prices. Arbitrage only ceases when prices are driven into line. Across exchanges this can happen in two ways, by domestic prices changing, and by exchange rates changing. So in the first case, when Doris can buy 20 knobs in England and 25 in Moldavia, her demand for Moldavian knobs will tend to drive their price up, while her lack of demand for English knobs will push their price down. At the same time, however, Doris's demand for dinars to buy the knobs, and her desire to supply sterling, will tend to drive the dinar–sterling exchange rate down. The equilibrium will come when there is purchasing power parity. In the present case, this will occur when the exchange rate is 8.

The question of whether it is domestic prices, or the exchange rate, which does the adjusting is rather important. The assumption behind the gold standard was that it would be domestic prices which did all the adjustment, so the exchange rate could be fixed. But the heyday of the gold standard corresponded with a period of economic stability. In more recent times the volatility of the world economy would have required much greater adjustments in domestic economies; and social and political changes meant that the necessary adjustments were less acceptable, hence the burden fell on exchange rate adjustment.

Of course our Doris example was excessively simple. In reality there is a variety of barriers to arbitrage:

- — There are costs to finding out about international prices, to converting currency, and to importing and exporting.
- — Some goods and services are hard to trade internationally, and so are partly sheltered from international competition: transport, education, labour are examples.

— National governments sometimes control competition by limiting the freedom to import and export, or by limiting the freedom to exchange currency. And if imbalance between demand and supply of a currency does put exchange rates under pressure governments will sometimes hold out against a change by borrowing and funding the deficit.

However, the underlying pressure towards purchasing power parity remains. So once an equilibrium system of exchange rates is established why cannot rates remain fixed? Where does the disequilibrium come from? The main factor which destabilises exchange rates is differences in domestic inflation rates.

Suppose the English and Moldavian brass door knob prices were £5 and 40 dinars in January 1986, with an exchange rate of 8 giving purchasing power parity, but during the next year English and Moldavian prices inflate by 5% and 15% respectively, to £5.25 and 46 dinars. By the end of 1986 an exchange rate of $\frac{46}{5.25} = 8.76$ will be needed to maintain purchasing power parity. The exchange rate must inflate to keep pace with domestic prices, i e,

$$8 \times \frac{1.15}{1.05} = 8.76$$

To summarise, for equilibrium we require purchasing power parity, but with differential domestic inflation this is inconsistent with exchange rate parity.

II CURRENCY HEDGING

We call the rate at which one currency can be exchanged for another *today*, the *spot* exchange rate. The rates you see hanging on the wall in the bank or bureau de change are spot rates. However you can also make a contract to buy or sell currency forward, and the rate at which you agree to exchange in the future is the *future rate*. You can get a forward rate for any term, but rates are commonly quoted for 1-, 3-, 6- and 12-months ahead. For example for 14 July 1994 the Financial Times showed the following dollar/sterling rates:

Spot	*Close*	*Day's spread*	*One month*	*% pa*	*Three months*	*% pa*
1.5660	1.5657 – 1.5662	1.5736 – 1.5650	1.5656	0.3	1.5652	0.2

Hence for immediate delivery on the 14 July you could buy sterling at the spot rate of 1.5660. The three-month forward rate was 1.5652, which, as the Financial Times tells us, represents an annualised rate of 0.2%.

This immediately leads us to some conclusions about relative interest rates. *Interest rate parity* requires that the difference between the interest rates on loans in the two currencies should be the same as the % difference between the spot rate and the forward rate of the same duration. We can check this, because the FT of 14 July 1994 also shows that three-month sterling loans on the Euromarket paid $4^{29}/_{32}$–$4^{31}/_{32}$, while three-month dollar loans were quoted at $4^{13}/_{16}$–$4^{15}/_{16}$, a differential of 0.24%, close to the 0.2% we noted earlier.

Purchasing power parity said that a given amount of wealth should be able to purchase the same bundle of goods in any country. Interest rate parity is just an inter-temporal extension of purchasing power parity, and in the same way there will be arbitrage possibilities unless it holds.

Derek

Derek has £1,000 and needs dollars in three months: he has two routes to getting them, both of which involve no uncertainty about future exchange rates. He can:

(1) buy dollars spot, and invest them at the dollar rate for three months, or

(2) make a forward contract and invest at the sterling rate for three months.

These should yield as follows:

(1) £1,000 converted at 1.5660	=	\$1,566.00
\$1,566 invested at $4\frac{13}{16}\%$ for three months	=	\$1,584.73
(2) £1,000 invested at $4\frac{29}{32}\%$ for three months	=	£1,012.06
£1,012 converted at 1.5652	=	\$1,584.07

Though there is some difference between the outcomes, it is too small to exploit, relative to the transactions costs involved. The market for Eurocurrency loans and the foreign exchange markets are highly competitive, and given that both the rates we observed are riskless means that we always observe interest rate parity to hold in practice. Indeed it almost holds by definition since dealers in the Eurocurrency markets fix relative currency loan rates by observing differences in spot and forward rates.

One lesson to emerge clearly is that currency risk – the problem that future cash flows in foreign currencies are dependent on unknown exchange rates – can be eliminated by hedging using forward markets. Moreover the cost of this insurance is low, so firms are free to make overseas contracts and appraise foreign ventures without having to worry about exchange rates. Of course it is only possible to hedge *expected* cash flows this way. If future cash flows have some uncertainty, as they often have with real investment projects, then there will be an associated risk of over- or under-covering the cash flows, so to this extent a currency risk will remain.

The role of expected inflation

We started by noting that if two countries are expected to have different domestic inflation rates exchange rate parity will not be possible. Their exchange rate will have to inflate at the difference between their domestic inflation rates to maintain purchasing power parity. But the forward rate is simply the market's expectation, its current best guess, of the future spot rate, so the differences between spot and forward rates, and thus interest rates, which we discussed in the last section reflect these differences in domestic inflation rates:

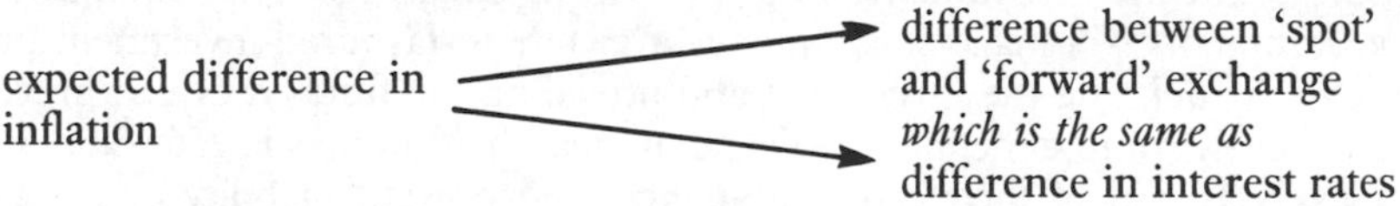

Notice we say *expected* inflation. In the figures we looked at the sterling interest rate was $4\frac{29}{32}\%$, and the dollar, $4\frac{13}{16}\%$, which seems to imply that on the day those rates were fixed the market expected UK prices to deflate 0.20% per annum faster than US prices over the next three months. The reader may recall that we encountered the relationship between inflation and interest rates in a domestic setting earlier in the book. We found that according to Fisher, the nominal interest rate, r, has two components, the real rate r′, and the inflation rate, i. Now, since we are saying that differences in international interest rates are accounted for by differences in inflation, we are implicitly saying that all countries have the same real interest rate, r′. This, however, would be going too far. Though it probably applies to rates in the Eurocurrency market, which is a particularly free market, it does not always hold between domestic interest rates. Between these rates we can find the same sorts of obstacles to interest rate parity as we did to purchasing power parity: constraints and costs to the individual's ability to borrow and lend freely internationally; and governments intervening to maintain disequilibrium rates. Between domestic interest rates we now and then observe differences that do not seem explicable in terms of expected inflation.

Another important question for our understanding of prices across exchanges, is whether the market gets its expectations right. Are forward rates a good predictor of future spot rates? The evidence is that forward rates do tend to predict future spot rates correctly on average, but they are not strong predictors and tend to overstate future changes in spot rates. So although forward rates seem to be set efficiently, they simply reflect the very great uncertainty associated with predicting exchange rates.

Financial policy across exchanges

Our analysis of interest rate parity and purchasing power parity resembles our 'perfect market' discussions in other parts of the book and taken literally it yields the familiar conclusion that financing policy is 'irrelevant' across exchanges. In a world of interest rate parity and purchasing power parity, real interest rates are the same everywhere, so it does not really matter where you borrow, and exchange rates always ensure the same real consumption opportunities, so it does not really matter when you remit funds. In reality we need to temper these conclusions somewhat.

International capital markets

We can view the world's capital markets as consisting of a set of more or less regulated domestic markets and a free international market. The 'Eurocurrency' market is an international market which arose partly to escape from the constraints of domestic governments. It is a market without a formal location, though a lot of its transactions take place in London. The characteristic of a Eurocurrency transaction is that a deposit is created in a bank outside the country whose currency it is denominated in. So a Eurodollar deposit is a dollar deposit outside the US. The Eurocurrency market deals in shorter-term loans. The longer end of the market is referred to as the Eurobond market.

The Eurocurrency market is unrestricted and very competitive, and real interest rates appear to be uniform across currencies in the market. But this may not apply between domestic markets: governments pursue policies which mean domestic rates can diverge from world rates; and they create barriers to prevent arbitrage restoring equilibrium. Sometimes governments will make cheap money available to favoured investment projects. In this case by defining the investment and providing the funds they can prevent mobility of the funds. More generally, governments may hold domestic rates above or below world levels as part of their economic policy, and prevent mobility by running exchange controls. Many countries run foreign exchange controls, as did Britain until recently, and particularly in developing countries for whom investment funds are particularly important, the illegal import or export of finance, often attracts Draconian penalties. Hence it may well be beneficial to look carefully at where to source the financing of a project.

Financing risk and repatriation

Purchasing power parity should ensure that a project's cash flows retain their home currency value even if the country in which the project is located devalues relative to the home currency. However many companies prefer not to rely on this, and consider carefully the effect of winding up the project and repatriating it after a devaluation. This often argues for only financing from home those assets with a buoyant world market value, and financing other assets locally.

Another complicating factor is differing international tax systems. Though the rules differ, in general we can expect overseas projects to be taxed in the country in which they are located. The parent will be subject to further home tax on payments remitted from overseas, though there may be some relief of domestic tax if there is a double taxation agreement between the two countries. Needless to say there are considerable opportunities for exploiting the diversity of tax rules by choice of structure, and of location for the parent and the subsidiary.

The main cash flows between subsidiary and parent tend to be for management fees, royalties, payment for goods and other services supplied, dividends and interest and repayment of principal. Though all of these appear to offer a vehicle for moving cash, to combat tax avoidance and to help enforce exchange controls domestic authorities keep a close check on the repatriation of funds, and expect to see these amounts as reasonable.

III THE NATURE OF OPTIONS

The option to *buy* something is known as a *call* option, and to sell, a *put*. The price at which the purchase or sale is to be made is the *exercise price*. As to the date of exercise there are two possibilities. We call an option that must be exercised on a specific date a *European* option, and one that may be exercised anytime up to and including the exercise date, an *American* option. You can write options to buy or sell any asset, and there are highly developed markets in closely related areas such as commodities futures. But our interest is in options on shares. We can get a good idea of how share options work by looking at the traded-options market.

Table I shows the prices at which options on GEC were being traded on 14 July 1994. On the London Market 'American' options are traded with a life of nine months, and there are expiry dates every three months, so investors always have options with at least two different dates to choose from. In July 1994 you could buy GEC options expiring in August or November 1994, and you could choose seven different exercise prices, between 240p and 390p, compared to the current price of a GEC share which was 278.5p. The

Table I Options on GEC shares

GEC share price on 14.7.94: 278.5p

	Option prices			
	Call		*Put*	
Exercise price	August	November	August	November
240	42.0	42.0	1.0	1.3
260	22.0	24.5	2.0	6.5
280	6.0	11.5	10.5	15.5
300	1.5	7.0	28.0	29.5
330	1.0	2.5	58.5	57.0
360	1.0	1.5	88.0	87.5
390	1.0	1.0	117.0	117.0

Source: Financial Times, 12 July 1994

exercise price can be above or below the current share price. Options with exercise prices below the current share price are commonly known as *in the money* and if the reverse applies they are *out of the money*. Option prices or *premiums* are quoted per share and options are traded in units or *contracts* of 1,000 shares.

Phil Smith

Phil Smith believes that by November 1994 GEC shares will be sufficiently above 300 to justify paying 7p now for the option to buy them. He instructs his broker to buy one contract for 1,000 November call options, at a total cost of 7p × 1000 = £70. When November arrives there are two possibilities. If GEC shares are, say, only 280 Smith will have to tear up his option and forget about it – no-one wants an option to buy 300 something that is only worth 280. But suppose Smith's hunch was correct and GEC shares are now 350. Smith can exercise his options and buy the shares for 300, or he can just sell the options to someone else. Most often, in fact, people buy calls with no ultimate intention of taking the shares. Either way he can calculate his profit as follows:

Share price	350
Exercise price	(300)
	50
Cost of option	7
Profit	43p × 1,000 = £430

In reality Phil Smith's profit will be less than this because of transactions costs. His broker will charge a fixed commission per contract, and since time elapsed between buying the options and exercising them, he has foregone some interest on the premium money as well. Also he will have to pay capital gains tax on the profit. But leaving these points aside Figure I shows Smith's payoff. The solid line shows how the option's payoff is related to the share price on the day the option expires. If the share is worth less than the exercise price, 300, then the option is worth nothing. After that, the payoff increases pence for pence with share price, as the 45° line. Since Smith paid 7p to buy the option in the first place his return is given by the lower broken line. If share price fell to zero, he would lose 7p, and he breaks even when share price is 307. Any increase in share price after that goes straight onto his return.

One difference between options and the underlying shares is where they come from. All GEC shares were, at some time or other, issued by GEC. But options on GEC shares have nothing at all to do with GEC. They are created by another investor being prepared to sell GEC shares at a fixed price sometime in the future. Suppose in the present case that person was Sharon Brown. All Brown had to do to sell or *write* options at 300 for April was to instruct her broker to do so for her. The day after the options are sold Brown will receive £70 for the options from her broker. Figure II shows Brown's return. It is the mirror image of Smith's.

When the GEC share price goes above 300 and Brown is forced to deliver them at 300 she is going to be sorely tempted to run away and renege on the deal. Because of this risk there are market rules which force the writer to lodge some *collateral* with his broker. This could be the share certificates, or if as is likely, Brown does not actually own any GEC shares, she can put up her collateral or *margin* in the form of government securities or cash. It is important, by the way, not to confuse selling a call with buying a put. If Brown had bought a put she would have *bought* the right to *sell* for, say 300 in November, rather than *selling* the right to *buy* to someone else. In the first case, if the price of GEC shares falls

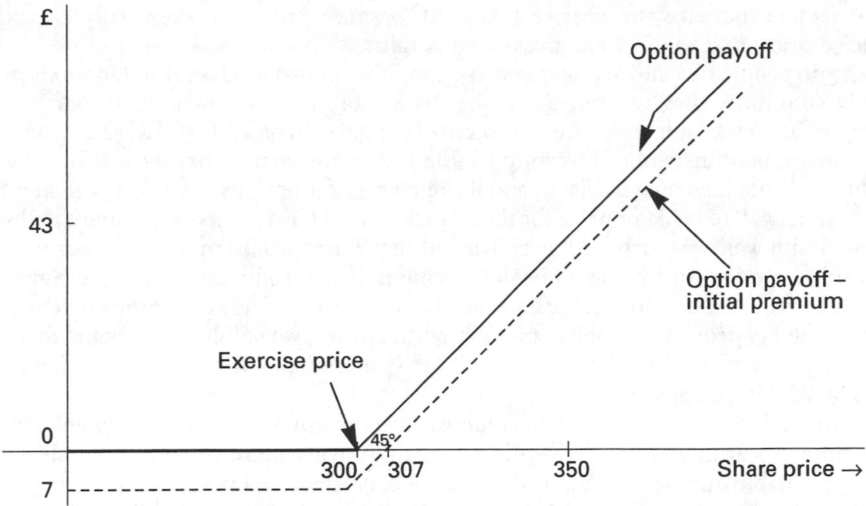

Figure I Smith's payoff to buying a GEC call

below 300 she *can* sell for 300, in the second case, if the price of GEC goes above 300 she will have to sell at 300.

The writer of a call option need not own the underlying shares nor the buyer of the option want to buy them. The option itself is the object of the transaction and both parties trade on the belief that the option will subsequently be worth less, or more, than its current price. Hence the option never needs to be exercised; either party can close his position before the exercise date by buying or selling the options to someone else.

What determines option prices? This will be our major concern in the rest of the chapter, but two factors are already clear in Table I. GEC call options have a higher price the lower the exercise price and the longer the period to expiry. This makes sense. Both

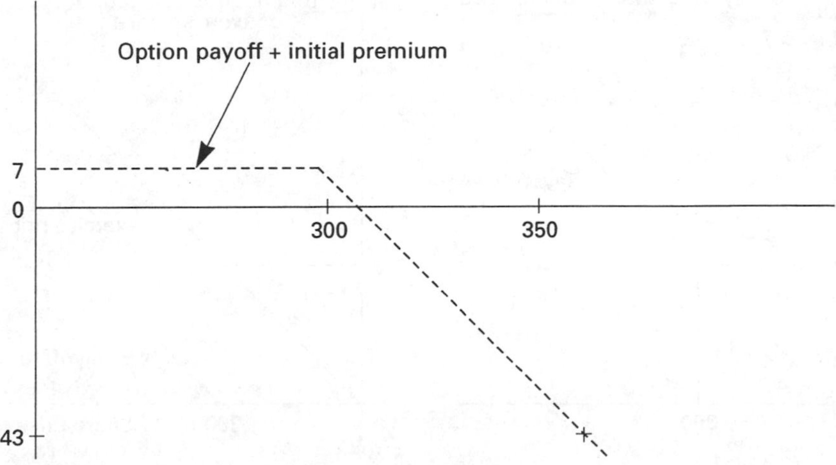

Figure II Brown's return to selling GEC calls

these factors increase the chance that GEC's share price will eventually exceed the exercise price, and this is what gives options value.

Why do people buy and sell options? We can think of two motives. First, options permit people who think they can out-guess the market to invest at low cost. In our previous example Smith was able to secure the potential capital gain on 1,000 GEC shares with only a £70 investment instead of investing £2,785 to buy the shares themselves. But the gain might easily not have materialised, and if the market for options is working efficiently we must expect £70 to be a fair price for the chance it would. For every buyer there is always a seller. Smith was obviously just as convinced the shares would move the other way.

Another motive for buying and selling options is risk reduction. Suppose Smith had already owned 1,000 shares in GEC, which he bought at 235 as against the current 278.5. If he wanted to protect his capital and part of that profit, yet still back his belief that GEC was going to carry on rising he could sell his GEC shares, and buy options, yielding 278.5p − 7p = 271.5p per share in cash.

It is possible to *hedge* all the risk in holding shares by using options. This exploits the fact that option prices increase with the price of the underlying share. So by holding shares and selling a suitable number of options the investor can balance increases in his share position by falls in his option position, and vice versa. We look at hedging portfolios in more detail later on.

Put options and put–call parity

The value of a put option is closely linked to the value of the equivalent call. Figure III(a) plots the payoff to owning one GEC share and a put option on it with an exercise price of 300. If the share price is above the exercise price we keep the share – the payoff is the share price. But if the share price is below the exercise price we exercise our right to sell the share for 300, so 300 is the lower limit of our payoff. The payoff in Figure III(a) is the same as the solid line in Figure I which was the payoff on a GEC call, but displaced upwards by 300. However we could recreate the payoff from holding a share plus a put *exactly* by holding a call and investing enough to yield the exercise price on the day the option expires, that is, holding the call and investing the present value of the exercise price.

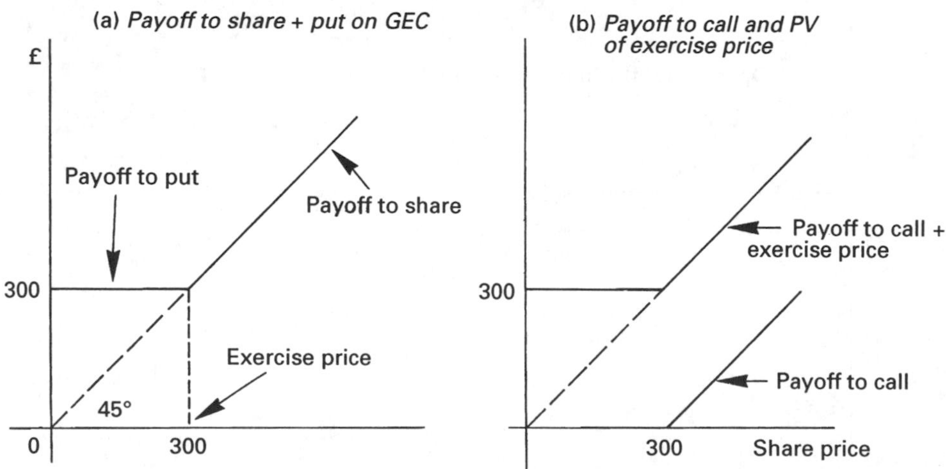

Figure III Put-call parity

Figure III(b) shows that this would give identical payoffs to buying a put and holding the share.

Since portfolios that give the same payoffs must have the same value we get:

value of put + value of share = value of call + present value of exercise price.

This is the expression of *put-call parity*, it means that once we know how to value calls this will permit us to value puts as well.

A simple 'states of the world' model of option value

We saw in Chapter 5 that the value of a share, S_o, is the present value of the future dividend stream, DIV_t, discounted at the shareholders' required return, r_e:

$$S_o = \sum_{t=o}^{\infty} \frac{DIV_t}{(1+r_e)^t}$$

This is the 'dividend valuation model'. The big problem facing investors in valuing shares is that the dividend stream, and the underlying earnings, are uncertain. It is helpful to restate this problem in terms of 'states of the world'. A *state of the world* is an exhaustive description of the firm's environment at a given time – we are thinking of the state of competition, technology, tastes, government policy, the macroeconomic environment, the internal environment of the firm, its financial policies, and so forth. We will say that each state of the world uniquely determines the firm's earnings, in other words, *given* the state of the world the firm's earnings are *certain*. All the uncertainty about future earnings and dividends, therefore, is uncertainty about states of the world. Take a simple case in which we are valuing a share and there are three possible states of the world. Figure IV depicts the problem.

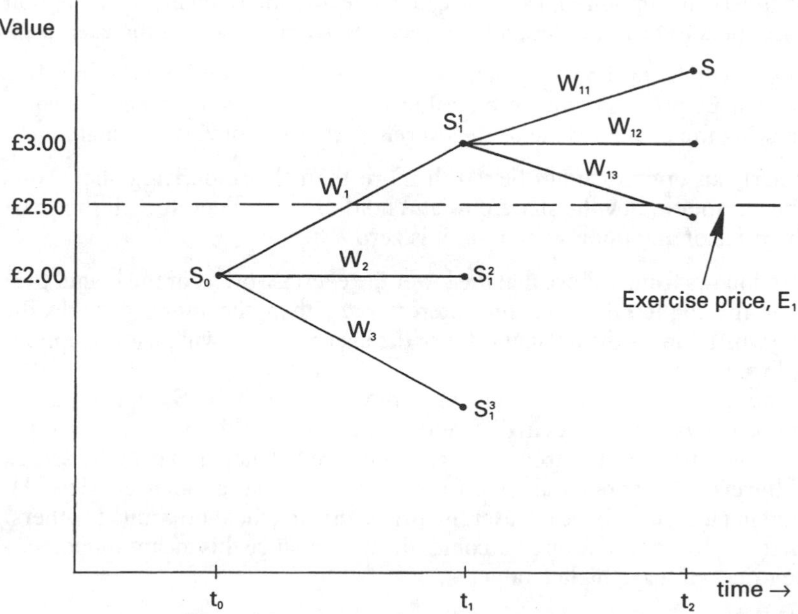

Figure IV Share value in different states of the world

The present value of a share (at t_o) is S_o. This value reflects the market's evaluation of the firm's earnings subject to future states of the world. If between $t_o \rightarrow t_1$ state of the world W_1 occurs, then at t_1 the value of the share will be S_1^1; if it is W_2 then the value will be S_1^2, and so on. And in subsequent periods there will be further branching. We can put some numbers into the picture. Suppose the value of the share at t_o is £2. How much would we be prepared to pay for the option to buy the share at t_1 for an exercise price, E_1, of £2.50? Clearly the option will only be worth exercising if S is greater than £2.50 at t_1. This is a question of whether W_1 occurs in the next time period. Suppose, in fact, we know that is a .3 probability of W_1, and if W_1 does occur, S_1^1 will be £3. If we exercised the option at t_1 we would be (£3 − £2.50 =) 50p better off. Since the probability of W_1 is .3, the expected value of this outcome will be 50p × .3 = 15p. So we should be prepared to pay the present value of 15p to secure the option.

On the face of it, option valuation looks just as hard as valuing shares. It requires the same sort of information about the future. But all the information relevant to valuing the option should already be embodied in the value of the share, *which is known*. The trick in option valuation is to disentangle that proportion of the overall share value that relates to the option. In the simple example we just looked at this was easy, there were only three possible states of the world, and we knew their probabilities. In practice the possibilities for future states of the world, and for future share values, are infinite and we have to make some assumptions about the process of share prices through time to generate the future distribution. This is what Black and Scholes do in the option valuation model we look at next. But before examining Black-Scholes we can quite easily deduce some general properties an option price must have.[1]

Some properties of an option pricing model

1 Option prices cannot be negative. If the exercise price turns out to be below the share price on the day the option expires, you can just tear it up. So on expiry, an option is worth the greater of zero or the difference between the share value and the exercise price.

2 An option price must not be less than the greater of zero or the difference between the underlying share price and the present value of the exercise price, otherwise you are better off borrowing the present value of the exercise price and buying the share.

3 Similarly an option cannot be worth more than the underlying share, otherwise it would be cheaper to buy the share now and hold on to it. Therefore, if the share price is zero, the price of an option written on it is zero.

4 It also follows from 2 above that the lower the exercise price, or the longer the period to expiry, or the higher the risk-free interest rate, than the more valuable the option. Anything which lowers the present value of the exercise price will raise the option value, all other things being equal.

The intuition of this is simple. The present value of a share, S, represents an expectation of good and bad outcomes in different states of the world. In the case of a riskier share with the same value more extreme future values are balancing to give the same expected value. However the option valuer does not need to take a balanced view. He is only interested in outcomes above the exercise price, and attaches zero value to others. For him the higher the variance of future outcomes the better, since this means outcomes above his exercise price will have higher value.

1 In this, as in most of this section we are following Merton (1973). Merton's account is invaluable reading for anyone requiring to deepen their knowledge of option pricing.

The pricing of American calls and dividends

An American call can be exercised on or before the exercise date, whereas a European option can only be exercised on the exercise date. What difference does this make to the valuation of an American option? The key thing to note is that if an American option is not exercised until expiry it is effectively a European option. Since it is always worthwhile to keep an option live rather than exercise it, so long as the underlying share does not pay dividends our previous theorems on European options will apply to American options too.

So far we have *assumed* that dividends are not paid on the underlying share. This is clearly unrealistic, so what effect will dividends have on option valuation? Share price falls after a dividend, 'ex-div'. This is simply because part of the assets whose value was embodied in the cum-div share price have now been distributed to the shareholders. Since we know that option value is an increasing function of the value of the underlying share, we would expect this drop in share value to engender a corresponding drop in option value. We know that the value of an option kept 'live' is always more than its value exercised, but if the loss in value due to the dividend is greater than this premium it might be rational for the holder to exercise it early, if he can. Hence the existence of dividends may lead to the premature exercise of American options. Furthermore, since the European call holder would have preferred to exercise early too, but could not, we can expect American calls to sell for a higher price in a world of dividends.

In practice it is feasible to build clauses into option agreements protecting them from dividend payouts. The value of a fully-protected option is unaffected by dividend payouts, however, in practice few options are fully-protected. But dividend policy is just one of the management decisions that can affect the value of the option by affecting the value of the underlying share. In this respect options are vulnerable like all other claims on the firm, to management decisions.

IV USING OPTIONS TO HEDGE

We know the general relationship between the price of a share and the value of an option on that share. The option value is an increasing function of the riskless interest rate, r_i, the time to exercise, t, and the variance of the share's return, σ^2. It is a decreasing function of the exercise price, E. In a seminal paper Black and Scholes (1973) derive an option valuation model which has these properties, by making assumptions about the process linking present and future share prices. Their model provides a deterministic option value, and can be used to build hedges using options.

The Black–Scholes model

The value of an option, O, is:

$$O = S \,.\, N(d_1) - \frac{E}{{}_{e}r_i t} \,.\, N(d_2)$$

$$\text{where } d_1 = \frac{\ln(S/E) + r_i t + \sigma^2 t/2}{\sigma\sqrt{t}}$$

$$d_2 = \frac{\ln(S/E) + r_i t + \sigma^2 t/2}{\sigma\sqrt{t}}$$

N(d) = 'cumulative normal density function' i e the area to the left of d under a normal distribution of unit variance and zero mean; ln is the natural log.

In words, BS are saying that the value of a European call option is the difference between share price and present value of the exercise price, but with weights N(d) attached. The model is deterministic, it gives a unique value for the option, and it has all the properties we derived in the last section. The assumptions Black and Scholes make in addition to the ones we have made already are that a) the share price follows a random process known as 'geometric Brownian motion' and b) there is continuous trading, and there are no restrictions on 'short-sales', that is, on having a negative holding.

Assumption a) permits BS to estimate the future distribution of share values using knowable parameters, the present share price and variance of return. But perhaps the key insight Black and Scholes had was that combining shares and options investors could build 'perfectly hedged', riskless, portfolios. For this they required assumption b).

Hedging

The existence of call options permits an investor to construct a perfectly *hedged* portfolio, i e a portfolio with zero risk. The overall return on such a portfolio must be the risk-free rate, r_i. The formula for creating such a portfolio is simple, and will be discussed below.

Figure V plots the relationship between option price and share value. The slope shows how much the price of the option increases as the price of the share rises by one unit. Consider a discrete increase in share price from 50p to 54p. We see that the option on the share responds by increasing in price from 20p to 22p. An investor holding one of these shares has a risky asset – an asset whose price fluctuates over time. Suppose he would rather hold a riskless position. The existence of a separate security, an option, whose price moves in concert with the share permits him to achieve this. All the investor needs to do is

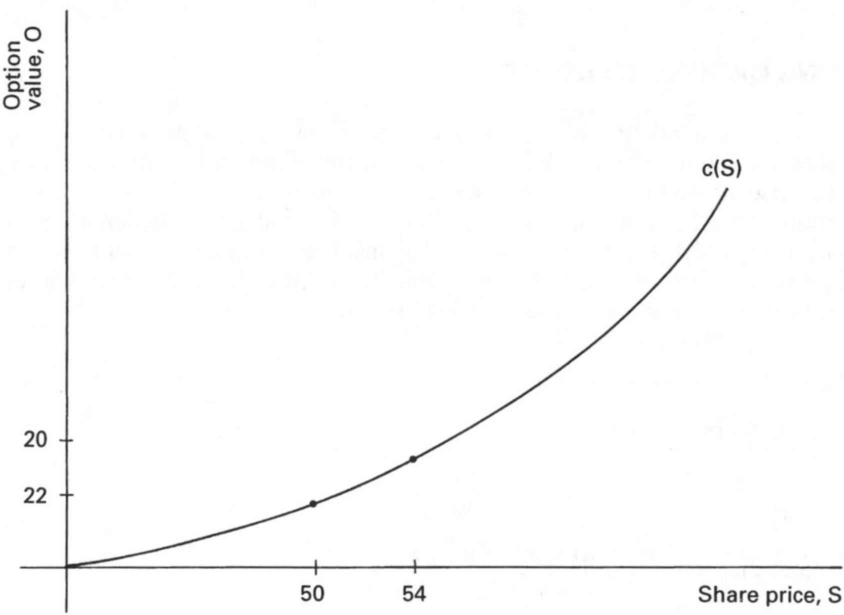

Figure V Relationship of option price to share value

sell short two options. Now when the value of the share increases by 4p this gain is exactly compensated by the loss on the short position in options – it will cost our investor an extra 4p to replace the two options. Similarly, if the share price falls the investor is also protected. He loses 4p on his share, but will need to pay 2p less to replace each of the two options he has sold. This is the hedging process, and it depends on the investors ability to sell short; hence the necessity for the assumption that there are no restrictions on short sales.

We looked at small changes in share price, and assumed the effects on option price were symmetrical. However the hedge ratio – the number of options you need to sell for each share – is the slope of the option valuation curve, and since this curve is convex its slope changes over the range of share price. The implication is that the investor will need to keep constantly rebalancing his portfolio as the hedge ratio changes with share price. Hence the need for the assumption that there is continuous trading in the market.

Primal plc

Shares in Primal plc are presently selling for 300p and the standard deviation of Primal returns is 40%. The riskless interest rate is 10%. What is the value of a 90 day call option on Primal with a 250p exercise price?

We can feed the following values into the BS model:

$$\begin{aligned} S &= 300 \\ E &= 250 \\ r_i &= .10 \\ t &= .25 \\ \sigma &= .4 \end{aligned}$$

It will also be useful to work out:

$$PV(E) = \frac{E}{e^{r_i t}}$$

$$= 243.82$$

The natural log of S/E, where $S/E = \frac{300}{250} = 1.2$, we can find natural log tables.

In (1.2) = .1823

$$\text{So } d_1 = \frac{.1823 + .10 \times .25 + (.4)^2 \times .25/2}{.4 \times \sqrt{.25}} = 1.1365$$

$$d_2 = \frac{.1823 + .10 \times .25 - (.4)^2 \times .25/2}{.4 \times \sqrt{.25}} = .9365$$

N (d_1) and N (d_2) are the areas under the unit normal distribution 'to the left' of d_1 and d_2. From Table II below we get:

N (d_1) = .8713 N (d_2) = .8246

So the value of the call option in Primal is

$$\begin{aligned} O &= 300 \times .8713 - 243.82 \times .8246 \\ &= 261.39 - 201.05 \\ &= \underline{60.34p} \end{aligned}$$

The BS formula is straightforward to operate, but an alternative is to use 'option tables'. The user 'plugs in' the key parameters, and the tables show the premium, as a percentage of S, that should be added to $S - E/_{e}r_{i}t$ to get the option value.

The hedge ratio

The Black–Scholes formula gives us the *hedge ratio* – the number of options the investor must sell short to create the perfectly hedged portfolio. In the example we had earlier the option price rose from 20 to 22 when the share moved from 50 to 54. The slope of the curve in this vicinity was 2/4 = ½, and the hedge ratio was 2, which was 1/slope. Actually, ½ was only an approximation of the slope over a discrete interval, in reality, the slope changes continuously round the curve. The BS formula tells us what the slope is at any point. We know that:

$$O = S.N\,(d_1) - \frac{E}{e^{r_i t}} . N\,(d_2).$$

The slope of this curve is $\frac{dO}{dS} = N\,(d_1)$.

To see whether this tells us how to build a hedged portfolio we can use the Primal example.

$N\,(d_1)$ for Primal was .8713. This implies a hedge ratio of $\frac{1}{.8713} = 1.1477$.

So if we owned 1,000 shares of Primal we could hedge by *selling* 1,000 × 1.1477 = 1147 calls.

The value of our portfolio will now be:

$$\begin{aligned} &1{,}000 . S - 1148 . O \\ &= 1{,}000 \times 300 - 1147 \times 60.34 = \underline{£2{,}307.90} \end{aligned}$$

If the share price rises to 301, the option price will rise to £61.24 (you can check this using the BS formula).

The value of the portfolio will be:
1,000 × 301 − 1147 × 61.24 = £2,307.56

The decrease in the value of the short position in options has almost perfectly offset the increase in share value. And readers can check for themselves that if share price falls to 299p the portfolio value will be £2,307.35.

The discrepancy of a few pence in each case is explained by the fact we explored a change of 1p around the share price. This may seem a small enough interval, but for perfect hedging one would need to readjust the hedge ratio continuously, as assumed by BS.

Valuing a put

Now we can value a call we can value a put, using the *put-call parity* result:

Put + share = Call + PV (exercise price)

In the case of Primal:

$$\begin{aligned} \text{Put} + 300 &= 60.34 + 243.82 \\ \text{Put} &= 4.16\text{p} \end{aligned}$$

The value of a put in Primal, if the share price is 300, is 4.16p.

TABLE II – AREA UNDER THE NORMAL CURVE

x	N(x)	x	N(x)	x	N(x)	x	N(x)	x	N(x)	x	N(x)
0.00	0.5000	**0.50**	0.6915	**1.00**	0.8413	**1.50**	0.9322	**2.00**	0.9773	**2.50**	0.9938
.01	.5040	**.51**	.6950	**.01**	.8438	**.51**	.9345	**.01**	.9778	**.51**	.9940
.02	.5080	**.52**	.6985	**.02**	.8461	**.52**	.9357	**.02**	.9783	**.52**	.9941
.03	.5120	**.53**	.7019	**.03**	.8485	**.53**	.9370	**.03**	.9788	**.53**	.9943
.04	.5160	**.54**	.7054	**.04**	.8508	**.54**	.9382	**.04**	.9793	**.54**	.9945
.05	.5199	**.55**	.7088	**.05**	.8531	**.55**	.9394	**.05**	.9798	**.55**	.9945
.06	.5239	**.56**	.7123	**.06**	.8554	**.56**	.9406	**.06**	.9803	**.56**	.9948
.07	.5279	**.57**	.7157	**.07**	.8577	**.57**	.9418	**.07**	.9808	**.57**	.9949
.08	.5319	**.58**	.7190	**.08**	.8599	**.58**	.9429	**.08**	.9812	**.58**	.9951
.09	.5359	**.59**	.7224	**.09**	.8621	**.59**	.9441	**.09**	.9817	**.59**	.9952
0.10	0.5398	**0.60**	0.7257	**1.10**	0.8643	**1.60**	0.9452	**2.10**	0.9821	**2.60**	0.9953
.11	.5438	**.61**	.7291	**.11**	.8665	**.61**	.9463	**.11**	.9826	**.61**	.9955
.12	.5478	**.62**	.7324	**.12**	.8686	**.62**	.9474	**.12**	.9830	**.62**	.9956
.13	.5517	**.63**	.7357	**.13**	.8708	**.63**	.9484	**.13**	.9834	**.63**	.9957
.14	.5557	**.64**	.7389	**.14**	.8729	**.64**	.9495	**.14**	.9838	**.64**	.9959
.15	.5596	**.65**	.7422	**.15**	.8749	**.65**	.9505	**.15**	.9842	**.65**	.9960
.16	.5636	**.66**	.7454	**.16**	.8770	**.66**	.9515	**.16**	.9846	**.66**	.9961
.17	.5675	**.67**	.7486	**.17**	.8790	**.67**	.9525	**.17**	.9850	**.67**	.9962
.18	.5714	**.68**	.7517	**.18**	.8810	**.68**	.9535	**.18**	.9854	**.68**	.9963
.19	.5753	**.69**	.7549	**.19**	.8830	**.69**	.9545	**.19**	.9857	**.69**	.9964
0.20	0.5793	**0.70**	0.7580	**1.20**	0.8849	**1.70**	0.9554	**2.20**	0.9861	**2.70**	0.9965
.21	.5832	**.71**	.7611	**.21**	.8869	**.71**	.9564	**.21**	.9865	**.71**	.9966
.22	.5871	**.72**	.7642	**.22**	.8888	**.72**	.9573	**.22**	.9868	**.72**	.9967
.23	.5910	**.73**	.7673	**.23**	.8907	**.73**	.9582	**.23**	.9871	**.73**	.9968
.24	.5948	**.74**	.7704	**.24**	.8925	**.74**	.9591	**.24**	.9875	**.74**	.9969
.25	.5987	**.75**	.7734	**.25**	.8944	**.75**	.9599	**.25**	.9878	**.75**	.9970
.26	.6026	**.76**	.7764	**.26**	.8962	**.76**	.9608	**.26**	.9881	**.76**	.9971
.27	.6064	**.77**	.7794	**.27**	.8980	**.77**	.9616	**.27**	.9884	**.77**	.9972
.28	.6103	**.78**	.7823	**.28**	.8997	**.78**	.9625	**.28**	.9887	**.78**	.9973
.29	.6141	**.79**	.7852	**.29**	.9015	**.79**	.9633	**.29**	.9890	**.79**	.9974
0.30	0.6179	**0.80**	0.7881	**1.30**	0.9032	**1.80**	0.9641	**2.30**	0.9893	**2.80**	0.9974
.31	.6217	**.81**	.7910	**.31**	.9049	**.81**	.9649	**.31**	.9896	**.81**	.9975
.32	.6255	**.82**	.7939	**.32**	.9066	**.82**	.9656	**.32**	.9898	**.82**	.9976
.33	.6293	**.83**	.7967	**.33**	.9082	**.83**	.9664	**.33**	.9901	**.83**	.9977
.34	.6331	**.84**	.7995	**.34**	.9099	**.84**	.9671	**.34**	.9904	**.84**	.9977
.35	.6368	**.85**	.8023	**.35**	.9115	**.85**	.9678	**.35**	.9906	**.85**	.9978
.36	.6406	**.86**	.8051	**.36**	.9131	**.86**	.9686	**.36**	.9909	**.86**	.9979
.37	.6443	**.87**	.8078	**.37**	.9147	**.87**	.9693	**.37**	.9911	**.87**	.9980
.38	.6480	**.88**	.8106	**.38**	.9162	**.88**	.9699	**.38**	.9913	**.88**	.9980
.39	.6517	**.89**	.8133	**.39**	.9177	**.89**	.9706	**.39**	.9916	**.89**	.9981
0.40	0.6554	**0.90**	0.8159	**1.40**	0.9192	**1.90**	0.9713	**2.40**	0.9918	**2.90**	0.9981
.41	.6591	**.91**	.8186	**.41**	.9207	**.91**	.9719	**.41**	.9920	**.91**	.9982
.42	.6628	**.92**	.8212	**.42**	.9222	**.92**	.9726	**.42**	.9922	**.92**	.9983
.43	.6664	**.93**	.8238	**.43**	.9236	**.93**	.9732	**.43**	.9925	**.93**	.9983
.44	.6700	**.94**	.8264	**.44**	.9251	**.94**	.9738	**.44**	.9927	**.94**	.9984
.45	.6736	**.95**	.8289	**.45**	.9265	**.95**	.9744	**.45**	.9929	**.95**	.9984
.46	.6772	**.96**	.8315	**.46**	.9279	**.96**	.9750	**.46**	.9931	**.96**	.9985
.47	.6808	**.97**	.8340	**.47**	.9292	**.97**	.9756	**.47**	.9932	**.97**	.9985
.48	.6844	**.98**	.8365	**.48**	.9306	**.98**	.9761	**.48**	.9934	**.98**	.9986
.49	.6879	**.99**	.8389	**.49**	.9319	**.99**	.9767	**.49**	.9936	**.99**	.9986

V SUMMARY

This chapter has shown how firms can reduce the riskiness of their cash flows by hedging. We described the nature of currency risk and showed how it can be hedged using forward contracts. We also saw how options are valued, and how they can be used to hedge equity risk.

REFERENCES AND BIBLIOGRAPHY

Black, F, and Scholes, M	'The Pricing of Options and Corporate Liabilities', Journal of Political Economy, May/June 1973, pp 637–659.
Eiteman, D K, Stonehill, A I, and Moffett, M H	*Multinational Business Finance* (6th edn, 1992) Addison Wesley, NY.
Hull, J	*Options, Futures and Other Derivative Securities* (2nd edn, 1993) Prentice-Hall Inc, Englewood-Cliffs, NJ.
Merton, R C	'Theory of Rational Option Pricing', Bell Journal of Economics and Management Science, Spring 1973, pp 141–183.

CHAPTER 11

Project choice in practice

The value-maximising firm should choose all projects with a positive net present value, but in practice firms often seem to make their investment decisions in rather different ways. We start this chapter by considering evidence on how one large corporation, Unilever, makes its investment decisions. In Section II we examine the findings of a work by R H Pike of investment practices in the UK. He found, as others have, that although the use of DCF analysis seems to be on the increase, other apparently conflicting decision-rules are also widely used. Amongst small and medium-sized firms, and even in large corporations it is common for projects to be chosen on the basis of rather simple criteria such as their *payback period* or their *average accounting rate of return*. It is easy to devise situations in which these criteria will lead to choices which do not maximise value. But it is not just these so-called *rules-of-thumb* that pose this threat. Many major corporations structure their investment decision-making using strategic planning models which seem to emphasise variables such as market share, and growth rate in sales, rather than value. These alternatives to DCF are too widespread to be lightly dismissed and in Sections III and IV we examine their relationship to DCF analysis in more detail and consider the reasons for their popularity.

I INVESTMENT DECISIONS AT UNILEVER

Unilever is one of the UK's largest and most successful industrial firms. When it submitted evidence[1] to the Wilson Committee nearly twenty years ago it gave some interesting insights into the way a firm of this size and sophistication makes its investment decisions and how its practice matches up with the theory we have been describing. Its practice was still fundamentally the same in the early 1990s.

In terms of basic technique Unilever uses a mixture of DCF and payback period. The prime measure of project performance is internal rate of return or 'DCF yield' which it calculates in constant prices. Net present value may be used when a choice has to be made between alternatives. Unilever later commented:

> All capital investment, whether for expansion or straight replacement, has to be evaluated in the same way and has to show a DCF yield compatible with the risk involved. Proposals heavily dependent upon market share/volume growth have to include sensitivity analysis to show the impact on the DCF yield if the growth does not occur. We are particularly sceptical about the benefits of favourable tax incentives which can vanish overnight!

When it comes to risk, Unilever said the following:

> To assist the assessment of risk, we test the sensitivity of the DCF yield to variations in the main assumptions. We also calculate the payback period and give particular attention to this measure in situations of high risk. A considerable part of the assessment of risk, however, is a judgement of

1 Unilever's submission to the Wilson Committee (1977).

> the credibility of the yield calculation. We have found from bitter experience that project profitability obtained in the event is on average significantly below project profitability estimated in advance . . . It must be stressed that in modern conditions, the allowance for risk in even an average risk proposal has to be substantial. Moreover, although formal methods of evaluation of risk can help in a number of cases the overall assessment of risk has to be mainly a matter of judgement rather than scientific calculation.

There is no mention here of variance and portfolio effects! If projects are perceived as risky, Unilever relies on the techniques of sensitivity analysis and payback. But a new dimension to risk emerges from Unilever's statement, the problem of 'reliability of source'. Unilever recognise that managers tend to be optimistic, and some are more optimistic than others.

Our main thrust in Chapter 9 was to find a robust way of adjusting the cost of capital for risk, but Unilever does not use a risk-adjusted discount rate. Indeed one reason Unilever favours IRR may be that, unlike NPV, it does not require a specific measure of the cost of capital. Unilever was sceptical about the cost of capital:

> The cost of capital also cannot be scientifically established. Working in constant prices, the marginal cost of capital in the form of extra borrowing is often negative, i e interest rate less tax is less than the inflation rate . . . Calculations of average cost of capital taking account both of shareholders funds and of borrowings are highly theoretical and controversial and can produce a wide range of answers depending on definitions. Partly for this reason we have never set any rigid minimum DCF return. (ibid)

Some time after, Unilever added the following comment:

> We do not formally calculate a cost of capital nor do we set hurdle rates for DCF yields. Operating management is encouraged to bring forward a wide range of investment proposals and setting a hurdle rate and/or publishing internally a cost of capital could stifle the flow of proposals . . .

Another issue which comes out strongly in the Unilever submission is the question of strategy. In practice, project appraisal in the sense we have been discussing it is the second stage in the overall investment decision. Firms do not choose projects in a vacuum, they choose them in the context of a *strategy*. Unilever were clear about this:

> In making decisions on investment proposals, the main criteria are:
>
> 1 Does the proposal fit into the agreed strategy for the company involved?
> 2 Is the prospective yield adequate in relation to the risks involved and the cost of capital?

In deciding strategy at Unilever, 'current and prospective profitability . . . are overwhelmingly the most important considerations'. In theory if the capital market is efficient firms can always borrow more money, albeit at a higher price. In practice, as we see later in the book, firms tend to put a high priority on using internally-generated funds and if these are not available investment may get postponed. Unilever has stated that it continues to expect to generate sufficient funds internally to finance capital expenditure programmes but is prepared to borrow for strategic acquisitions.

The third issue that Unilever raised is the question of timing in capital investment. This is another area which can be important in practice, but about which theory does not have much to say.

> . . . although we do our utmost to maintain stability in our capital expenditure programmes, they are influenced particularly in their timing by liquidity considerations. The strength of our balance sheet makes this factor less important for us than for the majority of companies. Nevertheless, major funds outflows . . . undoubtedly cause some low priority capital expenditure to be deferred.

II PIKE'S EVIDENCE ON INVESTMENT DECISION MAKING

R H Pike (1988) has surveyed the capital budgeting practices of 100 large UK manufacturing and retail companies between 1975 and 1986. As the survey response rate was very high (72%) and the same firms took part in each survey, Pike's work provides a fairly reliable basis for comparison. We present some of his results in Table 1. They throw some interesting light on how large firms make their investment decisions in practice.

In terms of administration, Pike found relatively few companies had a full-time capital budgeting staff, though by 1986 83% had a formal review body for projects. 64% of his sample were budgeting more than two years ahead in 1986. Finance theory gives some clear instructions on how to appraise projects, but is silent on how to generate worthwhile projects in the first place. About half Pike's respondents said they had difficulty in finding enough projects to meet their investment plans. Having generated proposals, all large firms subject them to some form of financial appraisal. By 1980 only 38% of firms also required a formal analysis of risk, risk assessment being mainly subjective. However, by 1986 a dramatic change had taken place; 86% of firms having a formal risk analysis requirement. As we saw in the case of Unilever, one 'risk' factor that concerns firms is the reliability of managerial forecasts and the tendency to optimism among some project sponsors. The only way to check for biases of this sort is the conduct of post-completion audits. While 84% of firms monitored past performances, Pike found that only 64% conducted post-completion audits – although this proportion had virtually doubled since 1975.

Table I Investment practices of 100 large UK firms

	% of companies		
	1986	*1981*	*1975*
ADMINISTRATION			
Full-time capital budgeting staff*	26	33	31
Formal review body	83	84	78
Budget more than two years ahead*	64	64	57
EVALUATION AND CONTROL			
Formal financial evaluation	100	95	93
Formal analysis of risk*	86	38	26
Monitor performance	84	76	69
Post-completion audit on major projects	64	46	33
EVALUATION TECHNIQUES			
Inflation ignored	2	11	30
Risk:			
Shortened payback	61	30	25
Increase rate of return	61	41	37
Sensitivity analysis	71	42	28
Probability analysis*	40	10	9
Financial appraisal:			
Payback	92	81	73
Accounting rate of return	56	49	51
Internal rate of return*	75	57	44
Net present value*	68	39	32

* indicates size is a significant factor

Source: Pike (1988)

The technical aspects Pike investigated were the treatment of risk, of inflation, the use of subjective judgement, and most fundamentally, the investment criteria themselves. While in 1975 it was still fairly common to ignore inflation in capital investment analysis, this is now extremely rare in larger firms. A fairly even spread of ways of handling inflation are adopted, with the largest firms tending to favour the specification of different rates of inflation, for different costs and revenues and other firms either forecasting at constant prices with a 'real' required return or making a general inflation adjustment. A number preferred to analyse inflation at the risk analysis/sensitivity analysis stage.

Many firms seemed averse to sophisticated risk analysis approaches, the preferred method of adjusting for risk amongst the smaller firms was to shorten the payback period, with larger firms opting for sensitivity analysis and increasing the required rate of return. Pike found a dramatic increase in the use of all the main risk analysis methods between 1980 and 1986 with probability analysis and sensitivity analysis showing the fast rate of growth. However, probability analysis, although employed by 40% of firms, is still only applied to a few major projects within those companies.

Table II Combined evaluation methods used (100 companies)

	1985–86	*1980–81*	*1975*
No method	0	0	2
Single method			
PBK	6	12	14
ARR	0	7	12
IRR	2	4	5
NPV	0	1	0
	8	24	31
Two methods			
PBK + ARR	10	13	14
PBK + IRR	8	14	14
PBK + NPV	5	6	4
ARR + IRR	2	2	0
ARR + NPV	1	1	1
IRR + NPV	3	4	1
	29	40	34
Three methods			
PBK + ARR + IRR	5	10	7
PBK + ARR + NPV	3	4	4
PBK + IRR + NPV	21	9	10
ARR + IRR + NPV	0	1	1
	29	24	22
Four methods			
PBK + ARR + IRR + NPV	34	12	11
Total	100%	100%	100%

Key PBK = payback
ARR = accounting rate of return
IRR = internal rate of return
NPV = net present value

Source: Pike (1988)

In earlier chapters we have emphasised the importance of judgemental factors in investment decisions. Pike's research bears this out. He asked firms to weigh on a semantic scale the importance they attached to judgemental aspects in decision making. Very few respondents discounted it as of little importance, and overall he found amongst firms approximately equal weight being attached to qualitative and quantitative aspects of appraisal.

Pike's empirical studies offer two important findings. First, there has been a significant increase in the adoption of more sophisticated capital budgeting practices during the 1980s, the primary explanation being the rapid development in end-user computing and application of computer-based financial packages in the investment area. Second, unlike most previous studies which have been unable to detect a positive link between capital budgeting sophistication and corporate performance, Pike found a significant positive association between the change in use of investment methods and the perceived change in capital budgeting effectiveness. In other words, senior financial executives generally believe that it pays to employ more sophisticated investment techniques and control procedures.

In the next section we concentrate on one aspect of quantitative appraisal, the choice of investment criteria.

III RULES OF THUMB

While DCF analysis has gained in popularity over the years there is plenty of evidence that many firms, including large corporations, are still using 'rules of thumb' for investment decisions. These are simple statistics such as *payback period* or average *accounting rate of return*. Tables I and II show Pike's findings. Pike found, as previous studies had done, a gradual growth in the adoption of DCF. But payback still emerges as the most popular technique, used in 92% of firms. Only 8% of firms were using single criteria, with payback the most popular. Most firms, in fact, used a combination of DCF and rules of thumb techniques. Also, it is worth noting that of the DCF techniques, firms seem to prefer IRR to NPV despite the fact that, as we showed earlier in the book, NPV is theoretically stronger. A survey by Schall, Sundem and Geijsbeck (1978) found a continuing trend towards the use of DCF techniques in the US also. They found 86% of firms in their sample now using NPV or IRR, but that the DCF techniques have not displaced rules of thumb but are used alongside. Only 16% of their sample used a DCF technique without also using a rule of thumb. In small and medium-sized firms the proportion is probably much higher.

There have been many studies of investment criteria over the years. What emerges so strikingly from them is the major role rules of thumb still play in the appraisal tool kit. This is particularly so when we note that it is nearly always the largest firms that are being surveyed, and we would expect these firms to be most likely to use 'sophisticated' techniques. The Wilson committee surveyed the investment practices of 'medium-sized' companies. They concluded:

> DCF techniques were used by only a fifth of companies, usually for the larger incremental projects. These were nearly all the larger companies. But even in cases where DCF was used there was often some scepticism about its value in practice . . . So investment appraisal in the majority of companies combined a relatively unsophisticated – or rule of thumb – assessment of payback and 'flat' (accounting) return on capital which were largely seen to go together. Other smaller companies, as we have said, did not even go this far in their financial quantification. (Wilson 1978)

We know that NPV is a robust and reliable investment criterion and that if the firm undertakes projects on the basis of NPV it will maximise value. The trouble with simple rules of thumb like payback and accounting rate of return is that they may not give results that are consistent with NPV.

Payback

The 'payback' period of a project is the number of years it takes to recover the initial cash outlay. It is found by summing the annual cash flow until the initial outlay is recovered. It has an associated decision-rule – *accept the project or projects with the shortest payback period.* Consider Exhibit I, where the cash flow of two projects X and Y are displayed.

Exhibit I

CASH FLOWS

	Project X		*Project Y*
t = 0	(500,000)		(500,000)
1	300,000		200,000
2	300,000	← payback	200,000
3	–	payback →	100,000
4	–		100,000
5	–		100,000
6	–		100,000

The payback period of the two projects is X = 1.7 years, Y = 3 years.

So under the payback criterion project X is preferred. However, the NPVs of the two projects (at 10%) are X = £20,650, Y = £109,080. On this criterion project Y is vastly superior.

The key defect of payback is that in setting up the speed of recovery of the outlay as the choice criterion, it ignores the rest of the project's life. In the example the subsequent cash flows of project Y were decisive.

Another defect of payback compared to DCF is its failure to discount the future cash flows. Some firms calculate *discounted payback* to cure this defect: the *discounted* cash flows from the project are summed and compared with the initial outlay.

Of course payback does not always give contrary results. Sarnat and Levy (1979) showed that in certain circumstances payback is consistent with IRR: for investment proposals with an IRR greater than 30% and with project lives exceeding ten years the 'payback reciprocal' provided a good estimate of the discounted rate of return. The problem with payback is that it concentrates on just one aspect of a project's performance and ignores others. NPV, on the other hand, is all embracing.

Accounting rate of return

The *accounting rate of return* (ARR) is the accounting profit of the project divided by the book value of the assets employed in it. Though it is usually called the ARR in the rules of thumb literature, it is nothing other than the return on capital employed we encounter in financial analysis.[2] The ARR can be calculated annually or as an average over the life of the

2 Also known as return on investment, return on net assets.

project, and in the context of investment appraisal it is common to calculate it on the average investment in the project. ARR tends to have associated decision-rules such as *accept the project or projects with the highest ARR* or *accept projects with an ARR above the predetermined cut-off rate*.

Suppose project X has an annual accounting profit of £5,000 net of depreciation, and there are no taxes. The initial investment is £24,000 which is written-down, straight-line, to zero over the four-years of the project life. The average investment in the project is £12,000 $\left(= \frac{24{,}000 + 0}{2}\right)$ and the average ARR will be 5,000/12,000 $\simeq$ 42%. This project will be accepted or rejected on the ARR criterion by comparing this 42% with the ARR from other projects or with the firm's cost of capital.

Is this sort of procedure likely to lead to the right projects being chosen? Again, the best approach is to investigate the relationship of ARR and IRR; IRR is not always a reliable signal of value but at least we know its shortcomings and its relation to NPV. We investigate this question in Chapter 20 and will see that we *can* relate the IRR of a project and its series of ARRs, but the IRR turns out to be a fairly complicated weighted average of the annual ARRs plus an error term which depends on the discrepancy between book and market values at the beginning and end. In a project which fully consumes its capital we can ignore the error term, but the IRR only becomes the simple mean of the ARRs when, additionally, the ARR is constant throughout the period. We cannot rely on the simple averages of forecast ARRs that firms commonly use for investment appraisal to be a good proxy for IRR. Still less can we rely on a single-year's ARR.

What is the appeal of rules of thumb?

If rules of thumb can lead firms to choose the wrong projects, why do firms use them? The first thing to note is that it is *inevitable* that rules of thumb give the wrong answers sometimes. If we could find a simple rule that *always* gave the same answer as a more sophisticated rule, then the more complicated rule would disappear – no one would ever talk about it. The question is, does the cost of using rules of thumb, which is the cost of choosing inferior projects sometimes, outweigh their appeal? Various explanations for the appeal of rules of thumb have been proposed.

First, of course, they are more *simple* to operate. Payback and ARR are fairly intuitive concepts while to know about DCF the manager will need some management education. The growth in such education during the last decade probably explains the spread of DCF. But why do many large firms, with procedural manuals and training departments, still use rules of thumb, often alongside DCF?

Payback emphasises the *liquidity* rather than the profitability aspect of investment decision making. It tells the decision-maker how soon he or she will get his cash back. This fact should be of no significance to the 'rational' decision-maker, since the DCF approach incorporates accurately the cost of capital, the cost of 'laying out cash'. However some managers persist in attaching importance to speed of payback. And if they perceive capital as tightly rationed, this will not be so irrational since the opportunity cost of funds will be high and will favour early payback.

The key factor which induces managers to calculate speed of payback, in particular, is *uncertainty*. We can make allowance for uncertainty when calculating NPV – by increasing the discount rate or adjusting downward the expected value of later cash flows. But the more uncertain we are about later cash flows the more we will prefer early payback projects. Since 'payback' in effect puts a terminally high discount rate on cash flows beyond the payback period, it may be a rough and ready way of screening out uncertainty, and this is why some firms use it alongside DCF.

Firms which calculate ARR are trying to assess the impact of the project on the firm's accounting statements, and might avoid projects which would dilute the firm's overall accounting return. Though the logic of finance attaches no weight to this, it is in reality a preoccupation of many firms.

In terms of the value-maximising model of the firm, one of the attractions of DCF analysis is that it forces managers to quantify projects fully. You cannot calculate NPVs without being very specific about your expectations of future cash flows. But this may be precisely why managers are unhappy with DCF. A lot of organisational literature has discussed the politics and psychology of decision making. It is suggested that decision-makers are uncomfortable with sophisticated and specific decision-rules. Investment projects are often initiated by relatively junior managers and the initiation of successful projects will enhance a manager's prospects. The less specific she or he is about the project at the outset the less chance there is of it conflicting with the personal objectives of superiors whose sponsorship it will need, and the less damaging will be the subsequent revisions of assumptions to the reputation of those involved. Firms tend to require full quantification of de-centralised decisions for control purposes. But for the same reason individual decision-makers tend to resist quantification in order to increase their freedom.

Maybe one unfortunate side effect of the dramatic improvement in analytic techniques and computational power available to the decision-maker is that successful decision making can appear to be measured by the sophistication of the techniques. We firmly believe that the decision-maker should use the best techniques available, nor is DCF too sophisticated for any manager to employ.

But one thing is worth remembering. Given a set of bad projects the most sophisticated choice rule will choose a bad project, but stick a pin into a set of good projects and you get a good project. If a firm has resources to invest in either inproving its decision techniques or improving its performance in generating ideas for new projects it might be better to choose the latter.

IV BUSINESS STRATEGY AND FINANCIAL RATIONALITY

Once we consider the practicalities of project choice we run up against the question of strategy. Given a set of potential investment projects the value of the firm will be maximised by choosing the ones with a positive NPV. But how does the firm *find* these projects? How does it develop its choice of activities, of products and markets, so as to ensure the best supply through time of valuable projects? This is the question students of *business strategy* attempt to answer, and it is closely linked to the investment appraisal issue.

Strategic portfolio matrices

One popular approach to strategy formulation has been the strategic portfolio matrix. Strategy models are decision-rules for detecting areas of sustainable competitive advantage. One of the best known of these is the so-called 'Boston-Box' model developed by the Boston Consulting Group (BCG). In strategic portfolio matrices two key strategic variables are emphasised: *market share*, and *market growth rate*. To understand why this is so, we need to sketch in some background.

Strategy models get part of their intellectual support from the 'PIMS' ('Profit impact of market strategies') research project carried out at Harvard in the 1970s. The key issue in business strategy is what sort of strategies yield maintainable profits. PIMS addressed itself to just this question; its aim was to identify and measure 'the major determinants of return on investment (ROI) in individual businesses'. PIMS collected data from 57 large US corporations on 620 individual businesses they owned. The data covered financial and market information for the separate businesses, and firms were asked to provide estimates of other variables including market share. The major conclusion of PIMS was that return on investment is strongly related to market share. These results are shown in Figure I.

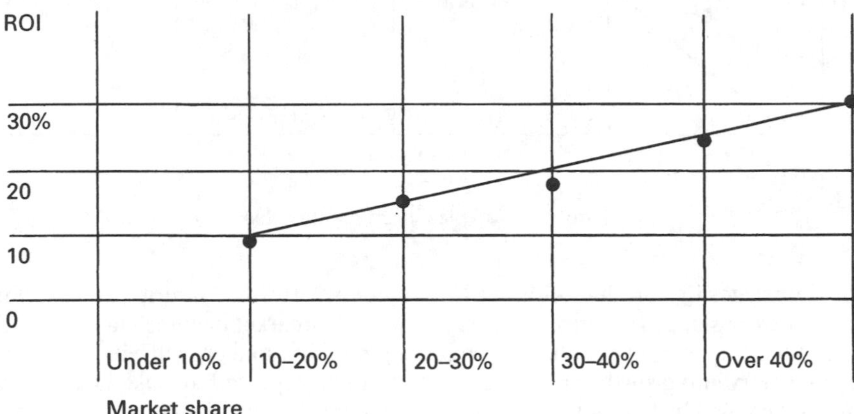

Source: Buzzell, Gale and Sultan (1975).

Figure I The relationship between market share and pre-tax ROI

On average a 10% difference in market share entailed a 5% difference in pre-tax ROI. PIMS found several factors contributing to this phenomenon. As market share rose asset turnover tended to stay steady but profit margin tended to rise sharply. The main cost difference between high and low share businesses was in the purchases-to-sales ratio, but marketing costs also appeared to decrease relatively as market share rose. Finally PIMS found that higher share business tended to have developed 'unique competitive strategies' and to be able to charge higher prices and sell higher quality products. In terms of *where* the market share/ROI relationship was most likely to hold, PIMs found market share to be more important for infrequently purchased products, and in businesses where buyers are fragmented.

To gauge the significance of market growth rate as a strategic variable we look at the notion of the *product life cycle* (PLC). PLC is a widely used concept in marketing.[3] It attempts to identify four stages in a product's sales history, each stage having distinctive characteristics.

3 All standard marketing texts carry a section on the PLC. See, for example, Kotler (1990).

Figure II depicts these stages as they are usually conceived for a 'typical' product.

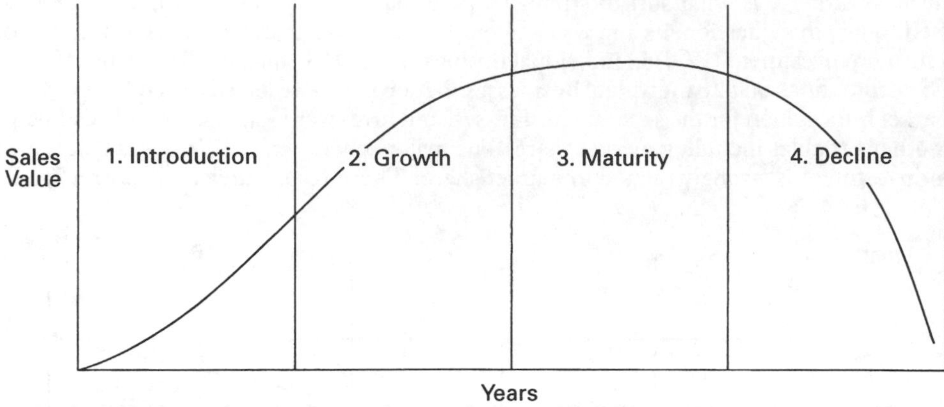

Figure II A typical product life cycle

The four stages in a product's life are Introduction, Growth, Maturity, and Decline. In the introductory stage, sales growth is very slow as the market becomes familiar with the product. Once the market accepts the product a period of rapid growth will ensue. In both the introductory and growth stages, the product can be expected to make heavy demands on cash – there will be high investment in research, marketing, plant, and stock-building. Only later in the growth stage will buoyant revenues start to recoup this cash outflow. The introductory stage is conventionally depicted as having low, even negative, profitability as the periodic write-off of the initial investment is set against low revenues, but in the growth stage profitability increases. In the maturity stage sales flatten out as the potential for new customers is exhausted. The product now generates a lot of cash as investment is confined to replacement investment, and 'profits peak in this period and start to decline because of increased marketing outlays to sustain the product's position against competition' (Kotler (1990) p 290). In the decline stage sales, profits and cash flow fade away to zero.

Strategic portfolio matrices offer users a technique for analysing and structuring their product portfolio. The two key dimensions of strategy, market share and market growth rate, are depicted on a two-dimensional matrix as depicted in Figure III. We have seen that these two variables can be considered in some ways as proxies for profitability and cash flow. The firm inserts activities into the matrix as circles, with the diameter of each circle proportional to the sales volume of the activity. The matrix is commonly divided into four boxes assigned names that have now entered business strategy jargon:

'problem children' = low share, high growth
'stars' = high share, high growth
'cash cows' = high share, low growth
'dogs' = low share, low growth

The firm's strategic objective can now be defined. The firm's long-term objective is to develop and maintain a *balanced portfolio*. Cash cows should generate cash, while problem children will probably use cash. Stars and dogs are expected to break even on the whole. In a balanced portfolio, there will be enough cash cows to support the problem children, and enough stars to provide the cash cows of the future. So the matrix generates investment and disinvestment strategies, known as 'holding' and 'building', and 'divesting' strategies in popular parlance. The firm will want to build or expand chosen problem children, divest the remainder of its problem children and dogs, and hold its investment in stars and cash cows.

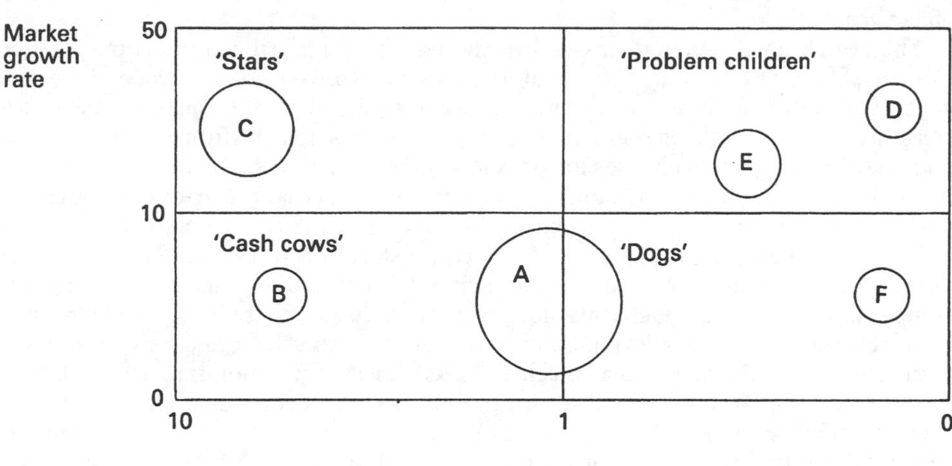

Figure III An example of a strategic portfolio matrix

The imaginary firm whose projects we have marked on Figure III has two cash cows, A and B. A, in particular, is a major source of revenue and cash, though its market share is only marginally greater than its nearest competitor. (Note that it is conventional in this context to measure the market share axis in terms of market share proportional to the market leader.) However project C combines high growth and a commanding market position and this could become a major cash generator in the future. The firm needs to decide whether to invest in one or both of E and D in order to enhance their market share. These decisions could not be made without more information on the competitive structure of the markets, and thus the likely costs of buying more market share. The same applies to F, but the presumption must be that in a low growth market the costs of buying more market share is unlikely to be justified.

A financial analysis of strategy models

Like all strategic analysis strategic portfolio matrices confront the most fundamental question of all – how to succeed in business. But despite their popularity they received some fundamental criticisms. A major thrust of criticism has been that the world is far more complex than the simple prescription suggests, and that the underlying relationship between market share and market growth is not sufficiently strong to merit the role it is given in the analysis.[4] We have described a particular strategy model, but there are several

4 For some of these criticisms see Wensley (1981a) and Wensley (1981b).

portfolio models that firms can currently choose from, and each has its own emphasis and method of scaling the key variables. Wind, Mahajon and Swire (1983) applied various models to 15 sample businesses, and found that only one business was classified the same, as a 'star', by all models. Indeed it seemed that a given business could emerge as any of dog, star, cash cow or problem child depending on the model. They concluded the 'any strategic generalisations concerning them [are] suspect and at best unstable', and suggested that each user would tend to choose the model which met its organisational objectives.

The search for the ingredients and recipe for above-normal returns is the modern alchemy. However the merits of the rival strategy models are outside our scope. But we *are* concerned with how these strategy models relate to the logic of business finance. It is convenient to think of the investment process in two stages: first the firm generates a set of potential projects, then it chooses the ones it is going to undertake. In finance books, and certainly in this one, we talk as though this distinction is nice and clear-cut, and financial analysis only enters the picture when the finance manager is presented with a set of well-quantified projects to evaluate. But once we start to consider strategy models the distinction ceases to be so clear-cut. By telling the firm where it should be going, the strategy model effectively opens up some options and closes off others. So, even if most or all of the corporations employing strategy models are using DCF analysis as well, the bundle of potential projects that reach the DCF investment appraisal stage will be a pre-selected one. We found just the same problem with 'rules of thumb'. Some firms use 'rules of thumb' alongside DCF, but using DCF *as well* does not render the rules of thumb harmless. If rules of thumb are used at any stage in the process there is a chance that positive valued projects will be rejected. Finance theory indicates that firms should choose projects on the basis of their NPV, evaluated making suitable allowance for risk. The question is, does a strategic portfolio matrix select on a consistent basis with NPV? If not, the firm may be overlooking valuable activities.

The model described advocates a portfolio which is 'balanced' in terms of market growth rate and market share. There is a link between these and financial variables if market share is a proxy for return on investment, and market growth rate is a proxy for financing requirements. *If* market share is a good proxy for ROCE, and ROCE a good proxy for value then it will make sense to hunt down valuable projects by looking for high market share. We note the limiting conditions under which ROCE is a proxy for value in Chapter 20 and a main thrust of criticism of the strategic portfolio matrix has been that the world is not so simple – market share is not a perfect proxy for value.

However, there are two other respects in which strategy models run counter to the logic of finance. First, they usually make no allowance for the *riskiness* of alternative activities, whereas putting a proper price on risk is one of the central preoccupations of finance. Second, the notion of a 'balanced portfolio' in terms of cash requirements has no financial rationale. Implicitly, in the model, all new investment must be financed from retained earnings and the portfolio is balanced to yield sufficient cash-generating projects to support projects with high investment needs. In reality, as we see in Part IV of the book, firms do raise most of their cash internally. But there is no reason why this should be the limiting factor on investment. If the capital market is efficient new funds will be available to finance valuable projects and a positive NPV on a project is evidence that it should yield a surplus after covering its cost of capital. The logic of finance is to cost capital directly rather than leave the supply of capital as a constraint on the investment decision.

In terms of financial logic, therefore, strategy models seem to have some key deficiencies. But how can we explain the fact that firms, in this case some of the most sophisticated corporations, use them and seem happy with them? What benefits do strategy models offer to make up for their limitations? Perhaps the overwhelming attraction of strategy models is that they help the firm *think*. The task of deploying the firm's resources today so as to ensure the best supply of valuable projects in the future is, particularly in a large diverse corporation, complex and beset by uncertainty. Strategy models attempt to structure this problem and to deploy research results that might be useful. They focus the firm's attention on apparently important variables. The limitations of such models are perhaps inevitable given the difficulty of the problem, but strategy models can help in the formulation of strategy even if the firm does not adhere slavishly to their prescriptions. As usual, where we find actual management practice diverging from finance theory, we have to hope the leeway is made up by sound judgement.

V SUMMARY

In this chapter we considered the practice rather than the theory of project decision making. We examined the findings of Pike about the practice of large UK firms. Though companies do seem to be growing more sophisticated, judgement and rule of thumb still play a major part.

In the third and fourth sections we reviewed two approaches to investment decision making that appear at odds with DCF analysis. Even in sizeable firms 'rules of thumb' such as payback and accounting rate of return maintain considerable support, despite their apparent shortcomings; and many of the largest companies develop their investment strategy using 'strategy models' which seem out of line in some respects with the logic of finance. We accounted for this behaviour in various ways, but the common theme was that they are both responses to the extreme uncertainty and complexity facing decision-makers in practice.

REFERENCES AND BIBLIOGRAPHY

Bierman, H Jr, and Schmidt, S — *The Capital Budgeting Decision* (1988) Macmillan, New York.

Buzzell, R, Gale, B T, and Sultan, R G M — 'Market Share – A Key to Profitability', Harvard Business Review, 1975.

Kotler, P — *Marketing Management. Analysis, Planning and Control* (1990) Prentice-Hall International, Englewood-Cliffs, New Jersey.

Moore, J S, and Reichert, A K — 'An Analysis of the Financial Management Techniques Currently Employed by Large US Corporations', Journal of Business Finance and Accounting, Winter 1983, pp 623–646.

Petty, J, Scott Jr, D F, and Bird, M M — 'The Capital Expenditure Decision-Making Process of Large Corporations', Engineering Economist, Spring 1975.

Pike, R H — 'An Empirical Study of the Adoption of Sophisticated Capital Budgeting Practices and Decision Making Effectiveness', Accounting and Business Research, Autumn 1988, pp 341–351.

Pike, R H, and Wolfe, M — *Capital Budgeting for the 1990s* (1988) Chartered Institute of Management Accountants.

Sarnat, M, and Levy, H — 'The Relationship of Rules of Thumb to the Internal Rate of Return: A Restatement and Generalisation', Journal of Finance, June 1979.

Schall, L D, Sundem, G L, and Geijsbeck Jr, W R — 'Survey and Analysis of Capital Budgeting Methods', Journal of Finance, March 1978, pp 281–292.

Wensley, R — 'Strategic Marketing: Betas, Boxes or Basics', Journal of Marketing, Summer 1981(a).

Wensley, R — 'The Market Share Myth', London Business School Journal, Winter 1981(b).

'Wilson Committee' — 'Committee to Review the Functioning of Financial Institutions – Survey of Investment Attitudes and Financing of Medium-Sized Companies', Research Report No: 1, HMSO, 1978.

Wind, Y, Mahajan, V, and Swire, D J — 'An Empirical Comparison of Standardised Portfolio Models', Journal of Marketing, 1983, pp 89–99.

QUESTIONS

1 For each of the following projects calculate the payback period, and the accounting rate of return using straight-line depreciation:

Year	*0*	*1*	*2*	*3*	*4*	*5*
Project						
1	(5,000)	1,400	1,400	1,400	1,400	1,400
2	(10,000)	3,300	3,700	3,000	1,000	
3	(15,000)	2,000	2,000	4,000	4,000	12,000
4	(20,000)	15,000	5,000			

Find the NPV of the four projects using a 10% discount rate.

2 Researchers have found that although there has been a trend towards the use of 'rigorous' DCF techniques of investment analysis in recent years many large firms still retain judgemental and rule of thumb methods for project choice. Explain why firms might use payback period in preference to DCF in investment analysis.

3 Finance theory suggests choosing those projects that yield the maximum net present value, subject to any capital constraint the firm might be under. However, many major companies use strategic portfolio matrices to choose their product portfolios alongside DCF techniques. Contrast these two approaches and explain whether they are in fact consistent.

Part IV
Financing

CHAPTER 12

The structure of the capital market

This chapter examines the capital market as it affects firms. First, we identify the main 'types' of finance the firm can raise which are in effect different types of contract the firm can make with its suppliers of funds. In the second section we look at the flow of funds between the main sectors of the economy. The factors that determine the supply of these funds and determine the demand of other sectors, determine the financial environment of the firm. The third section introduces the intermediaries – banks and institutions – through which most transfers of finance in the capital market pass. We try to explain the existence of intermediaries and to assess their role. In the fourth section we discuss the stock market, which is a particularly important part of the capital market. As in all markets demand and supply in the capital market are balanced by a market price, which is the 'return' to the saver and the 'cost of capital' to the investor. In the final section we examine the nature of the return in the capital market and what determines it.

I THE TERMS OF A FINANCING CONTRACT

In practice there is no limit to the variety of financing contracts that can be made, but for analysis we categorise them. The prime distinction is between equity and debt.

Equity is finance which gives ownership rights on the firm. There are two sources of equity finance: new money raised from outside by *share issues*; and the savings of the firm, including depreciation provisions, held back from shareholders as *retained earnings*. In the main, equity finance is permanent – the law severely limits the firm's ability to repay equity.

Debt is finance which makes the supplier a creditor of the firm. Under 'debt' we include medium and long-term loans at fixed interest. One form of this is the *debenture* or *loan stock* which is a security that can be bought and sold on the market. Debt also includes short-term arrangements such as *bank overdrafts*. But we can also identify a variety of other arrangements that effectively constitute debt financing – for example, stretching trade creditors, and the use of factoring and leasing. We will refer to these as 'quasi-debt'.

When a firm raises finance it makes a contract with the suppliers of the funds, and when we talk about the different *types* of finance a firm can get we are really talking about different terms that that financing contract can have. These should determine the following:

— QUANTITY: the amount of finance provided.

— TERM: how long the finance has been provided for. Finance can be provided over any period but people commonly distinguish short-term, medium and long-term, and permanent finance. *Short-term* finance is provided initially for less than a year. *Medium* and *long-term* is finance of fixed or finite duration but longer than a year. *Permanent* finance is issued with the intention it will never be repaid.

— RISK: the risk associated with the returns on the finance. The underlying riskiness of the firm's income stream is determined by economic factors, but the distribution of this risk to the various suppliers of finance is contractual and is determined by their respective claims over the firm's assets and income stream. So the contract might make the supplier an *owner* of the firm or a *creditor* of the firm. Finance which acquires ownership rights is called *equity* and to equity belong any surpluses or deficits the firm makes, and in most cases some influence on the policy of the firm through voting rights. All other finance is *debt*. Creditors are entitled to recover their interest and capital in priority to equity, but there is a pecking order within creditors. For example, *secured* loans acquire a lien over a particular asset or class of assets, giving them priority over other creditors.
— RETURN: the terms for payment of interest and repayment of principal. Some finance – for example postponed payment to trade creditors or the Inland Revenue – has no overt cost. Debt finance usually involves regular *interest* payments, but again the terms of the contract may differ, for example the rate of interest may be fixed at the outset or may be variable at the discretion of the supplier. In the case of equity the periodic payment is called a *dividend* and the level of dividend is set by management.

Table I UK industrial and commercial companies – main sources and uses of funds (£m)

	1989	*%*	*1991*	*%*	*1993*	*%*
SOURCES OF FUNDS						
Undistributed income and unremitted profits	35,727	33	34,904	49	49,862	62
Credit received, tax balances, capital transfers	1,339	1	1,229	2	692	1
Ordinary share issues	1,880	2	9,761	14	14,370	18
Debenture and preference issues, other capital issues	14,012	13	11,685	17	9,524	12
Bank borrowing	33,952	32	(918)	(1)	(11,386)	(14)
Loans and mortgages	10,156	9	4,253	6	4,581	6
Overseas	10,959	10	9,186	13	12,328	15
TOTAL SOURCES	108,025	100	70,100	100	79,971	100
USES OF FUNDS						
Fixed capital formation (gross)	52,538	49	50,042	71	48,693	61
Stock-building	9,283	9	(2,731)	(4)	2,326	3
Bank deposits cash and securities	28,444	26	8,802	13	10,042	13
Credit given	(404)	—	29	—	(438)	(1)
Overseas	15,199	14	6,042	9	12,624	16
Capital transfers	1,433	1	979	1	679	1
Other + balancing item	1,532	1	6,937	10	6,045	7
TOTAL USES	108,025	100	70,100	100	79,971	100

Source: CSO Financial Statistics, HMSO

Table I shows the relative importance of some of these types of finance to industrial and commercial companies. Retained earnings usually emerge as the major source, with bank borrowing second, while despite the importance given to them in finance books, including this one, new issues of shares are a relatively minor source of finance. However, as Table I shows, 1989 was quite exceptional with a high corporate investment and relatively low profits. Companies were still reluctant to issue shares following the market crash in late 1987, so the financing need was largely met by bank borrowing and debenture and preference share issues.

II THE FLOW OF FUNDS ON THE ECONOMY

Once upon a time economic transactions were restricted to barter – to the exchange of tangible goods or labour services, and the wealth of a man was restricted to the tangible goods physically in his possession. The constraints of this cumbersome way of doing things were eased in due course by the use of very compact and durable goods like gold, but were removed altogether by the use in transactions of 'claims' on resources, rather than resources themselves. A claim on resources is a legally enforceable property right – banknotes and cheques are examples of generalised claims – and this final stage awaited suitable social institutions, notably a legal system which could enforce claims. The purpose of this story is to make it clear that by the 'flow of funds' in the economy we mean the transfer of claims on resources.

Examining the flow of funds in the economy is a good way to get a clearer idea of the factors that might influence the supply of finance to firms. Following national income accounting, we can classify economic units in the economy into four sectors:

The BUSINESS sector, comprising industrial and commercial firms, and financial and banking firms.

The PERSONAL sector, representing households but also unincorporated business, sole-traders and partnerships. In theory, unincorporated businesses should be included in the business sector, but government statisticians have insufficient data to reclassify them.

The PUBLIC sector, consisting of central government, local authorities and public corporation such as nationalised industries.

The OVERSEAS sector, comprising flows of funds to and from abroad.

It is also conventional to divide the funds flow in the economy into two 'accounts'. The CURRENT account concerns the flows of income and expenditure of the sectors. The difference between the income and expenditure of a sector is its saving, and the CAPITAL account concerns the transfer of savings between sectors. Although we are concerned with capital transactions it is useful to start by examining the current account.

These are some examples of current account transactions:

The business sector buys labour or 'work' from the personal sector and there is a flow of wages in return. The personal sector will pay part of this income to government as tax, spend part and save the rest. The spending results in a flow of funds to business in exchange for goods and services, and also in a flow to the public sector since some goods and services are bought from public sector firms and since expenditure taxes are paid on some of the expenditure. By the same token the public sector pays wages to the personal sector and trades goods and services with the business sector. The surplus of the business sector receipts over its expenditure, its 'profits', are subject to tax, and the remainder constitute its savings. The personal sector similarly pays tax on its income. These flows are depicted in Figure I.

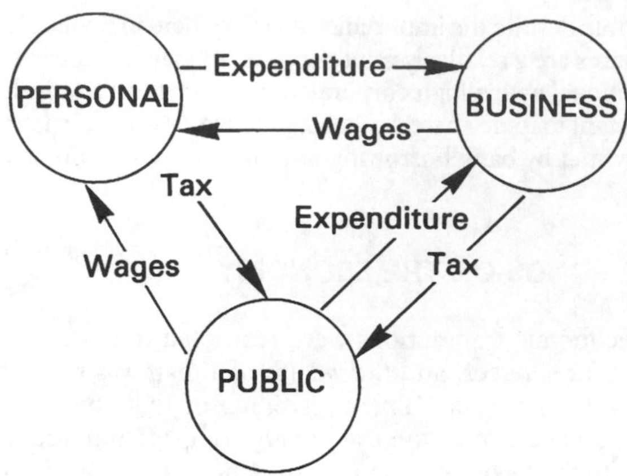

Figure I Some current flows between domestic sectors

The capital account

All three domestic sectors, personal, business and public, invest. But there is no reason why a sector's investment should match its saving. To the extent that its investment is not covered by its saving a sector must raise *finance*, i e use the savings of another sector.

Table II shows how much the three domestic sectors invested and saved in 1990. The personal and public sectors emerge as net savers, as are financial companies. Industrial and commercial companies are net investors and the business sector as a whole is a net investor.

Table II UK domestic sectors' savings and investment 1990/93 (£m)

		Business		
1990	*Public*	*Financial*	*Industrial & commercial*	*Personal*
Saving	15,694	8,463	36,833	31,883
Fixed investment + stock-building	17,636	6,793	58,475	29,004
Surplus	−1,942	1,670	−21,642	2,879
		Business		
1993	*Public*	*Financial*	*Industrial & commercial*	*Personal*
Saving	−32,452	9,950	51,554	59,918
Fixed investment + stock-building	−15,920	4,414	50,637	25,906
Surplus	−48,372	5,536	917	34,012

Source: UK National Accounts, CSO Blue Book, 1994 edn, HMSO

It is the function of the *capital market* to transfer savings between sectors, and also within sectors since individual units within a sector may be net savers or investors. For example, within the business sector one firm may finance another, and within the public sector profitable nationalised industries may subsidise government. In the personal sector a popular destination for personal savings is building societies. Building societies mainly reallocate savings within the personal sector to households which wish to invest in housing. To some extent the personal sector transfers funds direct to business by buying shares and debentures, but nowadays most flows of household and other funds for investment pass through *financial intermediaries*, the 'financial firms' part of the business sector – banks, unit trusts, pension funds etc.

An important factor has been the role of government as a competitor of business for personal savings. Governments often need to finance not only their investment but also their dis-saving – the excess of their current expenditure over their current income (which is largely tax revenues). This is the 'public sector borrowing requirement' (PSBR). Again, although the personal sector can lend direct to government by buying government bonds, government, like business, tends to go through financial intermediaries for its funds. The overseas sector is also significant in the capital account both as a destination for the savings of the UK personal sector, and as a source of finance for government and business.

Figure II depicts the capital account flows that we have been talking about.

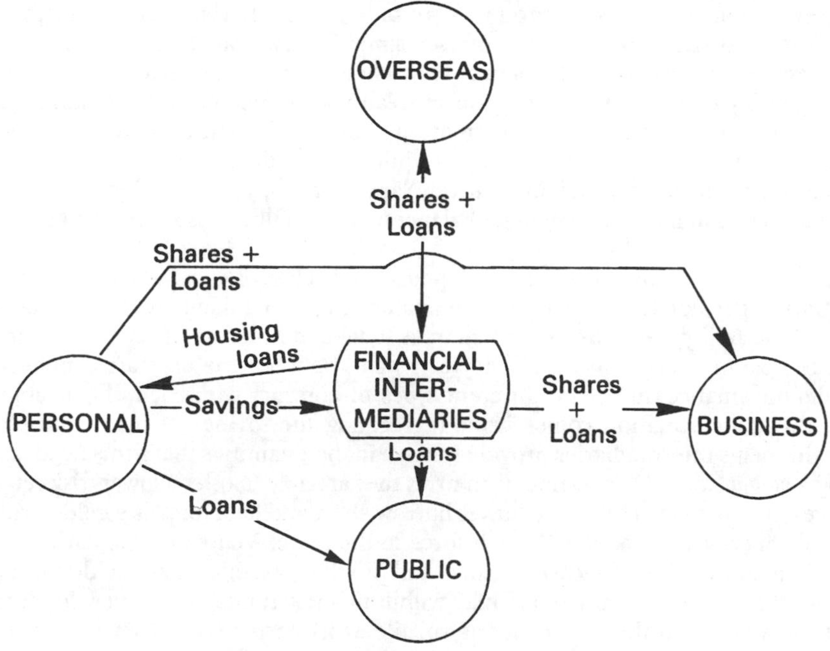

Figure II Some capital flows between sectors

Some influences on the supply of finance

Thinking about the flow of funds in the economy helps in understanding the environment in which the overall supply of funds to the firm, and the terms on which they are supplied, are set. Amongst other things the financing of firms will be influenced by:

— the level of saving by households, which will be influenced by the level and distribution of incomes, and by government tax policy.

— the competition for these household savings from other sectors, notably the government's borrowing requirement and the personal sector's own house-building plans.

— the role of the overseas sector in taking or providing funds, which will be influenced by the relative returns available in the UK and abroad.

— the firm's need for outside financing in the first place will be determined by the level of its retained earnings relative to the investment opportunities available.

III CAPITAL MARKET INTERMEDIARIES

Demand and supply in the capital market are brought into equilibrium by the price mechanism – we look at the role of *price* in the capital market later on. Various institutional arrangements have also developed in the capital market to help match supply and demand.

Consider the following problem: it is not that the overall amounts people want to save and to invest are out of line, but that savers and investors do not want to write the same types of financing contract – ie savers desire to lend on different terms from those on which investors seek to borrow. At risk of over-simplifying we can develop a plausible case for this eventuality occurring in practice. Households may be characterised as saving in relatively small parcels, either for long-term wealth accumulation or for building short-term 'transactions balances' – money temporarily stored with some expenditure in view. In either case we might expect households to require a good deal of security. Firms, on the other hand, tend to need funds in relatively large parcels, either for long-term capital expenditure or to finance current asset balances, and in either case subject to economic risk.

Between savers and investors has developed a whole class of *financial intermediaries*: the 'institutions' – pension funds, insurance companies etc; the banking system; and specialist agencies. The ability these institutions share is to take in funds and transform them with respect to quantity, term and risk. They can stand between the ultimate suppliers and demanders of finance and write different types of contract with each. Their ability to achieve this transformation comes from aggregating the savings of many households. Clearly this helps intermediaries provide finance in the quantities that firms need, and by building a *portfolio* of risky investments in firms they are able to offer a lower-risk return to their investors. As to term, the rule 'never borrow short and lend long' is a golden rule for individuals but does not hold with such force in the large. Many intermediaries borrow shorter than they lend. In the case of banks and building societies they can do this on the basis that, though individual lenders may withdraw their funds at will, new lenders will present themselves, so the sum is not as volatile as its parts. Also they take care not to commit themselves to fixed borrowing and lending rates, and in extremis are able to rely on the support of other banks and building societies.

This ability to 'transform' the terms of financing contracts is the customary explanation of the function of financial intermediaries; but it does not actually explain why they exist. In the study of finance, when we are confronted by some institutional arrangement we always have to ask ourselves what it does that the people it serves could not have done equally well for themselves. This is a particularly pertinent question with intermediaries. A little thought suggests that firms themselves could collect together the savings of many households into the quantities they need. If they want longer-term finance than savers wish to provide, they could always refinance with new short-term securities when the previous capital is withdrawn. As for savers, if they are unhappy with the risk associated with investing in a single firm they can build their own portfolios of securities. In other words all the benefits provided by intermediaries could, on the face of it, be 'homemade' by households and firms. In a perfect capital market this would be the case, but in reality households and firms find it advantageous to use intermediaries. We can interpret this in terms of the information costs and transactions costs associated with the capital market in practice. Many savers would find it prohibitively expensive to acquire or buy the necessary expertise to appraise investments and monitor firms, and the fixed costs associated with buying securities tend to make very small holdings uneconomic. Similar considerations will influence the firm.

The institutions

The 'institutions' are collectors of long-term savings: pension funds, insurance companies,[1] investment trusts and unit trusts. By the end of 1992 institutions had net assets of £850 billion, and pension funds alone accounted for £380 billion of this. Over the past decade households have reduced direct investment in company securities in order to save through institutions. There are several reasons for the appeal of the institutions to household savers. They may provide other services – such as insurance – as well as a method of saving. There are tax incentives to this form of saving, pension contributions are usually tax deductible while the pension and assurance companies are effectively free of tax. In the case of pensions, employees often have little choice but to contribute since contributing to the pension scheme is often a condition of the job, and employers usually provide an incentive by at least matching the employee's contribution. Unit and investment trusts dispose less funds than pension and insurance companies, and they use the funds in a rather different way, as can be seen in Table III. The investment policies of the pension and insurance companies derive from their particular business objective: maintaining a fund which will generate cash flows up to a fairly long time-horizon, sufficient to meet forseeable pension or insurance liabilities and improve them if possible. Hence these institutions feel no special compunction to invest in the business sector, or at least in company securities, and their portfolios contain significant proportions of property and property loans and of government securities.

Unit and investment trusts take a different approach. Households invest in particular trusts on the basis of the specific range of assets in which the trust will invest. The higher proportion of company securities in the portfolio of unit and investment trusts reflects the wishes of their investors. Households may find less difficulty in investing in property and government securities for themselves, and may feel that their pension and life assurance rights represent fairly riskless assets, so they look to unit and investment trusts to provide investments in more risky company securities.

In the 1980s overseas securities accounted for an increasing proportion of all transactions by investing institutions. In 1986, transactions in overseas securities, averaged across institutions, amounted to 27% of all business. In 1994, this figure was 20%.

Since the institutions effectively account for all of the personal sector's net investment in company securities, their investment policies are important, and there was some evidence that the criteria the institutions apply in choosing investments implied a bias

1 Strictly speaking it is life *assurance* companies who take household savings, but since insurance companies have tended to be net investors these two are usually grouped together.

Table III Pattern of asset holdings of investing institutions at end 1992

	Pension funds	%	*Insurance long-term*	%	*Insurance general*	%	*Investment trusts*	%	*Unit trusts*	%
Cash and other short-term assets (net)	12,237	3	14,150	4	2,819	5	442	2	2,432	4
Overseas short-term	1,250	0	674	0	658	1	132	0	70	0
Public sector securities	25,230	7	51,676	16	8,427	16	739	3	660	1
Company securities UK	208,216	54	144,297	44	10,334	19	13,613	48	34,616	57
Company securities overseas	65,063	17	32,101	10	3,747	7	12,457	44	22,820	38
Unit trusts	8,569	2	27,907	9	146	0	246	1	0	0
Government securities overseas	10,529	3	8,793	3	4,660	9	656	2	0	0
Mortgages and loans	273	0	8,295	2	977	2	0	0	0	0
Property	21,659	6	30,074	9	2,299	4	0	0	0	0
Other investments	28,998	8	9,488	3	20,431	37	0	0	0	0
TOTAL ASSETS	382,024	100	327,455	100	54,498	100	28,285	100	60,598	100

against smaller firms. Institutions prefer to hold securities that are readily marketable, hence they have a preference for quoted securities. Also they prefer minimal transactions costs – which implies large holdings, but holdings which can be sold without too much disruption – which thus implies large companies. Many institutions made a conscious effort to improve their smaller firm exposure through venture capital and enterprise funds during the 1980s.

The banks

Banks are major suppliers of finance and financial services to the business sector. The name 'bank' can be used by an institution which has obtained permission from the Bank of England to take deposits from the public.

Clearing banks ('commercial banks' in the US) are the 'high-street' banks, Barclays, Nat West, etc. These banks offer a wide range of financial services but it is their role in providing 'current account' banking, the clearance of receipts and payments, which explains their importance in financing. It is a natural development from this to providing an overdraft facility, which permits the customer to spend more than he has. The overdraft is a very flexible and convenient type of finance. Overdraft limits can be raised quickly and cheaply, and interest is only paid on the daily balance. The current account service also means that all firms already have a relationship with a clearing bank whether or not they need finance. For these reasons it is easy to seen why bank finance is the most popular type after retained earnings.

Merchant banks ('investment banks' in the US) provide a variety of services. They take deposits from the personal and business sectors and lend these funds, though in the main they only deal in 'large amounts'. They provide investment and portfolio management services to clients. They are the prime advisers of firms on 'new issues' of long-term finance, and if they are 'issuing houses' they are able to take up whole issues of shares for subsequent sale to clients, other institutions or the public. Many merchant banks are subsidiaries of clearers.

Finance houses are intermediaries which fall in the banking area, since in many cases they are subsidiaries of banks. Finance houses purchase assets on behalf of clients and lease them to the client, or sell them under hire purchase or deferred sale agreements. Thus they provide a form of indirect or 'off-balance-sheet' finance.

IV THE STOCK MARKET

We have been talking about institutions and intermediaries in the capital market. The word 'market' in this sense connotes the whole network of exchanges between the suppliers and demanders of funds. It is usual to subdivide this into two, reserving the title 'capital market' for the market in long-term claims and distinguishing the short-term 'money market'. One part of the capital market, the STOCK MARKET, requires special attention. The stock market is a market in the securities of domestic and foreign companies and of local authorities and the UK government. It is a market in the everyday as well as the economic sense. It has a physical location: there are number of regional exchanges in the UK, but The London Stock Exchange (LSE) is by far the biggest.

Prior to deregulation ('Big Bang') the London market operated a fixed commission 'single capacity' system, containing *jobbers*, stall-holders who specialised in buying and selling particular classes of shares, and *stockbrokers*, agents buying from, and selling to, jobbers on behalf of clients. The jobbers' income came from the 'turn' or 'spread' they could make on buying and selling, that is the difference between the prices at which a share was bought in and sold out again. The brokers' income came from a percentage commission on the value of the transactions they handled.

The 1986 deregulation of the London market had three main elements: the abolition of minimum commissions and of single capacity, and the admission of corporate members to the market. The immediate effect was a concentration of business among fewer, dual-capacity, *market-makers*. During the summer of 1987 after Big Bang, equity turnover nearly doubled while commission rates on larger deals had halved for institutional business to around .2%. The result was that commission incomes remained virtually unchanged. The full force of the changes was felt in the wholesale markets, for smaller deals the commission rate was the same or slightly higher than in 1986.

The stock market is both a *primary* market and a *secondary* market, that is a market where new securities are issued and where existing securities are traded. The volume of secondary business far exceeds the primary. The relatively small amount of new finance that firms raise through stock market issues reflects the fact that there are less costly types of finance available that firms prefer to use. This is sometimes taken as an indictment of the stock market, but this view is misplaced. The secondary market provides services of great importance. First, the market prices of shares traded on the stock market provide a measure of the economic value of firms. This piece of information is the linchpin of the capital market investment process – it signals the return shareholders will receive by providing finance to the firm, and it signals the cost of capital to the firm. Second, the existence of a secondary market enables the stock market to perform its vital intermediation function. All the securities traded on the stock market represent permanent or long-term finance. Equity finance is in principle permanent, most loan-stock is long in term. Investors may not want to provide finance for this length of time, or at least will not be certain they will want to, but if the financing contract is in the form of a security with a ready market this does not matter too much. The supplier of funds can enter into the financing contract with confidence that he will be able to sell the security whenever he wants to withdraw. The existence of a securities market provides *liquidity*. Finance can be simultaneously permanent from the point of view of the firm yet liquid as far as the investor goes.

The costs and benefits of listing

Only the securities of quoted companies can be traded on The Stock Exchange. Companies that appear on The Stock Exchange Daily Official List are described as 'listed'. The requirements of stock exchange listing tend to restrict the market to larger companies. To be listed a firm must meet the following requirements, amongst others:

Size

The firm must have securities with an initial market value of at least £700,000.

Securities on the market

At least 25% of each class of equity or convertible must be owned by the public, though large firms may be exempted from this.

Stock Exchange rules

The Stock Exchange information requirements are rather more demanding than company law. Firms have to report to shareholders twice a year instead of once, and a new issue has to be accompanied by a *prospectus* which provides potential investors with some information about the present state and future prospects of the firm.

History

Applicants for full listing normally need a three-year trading history with audited accounts to support it.

The initial costs of listing vary with the amount raised, but The Stock Exchange[2] estimated that there is a fixed element of around £350,000, largely consisting of fees to advisers.

Against these costs the company must weigh the advantages of listing. In terms of new finance, the company will find its securities much more attractive to the all-important institutional investor. Similarly, owners of existing securities will find their assets more marketable. This can be particularly important in family-owned firms where the family is planning a move away from the business or preparing for inheritance taxes. Company law used to allow a degree of privacy to private as against public companies, but this is no longer the case. However, listing does imply greater public access to information about the company and greater public interest. Some companies will welcome this, others may not.

The junior markets

The idea of the junior markets is to give smaller companies the advantages of listing. These markets, with their less stringent entry requirements, could act as a stepping stone for a growing company, allowing it eventually to transfer to the main market. But it has not proven easy to find a cost-effective situation.

The Third Market operated between January 1987 and December 1990. The requirements for a quotation on the Third Market were minimal. There was no minimum market capitalisation. The company must have been trading for at least a year, and have the sponsorship of a member of The Stock Exchange. Companies were regulated by their sponsors and not by the Exchange. Of the 92 companies which had been quoted on the Third Market during its life, 38 moved onto the USM, 40 had their listing cancelled and two were transferred to full listing. The remaining 12 were reorganised or acquired.

The Unlisted Securities Market (USM) was launched by The Stock Exchange in 1980 to deal in the securities of smaller companies, and to assist them to obtain a full LSE listing. What was then known as the 'Over The Counter' (OTC) market had existed since the early 1970s. It dealt with shares of companies which were too small to qualify for the official list. Dealers would match buyers and sellers for these shares, or deal in the shares as principals (as market-makers). The qualifying conditions for the USM are less stringent than for a full listing. For a company to qualify, it must have been trading for two years, and 10% of quoted shares must be in public hands. Shareholders must receive interim reports half-yearly.

However, the fixed costs of joining the USM turned out to be as high as for full listing. Moreover, the market for small firms has turned out to be perilously illiquid – 64% of London stocks with a market capitalisation under £50 million have less than two market-makers, and they traded less than five times a day on average (Stock Exchange (1994)). As a result in the early 1990s, though the demand for full listing remained buoyant, USM applicants fell to a trickle. In 1994 the LSE announced its intention to close the USM, but to attack the problem by promoting the ability of market-makers to trade unlisted securities

2 Stock Exchange Quarterly with Quality of Markets Review, Spring 1994.

occasionally under Rule 535.2 (redesignated Rule 4.2). This places no requirements on companies, apart from filing an annual report, and incurs the relatively small cost of issuing a prospectus.

The London Stock Exchange subsequently announced the creation of the Alternative Investment Market (AIM) to replace the USM. The AIM is based on the American NASDAQ – National Association of Securities Dealers Automated Quotation System. It is hoped AIM will have wider appeal than the USM though it will be more regulated. (see Financial Times, 17 February 1995).

Harmonisation in the EC

In line with moves towards standardised legislation throughout the EC, the structure of The Stock Exchange has been changed to bring it into line with the rest of Europe. The EC Directive aimed to ensure that companies would be accepted for listing on the stock market of any EC country if they fulfilled the listing conditions required by their home authority. The new listing requirements for The Stock Exchange, which came into effect in 1990–91, were less onerous than those required previously. In particular, the Mutual Recognition of Listing Particulars Directive specifies a minimum trading record of three years for companies whose securities are admitted to a country's main market. Until February 1990, The Stock Exchange required a five-year trading record for the official list. The requirement for the USM is now only two (previously three) years, to maintain a difference between the two markets.

Table IV Principal requirements for admission to formal Stock Exchange markets

	LIST		*USM*		*THIRD MARKET*[1]
	Former	*New*	*Former*	*New*	*Former*
Minimum market capitalisation (£000)	700	700	500	—	—
Minimum trading record (years)	5	3	3	2[2]	1[2]
Minimum proportion of shares held publicly (%)[3]	25	25	10	10	—

1 No companies were permitted to join the Third Market since January 1990. The market closed on 31 December 1990.
2 Waived for some green field projects.
3 The public is defined as excluding directors, connected persons and shareholders holding more than 5% of the company's equity.

Source: Bank of England Quarterly Bulletin, Vol 30, No 2, May 1990, page 245

The second important impact was due to the Public Offers or Prospectus Directive. From April 1991 all prospectuses were subject to a minimum standard. This tightening of requirements would have blurred the distinction between the Third Market and the USM. As a result, the Third Market closed at the end of 1990. Some Third Market listed companies transferred to the USM. Those who did not can still use the facility of Rule 4.2.

V THE MARKET PRICE OF FINANCE

As in other markets the supply of finance and the demand for finance are brought into equilibrium by the price mechanism. In this section we see what determines the market price in the capital market.

In general the ruling price in the capital market will be the return which brings into equilibrium aggregate saving and investment. We depict this using conventional demand and supply analysis in Figure III.

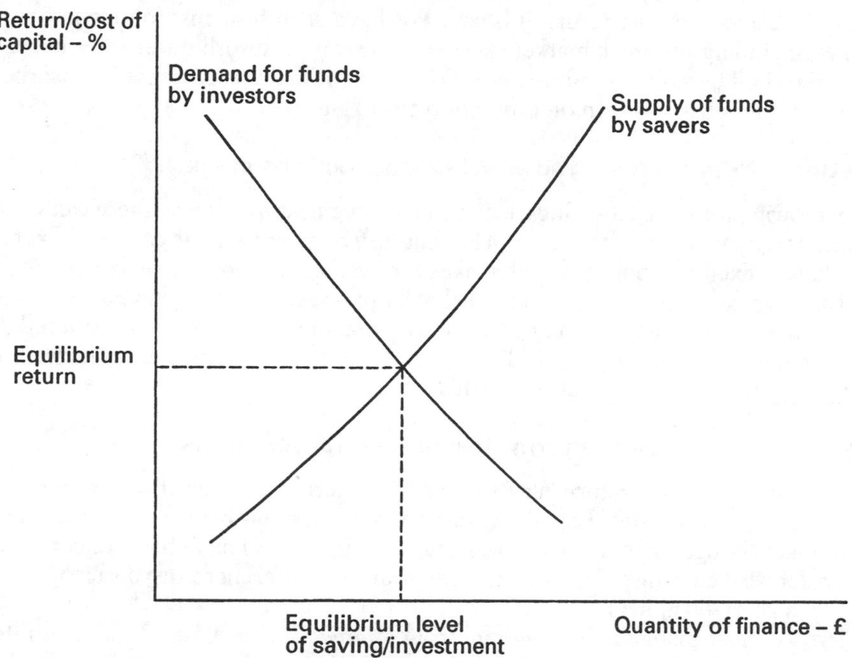

Figure III Saving and investment

The upward-sloping supply curve in Figure III reflects the willingness of savers to sacrifice more present consumption in response to higher returns. The downward-sloping demand curve reflects the increasing supply of projects that become worthwhile as the cost of capital falls.

To explain the actual level of the equilibrium return it is useful to recall the analysis by Fisher which we encountered in Chapter 6. Fisher said the market return or cost of capital, r, has two components. It comprises the investors required real return, r′, and the expected rate of inflation, i, so that

$$r = r' + i$$

Various researchers have investigated whether the Fisher theory actually explains the process by which the price of capital is formed. Fama (1975) showed that between 1953 and 1971 not only did changes in nominal interest rates in the US perform very well as predictors of inflation, but that the underlying real return, r′, was remarkably constant during the period. It seems clear, more generally, that expectations about inflation are a major determinant of observed nominal market returns.

The factors that determine the underlying *real* return are those real factors that determine the aggregate supply of savings and demand for investment funds in the economy. We identified some of them earlier in the chapter. Other factors include the level and distribution of incomes, government tax policy, demand for investment funds from government and from overseas, and so forth.

Having looked at the overall level of returns we now consider the variations in return on different types of finance. The terms of financial contracts can differ with respect to quantity, term and risk, and if the market is to be in equilibrium the value of each contract must be balanced by the return it offers. We have seen how institutions in the capital market, including the stock market itself, *intermediate*, i e absorb differences between the terms required by savers and investors. To the extent that these cannot be absorbed they will affect the relative return on different types of finance.

The quantity-premium – the effect of transactions costs

Even allowing for the cost savings achieved by using intermediaries, there can be significant transactions costs associated with lending and borrowing in the capital market. These costs have a fixed component which makes the average cost lower, the larger the amount involved. On the savings side we can see that large investors tend to have access to deposit rates which are a percentage point or two above what the general public are offered. On the cost side there has been a good deal of research into this topic since economies of scale in financing might inhibit the access of small firms.

The term-premium – the term structure of interest rates

In practice the market return may vary with the term of a loan, there may be a 'term structure' in interest rates. Explaining this phenomenon has been a major preoccupation of theorists, though as yet no neat consensus has emerged. The debate concerns whether and under what circumstances investors will require a different return on a long-term loan than on a short-term loan.[3]

First we must distinguish a *spot* rate from a *forward* rate. A 'spot' rate is a rate fixed today on a loan made today for some period, and a 'forward' rate is a rate fixed today for a loan to be made at some point in the future. We will denote a rate that applies to a loan running from time m to time n as ${}_mr_n$ so ${}_2r_4$ would be the rate on a loan starting at $t = 2$ and ending in $t = 4$. Hence spot rates all have a zero prefix, and forward rates a non-zero prefix.

The null hypothesis on term-structure is the EXPECTATIONS theory which expresses the relationship that would hold between interest rates of different terms if investors were indifferent as to term.

The expectations theory says that the relationship between spot rates of different terms must be such that any rate spanning several periods will be the geometric mean of the present and expected successive one-period spot rates covering those periods. This is less complicated than it sounds. Consider today's three year spot rate ${}_0r_3$. The expectations

3 For an introduction to this topic see Goodhart (1975). Cox, Ingersoll, and Ross (1981) provide a good critique of the main theories.

theory says it must relate to today's one year spot, ${}_0r_1$, and the spot rates that are expected to hold next year $E({}_1r_2)$, and the year $E({}_2r_3)$, as follows:

$$(1 + {}_0r_3)^3 = (1 + {}_0r_1)(1 + E({}_1r_2))(1 + E({}_2r_3))$$
$$\text{So } (1 + {}_0r_3) = ((1 + {}_0r_1)(1 + E({}_1r_2))(1 + E({}_2r_3)))^{1/3}$$

In other words, the return you get from investing long must be the same as would be expected on present information from a succession of short investments. If it were not, investors would move toward the higher return strategy until the rates adjusted to remove any advantage to investing either short or long. Hence if you observe an ${}_0r_1$ of 11% and an ${}_0r_2$ of 12% the only explanation for this under the expectations theory is that the future spot rate, ${}_1r_2$, is expected to be higher. Various arguments have been produced for the existence of a 'term-premium' independent of expectations. The LIQUIDITY-PREFERENCE theory of Hicks (1939) suggests that, even with the assistance of the intermediation process we described earlier, there may remain an imbalance between the desires of savers and investors. The risk aversion of savers will lead them to prefer to lend short-term, while the risk-averse firm will prefer to borrow long. A term-premium will be needed to balance supply and demand in these circumstances. And theories like the MARKET SEGMENTATION approach of Culbertson (1957) and the PREFERRED HABITAT theory of Modigliani and Sutch (1966) develop further the notion of savers who have strong preferences as to the maturity of loans they make in order to provide explanations for the emergence of a term-premium.

The risk-premium

We assume that the suppliers of finance in the capital market are risk-averse. Other things being equal they will require a higher return the more risky that return is. The question is exactly how much extra return will they require? Since the development of the capital asset pricing model (CAPM) this is a question that, given certain assumptions, finance theory is now in a position to answer. The CAPM was described in some detail in Chapters 8 and 9 and the reader might wish to review these chapters now.

We assume that risk can be measured in terms of *variance* of returns. Investors may own many return-yielding assets, company securities, government bonds, land, antiques and so on, and the first thing to perceive is that the rational investor will think in terms of the risk and return on his overall *portfolio* of assets rather than on each individual asset. Moreover we find that within a portfolio some of the riskiness of the individual assets cancels each other out. The extent to which this will happen depends on the extent to which individual returns are uncorrelated with each other and on the number of assets. We call this the degree of *diversification* of the portfolio. The only component of risk that cannot be eliminated by diversification is movements in the returns of the market as a whole – the so called *systematic* risk. But the investor can diversify the overall risk on his portfolio down to this level, and in a perfect capital market he can do this costlessly. So if he is a rational investor in a perfect capital market he will do this. In such a world we can calculate the required risk-premium on any asset, including company securities.

In the CAPM framework the return on a risky asset j, r_j, is given by:

$$r_j = r_i + \beta_j (r_m - r_i)$$

where r_i is the riskless interest rate, r_m is the return on the market portfolio and β_j is the coefficient measuring the responsiveness of the return of the asset j to the return on the market as a whole. A conclusion of Chapter 9 was that although analysis of the assumptions of the CAPM, and empirical work of asset pricing in practice, throws some doubt on the descriptive validity of the model, it remains the best simple model presently available for explaining the premium on the return of a risky asset.

VI SUMMARY

The capital market exists to allow the transfer of savings from net savers in the economy, such as households, to net investors such as firms. By studying the capital market we can understand the factors that determine the supply of finance to the firm, and which determine the market price of that finance – the cost of capital, which is the key statistic in financial decision making.

The overall supply of savings in the economy, and the overall cost of capital is determined by the factors that condition the saving and investment behaviour of the main economic sectors. The relative cost of different types of finance depends on the particular terms of the financing contract with respect to quantity, term and risk. There is a variety of arrangements in the capital market that help to transform the terms on which finance is supplied by 'intermediating' between savers and borrowers. The 'institutions' – pension funds, insurance companies, investment and unit trusts – perform this function, as does the banking sector. And the existence of a stock market within the capital market in which the securities of certain firms can be readily bought and sold enables firms to raise long-term finance in a form which is highly liquid from the saver's point of view.

Any residual differences in quantity, term or risk must be reflected in differences in return. In finance theory we assume that of these three, risk is the main determinant of relative returns.

REFERENCES AND BIBLIOGRAPHY

Briston, R M, and Dobbins, R	*The Growth and Impact of Institutional Investors* (1978) Institute of Chartered Accountants in England and Wales, London.
Carleton, W T, and Cooper, I A	'Estimation and Use of the Term Structure of Interest Rates', Journal of Finance, Sept 1976, pp 1067–1083.
Cox, J C, Ingersoll, J E, and Ross, S A	'A Re-examination of Traditional Hypotheses about the Term Structure of Interest Rates', Journal of Finance, Sept 1981, pp 769–780.
Culbertson, J	'The Term Structure of Interest Rates', Quarterly Journal of Economics, 1957, pp 489–504.
Fama, E F	'Short-Term Interest Rates as Predictors of Inflation', American Economic Review, 1975, pp 269–282.
Goodhart, C A E	*Money, Information and Uncertainty* (2nd edn, 1989) Macmillan.
Hicks, J	*Value and Capital* (1939) Oxford University Press, London.
Modigliani, F, and Sutch, R	'Innovations in Interest Rate Policy', American Economic Review, 1966, pp 178–197.
Van Horne JC	'New Listings and their Price Behaviour', Journal of Finance, Sept 1970, pp 783–794.
Wilson, Sir H (Chairman)	Committee to Review the Functioning of Financial Institutions, 'Report' (Cmnd 7937).

QUESTIONS

1 What are the main differences between equity and debt in a financing contract?

2 What types of equity and debt are most important for financing firms in practice, and why?

3 What role do financial intermediaries play in channelling savings to investment?

4 The stock market has been likened to a casino. Does it have a useful role in reality?

5 What are the relative advantages and disadvantages of a full stock exchange quotation, a junior markets quote, and being unlisted?

6 We believe the price of finance will reflect the risk, the term, and the quantity raised. How are each of these factors priced?

CHAPTER 13

Capital market efficiency

An important feature of a well-functioning capital market is that the prices of securities traded in the market should always fully reflect all available information. Markets with this property are informationally 'efficient' and the efficiency of the stock market has been subjected to a great deal of empirical testing. The results of these studies have suggested fairly convincingly that the stock market is efficient in pricing securities. In Section I we describe the notion of market efficiency in more detail and review the research evidence.

I MARKET EFFICIENCY

The *efficient markets theory* is the theory that *security prices always fully reflect all available information*. Suppose this were not the case, and that share prices only reflected new information slowly or not at all. By reacting more quickly and anticipating price changes, certain investors might be able consistently to make above normal returns through trading on the market. It is this potential for abnormal returns that researchers look for in testing market efficiency. The fact that some market operators might be able to gain at the expense of someone else is perhaps not particularly important in itself. Its significance is as an indicator that, for a period, a security was not correctly valued.

The present value of a security, V, is the future stream of cash flows from the security, C_t, to the investment horizon, n, discounted at the required return, r,

$$V = \sum_{t=0}^{n} \frac{C_t}{(1 + r)^t}$$

Information is relevant to the value of a security if it tells us something about the level and risk of the future cash flows. It is convenient to identify three levels of rigour in tests of the market efficiency reflecting different degrees of *availability* of information:

For WEAK-FORM market efficiency the set of available and relevant information is the price history of the security itself. The market is weak-form efficient if it is not possible to make abnormal trading gains by analysing past patterns of security prices. Tests of SEMI-STRONG efficiency investigate whether all publicly available information is embodied fully and instantaneously in share prices. The market is STRONG-FORM efficient if it is impossible to make abnormal gains using any information at all, including information that is not publicly available.

In the rest of this section we review the evidence on stock market efficiency. In the main, tests have shown the market to be weak, and semi-strong efficient, but not strong-form efficient.[1] People with inside information appear to be able to make abnormal gains. But there is also some evidence that does not fit so comfortably with market efficiency. We discuss these 'anomalies' in Section II.

1 The classic exposition of market efficiency and survey of its tests was Fama (1970). He updates this survey in Fama (1991).

Weak-form efficiency: share prices are random

The striking conclusion from research into weak-form efficiency is that share prices follow a *random walk* through time. But a moment's thought shows that this is just what we would expect in an efficient market. The market is weak-form efficient if it is not possible to make profitable predictions of share prices using the information implicit in past prices. The reason is simply that in such a market all the available information has already been used, and embodied in share prices. It follows that prices in an efficient market will be random, since random means unpredictable. If prices *are* random this directly contradicts the underlying assumption of much traditional investment analysis. The belief of 'technical analysis' or 'chartism' is that share prices can profitably be forecast by studying past movements in prices. Technical analysis is a widely practised art and it has a developed vocabulary with analysts looking for conventional patterns and trends in prices.

Researchers have used two sorts of test of weak-form efficiency. They have examined whether share prices actually do behave like a random series of numbers, and they have tested some of the investment rules implied by technical analysis.

Tests of randomness

There are two common ways of looking for randomness. One involves measuring the *serial correlation* between price changes in different time periods. The serial correlation between the price change in time t and the charge n periods previously, at time t–n, is known as the 'nth-order serial correlation'. For a random variable all orders of serial correlation should be zero, in other words there should be no discernible association between price changes at different times. Another approach to randomness is the *runs* test. A 'run' is a series of consecutive price changes of the same sign, and the 'runs test' investigates whether observed runs occur with the same frequency as would be expected in a random series.[2]

Many studies have used these tests to investigate price behaviour in the major stock markets. The earliest was by Louis Bachelier in a study of the French Bourse published in 1900. He found that commodity prices moved randomly. Nowadays this sort of work is made easier by the existence of computerised databases. Most researchers have found that in fact there are dependencies between successive price changes, but have usually concluded that they are too small to generate investment strategies that can cover their own transaction costs.

Mechanical trading rules

Researchers have also tested some of the mechanical trading rules with which practising investment advisers have claimed to successfully predict share prices. One example of a mechanical trading rule is the *filter rule*. A filter rule tells an investor when to buy and sell a share. It is of this form – 'buy when the price rises by more than X% from its last low point, sell when it falls by X% from a previous high'. The critical percentage, X, is determined by the analyst. Implicitly the filter rule is saying that past price movements are an indication of future movements so a successful filter rule would be evidence that the market was inefficient. Alexander (1964) and Fama and Blume (1966) examined the performance of filter rules. They found, as has often been found in weak-form testing of market efficiency, that prices are not perfectly random and in the absence of transactions costs it might be possible to make very small abnormal returns using filter rules. But once transactions costs are taken into account this ceases to be the case. Other trading rules have been investigated. In the

2 A fuller description of runs and serial correlation tests can be found in Foster (1986).

main they have been shown unable to yield price forecasts that are profitable after allowing for transactions costs.

Semi-strong efficiency: the effects of new information

The market is semi-strong efficient if prices always fully reflect all *publicly available* information. There is an impressive body of evidence that the market is semi-strong efficient.

It is fairly easy to check the speed with which share prices respond when new information becomes public; the evidence is usually that the market embodies new information in prices fully by the time it is formally announced. But it is rather harder to know if the market is getting prices 'right' and what the exact effect on prices of news about, say, a merger or dividend *ought* to be. The researcher would have to say he knew better than the market how the news affected expectations of future cash flows, and how those cash flows should be evaluated. It is easier to find situations where new information has apparently no economic content and check that prices do not change. One study of this sort was the study of 'stock splits' by Fama, Fisher, Jensen and Roll (1969). We will examine this study fairly closely as it is the seminal 'event study'.

Do stock splits boost value?

The *stock split* is an event whose theoretical impact we can calculate precisely – it should have no impact on the value of the firm. A stock split takes place when a firm gives its existing shareholders extra shares in proportion to the shares they already own.[3] In a stock split the company divides its share capital into smaller denomination shares, shares with a smaller 'par value'. Another way of issuing additional shares without shareholders contributing extra resources, is a 'bonus' or 'capitalisation' issue in which reserves are converted into more shares with the same par value as the existing shares. A stock split, per se, is not a 'real' event, merely a distribution of additional share certificates, so the total value of the firm should be unchanged by a stock split. However, there is a widespread belief amongst financial advisers and similar personnel that stock splits do increase the value of the firm, and on the face of it the evidence bears this out.

> *Splitz Ltd*
>
> Suppose Splitz Ltd has 200,000 shares in issue, selling for £5 each. Splitz decides to issue its shareholders with another share for each one they own. The total market value of the firm is £1m, and since the stock split should not change this value we would expect the post-split share price to be £1m/400,000 = £2.50. In practice Splitz share price settles at £3 after the split, giving a total market value of £1.2m.

This puzzling phenomenon was investigated by Fama, Fisher, Jensen and Roll (1969) in a classic study. Fama et al agreed that firms splitting their shares *did* experience abnormal value gains. But they explained this by hypothesising that stock splits carried valuable information about future dividends. One reason why dividend policy may be relevant to the value of the firm is that managers are known to dislike cutting dividends. Hence the setting of a new level of dividends is interpreted as a statement that this new level of dividends can be maintained in the future, and therefore provides important new information for outsiders. Since managers often try to maintain dividend *per share* when they split stock, a stock split is often accompanied by a dividend increase.

3 'Stock split' is the US terminology. In the UK stock splits are usually known as 'scrip' issues. On this occasion we find the US term more explicit.

The Fama, Fisher, Jensen and Roll (1969) study

Semi-strong tests are concerned with the impact of new information: they compare the share price which resulted with what it would have been without the new information. However the elapse of time causes a problem here. In practice investors are able to anticipate new information and start to embody it in share prices well before it is formally announced. There can be a gap of months between the true pre-information price and the post-information price, during which time many other relevant external factors may have changed. One way to handle this problem is to use the market model which provides a method of estimating what the price of a share 'would have been'. We know that under the assumptions of the CAPM there is a stable linear relationship through time between the return on an asset j and the market, m, such that:

$$r_j = r_i + B_j\,(r_m - r_i) \qquad (1)$$

where r_j = return on asset j
r_m = return on the market portfolio
r_i = riskless rate
B_j = coefficient specific to project j, reflecting the covariability between asset j and the market portfolio.

This theoretical model suggests the following linear estimating equation, known as the **market model**, to determine the relationship between the return on the market and return on a particular share j:

$$r_{jt} = a_j + b_j r_{mt} + e_{jt} \qquad (2)$$

where a_j, b_j are the parameters of the regression, and e_{jt} is an error term which is independent of r_m and has an expected value of zero.

The return on a share in the period ending at t:

$$r_{jt} = \frac{V_{jt} - V_{jt-1} + DIV_{jt}}{V_{jt-1}} \qquad (3)$$

where V_{jt} = Value of share j at time t
DIV_{jt} = Cash dividend paid in period t

The return on the market is calculated in a similar way, using a portfolio built for the purpose, or a published market portfolio such as the FT Actuaries.

Fama et al first had to establish that extraordinary returns were in fact associated with stock splits, and to abstract from the changes in the returns of a firm that occur anyway because of general market conditions. They had a sample of 622 different stocks that were involved in 940 splits from 1927 to 1959. For each security they estimated a version of the market model using data on the returns on the security and on the market for as many periods as were available, but excluding periods immediately prior to the split. (The last point is crucial in using the market model and we will explain it shortly.) Having estimated the model, the 'abnormal returns' earned on the share during any period can be calculated as the difference between actual returns and returns predicted by the model in each period, in other words as the residual, or error, terms, e_{jt}, in equation (2). (Hence the 'market model' technique is often known as 'residual analysis'.) For each month before and after the split Fama et al averaged the residuals across all the stock splits they studied, then found the cumulative total of these residuals month by month from 30 months before the effective date of the stock split to 30 months after. This is shown in Figure I.

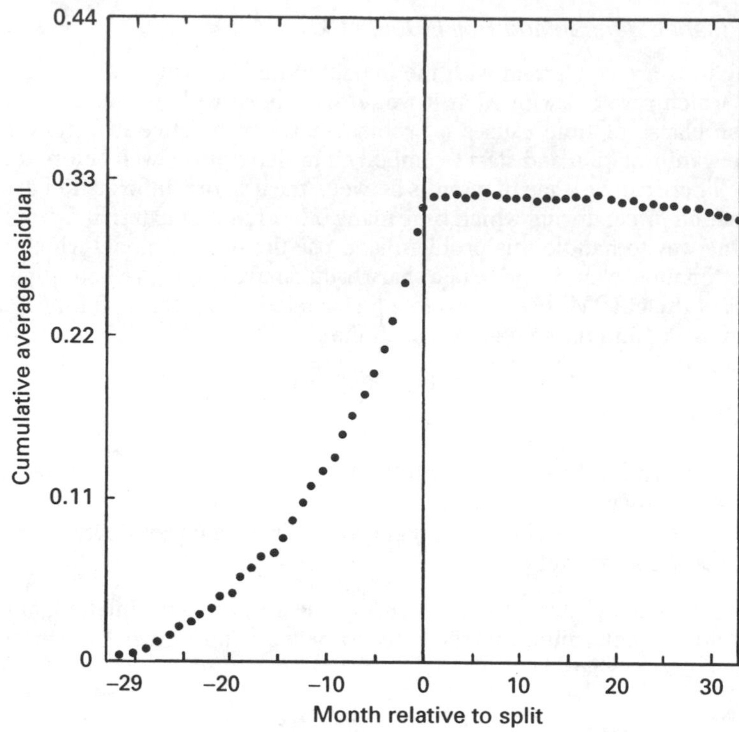

Reprinted with permission of the International Economic Review.

Figure I Cumulative average residuals from Fama et al (1969)

The shape of the cumulative average residual curve in Figure I is very much what we have now come to expect in event studies. The vertical height of the curve at $t = 0$ measures the extent of the extraordinary returns which had accrued by the time of the split. The flatness of the curve thereafter can be taken as evidence of market efficiency – the new information had been incorporated in share prices by the date of the split. The shape of the curve prior to the split is interesting, since it shows that the market started to anticipate gains up to 30 months in advance. It is common to find a good deal of anticipation of new information. Since splits were only announced a month or two in advance Fama et al concluded that these anticipated gains could not have been caused by the split, rather that the split *and* the extraordinary returns were jointly caused by '. . . a sharp improvement, relative to the market, in the earnings prospects of the company sometime during the years immediately preceding a split' (Fama et al (1969)).

Since extraordinary gains can start to arise well before the event with which they are associated it is important to restrict the estimation of the market model to the 'normal' period prior to the onset of these gains, otherwise there will be estimation bias. But the problem is that until the model is estimated the period of extraordinary gains cannot be identified. To overcome this, Fama et al estimated the model twice for each share, the first time to form an idea as to the likely period of extraordinary gains, and the second time excluding this period.

In order to test their hypothesis further Fama et al split their sample into shares whose dividend increased subsequent to the split, and those which failed to show the anticipated increase. They found that the latter showed rising cumulative average residuals in the months before the split, but once the anticipated dividend increase failed to materialise the market corrected its error so that the cumulative average residual 'plummeted' in the few months following the split.

The Fama et al study provides a good example of the use of the market model in finance research and it shows how careful investigation can unravel the inner logic in a situation in which even the participants themselves may not perceive it. But it remains unclear where the positive advantage lies to the firm in splitting its shares. When asked, managers tend to justify stock splits in terms of a lower share price being more 'convenient' for shareholders to transact, and having the appearance of a bargain. Both of these seem of dubious importance in a market dominated by institutional investors. Managers also justify splits in terms of their benficial effect on the value of the firm and as a way of signalling success to the market. Fama et al showed that in an efficient market the stock split itself is of no intrinsic value, it is only valuable for the dividend increases associated with it.

Creative accounting

Accounting profit reflects various accounting conventions and there seems to be a widespread view amongst managers that it can be worthwhile 'massaging' profits by a suitable choice of accounting methods. Also many firms give a good deal of thought and spend a good deal of money on the presentation of their accounting information to the outside world. But none of this affects the future cash flows of the firm, so in an efficient market it should not affect the firm's value either.

Beaver and Dukes (1973) studied the effect of choice of depreciation method on value. They compared the price-earnings ratios of two groups of firms, one employing straight-line depreciation and the other accelerated depreciation, a difference in practice with no apparent effect on value. The average P/E of each group differed, and Beaver and Dukes were able to show that the difference could not be explained in terms of risk or growth differences between the groups. But when depreciation, and thus earnings, were put on a comparable basis the difference in P/E was largely eliminated. Hence it appeared the market was efficiently peering through the veil of accounting practice and valuing the firms consistently. Kaplan and Roll (1972) used residual analysis to examine the share price behaviour of a group of firms that changed their depreciation method and a group that changed their method of accounting for investment tax credits. In both cases the market appeared to behave efficiently with respect to these changes in accounting method.

Other studies

We have considered the impact on values of some apparently irrelevant events – stock splits and accounting changes. Researchers have also studied the response of prices to the issue of information that *is* relevant to the valuation of shares, but we leave examination of these results to the appropriate chapters in the text. In Chapter 22 we consider how the gains or losses associated with merger are incorporated in share prices, and in Chapter 17 we consider the effect on share prices of dividend announcements. The evidence suggests the market handles this sort of information efficiently. In Chapter 14 we look at the behaviour of the market in valuing new issues, but here the efficiency conclusion is less clear.

Strong-form efficiency and insider trading

Strong-form tests of the efficient markets theory have considered two rather important and interesting questions. The first is whether certain people, 'insiders', have privileged access to information that can be used profitably in market trading. The second is whether any particular group appears to be consistently successful in trading.

Unsurprisingly, research has shown that it is possible to make abnormal gains on the stock market if you have access to relevant information ahead of the market. So the market does not appear to be strong-form efficient. The benefits from insider trading are hard to research fully because much of it is never publicised. But researchers have been able to examine some occurrences of insider trading. For example, Lorie and Niederhoffer (1968) were able to use SEC records in the US to identify trades in company shares by people with insider information. They found that these insider trades yielded returns above the market average. Jaffe (1974) found similar results when he investigated insider trades on SEC records.

After many years of discussion, the Companies Act 1980 finally made insider trading illegal in the UK. Under the Criminal Justice Act 1993, it carries a maximum penalty of seven years' imprisonment and an unlimited fine. The prohibition relates to individuals who have been 'connected' with the company either as a director, employee or shareholder, or through a business or professional relationship. Trading on information got from an insider is prohibited too, as is getting someone else to trade for you. However the Act does not create a civil offence, so aggrieved shareholders cannot sue for damages or have the share transaction made void.

The value of reputation

We are talking about the value of knowing before the market that a share price will rise or fall; but sometimes individuals may be in a position to make this happen. For instance it has been said that certain financial journalists have acquired a sufficient reputation to be able to affect the price of a share by recommending it; and that on occasion a City institution, or its chairman, acquires such a golden reputation that its buying and selling behaviour provides a trigger for the rest of the market. An individual who can affect the price of a share can profit by making appropriate purchases or sales on his own account at the same time. Such behaviour by a journalist is deemed highly unethical, and might indicate a semi-strong as well as a strong form breach of efficiency since the market would appear to be responding to irrelevant information. Unfortunately, or perhaps fortunately for the reader with faith in human nature and efficient markets, there is no systematic evidence on this topic. But some rather similar insider trading possibilities have been investigated.

The effect of buying and selling large blocks

Much buying and selling in the stock market is done by institutions with very large funds at their disposal. Institutions generally profess reluctance to take a holding which is so large that its purchase or sale could affect the share price. But institutional managers are sometimes in a position to do this, and this opens the sort of possibility for personal gain that we mentioned above. Similarly the broker handling a large transaction on the part of a private client might be able to make a personal gain if the share price were affected.

In principle it is unclear why the price of a share should be affected by a 'block trade', since if they are properly priced all shares should be perfect substitutes for one another, and the block could not be significant relative to the volume of all shares on the market. However various studies on the New York Stock Exchange have shown that block trades can lead to significant price changes, in which prices fall temporarily then regain some of their former level. Dann, Mayers and Raab (1977) chose a sample of 298 block sales between July 1968 and December 1969. They include any share which showed a significant fall in price between the opening of trading and the sale of the 'block'. Dann et al found that share prices did dip after a block sale but then returned very quickly to their new equilibium level. Indeed the return was so fast that they concluded the market was weak-form efficient in this respect. An investor in a position to invest $100,000, the maximum they considered, in *every* block trade they examined would have accumulated an annual return of 203% after tax and commission. But such is the speed of return of prices that had he bought at the price ruling exactly *one minute* later his annualised return would have been −4%! However Dann et al cautiously suggested that there might be a strong-form inefficiency here because New York Stock Exchange dealers could be in a superior position to capture any abnormal gains associated with block trades. First they would be better placed to participate at the 'bargain' block sale price; second, they have signficantly lower transactions costs, and in the Dann et al study trading profits were very sensitive to transactions costs.

The value of expertise

Insider trading is about people with privileged access to information, but what about people with special skills in analysing what information there is? Institutions such as investment trusts and unit trusts often claim such skills when advertising their services. Researchers have found that in general institutional investors do not achieve a superior performance to the market. For example Jensen (1968) examined the performance of 115 funds, and found they were not out-performing the market, even before deducting their costs of operation. The existence of institutions can be explained in other ways – they can transform the terms of financing contracts and can enable small investors to participate in a diversified portfolio, they provide pension and insurance services, and so forth – but this research casts some doubts on the wilder claims of institutional managers. Later studies, for example Henriksson (1984) and Ippolito (1989) find that mutual fund managers at least earn sufficient additional return to cover their costs.

One group of experts which does appear to beat the market is the well-known US Value Line Survey, and the Value Line predictions have received a large amount of attention from researchers. Value Line rank shares on the basis of a complex mixture of factors including the price history of the firm, and its earnings performance, through time and relative to other firms. While researchers have disagreed on what methodology to use, even the more unfavourable have found that *some* abnormal gains could be made using Value Line predictions, and this implies semi-strong market inefficiency. An example of a Value Line study is Copeland and Mayers (1982).

Research in this area is constrained by availability of data. There may also be other individuals who consistently beat the market, but keep it quiet.

The Briloff factor

It might seem that market efficiency paints a dreary picture of a capital market where security prices respond to new information with machine-like efficiency that allows no hope for the talented, and where only inside information can consistently beat the market. In practice few market participants see it that way, and the case of Abraham Briloff is worth considering. Dr Briloff was a leading American accounting professor at City University, New York. He believed that firms *do* mislead the market through accounting manipulation and he devoted a lot of effort to exposing these practices. Perhaps his best known prey was

McDonald's Corporation.[4] In an article in Baron's Magazine of 8 July 1974 entitled 'You deserve a break . . . McDonald's Burgers Are More Palatable Than Its Accounts' he accused McDonald's of various accounting ploys. For one thing Mr Kroc, the chairman of McDonald's, had distributed shares to friends and employees without declaring this in the accounts. More significantly, in pursuit of one of his favourite themes, Briloff accused McDonald's of 'dirty pooling' in accounting for acquisitions. In 1973 McDonald's brought new subsidiaries into the accounts at their 'book' value of $6 million even though they cost 'over £50 million' in terms of the value of the shares issued to buy them. This way, Briloff maintained, McDonald's would reduce the depreciation charge on these assets, and enhance profits in future years.

Briloff's revelations had an apparently dramatic effect on McDonald's share price. Foster (1986) notes that McDonald's price fell from 47⅞ on 7 May 1974 to 38⅜ on 7 August 1974. In June and July 1974 McDonald's shareholders experienced returns of minus 12% and minus 20%. Returns on the market fell too, but by only 1% and 7%, and McDonald's beta had been 1.7. Of course it cannot be proved that the fall in McDonald's share price was caused by Briloff – it may have been caused by something else. But if it was, it implies semi-strong and strong inefficiency. The market was misinterpreting publicly-available information; and it took an expert to point it out.

II AN ASSESSMENT OF MARKET EFFICIENCY

We now need to review some of the conclusions of the previous section. During the last decade a body of evidence has emerged that at first glance suggests real inefficiencies in share pricing – researchers have unearthed portfolio strategies that can yield significant abnormal gains relative to the return on the market as a whole. But rather than reject the hypothesis of market efficiency this has led researchers to re-examine the benchmarks they are using. Before we examine these 'anomalies' we describe an earlier controversy which points out the real difficulty in knowing if a share is incorrectly rated at any time.

Does inflation distort share prices?

Modigliani and Cohn (1979) claimed to find a major inefficiency in the valuation of shares in the US stock market. They noted that since the mid-1960s the nominal value of the Standard and Poor's 500 index of US stock prices had remained relatively constant, while in real terms its value had fallen to 60% of its 1965–66 level. The 'q' ratio, the ratio of value to replacement cost, of US non-financial corporations had fallen from over unity to less than two-thirds in the same period. Modigliani and Cohn argued that this fall did not reflect any underlying real change in the performance of the US economy but that the value of the S+P 500 was wrong, reflecting two inflation-induced errors made by investors in valuing shares. Investors were using the 'P/E' approach to valuing shares, but were multiplying the *wrong* measure of earnings by the *wrong* P/E ratio. To measure current-cost income it is necessary to make four inflation adjustments to historic-cost profit; three which we might normally expect to be negative, reflecting the need to replace fixed assets, stocks, and debtors and creditors at higher prices, and the fourth, normally positive, reflecting the eroding real liability of company borrowing. According to Modigliani and Cohn investors were deducting depreciation and stock adjustments but failing to add back a gearing adjustment, so understating profit.

The P/E ratio is the reciprocal of the required earnings yield. To capitalise a 'real'

4 This case is well written-up in Foster (1986) pp 409–420. For more good examples of the Briloff approach see his 'Unaccountable Accounting' (Briloff (1972)).

earnings stream it is appropriate to use a 'real' capitalisation rate, but Modigliani and Cohn believed that, moreover, investors were basing P/Es on the higher 'nominal' interest rates prevailing in the market and thus deriving P/Es that were too low. Correctly valued, Modigliani and Cohn claimed, the level of the S + P 500 would have been 200 in 1977, rather than 100.

The negative relationship between inflation and share value occurred in all developed countries in the 1970s (see Cohn and Lessard (1981)). But the key question is the link between the two events, and the Modigliani and Cohn argument in terms of market inefficiency is by no means universally accepted. Feldstein (1980) argued that the phenomenon can be explained in terms of the impact of certain features of the tax law, though his argument is specific to the US tax system. Moore (1980) has attempted to explain the UK experience in terms of an inflation-induced failure by companies to maintain the real value of dividends.

The Modigliani and Cohn hypothesis demonstrates the great difficulty in efficient markets research of knowing what share values *ought* to be. They produce published descriptions of the valuation procedures adopted by analysis to support their contention that shares were being wrongly valued. By substituting 'correct' procedures they restore the trend line for the S+P index very much to where they expected it to be. But this does not constitute *proof* of their hypothesis. The share valuation process is based on expectations of the future and is essentially unobservable. It remains possible that some sea-change in the future level and risk of the returns of companies, possibly associated with inflation, perhaps with the 'oil crisis', took place in the 1970s, and was correctly identified by investors. Cohn, in his 1981 paper with Lessard, draws a more tentative conclusion than before.

> The interesting question for further exploration is whether the observed relationship between interest rates, inflation and stock prices is the result of systematic errors in valuation on the part of investors or linkages between structural causes of inflation and factors that reduce long-term earnings potential for firms (pp 287–288).

Anomalies

We should treat the market efficiency tests described earlier with care. First, tests can never prove a theory, only falsify it. The work of the scientist is constantly to develop new tests. If the theory survives then the tests will add to our confidence in the theory, lend support to it, but not prove it. It is always possible that new observations will be made or new tests developed which falsify the theory. This certainly applies to the theory of stock market efficiency. For example, there may be trading rules in existence that can yield abnormal returns but about which their owner is wisely keeping quiet. And new tests are always being developed which may falsify the efficiency theory. Finally, the power of the efficient markets research is that its results describe the behaviour of large samples of share prices. But within those samples there may be local inefficiencies, such as the 'Briloff factor', which these tests cannot catch.

Tests of market efficiency examine the pricing of the securities of quoted firms. There are about 2,000 quoted firms in the UK, yet over 700,000 companies registered at Companies House. Of course quoted firms are the largest, and account for the major part of economic activity in the UK, but the concentration of research effort on these firms cannot be entirely explained this way. It also reflects availability of data. Only quoted firms have continuously recorded market prices, which are the necessary data base for rigorous testing of market efficiency. But there are a lot of other important questions we might want to ask about the performance of the capital market. Does the market discriminate against small firms? Are bank loans properly priced? Is the whole company sector correctly allocated its supply of funds?

But over the last decade we have become aware of a number of 'anomalies' in share prices. The most notable of these is the 'size effect'. Banz (1981) was one of the earliest to document the systematic tendency of small firms to earn a higher return than large firms. This is a durable and significant feature of returns, and has been confirmed by many other studies. The magnitude and persistence of the size effect is in itself suggestive that we are not dealing with an inefficiency here, but that the CAPM is failing to capture a factor in the returns required by investors which is related to the size of the firm.

Another body of evidence concerns the predictability of returns. In a weak form efficient market returns cannot profitably be forecast from the history of share prices. But De Bondt and Thaler (1987) find that a 'contrarian' portfolio strategy maintained over a number of years of buying losers and selling winners yields profits. On the other hand, Jegadeesh and Titman (1993) show that over shorter six-month, horizons relative-strength portfolios (buying winners, selling losers) are profitable.

A number of papers has shown that stock returns can be successfully forecast using variables such as dividend-yield, and price-earnings ratios. For example, Fama and French (1988) found that current dividend-yield could explain about 25% of returns over a two to four-year horizon. But the question of how to interpret this result raises a fundamental issue in research into market efficiency. Market efficiency tests require a benchmark against which to measure abnormal returns, so tests are always of the joint hypothesis that the market is efficient and that the equilibrium model of market returns, usually the CAPM, is appropriate. A failure can either indicate an inefficiency or that the benchmark is inappropriate. For example, the predictability of returns identified by Fama and French could be interpreted as an irrational bubble in prices, being slowly corrected, or that equilibrium returns vary through time in a way not captured by the CAPM.

Another class of anomalies concerns numerous 'seasonal' effects that have been documented. It seems that shares are more likely to earn negative returns on Mondays! This is the so-called 'weekend effect'. French (1980) looked at the returns on the 500 largest firms on NYSE from 1953 to 1977, and found a very significant negative Monday return overall, and in each five-year sub-period. There also appears to be year-end effect. Various studies, for example Reinganum (1982), have found a tendency for returns to fall in December, and rise the following January. Again, the response of researchers is to review the research design, in this case focusing on the 'bid-ask spread'. The spread between the prices at which market-makers will buy and sell can be quite large for smaller stocks. If there is a preponderance of sales at certain times this may create an appearance of seasonality.

We said earlier that researchers should always be seeking to falsify their theories. For Carl Popper, the philosopher, a potential for falsifiability was the test of a true science, so he would have been unimpressed by the reluctance of economists to relinquish their belief in market efficiency. But given the joint hypothesis problem they are probably right to see the market efficiency literature as evidence, instead of the limitations of single factor models of the return required by investors like the CAPM. The best evidence for market efficiency may be structural: given the competitiveness of modern, developed, capital markets it is simply implausible that large enduring phenomena such as the size effect could be due to inefficiency.

Efficient markets versus perfect markets

In thinking about what market efficiency does and does not imply, it is useful to clarify the difference between a *perfect* market and one which is simply *efficient*. The general conditions necessary for a market to be perfect are as follows:

1 There is full and costless information availabler to all participants.
2 There are no transaction costs and the tax system is neutral with respect to the market.
3 There are many buyers and sellers, so that participants are 'price-takers'.
4 Participants are 'rational': they behave in accordance with certain axioms of rationality such as preferring more to less of a good thing, and make their choices in a consistent way.

The appeal of the perfect market concept is that it can be employed to build models of economic systems from which powerful optimality conclusions can be drawn. If all the markets, for products, labour and capital are perfect in any economy than we can be sure the economy is 'Pareto-efficient', that is, there is no reallocation of resources that will make someone better off without making someone else worse off. In other words there is no gratuitous wastefulness. Market prices in such an economy carry a lot of information – they tell us the cost to the supplier of the marginal unit produced, and the consumer's evaluation of the marginal unit consumed.

But the perfect market economy is an unrealised ideal. In reality the necessary conditions for perfect markets do not hold and in the *capital market* it is particularly conditions 1 and 2 which appear unrealistic. In practice information is neither free not uniformly distributed. There is a gulf between the information about firms that 'insiders' – managers and their advisers such as stockbrokers, investment bankers, accountants, consultants – have access to, and the information shareholders are given. Shareholders have to spend money to narrow this gap. Secondly, raising finance and buying and selling existing securities is a costly process. We discussed some of the costs of new finance in a previous chapter. In addition, investors who buy and sell securities pay brokerage costs which reduce the gains from trading. Furthermore there are transactions costs in product markets that can have an impact on financial decisions, notably the costs associated with bankruptcy. Thirdly, companies and investors pay taxes of different sorts and at rates which depend on their individual tax-paying positions. Tax drives a wedge between what firms earn and investors receive.

As the reader of this book will find out, we usually assume a perfect capital market when we build models to analyse financial decisions. This provides a useful starting point from which we can develop an analysis of real situations by relaxing the perfect market assumptions. But though it is possible to figure out in general terms the effects of these market imperfections on financial decisions it is hard to quantify their effects.

Efficient is a much less demanding notion than *perfect*, and prices can always fully reflect all available information even when there are taxes, transactions costs and information costs. What makes for an efficient market? The real dynamic of efficiency is competition, and the capital market becomes competitive when there are many buyers and sellers constantly searching for information and reappraising security prices in the light of it, looking for the possibility of an abnormal gain. There is an apparent paradox here, which is why many practitioners find market efficiency hard to accept. They say 'How can you expect us to believe it's impossible to make abnormal gains on the stock market? For one thing the market is full of people hoping and striving to make an abnormal gain, and for another there is a large and well-paid profession of financial analysts and related experts whose job is to analyse company performance and identify profitable opportunities for investors'. In fact the existence of these people is entirely consistent with market efficiency – the market is efficient *because of* them rather than *in spite of* them. Market efficiency does not imply that abnormal gains cannot be made – good luck or the possession of inside information can both yield them. The point is that armed *only* with publicly available information you could not have an expectation of abnormal gain if you buy and sell shares in an efficient market. As for investors and analysts, it is the strivings of investors, and the close monitoring by analysts that create the competitive conditions under which new information is instantaneously capitalised into security prices.

III SUMMARY

The main implication of market efficiency is that, as far as we can tell, share prices can be trusted; given the existing stock of publicly available information shares will neither be over- nor under-valued. This is a very important conclusion. Supply and demand in any market are balanced by the price mechanism. In the capital market the 'price' is the cost of capital. The dividend valuation model suggests that the cost of equity capital is the discount rate which equates the value of the share and the future dividend per share stream. Thus if the share is under-valued the cost of capital will be too high, and vice versa. In general the firm can only be confident in its cost of capital if its shares are correctly valued. By exactly the same argument investors' return depends on the pricing of shares. But if the market is efficient investors and firms can participate in it with some confidence of getting a fair return and paying a fair price.

Market efficiency research yields a crop of more specific insights too. For instance, we now know that cosmetic accounting changes are unlikely to mislead the market, that stock splits are not a magical and costless method of enhancing share price, and so forth. Similarly investors should be duly suspicious of claims by experts and advisers to be able to beat the market.

REFERENCES AND BIBLIOGRAPHY

Alexander, S S	'Price Movements in Speculative Markets: Trends or Random Walks', Industrial Management Review, May 1961, pp 7–26.
Ariel, R A	'A Monthly Effect in Stock Returns', Journal of Financial Economics 18, 1987.
Ariel, R A	'High Stock Returns before Holidays: Existence and Evidence on Possible Causes', Journal of Finance 45, 1990.
Banz, R W	'The Relationship between Return and Market Value of Common Stocks', Journal of Financial Economics 9, 1981.
Beaver, W H, and Dukes, R E	'Tax Allocation and δ Depreciation Methods', Accounting Review, July 1973, pp 549–559.
Briloff, A	*Unaccountable Accounting* (1972) Harper and Row, New York.
Cohn, R A, and Lessard, D R	'The Effect of Inflation on Stock Prices: International Evidence', Journal of Finance, May 1981, pp 277–290.
Coutner, P H (ed)	*The Random Character of Stock Market Prices* (1964) MIT Press, Cambridge, Mass.
Copeland, T E and Mayers, D	'The Value Line Enigma (1965–1978): A Case Study of Performance Evaluation Issues', Journal of Financial Economics, November 1982, pp 289–321.
Dann, L, Mayers, D and Raab, R	'Trading Rules, Large Blocks and the Speed of Adjustment', Journal of Financial Economics, January 1977, pp 3–22.

De Bondt, W F M, and Thaler, R H — 'Does the Stock Market Overreact?', Journal of Finance, 1987, pp 557–581.

Dimson, E, and Marsh, P R — 'Event Study Methodologies and the Size Effect', Journal of Financial Economics, 1986, pp 113–142.

Fama, E F — 'Efficient Capital Markets: A Review of Theory and Empirical Work', Journal of Finance, May 1970, pp 383–417.

Fama, E F — 'Efficient Capital Markets II', Golden Anniversary Review Article, Journal of Finance, December 1991, pp 1575–1617.

Fama, E F, and Blume, M — 'Filter Rules and Stock Market Trading', Journal of Business, January 1966, pp 226–241.

Fama, E, Fisher, L, Jensen, M, and Roll, R — 'The Adjustment of Stock Prices to New Information', International Economic Review, 10 February 1969, pp 1–21.

Fama, E F, and French, K R — 'Dividend Yields and Expected Stock Returns', Journal of Financial Economics 22, 1988, pp 3–25.

Fama, E F, and French K R — 'The Cross-Section of Expected Stock Returns', Journal of Finance, June 1992, pp 427–465.

Feldstein, M — 'Inflation and the Stock Market', American Economic Review, December 1980, pp 839–847.

Foster, G — *Financial Statement Analysis* (2nd edn, 1986) Prentice-Hall, Englewood-Cliff, New Jersey.

French, C — 'Stock Returns and the Weekend Effect', Journal of Financial Economics, 1980.

Henriksson, Roy T — 'Market Timing and Mutual Fund Performance: An Empirical Investigation', Journal of Business 57, 1984.

Ippolito, Richard A — 'Efficiency with Costly Information: A Study of Mutual Fund Performance, 1965–1984', Quarterly Journal of Economics 104, 1989, pp 1–23.

Jaffe, J — 'Special Information and Insider Trading', Journal of Business, July 1974, pp 410–428.

Jegadeesh, N, and Titman, S — 'Returns to Buying Winners and Selling Losers: Implications for Stock Market Efficiency', Journal of Finance, March 1993, pp 65-92.

Jensen, M — 'The Performance of Mutual Funds in the Period 1945–64', Journal of Finance, May 1968, pp 389–416.

Kaplan, R S, and Roll, R — 'Investor Evaluation of Accounting Information; Some Empirical Evidence', Journal of Business, April 1972, pp 225–257.

Lorie, J H, and Niederhoffer, V — 'Predictive and Statistical Properties of Insider Trading', Journal of Law and Economics, April 1968.

Modigliani, F, and Cohn, R A — 'Inflation, Rational Valuation and the Market', Financial Analysts Journal, March/April 1979, pp 24–44.

Moore, A B — 'Some Characteristics of Changes in Common Stock Prices', from Cootner P H (ed) *The Random Character of Stock Market Prices* (1964) MIT Press.

Moore, B — 'Equity Values and Inflation: The Importance of Dividends', Lloyds Bank Review, July 1980.

Reinganum, M R — 'A Direct Test of Roll's Conjecture on the Firm Size Effect', Journal of Finance, 1982.

QUESTIONS

1 On the financial page of any daily paper you will see charts of the price history of individual shares and market sectors. What does weak-form market efficiency say about the value of charts like this?

2 When Bowtie plc had a 1 for 3 stock split, the share price fell from £2.40 to £2. Barry Bowtie, saw the value of his shares rise 11%. So he plans another stock split next year. Advise him.

3 Is the production by most large firms of expensive, glossy annual reports consistent with a semi-strong efficient market?

4 What difficulties exist in ever getting the necessary information for testing strong form efficiency?

5 Why is it sometimes claimed that inflation distorts stock market prices? How is this problem related to that of stock market efficiency?

6 What is the difference between an efficient market and a perfect market?

7 What is the significance of market efficiency for investors and financial managers?

CHAPTER 14

Equity

Equity is the finance the firm raises from the owners of the business. Equity can be raised in two ways: by issuing new shares and by retaining profits in the firm. In terms of importance, retained earnings are the major source of finance for most firms. We examine the firm's decision as to how much of its profit to put out as dividend and how much to retain later in the book. In the present chapter we concentrate on new issue finance.

Section I discusses some of the concepts and terminology of equity finance. Section II discusses the pricing of share issues and the nature and costs of different methods of issue. New issues entail costs of two sorts: there are transactions costs, and in addition shares are usually issued at a discount, which is effectively another cost of issue. Section III tells the story of a share issue by Hesketh Motorcycles in 1980. It shows the problems that can face investors in trying to decide the value of a new and 'unseasoned' share. Section IV shows the steps in determining the issue price and quantity of a new share issue.

A side effect of issuing shares to new shareholders at a discount is a dilution of the wealth of existing shareholders. This happens because the new shareholders are being allowed to buy cheap a part of something that currently belongs to the existing shareholders, namely the present and future earnings power of the firm. This problem can be avoided by giving pre-emptive 'rights' over the new shares to the existing shareholders. In Section V we consider the dilution problem and show how rights issues avoid it.

I EQUITY FINANCE – CONCEPTS AND TERMINOLOGY

Table I details the equity financing of the General Electric Company which is one of the UK's largest companies.[1] It is extracted from the group accounts at 31 March 1990.

Table I General Electric Company – shareholders' interest 31 March 1994

	%	*1994 (£m)*	%	*1993 (£m)*
Share capital[(a)]	3.6	137	3.8	136
Share premium account	2.8	108	2.6	94
Reserves	80.9	3,083	80.8	2,871
Shareholders' interest	87.3	3,328	87.2	3,101
CAPITAL EMPLOYED	100	3,813	100	3,555

	£
(a) Ordinary shares of 5p each issued at 31 March 1994 fully paid	136,848,300
Unissued	38,151,700
Authorised	175,000,000

1 UK General Electric is unrelated to the US company of the same name.

We can see that the equity or *shareholders' interest* was 87.3% of GEC's overall capital employed in 1994, of which *reserves*, which are the retained profit part of equity, accounted for 80.9%. The note says that the share capital is made up of *issued* and *fully-paid* 5p shares. Since the shares are 5p ones the number of GEC shares in issue must be £136,848,300 × 20 = 2,736,966,000. The *authorised* figure of £175,000,000 tells us what value of ordinary shares the company is allowed to issue by the terms of its memorandum of association. Companies sometimes issue shares *partly-paid* which means if the issue price is say 60p perhaps 35p will be payable on issue with the remaining 25p to be *called* at some specified or unspecified future date. The GEC shares are all 'fully-paid'.

The remaining term which needs explaining is *share premium* account. In terms of economics, this is a slightly meaningless figure which is related to the fact that the shares are '5p' shares. In the UK shares have to have a *nominal* or *par* value, 5p in the case of GEC. But the 5p tells us nothing about the shares since it is unrelated to their market value, or to the price they were initially issued at. Supposing GEC had initially issued its 5p shares for 22p. It must then show the 5p part of the proceeds as 'share capital' and the remaining 17p as 'share premium'. Not only do par values not seem to do anything useful, they may on occasions get in the way since the law says that shares cannot be issued at a price below par.

The key characteristic of equity is that it is a financing contract that gives ownership rights to the supplier of funds. We will be talking about *ordinary shares*[2] as though they are a homogeneous commodity possessing identical rights, notably a vote and an equal share in the profits and assets of the firm. In practice this is usually the case, but there are some variants on the standard ordinary share contract. One is the ordinary share with limited voting rights, commonly known as the *A-ordinary*, which were often issued by closely-controlled firms which sought to broaden their equity without losing control. The Stock Exchange now only permits issues of limited voting shares if they are clearly labelled as such, though some that were issued in a previous era still exist, lingering in the balance-sheets of companies. These now number less than 100 on The London Stock Exchange and in half of these the restricted nature of the shares is not evident from the name.

Some firms issue *deferred* shares which have the same rights as other equity, except they receive a dividend only when profits are above a certain level, or after a certain date. Another variant of the equity contract is the *preference share* which gives an entitlement to a fixed rate of dividend prior to other equity, and priority when the company is liquidated. Though preference shares are legally equity the fixed dividend makes them closer to debt, so we look at them in Chapter 15.

II ISSUING SHARES

When a company issues shares it has to decide what method of issue to use, and what price to charge. These are the subjects we consider in this section. The possibilities facing the firm when it issues shares depend rather on the nature of the firm and particularly on whether it is a *private*, *public*, or *public quoted* company. The private company cannot invite the general public to subscribe for shares. The public company is free to offer shares to the public, and the public company that also has a stock exchange listing can offer shares that have a ready market with a continuously recorded market price.

2 In the US these are called 'common stock', but in the UK the word 'stock' is used when the firm has taken the power for its share capital to be traded by value rather in units – hence rather than, say, 4,000 5p shares, the investor would buy £200 of stock.

Table II Common methods of issue of securities

	OFFER FOR SALE	PUBLIC ISSUE	PLACING	TENDER	STOCK EXCHANGE INTRODUCTION	RIGHTS ISSUE
METHOD	Company/Existing Shareholders → Issuing House → Public	Company/Existing Shareholders → Public	Company → Private clients of issuing house or broker, by arrangement	Company → Issuing House → Public (Company → Public)	Existing Shareholders → Public via The Stock Exchange	Company → Existing Shareholders
PRICE		Fixed before issue		Set by market	Fixed before issue	Fixed before issue
NOTES	Shares are bought by an issuing house or market-maker which sells them to the public. These may be new shares or a significant group of existing shares being sold by their owners.	Similar to offer for sale, but direct to the public. The issuing house acts as adviser, as agent rather than principal.	Cheaper than offer for sale, and not underwritten. Since placing limits on the public's chance to participate, The Stock Exchange limits the size of placings.	Identical to offer for sale, but public are invited to tender for a number of shares, and the shares are sold to the highest bidders at the price which clears the issue.	Company seeks to obtain a market for its existing securities on The Stock Exchange. No new money is raised.	New shares are offered to existing shareholders for cash in proportion to their existing holdings.

There are a variety of ways of issuing shares, and Table II provides a checklist of the main ones. The variety may seem confusing, but simply reflects different possibilities as to

1 Who the shares are going to be bought by – the public, or a known group of individuals or institutions (placing), or existing shareholders (rights).
2 Whether the shares will be sold in the first instance to an issuing house, then sold by them to the public (offer for sale, and sometimes a tender) or whether the issuing house acts simply as an adviser.
3 Whether the price is fixed before issue, or is set by competitive bidding (tender).

One event that looks like a new issue but is not is the *stock split*, or *bonus* or *capitalisation* issue as it is more properly called in the UK. In a stock split the firm simply issue existing shareholders with new shares in proportion to their existing holdings. Stock splits raise some interesting efficiency questions which we discussed in some detail in Chapter 13, but no new money is involved.

Another form of share issue is the *scrip dividend*, which is a dividend paid in the form of new shares instead of cash. Scrips were briefly popular in the UK after 1973 when the Revenue started taxing them as capital gains rather than as distributions of cash. This gave advantages all round. Shareholders were taxed at lower CGT rates, and firms got the cash-flow benefits of not having to pay advance corporation tax as well as avoiding a cash distribution. In 1975 however the system was changed, and the Revenue started taxing scrips as cash distributions. Without tax advantages there is no obvious point in a 'scrip', which becomes effectively a bonus issue. If shareholders want more cash they can make their own 'home-made' dividend by selling some shares, without having to be given more pieces of paper. Firms which want to pursue a high-retention policy might think scrips will make shareholders feel better, but in efficient capital markets we do not expect considerations like that to carry much weight. However, a tax advantage to scrips has reappeared for firms, including many multinationals, which have surplus dividend credits ('unrelieved ACT'). Companies do not have to remit ACT on scrip dividends, and this has led a number of UK companies to introduce a share alternative to the cash dividend.

We call a further issue of shares which are already on the market a *seasoned* issue. The Stock Exchange expects issues of seasoned shares to be made to existing shareholders as a 'rights' issue.

Table III shows annual share issues compared to the FA Actuaries Share Index.

Table III Annual share issues by UK listed industrial and commercial companies (£m)

	1982	*1983*	*1984*	*1985*	*1986*	*1987*	*1988*	*1989*	*1990*	*1991*	*1992*	*1993*
Ordinary share issues	946	1,723	993	3,253	5,350	12,706	3,873	1,833	2,852	9,761	5,272	12,326
FTA (industrial) index	397	463	612	713	860	892	942	1,206	1,034	1,249	1,441	1,677

Source: CSO Financial Statistics

Timing of issues

There is a well established tendency for the volume of share issues to follow the level of market prices. We would expect this if they both reflect an increase in profitable opportunities in the economy. But there seem to be other things happening as well, particularly a tendency to move to equity out of debt when the market rises. A good example of this was the aftermath to 1974. In 1974 the stock market plummeted and the new issues market dried up altogether. Firms were forced to turn to the banks for funds. The surge in new issues the following year was partly a refinancing of this bank borrowing. A similar dip in equity issues occurred following the October 1987 crash. This may sound like a plausible explanation of the fluctuations in new issues: it is essentially the notion that *timing* of new issues is something firms should attend to. But it does not square too well with the idea of an efficient market. We can understand firms thinking about the timing of new issues in one sense – the high fixed costs of issue mean they will want to issue new shares periodically rather than continuously, and in the meanwhile they will probably rely on borrowing. But these cycles for individual firms should cancel out in aggregate. The trouble is, 'timing' does not fit in too well with 'efficient markets'. In an efficient capital market shares are always correctly priced. They are never 'overpriced' or 'underpriced'. In retrospect we can spot peaks and troughs, but not whilst they are happening. The implication is that in an efficient market the firm could never rationally expect that share prices would be higher, and the cost of capital lower, in the future.

The costs of issue

The decisive factor in choosing between methods of issue is their relative cost, and the costs of issue vary both according to the type of issue and the amount of money being raised. There are two types of cost associated with a new issue: *administrative costs*, and *issue discounts*.

Administrative costs

Table IV gives estimates from Wilson (1978) of the cost of an ordinary share issue of £2 million on the stock market. We can see that some of the component costs were proportional to the value of the issue, but others were fixed. The existence of these fixed costs means that there are significant economies of scale in issuing shares. But the issue cost also depends on the type of issue. Table IV shows that although the administrative costs of a £2 million first issue of unseasoned shares were 7.6% of the proceeds, further issues of seasoned shares by placing of rights would only cost 2.6% or 4% respectively because certain listing costs would be avoided.

Underwriting

Whenever investors are invited to subscribe for shares there is inevitable uncertainty as to how many shares they will demand. Offers for sale and public issues are often oversubscribed, and in this case the company has to resort to some sort of *allotment* procedure to allocate shares pro rata to subscribers. Rights issues cannot be over-subscribed, but in common with others for sale and public issues they can be under-subscribed, and firms tend to insure against this possibility by writing *underwriting* contracts. An underwriter is someone who agrees, in exchange for a commission to buy any shares which are not subscribed. He, in turn, will spread his risk by writing similar contracts with sub-underwriters. Wilson (1980), talking about rights issues, said 'typically there will be 100 to 200 of these [sub-underwriters] none of whom will generally be asked to underwrite more than 2 or 3% of the issue'. The principle underwriter tends to be the issuing house or broker advising the company, while the sub-underwriters tend to be institutional investors. When it writes an underwriting contract the firm is effectively buying a put option from the underwriter, with an exercise price equal to the issue price of the share.

Table IV Typical costs of ordinary share issues to raise £2m

Item	New issues prospectus or offer for sale		Further issues	
			Placing	Rights
	£		£	£
Capital duty at 1%	20,000		20,000	20,000
Advertising	25,000		–	–
Accountancy fees (Note 1)	20,000		4,000	4,000
Legal fees (Note 1)	15,000		4,000	4,000
Listing fee	2,400	(Note 2)	1,000	1,200
Receiving bankers/registrars fees	15,000		2,000	5,000
Printers:				
Extel Card	2,000		–	–
Allotment Letters	2,000		1,500	1,500
Share Certificates	1,500		1,000	1,000
Offer for Sale	10,000		–	–
Circular	–		4,000	4,000
Underwriting commission at 1¼%	25,000		–	25,000
Broker's commission at ¼%	5,000		5,000	5,000
Issuing house ½% (Note 3)	10,000		10,000	10,000
Total cost of issue	152,900		52,700	80,700
Cost as percentage of proceeds of issue	7.6%	(Note 4)	2.6%	4.0%

Note 1 These figures may be higher depending on the amount of work to be done.

Note 2 This figure relates to the fee for bringing a new company to the market for the first time. Since the percentage of the company's market capitalisation offered to the market on the first occasion is normally a minimum of 35%, the total market capitalisation of the company in this example would be about £5.7 million. The 35% minimum is imposed by The Stock Exchange so as to ensure an adequate spread of shareholdings.

Note 3 This figure can rise to ¾% and the issuing house, whether broker or merchant bank, may also charge an additional fee for pre-issue corporate finance work.

Note 4 This figure appears to be high because it relates to the expenses of bringing a company to the market for the first time (see Note 2). Because of the need for a full prospectus, the advertising, legal, accountancy and printing fees are inevitably higher than would be the case for a company already listed. The figure is expressed as a percentage of the new money being raised but as a proportion of the total market capitalisation of the company is only 2.7%.

Source: Wilson Committee: *Evidence on the Financing of Industry and Trade*, Vol 3 (1978), p 257.

The risk of under-subscription depends on the relation between the issue price and the equilibrium market price of the share, i e on the size of the 'issue discount'. The cheaper the issue price of the shares the less chance of them not being taken up. So 'issue discount' and 'underwriting commission' are effectively substitutes, and some firms have issued at a 'deep discount' when they have had difficulty in getting underwriting on acceptable terms.

Issue discount

The ideal price for an issue of shares would be the price that just 'clears the market' – induces a demand from investors just equal to the number of shares being issued. A higher price means not all the shares are sold. A lower price means foregone revenue from the sale. Moreover, since the share price and the associated cost of capital are inversely related a lower price means an increased cost of capital. It also means a 'dilution' of the wealth of existing shareholders in the firm, and a transfer of wealth to the new investors. The issue discount – the difference between the market clearing price and the actual issue price – is the second major cost associated with new issues.

On the face of it, pricing shares should be like pricing most other products; however there are two special features of shares. First, we would expect the demand curve for any individual share to be horizontal, that is, demand should be perfectly (price-) elastic. This is because if properly priced so that the return on each share exactly reflects the riskiness of that share, all shares should be perfect substitutes for each other. If the demand curve for shares were absolutely horizontal then slight overpricing would result in no-one subscribing while a slight underpricing would lead everyone to subscribe. In practice of course it is not quite like that, and demand curves for shares do have some downward slope. Presumably this is because there is a good deal of uncertainty surrounding share valuation and investors may disagree on their valuations of the firm, and also because unless investors are in equilibrium in a perfect capital market, their marginal evaluation of an additional unit of risk may differ. But the 'horizontality' of demand curves in practice is quite impressive all the same, and explains why a small change in price may lead to a significant over or under subscription.

The second difference is the cost of overpricing a share. Initial overpricing of a product can usually be rectified by subsequent price cuts, discounts or simply by holding the price during inflation. In any case the damage may be cushioned by more successful pricing of other products. But a failure to set a market clearing price for a share issue is usually reckoned a near disaster, to be avoided at all costs. The loss is partly financial, though the firm can insure against this by writing underwriting contracts, but is mainly to do with reputation. At best a failed issue reflects badly on the price-setting skill of the company, but more likely it will be interpreted by the financial community as a market judgement on the quality of the firm itself. New issues are large, well-publicised and rarely-repeated events for the firm.

The problem is that the firm is short of information to guide its price-setting. Pricing an issue of seasoned shares is relatively straightforward since the firm already knows how the market values its existing shares. The main uncertainty concerns movements in the market as a whole that might take place between fixing the issue price and issuing the shares. But with an unseasoned issue the uncertainty is much greater for both the company and for potential investors. Not only are the shares new, but the firm itself may be new and have no substantive history to guide investors and possibly even no comparable firms with market prices that the price-setter can refer to. In the next section we describe an example of this problem; the Hesketh Motorcycle issue, and we include the relevant parts of the issue documents so that the reader can decide for himself what a reasonable price would have been.

Companies react in two ways to this uncertainty. First, they will usually employ experts to handle the issue and bring whatever experience is available to pricing it. Second, they tend to issue at a discount, preferring the cost of underpricing to the risk of overpricing.

Is the market efficient with respect to new issues? Ibbotson, Sindelar and Ritter (1988) found, as would be expected if most shares are being issued at a discount, that abnormal gains could be made in the first month of issue. Ibbotson et al studied good new issues in the US between 1960 and 1987 and found average underpricing of around 16%. In subsequent months, however, the market appeared to be efficient in pricing shares. So, though firms and their advisers appear to be underpricing issues and leaving abnormal gains to be made by subscribers, the subsequent pricing of newly issued shares appears to be efficient. The existence of positive market discounts had led to the existence of another market creature, the *stag*. Stags are people who subscribe for shares they do not intend to keep in order to take advantage of underpricing.

Tenders

The *tender* appears to be an ideal alternative to fixed price issues with all their attendant uncertainty. With a tender issue subscribers indicate how many shares they want and what they are willing to pay. The firm calculates the *striking price* which is the price that would just clear the market, and shares are allocated at the striking price to everyone who bid at or above this price. Competitive bidding systems such as this are in widespread use in countries such as France, and it is a puzzle why they are not more popular in the UK.

In the UK this topic became highly publicised after a spate of heavily over-subscribed issues achieved large discounts. One of these was the privatisation by the government of Amersham International, a high technology producer of radioactive materials. Amersham's offer price of 142p attracted subscriptions of £1.5 billion for £71 million of shares, a 20-fold over-subscription. On the first day of trading, the shares closed at 188p, a premium of 46p, or 32%.

Discussing the problem in the Financial Times of 26 March 1983, Barry Riley concluded that tender offers remained 'deeply unpopular'. One reason may have been that vested interests in the City like brokers and jobbers made good commissions from the active buying and selling that follows heavily-stagged fixed price issues. But a better reason was that tendering may be unfair to the small 'amateur' investor. Riley suggested that there were two types of applicant, the well-informed professional institutional investors who are in regular touch and tend to develop a consensus on the value of each new issue, and the amateurs with neither the advantages of expertise or of knowing what the market feels, and who will make a broader spread of bids. In a heavily-subscribed tender the price will tend to be set by the higher, outlying amateur bids, and the striking price will probably be above the subsequent equilibrium price for the share. The shares 'will tend to go to investors who have misjudged the price. They will stand in the market at a discount, possibly for several years, and the company will get a list of grumbling and frustrated shareholders'. However, tenders still represented the best hope according to Riley. He suggested that the tendering system would be improved if sponsors were more flexible in setting striking prices and if small investors were helped by being able, for example, to accept a striking price set by the institutional investor.

III HESKETH MOTORCYCLES: AN EXAMPLE OF AN UNSEASONED ISSUE

An example of the problems facing the firm and its potential investors in determining the appropriate price for an unseasoned new issue was provided by the Hesketh Motorcycles issue. For extracts from Hesketh Motorcycles' prospectus, see the Appendix to this chapter.

In 1980 the public were invited to subscribe for 1,800,000 ordinary shares in Hesketh Motorcycles Ltd. HML was a new company which had been formed to produce and sell a motorbike, the Hesketh V1000. The project was the brainchild of Lord Hesketh, then aged 29, who was well-known as the owner of a successful motor racing team. The bike had been developed initially by Lord Hesketh's company, Tristar, and another 1,060,180 shares, or 37.1% of the issued capital of HML had been issued at the same time to Tristar as settlement for the development costs they had borne. The HML shares had a nominal value of 50p, and were being offered at a price of 80p to the public. HML was not seeking a stock exchange quotation, but the shares could be traded under rule 163(2).

The interesting feature of the Hesketh offer was its highly speculative nature, which the offer document did not seek to conceal, and which gave it the flavour of venture capitalism. The bike did not yet exist in production-line form; its cost, reliability and customer appeal were essentially unknown. It was attempting to enter a market from which previous UK manufacturers had been expelled by the immensely powerful and efficient Japanese manufacturers.

When a company issues new shares it has to produce a *prospectus*, which is designed to give the potential buyer a reasonable idea of what he is letting himself in for. So, amongst other things it shows the asset position of the issuing firm and a five-year history of its profits and dividends, ten years if the shares are to be quoted. In Hesketh's case, of course, there was no history to show. If the issue is for the purpose of acquiring another company, similar information must be given about that company. If the money is wanted for an internal project it is usual to provide some estimate of the prospects for that project.

In the case of Hesketh the investor had to decide upon the future market prospects of a yet-to-be manufactured super-bike. Extracts from Hesketh's prospectus are included in the Appendix to this chapter and the reader can decide for himself whether he has enough information there to value Hesketh's shares and so make a decision about buying them. Compared to many, the Hesketh prospectus is informative about the project in hand. The problem for the investor was how to cope with the unavoidable uncertainty innate in such a project.

Hindsight

September 1980	The Hesketh issue attracted 925 applicants, and was just 3.1% over-subscribed. At close of business on the first day the shares were trading at 78p, compared to the 80p issue price.
September 1981	Hesketh announced the bike had run into engineering problems, and the sales launch would need to be delayed for six months. The owners were asked to subscribe another £590,000 of working capital.
February 1982	The bike went on sale, six months late. Dealers announced that 250 had been ordered. Hesketh shares rose to 54p from a low of 35p at the end of 1981.
May 1982	Hesketh shares were suspended at 22p. Since the launch 100 bikes had been sold. Hesketh's were 'looking for any options which appear to offer a secure future for the manufacturing operations of the company'.
June 1982	A receiver was appointed, and all production halted. The entire workforce was made redundant.

IV PRICING A NEW ISSUE – A WORKED EXAMPLE

To help envisage the steps in pricing a new issue consider a simple example:

Ralph Cooper

Ralph Cooper is an unquoted public company which wants to raise £1 million from an offer for sale of £1 ordinary shares. The number of shares Cooper has in issue already, N, is 5,000,000. Cooper recently reported the following figures:

Total earnings	£1.2m	Total dividend	£600,000
eps	24p	Dividend per share	12p
		Target payout	50%

The key questions are:

Question 1 How much does Cooper need to raise, £Q? The issue must cover its own transactions costs, and yield £1 million. The administrative costs of an offer for sale of this size are estimated at 6% of the gross. So Cooper must raise

$$Q = £1\text{m} \times \frac{100}{100-6} \simeq £1{,}065{,}000$$

Question 2 What will be the post-issue value of Cooper, V? To find the market value of Cooper we will use, for simplicity, the Gordon model described in Chapter 5. Cooper expects to continue to get a return of 12% from the new injection of £1m, hence earnings will be increased by £120,000 and since target payout is 50%, dividends will increase by £60,000. We elicit that Cooper believes it can maintain a growth rate of 6% indefinitely. A study of firms in the same industry suggests the market is requiring a return of 10% from firms of this risk.

$$\text{Hence, dividend post-issue} = £600{,}000 + .5 \times £120{,}000 = £660{,}000$$
$$\text{dividend-yield} = r_e - g = 10\% - 6\% = 4\%$$
$$\text{value of Cooper, } V = \frac{DIV}{r_e - g} = \frac{£660{,}000}{4\%} = £16{,}500{,}000$$

Question 3 What is the issue discount, DIS? It is felt that an appropriate issue discount on the expected equilibrium price for an offer for sale of this sort would be 10%, so DIS = 10%.

We can now find the issue price, P′, and the number of shares to be issued, N′. For convenience we will work with P, the equilibrium share price, rather than P′, where P′ is P less the issue discount, so $P' = P(1 - DIS)$.

P and N′ are two unknowns, but we have two expressions which determine them:
—We know that the proceeds of the issue, Q, is the number of shares issued, N′, times the issue price, P′.

$$Q = N' \times P'$$
$$= N' \times P(1 - DIS)$$
$$\text{Hence } \underline{1{,}065{,}000 = N' \times .9P} \qquad (1)$$

—We know that the value of the whole firm, V, is the number of shares in issue, N + N′, times the equilibrium price, P.

$$V = (N + N')P$$

Hence $16{,}500{,}000 = (5{,}000{,}000 + N')P$ (2)

Dividing (2) into (1) to eliminate P

$$\frac{1{,}065{,}000}{16{,}500{,}000} = \frac{.9N'}{5{,}000{,}000 + N'}$$

Hence $N' = 386{,}282$
$P = £3.06$

Cooper should issue 386,282 shares at an issue price of £2.75, which gives a discount of 10% on £3.06.

You may doubt that pricing a new issue can be so exact, with a unique issue price and quantity. We wanted to show the necessary relationships between issue price, the number of shares issued and so forth. But in practice there is much more room for manoeuvre because Q, V and D are not single-valued. The firm will not be committed to raising exactly a net £1 million, the post-issue value of the firm is a matter for estimation with a degree of inherent uncertainty, and the issue discount is a matter of choice. In practice pricing a new issue is an iterative process in which different assumptions about Q, V and D generate different values of N′ and P until the firm and its advisers find an acceptable strategy for the issue.

V RIGHTS ISSUES AND THE DILUTION PROBLEM

If an already quoted company issues new shares, Stock Exchange rules require it to make a *rights* issue. This means that the new shares must be offered to the existing shareholders in proportion to their existing holdings. Suppose a company has 1 million shares issued and wants to issue 200,000 more, it will make a 'one for five' rights offer to its existing shareholders. Each shareholder has the right to buy a new share for every five he already owns. He does not have to exercise the right, he can sell it, and if he prefers, the company must sell it for him. Rights issues are made at a discount on market value which can often be around 15%, which is why the 'rights' have a value in themselves.

The issue discount on rights is usually high. However the great virtue of 'rights' is that this does not damage the interests of existing shareholders, which is the reason The Stock Exchange insists on it. If we consider a simple numerical example we can see how giving existing shareholders pre-emptive rights avoids the reduction of their stake when new shares are issued at a discount.

Righteous plc

Righteous plc currently has 1 million shares issued and profits of £500,000 pa. The firm is valued at 10 × earnings, which is £5 million or £5 per share. It has a project in mind which will earn another £100,000 pa. The project will cost £1 million, and if the market continues to value the company in the same way it should add £1 million (10 × £100,000) to the value of the company.

To raise the £1 million, 250,000 new shares are to be issued at £4 each (transactions costs will be ignored throughout this example). After the issue the value of the company will be £6 million, and there will be 1,250,000 shares, so we can work out the new equilibrium share price as £6 million ÷ 1,250,000 = £4.80. The issue price of £4 is giving an effective discount of $\frac{4.80 - 4.00}{4.80} = 17\%$.

We will examine the implications of the above if the shares are issued (1) without, and (2) with pre-emptive rights to existing shareholders.

No pre-emptive rights As we see in the box, the old shareholders suffer an immediate loss of wealth because the value of their shares has fallen by 20p. In effect, by allowing new shareholders to buy an equal share in the earnings of the company cheaper than the new equilibrium market price part of the firm that previously belonged to the old shareholders have been given to the new. The existing shareholders' interest in the firm has been *diluted.*

RIGHTEOUS: WEALTH POSITION, NO PRE-EMPTIVE RIGHTS

	Before issue	After issue
Existing shareholders	£5 million	1,000,000 × £4.80 = £4,800,000
New shareholders	£1 million	250,000 × £4.80 = £1,200,000

With pre-emptive rights Suppose a rights issue is made of one for four (1,000,000 ÷ 250,000) and, since it makes no difference to the answer, assume that all existing shareholders SELL their rights. We would expect the market price of the right to buy for £4 something worth £4.80 to be 80p. So for selling their rights the existing shareholders should receive 80p × 250,000 rights = £200,000. This has the effect, as the box shows, of just restoring the initial positions.

RIGHTEOUS: WEALTH POSITION, WITH RIGHTS

	Before issue	After issue
Existing shareholders	£5 million	£4,800,000 + proceeds of rights, £200,000 = £5 million
New shareholders	£1 million	£1,200,000 − cost of rights, £200,000 = £1 million

One simplifying assumption in the Righteous example was that the value of the new project was the same as its cost, in other words that the internal rate of return of the project equalled the firm's required return, the project had a zero NPV. But suppose the project yields 15% compared to the required return of 10%, everything else as before so the project is worth £1.5 million and the market values the enhanced firm at £6,500,000. The new share price is £6,500,000 ÷ 1,250,000 shares = £5.20. The danger here is that existing shareholders might feel they have done well since, whatever happens, their wealth increases. In fact if the issue was made straight to the public without pre-emptive rights their loss would be even greater than before, in terms of opportunity cost. We can see this by calculating the value of the rights, were it a rights issue. Recall that the value of the rights measures the compensation the shareholders receive for their dilution if it is a rights issue, and thus their loss if it is not. In this case the rights should sell for £5.20 – £4.00 = £1.20 each, or 250,000 × £1.20 = £300,000 in total.

The important message in the Righteous example was that unless a rights issue is used, a new issue at a discount must lead to a transfer of wealth from old shareholders to new. But the corollary is that *the issue price, and the discount, is of no significance in a rights issue.* People sometimes worry about the equilibrium price after the announcement of a pending rights issue i e the *ex-rights* price being lower than the *cum-rights* price (the ex-rights price plus rights). This effect, known as 'dilution', is, however, predictable. In an efficient market the value of ex-rights shares plus the value of all rights outstanding should equal the value of the cum-rights. Marsh (1979) confronted this view in a study of 254 rights issues in the UK between 1962 and 1972. He found only a very small hiccup associated with the rights issue in the time-trend of the share price. On average share capitalisation fell by 0.5% in the months surrounding the rights issue.

Though the pre-emptive rights system avoids dilution, an increasing body of firms see it as a constraint, preventing them taking advantage of lower cost funding opportunities, such as using placing on the domestic or overseas markets. Hence there has been considerable pressure to relax the requirement for pre-emptive rights.

An example of a rights issue: BP

On 19 June 1981 British Petroleum Limited made one of the largest rights issues on record when it announced it was raising £600 million by offering 226,859,583 ordinary 25p shares to its existing shareholders. Since BP already had 1,588,017,084 shares in issue, the new issue was a one for seven rights issue. Shareholders could subscribe for one share for every seven they held on the 29 May. The offer price was 275p. The offer had to be accepted, and a first instalment of 125p paid, by 13 July. The balance of 150p had to be paid by the 2 December, but if the whole 275p were paid on 3 July the share would qualify for an interim dividend in November of 'not less than 6.25p per share'. So the shareholder had to decide if a net 6.25p received after four months was worth more than foregone interest on 150p for five months.

One novel feature of the issue was the role of the UK government. The government was a major shareholder in BP, but in line with its policy at that time of reducing its stake in enterprises, it told BP beforehand that it would not take up its rights. So private shareholders were offered the government's rights, another 1 for 8.69 they already held. But they had to pay 290p for these shares, the extra 15p going to the government for selling their rights.

VI SUMMARY

There are two sorts of cost involved in issuing equity – administrative costs and issue discount. Both costs vary with the size and method of issue. Issue discount, which arises when the firm sells shares at an issue price below their equilibrium market value, is perhaps the most perplexing. Firms regularly issue shares at a price which offers big gains to new shareholders at the expense of the existing shareholders. To avoid this problem The Stock Exchange requires 'seasoned' shares to be made issued by a 'rights issue' to existing shareholders. In a public issue the discount can be reduced by asking applicants to 'tender' for the shares, though in the UK this practice remains relatively unpopular.

APPENDIX HESKETH MOTORCYCLES: SHARE ISSUE PROSPECTUS

This prospectus has been prepared for the purpose of giving information with regard to Hesketh Motorcycles Limited ("HML"). The Directors of HML have taken all reasonable care to ensure that the facts stated herein are true and accurate in all material respects and that there are no other material facts the omission of which would make misleading any statement herein, whether of fact or opinion. All the Directors accept responsibility accordingly.

There is no listing on any stock exchange for the shares of HML and application is not being made to any stock exchange for a listing of any part of HML's capital. However, applications may be made to the Council of the Stock Exchange for permission to transact specific bargains in the shares of HML under Rule 163 (2) of the Rules and Regulations of the Stock Exchange. Persons wishing to deal in the Ordinary shares of HML in accordance with Rule 163 (2) should consult their stockbroker or other professional adviser.

A copy of this prospectus, having attached thereto copies of the documents referred to herein, has been delivered to the Registrar of Companies for registration.

The procedure for application and an Application Form are set out at the end of this document.

Hesketh Motorcycles Limited

(Incorporated under the Companies Acts 1948 to 1976. Registered in England No. 1178402)

OFFER
by
Venture Link Limited
on behalf of HML
for subscriptions for

1,800,000 Ordinary shares of 50p each, fully paid, at 80p per share, payable in full on application.

The Application List will open at 10.00 a.m. on Tuesday, 16th September, 1980 and may be closed at any time thereafter.

THE FUNDS RAISED BY THIS OFFER WILL BE USED TO PUT INTO PRODUCTION A NEW DESIGN OF MOTORCYCLE. BEFORE APPLYING FOR ANY OF THE SHARES HEREBY OFFERED, PROSPECTIVE INVESTORS SHOULD CONSIDER THE RISKS INVOLVED. AN INVESTMENT IN HML MUST BE REGARDED AS SPECULATIVE. ACCORDINGLY THE PARAGRAPH IN THIS DOCUMENT HEADED "RISK FACTORS" SHOULD BE READ CAREFULLY.

Share Capital

Authorised	Issued or to be issued fully paid
£1,750,00 in 3,500,000 Ordinary shares of 50p each.	£1,430,090 in 2,860,180 Ordinary shares of 50p each.

Indebtedness

At the close of business on 29th August, 1980 HML had an unsecured bank overdraft of £14,278 and a loan of £530,762 from Hesketh Tristar Limited ("Tristar") of which £530,000 has since been capitalised as described herein. Save as aforesaid, HML had no loan capital outstanding or created but unissued at that date and no outstanding mortgages, charges, borrowings or indebtedness in the nature of borrowings including bank overdrafts and liabilities under acceptances (other than normal trade bills) or acceptance credits, hire purchase commitments, guarantees or other material contingent liabilities.

Introduction

In 1972 Lord Hesketh, now Deputy Chairman of Hesketh Motorcycles Limited ("HML"), became involved on his own account in the business of Grand Prix motor-car racing under the name of "Hesketh Racing". In July, 1974 he promoted the formation of HML (then called Hesketh Racing Limited), which subsequently acquired the business of Hesketh Racing from him. On 1st May, 1979 HML became a wholly-owned subsidiary of Tristar, a company effectively controlled by Lord Hesketh and the Trustees of the estate of his late father. HML had at its disposal a group of talented designers and engineers who produced the Hesketh Formula I car which, driven by James Hunt, finished fourth in the 1975 Grand Prix World Manufacturers Championship.

The financial burden of maintaining a motor racing team without certainty of sponsorship is very heavy and it became evident that motor racing on its own was unlikely to prove consistently profitable. HML therefore eventually withdrew from direct involvement in Formula I racing. However, through its motor-racing experience, the production team had acquired considerable engineering skills which were used to build up a substantial and profitable specialised automotive engineering business involving the contract overhaul of Formula I and Formula II engines, the manufacture of specialist parts, including suspension components, complete chassis, oil tanks, water pumps and engine sumps, the production of high-precision steel and aluminium machinings and the contract testing, using dynamometers, of diesel and petrol engines for leading manufacturers. During 1977, HML began looking for other ways of exploiting its engineering skills, with the particular aim of developing a proprietary volume product. Among the many possibilities considered were various forms of transportation, of which the motorcycle, due to the rising cost of fuel, the increasing congestion of road traffic and the growth of leisure time, seemed to present the most attractive marketing opportunities.

The current share of the world motorcycle market held by British manufacturers had been reduced to negligible proportions, due mainly to the dominance of the large-volume Japanese manufacturers, with their technologically advanced and competitively priced products. Nevertheless HML's assessment was that an opportunity existed, and should continue to exist in both domestic and export markets for a British-made motorcycle in the high capacity (over 750cc), high-performance, 'superbike' sector. After an intensive and critical analysis of competitive designs and engineering, HML decided towards the end of 1977 to embark on the design of a new high-performance 'superbike' combining individuality and exclusivity with the best traditions of British engineering, with the aim of capturing a profitable share of the rapidly growing high-performance sector of the market.

Reason for the Offer

It was not possible for HML to bring the new motorcycle into volume production without the introduction of external capital. Accordingly it was decided to arrange this by way of an Offer of equity capital which would be underwritten by the group of investment trusts and investment trust management companies brought together by Venture Link Limited and listed in Paragraph 5 (b) of Appendix II of this prospectus.

To facilitate this Offer, the engineering business of HML has been transferred to a subsidiary of Tristar (see Paragraph 4 of Appendix II below), so that HML is now only concerned with the development and production of the new motorcycle.

It has taken some 2½ years from the original conception to produce a motorcycle which, following rigorous testing of several prototypes, is now ready for volume production. The overall specification, design, styling and engineering of this machine, the Hesketh V1000, were the responsibility of the HML team and a sub-contractor was employed to assist HML in the design and engineering of the completely new British engine and gear-box. The entire cost of the motorcycle project up to 30th June, 1980, amounting to approximately £530,000, has been borne by HML and finance by loans from Tristar which have since been repaid or capitalised. Expenditure from 1st July, 1980 to the date of this Offer has been financed by temporary bank borrowings.

The Offer will provide HML with funds of approximately £1,305,000, after allowing for the estimated expenses of the Offer, which will enable it to repay the temporary bank borrowings and to bring the motorcycle into production.

Technical Information on the Hesketh V1000

The 'Hesketh V1000' is a 90° in-line Vee-Twin motocycle of 1,000cc capacity. This configuration allows a low centre of gravity, making for better handling characteristics and permitting a slim compact motorcycle which presents a smaller frontal area, reducing wind resistance and assisting the performance and fuel economy. 90° in-line Vee-Twin engines give optimum smoothness, virtually free from the vibration frequently experienced with other types of 'superbike' engine, whilst four valves per cylinder produce exceptional power without detriment to fuel economy. The V1000 had a top speed of over 130 miles per hour and an average fuel consumption in excess of 50 miles per gallon is attainable under normal riding conditions. The Directors believe that the performance, handling and styling of the V1000 compare favourably with those of competing 'superbikes'.

The design of the V1000 combines a number of features not currently available on other 'superbikes' including a co-axial chain lay-out, which maintains a constant chain tension (greatly improving the life of the chain), and a parallelogram brake linkage system on the rear wheel, which allows the rider to apply the brake with greater safety when cornering.

Prototypes of the V1000 have been extensively road and bench tested and have been test driven by some of Britain's leading experts on high-performance motorcycles, who were consulted on its design and styling during all phases of its development. The V1000 has been shown to a number of leading British motorcycle dealers, all of whom subsequently expressed interest in obtaining dealerships for the machine. It has also received favourable comment in the motorcycle trade press and other media, both in the U.K. and overseas, and HML has as a result received numerous letters from individuals indicating an interest in acquiring a V1000 when a production model is available.

The Market For 'Superbikes'

The Motor Cycle Association of Great Britain Ltd ("MCA") circulates to its members monthly statistics relating to the sale and registration in the United Kingdom of motorcycles from which the following table has been compiled:

Year	Total all types (excluding mopeds)	'Superbikes' only (over 750cc) Units	% increase on previous period	% share of total market
1975	174,751	3,806	—	2.1
1976	188,627	4,804	26.2	2.6
1977	176,031	4,481	(6.7)	2.5
1978	174,095	7,747	72.9	4.4
1979	206,812	11,335	46.3	5.5
1979—6 months to June	94,742	6,041	—	6.4
1980—6 months to June	112,645	6,912	14.4	6.1

The estimated shares of the United Kingdom 'superbike' market during 1979 commanded by the various manufacturing countries were Japan: 64 per cent, Germany: 22 per cent, Italy: 12 per cent and others 2 per cent.

Over the period 1975/9 the share of the total U.K. motorcycle market held by 'superbikes' grew from 2.1 per cent to 5.5 per cent, representing an average compound rate of growth in the number of 'superbikes' sold in the U.K. of some 31 per cent per annum, compared with just under 3.5 per cent per annum for non-'superbikes'. The 'superbike' growth rate in the first six months of 1980, as compared with the corresponding period for 1979, dropped to 14.4 per cent, but this was mainly due to a sharp decline in sales of motorcycles with a capacity of between 751cc and 900cc; in the range of 901cc to 1050cc U.K. sales in the first six months of 1980 were up by over 50 per cent on the same period of 1979, although this rate of growth may have been exceptional and is not believed to have occurred in other European countries.

Statistics similar to those published by the MCA are not readily available in relation to the market for motorcycles on the continent of Europe. However the Directors believe that, whilst, as in the U.K., during the early part of the 1970's continental demand for motorcycles of all types grew very rapidly, there was virtually no growth in the demand for motorcycles below the 'superbike' category during the second half of the decade; in marked contrast, sales of 'superbikes' continued to grow at an impressive rate. 'Superbikes' are believed to have constituted about 2½ per cent of all continental motorcycle sales during 1975 but by 1979 estimated 'superbike' sales had risen to over 50,000 machines per annum, representing about 10 per cent of all continental sales. The Japanese manufacturers' share of the continental 'superbike' market appears still to be growing and is probably slightly higher than their share of the equivalent U.K. market.

The Marketing Plan

HML's marketing plan is based on the cautious assumption that the average rate of increase in sales of 'superbikes' in the United Kingdom and the rest of Europe from the beginning of 1981 onwards will only be about 5 per cent per annum. On this assumption, the number of 'superbikes' sold in the U.K. during 1981 to 1983 would be about 12,000 per annum and the number sold in the rest of Europe would be over 50,000 per annum. HML aims to capture between 5 per cent and 7 per cent of the available U.K. 'superbike' market and between 1 per cent and 2 per cent of the continental 'superbike' market during this period and also to make a limited number of sales into other countries such as Japan, Australia, South Africa and Canada, where a substantial demand for 'superbikes' exists. The United States, although potentially a very large market, is difficult for a foreign manufacturer to penetrate, due to the variety of regulations and legislation in force in the individual states; HML intends to restrict the initial marketing of its products in the U.S.A. to California. If the marketing plan is successfully achieved, HML will be exporting well over half its annual production by 1983.

At the present time only one model, the V1000 Sports Tourer, has been brought to the pre-production stage. However, HML intends to add other models to its range, all built around the same basic engine and gearbox unit. These will include:—

Cafe Racer—A machine with a more finely tuned version of the existing engine, a single seat, dropped handlebars and individual styling. The sales statistics of other manufacturers indicate a substantial worldwide demand for this type of machine, which HML plans to introduce in 1983.

Full Tourer—A machine with the standard engine, full weather-protection fairing and rear-detachable luggage. This configuration is very popular on the Continent and in the U.S.A. HML intends to introduce it in the latter part of 1982.

The above models, together with the existing V1000 Sports Tourer, will form the main Hesketh range which will be supplemented by the introduction, in the second or third year of production, of limited runs of specialised types of motorcycles such as low riders, production racer replicas and special-order personalised motorcycles. In addition, it is intended to enter the market for items such as police motorcycles, engine units for specialist frame-makers and accessories of various types, including clothing and headgear, which can be marketed, although not necessarily manufactured or assembled, by HML. A significant proportion of HML's turnover will also arise in due course from the sale of spare parts.

The Hesketh range of motorcycles will be sold through carefully selected dealers, who will be required to give contractual undertakings in regard to the maintenance of stocks of spares and the promotion of HML's product range in their dealership area. HML expects to appoint approximately 25 dealers to cover the British Isles. Overseas dealers will also be appointed in due course.

It is intended that the recommended retail price of the V1000, when first available, will be in the region of £4,000 including VAT. If it were available now, the price would be about £3,750 including VAT. The current prices of 1000cc production 'superbikes' range from approximately £2,050 to approximately £4,800, the price range reflecting widely differing specifications and performances.

The V1000 will be priced towards the upper end of the 'superbike' range, but the Directors believe that the 'superbike' market is not predominantly price-sensitive and that, having regard to its design and performance, there will be a ready market for the V1000. In addition, they are confident that its running costs will be lower than those of its competitors because of its fuel economy and of their intended policy of offering competitively priced spares. The latter policy should also result in U.K. insurance premiums being lower than those for comparable imported motorcycles.

The Production Plan

The first production models of the V1000 should be available for delivery in the early summer of 1981. No significant sales revenues are therefore expected in HML's current financial year ending 31st March, 1981. The sales effort in the following year, ending 31st March, 1982, will be concentrated mainly on the U.K. market; the first sizeable export deliveries are planned to take place during the year ending 31st March, 1983. The present production plan envisages assembly of sufficient motorcycles to permit the following total deliveries of all models in the Hesketh range:—

Year ending 31st March	Deliveries (Units)
1981	Demonstration models only
1982	1,000
1983	1,700
1984	2,000

HML will consider a further expansion of production, having regard to any additional capital expenditure involved, once a level of 2000 units per annum has been achieved.

Production of the V1000 and of subsequent models will be undertaken by means of an assembly operation and, initially, HML will not be significantly involved in the manufacture of components. A substantial proportion of the funds to be raised by the Offer will be used to purchase jigs and tools which will be made available to selected manufacturers for use in the volume production of the relevant components. A system of selective quality assurance testing will be allied to all deliveries of components before they are accepted. HML will then assemble, test, market and deliver the completed motorcycles. These will, in their turn, be subjected to rigorous final inspection and quality control procedures. The Directors will give consideration in due course to the manufacture of a greater proportion of components.

Premises and Staff

HML is currently negotiating to take an underlease for a period of 21 years on industrial premises at Daventry, Northamptonshire, comprising a factory with an area of 25,200 sq. ft., including 3,500 sq. ft. of office accommodation and a parking area sufficient for 60 cars, at a commencing annual rental of £44,000, subject to review every 5 years.

The Directors intend to sub-let, on an annual basis, a self-contained unit of 4,200 sq. ft., including 850 sq. ft. of office accommodation, at a proposed rental of £7,800 annually, until such time as HML requires the additional space. Subject to completion of the negotiations and legal arrangements, occupation of the factory and part of the office space is expected to begin in November, 1980; the remainder of the office space will be ready for occupation in the spring of 1981. These premises will provide sufficient space for HML's requirements in the immediate future. Daventry is some 10 miles from Easton Neston, Towcester, where the development of the V1000 has been carried on to date.

In the initial pre-production stage, following this Offer, the nucleus of the staff required by HML will consist of some 10 experienced employees who have all been engaged in the development of the V1000. Additional staff will be recruited locally, as required, and trained by HML. It is expected that HML will be employing a total workforce, including part-time workers, of some 30 by 31st March, 1981, rising to about 75 when a production rate of 2,000 machines per annum is achieved. Having regard to current employment conditions in the engineering industry in the Midlands, HML expects no difficulty in recruiting staff of the required calibre.

Management

Chairman

Sir Barrie Heath, aged 64, was appointed non-executive Chairman on 20th August, 1980. Until the beginning of 1980 he was Group Chairman of Guest, Keen & Nettlefolds Limited. He is a director of Barclays Bank Limited, Pilkington Brothers Limited, Smiths Industries Limited and Tunnel Holdings Limited and a member of the European Advisory Council of Tenneco Inc. He has wide experience of production engineering, particularly in the motor industry.

Deputy Chairman

Lord Hesketh, aged 29, has, since the appointment of Sir Barrie Heath as Chairman, become Deputy Chairman of HML. The development of the V1000 has been made possible by the financial support provided by Tristar, of which he is Chairman and which is effectively controlled by him and the Trustees of his late father's estate. Lord Hesketh intends to devote a large part of his time to the affairs of HML, particularly in regard to the marketing and promotion of its products.

Managing Director

Antony Horsley, aged 36, is the Managing Director of HML and has been responsible for the overall supervision of the V1000 programme. He was until recently Managing Director of Tristar and of other companies in the Tristar group of companies ("the Tristar Group"), but has now resigned his executive positions within the Tristar Group in order to devote his full time to the affairs of HML. He remains a non-executive director of Tristar and its subsidiary companies and is also a Trustee of the late 2nd Baron Hesketh's estate.

Technical Director

Geoffrey Johnson, AMIET, aged 45, is Technical Director of the Tristar Group. He will be devoting the major part of his time to the affairs of HML and is, and will continue to be, responsible for the design and engineering of the V1000 and for the technical programme required to bring it to the production stage and to introduce additional models to the range. He was formerly Chief Engineer of engine design in the Austin-Morris Division of British Leyland, and, before that, Chief Designer to British Racing Motors Limited (BRM).

Financial Director

Leslie Hartwell, FCCA, MBIM, aged 44, is Financial Director of the Tristar Group and of other concerns connected with the Hesketh family's interests. He has occupied senior executive positions with Slough Estates Limited and Richard Johnson & Nephew Group Limited. He will be responsible for controlling the financial affairs of HML and for introducing the production control, stock control and accounting systems needed to administer its operations. It is planned that a full-time Financial Director of HML will be recruited in the near future, whereupon Mr. Hartwell will relinquish his directorship of HML.

Non-executive Director

David Simpson, aged 46, was appointed a non-executive Director on 20th August, 1980. He is a Director of Heritable Group Holdings Limited and Managing Director of Heritable Industrial Holdings Limited. He is also Managing Director of Godwin Warren Holdings Limited, Chairman of Godwin Warren Engineering Limited and Chairman of Mokes & Co. Limited. Prior to other appointments, he was labour relations manager at Vauxhall Motors Limited, Plant Director of a manufacturing division of Chrysler (UK) Limited and Director of Manufacturing of Leyland Cars Limited.

It is expected that a further appointment to the Board, to fill the post of Production Director, will be made shortly and additional executives, at or below Board level, including a marketing manager, will be recruited as needed. The Directors have also agreed to give consideration to the appointment to the Board in due course of a further non-executive director to be nominated by Venture Link Limited.

To meet HML's short term requirements for administrative and technical assistance, Tristar and HML have entered into a Management and Services Contract (see paragraph 7 (d) of Appendix II). The cost to HML of the executive services of Lord Hesketh, Mr. Johnson and Mr. Hartwell, who will remain directors and employees of Tristar, but who will devote a large part of their time to the affairs of HML, will be covered by payments under this Contract. Apart from such payments it is not expected that any substantial trading will take place between HML and Tristar or any of its subsidiaries. Such trading as may occur will be strictly on an arm's-length basis.

Mr. Antony Horsley has entered into an Agreement to serve as Managing Director of HML for a period of three years commencing on 1st September 1980 (see Paragraph 7 (c) of Appendix II).

Proceeds of the Offer and Working Capital

The estimated net proceeds of the Offer, after expenses of £135,000, will amount to £1,305,000, the whole of which will be applied in the provision of working capital, including the repayment of temporary bank borrowings incurred since 30th June, 1980. It is expected that some £500,000 of this sum will be utilised during the pre-production period on the acquisition of jigs, tools, test equipment and other items of a capital nature.

The Directors of HML are satisfied that, having regard to the net proceeds of the Offer and to bank facilities which are available, HML will have sufficient working capital to enable it to achieve its present production plan.

Substantial Shareholding

Following the Offer, Tristar and a subsidiary of Tristar will respectively own 1,060,000 and 180 Ordinary shares in HML, representing in aggregate 37.1 per cent of the total issued capital. Tristar has given an undertaking to Venture Link Limited and to Grieveson, Grant and Co. (see Paragraph 7 (a) of Appendix II), that it will not, save in certain exceptional circumstances, dispose of any part of its holding of 1,060,000 shares before 30th September, 1983.

Preferential Applications

Of the 1,800,000 Ordinary shares which are the subject of this Offer, a total of 20,000 shares are reserved for allotment, at the issue price of 80p, against applications received from Directors and employees of HML and of the Tristar Group, numbering some 87 persons.

Employees' Profit Sharing Scheme

The Directors intend as soon as appropriate to establish an Inland Revenue-approved Profit Sharing Scheme to provide a continuing incentive to employees who have served an appropriate qualifying period of employment by assisting them to become shareholders in HML. Full details of the Scheme would be submitted to the Shareholders for approval.

Future Prospects and Profitability

Full production drawings of, or specifications for, all the components required for the manufacture of the V1000 have been prepared and submitted to possible suppliers for the purpose of obtaining written estimates. The estimates received, together with HML's own estimates of the size and cost of the direct and indirect labour force required and of the overheads and other expenditure involved, have been used to calculate the overall unit production cost of the motorcycle at different levels of production. All estimates have been adjusted, where appropriate, for the possible effects of inflation between the dates of the original estimates and the anticipated start of production. The unit cost would, of course, be affected by the introduction of different models into the range at a later date.

Volume deliveries of the V1000 are not likely to commence before May, 1981. HML will therefore make a trading loss in its current financial year ending 31st March, 1981, partially offset by interest earned on invested funds. Thereafter, profitability will depend on a number of factors including the selling price of the V1000 and associated spares, the number of motorcycles produced and sold, the volume of sales of spare parts and the cost of materials and labour.

However, on the assumption that production is confined to the V1000 Sports Tourer, the table set out below shows the expected profitability of the operation at different levels of production, assuming a constant recommended retail selling price of £3,950 per machine and making no allowance for Profits derived from the sale of spare parts or accessories or for interest earned on the temporary investment of surplus funds. The table, which is based on the historical cost convention, provides for the writing off of the deferred research and development expenditure incurred on the motorcycle up to 30th June, 1980, amounting to £494,681, at the rate of £60 per motorcycle sold. At that rate of amortisation it is expected that the whole of the £494,681 will be written off within a period of five years from the start of deliveries. Amortisation provided in this fashion, being in respect of expenditure already incurred, will not involve any additional cash outgoing.

No. of units sold per annum	1,000	1,500	2,000
Turnover	£2,836,000	£4,254,000	£5,672,000
Operating profit after charging current research and development expenditure	£310,000	£700,000	£1,050,000
Exceptional item: Amortisation of deferred research and development expenditure	£60,000	£90,000	£120,000
Operating profit after exceptional item	£250,000	£610,000	£930,000

The figures in the above table should not be taken to represent profit forecasts. However if they were to represent HML's pre-tax profits for any particular financial year, the following hypothetical earnings and ratios, based on the Offer price of 80p per share, would result:—

Pre-tax earnings per share:			
Before exceptional item	10.8p	24.5p	36.7p
After exceptional item	8.7p	21.3p	32.5p
Price/earnings ratios on nil tax basis:			
On earnings before exceptional item	7.4	3.3	2.2
On earnings after exceptional item	9.2	3.8	2.5
Price/earnings ratios on a notional 52 per cent tax charge:			
On earnings before exceptional item	15.4	6.8	4.5
On earnings after exceptional item	19.1	7.8	5.1

The Directors have been advised that the majority of the deferred research and development expenditure of £494,681 incurred on the motorcycle project up to 30th June, 1980 will be allowable as a deduction against future trading profits liable to Corporation Tax. Having regard to this and to tax allowances which will arise from future expenditure on development and on capital items, the need to provide for Corporation Tax in the accounts covering the first two years of production should be extinguished or significantly reduced.

Accounts and Additional Information

There is set out in Appendix I a copy of the Report by the Auditors and Reporting Accountants showing the financial position of HML as at 30th June, 1980 together with a Pro-Forma Balance Sheet showing the position following the outcome of this Offer. It is intended that HML shall prepare its accounts as at 31st March of each year. Interim reports will also be issued, but not in respect of the six months ended 30th September, 1980.

There is set out in Appendix II certain additional statutory and general information.

Dividends

It is the Directors' intention that HML should commence paying dividends once sufficient distributable profits are available. The timing and amount of the first distribution will depend partly on the results achieved and partly on the extent to which funds may be required to finance further expansion of production.

Risk Factors

Prospected investors in HML should recognise that since the motorcycle project is not an established manufacturing and trading operation, the following special risk factors apply:—

(i) the V1000 design is new and, in spite of extensive pre-production testing, the machine could still reveal design faults requiring rectification;

(ii) volume assembly and production has not yet commenced and "teething troubles" could be experienced, with consequent delays in meeting delivery targets; and

(iii) estimates of the potential market for the V1000 and other models to be introduced in due course, which the Directors believe to be realistic, may not be achieved.

REFERENCES AND BIBLIOGRAPHY

Asquith, P, and Mullins, D W — 'Equity Issues and Offering Dilution' Journal of Financial Economics 15, January–February 1986, pp 61–90.

Hansen, R S, and Pinkerton, J M — 'Direct Equity Financing: A Resolution of a Paradox', Journal of Finance 37, June 1982, pp 651–666.

Ibbotson, R G, Sindelar, J L, and Ritter, J R — 'Initial Public Offerings', Journal of Applied Corporate Finance, 1988, pp 37–45.

Masulis, R W, and Korwar, A N — 'Seasoned Equity Offerings: An Empirical Investigation', Journal of Financial Economics, 1986, pp 91–118.

Marsh, P R — 'Equity Rights Issues and the Efficiency of the UK Stock Market', Journal of Finance, 1979, pp 839–862.

Ritter, J R — 'The "Hot Issue" Market of 1980', Journal of Business 57, 1984, pp 215–240.

Rock, K — 'Why New Issues Are Underpriced', Journal of Financial Economics 15, January–February 1986, pp 187–212.

Smith, C W — 'Alternative Methods for Raising Capital: Rights versus Underwritten Offerings', Journal of Financial Economics 5, December 1977, pp 273–307.

'Wilson Report' — Committee to Review the Functioning of Financial Institutions, Report (Cmnd 7937).

Wilson, Sir H — *Evidence on the Financing of Industry and Trade*, Vol 3, (1980).

QUESTIONS

1 What are the distinguishing characteristics of equity and debt from the point of view of an investor?

2 Dombey plc is considering 'rights', 'offer for sale' and 'tender' as methods of share issue. Report to Dombey advising them on their new issue strategy. Indicate the advantages and disadvantages of the main alternative methods, and the relative costs of each.

3 Dombey currently has 20 million shares in issue and a share price of £1. The shares sell at a P/E of 10 and a dividend yield of 5%. Dombey's directors are planning to raise £4 million of cash through the share issue and they hope this new investment in the business will increase earnings by £500,000 per annum.

Making some reasonable assumptions about costs of issue, calculate the effect on shareholders' wealth of the three alternatives which Dombey is considering. State clearly any assumptions you have made.

CHAPTER 15

Debt

Debt finance comes in many forms: as loan stock, 'convertibles', and preference shares; as bank loans and overdrafts; but also in disguise in the form of leasing and factoring arrangements and trade credit. By far the main source of debt finance for UK firms is short-term bank borrowing, particularly in the form of 'overdraft' arrangements. Long-term debt has become a relatively minor source of company finance, though there is still some interest in loan-stock that is 'convertible' into shares.

Section I gives an overview of debt financing, and discusses the risks of debt and the valuation of a debt contract. Section II considers long-term debt including preference shares, and Section III considers the special problems in analysing convertible loan-stock and warrants. In Section IV we consider the raising of short-term loans.

I AN OVERVIEW OF DEBT FINANCE

In a *debt* contract the supplier of funds becomes a *creditor* of the firm for the principal and interest it owes him. The contrast is with equity where the supplier becomes an *owner* of the firm. The debt/equity distinction is only meaningful in an uncertain world. If the future were known with certainty everyone would receive a known stream of returns, and since there would be no risk involved, we would expect everyone to require the same rate of return. In reality though, financing firms is risky. Firms may prosper exceedingly, or they may fail and dissipate all their assets, and ahead of time we cannot be sure which is going to happen. By investing in firms the equity shareholder runs the risk of losing some or all of his money, but this risk is balanced by the possibility of sharing in any surplus the firm makes. The problem for the debt-holder is that he has 'downside risk' too, he stands to lose his money. But he cannot participate in the firm's positive variances since his claims have an upper limit.

We need to understand the various ways in which debt-holders can protect themselves from this asymmetry in their risk. First they write protective *covenants* into the debt contract to try and reduce the risk of the firm failing to meet their claims. Second they will often look to take a title over some of the firm's assets as *security* for the loan. Debt claims have, in any case, priority over equity and so third it might seem wise for debt to prevent the *gearing* of the firm, the ratio of debt to equity, from getting too high. This way there will not be too many people making prior claims on the same cake. Any residual risk after all this will be reflected in the cost of debt capital.

One of the fundamental lessons of finance is that risk cannot be *reduced* by writing financial contracts, but it can be *shifted* somewhere else. It is useful to bear this is mind when we look at the efforts of individual debt-holders to protect themselves.

Restrictive covenants

Debt-holders have a problem of downside risk, and this is compounded by the fact that, unlike equity, they have no general right to control the firm. Debt contracts often contain quite complex sets of *restrictive covenants* designed to give debt some control and the right to void the contract if the firm commits certain future acts that damage debt-holders' interests. Table I shows the sort of restrictions commonly found in debt contracts.

Table I Typical restrictions on debt agreements

- Limitations on the amount the firm may borrow, secured or unsecured; or undertakings that certain specified ratios will be maintained.
- A prohibition on the creation of any further charges on the assets of the business (sometimes known as a 'negative pledge').
- Limitations on the amount of remuneration that the directors may draw, and on dividends; and continuance of existing directors' loans to the business.
- The right of the investor or lender to monitor the performance of the business and to receive regular financial information.
- The right of the investor or lender to appoint a director to the board (this is more usual in the case of an equity investment).
- The right to be consulted about specific developments or unusual transactions.

Source: *Money for Business* (Fifth Edition, 1985, page 28) Bank of England

The problem facing debt-holders is that after writing the contract, with terms specifying the term and amount of the loan and the rate of interest, the firm can do things which materially alter the debt-holder's position. It may issue more debt of equal or greater *seniority*; it may distribute as dividends or salaries assets the creditors were looking to as security; it may develop a more risky investment strategy, the benefits of which would be reaped by equity but the costs of which might be borne by debt. Restrictive covenants attempt to limit the power of firms to do these things.

The effects of restrictive covenants can be dramatic. We see an example of this in Chapter 23 when we study the bankruptcy of Stone-Platt. Amongst other conditions, Stone-Platt's lenders had included a clause requiring a particular level of gearing to be maintained. When Stone-Platt wrote off some big losses against reserves this pushed gearing over the limit, and a good part of Stone-Platt's debt became repayable on demand. Stone-Platt also had *cross-default* covenants which mean that once it defaulted on one debt, other debts became repayable too.

Security

Debt-holders have priority over equity in the payment of interest, and in repayment of the principal if the firm is wound up. But if a debt is *secured* it has priority over other creditors too. Loans can be secured by a *fixed* or a *floating* charge. If the charge is fixed the debt contract identifies specific assets and restrictive covenants identify particular events which will permit the debt-holders to sell those assets to recover the debt. Once the sale is trigged the debt-holders or a *trustee* representing them will appoint a *receiver* to enter the firm and arrange for the sale of the assets.

Effectively, by securing an asset, a part of the ownership rights is being transferred to the debt-holder, namely the right to dispose of it in certain circumstances, though not the right to use it. And when he does dispose of it any surplus remaining after he has discharged his debt belongs to the shareholders. An alternative to the fixed charge is the 'floating' charge. Under a 'floating' charge there are no restrictions on the firm's right to dispose of its assets prior to default.

Because taking security puts a lender at the front of the queue of creditors it reduces his risk at the expense of other creditors by reducing the fund of assets available to meet their claims. To help creditors assess their risk, company law requires each company to make available at Companies House a list of the prior charges over its assets.

The firm's ability to offer security depends on having the right sort of assets, that is, assets with relatively secure realisable value and assets whose continued existence is easy to monitor. Offices and houses form good security, while highly specialised plant and machinery, or stocks of raw materials or bank accounts might not. The creditor will usually look for security whose face value is some multiple of the debt to be secured. Given the inherent uncertainty of future realisable values, and the transactions costs associated with selling assets, a creditor might well look for £100,000 or more of security to secure a loan of £50,000.

When the firm does not have adequate securable assets it is quite common, particularly in smaller firms, for creditors to accept personal security from directors or third parties. Directors might pledge personal property: houses, insurance policies, jewellery; or give a personal *guarantee*, which is effectively a floating charge on the individual's assets.

II LONG-TERM DEBT

In this section we discuss long-term debt, which we will call any debt with an initial term of over ten years. Firms can arrange *term loans and mortgage loans*. A term loan may have a fixed or variable rate of interest, will normally be secured, and have a term of up to twenty years. The prime sources of term loans are the clearing banks and merchant banks, and the institutions – pension funds and insurance companies. A mortgage loan tends to be of longer term and is usually raised from a pension fund or insurance company against the security of land or property. Alternatively the firm can issue securities such as loan-stock, preference shares or convertibles.

Loan-stock, 'debentures', or 'bonds' as they are commonly known in the US, are similar to share capital in some respects. The firm issues securities embodying a written acknowledgment of the loan. These securities can be traded by their owners and the company can change their marketability by having them listed on The Stock Exchange. Like shares, public issues of loan-stock must be accompanied by a prospectus. The holders of the loan-stock have their rights specified in a 'trust deed' rather like the articles of association which protect equity, and it is usual to appoint a *trustee* to monitor the firm and act on behalf of the holders if the terms are infringed.

Unlike equity capital loan-stock is usually repaid after a finite period though irredeemable loan-stocks is also found. Often the trust deed will give the firm a range of opportunities to *call* or *redeem* the loan-stock. So '7½% loan-stock 1997–99' indicates that the loan-stock is redeemable at the firm's option some time between these dates. However, the firm can repurchase its loan-stock and so effectively redeem it at any time. Unless the firm thinks it can outguess the market about future interest rates repurchasing loan-stock in the market is fairly uninspiring behaviour. It is simply a repayment of capital, a zero-NPV transaction which seems to imply the firm has insufficient positive-NPV projects in the offing. But redemption can be worthwhile. Redeemable loan-stock has a fixed redemption price. Falling interest rates can drive the market price of debt above the redemption price. When this happens the firm should redeem at the first opportunity and refinance at the new lower interest rates.

Preference shares are annoying analytically because they are on the margin between debt and equity; they look like equity, but are effectively debt. There are several variants of the preference share contract but in a 'basic' plain vanilla preference share the holder receives a fixed and predetermined 'dividend', and a repayment of capital if the firm is liquidated in priority to other equity but after the claims of other creditors, including loan-stock, have been met. In common with equity, the firm does not *have to* pay the agreed dividend on a basic preference share, and if it misses the dividend one year the missed dividend does not become a debt of the firm to be made up in future periods. But this characteristic is remedied in a *cumulative* preference share – in this case the firm must make good previous years' preference dividends before paying a dividend to ordinary shares.

Preference shares are usually permanent finance, i e irredeemable. But firms sometimes issue redeemable preference shares which are redeemable in a predetermined period in a similar way to loan-stock. Since company law views preference shares as equity and a basic tenet of company law is that equity should not be repaid, firms are only allowed to redeem preference shares under strict conditions, one of which is that the preference capital of the business should be replaced by an equivalent reserve so that the equity of the firm as a whole is not reduced.

Our criterion for equity was that it yields 'ownership' of the surplus or residue generated by the firm. On this criterion the basic preference contract does not qualify as equity but appears to have the features of loan-stock but with the lower priority in the distribution of income and capital. However another variant of the preference contract appears to qualify. Firms sometimes issue *participating* preference shares which give their owners a share in the surplus of the firm on top of a fixed dividend. If preference shares truly ranked equally with other equity for the surplus of the firm, they would be equity. In practice this is uncommon, and we treat preference shares as debt when analysing the capital structure of a firm.

We do not need to spend too much time agonizing whether preference shares are equity or debt. Debt and equity are truly points on a continuum, so it should be no surprise that we can find contracts combining elements of both. Preference shares ought to be unpopular. Because of their nominal 'equity' status of preference shares preference 'dividends' are not deductible for tax in the same way as interest payments, thus increasing the cost to the firm of servicing this form of finance relative to equivalent loan-stock. However, preference shares have undergone something of a renaissance, and firms seem prepared to pay a real price, in terms of tax efficiency, for a cosmetic gain in terms of an accounting classification as equity. In fact for a firm facing certain covenant restrictions, for a regulated firm, or for a bank trying to bolster its equity for capital-adequacy tests, this may make some sense; even more so if, as some firms have found, the tax cost can be reduced by issuing overseas.

The market for long-term debt

We can think of good reasons not to issue preference shares, but Table II shows that long-term debt has also varied in popularity with redemptions exceeding new issues in some years.

When inflation is running at a high level, firms are reluctant to commit themselves to long-term loans at high, fixed, interest rates because of the danger of being burdened with a crippling interest bill if the rate of inflation fell, and with it nominal returns. The obvious alternative would be floating-rate or *index bonds*, where the interest rate is linked to a general price index. These are in widespread use in some countries that have experienced chronic high inflation. In the UK the sticking point has been the government, whose

Table II Annual debt issues by UK listed public companies (£m)							
	1982	*1984*	*1986*	*1988*	*1989*	*1990*	*1991*
Preference shares (net issues)	8	42	65	744	898	420	793
Convertible loan capital & debentures	8	101	55	446	1,134	698	(78)
Other loan capital	187	180	851	349	1,511	(1,171)	(344)

Source: CSO Financial Statistics, HMSO

borrowing has set the culture in the bond market. Though the UK government has offered some index-linked arrangements to investors, there has been no major move to indexing, which may reflect the confidence that governments, free of the risk of bankruptcy, can have about their ability to meet future claims.[1] What action there has been in the market for long-term corporate debt has involved 'convertible loan-stock' which we analyse in the next section.

III CONVERTIBLES AND WARRANTS

The problem with debt is the 'downside risk' – the investor runs the risk of loss but cannot share in the success of the firm. In a world of high interest rates and uncertain inflation investors may be particularly reluctant to tie themselves to lending long-term at fixed interest. In finance theory our usual belief is that risk can be assessed and compensated by a suitable risk-premium, but in practice this may not be so. A way round this problem is to offer loan-stock that is *convertible* into shares or, similarly, loan-stock with *warrants* attached that give the investor the right to buy shares. We will start by looking at warrants.

Warrants

A *warrant* is an option which gives the holder the right to buy shares in the firm at a given exercise price at some time in the future. Firms issue warrants for various reasons; they can be attached to loan-stock, they are sometimes issued as part of the consideration for a merger or issued to favoured individuals associated with the firm. The share options that employees get under the share-participation schemes that many firms run are akin to warrants except that the employee's rights are usually limited – he cannot usually sell the share option and often has to hold the share for a certain period after he has exercised the option.

Warrants are options on the underlying share. The only difference between warrants and traded options is that warrants tend to have a longer term, usually several years, and they are issued by the firm rather than being sold by another investor. When the warrant is exercised, new shares come into being. We know from Chapter 10 that the value of the warrant will be as shown in Figure I.

On the day the warrant is exercised its value is the greater of the share price less the exercise price, and zero. Prior to that the warrant's value will be a convex function lying above this. A warrant with 'time to go' will always sell at some positive value. This value will

1 See the Bank of England Quarterly Bulletin, March 1981, for a fuller discussion of these issues.

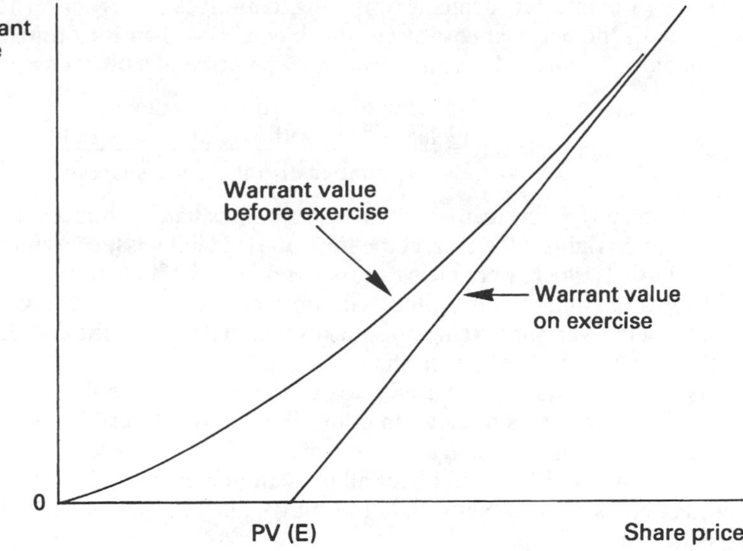

Figure I The value of a warrant

also be an increasing function of the time to expiry, the riskless interest rate, and the variance on the underlying share, and a decreasing function of the exercise price.

Convertibles

In a convertible issue the investor buys loan-stock, but has the option to convert it into shares at some time in the future. Issuing convertibles is rather like issuing loan-stock with warrants attached although there are some differences. For example the convertible-holder forfeits his loan-stock when he converts, while the holder of loan-stock with warrants retains his loan-stock when he exercises the warrants. So from the firm's point of view, it gets an extra cash injection when the warrants are exercised. Also, the holder can detach the warrant from the loan-stock and sell it separately. Another difference, as we see later, is that convertibles can get rather complicated to analyse.

In 1982 Habitat issued £37,502,847 of 9½% convertible unsecured loan-stock as part of the consideration for its purchase of the Mothercare chain of childswear shops. Interest on the loan-stock was payable on the 15 April and the 15 October each year and the loan-stock would be redeemed at par in four equal instalments from 1998 to 2001. However, before then the holder had the right to convert the stock into 10p ordinary shares at the rate of £145 per 100 shares. This right could be exercised on 30 November in any of the years 1985 to 1998.

To sacrifice £145 of loan-stock for 100 shares puts a price of £1.45 on each Habitat share. This is the *conversion price*. At the date of the issue Habitat shares were actually standing at 103p, 42p less than the conversion price. This difference is normally called the *conversion premium*. It is usual to issue convertibles at a positive conversion premium – the expectation is that by the time conversion is possible the price of the underlying share may have risen enough to make conversion worth while. On the other hand the convertible will sell at a premium over the value of equivalent 'straight' loan-stock, simply because the convertible is more attractive to investors. It is loan-stock plus an option. So the firm will raise more per £1 of interest payments by issuing loan-stock that is convertible, or put the other way round, the *apparent* cost of convertibles is less than for ordinary loan-stock. People sometimes calculate the *rights premium* to describe this difference, where

$$\text{rights premium} = \frac{\text{value of convertible} - \text{value of loan-stock without conversion rights}}{\text{number of underlying shares}}$$

In the UK, since very few loan-stocks are quoted it is hard to find a comparable stock without conversion rights. However, at the time of the Habitat issue, preference shares in ICI, a blue-chip UK stock, were giving a gross yield of 14.1%, compared to the nominal yield of 9½% on Habitat's convertible. The nominal rate on the convertible combined with the value of the warrant attached to it makes the total yield on the convertible package comparable to that of the preference shares.

Warrants and convertibles that have yet to be exercised are 'overhanging'. Recognising that *overhanging* convertibles threaten to dilute the equity interest, firms are required to publish earnings-per-share data in undiluted and fully-diluted form. In the latter case the firm works out what its EPS would be if all outstanding convertibles and warrants were converted. Habitat's 1982 EPS was 9.9p but 'fully-diluted', if all outstanding loan-stock were converted, it was 9.3p.

In the simplest case a convertible is just loan-stock with warrants attached. Figure II shows how its value will behave. Now the lower boundary which is the thick line has two components: the value of a 'straight' bond which is an increasing function of the share value because bond and share both depend on the underlying value of the firm, and the conversion value, which is the 45° line through the origin. We can see how the convertible's 'option' properties determine its value. The convertible with some life left will sell at a premium over the lower boundary and is shown by the dotted line in Figure II. We could find the specific value of such a convertible by valuing the 'straight' loan-stock, and using Black-Scholes (see Chapter 10) to value the warrant component. However the problem in practice is that convertibles are rarely so simple. Convertibles usually have two features

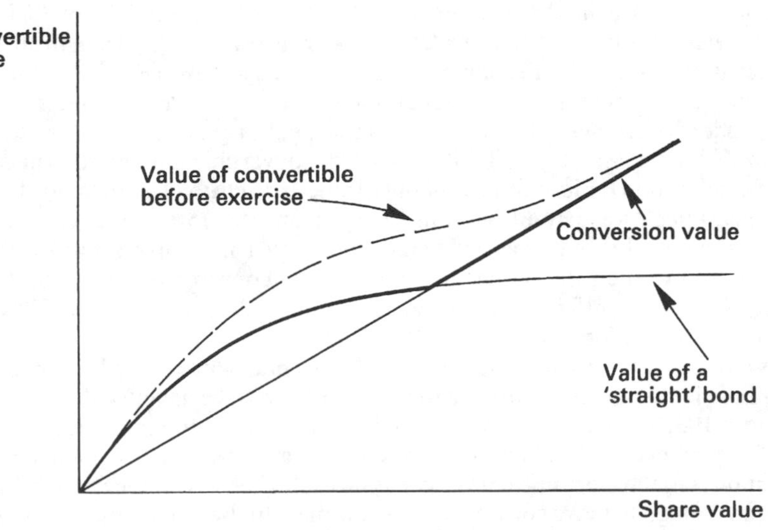

Figure II Value of a convertible

that make them rather complicated to value: they are *callable*, and the underlying share pays *dividends*. When we talked about a 'simple' convertible earlier, we meant a convertible without these features. Theorists are able to value convertibles with calls and dividends, but the solutions are rather complex. We will simply give some insights into the problem.

Dividends and dilution

In deriving the Black-Scholes model it was convenient to assume the underlying share did not pay dividends. Amongst other things this meant we could use the BS model for European call valuation to value the American options we usually meet in practice.

But if the underlying share pays dividends the option holder might want to exercise early, which he could with an American call. So she values the American call more highly, and the Black-Scholes model is no longer appropriate. Just the same problem arises in valuing warrants and convertibles as dividend-paying shares. If the share pays a dividend it might be in the bond-holder's interest to convert just before the share goes ex div. Once the share goes ex div the conversion value of the convertible will drop.

There is a general problem that all debt-holders face – the risk that management will subsequently make decisions, after the debt contract is written, that harm debt. We saw that debt-holders try to protect themselves by writing restrictive covenants into the debt contract. One particular risk for convertible holders is that the firm will make a stock split and so reduce the conversion value of the convertible. Convertible contracts usually *protect* holders from this risk by acquiring that conversion rights be adjusted after a stock split to maintain the value of the conversion rights. So if convertibles have a right to buy 100 shares for £145 stock, and the firm subsequently makes a 1 for 5 stock split, the conversion rights will need to be adjusted to 120 shares for £145 stock.

Sometimes however the convertible contract consciously specifies conversion rights that change over the life of the bond. The conversion value of the bond may be stepped-up or down at discreet intervals. A change in conversion rights has the same effect as a dividend on the underlying share, and can similarly lead bond-holders to convert early. Generally speaking there is a large range of managerial actions that can have the effect of changing the bond-holders' conversion rights by changing the value of the underlying share. Convertible contracts cannot provide full protection from these risks.

Calls

Another feature which complicates the analysis of convertibles is the call provision. The firm can usually *call* its convertibles in just the same way as it can redeem ordinary loan-stock. The firm has an option to call the convertible at a specified call price, and the convertible-holder must either accept the cash or convert immediately. So the call option has the effect of forcing conversion. Now, the convertible is a compound of three things: an ordinary bond plus a warrant to buy shares, less a call option sold to the firm.

Ingersoll (1977a) shows that the value-maximising policy for the firm is to call a convertible only when its conversion value equals the call price. To call earlier or later than that means that the firm is making its convertible-holders richer than it needs to. When Ingersoll investigated what firms actually do, in a subsequent paper (Ingersoll (1977b)), he found a strange thing. On average, the 124 US firms which called convertibles between 1968 and 1975 and which Ingersoll investigated did not call until conversion value was 44% higher than the call price. In other words they allowed convertible-holders to convert at a price 44% higher than they needed to. One explanation put forward for this has been that firms, conscious of future financing needs, do not want to leave their investors with a bad flavour in their mouths for the company's shares.

The appeal of convertibles

Convertibles, loan-stock-with-warrants, and other variants such as convertible preference shares are complex financing contracts combining elements of debt and equity. Convertibles look very attractive to all concerned. The investor apparently gets the best of both worlds; the relative security of creditor status plus the chance of participating if things go well. The firm raises finance at a cost apparently below even the cost of debt. There may be firms which analyse convertibles this way, but we expect firms to be more rational! When the investor buys a convertible he is effectively buying two things: an ordinary loan-stock plus an *option* to buy shares at a given price sometime in the future. It is the value of this option that accounts for the increased value of the convertible. But to calculate the cost of funds raised this way by relating it to the cost of servicing the debt-plus-option bundle, would be misleading. There is a hidden cost in issuing convertibles, it is the series of dividend payments, starting some time in the future, that the holder will become entitled to as and when he exercises the conversion option. Put another way, the 'something extra' the purchaser of a convertible pays for does not come from nowhere; it is taken away from existing shareholders. Shareholders are accepting that at some time in the future they may have to sell a share in the firm to outsiders at below its market value. In return for this they get a relative interest 'holiday' in the early years of the new money they are raising. The apparent cheapness of convertibles is an illusion that comes from ignoring the equity aspect. Correctly valued, convertibles do not offer cheap finance. So why do firms issue them?

Convertibles tend to be issued in situations where neither debt nor equity is, on its own, attractive enough. Convertibles are commonly issued as consideration in a merger. Here, there can be a great deal of uncertainty surrounding the future prospects of the merged firm, and if the firms involved are relatively small or relatively new there may simply not be enough information to permit investors to happily accept debt or equity on their own. Meyers (1993) analyses the dilemma which arises when management knows more about the true value of the firm's projects than shareholders do. If management issues equity, this is a signal to investors that the company's equity is over priced, and share prices will be bid down. If management issues debt, this is a signal that equity is underpriced and investors will bid share prices up. The convertible resolves this dilemma by committing management to compensate investors via the warrant if share prices rise and insure them via the face value of the debt if share prices fall. Hence the convertible takes away the motivation for management to 'play the game'.

IV SHORT AND MEDIUM-TERM LOANS

It is common to distinguish 'medium-term' finance of between three and ten years, and 'short-term' finance of less than three years' term. In either case the main source of this finance is the banks.

Term loans

In principle term loans provide a predetermined amount of finance for a fixed period, though often there will be provision for the borrower to draw less than the full amount or to repay early. The interest may be fixed, or periodically varied in line with the bank's base rate. Banks are capable of being fairly flexible about terms, and in the case of project finance may be prepared to offer an interest schedule that matches the cash flow of the project, with interest 'loaded' towards the end of the project. Conversely the borrowers tax position may indicate loading the interest towards the front of the loan.

Overdrafts

The basic term loan is for a fixed amount and term, but the *overdraft* works differently. The bank sets an upper limit to the amount the firm can borrow, in the form of a drawing limit on the firm's current account. The firm only pays interest on the daily balance outstanding. The duration of the arrangement is usually specified at the outset, and is typically 3, 6 or 12 months, with the possibility of renewal for further periods. The interest rate will vary with the bank's base lending rate. The beauty of overdrafts, from the point of view of the firm, or the individual for that matter, is that interest is only paid on the daily borrowing requirement. So it is very attractive to finance at least the fluctuating component of the total financing need this way. The problem with overdrafts is their short-term nature. The firm cannot be certain that the facility will be renewed, and because it operates on the firm's current account the bank is powerfully placed to hinder the normal operations of the firm until the overdraft is cleared.

Export finance

A whole host of special provisions has developed to help firms finance their exports. These have come about for two reasons. For one thing there are special financial problems associated with exporting: there is uncertainty as to exchange rates, and possibly as to the credit worthiness of the customer and to the political risks involved, and payment can take longer. But also, governments have seen exports as an important part of the national economic effort and worthy of support.

A large part of an exporter's risk can now be insured through the government's Export Credit Guarantee Department (ECGD). The firm is expected to insure a reasonable part of his business, and pays a premium based on his previous claims record. In return he gets coverage against the default of the buyer and political risks such as the blockage of remittances. ECGD is also prepared to guarantee export finance bank loans on behalf of its policy-holders for an additional premium. Certain insurance companies also offer these services.

The traditional instrument for financing foreign trade is the *bill of exchange*. A bill 'may be thought of as a post-dated cheque that can be sold for cash at a discount. It is a legal document covered by the Bills of Exchange Act 1881, in which the consequences of default are clearly defined. It enables the seller of goods to obtain cash for them as soon as possible after their dispatch, while allowing the buyer to defer payments until the goods reach him . . .' ('Money for Business' (1983)). Bills are usually for 30 or 90 days. They can be drawn by the seller ('trade bill') or the bank will attach its own name to the bill ('bank bill'). In the latter case the bank 'accepts' the bill and is said to have given the drawer a 'banker's acceptance' which will make the bill easier to negotiate. Upon receipt a bill can be *discounted* by another bank or more likely by one of the discount houses who specialise in this work. They pay cash to the extent of the future value of the bill less an appropriate financing charge.

Bill finance has several attractions; it is project specific, and the buyer's uncertainty about payment is resolved early. Because bill discounting takes place in a well developed market, the cost of bill finance is normally competitive with overdraft rates.

In looking for export finance the exporter is usually looking for expertise and advice, as well as funds. There are now many sources of export finance available to firms, including clearing banks, merchant banks, discount houses, export houses and finance houses.

V SUMMARY

Debt finance is commonly divided into short, medium and long-term. By far the most important type of debt in practice is short-term bank finance, and particularly overdraft finance. Next to retained earnings this is the major source of company finance in the UK. By contrast, probably because of high levels of inflation and uncertainty, the use of long-term debt has dwindled to insignificance in the UK in recent years.

The key to understanding debt financing is to think of debt's risk relative to equity. Like equity, debt runs a risk of losing its money, but unlike equity it cannot share in the success of the firm. Debt protects itself in several ways: by priority in distributions, by taking 'security', by writing protective covenants into the debt contract. Investors' evaluation of the risk that remains to debt after taking these measures will be reflected in the relative cost of debt finance. If the firm wishes to enhance the attractiveness of debt further it can issue 'convertibles' or 'loan-stock-with-warrants' to give debt-holders a participation in equity.

REFERENCES AND BIBLIOGRAPHY

Bank of England — 'Money for Business', Periodically.

Bank of England — 'UK Corporate Bond Market', Bank of England Quarterly Bulletin, 1981.

Ingersoll, J E — 'A Contingent-Claims Valuation of Convertible Securities', Journal of Financial Economics, 1977 (a), pp 289–321.

Ingersoll, J E — 'An Examination of Corporate Call Policies on Convertible Securities', Journal of Finance, 1977 (b).

Myers, S C — 'Determinants of Corporate Borrowing', Journal of Financial Economics, November 1977, pp 147–175.

Myers, S C — 'Still Searching for Optimal Capital Structure', Journal of Applied Corporate Finance, Spring 1993.

QUESTIONS

1 'Debt shares in the downside risk of the firm, but not in the upside, moreover the control of these risks belongs to equity.' How do debt-holders protect themselves?

2 What is the difference between the coupon-yield and the redemption-yield of a bond? On 1 January 1987 £1,000 of Arkwright plc 10% loan stock is selling for £750. The loan-stock is redeemable at par on 31 December 1990. What is the coupon-yield, and the redemption-yield on the debt? Ignore tax.

3 Suppose Arkwright pays tax at 40%, one year in arrears. What is its after-tax cost of debt in the above example?

4 When companies issue long-term debt, they usually do it in the form of convertibles. How do you account for the apparent popularity of convertibles, and unpopularity of straight debt?

5 How much does the Black-Scholes option pricing model help in valuing convertible loan-stock?

6 Cute plc has 1,000,000 Ordinary shares outstanding at present. Earnings per share are 25p, before tax, and the shares sell at a P/E of 12. The company plans to issue £500,000 of 10%, 20 year convertible loan stock, convertible at the stockholders' option at a conversion price of £4. The new capital is expected to generate increased annual earnings of £100,000. The company tax rate is 40%.

Compute the new earnings per share before and after conversion.

Compute the conversion premium on issue and explain under what circumstances it will pay stockholders to convert.

7 You work in the planning department of the High Street Bank. The bank is worried about the criteria its branch managers are employing in granting overdrafts and making term loans. Write a note to managers defining the information they should be getting from potential applicants.

CHAPTER 16

The capital structure decision

We have described two types of financing contract: equity – new issues and retained earnings; and debt of various sorts. The question is, what mix of financing should the firm use. What is the capital structure that maximises the value of the firm? As usual the best way to approach the capital structure problem is first to envisage what would happen in a perfect capital market, then to consider the effect of introducing realistic market imperfections into the analysis. In a classic study Modigliani and Miller (1958), 'MM', showed that in a perfect capital market it does not matter what capital structure the firm chooses, its value will be unchanged – in other words capital structure is *irrelevant* to the value of the firm. The argument is that different mixes of financing contract are merely different ways of cutting and distributing a given cake, the cake being the level and risk of the firm's earnings stream. Just as the nature of a cake is unaffected by who eats the cherries and who eats the sponge, so the total value of the firm is unaffected by the detail of the distribution of risk and return to providers of finance. This is the case in a perfect capital market, but when we introduce the market imperfections of tax, bankruptcy costs, and information costs we find the value of the firm *is* affected by capital structure.

In Section I we discuss the nature of financial and business risk while Section II compares two simple models of the link between financial risk and valuation. The analysis of the capital structure decision in a perfect market is presented in Section III. In Section IV we examine the effect of introducing market imperfections into this model. In the final section we examine the evidence on the capital structures that firms actually have, and try to generate some recommendations for choice of capital structure. At this point we concede that at the present state of knowledge we cannot fully explain the capital structures we observe in the real world.

I BUSINESS RISK AND FINANCIAL RISK

In previous chapters we saw that the future returns to projects cannot be known with certainty – what we face when looking at the future is a distribution of possible outcomes and we use the 'variance' of this distribution, a measure of dispersion, to measure the riskiness of future returns. The returns to the firm as a whole are also risky, being the aggregate of the returns from its individual projects. But this aggregate risk depends on how the component projects fit together as a portfolio and managers might try to diversify the component projects of the firm in order to achieve a relatively low-risk return from the firm as a whole.

The risk we have been talking about so far – the economic risk innate in the firm's operations – we now label *business risk*. Various factors cause some projects and thus some firms to have relatively more business risk than others including the structure of the market and the industry, the rate of change of tastes and technology, and the exposure to macroeconomic variables. The discussion of risk in the first part of the book was independent of financing. But when we consider financing alternatives we encounter a new aspect of risk: *financial risk*. Financial risk is a function of the proportion of debt in the total financing of the firm. We will use the word *gearing* for this proportion, though the US term *leverage* is also used. We define gearing as:

$$\text{GEARING} = \frac{\text{Debt}}{\text{Debt} + \text{Equity}}$$

$$= \frac{D}{D+S} = \frac{D}{V}$$

where D = market value of debt
S = market value of equity
V = D + S = market value of the firm

'Debt' includes all borrowing that is intended should form part of the long term financing of the firm. An alternative specification which is commonly used is

$$\text{GEARING} = \frac{\text{Debt}}{\text{Equity}}$$

The first definition is perhaps more convenient, since it has a possible range to 100% rather than to infinity. When analysing the impact of the firm's capital structure it can be useful to explore the 'income' aspect of gearing as well. We can define

$$\text{INCOME GEARING} = \frac{\text{Interest payments}}{\text{Earnings before interest}}$$

As we shall see the impact of gearing is related to the commitment of fixed interest payments relative to a varying underlying income stream – income gearing measures this directly. There is a close parallel between business risk and financial risk. The extent to which variability in a firm's revenues transforms into variability of operating profit depends on its cost structure. If costs are variable then much of any downturn in revenues will be passed on to suppliers, but the higher the '*operating gearing*', which is the proportion of fixed costs to total costs, the more of these costs the firm must absorb itself.

How gearing creates financial risk

ARC plc

ARC plc, is choosing between two alternative and rather extreme capital structures, a low-geared structure with £100,000 of debt and £1 million of equity (gearing = .09), and a high-geared structure with £1 million of debt and £100,000 of equity (gearing = .91). ARC can issue debt at a cost of 5%, which is below its cost of equity. ARC expects future profits to be either £100,000, £75,000 or £50,000, each equally probable, and Table I presents the return to equity and to debt under each of these outcomes and under each gearing situation, assuming all surplus profits are distributed to equity as dividends so that earnings per share (EPS) and dividend per share are the same.

At both gearing levels and at all levels of profit the return to debt is the same – a constant 5p in the £1, or 5% – this was our assumption. But in the second and fourth rows we see the impact on the returns to equity of gearing-up with lower cost debt. With high-gearing the average earnings per share, π, is 25p as against 7p with low-gearing – by importing more cheap finance the residual profits increase dramatically relative to the reduced number of equity shares. But the gearing also increases the riskiness of the equity return. At low-gearing, the standard deviation of EPS, σ, assuming all three profit outcomes are

Table I ARC plc: Interest and dividends

	Profit	*£100,000*		*£75,000*		*£50,000*		
LOW-GEARED		Interest per £1/EPS						
Interest on £100,000 debt		£5,000	5p	£5,000	5p	£5,000	5p	
Dividends on £1m equity		£95,000	9p	£70,000	7p	£45,000	4p	π = 7p σ = 2p
HIGH-GEARED								
Interest on £1m debt		£50,000	5p	£50,000	5p	£50,000	5p	
Dividends on £100,000 equity		£50,000	50p	£25,000	25p	£0	£0	π = 25p σ = 20p

equally likely, is 2p. At high-gearing it is 20p. The variability, which is risk per unit of return $\frac{\sigma}{\pi}$, is

$$\text{low-gearing, } \frac{2}{7} = .29\text{; high-gearing, } \frac{20}{25} = .8$$

Gearing has given equity a higher return but at the cost of bearing a higher risk. It is this extra risk which we call 'financial' risk. We can measure the extent of the financial risk component by finding the variation in equity returns in the no-gearing case. With no debt the whole financing will be provided by 1,100,000 £1 shares. Average equity earnings in total will be (100,000 + 75,000 + 50,000) ÷ 3 = £75,000. So average EPS is £75,000 ÷ 1.1 million = 6.8p. The standard deviation of this return is 1.87p, and the variability 1.87/6.8 = .28, and this is a measure of the underlying business risk of the firm. Now we can identify the components of the risk borne by ARC equity in the high-geared case as follows

variability with no gearing = .28 BUSINESS RISK
variability with high gearing = .80
Difference = .52 FINANCIAL RISK

Gearing increases the return to equity but also the risk, but these risk and return effects come from quite separate sources. Gearing pushed up the return to equity because we *also assumed* that debt was cheaper than equity. There are good reasons for this assumption in practice – the tax-deductibility of interest payments, and the lower risk associated with debt. But if debt happened to have a higher cost than equity, the effect of gearing would be to reduce the return to equity. The risk effect of gearing, on the other hand, occurs because the return to debt is fixed, irrespective of whether debt is cheaper or not. By agreeing to give debt a larger risk-free slice of earnings the firm is reserving all the variation in earnings for equity, but on a lower absolute return. Figure I depicts this under ARC's two gearing alternatives. For convenience we express the assumption that earnings of £100,000, £75,000 and £50,000 are equi-probable by showing earnings fluctuating between these values through time.

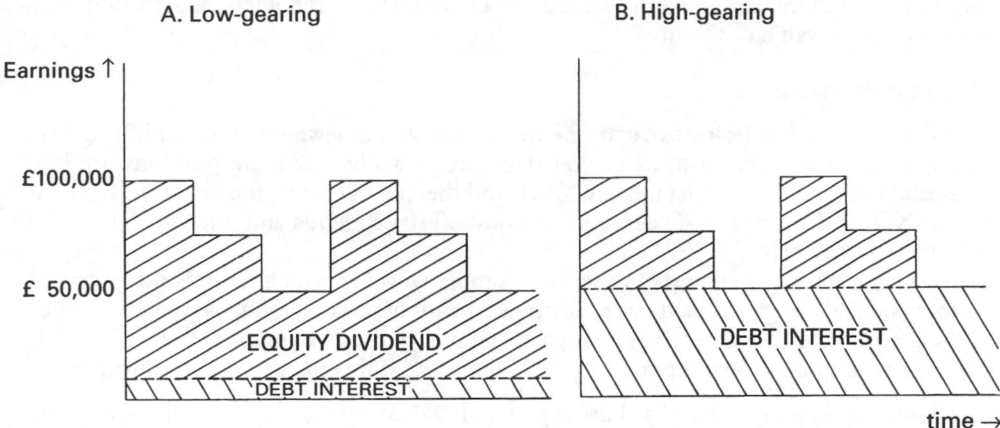

Figure I The division of ARC earnings between equity and debt

Equity as an option on the firm

Another way to think about this relationship between debt and equity is using option theory. Though the idea may seem rather strange at first, some thought will show that the returns to debt and equity are the returns they would receive if debt-holders owned the firm and had sold a call option on it to equity investors at an exercise price equal to the redemption value of the debt, which is the amount debt-holders receive when the debt expires. Suppose D is the redemption value of the debt, and V the value of the whole firm when debt is redeemed, with S the value of the equity. When the debt is redeemed, debt get D if $V > D$, but if the firm's assets are insufficient, i e $D > V$, debt get V. So the return to debt will be MIN (D, V). If $V > D$, equity get what is left, i e $V - D$, but if $D > V$ then equity get nothing. So the return to equity will be MAX $(0, V - D)$ which we can recognise as the payoff to a call option.

If we assume V is given and is invariant to the split between debt and equity (this is the assumption we will be exploring in the remainder of this chapter), once we know equity is an option we could use the Black and Scholes option pricing model to give us insights into the determinants of both S and D $(= V - S)$. Recall from Chapter 10 that, other things equal, the value of an option is an increasing function of the risk of the underlying asset. This was because the option value depends entirely on positive variances above the exercise price – the more risky the asset, the more of these there will be. Hence, once the debt contract is signed and sealed it is in the interests of equity to increase the riskiness of the firm. We can see exactly why this is so.

Option theory provides a method for evaluating the effect of changes in risk on the value of debt and equity, and of other financing changes the firm might have in mind, such as increasing the amount of debt (= the exercise price of the option) or the duration of debt (= the time to exercise).

II DOES FINANCIAL GEARING ADD VALUE?

It equity investors are risk-averse they will only be interested in gearing if they are compensated by higher returns. The key question to which we now turn is whether and under what circumstances gearing will lead to a net gain to shareholders, as signalled by an increase in the value of the firm.

Some naive models

We will start by considering two extreme views, and one somewhere in the middle, of how the firm is valued relative to its capital structure. Two two extreme positions are best described in terms of the 'net income' (NI), and the 'net operating income' (NOI), of the firm.[1] NOI is the firm's basic earnings stream before dividends and interest, NI is NOI less interest payments, I.

To start with we are going to describe a simple world in which there is no growth in earnings, all earnings are paid out as dividends, and the cost of equity is r_e, and in which debt is a perpetuity and receives a constant annual interest payment I. We will assume there is no taxation so that the cost of debt is simply r_d. If there is a constant growth rate in dividends, g, then the value of a share is $\frac{DIV}{r_e - g}$. If we assume further that all earnings are paid out as dividends, so $DIV_1 = NI$, and there is no growth in earnings, so $g = 0$, then the value of equity is $S = \frac{NI}{r_e}$. Similarly, $D = \frac{I}{r_d}$. The overall value of the firm is $V = D + S$

so

$$V = \frac{I}{r_d} + \frac{NI}{r_e} \tag{1}$$

Dragon plc

Suppose Dragon plc has an NOI of £3,600, pays interest of £600 and distributes the remaining £3,000 as dividend. Its costs of debt and equity are 5% and 12% respectively. In this case the overall value of the firm is

$$V = \frac{600}{.05} + \frac{3{,}000}{.12}$$
$$= 12{,}000 + 25{,}000 = £37{,}000$$

We can also say something about the average price a firm pays for its finance, which will be the cost of the individual types weighted by the proportions it uses of each. We define the *weighted average cost of capital*, WACC, or r_a, as

$$r_a = \frac{D}{D+S} r_d + \frac{S}{D+S} r_e \tag{2}$$

For Dragon

$$r_a = \frac{12{,}000}{37{,}000} \times .05 + \frac{25{,}000}{37{,}000} \times .12$$
$$= 0.016 \qquad + 0.081 \quad = 9.7\%$$

Our interest is in what happens to the value of the firm, V, and its overall cost of capital, r_a, when gearing changes. The NI model and the NOI model represent two different views about how equations (1) and (2) will respond. The NI model says that r_d and r_e are constant. If $r_d < r_e$ then switching to cheaper debt must reduce r_a, the average cost of

1 This follows the analysis by Durand (1952).

capital. And switching from dividends to interest must increase V as well, because in (1) we are capitalising interest at a higher value than dividends. The NOI approach is quite different. It says that the overall amounts, V and r_a, are constant, and r_d is constant too. Something must give if (1) and (2) are to hold at different gearing levels, and it is r_e which changes. We can see this in action with numerical examples.

The NI model

Table II shows the NI approach in Dragon plc with NOI of £3,000 and a cost of debt of 5% and cost of equity of 12%. In the first column we assume it has £12,000 of debt as before. In the second column it has £24,000 of debt and therefore pays £1,200 interest.

Table II The NI approach to valuation

	Gearing I	*Gearing II*
NOI	3,600	£ 3,600
Interest, I	600	1,200
NI	3,000	2,400
equity capitalisation rate, r_e	.12	.12
Value of equity, S	25,000	20,000
Value of debt, D	12,000	24,000
Value of firm, V	£37,000	£44,000

Because of the lower capitalisation rate on debt the total value of the firm is increased by issuing debt instead of equity. There is no limit on the benefits to this policy and the relationship between value and gearing are depicted in Figure IIa. The value maximising position appears to be 100% gearing, and this would also give the lowest overall cost of capital, which would just be r_d.

In practice most firms stop a long way short of 100% gearing. One reason for this could be a fear that extreme gearing will lead to bankruptcy. So when gearing is perceived as getting too high both debt and equity may increase their required return to compensate themselves for the increased risk, thereby causing a downturn in the valuation of the firm at high gearing levels. We depict this modified NI model in Figure IIb. This picture, with benefits to cheaper debt 'up to a point', is known as the *traditional view*. It will make a useful comparison later on.

The NOI model

Under the NI model debt and equity were valued independently, using appropriate capitalisation rates. The value of the firm was the sum of the two. Under the NOI approach the value of the firm is determined directly by capitalising the NOI of the firm using an overall capitalisation rate r_a, which is constant and given for the firm. Hence $V = \frac{NOI}{r_a}$. It follows immediately that, since NOI and r_a are constant and given, V is invariant to gearing. But it remains the case that $V = D + S$. If we still assume that r_d is constant then debt can be valued independently as $D = \frac{I}{r_d}$. Hence the value of equity, S, is the residual $S = V - D$ and r_e, the return on equity, is determined within the system since $r_e = \frac{NI}{S}$.

a The NI model

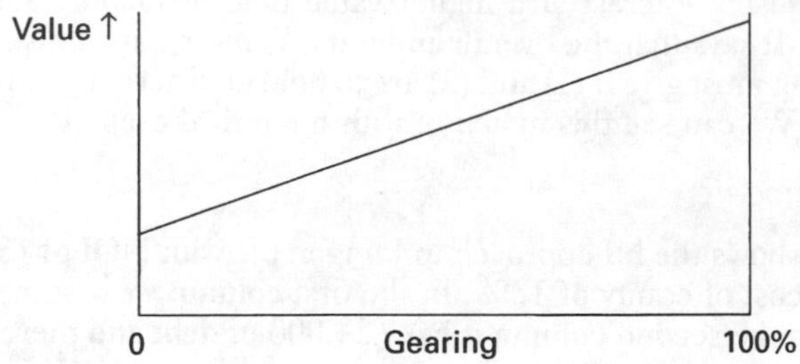

b The 'traditional' view

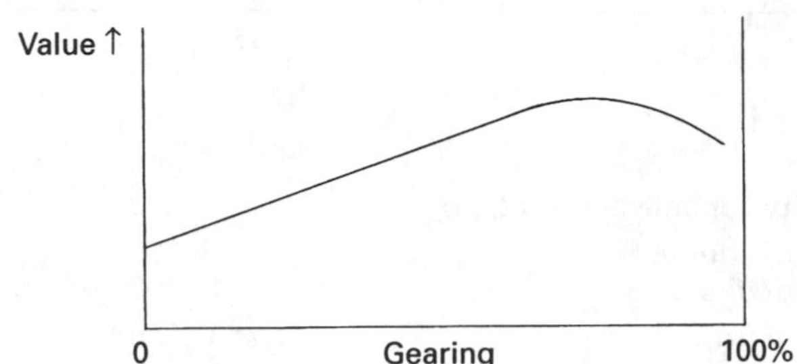

c The NOI model

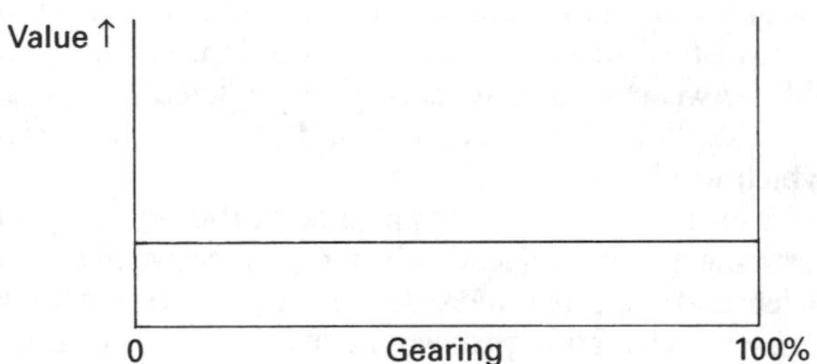

Figure II Different models of capital structure

We will use the NOI model on the Dragon example. We assume $r_d = 5\%$ as before, but this time assume an overall capitalisation rate for the firm, $r_a = 10\%$. The equity rate, r_e, is to be found. This time the valuation process is described in Table III. Under gearing 1 the implicit cost of equity is

$$r_e = \frac{NI}{S} = \frac{3{,}000}{24{,}000} = 12.5\%$$

Under gearing 2, $r_e = \dfrac{2{,}400}{12{,}000} = 20\%$

The value of the firm is thus invariant to gearing and is found directly by capitalising NOI. This is depicted in Figure IIc.

As they stand the NI and NOI models are just exercises in arithmetic, no more. Next we analyse which of them is likely to describe the workings of the real world.

Table III The NI approach to valuation		
	Gearing I	*Gearing II*
NOI	3,600	3,600
Overall capitalisation rate, r_a	.10	.10
Value of the firm, V	36,000	36,000
comprising		
Debt, at values as before, D	12,000	24,000
Equity, S	24,000	12,000
	36,000	36,000

III THE PERFECT CAPITAL MARKET: MODIGLIANI AND MILLER

In their classic 1958 paper Modigliani and Miller showed that in a perfect capital market the value of a firm is unaffected by its gearing – so the capital structure decision is irrelevant to valuation. In other words, they showed that in a perfect capital market firms will be valued according to the NOI model. The analysis of how firms are valued in perfect markets is the cornerstone of finance theory. This is not so much because we think the capital market is perfect but rather because the perfect analysis provides a framework into which we can systematically introduce and evaluate the imperfections of the real world. We will adopt this approach with the capital structure analysis, first presenting Modigliani and Miller's argument, then relaxing the perfect market assumption in the next section.

MM derive two 'propositions':

Proposition I The market value of any firm is independent of its capital structure and is given by capitalising its expected return at the rate r_a appropriate to its [risk-]class. Hence

$$V = \frac{NOI}{r_a} \tag{3}$$

Putting this the other way round: The average cost of capital to any firm is completely independent of its capital structure and is equal to the capitalisation rate of a pure equity stream of its class. Hence

$$r_a = \frac{NOI}{V}$$

Proposition II The expected yield of a share of stock is equal to the appropriate capitalisation rate r_a for a pure equity stream in the class, plus a premium related to financial risk equal to the debt-to-equity ratio times the spread between r_a and r_d. Hence

$$r_e = r_a + (r_a - r_d)\frac{D}{S} \tag{4}$$

In their original 1958 paper MM made a variety of assumptions in order to derive their propositions. Since then theorists have worked to reduce the assumptions that are necessary to support the theory. This process is central to the scientific method of economics. The fewer assumptions necessary for a theory, the stronger the theory.

One feature of the original MM work which looks rather strange now is their requirement that firms belong to homogeneous 'risk classes'. These are the classes MM refer to in the statements of their propositions we quoted above, and their overall capitalisation rate, r_a, is a rate appropriate to firms *in the risk class*. MM were writing before the CAPM gave us a method of directly evaluating differences in risk between firms, so they had to eliminate risk from their discussion by working with firms within a constant risk class. (This is more evidence, for the reader who might be doubting it, why the CAPM represented such a major advance in finance thinking.)

The necessary assumptions

The assumptions necessary for the MM propositions are those that define a perfect market. In particular, we need the following attributes of a perfect market.

1 The tax system is neutral with respect to capital structure.
2 Individuals and firms can borrow and lend at the same rate.
3 There are no costs associated with the liquidation of the firm.
4 Information is freely available to all participants in the capital market.

When we have established the MM propositions we will investigate the realism of these assumptions in turn.

Deriving the MM propositions

The proof of MM's proposition I is important because it employs two concepts that we use constantly in thinking about financial decisions: the concepts of *arbitrage* and of the *homemade alternative*.

The test of any financing or investment decision is whether it enhances value. Since the value of firms is set in the market place this means studying the market reaction to the decision. In a perfect market two identical commodities must sell for the same price. Indeed we can define a 'perfect market' this way. If the prices of two identical commodities are out of line in such a market owners will switch from the dearer to the cheaper to make a profit. But this process of selling and buying drives prices down and up respectively until in equilibrium the prices are equal and there is no more incentive to switch. We call the process by which prices are driven into line in this way the arbitrage process. In the case of the capital market the 'commodities' are the shares or debt of firms, both of which offer claims over an uncertain stream of future returns. For us to be sure that two different commodities in this market were identical we would have to be sure they gave the same return in every possible future state of the world. MM's proof of irrelevance does precisely this. It shows in the case of capital structure that the sum of the shares and debt of a firm remains an 'identical commodity' whatever the split between the two, hence the operation of arbitrage in the market will ensure that two firms different only in capital structure must have the same value.

Another concept MM employ in reaching their conclusion is the notion of the homemade alternative. Often we see firms, or intermediaries in the capital market, doing things which appear to benefit investors. But in general these will only add value to the firm if they are things the investor could not have done for himself. In the MM world investors can borrow just as easily as firms, and at the same cost. In this world no-one would pay more for a firm just because it borrows. Homemade gearing is a perfect substitute. Homemade alternatives may cease to be equally valuable once market imperfections enter the picture. In a world of taxes, transactions costs and information costs, capital structure and dividend policy may be relevant to the value of the firm.

Consider two firms, 1 and 2, with the same expected profit (NOI), X, and in the same risk class. Firm 1 has all-equity financing, firm 2 has some debt. Suppose also, in line with the 'traditional' view of capital structure, that the geared firm, 2, is accordingly more valuable. Figure III may help to envisage what is going on. The capital structure of the two firms is represented by two boxes and the height of each box indicates the total value of each firm, V_1 and V_2. In the case of firm 2 this value is made up of D_2 of debt and S_2 of equity.

Let Y_1, Y_2 be the incomes an investor gets from owning the proportion α of the equity of each firm. (We represent the proportion he owns horizontally in Figure III.) Hence $Y_1 = \alpha X$.

But because firm 2 has to pay interest at the rate r_d on its debt D_2 the equity profit is correspondingly reduced so $Y_2 = \alpha\ (X - r_dD_2)$.

Now, by assumption, firm 2 is more valuable than firm 1,

$$V_2\ (= S_2 + D_2) > V_1\ (= S_1)$$

This opens up a profitable strategy to the investor in firm 2. He can take the following steps:

1 Sell his equity stake in firm 2, αS_2.
2 Raise a loan, exactly equal in size to α of firm 2's debt, αD_2.
3 Spend the proceeds, $\alpha(S_2 + D_2)$ on shares in firm 1.

Step 2 should be no problem since he can offer as security his shares in firm 1, which represent claims on the same underlying assets that firm 2 could offer its debt-holders.

Using this strategy the investor increases his income at no cost. The investor's old

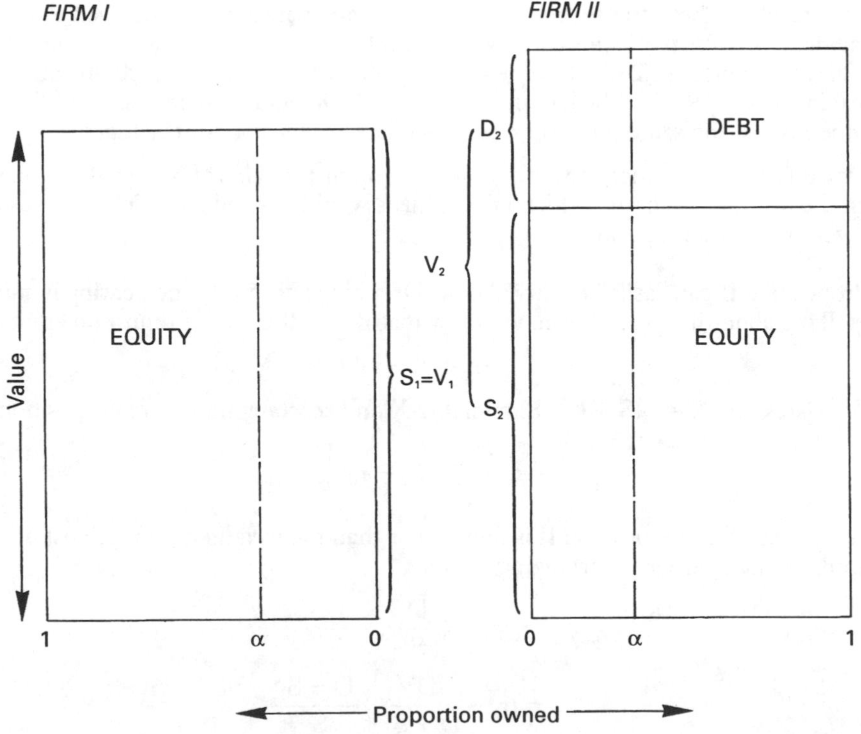

Figure III Value of the geared and ungeared firm

income was $\alpha(X - r_dD_2)$. If he had bought α of firm 1, his new net income would be the same: αX, less the cost of servicing his loan, αr_dD_2. However his income from firm 1 will be higher than αX, since his proceeds from the sale and the loan enable him to buy more than α of firm 1. We know this because, by assumption, $S_2 + D_2 > S_1$, so that $\alpha(S_2 + D_2) > \alpha S_1$. Though his income increases, his risk is unchanged since he now has personal borrowing in the same proportion $\frac{D_2}{D_2 + S_2}$ as firm 2 had. Arbitrage will take place, the value of 2 will be bid down, and the value of 1 bid up until $V_2(= S_2 + D_2) = V_1(= S_1)$. By an equivalent argument we could also show that the value of the geared firm cannot be lower than the ungeared.

Griselda Grasby

Suppose the two firms we just described are Argon plc and Neon plc, which are effectively identical in that they have the same expected NOI of £200,000, and this profit has the same risk. The market rate of interest is 12%. Argon is an all-equity firm valued at £1 million. Neon has £800,000 of equity and £400,000 of debt, so Neon's total market valuation is £1.2 million. Both firms pay out 100% of net income as dividends.

Griselda Grasby owns £80,000, or 10%, of Neon's equity and notices the valuation discrepancy, so she does the following:

— sells her Neon shares, realising £80,000
— takes out a loan equivalent in size to 10% of Neon's debt, £400,000 × 10% = £40,000
— invests £120,000 in Argon's equity

As a result of these transactions Grasby's income is increased. She used to receive a dividend of 10% of Neon's earnings, £15,200. She now gets 12% of Argon's NOI of £200,000, which is £24,000 and has to pay £40,000 × 12% = £4,800 of loan interest, leaving a net £19,200. She has an equity of £80,000 on underlying assets of £120,000, which is just the same proportion as Neon had, so her risk is unchanged.

One question we cannot answer is what the equilibrium value of Neon and Argon would be in the previous example. Which value adjusts would depend on which firm was out of line with the market as a whole.

Proposition II can easily be derived now. Dropping subscripts and bearing in mind we are talking about the geared firm, we know that if r_e is the rate of return on equity then

$$Sr_e = X - r_dD$$

We also know $X = r_a(S + D)$. Eliminating X and rearranging we get proposition II:

$$r_e = r_a + (r_a - r_d)\frac{D}{S}$$

We can see that Proposition II is none other than the weighted average cost of capital formula we met earlier. Rearranging we get

$$r_e = (1 + \frac{D}{S})r_a - \frac{D}{S}r_d$$

$$= (r_a - \frac{D}{D + S}r_d)\frac{D + S}{S}$$

so,

$$r_a = \frac{D}{D + S}r_d + \frac{S}{D + S}r_e$$

IV THE EFFECT OF MARKET IMPERFECTIONS

Under the MM assumptions the capital structure of the firm is irrelevant to its valuation. We now investigate the realism of those assumptions to see what modifications we may have to make to the irrelevance proposition.

Taxation

If there is a corporation tax against which debt interest is a deductible expense but equity dividends are not the tax system will not be neutral with respect to capital structure. The effect of corporation tax is to make the value of the firm an increasing function of gearing, and thus the cost of capital a decreasing function. To see why, we have to modify the NOI valuation model to allow for corporation tax. Now it is *after-tax* returns that investors will capitalise, using a capitalisation rate, r_a, which we will now assume to be an appropriate *after-tax* rate.

Consider two identical firms with NOI before tax of £2,000. Suppose the corporation tax rate is 35% and the after-tax capitalisation rate, r_a, is 20%. One firm is presently financed entirely by equity, the other has £3,000 of 12% debt. What will be the relative value of these two firms? We will proceed in two stages: first assuming corporation tax exists but interest is not tax deductible, second calculating the value-effect of the tax deductibility of interest payments, the value of the 'tax-shield' provided by interest.

When there is corporation tax but interest is not tax deductible, the picture is our usual NOI one – the total valuation of the firm is unaffected by gearing. What happens once interest is tax deductible? The value of the debt is unchanged, but now the Revenue rebates to the firm an amount which is the rate of corporation tax times the interest payment. If the interest payment is r_dD and the tax rate is T, then the tax rebate is Tr_dD. What discount rate should we use to value this rebate? It is effectively an increase in the after-tax NOI of equity, so maybe the overall capitalisation rate, r_a, might be appropriate? But tax rebates are, unlike NOI, a low risk stream. *Given* the continuation of the tax system, and assuming the company has sufficient taxable earnings, the tax rebate is as certain as the interest payments to which it relates. Except for the risk of bankruptcy we can consider interest payments a certain stream. In these circumstances it is appropriate to capitalise tax savings using the debt capitalisation rate, r_d.

Assuming the payment of debt interest is a perpetuity – the firm always intends to have gearing of this extent – then we can value the tax saving thus

$$\text{Value of tax saving} = \frac{Tr_dD}{r_d}$$

$$= TD$$

The value of tax savings is the value of debt times the corporation tax rate. In Table IV we see that this amounts to £3,000 × 35% = £1,050.

MM's after-tax propositions I and II

Using subscripts G, U for the geared ad the ungeared firm respectively, MM derived the following:[2]

After-tax proposition I $\qquad V_G = V_U + TD \qquad$ (3b)

2 MM's first attempt at incorporating corporation tax, in their 1958 article, was mis-specified. MM (1963) represents their corrected attempt.

Table IV The NOI approach with corporation tax

(1) Assuming corporation tax exists but interest is not tax deductible

	Ungeared firm	*Geared firm*
NOI	2,000	2,000
CT @ 35%	700	700
After tax NOI	1,300	1,300
capitalisation rate, r_a	.20	.20
Value of firm	£6,500	£6,500
Comprising equity	6,500	3,500
debt	—	3,000
	£6,500	£6,500

(2) Effect of tax deductibility

Interest paid £3,000 @ 12%	=	£360
Tax-saving £360 @ 35%	=	£126
capitalisation rate, r_d,	=	.12
VALUE OF TAX SAVING		£1,050

Hence value of geared firm = value of ungeared firm + value of tax saving = £6,500 + £1,050 = £7,550

The value of a geared firm is the value of the ungeared firm plus the value of the tax savings.

After-tax proposition II $$r_e = r_a + (1 - T)(r_a - r_d)\frac{D}{S} \quad (4b)$$

The after tax return on the equity of the geared firm is that for the ungeared firm plus a premium relating to the corporation tax rate, the return on debt and the degree of gearing.

If T = 0, these after-tax propositions reduce to the pre-tax propositions I and II.

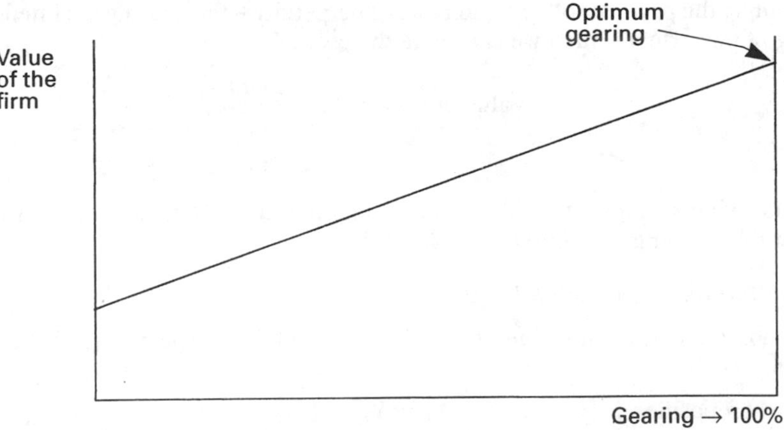

Figure IV The value of the firm under MM's after-tax analysis

As it stands, MM's after-tax proposition I implies the firm should have 100% gearing since value is an increasing function of gearing with a positive corporation tax rate – we have the 'extreme corner solution' depicted in Figure IV. Clearly this does not happen in practice. To understand why we must bring in some other market imperfections.

The effect of personal tax

One problem with MM's tax analysis is that it only considers corporation tax. But other taxes affect the after-tax receipts of debt and equity investors too – personal income tax on dividends and interest, and capital gains tax. Miller (1977) developed a more general model. He proposed the following modifications of MM's after-tax proposition I:

$$\text{let } A = \text{tax advantage of gearing} = [1 - \frac{(1 - T)(1 - T_{pe})}{(1 - T_{pd})}]D$$

where, now,

T = corporation tax rate
T_{pe} = personal tax rate on dividends
T_{pd} = personal tax rate on interest

We can see that MM were effectively assuming the special case where the rate of tax on dividends and interest are the same. If $T_{pe} = T_{pd}$, Miller's model for the tax advantage to gearing reduces to our earlier TD. So if the corporation tax rate were 35% the tax advantage to debt would be .35D.

Now consider a tax system in which, additionally, interest suffers personal tax, but dividends do not. This is effectively the situation under an 'imputation' tax system such as the UK one. In the UK, dividends are taxable, but the basic rate of tax is deemed to be already covered by the company's corporation tax payment since the company receives a dividend tax credit (known as ACT, or advance corporation tax). So if the investors are paying tax at the basic rate of 25% we might have:

$T = 35\%$
$T_{pe} = 0\%$
$T_{pd} = 25\%$

$$\text{in which case, } A = [1 - \frac{(1 - .35)\,(1 - 0)}{1 - .25)}]D = .13D$$

In this case the benefit to debt is reduced. The reason is clear – when we look at the whole tax system we see that the corporation tax saving on interest is partially balanced by personal tax on interest.

In general, to get an adequate picture of the tax effects of the firm's capital structure decision we need to look at the particular tax position of the firm and of its investors, and the effective rate of personal tax faced by a firm's clientele of investors can vary enormously depending on their personal circumstances. While charities are exempt tax, some individuals pay tax at the top personal rate. It is hard to generalise about the effect of a tax system on the basis of its statutory characteristics since tax systems allow so much variety of individual treatment. In this situation the best we can do is recommend each firm to evaluate the tax positions of its own investors in appraising its optimal capital structure.

Exactly the same doubts arise about the position of the firm itself. Though the nominal corporation tax rate might be 35%, the effective rate for many firms is considerably reduced because they are 'tax exhausted', they have zero taxable earnings in some periods. If the firm is not in a taxpaying position it cannot recover its ACT, and the tax credit on dividends becomes a real tax again. Consider the extreme case when the effective tax rates facing a firm and its investors are:

$T = 0, T_{pe} = 25\%, T_{pd} = 25\%$

then $A = (1 - \frac{1}{1})D = 0$. In this case the advantage to debt is zero, and capital structure is, again, irrelevant.

Miller uses his model to draw some general equilibrium conclusions. He suggests that in practice T_{pe} will be so low as to be effectively zero, and he points out that, for equilibrium, at the margin the tax advantage to debt must be zero. Looking at his equation we can see this will occur when $T_{pd} = T$, when the tax rate of the marginal debt-holder just equals the corporate tax rate. This will determine the overall amount of corporate debt, but since all companies will face the price of debt set by this marginal tax rate, there will be no optimum gearing for any individual firm, and gearing will again be irrelevant.

Bankruptcy costs

To escape from the extreme corner solution implied by MM's after-tax analysis theorists have also turned to bankruptcy costs. In an MM world there were no costs to bankruptcy. But if there are, and if gearing increases the risk of bankruptcy, then this will imply an interior solution, an optimal gearing just where the value loss from possible bankruptcy starts to outweigh the value-gains from tax savings. The argument is appealing since bankruptcy[3] is a bogey-word. In bankruptcy, investors lose their money, workers lose their jobs and managers lose their reputations. There is never any problem arguing the case that bankruptcy is a bad thing and that investors will shy away from it.

In Chapter 23 we identify several costs to bankruptcy. When a firm is liquidated its assets may be sold at a discount on their economic value, the proceeds of liquidation will be subject to transactions costs such as liquidator's fees, and the process of receivership and liquidation may impose managerial costs. All of these may cause the owners to lose a proportion of the value of the firm if it is liquidated. If this proportion is L and the value of the firm is V, then they will lose LV. However liquidation is an uncertain event, and we can express the expected value of these bankruptcy costs in terms of the probability of bankruptcy, p, which we assume to be some function of gearing. So expected bankruptcy costs = pLV. Hence we can extend our valuation formula for the geared firm thus

$$V_G = V_U + TD - pLV. \qquad (3c)$$

Now, assuming p only becomes significant at higher levels of gearing the relationship between value and gearing will be as depicted in Figure V.

The crucial intellectual step is to see that in a perfect capital market *bankruptcy is of no importance*. Firms will use assets just so long as their economic value within the firm exceeds their value outside. If the profitability of the assets declines to such an extent that this ceases to be the case, then they should be sold. If such a large proportion of the firm's assets fall into this category that the firm cannot continue to exist without them, then the firm will be liquidated. Since the realisable value is now the economic value of the firm, no loss will be associated with liquidation so far as owners are concerned, if the firm is liquidated in a perfect market.

How important are bankruptcy costs in practice? The evidence is very thin. The transactions costs in liquidation are real enough, though as a percentage of value they may not be large. A study by Warner (1977) of US railroad bankruptcies showed that they averaged only 3.5% of the value of the firm in question, though the percentage may be

3 We follow the American practice on this and use the word 'bankruptcy' interchangeably with 'liquidation' which is the correct word in the UK for company failure.

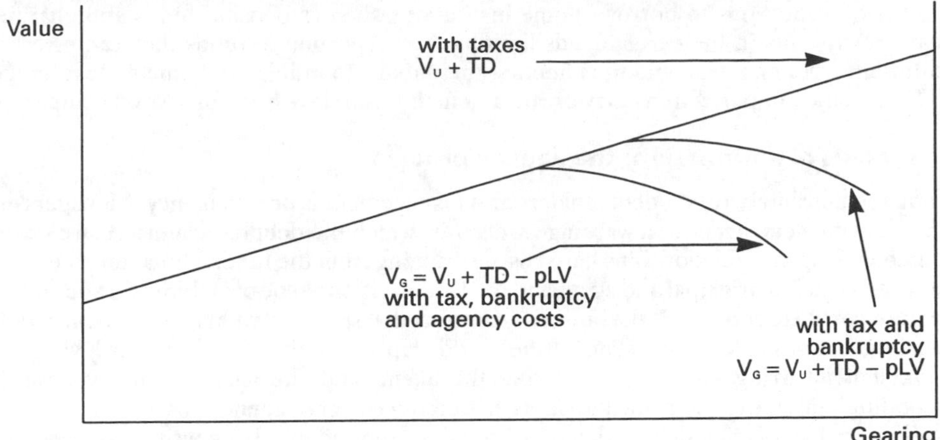

Figure V The effect of gearing on value with different market imperfections

much higher for small firms. Do the assets of liquidated firms sell at below their economic value? The implication is that asset markets are inefficient and perhaps that receivers do not seek out best prices when selling assets. There is no hard evidence on this topic. To some extent the problem may be one of perceptions. Investors may have lost touch with the real value of the firm and the event of bankruptcy may cause a sudden awakening to losses that have been accruing for some time. The managerial costs of failure – the extra time spend in dealing with receivers, liquidators, bankers; the lost opportunities embodied in the constraints on behaviour imposed by these people – are similarly hard to quantify. But costs that are hard to quantify may still be real.

The second question is the relationship between gearing and the probability of bankruptcy. One view is: 'Gearing increases the firm's fixed commitments to interest payments. These commitments are legally enforceable. Hence gearing increases the likelihood that outsiders can enforce liquidation on the firm'. The trouble with this view is that it ignores the *economics* of failure and looks only to the *legal* event. The task of a receiver is to explore alternative uses for a firm's assets and ascertain the best use. Though it is easy to see that higher gearing may trigger the appointment of a receiver sooner rather than later, it is not so clear why this will make bankruptcy more likely. The decision to liquidate should reflect the economic value of alternative possibilities, and this appears to be independent of the appointment of a receiver. Again the problem may be one of confusing cause and effect. A succession of losses will drive up gearing simply by eroding the equity base. The underlying cause remains the economic performance of the firm.

Can individuals and firms borrow and lend at the same rate?

The central plank of the MM propositions is the notion that homemade and corporate leverage are perfect substitutes. A necessary condition for this is that individuals and firms can borrow and lend at the same rate. In practice there may be market forces at work which lead investors to prefer firms to do the borrowing and which accordingly raise the value of geared firms. First, there are economies of scale in borrowing which make it cheaper for the firm to borrow rather than the individual. Second, there may be restrictions on the ability of institutions to borrow. Some institutions such as pension funds and charities have restrictions in their trust deeds limiting the proportion of funds they can invest in different types of assets, and thus limiting their ability to indulge in homemade leverage. These market imperfections may create a demand from investors for geared companies.

The costs of information: the agency problem

The relationship between debt-holders and management is one of agency. Managers are the debt-holders' agents, stewarding assets over which the debt has claims. As we saw in Chapter 2, agency relationships have costs, springing from the fundamental divergence in interest between principal and agent and the fact that it would be prohibitively expensive to write a complete contract at the outset – a contract that specified what management should do in every possible future state of the world. Up to a point it will be worthwhile the principal incurring costs in monitoring the agent, and the agent incurring costs in 'bonding' himself to the principal in order to reduce overall agency costs.

The problem facing debt is that, once the debt contract has been written, subsequent actions of managers may reduce the value of debt-holders' claims – the firm may issue other senior debt, pay large dividends to equity, increase the risk of the firm, and so forth. In response debt will try to protect itself by writing protective covenants into the debt contract, limiting the actions of management. But debt only partly protects itself this way: greater protection would require more complete contracts and prohibitive costs in monitoring the subsequent actions of managers. Since the risks to debt get greater with gearing and the agency costs of controlling those risks will be prohibitive, agency costs argue for limiting the gearing of the firm.

Figure V above shows the effects of corporation tax, bankruptcy costs, and agency costs, on value. The final picture is very similar to the 'traditional view' we presented earlier in the chapter.

The role of 'securable assets'

Firms differ in the assets they can offer as 'security' for debt. In practice we find companies such as property companies may have substantially more debt than firms with less securable assets. But the possession of securable assets is just one manifestation of the underlying business risk of the firm. What characterises the 'securability' of an asset is the degree of certainty that we can have about its future resale value. So while 'business risk' describes the variability of the returns from the firm's assets in their 'first-best' use, the resale value of the firm's assets reflects the forgone returns from second-best uses. The greater the security that can be given to debt financiers, the less the monitoring costs they will need to incur in protecting their debt.

V CAPITAL STRUCTURE IN PRACTICE

By starting from an MM world with no taxes then considering different market imperfections it is possible to build up a picture of the factors that are likely to determine optimal capital structure. These factors will differ from firm to firm, depending on the tax position of the firm and its particular clientele of investors, the scale of potential bankruptcy costs and the risk of bankruptcy, and the difficulty in writing financing contracts that protect debt. But the fact is, theory cannot at present fully explain why firms choose the capital structures they do.

Table V shows the average gearing of UK firms by sector in 1992. Gearing is defined as long and short-term borrowing divided by borrowing plus equity, all at book values. Defined this way the average UK firm borrowed 33% of its finance in 1992. However, there were large differences between industries. Conglomerates had gearing of 56% and leisure 43%, while transport companies borrowed 49%. On the other hand the average gearing in electronics, food retailing, rentals, telephones and water was below 25%.

Table V Gearing of UK firms in 1992

Equally-weighted average ratio of short and long-term debt to debt plus equity for companies on the Exstat database

Industry	*Gearing ratio (1992)*	*Industry*	*Gearing ratio (1992)*
1 Building materials	37%	14 Leisure	43%
2 Contracting & construction	35%	15 Packaging & paper	37%
3 Electricals	37%	16 Publishing & printing	32%
4 Electronics	22%	17 Stores	28%
5 Engineering: aero	36%	18 Textiles	28%
6 Engineering general	34%	19 Agencies	26%
7 Metals, metal form	18%	20 Chemicals	38%
8 Motors	35%	21 Conglomerates	56%
9 Other industrial	44%	22 Transport	50%
10 Brewers & Distiller	33%	23 Telephone network	22%
11 Food manufacturing	35%	24 Water	23%
12 Food retailing	24%	25 Miscellaneous	34%
13 Health & household	29%	26 Oil & Gas	25%

All companies 33%

Though it is interesting to see how different industries shape-up in terms of capital structure, data like this cannot be more than suggestive. The key question is how capital structure affects value, but this question is hard to research. No two firms are identical and firms differ in other ways that might affect value; the most notable being economic risk, and growth rates. Researchers have adopted various approaches to this problem. Modigliani and Miller (1958) chose two industries in the US which had fairly large populations of apparently homogeneous firms – electric utilities and oil companies. They regressed cost of capital on capital structure and found no apparent influence of capital structure. MM were unable to reject the null hypothesis of the irrelevance of capital structure. However MM's 1958 work was criticised in that their sample groups were not truly homogeneous in either economic risk or growth rates. Weston (1963) and MM (1966) made some allowance for this and got results which suggests there is a positive tax advantage to gearing. Masulis (1980) devised a different methodology. He studied 163 occasions between 1962 and 1976 on which firms had exchanged equity and debt. By studying financial exchanges within given firms he hoped to hold the effect of economic risk and of growth constant. He found evidence of statistically significant tax advantage to gearing. However, there is a good deal more research needed before we have a full explanation of the effects of capital structure on value.

Titman and Wessels (1988) used a form of factor analysis to explain the differences in capital structure across a panel of 469 US firms in the period 1974 to 1982. They found evidence that profitable firms have less debt, but also that firms with what they called 'unique' assets were likely to have lower debt. These firms were more likely to impose costs on customers, suppliers, and workers when they liquidated. They found no evidence that differences in growth rates, tax position, risk, or the presence of securable assets affected gearing.

VI SUMMARY

Finance theory cannot yet fully explain the capital structures that firms adopt in practice, but – with the help of Modigliani and Miller's analysis, and a careful inspection of real world market imperfections we can get a good idea of the factors that will affect the capital structure decision. In a perfect capital market the capital structure of the firm would be irrelevant to its value. But in reality the underlying tax subsidy on debt provides a strong incentive to 'gear-up', but it is impossible to generalise about the tax effects on gearing. The size of the tax advantage to debt depends very much on the particular tax positions of the firm and its shareholders. However, whatever the tax advantage to debt, there will be limits on the gearing of firms. Both bankruptcy costs, and agency costs, make debt-holders reluctant to provide high levels of gearing to firms.

REFERENCES AND BIBLIOGRAPHY

Durand, D — 'Cost of Debt and Equity Funds for Business; Trends and Problems of Measurement' in 'Conferences on Research in Business Finance', National Bureau of Economic Research, New York, 1952.

Jensen, M C, and Meckling, W H — 'Theory of the Firm's Managerial Behaviour, Agency Costs and Ownership Structure', Journal of Financial Economics Oct 1976, pp 305–360.

Marsh, P — 'The Choice between Equity and Debt: An Empirical Study', Journal of Finance, March 1982, pp 121–144.

Masulis, R W — 'The Effects of Capital Structure Change on Security Prices: A Study of Exchange Offers', Journal of Financial Economics, June 1980, pp 139–177.

Miller, M H — 'Debt and Taxes', Journal of Finance, May 1977, pp 261–275.

Modigliani, F, and Miller, M H — 'The Cost of Capital, Corporation Finance and the Theory of Investment', American Economic Review, June 1958, pp 261–297.

Modigliani, F, and Miller, M H — 'Corporate Income Taxes and the Cost of Capital: A Correction', American Economic Review, June 1963, pp 433–443.

Modigliani, F, and Miller, M H — 'Some Estimates of the Cost of Capital to the Electric Utility Industry', American Economic Review, June 1966, pp 333–391.

Modigliani, F, and Miller, M H — 'Reply to Heins and Spreckle', American Economic Review, September 1969, pp 592–595.

Myers, S C — 'Determinants of Corporate Borrowing', Journal of Financial Economics, November 1977, pp 147–176.

Myers, S C — 'Still Searching for Optimal Capital Structure', Journal of Applied Corporate Finance, Spring 1993.

Myers, S C, and Majluf, N S — 'Corporate Financing and Investment Decisions When Firms Have Information Investors Do Not Have', Journal of Financial Economics, June 1984, pp 187–222.

Titman, S, and Wessels, R — 'The Determinants of Capital Structure Choice', Journal of Finance, March 1988, pp 1–40.

Warner, J — 'Bankruptcy Costs: Some Evidence', Journal of Finance, May 1977, pp 337–348.

QUESTIONS

1 Ios and Knossos are identical firms with the same expected stream of net operating income, NOI. However, Knossos has some debt in its capital structure while Ios does not, and the market value of Knossos is higher as follows:

	Ios	*Knossos*
NOI	10,000	10,000
Loan interest	—	2,000
Net income	£10,000	£8,000
Value of debt (market rate of interest – 10%)	—	20,000
Value of equity (equity capitalisation rate – 20%)	50,000	40,000
Value of the firm	£50,000	£60,000

If the world is as described in MM's before tax capital structure analysis are these equilibrium values? If not, describe a profitable arbitrage strategy which will exploit the situation and suggest when equilibrium might be reached. Work out the existing, and equilibrium, costs of equity, debt, and the overall weighted average cost of capital in each case.

2 What difference would it make to your answer to 1, if there is a 35% corporate tax, but no personal tax?

3 What was Miller's expression for the tax advantage to debt in a world of personal and corporate tax? What tax rate would the marginal debt-holder need to have in a UK context for capital structure again to be irrelevant?

4 The following assumptions seem to be necessary to support the basic MM analysis: no taxes, no bankruptcy costs, freely available information, a single borrowing and lending rate. How does relaxing each of these assumptions affect our predictions for the existence of an optimal capital structure? Which of MM's assumptions seem *least* likely to hold in reality?

CHAPTER 17

The dividend decision

Retained earnings are the main source of finance for most firms, and since retaining earnings and distributing them are alternatives the dividend decision is a key financing decision. Moreover, investors see the dividend as a signal of managers' expectations about the future.

This chapter analyses the dividend decision. Section I introduces some of the concepts and terminology in dividend policy and examines the evidence on the actual dividend policies of firms. In Section II we examine two approaches to the analysis of the dividend decision. The first is the 'naive' though rather appealing idea that the firm should just hold on to the earnings it needs to finance its positive valued projects each period, and distribute the rest. The second is the classic demonstration by Miller and Modigliani that in a perfect capital market it does not matter what dividend policy the firm adopts – in such a market dividend policy is irrelevant to the value of the firm. As with the capital structure decision, the MM analysis provides a good basis for a systematic review of the effect of market imperfections on dividend policy. We provide this in Section III and draw some conclusions on the determinants of dividend policy in practice.

I DIVIDEND POLICY: CONCEPTS AND TERMINOLOGY

We use the word 'dividends' to describe the periodic payments which companies make to service their equity capital. We are interested in the dividends on ordinary shares; companies also pay dividends on preference shares if they have any, but though the Revenue taxes these like ordinary dividends, we treat them as akin to interest payments. There are no legal constraints on whether and when a company pays a dividend in the UK, except that the dividend cannot exceed the company's *realised* profits. So, for example, if the company has revalued a property and found that it is worth more than it cost, this surplus can only be paid out as a dividend when the asset is sold and the surplus 'realised'. But the company does not need to have adequate *current* profits to cover its dividend, a dividend can be paid from retained earnings (realised profits) of previous periods. Public companies commonly pay a dividend twice a year: an *interim dividend* during the year and a *final dividend* after the year-end when the firm has full information about the year's earnings.

GEC

In the financial year ended 31.3.1994 GEC paid the following dividends:

GEC, dividends for the year ended 31.3.1994

Interim	£ 2.81p
Final (proposed)	£ 8.01p
Total dividend per share	£10.82p

The final dividend was payable on 3 October 1994, but to qualify, the shareholder had to be registered as the owner of the share at the close of business on 4 August 1994. Hence we say the share was *cum div* up to that time, and *ex div* thereafter.

In analysing firms' dividend policies the key statistic is the *payout ratio* which is the proportion of distributable profit actually distributed:

$$\text{Payout ratio} = \frac{\text{Dividend per share}}{\text{Earnings per share}}$$

Alternatively we talk about *dividend cover* which is the reciprocal of the payout ratio – the number of times the dividend could have been paid from the earnings. Note that in calculating the payout ratio 'earnings' are defined as profit after tax, and after preference dividends and minority interests, before any 'extra-ordinary' items. That is, profit available to ordinary shareholders. In 1994 GEC's earnings per share (EPS) was 19.8p, so its payout ratio was 55% $(= \frac{10.82}{19.8} \times 100)$ and its cover was 1.8.

The UK shareholder who receives a dividend from a company is entitled to a tax credit, as thought the dividend was net of basic rate tax. We have assumed the 'imputation rate' to be 25% in general elsewhere in the book, but at the time GEC paid the final dividend in our current example the rate was 20%. Hence the amount of the tax credit is $8.01 \times \frac{20}{80} = 2.00$, which is also the amount GEC must pay to the Inland Revenue as ACT, an advance payment of its corporation tax bill. Hence the 8.01 final dividend is worth $8.01 \times \frac{100}{80} = 10.01\text{p}$ to the investor, and cover and payout ratios are sometimes calculated using this *gross* figure. When using payout figures it is useful to be clear whether you are dealing with gross or net dividends.

Many large UK firms, including GEC, offer their shareholders the alternative of taking extra shares instead of the cash dividend. This is commonly known as a *scrip* dividend. Unlike cash dividend the firm does not have to pay ACT on a scrip, but shareholders do not receive a tax credit either. This makes them unattractive to tax exempt institutions.

Firms are also permitted to repurchase their own shares so long as they get permission from their shareholders, and conceptually this is rather similar to paying a dividend; they are both methods of distributing cash. Though share repurchase is permitted in the UK it is much more energetically practised in the US. Apple Computer provides a good example of how share repurchase and dividend paying can fit together.

Apple Computer

It is not uncommon for US firms particularly in high-tech industries, such as computers, to pay no dividends. These are usually fast growing firms who argue that they can reinvest shareholders' money at a higher return than shareholders can get outside. In any case, as we note later in the chapter, the US tax system does not provide an incentive to distribute. So firms like DEC, Compaq and Microsoft have never paid a dividend. Apple did the same in its early years, but such was its profitability the company found itself generating much more cash than it could usefully invest. Apple was not tempted to diversify away from its core area of competence merely to use up cash, but started to pay the following relatively modest dividend.

	1985	*1986*	*1987*	*1988*	*1989*	*1990*	*1991*	*1992*	*1993*
Earnings ($M)	61	154	217	400	454	475	310	530	87
Dividends	–	–	15	40	50	54	57	57	56
Payout ratios	–	–	7%	10%	11%	11%	18%	11%	64%

However, these dividends were small next to Apple's cash pile, and Apple was at the same time returning cash to the shareholders on a far larger scale through stock repurchase, as follows:

	1985	*1986*	*1987*	*1988*	*1989*	*1990*	*1991*	*1992*	*1993*
Stock repurchase ($M)	–	54	154	299	13	570	185	213	273

Despite this, Apple still had cash and short-term investments of $892 compared to equity of $2,026 in 1993. Apple appears to pursue a policy of steadily increasing dividend, albeit at a low payout ratio consistent with its status as a high-growth, high-technology company. For getting significant amounts of cash back to investors in a way which is flexible, year-on-year, it prefers to repurchase stock. Note also that, even though earnings slumped in 1993, Apple maintained its dividend and also a high level of stock repurchase.

Lintner's study of dividend policy

The classic study of the dividend behaviour of firms was Lintner's (1956) study. Lintner proceeded in two stages. First he conducted a series of interviews with businessmen to form a view of how they went about their dividend decisions. He then formed a model on the basis of these interviews which could be tested on a larger data set. It emerged from the interviews that investment needs were not a major consideration in the determination of dividend policy, rather that the decision to change the dividend was usually a response to a significant change in earnings which had disturbed the existing relationship between earnings and dividends.

Lintner modelled this dividend behaviour as follows:

$$\Delta D_{it} = a_i + c_i\,(D^{\star}_{it} - D_{i,t-1}) + U_{it}$$

where ΔD_{it} = change in dividends per share of company i in year t
c_i = speed of adjustment factor
$D^{\star}_{it}$ = target dividend payout
$D_{i,t-1}$ = last period's dividend per share
a_i = constant
U_{it} = normally distributed random error term

Lintner fitted this model to dividends and earnings data from 1918 to 1941. He found that firms appeared to have a target payout ratio of .5 and to adjust towards this at a rate of 30% per year. His model explained 80% of changes in dividends in the firms he studied.

In a later study Fama and Babiak (1968) tested a variety of models of dividend behaviour against dividend data for 201 firms from 1947 to 1964. They found that Lintner's model performed well and was only improved by suppressing the constant term and introducing a lagged earnings term.

Lintner's findings suggest a pattern of dividends through time rather like the one depicted in Figure I. In Figure I dividends move in a lagged response to earnings, maintaining a constant payout ratio in the long term. Managers like a smooth and increasing dividend per share through time and are wary of increasing dividends if they might have to be reduced later on. This is not to say firms never cut dividends, they sometimes have to. If there is a general slump in earnings across the economy so that many firms are cutting dividends, then the embarrassment is reduced though it is still an agonising decision for the first few firms to take the plunge. GKN was in just this position in 1980. Lack of earnings meant it could not offset against corporation tax the ACT on its dividends, so increasing their cost, and GKN would have had to borrow cash at high

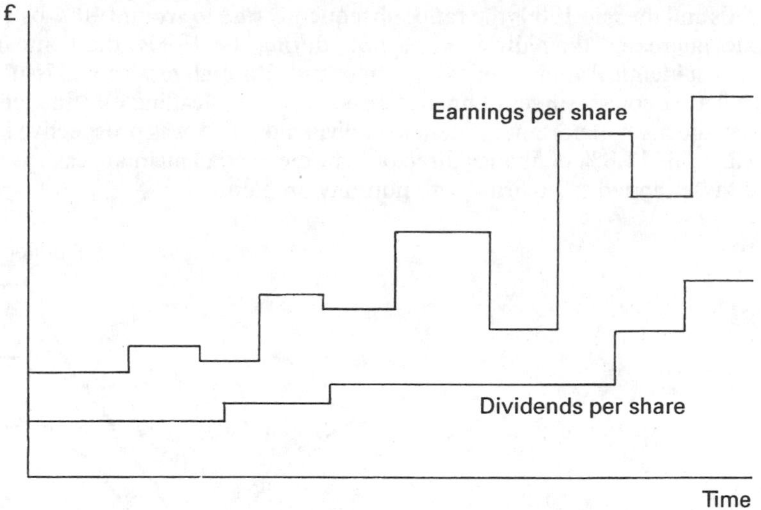

Figure I Relationship of dividend to earnings

interest rates just to maintain the previous year's dividend. Moreover GKN was in the process of making 10,000 workers redundant, so it was not clear why shareholders should not share some of the misery. In the end GKN cut its interim.

Dividend behaviour in the UK

In the UK the Bank of England tracks the payout ratio of industrial and commercial companies. In its Quarterly Bulletin of August 1993 the bank charts the UK payout ratio from 1970 to 1993 (Figure II). Having sustained a payout ratio of around 20% between

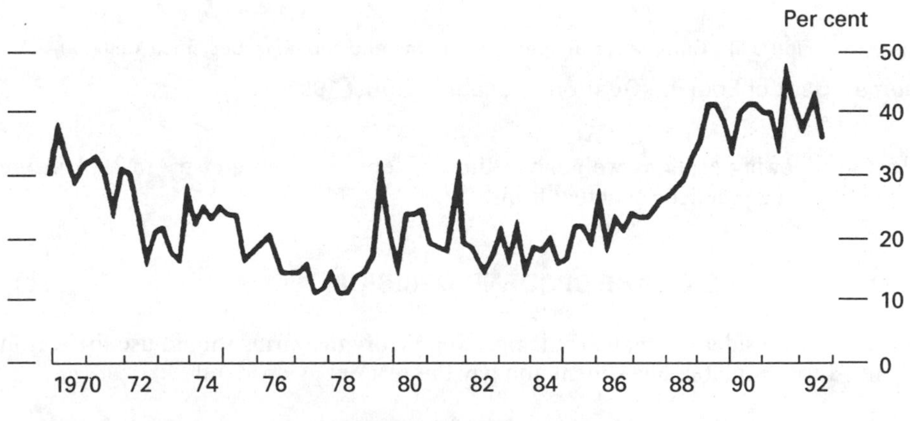

Figure II Dividend payout ratio[1]

Source Bank of England Quarterly Bulletin, August 1993

1 Dividend payments as a percentage of post-tax income.

the mid 1970s and the mid 1980s the ratio subsequently rose to around 40% by 1993. But, as companies increased their dividend payouts during the 1980s, the company sector raised an almost identical amount of cash from outside through new capital issues (Figure III). The Bulletin quotes a survey of finance directors by 3i, a leading UK financing house. Far and away the most important influence on dividend policy was prospective long-term profit growth. Only 14.8% of finance directors saw the need to maintain cash as the prime factor, and these tended to be firms with liquidity problems.

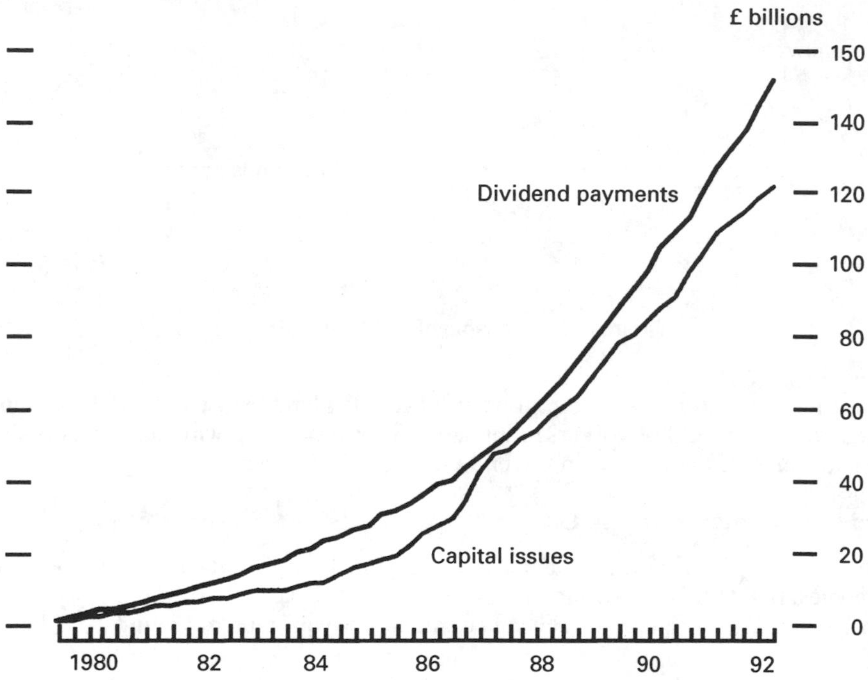

Figure III Cumulative dividend payments and capital issues since 1980

Source Bank of England Quarterly Bulletin, August 1993

In the following sections we analyse the dividend decision and try to explain these dividend-paying practices of actual firms.

II THE ANALYSIS OF THE DIVIDEND DECISION

First we will consider the 'naive' but appealing theory that firms should use the earnings they need for profitable investment and pay the rest out as dividends.

A naive model: dividends as a residual

Gordon Grub

Gordon Grub Ltd is a manufacturer with profit after tax this year of £1 million and the following set of investment projects available:

Gordon Grub Ltd
Available investment projects

Project	Capital required	NPV
	£	£
A	250,000	50,000
B	150,000	40,000
C	100,000	35,000
D	100,000	30,000
E	100,000	(20,000)

We know that to maximise the value of the firm, Grub should select projects A, B, C, D. If the projects have been properly appraised using a discount rate which measures the return that shareholders could earn elsewhere, their NPV measures the value created by using the funds inside the firm rather than distributing them for investment outside. This investment decision appears to imply a dividend decision. Surely the firm should hold on to the capital it needs, namely the capital required for projects A, B, C, D which is £600,000 (£250,000 + £150,000 + £100,000 + £100,000) and distribute the rest as dividend? To do anything else would be to reduce the value of the firm, either it would imply holding on to funds which could be better invested outside, or distributing funds that could be better invested inside. In this world the payout ratio would be determined year by year by the investment projects available to the firm that year. Dividends would be a residual. Figure IV depicts this idea.

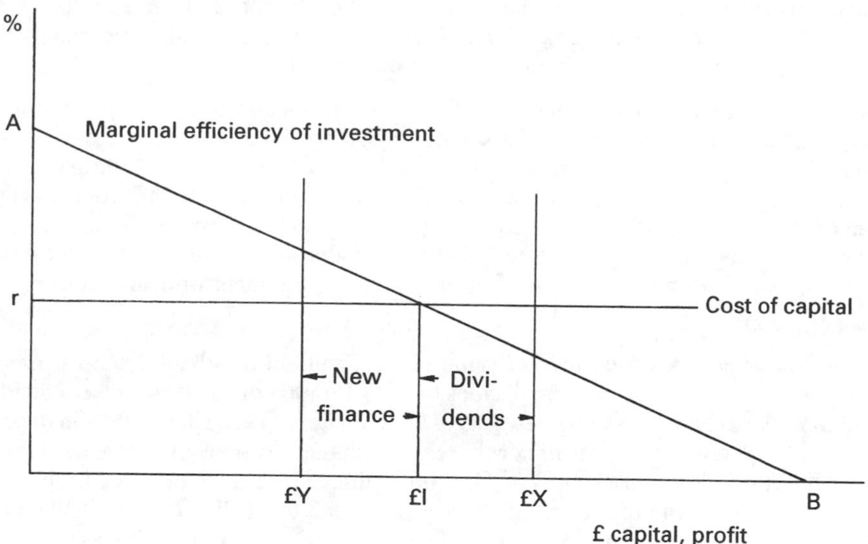

Figure IV A naive model of the dividend decision

Line AB in Figure IV depicts the investment projects the firm has available in the year, ranked in order of return – this is the familiar 'marginal efficiency of investment' schedule. Efficient investment dictates investing up to the point where the return on the marginal investment just equals the cost of capital, r, implying an investment outlay of I. If profits in the year are X a surplus of X−I can be distributed as dividend. If profits are only Y, new financing of I−Y will be needed.

In practice retentions *are* the major source of finance, and Wilson (1980) reported 'In the evidence we have received from companies there are frequent allusions to external finance being regarded essentially as a means of making good any shortage of internal funds . . .' (p 148). But Lintner showed that firms do not appear to behave in line with the 'naive' model. Their preoccupation seems to be with maintaining a long-run target payout ratio. Moreover, as Figure IV shows, firms not only pay dividends and raise new external finance at the same time – a bizarre activity under the 'naive' theory – they are often inclined to *increase* dividends around a new share issue. To understand this behaviour we need to analyse the determinants of dividend policy carefully.

The perfect market model: Miller and Modigliani

In their 1961 paper Miller and Modigliani (MM) analysed the effect of dividend policy on the value of the firm in a perfect capital market. Just as they had with capital structure, they showed that dividend policy is irrelevant; given their assumptions 'the current value of the firm must be independent of the dividend of the firm'. MM made the following assumptions:

1 *Perfect capital markets* That is, markets in which buyer and seller are price takers, free and fully available information, no transactions costs, neutral taxation.
2 *Rational behaviour* MM define this as 'investors always prefer more wealth to less and are indifferent as to whether a given increment to their wealth takes the form of cash payments or an increase in the market value of their holdings of shares'.
3 *Certainty* MM also demonstrated that their conclusions hold under uncertainty about the future profits and investment programme of the firm.

In such a world homemade financial policy is a perfect substitute for corporate financial policy, and there are no obstacles to market arbitrage driving into line the values of firms that pursue different policies. The investor is left exactly as well-off whether the firm pays him a dividend or not. If he gets a dividend the value of his shares will be less than if he does not by just the amount of the dividend. And if he does not get a dividend he can create his own homemade altenative by selling shares: he will be left with the same value of cash and shares as if the firm had paid a dividend. We can get the main features of MM's argument with an example:

Irrelevance plc

Irrelevance plc has a total market value of £1.2 million in 300,000 shares presently worth £4 each. Suppose the firm decides to pay £150,000 of its assets out as a dividend, and to replace them by issuing new shares. The owner of each share gets 50p dividend, but what happens to the value of her share? In exchange for their £150,000 cash the new shareholders will require shares of £150,000 value. Since the total value of the firm is £1,200,000 the value of the existing shares must fall to £1,050,000, or £1,050,000 ÷ 300,000 = £3.50 per share. (We can work out, in passing, how many shares would need to be issued to the new equity, £150,000 ÷ £3.50 = 42,857.) Hence the owner of one share in Irrelevance plc is in the same position whether or not the firm pays a dividend:

	Dividend paying	*No dividend*
Value of dividend	.50	–
Value of share	3.50	4.00
Shareholder's wealth	£4.00	£4.00

What would have happened to the value of a share if Irrelevance had decided to pay the dividend but *not* to replace the cash from outside? We cannot say, because that would require knowing the NPV of the £150,000 used in the firm. By assuming that the cash is *replaced* we are leaving the firm, its assets and earnings capacity, unchanged, and thus can expect the value of the firm to be unchanged. Reducing the size of the firm would be an investment decision, and that would obscure the analysis of the dividend decision.

There are two points to note in the argument. First, the firm's investment plans were unaffected by the dividend policy, so that the distributed cash had to be replaced; this is probably the main psychological barrier to accepting the irrelevance proposition since we tend to associate retention with reinvestment. Second, that replacing the cash meant transferring an identical amount of share value to new investors. However, both these depend on the proposition that the total value of the firm is unaffected by the dividend.

To demonstrate that the irrelevance proposition holds under uncertainty as well as certainty MM extend their rationality assumption. They assume 'symmetric market rationality' that is, every trader in the market is rational and imputes rationality to every other trader in forming his expectations. In this case MM suggest that two otherwise identical firms with different dividend policies could not sustain different values in the market. It is important to note that uncertainty introduces the possibility of the firm replacing cash through issuing debt, as an alternative to equity. Does the use of debt affect the value of the firm? This of course is the subject of MM's 'other', 1958, article in which they show that under similar perfect market assumptions the level of gearing does not affect the value of the firm.

III THE EFFECT OF MARKET IMPERFECTIONS

We can now assess systematically the impact of certain market imperfections that may occur in practice.

Taxation

The UK system of company taxation, the imputation system, is often held to be neutral with respect to dividends. Consider a firm wondering whether to distribute £100. The appropriate comparison is between (a) distributing £100 while issuing £100 of shares, and (b) retaining £100. If the firm distributes £100, it must remit £100 × 25/75 = £33.33 to the Revenue in the next quarter as a payment of advance corporation tax (assuming a rate of imputation of 25%). The Revenue deems the advance corporation tax to cover the shareholders' basic rate tax. So the £100 is 'net' to the shareholders, and the £33.33 paid by the firm is an advance payment of a corporation tax liability the firm would have had to pay anyhow. Under the imputation system, therefore, the dividend costs the firm £100 and the shareholder receives £100. If he reinvested this money by buying £100 of shares, he and the firm would be just as well off as if the firm had retained the £100 in the first place.

In practice this simple account of the neutrality of the imputation system needs qualifying in various ways. For one thing there is a cash-flow cost. The time-lag between paying advance corporation tax and paying mainstream corporation tax can be considerable. In the present example, if the lag were only one year and the firm's cost of capital was 10%, then the cost of the early payment is £33.33 × 10% = £3.33. (Additionally there may be some small tax costs associated with issuing the £100 of new shares such as VAT on brokerage.) On the other hand, if the £100 is retained the shareholders incur a potential liability to capital gains tax, though if the shareholders do not plan to sell in the near future the present value of the capital gains tax liability may be substantially reduced.

However, the fundamental difficulty is that we assumed a tax-paying firm, with investors who pay basic rate tax. For realism, as we did with capital structure, we have to take account of the diversity of tax positions of the firm and its investors, and this makes it hard to generalise about the impact of the tax system on dividend policy.

In so-called 'classical' tax systems, which are found in the US, Holland, Belgium, and some other countries, firms do not receive a tax credit when they pay a dividend. But something similar can arise in the UK. If the firm is not in a tax-paying position then the advance corporation tax cannot be offset, at least until the firm returns to a tax-paying position. At the limit this could be never, and the £33.33 will become surplus advance corporation tax, an incremental tax. Firms in this position might be unprofitable but they might also be high-growth, with a lack of mainstream corporation tax due to high capital allowances. As to the shareholders, we assumed they were paying basic rate income tax. An important group of shareholders is tax-exempt; institutions like pension funds and charities do not pay tax and can reclaim the advance corporation tax paid on their dividends. On the other hand, wealthy individual shareholders may be paying higher rates of tax.

Each firm will have to assess the composition of its shareholding and weigh their tax-paying positions and its own in determining its dividend policy. The outcome may be on either side of neutrality. So while the imputation system is neutral for basic rate taxpayers when the firm is tax paying and can recover the advance corporation tax, tax exempt investors will prefer distribution and higher-rate taxpayers will prefer retention. Using our earlier numbers, the tax exempt investor can recover tax of £33.33 on his £100 dividend, and so receives £133.33 at a cost of £100 to the firm.[2] If the UK firm only has tax exempt investors it would be worth paying dividend right up to the point where the firm had permanent surplus advance corporation tax, so was effectively being taxed under classical rules – at this point the credit is worthless to the firm, so it is costing the firm £133.33 to provide the dividend. In the UK the tax exempt group includes overseas investors, and individuals investing through tax-free vehicles such as 'personal equity plans'. This, and the fact that an increasing proportion of firms were tax-paying and thus able to recover the advance corporation tax credit in the 1980s may explain the rise in payout ratios we observed in Section I.

A clientele effect?

Since investors' tax positions may give them positive preferences for dividends or for growth, we can expect a company to develop a clientele of shareholders who like its dividend policy. There are other market imperfections which generate this sort of preference, besides taxation. For example some institutional investors are constrained by their trust deeds from making current expenditures from capital. And though the hard logic of finance implies indifference between dividends and capital gains, it is easy to conceive of individual investors who impose a similar constraint on themselves. They prefer high income shares and shudder at the thought of 'living off capital'. They conflict with MM's assumption of rationality.

MM themselves suggested that the formation of clienteles would permit the market to absorb certain tax imperfections, and that even if there was not a perfect match between the distribution of shareholder preferences and the distribution of company payout ratios,

2 The contrast is with the US where the firm does not get a tax credit when it pays a dividend; hence in a country with a classical tax system it is tax exempt investors who are neutral.

investors could build their own payout ratios by buying appropriate proportions of what was available. Only if the distribution of preferences was heavily skewed to one end would the perfect market results be impaired.

Do firms develop clienteles? Research in the US by Llewellen, Stanley, Lease and Schlarbaum (1978) shed some light on the significance of the clientele effect in practice. Llewellen et al surveyed 2,500 clients of a large broker by questionnaire, and received 914 responses from investors holding interests in 1,869 different shares in all. They ranked the dividend-yields of these shares into ten groups then used multiple discriminant analysis to determine any significant differences between the characteristics of investors in the groups. They conclude

> it seems to us, that a substantially sharper profile of differences would be necessary to raise much of a concern about investor specialisation along tax lines, or to suggest to corporations a 'tax-tailored' dividend policy . . . [and] we . . . are unable to find in the data much evidence to support the notion that an important dividend-tax-clientele effect is in fact present.

But other studies in the US concluded the opposite. Pettit (1977) who also studied the portfolios of brokerage clients concluded that there was a portfolio effect since he was able to explain a significant part of the variation between the dividend-yields of individual investor's portfolios in terms of factors such as the investor's age, family income, and marginal tax rates. In an earlier study Elton and Gruber (1970) also found support for a clientele effect using a rather different methodology.

Transactions costs

One market imperfection which creates a bias towards retention is the existence of issue costs on new shares. As we see in Chapter 14 these are of two sorts, *administrative* costs which for a relatively small 'issue for sale' can be of the order 6% and *issue discount* which can be 15% or more if shares are issued to new equity. In a rights issue the costs are less – issue discount is not a cost, and the administrative costs may be lower. These costs make retained earnings a cheaper source of finance than new issue finance. Also, if firms do build up clienteles of investors, the transactions costs associated with the purchase and sale of shares will provide an incentive for firms to maintain a stable dividend policy – *homemade dividend policy* will have a cost attached to it.

Uncertainty and the supply of information

The future cash flows from firms are uncertain, and it is sometimes argued that dividends are 'relevant' because they resolve some of this uncertainty. On the other hand MM claimed that their irrelevance proposition still held under uncertainty. We need to distinguish two things – first, that the future is uncertain, second, that the information which can help form expectations about this uncertain future may not be freely and equally available to everyone. The first is an immutable fact about the world, the second is a potential market imperfection.

The evidence from testing of the efficient markets theory suggests that information is not 'equally' available in practice. In particular we distinguish two levels of access – the *insider* level and the *outsider* level. The insiders are management and their advisers who should have the best access to the relevant information for forecasting the firms' future cash flows, and who in part determine it by their decisions. The outsiders are shareholders who receive a limited diet of highly aggregated information about the past performance of the firm. Shareholders employ analysts to try and bridge this gap by close scrutiny of the firm, but analysts are unable to completely bridge the gap and as tests of strong-form market efficiency indicate, possession of inside information remains a thing of value. In this context the dividend decision is a significant signal of future prospects. Its significance as a signal springs from a general belief that managers do not like reducing dividends below the previous year's level. So when management sets a dividend it is implicitly making a statement that the dividend can be maintained in future periods, and thus a statement about expected future profit levels. On this view the dividend decision becomes a quasi profit forecast.

MM recognised the informational role of dividends. They noted

> . . . in the real world a change in the dividend rate is often followed by a change in the market price (sometime spectacularly so). Such a phenomonon would not be incompatible with irrelevance to the extent that it was merely a reflection of . . . 'the information content' of dividends . . .
>
> . . . where a firm has adopted a policy of dividend stabilisation with a long-established and generally appreciated 'target payout ratio', investors are likely to (and have good reason to) interpret a change in the dividend rate as a change in management's view of future profit prospects for the firm. The dividend change, in other words, provides the occasion for the price change though not its cause . . .
> (MM 1961)

MM are saying that the test of relevance is the effect of dividend policy on the value of the firm, but dividend policy does not alter the value of the firm, only the timing of the recognition of its value. Of course if dividends have an information role which management and shareholders recognise as important this will lead to a dividend policy that is different some or all of the time from what it would otherwise have been. In this case the firm will be retaining more, or on the other hand raising more from the other sources, than it would have done. Surely this entails a cost? Not per se, only if some of the other market imperfections we have discussed, such as tax costs and transactions costs, are real.

Various writers have investigated if dividend change announcements affect share value. Watts (1973) concluded that no significant value gains could be made with prior access to dividends announcements but Pettit (1972) concluded that dividend information was used by the market in determining the value of shares. These studies seem to imply that dividend announcements do have an information content, and the stock market appears to be efficient in using this information. Of course dividend information is not the only data used by the market in determining share prices.

IV SUMMARY

Dividend policy is a key financing decision, since dividends determine retentions and these are the main source of finance for most firms. The most obvious dividend policy would be the one which just distributed those earnings the company could not profitably reinvest. MM showed that under perfect market assumptions it would not matter what dividend policy the firm chose, the value of the firm would be unaffected by whether it used retentions or new issue finance for its investment. In practice firms have target payout ratios in the long term, and these tend to reflect their financing needs. In the short term firms do not pay out a set proportion as earnings rise and fall. They like a smoothly rising dividend per share and strongly dislike cutting dividends. This gives dividends a signalling role: it indicates that management think current dividends can be maintained. The neutrality of the tax system with respect to dividends depends very much on the particular tax situation of the firm and the shareholders. There is no doubt, however, that the cost of new issue finance provides a strong incentive to retain earnings.

Putting together the observations of Lintner and others, the arguments of MM, and our knowledge of real world market imperfections, we can get a picture of the factors that will shape the dividend policy of the firm:

1 High-growth firms will probably have lower payout ratios. Issue costs make retained earnings a cheaper source of finance than new issues, other things equal. Hence the firm's target payout ratio will reflect investment needs in the long run, in line with the 'naive' model.
2 In the short run, the firm will be conscious of the information signalling properties of dividends. The firm will be keen to show a regular advance in dividend per share, but be aware of the risk of having to reduce dividends in the future.
3 Around these general conclusions, the relative preferences of the firm and its shareholders as to dividend policy will depend very much on their individual tax positions. High retention policies will appeal to shareholders with high personal tax rates, and to firms which cannot offset their advance corporation tax, but the UK tax system provides a strong incentive to distribute dividends in normal circumstances.

REFERENCES AND BIBLIOGRAPHY

Bhattacharya, S — 'Imperfect Information, Dividend Policy, and the "Bird in the Hand" Fallacy', Bell Journal of Economics, Spring 1979, pp 259–270.

Elton, E J, and Gruber, M J — 'Marginal Stockholders' Tax Rates and the Clientele Effect', Review of Economics and Statistics, February 1970, pp 68–74.

Lintner, J — 'Distribution of Incomes of Corporations Among Dividends, Retained Earnings and Taxes', American Economic Review, May 1956, pp 97–113.

Llewellen, W G, Stanley, K L, Lease, R C, and Schlarbaum, G G — 'Some Direct Evidence on the Dividend Clientele Phenomenon', Journal of Finance, December 1978, pp 1385–1399.

Miller, M H, and Modigliani, F — 'Dividend Policy, Growth and the Valuation of Shares', Journal of Business, October 1961, pp 163–196.

Miller, M H, and Scholes, M S — 'Dividends and Taxes', Journal of Financial Economics, December 1978, pp 333–364.

Pettit, R R — 'Dividend Announcements, Security Performance and Capital Market Efficiency', Journal of Finance, December 1972, pp 993–1007.

Pettit, R R — 'Taxes, Transactions Costs and Clientele Effect of Dividends', Journal of Financial Economics, December 1977, pp 419–436.

Wilson, H — Report of the Committee to Review the Functioning of Financial Institutions, 1980, Cmnd 7937.

QUESTIONS

1 According to the MM model, the shareholder is just as well-off if the firm retains £1 as if they pay him a dividend of £1 and replace it with a new share issue. What assumptions are necessary for this conclusion? Does irrelevance hold under realistic assumptions?

2 MM say dividend policy is 'irrelevant' and so should not affect share prices. But earlier we showed that the value of a share is the present value of the future dividend stream. Is there a conflict here?

3 The following in condensed form is a letter published in Accountancy Age on 3 February 1983 on the topic of current cost income, dividends and the capital market:

> I have yet to see a company report which says that because of CCA figures the dividend has been proportionally reduced and in fact, in many instances, dividends have been maintained out of historically calculated profits when the CC accounts have shown an apparent loss. Neither does it appear that the stock market in general pays much attention to CCA figures otherwise prices would be dramatically reduced. If companies were to base their dividends on CCA there would inevitably be a collapse of stock market prices.
>
> Therefore management will continue, so long as historically produced profits permit, to maintain dividends in order to protect themselves. In the meantime industry will, as it always has, keep its shareholders happy and the wolf from the door by over distribution and will rely on raising new capital from its happy shareholders to finance the replacement of assets and working capital.

Comment on this letter.

CHAPTER 18

The cost of capital

The cost of capital is the vital link between a firm's financing and its investment. It measures the return the firm must earn on its assets to meet the requirements of investors. So the cost of capital provides the discount rate for evaluation of new projects and for valuing the firm as a whole, and it provides a benchmark for the return from existing activities.

In this chapter we show how to find the cost of capital. Since the firm may use both debt and equity finance, and these have different costs, we calculate the weighted average cost of capital or WACC. Section I assembles the raw materials for an analysis of the cost of the capital and Section II uses them to calculate the WACC. Section III describes an alternative which can be useful in some situations. This is the 'adjusted present value' (APV) approach in which we value the project or firm as though it were all-equity financed, then explicitly quantify the benefits from using debt. WACC is widely used: it is easy to calculate, decentralisable, and it fits nicely with theory, but it has limitations. We discuss these in Section IV.

I THE PRICE OF FINANCE IN THE MARKET PLACE

We have a good idea from previous chapters what factors determine the price of finance. Take as a base point the real, riskless interest rate, which is the return investors would want on a completely riskless loan if no inflation was expected. Onto this, investors will add a premium for anticipated inflation and a risk premium for the relative risk of the return. For loans of different term there will be a discount or premium reflecting the term-structure of interest rates. For some types of finance the cost to the user will be raised further by the market costs of raising finance.

We can get an idea of the term-structure and the shape of the *yield curve* by looking at the yield on riskless loans of different terms. Table I shows interest rates on a selection of inter-bank loans and redemption yields on government bonds in October 1994. Treasury-bills or 'T-bills' are three-month loans to the government, and are widely used as an indicator of the short-term interest rate. The UK T-bill rate was 5.72% in October 1994. By contrast Treasury stock, or 'gilts', redeemable in 2002, were yielding 8.8%. A commercial rate which is widely used as the basis of transactions is 'LIBOR', the London inter-bank offer rate. Table I shows that LIBOR was around 6% at that time.

Inflation and real returns

These yields are 'nominal'. How much of this is expected inflation? We can gauge this by looking at the yield on *index-linked* bonds. In index-linked bonds inflation is taken care of because the repayment of principal is indexed, so the observed yield on the bond is a real return. In October 1994, 2% Treasury Index-linked Bonds 1996 were yielding 2.92%. Historically, this figure is rather high. Over the years the real rate of return has been

Table I Yields in the UK money-market and on government bonds at 11 October 1994

Money Market	%		*Government Bonds*	%
Inter-bank overnight	4¾–6½	12¾	Treasury Stock 1995	6.89
7 days	5³⁄₁₆–5⁹⁄₁₆			
1 month	5⅜–5½	12	Exchequer Stock 1998	8.59
2 months	5³⁄₁₆–5¹⁵⁄₁₆	13	Treasury Stock 2000	8.83
3 months	6⁵⁄₁₆–6⁷⁄₁₆	9.75	Treasury Stock 2002	8.87
Treasury Bills				
1 month	5³⁄₁₆–5¼%			
3 months	5¹¹⁄₁₆–5¾%			

Source: Financial Times, 11 October 1994

between 0% and 1%. The vital attribute of index-linked bonds is that they enable us to discover what the market expects inflation to be in the future, and to back the market's expectations about inflation out of nominal rates.

We know that the relationship between the nominal interest, r, the real rate r′, and expected inflation, i, is[1]

$$1 + r = (1 + r')(1 + i)$$

Suppose that the redemption yield on Treasury Stock with a two-year term is 5.5% and the yield on an index-linked government stock of similar term is 2.9%, then

$$(1.055)^2 = (1.029)^2(1 + i)^2$$
$$1 + i = 1.055/1.029$$

Expected inflation i = 2.52% per annum over the next two years.

The market premium

The default risk on UK government bonds is effectively zero, but this does not mean these loans are risk-free. The main component of nominal returns is expected inflation and since actual inflation is uncertain, to this extent government bonds are a risky investment. But we would expect corporate bonds to yield more than government bonds, and ordinary shares, which bear the residual risk of business, to give a higher return still. The return on the equity market as a whole has two components, the dividend-yield and the capital gain, which is the percentage increase in the market index over the period. We show this in Table II for the years 1988–92, and also the redemption yields on more senior (less risky) company securities – debentures and loan-stock.

Clearly company debentures and loan-stock yield more than government bonds. Clearly also *redemption yields* on bonds are higher than the dividend yields on equities. This difference is sometimes known as the *reverse yield gap*, the implication being that yields are somehow the wrong way round, given the relative risks. Of course there is only a paradox in the reverse yield gap because we ignore the capital gain component of the return to equity. The reason bond-holders need higher yields is that they do not get capital growth, as equity may.

1 So $r = r' + i + r'i$, and since the magnitudes of r′ and i can make the cross product term r′i insignificant, a common rule of thumb is $r = r' + i$, the nominal rate is the sum of the real rate and inflation.

Table II Returns on FT Actuaries All Share Index

	Ordinary shares			Debenture and loan-stock
	Capital gain %	*Dividend-yield* %	*Total return* %	*Redemption yield* %
1988	−9.1	4.3	−4.8	10.80
1989	19.2	4.2	23.4	11.31
1990	−1.6	5.0	3.4	12.80
1991	8.7	4.9	13.6	11.34
1992	3.1	4.9	8.0	10.37

Source: CSO Financial Statistics, HMSO

However Table II shows how very erratic the total return to equity can be. Over the five-year period 1988 to 1992 it ranges from −4.8% to +23.4% annually. Because equity have the residual claim on business income, ex post returns to equity, the returns equity actually got, are a very noisy indicator of what they required, ex ante.

Valuation is a forward-looking exercise, so to estimate the CAPM we need at estimate of what the market risk-premium, $r_m - r_i$, *will be.* The best estimate of this is the historic premium measured over a very long period, that embraces wars, slumps and booms. Brealey (1990) measured the excess of the return on equities in the FTA All Share Index, r_m, over the return on treasury bills, r_i, for the years 1919 to 1989. The arithmetic average risk premium was just under 9%. This is an after-tax risk premium; Brealey assumed that the dividend-yield element was taxed under prevailing rules. Updated to 1993 the average is around 8.75%.

II THE WEIGHTED AVERAGE COST OF CAPITAL

If the firm uses finance of different types we want to know what it pays for its finance on average. We can find this by calculating the *weighted average cost of capital* (WACC), where

$$r_a = g \times \text{after-tax cost of debt} + (1 - g) \times \text{after-tax cost of equity} \qquad (1)$$

here r_a is the weighted average cost of capital, and g is the firm's gearing ratio and g = D/D + S where D is the value of debt and S is the value of equity. For convenience of exposition we assume just two sources of finance, but if the firm uses various types of funding with differing costs we simply take the weighted average across these. We now look in more detail at how to measure the gearing and how to find the cost of debt and the cost of equity.

Gearing

Market not book values

Gearing should be measured at market values, not at the book values of the debt and equity. Book values taken from balance-sheets are historic figures which do not measure the current capital structure of the firm. In measuring the WACC we want to know what it would cost to deploy another £1 of finance today – maintaining today's capital structure and using today's costs of capital.

In practice we do not always have market values available – often we find ourselves calculating WACC for an unquoted firm and will need to estimate the market values. And even with a quoted firm there is a strong chance the debt will not be quoted, so that we have to estimate the market value of debt. We could do this by capitalising the firm's interest expense using a capitalisation rate culled from a similar firm which does have its debt quoted, i e D = interest/x, where x = interest/value of debt, for a similar firm. But this begs the question, are the two firms similar in the risk of their debt? Common practice is to use market equity but book debt for simplicity.

Wide or narrow gearing?

How should gearing be measured – 'narrowly' to include only long-term debt, or 'widely' to include 'short-term' finance such as overdrafts? This really depends on what the permanent capital structure of the firm is expected to be. If short-term sources of finance are expected to be a permanent feature of the balance-sheet, as is often the case in practice, then it would be appropriate to use a concept of gearing which includes them.

Companies which have a significant cash holding in their balance sheet commonly net this against debt when calculating gearing and WACC. The issue, as we note next, is one of targets – if the ratio of net debt to equity is the proportion in which future investment will be financed then this WACC will be appropriate. If used as a benchmark for returns for existing activities, for consistency, these need to be operating returns excluding returns from financial assets.

Target not actual gearing

Similarly, if the firm is not presently at its optimal capital structure it is the firm's *target* rather than its *actual* gearing we should use. This can seem perplexing at first. But a similar situation arises when the firm *is* on target, but does not raise finance in those proportions.

Zoom Ltd

Zoom Ltd has a capital structure containing 50% debt, and feels its present gearing is optimal. Its specific cost of debt is 5% and of equity 15%. Zoom is planning an expansion programme which involves investing £1 million this year, and £1 million next. Because of the high fixed costs associated with issuing capital Zoom's finance director has decided to finance this year's investment by an issue of debt, and next year's by an issue of equity. She is wondering whether to appraise this year's investment using the actual cost of the funds they will use, 5% or the WACC, 10%.

The finance director must use 10% as her discount rate, reflecting her *target* gearing. Suppose she uses 5% this year, then, for 'consistency', 15% next year. She will be accepting projects with, say, an IRR of 8% this year but rejecting 12% projects next year. The point is that 5% is not Zoom's cost of capital. Zoom does not plan to continue raising finance at this cost, *nor could it*. The capital market only allows Zoom debt at 5% because Zoom is also raising half its finance in the form of equity yielding 15% – the costs of the component types of finance a firm uses are interdependent.

Costs of debt and equity: the effect of taxes

In previous chapters we have seen what drives the costs of debt and equity. In bringing these together to build the WACC the main area which needs care is the tax treatment. The question, as always, is one of opportunity cost. In all tax systems (that we are aware of) interest payments by companies are deductible for corporation tax. So if the tax rate is 35% it costs the firm £6.50 to put £10 of interest in the pocket of investors – the firm pays £10 but saves £3.50 to tax. The investor would then have to pay personal tax on the £10. In notation, if the corporate tax rate is T, and the cost of debt is a r_d, the after-corporate tax cost of debt is $(1-T)r_d$.

The difference comes on the equity side. Assume we calculate the cost of equity using beta, $r_e = r_i + \beta\ (r_m - r_i)$, where r_i is the riskless interest rate, and $(r_m - r_i)$ the market risk-premium. In 'classical' tax systems such as the US, dividends are not tax deductible for the company, they are 'double-taxed'. So the WACC in a classical tax system is

$$r_a = g[(1-T)r_d] + (1-g)[r_i+\beta\ (r_m-r_i)] \quad (1a)$$

But in many countries there is now some tax deduction for equity too. For instance in the UK system, when it pays a dividend the firm effectively purchases a tax credit for shareholders at the basic rate of personal income tax for dividend income. If P is the rate of imputation, that is, the rate of tax credit, then the WACC in an imputation system is[2]

$$r_a = g[(1-T).r_d] + (1-g)[(1-P).r_i+\beta\ (r_m - r_i)] \quad (1b)$$

Obstreporous and Son

Obstreporous and Son had recently used the proceeds from divesting of a subsidiary to retire £250 million of short-term debt. They now want to calculate the required return based on the new capital structure. The company balance-sheets showed the outstanding debt to fall into three categories:

	Amount	*Rate*
Short-term overdrafts	£57m	7.5%
Short-term bank loans	£80m	6.0%
Short-term finance leases and hire purchase contracts	£20m	6.5%
Long-term bank loans	£89m	6.5%
Long-term commercial paper	£795m	5.5%
Long-term debentures	£454m	6.25%
Interest-bearing share capital	£2m	8.5%
Total	£1,497m	

The pre-tax weighted average cost of debt (calculated by taking the sum of the coupon payments as a percentage of the total outstanding debt) turns out to be 6%. The corporate tax rate (T) is 33%, so the after-tax cost of debt is 6% × (1−.33) = 4.02%. £1,497 million is the book value of the debt. Since Obstreporous' corporate bonds are rated AA3, the risk of the company debt is considered negligible.

The market value of equity is easy to calculate. The company has 1,310m shares outstanding (fully diluted) which trade at a share price of £8.20. The market value of equity is therefore 1,310 million × £8.20 = £10,742 million. The return on equity is calculated by the after-tax capital asset pricing model: $r_e = (1-P)r_i + \beta(r_m-r_i)$. With the return of Treasury bills at 5%, the personal tax rate at 25%, the beta of Obstreporous at 1.15, and the historic market risk-premium at 8.75%, the after tax cost of equity was calculated to be 13.8%.

Obstreporous' gearing is 1,497/(1,497 + 10,742) = 12.2%

So WACC = 12.2% × 4.02% + 87.8% × 13.8% = 12.59%

2 Though the tax credit, S, only appears to apply to the riskless element of the cost of equity in (1b) this is because the market risk-premium of 8.75% we assume for the UK is already net of tax.

Inflation: some pitfalls

Some of the commonest pitfalls in using the cost of capital concern inflation. Most importantly, *you must use the real cost of capital to discount real cash flows, and nominal for nominal.* The numbers that come most readily to hand are the nominal cost of capital, and cash flows forecast at today's prices, i e real cash flows. This is a lethal mix which would lead to the rejection of many virtuous projects.

To get the real cost of capital calculate the nominal as (1a) or (1b) above, and deduct expected inflation as the final step. We have encountered companies calculating the real rate directly by using a real interest rate, say the yield on index-linked bonds, as r_i and in r_d. This leads to overstating the cost of capital by understating the tax saving. The Revenue give a tax deduction for the nominal cost of capital, not just the real.

Something which causes a lot of anxiety is whether to use the short, medium or long-term government rate as the riskless rate in the WACC formula. Some argue for a longer rate to match the maturity of the investment. Others point out that for investors, equity, at least if it is quoted, is highly liquid so that a short-term rate is appropriate. Moreover the market risk premium which we use is calculated as the excess return over the Treasury bill rate. In fact this problem is more apparent than real – the issue again is inflation. The main driver of the term structure of interest rates is inflation expectations over different horizons. What matters is that the inflation assumption built into the cash flows is consistent with that inflation rate implicit in the cost of capital you are using.

Asset betas

A potential difficulty in using WACC with a CAPM-based cost of equity is that the firm may not be quoted or have sufficient share-price history to calculate a beta. In this case we can use the beta of a firm with similar business risk. But likely as not that firm will have a different capital structure, imparting financial risk to its beta. A simple formula permits us to 'ungear' the beta, and regear it.

Because in the CAPM world the relationship between return and risk is linear, it follows that the beta of a portfolio of securities is simply the weighted average of the betas of the component securities. Similarly, the overall beta of a firm, which is often known as its *asset beta* is the weighted average of the betas of its debt and equity, as follows:

$$\text{asset beta} = \frac{D}{D+S}\,\beta\text{ debt} + \frac{S}{D+S}\,\beta\text{ equity}$$

We will assume the beta of the debt is zero, ie the debt is riskless. This is by no means necessarily the case, especially for highly geared firms in which debt is bearing significant risk, but it will serve as a useful approximation. Hence

$$\text{asset beta} = \frac{S}{D+S}\,\beta\text{ equity}$$

This gives us an expression for ungearing the observed equity beta of one firm, to find a suitable beta for an otherwise similar project or firm, with different gearing.

Court Ltd

Suppose we want to estimate a beta for Court Ltd. We notice that Ball plc is a similar company with similar business risk, and its shares have a beta of 1.2. Ball has 30% gearing, while Court has 50% debt in its capital structure. We can find the underlying asset beta by ungearing Ball's beta,

$$\text{asset beta} = \frac{7}{10} \times 1.2 = .84$$

This is the beta which an ungeared firm with this business risk would have. Gearing up the beta for Court gives

$$.84 = \frac{5}{10} \times \text{Court's beta, so}$$

$$\text{Court's beta} = 1.68$$

Adjusting WACC for local risk

The firm is effectively a bundle of projects. If those projects have different risks the WACC will be an average of the risky discount rates for the firm's component projects. Figure I shows the problem of using WACC as a discount rate when project risks differ. It plots project return against project beta. The WACC implies a constant discount rate whatever the project beta, hence in Figure I it plots as a horizontal line. We contrast this with the CAPM line, where now the β is different for each project j. The problem with using WACC is now clear. For certain projects, such as X and Y, WACC will yield the wrong investment decision. X would be rejected and Y accepted, since their expected returns are below and above the firm's average cost of capital respectively. But projects X and Y are significantly less, and more, risky than the firm as a whole, and using the CAPM to get a project cost of capital we can see X is earning a more than adequate return, and Y a return less than its cost of capital.

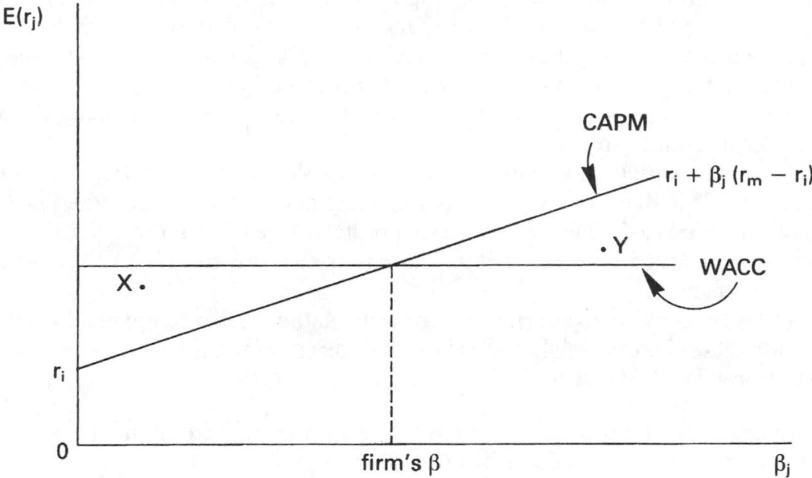

Figure I How WACC may lead to wrong investment decisions

In principle, the WACC can be adjusted, using a beta appropriate for each project. But the WACC is effectively a rule of thumb embodying a trade-off between accuracy and economy of operation. Immediately we start combining it with project betas, we lose the advantage of convenience. For large projects this will be worthwhile, but an effective compromise is to work out *divisional* betas and costs of capital. There will not be much loss of efficiency in this so long as most of the diversity in the firm's risk lies between its divisions, while within divisions projects are fairly homogeneous as to risk. The extent to which most risk-differences *are* inter-divisional will vary from firm to firm and will reflect the type of economic logic behind the firm's organisational structure. We know the sort of factors that are likely to cause differences in business risk and thus in beta; the operating leverage, the competitive structure of input and output markets, the rate of technological change, the sensitivity of demand to macroeconomic fluctuations, and so forth. So long as projects are fairly homogenous in factors like this within divisions, it will be safe to use a divisional cost of capital for appraising projects.

III ADJUSTED PRESENT VALUE

The WACC provides an average cost of capital for use across the firm's activities, and through time. We saw how to adjust WACC for risk, but there are other ways besides risk in which a project or divisional cost of capital can diverge from the average for the firm.

For one thing, the project's particular cash flow profile will determine the contribution it makes to the firm's overall financing requirement, and thus the amount of external financing it will require. If this external financing has to be by new issues of securities there will be *issue costs* which can add a hefty premium to the cost of capital, relative to retained earnings. Second, and perhaps most important, there can be tax advantages to gearing, and projects may differ in the extent to which they can be financed by debt. This can happen if individual projects create assets which are more or less able to form security for loans than the average for the firm. For example, suppose a firm with overall gearing of 50% undertakes an investment involving highly securable assets which can be financed 75% by borrowing. The project will bring tax advantages to the firm which would be understated if it were evaluated using a WACC with 50% gearing. Of course issue costs, and the tax advantages to borrowing, are already reflected in the WACC. But we cannot assume that all activities are average in these respects, as we would be doing if we used WACC as the discount rate.

Another problem which arises whether we are using WACC to value projects or to value the firm as a whole is that the tax effects of financing may vary through time. Perhaps on the basis of a detailed cash-flow projection we predict the gearing of the firm to change, or the firm to move in and out of tax-paying. There is no easy way to adjust WACC to reflect these changing factors.

Myers (1974) suggested an alternative approach. Rather than attempt to adjust the cost of capital for these factors we should value them directly by calculating *adjusted present value*. We proceed in two stages:

1 Find the value of the project or firm as though it were all-equity financed, using an equity rate that properly reflects business risk.
2 Find the value of the tax savings associated with borrowing, and any other unique financing costs and benefits the project or firm brings. Add 2 to 1 to find the Adjusted Present Value.

Prenderville Ltd

Prenderville Ltd is thinking of investing £500,000 in a project against which it can secure loans of 75% of the written-down value of the assets. The project generates net cash flows of £135,000 per annum for 5 years. The asset value declines on a straight line to a zero resale value after 5 years. The company's marginal tax rate is 35%, it can get

25% per annum writing-down allowances on the asset, and pays tax with a one-year lag. Prenderville's pre-tax cost of equity is 12%, and of debt 7%, and it has 50% gearing. For simplicity of exposition, we assume Prenderville is taxed under classical rules, so there is no tax deduction for equity. This is plausible for a UK firm with surplus advance corporation tax. First we will appraise the project using conventional WACC, then using Adjusted Present Value.

Weighted average cost of capital

In Prenderville's case we have $r_e = 12\%$, $r_d = 7\%$, $T = 35\%$, and $\frac{D}{D+S} = .5$

So $WACC = (1 - .35) \times .5 \times 7\% + .5 \times 12\% = 8.3\%$

Prenderville will get the following capital allowances, at 25% of the reducing balance:

Year	0	1	2	3	4	Total
	125	94	70	53	158	500

Using 8.3% as a discount rate we can find the project NPV as follows:

Project appraisal using WACC (£000)

Year	*0*	*1*	*2*	*3*	*4*	*5*	*6*
Asset cost	(500)	–	–	–	–	–	–
Tax on capital allowances (at 35% lagged 1 year)		44	33	25	19	55	–
Revenues		135	135	135	135	135	–
Tax on revenue			(47)	(47)	(47)	(47)	(47)
Annual cash flows	(500)	179	121	113	107	143	(47)
8.3% discount factors	1	.923	.853	.787	.727	.671	.620
PRESENT VALUES	(500)	165	103	89	78	96	(29)
						NPV =	2

Using WACC the project has a marginal positive NPV of £2,000.

Adjusted present value

Given its atypical debt structure it would be safer to calculate the project's APV. We do this in two steps.

(1) What would be the value of the project, all-equity financed? To find this we can use the same annual cash flows we had before. But discounted at what rate? The all-equity discount rate is *not* 12%, but the return equity would require if the firm *were* all-equity financed. For convenience we will assume the project has the same risk as the whole firm. We can disentangle the appropriate all-equity rate for the firm from the data we have, using MM's after-tax proposition II:

$r_e = r_a + (1 - T)(r_a - r_d)\frac{D}{S}$, where r_a is the all-equity, or 'ungeared' cost of equity.

Substituting, $.12 = r_a + .65(r_a - .07)\frac{1}{1}$, $r_a = 10\%$

The fact that r_a is less than 12% provides a check we have got the answer right. When the firm is ungeared the equity is relatively less risky, so we expect equity-holders to accept a lower return.

Discounting the annual cash flows at this new rate gives

Year	*0*	*1*	*2*	*3*	*4*	*5*	*6*
Annual cash flows	(500)	179	121	113	107	143	(47)
10% discount factors	1	.909	.826	.751	.683	.621	.564
PRESENT VALUES	(500)	163	100	85	73	89	(27)
							NPV = (£17)

If the project were all-equity financed it would have a negative NPV of £17,000.

(2) What is the value of the tax advantage to debt? We can find this as follows. We know that each year the firm borrows 75% of the asset value of the project, and that the asset value is depreciating at 20% per year. We find the value of the tax saving as the discounted present value of the annual tax savings on interest, using $r_d = 7\%$ as the discount rate since this is a low risk stream.

Tax saving on debt

Year	*1*	*2*	*3*	*4*	*5*	*6*	*TOTAL*
1) Written down value of assets (£000)	500	400	300	200	100	–	
2) Debt (.75 of 1))	375	300	225	150	75	–	
3) Interest (.07 of 2))	26.25	21	15.75	10.5	5.25	–	
4) Tax saving (.35 of 3))	–	9.19	7.35	5.51	3.68	1.84	
PV of Tax savings at 7%		8.03	6	4.2	2.62	1.23	22.08

The value of the tax savings is £22,080. Added to the all-equity NPV this gives the following APV:

adjusted present value = −£17,000 + £22,080 = £5,080

The tax saving has been sufficient to make this project worth undertaking.

APV versus WACC

The idea behind APV is simple and elegant. The reader who recalls Chapter 16 will recognise that we are just using MM's proposition I, rather than II, to appraise projects. MM's after tax proposition I was $V_G = V_U + TD$. The value of the geared firm is the value of the ungeared firm plus the value of tax savings. We can apply this to projects too, and avoid the averaging assumptions of WACC.

The problem with APV is that, though conceptually sound, it is less simple and more time consuming to implement in practice. WACC is essentially a *rule of thumb*. Like all rules of thumb it embodies a trade-off between accuracy and economy. There is a danger that using WACC will lead the firm to make some wrong investment choices. But the great virtue of WACC is that it is easy to calculate and to pass to subordinates to permit decentralised decision-making. The firm has to weigh the costs and benefits. We suspect that APV will be attractive when valuing firms, or when valuing a project which is sizeable and where the firm believes its financing costs – tax advantages, issue costs, and so forth – are significantly out of line with the rest of the firm.

IV THE COST OF CAPITAL: FINAL COMMENTS

In recent years, the use of WACC with a CAPM-based cost of equity has become widespread, particularly in medium and large companies where there are people in the planning or finance area who have been trained in these concepts. This is good, because it means that the company is embracing some fundamental and important ideas: that the firm only adds value when it earns a return at least as good as investors can get from other investments of similar risk; and that the systematic risk that investors care about and which is captured by the CAPM may be not at all what we mean by risk in an everyday sense.

But the cost of capital is such an important number in the financial management of a modern company that it needs handling with extreme care, and by and large the required care lies in the direction of applied common sense, rather than increased technical precision. The ability to calculate the cost of capital in a rigorous and objective way is important for the firm, not least because if we are setting different targets for different business units, these need to be credible and defensible. But it is important to be aware of the inherent difficulties, and of the questions to which economists do not yet have clear answers. Two of these concern tax, and the market premium.

Tax

Our WACC equations for the classical, and imputation system, equations (1a) and (1b) capture the corporate tax incentives associated with financing; the implied benchmark is the return the investor could earn on other securities of similar risk *before personal tax*. But what investors actually care about is after-tax income, and our WACC will fail to measure the opportunity cost of capital to the extent that personal taxes differ systematically on different classes of security, in other words if personal taxes reduce or enhance the effect of corporate taxes. We saw in a previous chapter how theorists have described 'worlds' in which precisely this will occur. Both Modigliani and Miller, and Miller were assuming a classical tax system. In the MM world there were no personal taxes so the corporate tax advantage to debt carried through. In the Miller world there were personal taxes, and taxable investors held debt while tax-exempt investors held equity, in equilibrium completely eliminating the corporate tax advantage to debt. Again, amongst equity investors clienteles might form around dividend policy, with high-tax investors preferring low payout stocks that deliver more return in the form of lightly-taxed capital gains. The trouble is, we are not entirely sure if the real world is MM or Miller, nor do we have much evidence about dividend clienteles. For this reason, unless the firm knows the idiosyncratic tax profile of its investors, we recommend it use a WACC that simply embodies the primary corporate tax savings to financing.

Sometimes the firm may not be able to capture the corporate tax savings in full. We saw in Chapter 3 how tax loss carry-forwards, and in the UK unused imputation credits ('surplus advance corporation tax'), create a situation where the effective tax rates, T and S, are below the statutory rates. In this case if the firm can estimate these effective rates, it should use the effective rates in its WACC.

The market premium

The market premium is the largest single element in the WACC, and the most controversial. The aim is simple, we want to know what return equity investors will get on average in the future – this is their opportunity cost when they invest in the particular project or firm under review. In the absence of a theory of the animal spirits which determine the compensation investors require for equity risk, it is wise to base expectations on the largest possible history of data. Copeland, Koller and Murrin (1990) highlight the danger of taking too short a period. They suggest that the very high prices observed on the stock market before the 1987 crash may have been explained by analysts using as a risk-premium the very low average of the previous two decades, which in the US was between 2.6% and 3.5%.

The real controversy concerns the averaging method, not the estimation period. The 8.75% estimate which we use for the UK is an arithmetic mean. But using a geometric mean typically yields a rather smaller premium and many US commentators recommend this. So Copeland et al recommend a geometric mean risk-premium of 5–6% for US companies though the arithmetic mean in the US has been 7–8%. There are, in other words, different views on what is reasonable expectation about the return which investors will require.

V SUMMARY

WACC is a very convenient way to get a discount rate. The company treasurer can figure out the target gearing for the firm and the costs of its specific sources of finance, and the resulting discount rate can be promulgated round the firm, permitting decentralised investment appraisal. But this convenience is bought at a price. The WACC is an average for the whole firm, whereas the capital used by each individual project may have its own cost, in particular projects may have different risk levels, project financing may bring differing tax advantages and issue costs. In some cases, when valuing larger projects or whole firms, it may be preferable to calculate the 'adjusted present value' – value the project or firm as though it were all-equity financed, then estimate the value of the tax and other financing savings from borrowing separately.

REFERENCES AND BIBLIOGRAPHY

Brealey, R A — 'Notes on UK Risk Premium 1919–89', unpublished paper, London Business School, 1990.

Copeland, T, Koller, T, and Murrin, J — *Valuation, Measuring and Managing the Value of Companies* (1990) Wiley.

Ibbotson, R G and Sinquefield, R A — 'Stocks, Bonds, Bills and Inflation: Year-by-Year Historical Returns (1926–1974)', Journal of Business, January 1976, pp 11–47.

Miller, M H and Modigliani, F — 'Some Estimates of the Cost of Capital to the Electric Utility Industry; 1954–1957', American Economic Review, June 1966, pp 333–391.

Modigliani, F and Miller, M H — 'Corporate Income Taxes and the Cost of Capital; A Correction', American Economic Review, June 1963, pp 433–443.

Myers, S C — 'Interactions of Corporate Financing and Investment Decisions – Implications for Capital Budgeting', Journal of Finance, March 1974, pp 1–25.

QUESTIONS

1 The balance-sheet of Rodent plc gives the following information about share capital, reserves and long-term liabilities:

	£m
Share capital, 1,000,000 shares of £1	1.0
Reserves and retained profit	0.5
	1.5
4% irredeemable debentures	1.0

The dividend paid by the company has been 20 pence per share for many years and is expected to remain at this level indefinitely if no investment is made this year. A dividend of 20p has just been paid and the current market price of the shares is £2 each. The market price of £100 nominal of debentures is £40. The company's marginal tax rate is 35%.

The company has an investment project available with the following cash flows:

	Now £	*End of each year in perpetuity* £
Cash flow	−100,000	8,000

Report to Rodent's directors on the company's cost of capital, and whether the project should be accepted.

2 Rodent's managing director replies to your report. He says that, because debt is manifestly cheaper he intends to finance only with debentures from now on. Reply to him.

3 Tobin plc has asked you to calculate its required rate of return for project appraisal. You do some preliminary work and discover that the standard deviation of the returns on Tobin's equity has been 14%, and on the market equity as a whole, 8%, and the coefficient of correlation between the returns on Tobin and on the market is 0.5. Tobin has 40% debt in its capital structure.

Estimate Tobin's beta coefficient.

Indicate how you would estimate the remaining information needed to calculate the required rate of return.

Estimate a beta for an otherwise similar company with 30% gearing.

4 Alberto Industrial Fasteners is planning to invest £80,000 in an automated widget nurdler. Under a technology support scheme the government will lend 75% of the cost at normal market interest rates, the loan to be repaid in equal instalments over the asset's life. The machine is expected to generate a net cash flow of £36,000 per year and to be scrapped after three years with no residual value. The corporation tax rate is 35% and the machine will qualify for a first year allowance of 50% and 25% writing-down allowances subsequently.

Alberto is 30% financed by borrowing, and its debt and equity investors require 12% and 18% returns respectively. The costs of raising debt are considered to be more-or-less zero, whereas issuing new equity involves 5% issue costs.

Value this project using the APV method, and the weighted average cost of capital.

5 What are the relative merits of WACC and APV for investment decision making?

Part V
Performance measurement

Chapter 19

Accounting numbers

In this chapter we examine the relationship between accounting measures of income and value, and financial valuation. We want to known how accounting values relate to economic values, and how accounting profit relates to cash flow.

Section I explores the relationship between different measures of the cost and value of assets, and examines how these measures are used in financial decisions. Section II examines how the company's balance-sheet reports its assets. Section III contrasts accounting profit with economic income and describes the content of a company's profit and loss account and its cash flow.

I COST AND VALUE – THE BASIC IDEAS

The company balance sheet provides the raw material for several important pieces of financial analysis. In valuing a firm we want to know what its assets would fetch if they were sold individually. This break-up value or realisable value, when compared to the value of the firm as a going concern, tells us about the wisdom of keeping the firm going. A slightly different question is, what investment would be required to re-create the firm today? This is the replacement cost of the firm and when we compare this replacement cost to the value of the firm as a going concern it tells us about the value added by the current firm and its management.

In other words investment decisions, and judgements about performance, depend on the relationship between the Economic Value (EV) of the project or firm, which is the present value of the future stream of cash flows it is expected to generate, its value as a going concern and two measures of the cost of the assets employed. The replacement cost (RC) is the current cost of acquiring the assets, while the realisable value (RV) is the proceeds of selling them, net of the costs of selling.

Some decision-rules for investment

In the case of *investment* decision, investment is worthwhile if the present value of the cash flows is greater than the initial cost of acquiring the necessary assets that is, if $EV > RC$. Clearly this is simply another way of stating our project decision rule, accept all projects with a positive net present value, since $NPV = EV - RC$.

In the case of *disinvestment* decisions, which we examine in Chapter 23, the rule is parallel except that now the question is whether the present value of cash flows from assets in their present use is greater than in alternative uses, as measured by what we could dispose of the assets for. So disinvest if $EV < RV$.

If asset markets were perfect the buying and selling price would be the same, but usually $RC > RV$, and in practice replacement costs exceed realisable value by some margin. Transactions in an asset will incur transactions costs which must be borne by buyers and sellers. These will include the costs of market intermediaries who provide the necessary expertise and organisation. For regularly traded items like vehicles, workshop machinery and office buildings these transactions costs are the main source of the margin between buying and selling prices. But other assets may be more 'thinly-traded' and in this case the gap between RC and RV can widen dramatically. The realisable value of an asset depends on its value in its next best use, which may be well below its replacement cost. As an extreme case, consider a chemical plant which costs £100 million to construct but whose design is totally specific to the manufacture of one chemical. If demand for that product disappears, perhaps because it becomes technically obsolete, there are likely to be no other uses for the plant, except perhaps as a museum of industrial archaeology. If the site value is low and the authorities insist the plant is demolished on environmental grounds the realisable value could even be negative.

But the big question is how EV relates to RC. Why do positive net present values occur? Put another way, what enables firms or projects to create value, yield 'rents', that is, yield a return above the cost of capital? The search for profitable opportunities is the central quest of economic life. But it *is* possible to describe the relationship of EV and RC at an abstract level. In a world with perfect markets EV, RC and RV will all coincide. If all markets are perfect and all inputs in competitive supply, there are no positive NPVs, no abnormal profits. As soon as any appear they are eliminated by competition. Positive NPVs arise when markets are not perfect, and the search for positive-valued projects could be described as the search for exploitable market imperfections.

Tobin's q and the valuation ratio

We can take a measure at the level of the whole firm, equivalent to the NPV of a project, to reveal if the firm is 'adding value'. The relationship between the economic value and the replacement cost of the whole firm is usually expressed as a ratio rather than a difference, in the statistic known as *Tobin's q*[1] where

$$\text{`q'} = \frac{\text{MARKET CAPITALISATION OF THE FIRM}}{\text{REPLACEMENT COST OF ASSETS}} = \frac{\text{EV}}{\text{RC}}$$

At the level of the firm, the market capitalisation of the firm's equity measures the investors' evaluation of the future income it will generate, equivalent to the economic value of a project's cash flow.

A 'q' of unity is the equivalent at the level of the firm, to an NPV of zero in the case of a project. The firm with a 'positive NPV' will have 'q' > 1, and is earning a return above the required return of shareholders. Conversely, the firm with 'q' < 1 is not covering its cost of capital.

When we look at Tobin's q for the UK industrial sector an interesting picture emerges. Figure I plots the aggregate 'q' for the UK from 1966 to 1993. In the early 1970s the market valuation of UK industrial and commercial companies fell below the replacement cost of their assets and q remained below one until the late 1980s. The implication was that the average return of UK companies was below the cost of capital, providing what the Bank of England Quarterly Bulletin described as a 'very weak inducement to invest'. Put another way, the aggregate NPV of UK firms appeared to be negative. One source of comfort was that just the same phenomenon occurred in the other developed countries. Modigliani and Cohn (1979) argued that the falling 'q' reflected inflation-induced errors in share valuation. They asserted that Western stock markets were under-valuing shares so that a truer 'q' would be above unity. However, this theory did not receive widespread support.

1 The 'q' notion is usually attributed to James Tobin; see, for example, Tobin (1971).

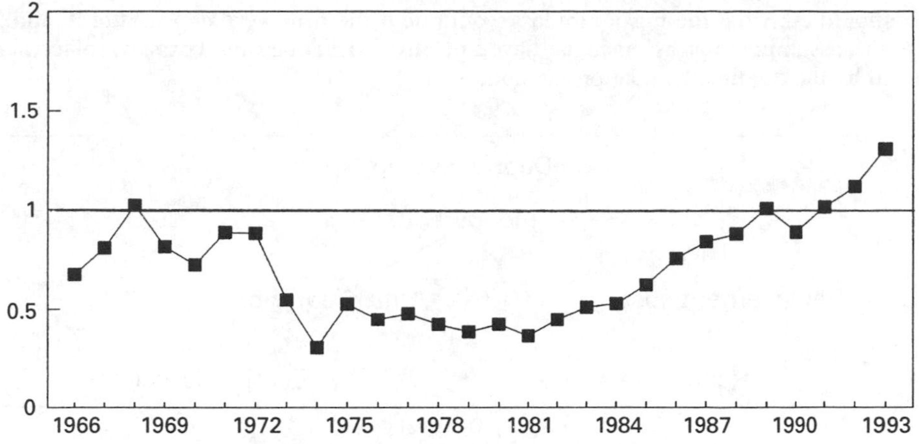

Figure I 'Tobin's q' for UK industrial and commercial companies, 1966–93

Source: Bank of England

The question is whether the equilibrium value of 'q' really is unity. For one thing the replacement cost of the individual assets of a firm drawn from current cost balance-sheets may not adequately measure the cost of reproducing the whole firm. For another, the gap between replacement cost and realisable values means we would not necessarily want to dismantle a firm just because EV/RC<1.

Because firms do not report replacement costs it is more common to encounter this ratio with 'book' equity from the balance-sheet in the denominator. This accounting ratio of market capitalisation to book equity is known as the *valuation ratio* or *market to book* ratio. So long as the carrying value of the fixed assets in the firm's balance-sheet is reasonably current, and so long as the firm does not use significant unrecorded intangibles, then the denominator may proxy opportunity cost adequately. Even when the denominator is pure historic cost, some analysts use the market to book ratio to compare current value to 'invested capital' contributed by shareholders over the years. This can be interesting, but we certainly cannot conclude that a ratio greater than unity represents 'virtue' in this case. It begs the very large questions, over how long was the equity invested, and how much of the equity required return has been taken out as dividend?

Deprival value

EV, RC, and RV can be combined to yield a measure of the opportunity cost of the firm's assets, that is to give an answer to the question 'what would be the maximum loss if the firm were deprived of the asset?'. Bonbright (1965) showed that you can get an accounting measure of the opportunity cost of an asset by combining, EV, RC, and RV. This composite measure is usually known as *deprival value* or *value to the business*, and in 1980 UK firms were briefly asked to produce a supplementary current cost balance-sheet and income statement under accounting standard SSAP16 using this measure of cost. SSAP16 defined deprival value or value to the business as 'net current replacement cost; or if a permanent diminution to below net current replacement cost has been recognised, the recoverable amount . . . [which is] the greater of the net realisable value of an asset and, where applicable, the amount recoverable from its further use'.

Figure II depicts this. All it says is that to find the opportunity cost of an asset to the firm you should ask what the maximum loss would be if the firm were deprived of it, and in practice, assuming most assets in use have a positive NPV, one would expect replacement cost to be the dominant valuation method.

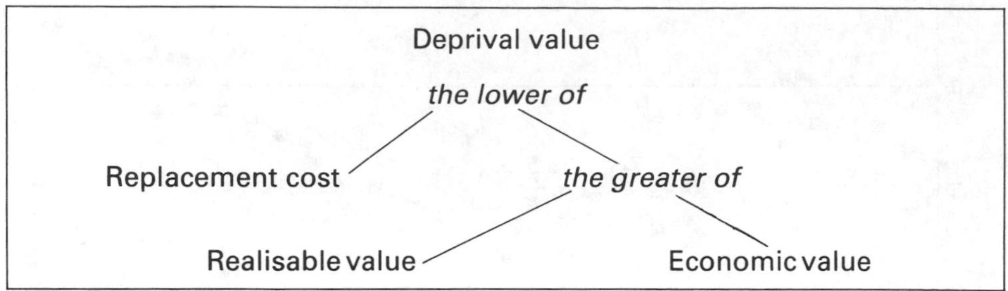

Figure II Deprival value

Gomez Garment

The Gomez Garment Manufacturing Co uses a computer controlled cutting table. Gomez reckons it could get £30,000 for the one it has, though it would cost £40,000 to replace. Suppose the economic value of the machine to Gomez, the present value of the contribution the machine will earn, were in turn, £20,000, £35,0000 or £60,000.

If the EV is only £20,000 Gomez would be better off selling the machine for £30,000. So if Gomez were deprived of the machine, it would lose the opportunity to sell it, and its opportunity cost is £30,000. Deprival value is £30,000 in this case. If the EV is £35,000, however, it would not be worth Gomez's while replacing the machine, but since it has one, Gomez is better off using it. In this case the deprival value is £35,000. Hopefully the 'normal' situation is the third one, where EV is £60,000. In this case EV > RC, and the machine has a 'positive net present value' of £60,000 − £40,000 = £20,000. If Gomez were deprived of the machine it would want to replace it and so the deprival value is £40,000.

II THE BALANCE-SHEET

We now examine the *balance-sheet*, in which a company lists the assets it has, and the claims outstanding against those assets. If the balance-sheet gave us a complete list of the assets and liabilities of the firm valued in terms of their replacement cost or deprival value this would create a neat division of labour, with the accountant measuring the opportunity cost of the firm's assets, and the stock market measuring the economic value of the firm. In practice, firms present a possibly incomplete list valued on a mixture of bases but, fundamentally, at 'historic cost', which is what the assets originally cost. So to interpret a balance-sheet, and use it as the basis for the sort of judgements we wish to make, we need to ask these questions:

- On what basis are the assets and liabilities valued?
- Is the balance-sheet complete?

Some vocabulary

The main barrier to entry in reading accounting statements is vocabulary, the terminology and layout of the numbers. This is not helped by the fact that accountants can use several different words for the same thing, and sometimes mean different things by the same words. So we start with a brief introduction to the vocabulary of the balance-sheet. We do this using as an example The Body Shop International plc. Body Shop, in the words of Anita Roddick, the founder, produces products that cleanse, polish and protect the skin and hair. From beginnings in a single shop in Brighton, England in 1976 it has grown to a group with international sales of £195.4 million in 1994, largely through franchises. The ICC Business Ratio Report ranked Body Shop the second most profitable UK company in terms of profit margins in 1991. Exhibit I shows financial data for Body Shop for the year ended 28 February 1994. We will be using this data in the next chapter to calculate some financial ratios for Body Shop.

In its balance-sheet the company lists its assets, and lists how those assets are financed, in other words lists the claims on those assets, the liabilities of the firm. There are five building blocks in a balance-sheet conventionally. The firm classifies its assets into *fixed* and *current*, and shows *current* and *long-term* liabilities to third parties, and the residual, the *equity* claim, which is the investment of shareholders in the business. So in essence the balance-sheet looks like this.

FIXED ASSETS		EQUITY
CURRENT ASSETS		LONG-TERM LIABILITIES
		CURRENT LIABILITIES
TOTAL ASSETS	=	TOTAL LIABILITIES and EQUITY

Though US companies helpfully show assets and liabilities separately, these elements may be displayed in a different order. For instance European companies such as Body Shop typically show their balance-sheet in the so-called 'net assets' format with the current and long-term liabilities netted against assets to balance with equity (see Exhibit I).

Exhibit I

The Body Shop International plc – Selected group financial data

Consolidated balance-sheet data

As at 28 February 1994

	1994 £m	1993 £m
Fixed assets		
Intangible assets	3.7	5.2
Tangible assets	67.9	64.8
	71.6	70.0
Current assets		
Stocks	34.6	35.3
Debtors	37.2	33.6
Cash at bank and in hand	24.9	14.0
	96.7	82.9
Creditors: amounts falling due within 1 year	35.6	31.2
Net current assets	61.1	51.7
Total assets less current liabilities	132.7	121.7
Creditors: amounts falling due after more than 1 year	32.4	35.2
Deferred tax	3.4	3.8
Minority interests		0.5
	96.9	82.2

Capital and reserves		
Called up share capital	9.4	9.4
Share premium account	35.7	33.5
Profit and loss account	51.8	39.3
	96.9	82.2

Consolidated profit & loss account data for the year ending 28 February 1994	**1994**	**1993**
Turnover	195.4	168.3
Cost of sales	89.5	78.0
Gross profits	105.9	90.3
Distribution costs	43.0	37.5
Administrative expenses	32.8	28.5
Total administration and distribution	75.8	66.0
Profit before interest payable	30.1	24.3
Profit on asset sale	1.1	
Interest receivable (per note to the P&L)	1.0	0.7
Interest payable (per note to the P&L)	2.5	3.5
Net interest	1.5	2.8
Profit on ordinary activities before taxation	29.7	21.5
Taxation on profit on ordinary activities	10.1	7.6
Profit on ordinary activities after taxation	19.6	13.9
Minority interests	0.2	0.1
Profit attributable to members of holding company	19.4	13.8
Dividends	3.8	3.2
Retained profit for year	**15.6**	**10.6**
Earnings per share	**10.3p**	**7.4p**

The Body Shop International plc – Selected group financial data: notes

15 Debtors	**1994 £m**	**1993 £m**
Amounts falling due within one year		
Trade debtors	24.7	22.6
Assets held for sale	0.2	0.6
Other debtors	5.1	4.4
Prepayments	3.0	3.3
	33.0	30.9
Amounts falling due after more than one year		
Finance lease and hire purchase receivables	1.8	2.1
Other debtors	1.3	0.1
Prepayments	1.1	0.5
	4.2	2.7
	37.2	33.6

16 Creditors

	1994 £m	1993 £m
Amounts falling due within one year		
Bank loans and overdrafts – unsecured	2.3	4.1
Variable rate loan-stock – unsecured	2.1	1.1
Other loans – unsecured	–	2.0
Trade creditors	8.2	8.9
Corporation tax	8.9	5.0
Other taxes and social security costs	1.3	1.2
Proposed dividend	2.4	1.9
Other creditors	4.1	1.3
Accruals	6.2	5.7
Obligations under finance leases and hire purchase contracts	0.1	–
Amounts due to subsidiary undertakings	–	–
	35.6	31.2

17 Creditors

	1994 £m	1993 £m
Amounts falling due after more than one year		
Variable rate loan-stock – unsecured	1.8	–
USA loan notes – unsecured	30.5	31.7
Other loans – unsecured	–	2.1
Deferred consideration	–	1.2
Obligations under finance leases and hire purchase contracts	0.1	0.2
	32.4	35.2

The distinction between fixed and current is usually made on the basis of liquidity – if an asset (or liability), will be liquidated within twelve months, it is current. But the more fundamental issue is of purpose: current assets represent stages in the productive cycle: the firm acquires *stock* or inventory of raw material. If it buys inputs on credit, it will have a *creditor* or payable in its liabilities as a result. The raw material is processed into work-in-progress, then finished goods stock. When the finished goods are sold a *debtor* or receivable is created. The cycle is completed when the debtor pays *cash*. Fixed assets are held for use rather than resale: they are the productive capacity of the business and include *land and buildings*, and *plant and machinery*.

The Body Shop

We can see that Body Shop's net assets of £96.9 million were made up of fixed assets of £71.6 million and current assets, including stocks, debtors, short-term investments, and bank balances, of £96.7 million. Netted off against the total or 'gross' assets to give the net assets figure are the firm's current liabilities: short-term creditors' loans and overdrafts of £35.6 million, and longer-term liabilities, and deferred tax of £35.8 million.

How are assets valued?

The fundamental basis of valuation in balance-sheets is *historic cost* which is the price at which the assets were acquired. Clearly, with positive inflation in prices, a historic cost balance-sheet understates the cost of replacing assets, to an extent which depends on when the assets were acquired. In practice the historic cost principle is much modified, and what we get in balance-sheets is a mix of historic and current costs. This happens for two reasons. Current assets have to be marked down to realisable value when it is below cost, and in some countries fixed assets may be revalued upwards.

Lower of cost and realisable value

The fixed asset/current asset distinction is important when it comes to valuation. Since current assets are by assumption going to be realised in the short-term, accountants have to write them *down* to realisable value whenever this is below historic cost. This happens annually through the process of identifying obsolete or slow-moving stocks, of providing against bad and doubtful debts, and of checking the market values of any marketable securities the firm has. So current assets, at least, are 'marked-to-market' but only when this is below historic cost. On grounds of 'prudence' firms are not allowed to reflect in the balance-sheet when realisable value of current assets is above cost. Hence the valuation rule for current assets is 'the lower of historic cost and realisable value'.

Most firms write-down stock rigorously, but the firm which is in difficulties may be reluctant to do so. It has a dilemma – it can least afford to write stocks off, but it is most likely to have redundant stocks since its failure, and its low stock values, may well spring from the common source of insufficient demand. A similar problem arises with debtors. Some debtors never pay, for good or bad reasons. They may genuinely dispute the quality or delivery of the goods, or they may not have sufficient funds to pay. The firm should constantly be looking out for debts that will turn 'bad' in this way and should eliminate them. But, again, to write off a £100 debt means sacrificing £100 of profit. Most firms write off their bad debts, but the occasional firm will be reluctant or slow to do this, particularly if the firm is failing.

Finding the cost of stocks

In the particular case of stocks or inventories it is not always easy to ascertain what historic cost was. Stocks are the raw materials, partly completed work (work-in-progress) and finished goods that the firm is holding. Firms can have thousands, even millions of items in stock and keeping individual records of the cost of all these items would be prohibitively costly, so in order to value them it is usual to make some arbitrary assumptions. The firm may assume that the stocks on hand are the ones most recently acquired, thus they can be valued at current prices. This is the 'FIFO' (first in, first out) assumption. An alternative is to assume that the final stocks are representative of the whole year's purchases, then they can be valued at average prices for the period. With positive inflation, LIFO shows the lowest balance-sheet value, but charges correspondingly more against profit. For this reason it is unpopular with tax authorities, outside the US.

Fixed asset revaluation

By contrast fixed assets, which by assumption are held for use rather than to be liquidated, are carried at depreciated historic cost. If the realisable value of a fixed asset falls below cost the firm does not have to write the asset down unless the fall is permanent.

It is in long-lived fixed assets such as property that the greatest divergence between historic cost and opportunity cost can occur. If a company revalues its property assets this clearly increases the usefulness of its balance-sheet. To revalue means to show the assets at some measure of current cost. However, in many countries firms are permitted to revalue their fixed assets, in particular land and buildings. In the US this is not permitted, and strict historic cost is required; some other countries have a balance-sheet based corporate tax system so that to recognise an increase in the value of assets might be to generate a tax liability, providing a disincentive to revalue assets. In the UK it is not uncommon for firms with property assets to regularly revalue them, perhaps every three or four years. But there is no requirement to do so, and no rules as to how frequently it should be done or what basis of valuation should be used.

Young & Company

Young & Co is a medium-sized publicly-quoted brewing company in the South-East of England. Young's 1993 annual report shows total assets of £163 million, of which £152.6 million were tangible fixed assets, mainly properties including a brewery and pubs. Over £87 million of this value is the result of revaluations, the most recent of which was in 1992. The basis on which the properties are valued are:

1 The brewery: existing use, on the depreciated replacement cost basis.
2 The licensed properties: valued by the directors at open market value for existing use, having regard to trading potential.
3 Other properties: open market value, on an existing use basis.

Dimitri

Dimitri regularly buys 1,000 items of a particular component each month. At the annual stock check on 31 December the storeman finds they have 2,000 in stock. The price of this component has gone up three times during the year as follows:

	Period	*Price (£)*
	→ 31 March	2.56
1 April	→ 31 May	2.90
1 May	→ 30 November	3.00
1 December	→	3.10

How should the components be valued? If we make the FIFO assumption, that the ones on hand are the most recent, then the stock represents November and December purchases and would be valued thus:

FIFO basis

		£
Bought in November:	1,000 @ 3.00	3,000
Bought in December:	1,000 @ 3.10	3,100
	2,000	£6,100

But if the firm feels its stock comprises items bought throughout the year it might value at an average price:

Average basis

Average price of three months @ 2.56, 2 @ 2.90, 6 @ 3.00, 1 @ 3.10 = 2.88
2,000 items @ 2.88 = £5,760

Is the balance-sheet complete?

Once we reflect on the process by which a balance-sheet is produced, it is clear that it may not give a complete listing of the assets and liabilities of the firm. The accountant does not sit down and say 'what do we have and what do we owe?'

First, the balance-sheet is transaction-based, which means that assets and liabilities are recorded at their historic cost. It also means that they are *only* recorded if they were acquired in a transaction. So assets acquired as windfalls or gifts will not be there: if the firm one day discovers an oil-well under its (freehold) head office this will not find its way into the balance-sheet in the normal course of events. Second, the accounting principle of prudence or 'conservatism' means that even when a transaction has created an asset the expenditure may be written off against profit rather than recorded as an asset in the balance-sheet. Obvious examples are expenditure on training employees, expenditure on advertising and promotion which creates 'brand equity', expenditure which creates strategic options, and investment which creates intellectual property such as publishing rights or R & D. Accounting standards permit companies to 'capitalise' or to carry in the balance-sheet R & D expenditure but only to a limited extent, insofar as it is expenditure on developing a product with a secure market.

Pilkington Group

The Pilkington Group is an international glass and plastic products company servicing principally the building, transportation and opthalmic markets. In the early 1950s, Alastair Pilkington developed the float glass process which revolutionised the way in which sheet glass was manufactured worldwide. Pilkington decided to exploit the invention by licensing other people to use the process. In 1968, licensing income, technical fees and commissions accounted for over 25% of Pilkington's pre-tax profits. As licensing agreements began expiring in the early 1980s and as Pilkington's business expanded, reliance on licensing income diminished. Nonetheless, by 1993, licensing fees still accounted for virtually 20% of operating profit. Even though the float glass process was a piece of intellectual property of immense value, accounting standards permitted little or none of this asset to show in Pilkington's balance-sheet.

Though human capital, brands and intellectual property are clearly assets, there is a reluctance to capitalise intangible assets such as these because of 'uncertainty' about their value. In fact this is a symptom of something else. When a firm identifies an intangible asset such as a brand it is effectively labelling or packaging its own value-added. The asset is not one in competitive supply, but is specific to the firm and possibly unique. We talked about a 'neat division of labour' in which the firm shows the opportunity cost of its assets in its balance-sheet and the market puts a value on the firm as a going concern. The difference between the two is the value added by the firm. Clearly this distinction becomes harder to make if firms put their own value in the balance-sheet.

Just as it is worth reflecting whether the balance-sheet gives a complete list of the assets of the firm, it is also important to be sure we have a full list of its liabilities. This should not be such a problem, since the conservatism principle of accounting which discourages firms from counting chickens before they are hatched – from recognising unrealised profits or contingent assets – does require firms to recognise potential or contingent liabilities. However, they may merely do this in a note, rather than in the balance-sheet itself. Sometimes the firm can arrange for an asset and the associated liability to be 'off balance-sheet'. We look at ways of achieving this in a subsequent chapter.

III INCOME MEASUREMENT

In this section we discuss income measurement at an abstract level, to help understand what the profit and loss account of a company actually says.

We will define the income of an individual during some period as the increase in his wealth plus his consumption in that period. So his income is what he consumes, and what he could have consumed without reducing his wealth. This idea becomes more concrete if we think specifically about the income from a firm. Defined this way the shareholders' income from a firm is the increase in the value of the equity of the firm over the period plus the assets shareholders have consumed. By 'consumed' we mean taken out of the firm as dividend, net of any further cash they have contributed to the firm during the period. So income is defined by the basic accounting identity:

$$I_t \equiv C_t + A_t - A_{t-1} \tag{1}$$

I_t = income in period from t−1 to t, and in the case of a firm A_t = equity at time t, C_t = distribution to shareholders, net of further equity contributed.

If A is the *market value* of the equity then (1) is our familiar expression for the numerator of the return to shareholders measure; the income from holding shares is the dividend plus capital gain. Strictly, this is the measure of shareholders' income only so long as their *capital is maintained.* If A_t and A_{t-1} are not measured at the same prices, if there has been inflation during the period, allowance should be made for this by indexation of the initial investment. With this modification, (1) is precisely the measure of the income from owning shares used by tax authorities (in the UK). Shareholders pay income tax on the dividends they receive, and capital gains tax at the same rate on the excess of the final value of their shares, over the initial cost increased by the subsequent change in the retail price index, plus any further capital contributions they have made. The only difference is that the capital gain element in the income is only measured when the shares are sold, rather than periodically as it accrues.

Since the market value of the firm embodies expectations about the future a component in economic income is likely to be the value of changed expectations about the future. These are therefore unrealised income to the firm, though the shareholder can realise it by selling his claim. When A is a balance-sheet, rather than a market, measure of assets the income of shareholders will be the change in 'book', ie balance-sheet, equity plus net dividend distributions. We now know enough about the balance-sheet to know that the interpretation of this number depends on the *completeness* of the balance-sheet, and the way in which assets are *valued.* If the balance-sheet provided a complete listing of assets and liabilities at realisable values, then the income measured according to (1) is the income which could be realised immediately by breaking up the firm. In practice, as we saw, balance-sheets do not do this. Instead accountants prepare a profit and loss account to explain how the firm's assets have increased during the period as a result of trading.

Historic cost profit

We know that to find the value of a *project* we predict the cash flows it will generate in the future and discount them to the present. The firm can be viewed as a bundle of projects, and Table I represents this, as though we could identify all the projects that make up the firm, Kawalski and Co, and lay out the cash flows associated with them in a table.[2] So project h, for example, is a project with a five-year life, starting in year 6. The NPV of project h at its commencement at the beginning of year 6 is £1,601 (discounted at 10%).

In project appraisal we take a single project and evaluate it by looking at all its cash flows through time. The accountant who is asked to measure historic cost profit has to do the opposite. His job is to produce a useful picture of the performance of the firm based on the

2 In practice of course it will usually be impossible to identify separately the component projects in a firm, because of the interrelationships and dependencies, the joint costs and benefits, between projects.

Table I Table of cash flows for Kawalski and Co

Project No: ------	d,	e,	f,	g,	h,	i,	l,	k ------
Year							the project appraiser's view. NPV = £1,601 (at 10%)	
5				−ve				
6				+ve	−1,500	−ve		
7				+ve	+1,000	+ve		
8				+ve	+1,000	+ve	the profit measurer's view	
9				+ve	+1,000	−ve		
10				+ve	+1,500	−ve		
				−ve		+ve		
						+ve		
						−ve		

cash flows of the whole firm in just one year. So the accountant measuring, say, the year 8 profit of Kawalski has as his starting point a series of cash flows reflecting inflows and outflows at different points on the life-cycles of the various projects that are alive in year 8. The problem with taking this sideways view of the firm is that just as one year's cash flow might not in isolation tell you much about the worth of a project, one year's cash flow for the firm as a whole may not be representative of the performance of the firm through time. So accountants try to make a more representative income figure by reallocating costs where necessary to the period in which the matching revenue was earned. This is the 'accruals' convention of accounting. However since the 'accruals' convention seems to allow plenty of scope for subjectivity, accountants are expected to be guided by the *prudence* concept. Under the prudence concept revenues and profits are not anticipated, but are recognised '. . . only when realised in the form either of cash or of other assets the ultimate cash realisation of which can be assessed with reasonable certainty' (see Statement of Standard Accounting Practice (SSAP2)). The resulting figure is *historic cost profit*. The costs that have not been expensed in the period, and are expected to generate revenue and so be expensed in future periods, are assets at the end of the period valued at historic cost. So in historic cost accounting asset values are accumulated unused costs.

The effect of price changes

There are lags in the productive process between buying the inputs and selling the outputs, and it is because of these lags that financing is needed. These lags have implications for profit measurement as well. Historic cost accounting measures profit by reallocating costs between time periods so that revenues are matched with the actual, 'historic' cost of the relevant inputs. If price levels are in general rising through time, the longer the lag between purchase of inputs and sale of outputs the higher the apparent profit of the firm. Historic cost profit may provide a misleading signal for financial decisions in this situation. It will become harder to make meaningful comparisons between firms because the measured return of a firm will reflect both its operating performance in converting inputs into outputs, *and* the set of prices in which those inputs and outputs are measured, reflecting the firm's particular 'lag structure' and any intervening price changes.

Examine project h in more detail. Table II shows the underlying cash flows of project h that generated the net cash flow we saw in Table I. The project involves initial investments

Table II Table of cash flows for project h (£)

Date incurred	*beginning year 6*	*end year 6*	*7*	*8*	*9*	*10*	total
Machinery	(2,000)						
Working capital	(500)					500	
Revenue		2,500	2,500	2,500	2,500	2,500	
Labour and materials		(1,500)	(1,500)	(1,500)	(1,500)	(1,500)	
	(2,500)	1,000	1,000	1,000	1,000	1,500	3,000
Year 6 cash flows	(1,500)						
NPV of project h at 10% = £1,601							

of £2,000 in machinery with a five-year life and with no resale value, and of £500 in working capital. Each year the output is sold for £2,500 and expenses of £1,500 are incurred for material and labour. There is no tax. Recall the problem facing the accountant required to produce a profit figure for year 8. His starting place is the cash book which shows the project h cash flow to be £1,000 in year 8. Is this 'representative' of the performance of project h? Clearly not, since it required an outflow of cash at the beginning of the project to create the necessary investment in fixed and working capital. The response of the accountant is to convert the cash-flow series into 'historic cost profit' by smoothing out some of the lumpy cash flows over time. Consider the machine. The cost of the machine is spread over the five years by deducting annual depreciation (calculated here on a 'straight-line' basis) thus:

$$\text{Depreciation} = \frac{\overset{\text{Purchase cost}}{\overset{\downarrow}{2{,}000}} - \overset{\text{Terminal value}}{\overset{\downarrow}{0}}}{\underset{\text{Useful life}}{\underset{\uparrow}{5}}} = £400 \text{ per annum}$$

This gives an annual profit figure of:

revenue	2,500
labour and materials	(1,500)
depreciation	(400)
Historic cost profit	£600

But suppose that the purchase price of the machine the firm uses is inflating at 20% per annum so that by year 8 a new machine to replace the old one would cost £2,000 × $(1 + .2)^2$ = £2,880. Recall that our firm consumes one-fifth of such a machine each year, so if it valued the machine at replacement cost it would have had annual depreciation of £2,880 × ⅕ = £576 and an annual accounting profit of £1,000 − £576 = £424 in year 6. Assuming none of the other cash flows were affected by inflation, £424 is the *replacement cost profit* of the project in year 6.

The profit and loss account and cash flow

The *profit and loss* is best thought of in two halves. The first half explains how the company made its profit, while the second half explains how this is shared between the three groups with a claim on it: lenders, the tax authorities, and equity.[3] The P+L starts by showing the value of the *sales* made in the year (also known as *revenue* or *turnover*). It then deducts the costs incurred to achieve these sales to give the *operating profit* (sometimes called *trading profit*). It is common, when the business involves buying in significant inputs from other firms and/or adding value to these by manufacturing, to identify two levels of cost. The *cost of sales*, which accountants call 'direct costs', typically include purchases from outside, and factory labour and overhead. The remaining costs are *sales and administration*, or indirect costs. The difference between sales and cost of sales is *gross profit*.

Though gross profit is commonly reported, it is a slippery concept. For one thing, there are no rules as to what costs a firm should call 'cost of sales', which means that care is required when comparing companies. Secondly, there is a temptation to interpret cost of sales and sales-and-administration as variable cost and fixed cost respectively, but this is unsafe. Most firms have fixed and semi-fixed elements such as factory overhead and labour in the costs they call cost of sales, but costs that are fully variable with sales, such as salespersons' commission, in sales-and-administration. Alongside operating profit, the firm may have income from non-operating sources – interest and dividends received on investments, rental income, shares in the profits of joint ventures. We call the sum of income from operating and other sources, *profit before interest paid and tax* (PbIT).

The Body Shop

Body Shop (see Exhibit I) reports gross profit of £105.9 million in 1994 on sales of £195.4. It calls its sales-and-administration costs 'net operating expenses'. These were £75.8 giving an operating profit of £30.1. Body Shop also had a profit of £1.1 on sale of a subsidiary, and within the net interest paid of £1.5 was interest received of £1.0 and interest paid of £2.5. So PbIT was £32.2 (30.1 + 1.1 + 1.0).

There are three main claimants on the profit of a firm. The firm will have to pay *interest* on any borrowings and will pay *tax*, on what remains. The *profit after tax* or as it is commonly known, the *earnings* of the firm, belongs to equity, who are the residual claimants. They either receive it as *dividend* or it is reinvested in the firm on their behalf as *retained earnings*.

The Body Shop

Body Shop's PbIT of £32.2 is shared between interest paid of £2.5, and a tax charge of £10.1, but also *minority interests* of £0.2. These are third parties with a stake in a subsidiary whose profit has been fully consolidated into the Body Shop results. £19.4 is left for Body Shop shareholders, of which they receive £3.8 as dividend.

Current cost profit

We saw in the previous section that historic cost profit can be misleading when there is inflation. Profit tends to be flattered because historic cost does not fully reflect the cost of replacing assets. Some utilities account for this by revaluing their balance-sheets at replacement cost, and making, typically, four adjustments to historic cost profit to correspond to four main categories in the balance-sheet: fixed assets, stocks, monetary working capital and net borrowing:

— An additional *depreciation* charge to bring depreciation up to what it would be if it were calculated on the replacement cost of fixed assets.

3 The profusion of vocabulary is particularly marked here. The P+L is commonly known as the Income Statement.

- A *cost of sales* adjustment to provide for the cost of replacing at current prices the stocks consumed during the year.
- A similar adjustment for *monetary working capital*, which is essentially debtors and creditors, to reflect the fact that changing output and input prices will require the firm to maintain proportionately changed levels of debtors and creditors.
- A *gearing* adjustment. Since the amount of loans made to and by the firm is fixed in money terms the real value of the firm's net borrowing will fall during a period of inflation. The market interest rate r has two components, $r = r' + i$, where r' is the real rate of interest, and i is the expected rate of inflation during the period of the loan. In historic cost accounting the full interest payment r is deducted as an expense, but to find current cost profit the firm adds back an amount to reflect that part of r which is in effect an early repayment of capital.

Normally, if price levels are increasing, the depreciation, cost of sales, and monetary working capital adjustments will be negative ie deductions from profit, reflecting the increased cost of replacing the respective inputs. Since net borrowing is effectively a negative asset, the reverse applies to the gearing adjustment. If the firm is a net borrower the nominal interest charge overstates the real cost of borrowing and this is reflected in a positive gearing adjustment.

British Gas plc

British Gas shows its assets at replacement cost in the balance-sheet. Its total assets are in excess of £30 billion, of which £17.3 billion is due to revaluation. The effect of measuring profit on a current cost basis was a reduction of £208 million in 1992 and £248 million in 1993, see below:

For the year ended 31 December	**1993** **£m**	**1992** **£m**
Current cost profit/(loss) on ordinary activities before taxation	(613)	846
Current cost adjustments:		
Cost of sales adjustment	12	2
Monetary working capital adjustment	48	48
Supplementary depreciation	251	195
Profit on sale of tangible fixed assets adjustment	2	4
Gearing adjustment	(65)	(41)
	248	208
Historic cost profit/(loss) on ordinary activities before taxation	(365)	1,054

Cash flow

We saw that accountants reallocate cash flows through time to derive a 'profit' measure. We need to understand the precise link between cash and profit for at least two reasons. In valuation, it is cash flow we are interested in. Second, firms fall into financial distress for lack of cash, not lack of profit. Particularly in the short term, cash flow and profit can give contrary signals. While products reaching the end of their life-cycle and requiring little further investment can be large cash generators – the so-called 'cash cows', fast-growing and heavily investing firms may be profitable but be heavy users of cash.

In addition to the profit and loss account and balance-sheet, firms have to provide cash flow data. To interpret this it is useful to recognise that there are five key elements in the firm's cash flow:

1 Cash from profit – we need to add back the non-cash elements in the profit calculation.
2 Claims – a part of the cash generated has to go in paying interest, tax and dividends.
3 Investment in working capital – if the firm is growing it will probably have to use cash to grow its current assets, though current liabilities will pay for part of this. Similarly it will need cash for –
4 Investment in fixed assets.

We say the firm is cash-positive or cash-negative if it has a surplus or deficit of cash from items 1 + 2 + 3 + 4. This must be financed, so the final item in the cash flow is:

5 Financing.

The Body Shop

The Body Shop's 1994 cash-flow statement can be summarised as:

			£m
(1)	Operating profit		30.1
	add depreciation etc		10.2
			40.3
(2)	Interest, tax, dividends		(11.4)
(3)	Increase in stocks and debtors	(5.1)	
	Increase in creditors	5.1	–
(4)	Fixed assets investment		(12.0)
			16.9
(5)	Changes in debt and equity		4.2
	Increase in cash		12.7
			16.9

So Body Shop was cash positive in 1994 and its working capital was entirely self-financing. Its operating profit of 30.1 translated into a cash inflow of 16.9, part of which was used to pay off debt, and the rest, 12.7, put in the bank.

IV SUMMARY

This chapter described the structure and vocabulary of a company's accounting statements. We showed how alternative measures of the cost and value of assets are used in decisions and how they link to the balance-sheet data provided by companies. We also showed how the income measured by a company in its profit and loss account relates to economic income.

REFERENCES AND BIBLIOGRAPHY

Elliott, B E, and Elliott J — *Financial Accounting and Reporting* (1993) Prentice Hall.

Ernst and Young — *UK GAAP* (1994, regularly updated).

Hicks, J R — *Value and Capital* (1939) Oxford University Press.

Modigliani, F, and Cohn, R A — 'Inflation, Rational Valuation and the Market', Financial Analysts Journal, March/April 1979, pp 24–44.

Tobin, J — 'A General Equilibrium Approach to Monetary Theory', in *Essays in Economics: Macroeconomics* (Vol 1, 1971) Chicago.

Tweedie, D, and Whittington, G — *Capital Maintenance Concepts* (1985) ASC.

QUESTIONS

1 What accounting issues should the analyst be aware of in using the balance-sheet value of the shareholders' interest as a basis for valuing shares?

2 Explain the terms – 'economic value'; 'historic cost'; 'replacement cost'; 'realisable value'. What do the relative values of these numbers tell us about a firm?

3 We have the following information about Brassdock Ltd, as at 31.12.1994:

Balance-sheet			£
Fixed assets			100,000
Goodwill			10,000
Current assets	Debtors	60,000	
	Stock	20,000	
	Cash	20,000	
		100,000	
Current liabilities		(60,000)	40,000
			150,000
Share capital (£1 ord shares)			50,000
Reserves			80,000
Shareholders' interest			130,000
Long-term debt			20,000
			150,000
Net profit after tax for year ended 31.12.1994			£20,000
Proposed dividend for year			10p

£40,000 of fixed assets represents the cost of a town centre property recently revalued at £140,000.

Debtors included £10,000 due from X Ltd, now in receivership. Brassdock owns a patent, not shown in the balance-sheet, for which an American electronics firm offered £14,000 during 1990.

The average dividend-yield in the industry is 3% and the average P/E is 12.

Value a Brassdock share on the basis of its assets, its earnings and its dividends. How do you account for the difference? Which basis should an analyst use? What other information would you have liked?

4 From the following data derive a 'current cost' profit for Zoo Ltd for year ended 21.12.94:

Balance-sheets	*31.12.94*	*31.12.93*
Machine (cost 1,500 on 1/1/93; 10-year life)	1,200	1,350
Stock (valued on FIFO basis)	400	250
Debtors	400	200
Creditors	(150)	(100)
Cash	770	250
	2,620	1,950

CHAPTER 20

Return on capital employed

Return on capital employed (ROCE) is an accounting measure in widespread use by financial analysts for assessing the performance of companies, by government agencies in regulating the profitability of firms, and within firms for assessing divisional performance and as a factor in reward schemes. In Section I we discuss the measurement and analysis of ROCE. In Section II we consider some issues that arise in its interpretation.

I THE MEASUREMENT AND ANALYSIS OF RETURN ON CAPITAL EMPLOYED

Measuring ROCE

From a financial perspective, a company is a bundle of net assets, against which the people who provided the finance for the assets have claims. The balance-sheet provides a (possibly incomplete) list of these assets and claims. Conventionally we distinguish two sorts of financing claims, equity and debt (= borrowing), so we define *capital employed* as the finance provided by equity and by debt. Performance analysis proceeds by, first, identifying the capital employed in the balance-sheet; then using accounting data identifying in the profit and loss account the profit the company has made for its equity and debt investors, so as to calculate the *return on capital employed*. Finally, the analyst decomposes the return on capital employed to understand how it is generated.

Though we will describe one specification, there are many variants of this ratio and many names for this ratio are used in practice, including *accounting rate of return* and *return on net assets*. From what we learned about the structure of the balance-sheet in the last chapter it is clear that RONA and ROCE will be the same so long as net assets are defined as fixed plus current assets less non-financial short and long-term liabilities. Some firms use *return on total assets* and others define the asset base according to their own priorities. For many purposes it will not matter too much which measure is used if it is used consistently.

Capital employed

Clearly, any liability of the firm finances the firm and we would expect a well-run firm to make best use of the financing potential of trade creditors, tax liabilities and so forth. These all serve to reduce the bundle of net assets the firm needs to finance externally. Capital employed measures this external financing. We use two tests to resolve hard cases: (a) is the claim interest-bearing, and (b) did the claim arise primarily with a financing motive, rather than as a by-product of some other transaction?

Long and short-term borrowing are both included in capital employed. Some analysts include only long-term, however the short-term/long-term distinction is rather arbitrary and many companies appear to include short-term instruments such as overdrafts in their planned capital employed. Separating the transitory from the permanent components of short-term borrowing could be difficult, and it is not always easy to identify the long-term component of interest payable.

Unless they have equity features, for instance are non-cumulative, participating and irredeemable, preference shares are treated as borrowing. Finance leases are also included in borrowing. Other long-term liabilities, and provisions are excluded from capital employed and so are treated as negative net assets. Hence, for example, we treat deferred tax as a tax liability rather than an equity reserve. Intangibles such as goodwill can be removed from net assets, and capital employed, if they are likely to be a significant source of bias in comparison. We have not set off cash against borrowing, as is the practice of some analysts. To do so deflates the apparent borrowing of the firm and implies a set-off which usually has no contractual basis.

Profit before interest and tax

Since capital employed includes funds provided by both debt and equity, the corresponding income measure is profit before interest paid and tax (PbIT), sometimes known as EBIT or earnings before interest and tax in US parlance. So

$$\text{Return on capital employed} = \frac{\text{Profit before interest paid and tax}}{\text{Capital employed}}$$

The Body Shop

We see from the Body Shop balance-sheet (Exhibit I in the previous chapter) that it had shareholders' equity ('capital and reserves') of £96.9 in 1994 and £82.2 in 1993. We also include minority interests, of which there were £.5m in 1993, this is capital controlled by the Body Shop management, and PbIT is measured before the minority claim is identified. Like many companies, the detail of Body Shop's borrowing is contained in creditor notes to the balance-sheet. Body Shop has short-term borrowings of £4.4 million (= 2.3 + 2.1) in 1994, and £7.2 in 1993. It also has finance lease obligations of £.1 in 1994. It has longer-term liabilities including finance leases in 1994 of £32.4, and £35.2 in 1993.

So capital employed in 1994 is £133.8 (96.9 + 4.5 + 32.4) and in 1993 £125.1 (82.2 +.5 + 7.2 + 35.2). Since PbIT was £32.2 in 1994 and £25.0 in 1993, we have

	1994	*1993*
ROCE	$\frac{32.2}{133.8} = 24.1\%$	$\frac{25.0}{125.1} = 20.0\%$

Many financial ratios relate a 'flow' to a 'stock', for example, PbIT/Capital Employed; Sales/Debtors. The flow arose over a period but the stock is measured at a particular date. For convenience we use year-end figures, but there is a danger of bias arising. The use of closing figures is easier, avoids having an extra year's data, and will not distort if the true profile is comparable between the firms or years under review. The average of opening and closing capital employed, debtors, etc is sometimes used, but even this will only be exactly right if the flow accrues evenly through the year, and the asset grows at a constant rate.

We suggested earlier that it is not generally a good idea to net cash off against capital employed. But where the firm has significant cash and financial assets it is informative to calculate a separate return on these assets and on the remaining 'operating' or 'business' assets. For cash-rich companies a failure to exclude the cash can seriously distort the measured return on the underlying business, so in this case one can split PbIT into operating profit and other income, and split capital employed into cash and liquid assets, and other, ie operating, assets. Tho two elements of ROCE are then

Operating return = Operating profit/operating assets

Return on financial assets = Other income/cash and liquid assets.

Margins and asset turnover

It can be revealing to break the ROCE down into two elements, the *net margin* and the *asset turnover*. Clearly, in terms of arithmetic

$$\frac{\text{PbIT}}{\text{Capital employed}} = \frac{\text{PbIT}}{\text{Sales}} \times \frac{\text{Sales}}{\text{Capital employed}}$$

$$\text{so ROCE} = \text{'net margin'} \times \text{'asset turnover'}$$

The return a company earns, which is its profit per unit of capital employed, is a function of the profit margin on sales, and the efficiency with which it uses its capital to support this level of activity.

The Body Shop's sales were £195.4 in 1994 and £168.3 in 1993 so

	Margin		*Asset turnover*	
1994	$\frac{32.2}{195.4}$	= 16.5%	$\frac{195.4}{133.8}$	= 1.46
1993	$\frac{25.0}{168.3}$	= 14.9%	$\frac{168.3}{125.1}$	= 1.35

Consistency check: 1994 ROCE = 16.5% × 1.46 = 24.1%. Note that, because the amounts are small in the Body Shop's case, we have included other income in the net margin calculation.

We can see that Body Shop's improvement in ROCE in 1994 came both from improved margin, and a small improvement in asset utilisation as measured by the asset turnover ratio. The net margin in 1994 was helped to a small extent by our inclusion of the £1.1 profit on an asset sale.

The ratio pyramid

The final step is to try and track down, from the data available, what is driving net margin and asset turnover. Clearly net margin is a function of gross margin (= gross profit/sales) and of expenditure on sales and administration.

Body Shop had:

	1994		*1993*	
Gross margin $= \frac{\text{Gross profit}}{\text{Sales}}$	$\frac{105.9}{195.4}$	= 54.2%	$\frac{90.3}{168.3}$	= 53.7%
S&A/Sales	$\frac{75.8}{195.4}$	= 38.8%	$\frac{66.0}{168.3}$	= 39.2%

So Body Shop's net margin improved due to a .5% improvement in gross margin and a .4% reduction in expenditure on S&A relative to sales.

Asset turnover depends on how effectively the firm is managing the main asset and liability categories in the balance-sheet. We can get a feel for this by calculating sales/asset ratios and, commonly for working capital, 'asset days'. We will spell out how to find trade debtor days and stock days in a little more detail. The usual indicator of debtor efficiency is

$$\text{Debtor days} = \frac{\text{TRADE DEBTORS}}{\text{SALES}} \times 365$$

This tells us how many days' credit the firm's debtors are taking on average. As a numerator, trade debtors, ideally with VAT excluded from UK debtors, is used. Strictly, to assess the latest debtor policy, closing debtors would have to be related to annualised sales for the last month or two, but these figures are not normally available. Ideally sales should be *credit sales*, but this figure is, again, not normally available. If a firm with significant cash sales is being appraised but the overall sales figure is used in the debtor ratio, there will be no distortion for comparative purposes so long as the proportion of cash sales can be assumed to be constant.

A similar ratio can be calculated for stocks, and similar comments apply.

$$\text{Stock days} = \frac{\text{STOCKS}}{\text{COST OF SALES}} \times 365$$

Cost of sales is used as a denominator since stocks, unlike debtors, are carried in the balance-sheet at cost, or input prices, excluding profit. The stock ratio is sometimes calculated using sales rather than cost of sales. Using sales will be distorting only if the relationship between purchases and sales is changing, that is if the gross profit margin is not constant.

Figure I displays the relationship between these ratios.

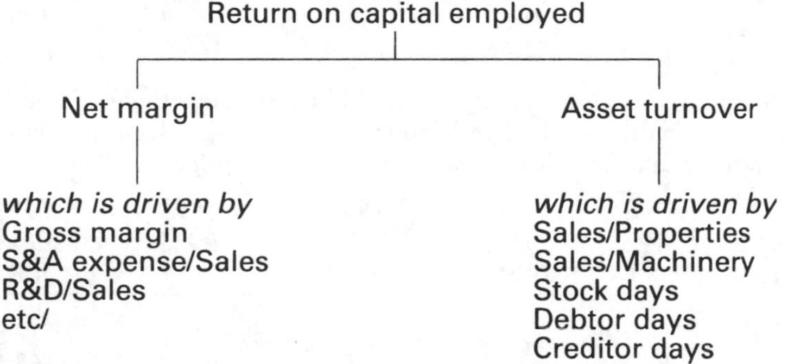

Figure I Performance analysis, ratio pyramid

Reviewing Body Shop's numbers we get the following,

		1994		*1993*
$\frac{\text{Sales}}{\text{Tangible assets}}$	$\frac{195.4}{67.9}$	= 2.88	$\frac{168.3}{64.8}$	= 2.60
Stock days	$\frac{34.6}{89.5}$	× 365 = 141 days	$\frac{35.3}{78.0}$	× 365 = 165 days
Trade debtor days	$\frac{24.7}{195.4}$	× 365 = 46 days	$\frac{22.6}{168.3}$	× 365 = 49 days
Trade creditor days	$\frac{8.2}{89.5}$	× 365 = 33 days	$\frac{8.9}{78.0}$	× 365 = 42 days

These ratios suggest that Body Shop improved utilisation of tangible fixed assets, stocks and trade debtors during the year. There was an increase in the value of sales supported by a £1 of each of these categories of asset. On the other hand Body Shop took significantly less trade credit, thus increasing the required capital employed.

Time-series comparisons

A prime motive for studying historic accounting numbers is the search for regularities that might continue into the future: the forecasting motive. One problem in time-series is dealing with changing price levels. There are two things to attend to here:

(1) Current cost One great virtue of current-cost figures for comparative purposes is that they attempt to be *internally consistent*, and this removes some of the uncertainty the analyst faces in interpreting accounting numbers. So where possible current-cost numbers should be used.

(2) Inflation There is still a need to take account of inflation even when current-cost figures are being used. If a financial report has been drawn up using current-cost accounting we can rely on the report being internally consistent in terms of prices. But the current-cost prices will be specific to the date of the report, and if we want to compare with other year's results or with a firm using a different reporting date, then we must 'index' the figures we are using to eliminate any inflationary distortions.

The Body Shop's sales over a five-year period were:

	1990	*1991*	*1992*	*1993*	*1994*
(£m)	84.5	115.6	142.4	168.3	195.4

Before we can interpret these figures it would help to index them. Table I shows the retail price index (RPI) over the five calendar years 1990–1994. From this, coefficients can be derived to calculate all the sales figures in 1990 prices.

	1990	*1991*	*1992*	*1993*	*1994*
Reported sales	84.5	115.6	147.4	168.3	195.4
Price deflator	×1	×.92	×.88	×.87	×.85
SALES AT 1990 prices	84.5	106.2	123.6	146.4	165.9
% growth in 'real' sales		+25.7%	+16.4%	+18.5%	+13.4%

Once we index the Body Shop's sales, by recalculating them at 1990 prices in this case, we get a clearer view of the trend of 'real' sales.

Table I Retail Price Index

Year	*1990*	*1991*	*1992*	*1993*	*1994*
Index	474	516	538	546	558
Deflator to convert to 1990	474/474	474/516	474/538	474/546	474/558
=	1	.92	.88	.87	.85

Source: CSO/Eurostat, Employment Gazette

Indexation is only needed when comparing *values* at different times, such as 'sales revenue' in different years or between firms with different reporting dates. Obviously it is not necessary to index *real* figures, such as 'number of employees'. But remember that the ratio of two values is a real figure, while the ratio of a value and a real figure is a value. So if we are comparing Fixed asset turnover $= \frac{\text{Sales}}{\text{Fixed assets}}$ we do not need to index, but if we are calculating, say sales per employee $= \frac{\text{Sales}}{\text{No of employees}}$ we must index.

In the previous example RPI was used to index 'sales'. We could have used the specific price index relating to the particular types of goods and services the Body Shop produces. But a general index such as RPI has certain advantages:
— specific indices may not be readily available;[1]
— in a multi-product firm an appropriate composite index would have to be calculated. This requires information about the composition of published figures that the outsider does not have.

Cross-sectional analysis

Since we cannot know in isolation whether a firm is efficient we might try to form a judgement by comparing it with other firms. But what is a comparable firm? There are few single-product, single-market firms. Most firms produce multiple products and sell them in several markets, and each product can be expected to require a different configuration of assets and costs for its production, and each market for inputs and outputs to set prices under potentially different conditions of demand and competition. A useful comparison of efficiency or performance between two firms must hold these factors constant. The usual way of doing this is to use as a 'control' a firm producing similar products in similar markets. But there may be few if any firms with a similar range of activities. The problem is compounded by the fact that firms are not obliged to report to outsiders on their separate activities. The outsider may hope for some breakdown of sales revenue into activities, but he will not often find disaggregated data on assets and costs.

There are several levels at which the analyst can look for comparable data.

(1) The individual firm Data on individual firms is available as follows:

— ANNUAL REPORTS The annual report of all registered companies can be inspected at Companies House in London or Cardiff.[2] To reduce the inconvenience, 'search agencies' advertise in the financial press who will make the visit and post the results, in exchange for a fee.

— DATABASES The financial data of larger firms are collected and published by various agencies. EXTEL publishes cards containing financial, and some historical and institutional data on 8,000 firms. It also produces EXSTAT, a computerised source of financial data to subscribers. The DATASTREAM teletext service is another source of data on individual firms.

(2) Aggregate data There are various sources of financial data aggregated over industries. Datastream and Extel provide this. The government provides industry

1 The RPI is published monthly in the Employment Gazette, by the Department of Employment. It gives a monthly RPI for the past two years, and an annual index for more than ten years. Specific indices are produced by a variety of agencies. *Price Indices for Current Cost Accounting*, published by HMSO in the Business Monitor series give current cost indices for a variety of specific goods and services. Failing this, many trade associations produce their own price indices.

2 If the company has filed them. Some companies fail to.

averages in *company finance*, a publication in the Business Monitor series. Many industry and trade associations compile average financial data on members.

(3) Inter-firm comparisons One problem, with aggregate or firm-level published data is that it contains only the information that firms are required to publish – it is 'outsider' information. A firm can get access to more detailed information about competitors by joining an inter-firm comparison agency such as PIMS, or the Centre for Inter-firm Comparisons. In return for providing confidential information that it would not normally publish, the firm receives an analysis of similar data provided by other firms.

II ECONOMIC INTERPRETATION OF ROCE

ROCE is a commonly used accounting ratio. Within the firm managers make judgements about the performance of single projects and divisions using ROCE, and outsiders evaluate the performance of whole firms this way. Accounting numbers are commonly used in *comparison*, and we have already encountered some of the problems in using ROCE this way. Comparisons rely on consistency in terms of price data and accounting treatment, and the outsider may have some difficulty ensuring this.

In this section we review the role of ROCE in some of the uses to which it is put. We start by asking whether, and in what situations, ROCE is a good proxy for the internal rate of return, IRR. If we can establish the status of ROCE this way then it will make some sense to compare the ROCE of projects, divisions and firms with the cost of capital. We know from Chapter 7 that IRR itself can be troublesome and provide an inconsistent signal on occasions, but we leave these problems to one side in this discussion.

ROCE as a proxy for IRR

The relationship between ROCE and IRR was explained by John Kay in Kay (1976). We will describe the version of the relationship produced by Peasnell (1982). The building blocks for Peasnell's theorem are two accounting identities we are familiar with already plus the definition of net present value. The first is the profit identity.

$$P_t \equiv C_t + (A_t - A_{t-1}) \qquad (1)$$

where P_t is profit in period t, C_t is the dividends or cash distributed by the project or firm in the period, and A_t is the accounting or book value of the firm's assets at time t. The second is his definition of return on capital, a_t, where

$$a_t \equiv \frac{P_t}{A_{t-1}} \qquad (2)$$

We can define net present value as the present value of the net cash flows plus the present value of the terminal realisable value of the assets, less the initial cost.

$$NPV = \sum_{t=1}^{N} \frac{C_t}{(1+r)^t} + \frac{R_N}{(1+r)^N} - C_o \qquad (3)$$

Where C_o is the initial outlay on assets, and R_N is the terminal value of the assets. We will not reproduce Peasnell's proof, but it is quite simple and proceeds by noting that both the accounting identities and the NPV formula contain the cash flows, C_t, so one can be substituted into the other by eliminating C_t. Also we know that the internal rate of return, which we will call r*, is the discount rate that gives NPV = 0. By some manipulation Peasnell derives the basic theorem, which shows the internal rate of return from a firm or a project over a number of periods to be a weighted average of the periodic accounting rates of return, plus an error term relating to the discrepancy between book value and market value of assets at the beginning and the end.

$$r^* = \sum_{t=1}^{N} W_t a_t + E \tag{4}$$

where the period weights and the error term are defined as

$$W_t = \frac{A_{t-1}/(1+r^*)^{t-1}}{\sum_{j=0}^{N-1} A_t/(1+r^*)^j} \quad \text{where} \sum_{t=1}^{N} W_t = 1 \tag{5}$$

$$E = \frac{E_N - E_o}{\sum_{j=1}^{N} A_{j-1}/(1+r^*)^j} \tag{6}$$

$$\text{where } E_N = (R_N - A_N)/(1+r)^N$$
$$E_o = C_o - R_o$$

Taken together the theorem embodied in (4), (5), and (6) looks fairly intimidating, but it contains within it some interesting results:

1 If $E = 0$, then $r^* = \sum_{t=1}^{N} w_t a_t$

if there are no opening and closing valuation errors, or they cancel out, the internal rate of return is a weighted average of the return-on-capital series. There will be no opening and closing valuation errors if the market values of the assets equal their book values at the beginning and end.

2 If $E = 0$, and $a_1 = a_2 = a_3 \ldots = a$, then
$r^* = a$
if the ROCE is constant and there are no opening and closing valuation errors then the ROCE is a good proxy for IRR.

Kay and Peasnell derive various other special cases, but an interesting one is

3 If $E_N = E_0$ and if the book value of the firm's assets grows at a constant rate which is less than the IRR, the IRR will be more closely related to earlier ROCEs. If the rate of growth is greater than the IRR, the IRR is more closely related to later ROCEs.

The key implication of Peasnell's theorems is that a series of ROCE or the ROCE of a single period provide a good proxy for IRR only under apparently limiting assumptions: only if the differences between the book value and market value of the firm's assets at the beginning and end of the period are either zero, or cancel each other out. Otherwise an adjustment has to be made to allow for the opening and closing valuation discrepancy. The logic of this is clear – if there is effectively no change in the value of assets during a period, then the ROCE of the period will tell us all we need to know about economic performance. This has implications for the various uses people put ROCE to.

ROCE in company and project appraisal

In Chapter 11 we saw that managers commonly use 'rules of thumb' to make project investment decisions. One of these involves deriving either the average accounting ROCE from a project, or the ROCE for a single year, and comparing this with the cost of capital. We can see now that we can only be sure the average ROCE will be a good proxy for IRR if the average uses the weights in expression (5) and if the assets are fully consumed on the project and have no resale value at the end so that there is no valuation discrepancy.

To show how the formula for calculating IRR would work in project appraisal, Peasnell produces a simple example. Consider a machine which costs £10,000 and which has a useful life of six years with no terminal value. The machine produces cash flows of £2,296 each year. DCF analysis of the project would show that it has an IRR of 10%, and an NPV of £614 using an 8% discount rate. However, using Peasnell's formula we can get the same result by analysing its stream of accounting rates of return. Table II shows how this works out.

Net profit each year is £629, the annual cash flow less the annual depreciation. To find ARR this is divided by the *opening* asset value (as Peasnell's formula requires). So in year 1, ARR is 629/10,000 = 6.29%. The weights are calculated using expression (5) and the IRR is simply the sum of these, since, because the machine is completely consumed on the job, there is no valuation error term.

Peasnell's formula shows that a series of ARRs can be meaningful economically, but he is not necessarily recommending we should calculate IRR this way. In the example, it would have been more straightforward to calculate it conventionally.

Table II Peasnell's formula applied to a project

Year	*0*	*1*	*2*	*3*	*4*	*5*	*6*	
Cash flow	(10,000)	2,296	2,296	2,296	2,296	2,296	2,296	
Profit before depreciation		2,296	2,296	2,296	2,296	2,296	2,296	
Less: depreciation		1,667	1,667	1,667	1,667	1,667	1,667	
(1) Net profit		629	629	629	629	629	629	
(2) Written down value of machine	10,000	8,333	6,667	5,000	3,333	1,667	0	
ARR (1) ÷ (2)		6.29%	7.55%	9.44%	12.58%	18.88%	37.78%	
Weights		.332	.251	.183	.125	.075	.034	
total		2.09	1.90	1.73	1.57	1.4	1.28	= 10%

Does it make sense to compare the ROCE of a firm with the firm's cost of capital? Exactly the same comments apply. If there are no valuation discrepancies, the ROCE will be a good proxy for IRR and we can compare it with the cost of capital, embodying the market's perception of the firm's riskiness. But if the value of the firm is changing as well we cannot rely on ROCE as a measure of IRR. For example if the firm is 'building for growth', investing heavily now in the anticipation of future profits, its current ROCE may be low but its market value will be increasing and this will generate a positive error term so that the IRR will be above ROCE.

ROCE as a target for individuals and divisions

Perhaps the most common method of organising a large firm is as a group of more or less autonomous 'divisions'.

The question arises of how to ensure that the behaviour of the autonomous divisions will conform to the assumed objective of the firm as a whole – value-maximisation. One practice is to appraise the achieved ROCE of each division and since the rational and ambitious divisional manager will respond to this appraisal system by maximising ROCE, this is tantamount to setting the maximisation of ROCE as the divisional objective. Commonly the manager's pay will be linked to ROCE on assets under his control.

Some of the problems in making ROCE an objective should be clear by now. It is important that the prices of inputs and outputs should reflect the opportunity costs to the firm of the resources involved. This may not happen unless divisions sell goods and services to each other at the right *transfer prices*. Unless transfer prices are carefully set the performance of different divisions may be over or understated and they may well over- or under-produce in response. This applies particularly to finance. If capital is not priced at its opportunity cost it may be inefficiently allocated within the firm and the situation can arise where one division is starved of funds for projects which have a higher return than some that actually get undertaken in other divisions. The allocation problem can be helped by requiring divisions to bid competitively for the available supplies of capital within the firm. In many organisations investment decision making is retained at head office, but when divisional managers can control their own investment base it has been suggested they should be appraised on the basis of the *residual income* they generate, where residual income is accounting profit less a charge for the cost of the capital used by the division.

But the real problem with appraising managers in terms of ROCE can be seen from studying equation (4). It imparts a bias in favour of projects with positive returns in early years and against projects which may have a positive value but earn their returns in subsequent periods. In fact given high rates of job turnover amongst managers, the cynical manager can enhance his own reputation and tarnish the reputation of his successor by choosing just these projects! In terms of equation (4) managers will have an incentive to choose projects with high a and low or negative E.

Even if ROCE is a good proxy for IRR, this does not imply we should *maximise* it. Consider Table III which shows three projects A, B, C, yielding differing profits in perpetuity. Suppose the firm can choose to undertake any or all of the projects A, B and C, which should they choose?

The reader will recall that the rational firm would invest until the IRR of the marginal project equals the cost of capital. Such a firm will choose all three projects, since they all yield a return which covers the cost of capital. But the ROCE maximiser will choose only A. B and C are both worthwhile but will be rejected because of their tendency to dilute the achieved ROCE.

Table III

Project	*Annual profit (£)*	*Capital employed (£)*	*ROCE*	*Cumulative ROCE*
A	300,000	1,000,000	30%	30% (A)
B	200,000	1,000,000	20%	25% (A & B)
C	100,000	1,000,000	10%	20% (A & B & C)

Cost of capital: 8%

There is no easy solution to the divisional control problem, for two reasons. First, we are trying to find a measure of present performance, when what we really want is a measure of value performance which depends on effects which lie partly in the future and are as yet unknown. Second, we want a control on divisional performance which preserves as far as possible the benefits of autonomy. By virtue of its inside position head office is in a position to monitor the detailed plans and budgets of the division, and to exercise more direct control than the shareholder. But the closer this control, the less autonomy remains.

ROCE as a measure of efficiency

Are firms with higher ROCE necessarily more efficient?

Arthur Shaw Ltd

Arthur Shaw Ltd is a general manufacturer whose income statement last year was as follows:

	£m
Sales	1.0
Materials	(.2)
Labour	(.3)
Overheads	(.1)
Profit	.4

Capital employed was £1m, and ROCE 40%.

Arthur Shaw, the chairman and owner of the firm was pleased with the results, but was well aware of the importance in achieving this result of the loyalty of the customers and the diligence of the workers. So he decided to reward them this year with a 15% price cut and a 30% bonus respectively. Nothing else changed this year, either in quantitites of inputs or outputs, or in their prices, so the results were

	£m
Sales	.85
Materials	(.20)
Labour	(.39)
Overheads	(.10)
Profit	.16

Capital employed was £1m, and ROCE 16%.

Was Arthur Shaw less efficient this year?

The answer depends on what 'efficiency' we are talking about. Since the fall in profit will presumably lead to a fall in the value of the firm, it seems that the change in ROCE does signal a reduction in efficiency. The reason this conclusion may feel uncomfortable is that there was no change in the 'efficiency' with which the firm converted physical inputs into outputs, and the profits change simply reflects a voluntary redistribution of the surplus, which may well have led to an increase in social welfare overall.

We might be happier with the conclusion that efficiency had fallen if the changes in sales price and wages had not been voluntary, but forced by changes in the respective output and input markets, that is, if Arthur Shaw Ltd had been forced to trim its prices by increased competition, and to pay higher wages by increased outside demand for this type of labour. In general, changes in the return of firms will signal a parallel change in welfare of society as a whole, as well as in the welfare of shareholders, only if the prices of inputs and outputs measure their relative utility and scarcity. If prices are of this sort it will be feasible to make comparisons between firms to judge relative efficiency. But do prices do this job? The only world that economists have identified in which one could be confident that prices are accurately measuring the relative utility and scarcity of resources is the world of perfect competition in input and output markets. If this does not obtain, it may be the case that comparisons between firms will mislead.

The arbitrary price changes that Arthur Shaw imposed could not have happened in a world of perfect markets because his return on capital would then be the competitive return, just sufficient to stay in business, and his act of generosity would have driven his return below this necessary level. In the example Arthur Shaw was fixing the prices of his inputs and outputs, whereas in a perfect market all participants must 'take' prices and accept the market prices.

In practice markets are not perfect, and it follows that it is dangerous to conclude that a firm with higher ROCE is necessarily more efficient or desirable in a social sense. The difference in results may simply reflect the fact that one firm is a monopolist in its input or output markets while the other operates in highly competitive markets.

III SUMMARY

In this chapter we showed how return on capital employed is calculated and how other financial ratios can help explain the ROCE performance of the firm. We also examined some of the pitfalls using ROCE and saw when ROCE is, and is not, likely to provide a good proxy for IRR.

REFERENCES AND BIBLIOGRAPHY

Drury, C R — *Management and Cost Accounting* (3rd edn, 1992) Chapman and Hall, London.

Foster, G — *Financial Statement Analysis* (2nd edn, 1986) Prentice-Hall Inc, Englewood-Cliffs, New Jersey.

Kay, J A — 'Accountants, Too, Could Be Happy in a Golden Age', Oxford Economic Papers, 1976.

Peasnell, K V — 'Some Formal Corrections Between Economic Values and Yields and Accounting Numbers', Journal of Business Finance and Accounting, 1982 Autumn, No 3, p 361.

Scherer, F M — *Industrial Market Structure and Economic Performance* (2nd edn, 1980) Rand McNally, Chicago.

Skinner, R C — 'Return on Capital Employed as a Measure of Efficiency', Accountancy, June 1965.

Skinner, R C — 'The Role of Profitability in Divisional Decision Making and Performance', Accounting and Business Research, Spring 1990, pp 135–141.

QUESTIONS

1 What difficulties arise in using ROCE to compare the performance of two firms?

2 What difficulties arise in setting ROCE as a target for managers?

3 You are personal assistant to the manager of a large branch of a leading commercial bank. Thrusting the file into your hand, your manager explains that tomorrow the

chairman of Northampton Engineers Ltd is coming to discuss their loan facility. Northampton are seeking to increase their overdraft by £200,000 to finance the acquisition of badly-needed modern equipment. Your manager is very concerned about the existing level of the overdraft. As background he tells you that Northampton have been associated with your bank for 40 years, and that they are an important employer in the town.

The file contains the recent accounts of Northampton. You also obtain from the bank's economics section some performance indicators for Northampton's sector of the engineering industry as a whole.

Industry sector figures: 1986

Return on total assets	10%
Debt ratio	45%
Profit margin on sales	4%
Acid test ratio	1.2
Current ratio	2.5
Stock turnover	8 times
Debtors' turnover	14 times

NORTHAMPTON – Balance-sheets (31 December)

ASSETS EMPLOYED	*1993*	*1994*
Land and buildings	293,700	275,400
Machinery	284,580	243,180
Stocks	1,147,500	1,859,040
Debtors	624,240	872,100
Cash	64,260	42,900
Creditors and accruals	477,360	862,920
Overdraft	229,500	642,600
	1,707,420	1,787,100
FINANCED BY		
Ordinary shares (£1 at par)	826,000	826,000
Retained earnings	789,480	881,280
Debentures	91,940	79,820
	1,707,420	1,787,100

– Income statements (year ended 31 December)

Sales	6,196,500	6,426,000
Cost of sales	4,957,200	5,140,800
Gross profit	1,239,300	1,285,200
General expenses	698,040	826,200
Depreciation	229,500	275,400
Net income	£311,760	£183,600

Prepare a brief for your manager suggesting how he should respond to Northampton. Consider what further information would be useful.

CHAPTER 21

Balance-sheet management

This book is, in large part, about how to make investment and financing choices which add value. But *given* its mix of business activities, the firm can often choose alternative ways of structuring its assets and liabilities to achieve the same business end. Sometimes this adds value, for example when leasing rather than owning an asset is tax-efficient. But other times the effect is merely cosmetic, to make the balance-sheet look different. In this chapter we analyse the ways in which 'balance-sheet management' may and may not add value.

Section I decribes the effect which management action can have on book gearing, and considers the logic of matching the term of borrowing to the life of assets. Section II reviews other arguments for using leasing and factoring. Section III shows how to conduct an economic analysis of a tax-driven leasee.

I BALANCE-SHEET STRATEGIES

Flattering the gearing ratio

We have seen how to calculate the *gearing* ratio, which we defined as the ratio of the firm's borrowing and equity finance, alternatively the debt to equity ratio. Of all financial ratios, this is the one which seems to preoccupy firms the most. Chapter 16 showed that there can be tax advantages to borrowing, but that borrowing brings financial risk and increases the risk of financial distress. Other things equal most firms would like their borrowing to *look* as low as possible.

Usually gearing is measured from the balance-sheet, that is at 'book', but we saw in Chapter 19 that the balance-sheet may be incomplete and may use values which are out-of-date and inappropriate. One response is to measure gearing at market values rather than book values. But book gearing is still the measure predominantly used in practice. There are several actions firms can take which change the appearance of the balance-sheet and reduce book gearing.

Enhancing equity

Inge

Inge's gearing is 66% (200/(100 + 200)) and her balance-sheet is as follows:

Assets		*Liabilities*	
Fixed assets	200	Equity	100
Debtors	100	Borrowing	200

(1) Inge revalues some property fixed assets, which are currently included at cost of 100, to 300; this revaluation adds a corresponding 200 to the residual claim, equity. (2) Inge recognises some hitherto unrecorded intangible assets at 100. So the new balance-sheet has gearing of 33%:

Fixed assets	400	Equity	400
Intangible assets	100	Borrowing	200
Debtors	100		

Revaluation is feasible in many countries, and managers may be able to capitalise expenditure on RD, or to carry acquired goodwill in the balance-sheet. For these reasons, economists argue that gearing should be calculated using the market value of equity. If there are omitted assets or the book value of assets is understated then this should be reflected in the market value of equity and a value-based measure of gearing would be unaffected by Inge's accounting policy.

Off balance-sheet

An alternative strategy for a company is to write a contract with a third party to take some of the assets, and the corresponding borrowing, 'off balance-sheet'.

Jochen

Jochen has the same balance-sheet as Inge. (1) He transfers ownership of 100 of the fixed assets to a leasing company, and leases them back, and (2) sells 50 of the debtors to a factoring company. He uses the 150 proceeds to reduce borrowings. Jochen's new balance-sheet is

Fixed assets	100	Equity	100
Debtors	50	Borrowing	50

We can reasonably assume that nothing of substance in the business is changed. Clearly Jochen still has use of the fixed assets, and is still able to offer credit to his customers. Moreover the risk profile will be unchanged if the borrowing was already secured on the fixed assets, and the factoring company still has recourse to Jochen if the debtors do not pay. Jochen has reduced his gearing to 33% (50/(100+50)) by making the balance-sheet less complete. Since Jochen's approach is to take borrowing off the balance-sheet, whereas Inge's was to recognise more book equity, a value-based measure of gearing will be less help.

Dressing debt as equity

A final strategy which some firms have adopted in order to flatter book gearing is to issue securities which in substance may be debt, or near-debt, but which are legally equity or may be accounted as equity. Favourites are preference shares, and convertible loan-stock with an exercise price which assures conversion. These are discussed elsewhere in this book.

Regulators go to some lengths to control balance-sheet management. In most countries, companies which write 'finance' or 'capital' leases, that is leases which in substance give the rights and rewards of ownership, in contrast to short-term operating leases, are required to capitalise them. That is, they must record the leased asset in the balance-sheet as though they owned it, and record the underlying borrowing as debt. Most countries have strict rules about recognising intangible assets in the balance-sheet, and some countries outlaw revaluation. Some countries are introducing broader catch-all requirements that company reports show the economic 'substance' of transactions rather than the legal 'form'.

The financial analyst who compares the financial structure of companies will typically be aware of the effect of balance-sheet strategies and will be on the lookout for them. The main instruments of 'creative accounting' in this area are well-known and well-documented,[1] and

1 For a stimulating recent treatment see Terry Smith *Accounting for Growth* (1992).

because analysts do not always have the data to adjust the balance-sheet accounting, there has been a tendency towards the use of the cash-flow statement, and profit and loss account measures such as interest cover, to assess solvency and credit risk. Moreover many analysts treat preference shares as borrowing by default, unless they are convinced otherwise. As a result, though there are doubtless exceptions, there is no evidence that firms can systematically affect their value or their credit-rating by balance-sheet management. There can be good reasons for several of the actions we have mentioned in this section, for revaluations, leasing, and the use of preference shares and we examine some of them later in the chapter. But flattering book gearing is not a good reason and cannot be expected to add value in an efficient market.

Matching assets and liabilities

A rather different sort of strategy which needs to be considered concerns the term of the company's liabilities. There is a traditional rule of thumb which says the firm should match the term of its financing to the life of its assets. The rule says that the long-term finance of the firm should be at least as great as its fixed or long-term assets. In terms of the simple balance-sheet below, the difference x should always be positive and the firm should never finance any part of its long-term assets with short-term finance.

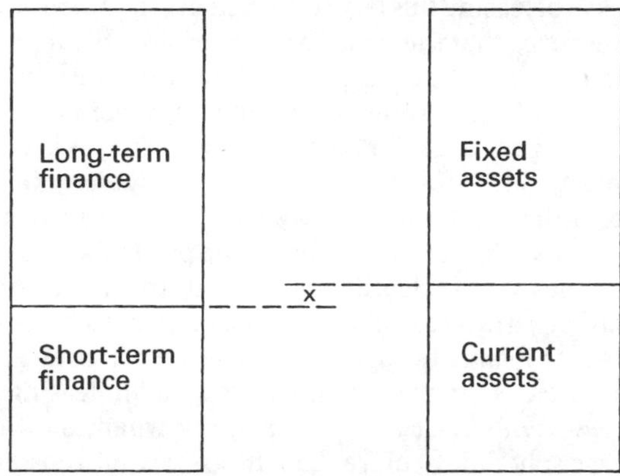

In its *Money for Business* (Fifth Edition, 1985), the Bank of England stated a similar principle.

> For a business with a sound balance-sheet, long-term funds are in general appropriate to help finance investment in productive assets with a long-life, such as industrial buildings or heavy plant machinery. . . . Medium-term finance . . . is appropriate for the purchase of most plant and machinery, and to finance a proportion of working capital. Short-term funds are appropriate to meet fluctuations in working capital and for the finance of trade.
> (p 11–12)

This principle is the equivalent of the old banking adage 'never borrow short and lend long. At first glance it sounds eminently sensible, but subjected to the hard logic of finance, it loses some of its force. The aim may be to avoid the danger that the firm will be unable to repay if short-term finance is withdrawn, without selling off fixed assets and thus dismantling the fixed capital of the firm. In an efficient capital market it is hard to see the logic in this. For one thing, if finance were withdrawn there should be no more reason to consider a loss of fixed capital more significant than a loss of current assets. In a firm which is not carrying redundant assets both are vital. But anyhow in an efficient capital market we find it hard to conceive that short-term finance would be withdrawn yet the firm be unable to replace it, unless there had been a deterioration in the economic value of the firm. If the effect of gearing up with long-term finance is to limit the option the investor has to withdraw his funds, should there be a fall in the value of the firm, then we can expect him to want compensating for this reduction in his options.

II OTHER MOTIVES FOR LEASING AND FOR FACTORING

Leasing

The essence of a lease contract is that the user and owner remain separate and the former pays the latter a regular rental for the use of the asset. Some lease contracts give the user the right to buy after a certain period, and in this case leasing becomes similar to *hire purchase*. In an HP contract both parties set out with the intention that ownership will transfer at the end of the hire period. Another sort of contract which can generate a similar profile of cash flows is the *instalment sale*. In this case the user of the asset acquires ownership at the outset, but pays the purchase price in instalments. In terms of economics there may not seem much difference between these arrangements. But there is a legal difference concerning ownership, and in the case of leasing this legal difference turns out to be all important since it determines the tax allowances that the lessor and lessee are able to claim. The drafters of lease contracts have to take care to differentiate them from instalment sale agreements robustly enough to withstand the scrutiny of the Inland Revenue.

If the lessee is only leasing the asset for part of its useful life, as is normally the case with property, or equipment like a bulldozer required for a particular job, and the asset is then leased to someone else, the lease is known as an *operating* lease. But in many leases the lessee intends to use the asset for its full useful life. There is no particular expectation that the asset will be leased again after the first user has finished with it, and the lessor may well then sell it on the second-hand market. In this case the user is making a real choice between leasing and buying the asset. It is these *finance* or *capital* leases that we are interested in.

The lessee makes a series of payments to the lessor, and in leasing jargon this series of payments is called the *lease schedule*. Leasing is worthwhile when, allowing for the tax effects, the lessor values the lease schedule at more than the asset would cost him to buy, while the lessee values it at less than it would cost him. This happy situation can arise when lessor and lessee are in different tax positions, and in the next section we analyse 'lease-or-buy' as a purely tax-driven decision, but are there any other motives for leasing? Lessors will usually quote a list of advantages, with tax benefits as perhaps the main but not the only one. Usually these other arguments are saying that there may be *imperfections* in either the *product* or *capital* markets and the lessor may be better placed to capture them than the lessee. Finance books tend to ignore these arguments. The reason is that market imperfections can be more apparent than real, and where they do exist there is usually some way other than leasing of capturing the benefit so they are irrelevant as far as the leasing decision goes.

- Through leasing the lessee can avoid the risk of owning an asset which may become technologically superseded or otherwise redundant at some time during its life.

Leasing a micro-computer sounds like a better idea than buying while technological change is still so rapid in that area – risk of obsolescence is transferred to the lessor. But the lessor is likely to have noticed this, and if he is rational he will have raised the lease payments to compensate himself for the risk that the resale value of the equipment might slump. This is not a good reason for leasing, nor is the following capital markets argument.

- The lessee may not have been able to raise the cash to buy the asset outright, OR he could only get the cash at a higher cost of capital than the lessor. Also a leasing contract finances 100% of the asset and is secured only on the asset.

The inability of a firm to finance an asset purchase at all, or to finance it on reasonable terms, may be due to capital market imperfections, or it may simply reflect the risk of the venture. In the latter case the rational lessor will 'cost' the capital involved in the lease at a rate appropriate to the riskiness of the lessee, rather than at his own marginal cost of capital. Anyhow the view that leasing is an easy way to get 100% financing of an asset, and that it leaves the gearing and borrowing power of the firm intact, does not take account of the mechanisms of an efficient capital market. Most leasing companies are subsidiaries of the big banks. The leasing company is likely to subject the lessee to just the same credit review, and subsequent monitoring, as any other provider of finance would.

However, some product market imperfections *may* be important:

- The lessor may be able to buy the asset cheaper, perhaps because he writes a lot of leases for this sort of asset and gets volume discounts.
- The lessor may be able to provide servicing and maintenance more economically than the lessee could because of indivisibilities in the provision of a service department. So, for example, it may not be worthwhile for the lessee to employ and equip a full time service engineer.
- The lessor may have better access to the second hand markets and thus be able to dispose of the asset at a higher price.

In principle, even if economies of scale confer these benefits, the lessee can share them in other ways than by leasing. The lessee has the alternative of buying through a large wholesaler arranging a service contract, finding a second-hand dealer to dispose of the asset. But in practice we suspect that a significant reason for leasing is to use the lessor's market expertise and access.

Leasing as project finance

We can suggest another reason for leasing that also fits in with our usual approach to financial decision making. The models of MM and Miller showed that a company's financing and investment decisions are quite independent of each other, under certain assumptions. When we relax these assumptions we see financing and investment as interrelating with the cost of capital as the messenger, but even so we tend to treat them as sequential – the company raises a tranche of capital, and the cost of capital then serves as a cut-off rate for investment decisions. However, particularly in small and medium-sized firms, but sometimes in the largest firms too, managers tend to think in terms of *project finance*. In other words they identify a project or asset for investment, then go and raise the funds specifically to finance it. Firms like this may be investment rather than finance oriented, and may not feel they have the skills or time required for a sophisticated search for financing. Leasing offers an exceptionally convenient way of raising project finance. A final reason that, even in larger firms with conventional financing operations, we find managers leasing, is that it can provide a convenient way round head office limits on capital expenditure.

Factoring

In leasing some of the fixed assets one firm uses are owned by someone else. Many firms do something similar with their debtors by *factoring* or *invoice discounting*. In a factoring contract the firm sell its book debtors to a factoring company, usually for immediate cash and on a continuing basis.

By factoring its debts the firm is doing two things. First, it is buying certain services it would otherwise have to provide for itself. The factor runs its debtor ledger for it: keeps accounting records and pursues debtors for cash; and most factors will accept the risk of bad debts on behalf of clients as well, though credit risk is not always transferred. The cost of the service is expressed as a percentage of the debts factored and depends on the services the factor is providing and, if he is insuring against bad debts, on the riskiness of the debts. Second, the firm is raising finance to the extent of the early payment it receives from the factor. The cost of the financing component is usually a little above bank overdraft rates. As with leasing, the main factoring houses tend to be subsidiaries of the large banks.

The firm can take the ledger management service of factoring without the financing. Conversely, if it has its own sales ledger department but wants to raise finance on debtors it can use 'invoice discounting'. Institutions which provide this service are often factoring houses. They agree to buy the whole sales ledger, or just invoices relating to approved debtors, and the firm assigns these invoices to the discounting house in exchange for an agreed proportion of their value. The firm itself collects the debts in the normal way, and retains responsibility for bad debts, and when it receives the cash it reimburses the discounting house. Invoice discounting is a parallel system to the bill discounting which is long established in international trade. Again the discount rate in these arrangements is closely related to the bank overdraft rate.

It is rather harder to find a powerful rationale for factoring than it is for leasing. The decisive argument for leasing is a tax one: by postponing tax payments lessor and lessee could jointly generate economic value at the expense of the Inland Revenue. But there is no tax argument for factoring, so factoring has to justify itself in terms of exploiting market imperfections. The ledger management service is likely to appeal to firms that are too small for it to be economic to have their own bookkeeper and credit controller, or are growing fast and want to avoid the disruption of reorganising the sales-ledger function. Otherwise we would not expect there to be much to choose between the firm running its own sales ledger and paying another firm to run it. Insurance against bad debts might similarly be attractive to the firm which is too small to withstand the default of a major customer, though there are other ways the firm could insure itself against this.

On the financing side, we usually consider that capital market imperfections are more apparent than real. If the firm sees factoring or invoice discounting as an easier or cheaper source of finance, it is probably deluding itself. Factoring is essentially bank borrowing secured against particular assets, debts in this case. As we saw, most of the factoring houses are bank subsidiaries, and the cost of capital is closely related to the bank overdraft rate. The factoring house is likely to apply typical bank lending criteria in assessing the client. Like leasing, factoring is off balance-sheet finance. But we would not expect the financial community to be misled by that. Aware that existing factoring agreements will reduce the potential security for further loans, borrowers commonly ask for full disclosure of existing agreements when assessing further loans.

When they are advertising their services factors tend to play up two financing advantages. It is a 'flexible' source of finance, and it helps to avoid cash shortages. They emphasise that, being linked to turnover, the finance from factoring grows with the business. In practice the factoring agreement will often contain credit limits which the firm will need to negotiate periodically as debtors grow, so the difference with an overdraft may not be so great. In general we recommend the firm to ask two questions when it contemplates factoring. What am I getting that I could not get some other way? What is it costing me?

Squeezing debtors, stretching creditors

A message of this chapter is that sometimes things that look like investment decisions are actually financing decisions. When we look at working capital investment in Chapter 24 we see that it would pay the firm to make debtors pay as early as possible and to postpone paying creditors as long as possible. This is certainly true so long as these operations are costless and represent merely more efficient working capital management. But beyond a certain point real costs will set in, and with hindsight we can see what they are. Squeezing debtors and stretching creditors are effectively financing operations, and impose financing costs on outsiders. It is likely that eventually, and if they have the market power to do it, debtors and creditors will pass these costs back to the firm. Suppliers will ask a higher price for their goods and services and customers will want a discount for early payment. And as we see in Chapter 24, in terms of the equivalent loan, offering discounts for early payment can be very expensive finance.

III ECONOMIC ANALYSIS OF TAX-DRIVEN LEASING

In Chapter 3 we discovered that the Inland Revenue allows companies to deduct 'capital allowances' in calculating taxable profit. Let us assume a simple world in which the capital allowance is 100% in the first year, and the corporation tax rate is 35%, and companies pay tax a year in arrears. Consider the situation where a firm qualifies for capital allowances, but cannot use them because it has not got enough taxable profits.

Reagon plc

Exhibit I describes two alternative states of Reagon plc, which is buying a £3,600 machine. Cases A and B show Reagon's tax position if its taxable profit before capital allowance is £10,000 and £900 per annum respectively. The only difference between the two cases is that in the low profits case, profits are insufficient to absorb all the allowance in the first year, so it has to be used up gradually over four years. So what? Reagon seemingly cannot complain because, either way, it ends up saving £1,260 tax, indeed in Case B Reagon pays no tax for four years. But in columns 8 and 9, we calculate the present value of the cost of the machine in each case, assuming a 10% discount rate. Since the outlay of £3,600 is made in year 0 in each case, the PV is simply the discounted tax savings less £3,600. The effect of postponing the tax relief is that the relief is worth less in PV terms, so that the PV of the machine's cost is £2,601 in Case B but only £2,455 in Case A.

The way is now open for a mutually advantageous trade. Suppose in Case B Smith, with £100,000 of taxable profit per annum, arrives on the scene and offers to buy the machine and lease it to Reagon for five annual payments of £900, payable in advance. The PV of this lease schedule is:

Time	*10% PV factors*	*Lease payments*	*Tax paid/ saved at 35%*	*Present values*
0	1	(900)		(900)
1	.9091	(900)	315	(532)
2	.8264	(900)	315	(483)
3	.7513	(900)	315	(440)
4	.6830	(900)	315	(400)
5	.6201		315	196
				(2,559)

So if Reagon leases the machine at £900 per annum from Smith, it saves £2,601 and pays £2,559 instead, a net gain of £42. Since Smith has plenty of taxable profit it is in the same position as Reagon in Case A, so the machine costs £2,455 and it receives £2,559,

Exhibit I

	CASE A			CASE B					
	Reagon with high profits			Reagon with low profits			Present values		
	(1)	(2)	(3)	(4)	(5)	(6)	(7)	(8)	(9)
Time	*Profit per annum*	*Capital allowance*	*Tax saved 35% of (2)*	*Profit per annum*	*Capital allowance*	*Tax saved 35% of (5)*	*10% PV factors*	*A (3) × (7)*	*B (6) × (7)*
1	10,000	3,600	1,260	900	900	315	.9091	1,145	286
2	10,000	–	–	900	900	315	.8264	–	260
3	10,000	–	–	900	900	315	.7513	–	237
4	10,000	–	–	900	900	315	.6830	–	215
		£3,600	£1,260		£3,600	£1,260			
							Less initial outlay	(3,600)	(3,600)
							PV of COST	(2,455)	(2,601)

so its net gain is £104. When firms are in different tax-paying positions they may both be able to benefit by writing a lease contract. The loser is the Inland Revenue.

First we will consider how people in different tax positions will value a *given* lease schedule, then we will consider how to find the *optimal* schedule from the point of view of either or both parties. Lease evaluation is simple so long as we remember that leasing is a *financing* decision not an *investment* decision. On occasion the financial benefits to leasing might be enough to tip a negative NPV project into surplus. But in general by the time the lease analysis is undertaken, the investment appraisal should already have been done. The alternative to leasing is to buy the asset, financed by a loan secured on the asset. Since the comparison is with borrowing, two things follow:

— The relevant numbers to compare are the cash flows associated with leasing and with purchasing. The operating flows of the underlying assets are *irrelevant* since they are the same in each case.
— The appropriate discount rate is the firm's marginal borrowing rate on secured loans. The rationale is that lease payments are a low risk stream and, given the prevailing tax system, so are the tax effects. Of course, the ability of the firm to *take advantage* of tax effects depends on its uncertain future profits, so it could be argued we should discount tax effects at a rate which reflects this risk. We will follow usual practice and use a single low risk borrowing rate throughout.

We will develop our analysis step-by-step, making different assumptions about the lessee's tax position.

When the lessee is a permanent non-taxpayer

A lessee can be permanently non-tax-paying either because, like local authorities or pension funds, it is tax-exempt, or because it does not expect to earn taxable profits in the foreseeable future.

Dean

Dean is a firm, and is choosing between the purchase of a £9,500 lathe today, and a lease contract for the same asset involving an annual payment of £2,200, payable in advance, for five years. Dean's marginal borrowing rate is 8%.

Cost comparison method

The analysis of Dean's decision is relatively simple and is shown in Exhibit II. We can find

Exhibit II Lessee in a permanent non-tax-paying position

Year	*0*	*1*	*2*	*3*	*4*	*TOTALS (£)*
PURCHASE	9,500					9,500
LEASE	(2,200)	(2,200)	(2,200)	(2,200)	(2,200)	11,000
	7,300	(2,200)	(2,200)	(2,200)	(2,200)	
Discount factor	1	$\frac{1}{(1+.08)}$	$\frac{1}{(1+.08)^2}$	$\frac{1}{(1+.08)^3}$	$\frac{1}{(1+.08)^4}$	
PRESENT VALUES	7,300	(2,037)	(1,886)	(1,746)	(1,617)	13

NPV = £13 DECISION-LEASE

the NPV of the difference between the lease payments and the purchase payment using the firm's marginal cost of borrowing, 8% as the discount rate. The calculation is presented in terms of what happens if Dean leases: it saves the purchase cost of the machine but has to incur the cost of the lease payments. Since we did it this way round, a positive NPV of £13 indicates a preference for leasing, because its discounted cost is the lesser of the two.

Equivalent loan method

Our method, here, was to find the *NPV* of the difference between the lease and purchase alternatives. Another way of going about the analysis is to find the 'equivalent loan' to the lease contract directly and compare this with the purchase cost. The equivalent loan is the loan which would generate the same schedule of interest and repayment as the lease schedule. In Exhibit III we see that the lease payments would service a loan of £9,487. If Dean borrowed £9,487 at the outset, the initial repayment of £2,200 would give a balance at the end of the first year of £7,287. Dean would pay interest on this of £583 = £7,287 × 8%) so the rest of the year's £2,200 can repay £1,617 of principal giving a new balance of £5,670 (= £7,287 – £1,617) and so forth. How did we find the £9,487 to start with? In this case we could cheat – the lease schedule is simply a four-year, 8% annuity of £2,200 plus the initial £2,200 and we can find the PV of this from annuity tables as £7,287 + £2,200 = £9,487. Usually though, when tax and other complications yield an uneven stream of cash flows for the lease, we have to find the loan equivalent by trial and error, trying different initial amounts until we find the one that generates a final balance of zero.

Exhibit III

Year	*0*	*1*	*2*	*3*	*4*	*5*
Balance on loan	9,487	7,287	5,670	3,924	2,037	0
Interest at 8%	–	583	454	314	163	
Repayment of principal	2,200	1,617	1,746	1,886	2,037	
Lease payments	2,200	2,200	2,200	2,200	2,200	

The NPV we calculated earlier was simply the purchase cost less the loan equivalent of the lease, £9,500 – £9,487 = £13. Whenever we calculate an NPV, be it for a lease or a project, we are effectively calculating a loan equivalent. Projects are worth undertaking when the future cash flows from the project could service a loan which is larger than the initial outlay on the project. This is what a positive NPV means, and is an important insight. Finding the loan equivalent directly is just another way of doing the same computation, and in the present case it does not offer any benefits. However, it can be a more convenient way of analysing the lease when tax effects are more complicated.

Where the lessee is fully tax-paying

The case of the fully tax-paying lessee is not very interesting in practice since the lessee does not benefit from leasing; but it helps us develop our analysis of tax effects. Assume the lessee has plenty of taxable profits so that the tax effects of the purchase and lease alternatives result in cash flows with a payment lag of one year. We assume capital allowances are 25%, reducing balance. There is another point to note here:

— When the firm is paying tax the *after-tax* discount rate should be used. In this case the after-tax cost of capital is 5.2% which taxed at a corporation tax rate of 35% is 8% × (1–.35) = 5.2%.

Exhibit IV shows how Dean will evaluate the lease when it is fully tax-paying. With the introduction of tax, leasing has become less attractive than purchasing. However a moment's thought shows that when both are fully tax-paying there can never be a lease schedule at which lessor *and* lessee will find it worthwhile to lease for tax reasons. If the lessee is a normal taxpayer, the lessor's and lessee's analysis will be the mirror image of each other. In the present example, the lessor's evaluation will be Exhibit IV with the signs reversed. It has an outlay of *£9,500* on the machine, and *receives* the lease payments. Its NPV will be plus £8 and it will want to lease, but unfortunately the lessee will not accept its proposal, nor any lease schedule that gives the lessor a positive NPV.

Where the lessee is temporarily non-tax-paying

When the situation arises, which is not uncommon, that the firm is in a temporary non-tax-paying position, we have a combination of the previous two cases. Suppose in our example that Dean's tax advisers estimate the firm will start to be in a tax-paying position after two years. Exhibit V shows the revised analysis.

There are two new points to note:

- The backlog of tax allowances can be claimed as soon as the firm resumes tax-paying and it enters the analysis as a cash flow of that period. So tax of £1,922 (= £831 + £623 + £468) and £2,310 (= 3 × 770) are entered in year 3.
- Cash flows are discounted at the rates prevailing year-by-year until they are received. So taking the fourth-year cash flows as example they are discounted by $\dfrac{1}{(1+.08)^2(1+.052)^2}$ because during two of the years before they are received the firm's marginal borrowing rate is 8% since it is not in a tax-paying position and so cannot get tax relief on interest payments. In the third and fourth years, however, the after-tax rate can be used.[2]

Given the lessee's particular tax-position, leasing has a positive NPV of £313.

Finding the optimal lease schedule

When we discuss *merger* we will see that there are often other more efficient ways of achieving the same economic ends. Leasing is a good example. Leasing is an arrangement whereby two firms write a contract which is mutually profitable, at the expense of the Inland Revenue. Mergers have sometimes been argued on the grounds of tax benefits, but merger is a permanent and all embracing solution that can be costly, disruptive and uncertain in its effects. In leasing a specific benefit is perceived, and a specific contract written to exploit it. When looking at merger we ask two questions: How large are the gains? Who gets them? We can ask the same questions about leasing, and will start with the second.

Sharing the gains

The gains to leasing come from the differences in tax position of lessor and lessee, but the share of the gains to each party depends on the particular schedule of lease payments they

2 Strictly speaking our analysis here is incomplete, because there is a backlog effect on interest payments to be recognised as well. In the third year the firm can claim tax relief on the interest implied in the discount factor for the earlier years. Calculating the appropriate tax effect to include in year three is a little complicated though, since it depends on the size of the cash flows which were discounted back through the first three years, of which it is itself one. Franks and Hodges (1978) suggest a method for calculating this tax effect.

Exhibit IV Lessee fully tax-paying

	Year	*0*	*1*	*2*	*3*	*4*	*5*	*TOTALS (£)*
PURCHASE	Cost	9,500	–	–	–	–	–	9,500
	Capital allowances	–	(831)	(623)	(468)	(351)	(1,052)	(3,325)
LEASE	Payments	(2,200)	(2,200)	(2,200)	(2,200)	(2,200)	–	(11,000)
	Tax on payments	–	770	770	770	770	770	3,850
		7,300	(2,261)	(2,053)	(1,898)	(1,781)	(282)	
Discount factor		1	$\frac{1}{(1+.052)}$	$\frac{1}{(1+.052)^2}$	$\frac{1}{(1+.052)^3}$	$\frac{1}{(1+.052)^4}$	$\frac{1}{(1+.052)^5}$	
PRESENT VALUES		7,300	(2,149)	(1,855)	(1,630)	(1,454)	(219)	(8)

NPV = (£8) DECISION-PURCHASE

NOTE: The capital allowances have been calculated as 25%, reducing balance, with a balancing allowance in the final year. We have assumed a tax rate of 35%, so it is useful to check that the total capital allowances are 35% of the purchase cost (£3,325 = 35% × £9,500), and the tax relief on lease payments is 35% of the total payments (£3,850 = 35% × £11,000). Note that if the assets are 'pooled' (see Chapter 3) there is no balancing allowance or charge, and capital allowances continue to accrue indefinitely. Throughout this chapter we are assuming assets are not pooled.

agree. Take the example of the previous section where a machine costing £9,500 was to be leased for five annual payments of £2,200 payable in advance. Our lessee, who was a temporary non-taxpayer for three years, found this lease to have a positive NPV of £313, and it gave the lessor a positive NPV of £8.

We can find the range of acceptable lease schedules by seeing what is the minimum the lessor would accept and the maximum the lessee would pay, i e the schedule of payments that just give each party a zero NPV. Exhibit IV, with the signs reversed, gives us the layout of the lessor's analysis, and Exhibit V the lessee's. One way of proceeding is to replace £2,200 by x in each calculation, then get an expression for the present value of the lease in terms of the lease payment x. The present value is then set to zero to find the break-even x. A quicker way is to inspect Exhibits IV and V and to ask in each case what difference an incremental rental of £1 makes to the present value of the lease. This involves adding up discount factors, and not forgetting the tax effects. We find that decreasing the lease payment by £1 makes the lessee £4.38 better off, increasing it makes the lessor £3.02 better off. Conversely, a reduction in the lease payment of $\frac{8}{4.38} = 2$ will just wipe out the lessor's present value, while an increase of $\frac{313}{3.02} = 104$ will wipe out the lessee's. Hence:

Annual payment	*Lessor's NPV*	*Lessee's NPV*	*Total NPV*
£2,198	0	314	314
£2,200	8	313	320
£2,304	111	0	111

£2,198 and £2,304 are the limits within which a mutually advantageous leasing contract can be written. The *actual* payment will depend on relative bargaining strength. If there is strong competition amongst lessors then we can expect the lease payment to be at the lower end. Edwards and Mayer (1983) examined 100 UK leases written by the banks between 1977 and 1982 and computed their value in terms of an equivalent loan, assuming the lessees were permanently non tax-paying. They found that 80% of the value gains went to lessees and 20% to lessors. The best piece of advice we can give the lessee is to calculate the lessor's NPV as well as his own. That way he knows the total gain available to be shared.

Increasing the gains to both parties

We have seen how the leasing schedule determines the split of the overall gains to leasing between lessor and lessee. The previous arrangement with five annual payments yielded tax advantages to both parties, but they could do better still by pursuing the logic of leasing even further. So far in our example we have assumed a particular *profile* of lease payments, i e equal payments in advance over five years. But suppose lessor and lessee were to agree a lease schedule which involved no payment at all until the end of year three, then two annual payments of, say, £6,000. The reader can confirm, assuming tax positions as before, that this will give the lessor an NPV of £106 and the lessee £499, a total of £605. The problem with the former lease schedule was that for the first three years the lessor was receiving lease payments and paying tax on them though the lessee was not able to claim the equivalent tax relief until after the three years had elapsed. In the interim, the Inland Revenue holds the cash. By agreeing to postpone lease payments the lessor and lessee capture this cash flow benefit for themselves. They generate a value gain which they can share between them. As a general rule the gains to leasing are maximised if *no lease payments are made until the lessee is paying tax*. In the case of a permanent non-taxpayer, it

Exhibit V Lessee temporary non-tax-paying

	Year	*0*	*1*	*2*	*3*	*4*	*5*	*TOTALS (£)*
PURCHASE	Cost	9,500	–	–	–	–	–	9,500
	Capital allowances	–			(1,927)	(951)	(1,052)	(3,930)
LEASE	Payments	(2,200)	(2,200)	(2,200)	(2,200)	(2,200)	–	(11,000)
	Tax on payments				2,310	770	770	3,850
		7,300	(2,200)	(2,200)	(1,812)	(1,781)	(282)	
Discount factor		1	$\frac{1}{(1+.08)}$	$\frac{1}{(1+.08)^2}$	$\frac{1}{(1.08)^2(1+.052)}$	$\frac{1}{(1+.08)^2(1+.052)^2}$	$\frac{1}{(1+.08)^2(1+.052)^3}$	
PRESENT VALUES		7,300	(2,037)	(1,886)	(1,477)	(1,379)	(208)	313

NPV = £313 DECISION-LEASE

will be profitable to postpone for ever! This strange and rather impractical result follows once we see we are simply postponing the tax payment and so reducing its present value. In reality we do not find many lessors and lessees agreeing to settle up on the Day of Judgement, but schedules in which payments increase, or 'balloon' at the end of the lease, are found.

In this section we have discussed the determination of the lease schedule. But for smaller leases the lessee usually faces a fixed schedule, the lessor's standard terms. It is usually only for larger leases that the parties find it worth negotiating a specific schedule, tailored to the lessee's needs.

IV SUMMARY

In this chapter we looked at some strategies that change the appearance of the balance-sheet, and in particular at leasing and factoring. The most important of these is leasing, which now accounts for a significant proportion of the new assets that firms acquire. There are two sorts of arguments for leasing, one is that it confers tax advantages, the other is that it permits the firm to exploit market imperfections, and flatters book gearing. In practice market imperfections are often more apparent than real, and when they do exist there may be other ways in which they can be exploited.

Once we have examined leasing we can view arrangements such as factoring and invoice discounting with a fairly cool eye. They do not offer tax advantages, and the firm which uses them ought to think hard about the benefits they yield.

REFERENCES AND BIBLIOGRAPHY

Bank of England	*Money for Business* (4th edn, 1983) Bank of England and City Communications Centre, London.
DeMetz, G L R	*Off Balance Sheet Finance* (1985) Graham & Trotman.
Ma, R	'Comparative Analysis of Lease Evaluation Models: A Review Article', Accounting and Business Research, Spring 1981, pp 153–162.
Myers, S, Dill, D A, and Bautista, A J	'Valuation of Financial Lease Contracts', Journal of Finance, June 1976, pp 799–819.
Smith, T	*Accounting for Growth: Stripping the Camouflage from Company Accounts* (1992) Century Books.

QUESTIONS

1 Assuming rational and fully-informed lessors and lessees, where does the mutual advantage in leasing come from? Why do textbooks treat leasing as a 'tax-induced' phenomenon?

2 Guest and Smith are considering whether to buy or lease their own lathe. If bought, it will cost £5,000 and qualify for a first-year allowance of 100%. It is expected to have a useful life of five years, and no terminal value. If leased, there will be five annual payments of £1,150, payable in advance and qualifying for tax relief. The rate of corporation tax is 35% and the firm has a one-year lag in tax payments. The firm's

marginal cost of borrowing is 8% before tax, and it uses an after-tax discount rate of 12% for appraising risky projects.

Advise the firm whether they should buy or lease, showing your calculations.

Suppose Guest and Smith are not in a tax-paying position in the first two years. Without calculating the outcome, set out the cash flows to show how this will affect the analysis.

3 Loose Ltd is wondering whether to lease or buy a new laser printer. The printer costs £2,000 to buy. Alternatively it could be leased from Lois Leasing Ltd for four equal annual rentals payable in advance. The machine qualifies for 25% writing-down allowances. Lois is a full taxpayer, but Loose is non-tax-paying for the first two years. The corporation tax rate is 35%. Loose's cost of borrowing is 10% and its cost of equity is 17%.

What is the minimum lease payments Lois would accept, and the maximum it would be worth Loose's while paying? Can you suggest a strategy that might improve the value of the lease to the two parties?

Part VI
Topics in investment and disinvestment

CHAPTER 22

Merger and growth

Previous chapters have talked about investment in terms of building *new* projects. This is 'internal' or 'organic' growth. But very often firms choose to grow by *merger* – by buying *existing* projects through the acquisition of the whole or part of another firm. As with organic investment, merger is worthwhile if it leads to an increase in the *value* of the firm.

In Section I we introduce the necessary terminology and concepts for talking about merger. We look at some of the 'stylised facts' of merger: the prevalence of merger activity and the nature of the firms that merge, and we consider the legal and institutional constraints on merging. Section II provides details of the mechanics of a merger and in Section III we describe an example of a hostile bid, the attempted take-over of BAT by Sir James Goldsmith's Hoylake consortium.

To have any chance of making good merger decisions managers need a clear understanding of the effect of merger on the value of the firm. We examine the potential costs and benefits of merger in Section IV and in Section V review the evidence on the success of mergers in practice. In considering this question we shall be throwing some light on the economics of organic growth, too, and on an issue that is widely debated – the rationale for the larger firm. Section VI discusses leverage buyouts. Section VII outlines an approach to valuing the target firm. In the final section we discuss the arithmetic of the merger decision, and contrast how a merger should and should not be evaluated.

I THE BACKGROUND TO MERGER

Concepts and terminology

There are various terms for merger. In this chapter we use the word *merger* to cover a range of situations from a simple change in ownership of a firm to the situation where the operations of a firm, its physical and human assets, are fully integrated into those of another firm. People sometimes talk about *take-over* or *acquisition* when the main feature of the investment is a change in control, where one firm is fairly clearly buying another and perhaps the merger is contested by one party, and save the word *merger* for the situation where the two firms are of similar size or perhaps the merger is not contested. However, this distinction is not easy to apply in practice. We will use the words interchangeably, and also will talk as though there is an *acquirer* which initiates the merger and an *acquiree* or victim.

But it *is* useful to distinguish mergers according to the association between the *activities* of the firms involved:

—A *horizontal* merger occurs when the merging firms produce in the same industry, and a *vertical* merger where one firm produces inputs to the production of the other. For example a brewery which buys up another brewery is growing horizontally; if it buys a hop farm it is pursuing 'backward' vertical integration, and if it buys a chain of pubs, 'forward' vertical integration.

—A *concentric* merger involves the extension of a range of products or services, using the same core of expertise in, say, production, engineering, R & D, and marketing. For example a computer manufacturer which buys an office equipment firm or a software house, is growing concentrically.

—A *conglomerate* or *diversification* merger is one between firms in unrelated product areas. In this case there is no core of technical or product expertise common to the firms involved. Within conglomerate mergers we can make a further distinction between *managerial* conglomerates, where the new group shares management skills, probably at the strategic control level, and *financial* conglomerates which are the loosest groupings of all – here the conglomerate is effectively just a holding company, a portfolio of autonomous firms. For example a building group which buys a newspaper chain is indulging in conglomerate merger. Whether it is 'financial' or 'managerial' depends on the degree of control exercised over the operations of the new subsidiary.

This distinction is useful because, as we will see in the next section, the degree of association dramatically affects the potential benefits from merger. Because the economic logic of vertical/horizontal and concentric mergers is rather plainer to see, firms sometimes go to some pains to label their mergers this way. The Financial Times described the expansion of certain oil companies into mining thus:

> Oil companies, which . . . now like to be known as 'energy' or 'resource-based' undertakings, thus argue that diversification into mining and minerals operations is logical.

In practice it is not always very easy to classify a merger. The merging firms may have a variety of activities, some of which are associated and some of which are not.

The Office of Fair Trading looks at merger proposals and classifies them as horizontal, vertical or diversified. Over the period 1970–84 the proportion of merger proposals which were diversified averaged out at about 27%. Littlechild (1989) reports the changes in the pattern of mergers. In the late 1960s diversified mergers (conglomerates) accounted for 7% of mergers, rising to 29% (in the 1970s), then rising to 40% (in the 1980s) with a peak of 54% in 1985. The trend in horizontal mergers is its mirror image with 89% in the late 1960s, falling to around 66% (in the 1970s), then to 57% (in the 1980s) with the lowest proportion of 42% in 1985.

The scale of merger activity

Table I shows the scale of merger activity in the UK in recent years, and how it was

Table I UK mergers 1985–93

Year	*Number of companies acquired*	*Expenditure (£m)*		*Cash as %*	*Ordinary shares*	*Preference and loan-stock*
		Total	*Cash*			
1985	474	7,090	2,857	40	3,708	525
1986	842	15,370	4,062	26	8,761	2,548
1987	1,527	16,529	5,705	35	9,969	853
1988	1,499	22,834	15,990	70	4,990	1,853
1989	1,330	27,249	22,359	82	3,520	1,373
1990	776	8,235	6,325	77	1,522	389
1991	506	10,434	7,278	76	3,034	121
1992	432	5,941	3,772	64	2,122	47
1993	526	7,063	5,690	80	1,162	211

Source: CSO Financial Statistics, HMSO

financed. There was a dramatic swing in this period from equity to cash as the preferred means of payment for acquisitions.

Merger waves

Table II extends the merger statistics from Table I back to 1963 and shows that merger activity appears to go in waves. In the UK peaks of merger activity have occurred around 1964–65, 1972–73 and 1987–89.

Table II Mergers of industrial and commercial companies 1963–93

Year	*Number of mergers*	*Year*	*Number of mergers*
1963	888	1979	534
1964	940	1980	469
1965	1,000	1981	452
1966	807	1982	463
1967	763	1983	447
1968	946	1984	568
1969	907	1985	474
1970	793	1986	842
1971	884	1987	1,527
1972	1,210	1988	1,499
1973	1,205	1989	1,337
1974	504	1990	776
1975	315	1991	506
1976	353	1992	432
1977	481	1993	526
1978	567		

Source: CSO Financial Statistics, HMSO

Researchers have tried to explain these merger waves. There seems to be no association between merger activity and the business cycle, however it is firmly established that mergers are most likely to occur at stock market peaks, though we have no clear explanation why this is so from orthodox theory.

The characteristics of acquirers and acquirees

Numerous studies have attempted to ascertain what makes a firm vulnerable to a take-over bid. At least part of the answer depends on the underlying motives of the bidding firm. The simple explanation of take-over as a sanction on under-performing firms suggests that target firms will have lower than average profitability. However, studies which have examined the pre-merger profits of target firms have variously shown them to have poor, average or above average profitability.

Singh's two studies (1971 and 1975) of UK mergers between 1955 and 1970 attempted to determine the characteristics of acquirer and acquiree firms and thus discover which firms were most likely to be taken over, or to take over others. He concluded that bidders were on average bigger, more profitable, faster growing, more liquid and more highly geared than those they acquired, also that they showed greater recent improvement in profits and retained more profits. In the later study, Singh found *size* to be the main distinguishing factor between acquirers and acquirees. As to *profitability*, the difference between the average levels of the two groups was not very big but there was a 'very marked' difference between the rates of change in profitability – 'acquiring firms, on average, showed a small improvement [over the last two years] in their profit records while acquired ones showed a marked decline'. The earlier study had found growth to be a more important distinguisher, but liquidity less so. Singh's results suggested a survival strategy – above a certain minimum size class, varying from industry to industry, the best way a firm could avoid being taken over would be by growing.[1]

A different approach was taken by Jensen and Ruback (1983), who was the first to identify a target firm's cash flow as a possible motive for take-over. He found that firms with a mismatch between growth and resources were vulnerable: firms with high growth and low liquidity, as were those with low growth, high liquidity, and low leverage. Jensen pointed out that as well as the traditional 'under-performers', there were targets which were performing exceptionally well when they were acquired. Firms with a high free cashflow that was not being paid out to shareholders, and an under-used borrowing capacity made attractive take-over targets Their acquirers were highly geared and short of cash, or, having reached the limits of organic growth, were seeking to use up spare cash of their own.

The term 'take-over' implies unwillingness on the part of the acquired firm. In fact, most take-overs are 'friendly', in that the directors recommend shareholders to accept the offer, and the potential synergies from the amalgamation are clear to all. Morck, Shleifer and Vishny (1987) divided targets into 'hostile' and 'friendly' and successfully isolated attributes specific to the targets of hostile take-overs. Targets of friendly acquisitions were found to have a Tobin's q comparable to that of non-targets (making them virtually indiscernible from the population of firms as a whole), whereas hostile take-over targets had a lower Tobin's q and were concentrated in low-q industries.

Morck, Shleifer and Vishny's evidence suggested the existence of entire industries where capital may be profitably redeployed. Targets of hostile take-over bids were found to have a lot of old tangible capital, to grow slowly, and in many cases to have heavy debts. Friendly targets however were basically indistinguishable from the sample as a whole in terms of profit performance, they tended to be smaller, younger and faster growing than hostile targets, with higher interest and dividend payments.

II THE MECHANICS OF A MERGER

Usually in a merger one firm is buying the other – there is an acquirer and an acquiree. This will happen simply for legal convenience even in a marriage of equals, though sometimes in this case a new company might be formed to buy the two existing firms. Whether the acquiree remains a separate legal entity is of no great consequence economically except for one fact: by maintaining a subsidiary's company status the parent is protected by limited liability for the subsidiary's debts. At worst the subsidiary can be allowed to go bankrupt – though few parents, conscious of their business reputation, would allow this.

The consideration

The consideration for mergers is either shares, or loan-stock, in which case the acquirer issues its own shares or bonds in exchange for the acquiree's shares, or cash, in which case

1 Below this minimum size Singh suggested, the best thing would be to get smaller, though he recognised this to be impracticable in a dynamic economy. Increasing the firm's profitability, on the other hand, would not be a very useful survival strategy.

the offer is made in cash either from the acquirer's reserves or raised specially by borrowing or by a public issue of shares. Often the acquiree's shareholders will be offered a choice or a mixture of these.

The acquirer's decision whether to offer cash or shares will depend on several things. The obvious one is the size of his cash reserves. If these are insufficient he would have to incur issue costs in raising cash, as well as the transactions costs associated with the merger. A second is the degree of confidence the acquiree-shareholders have in the value of the acquirer's shares – cash has a certainty about it which may appeal to shareholders. A third factor is the tax position of the acquiree shareholders – to the extent that if the offer is for cash it becomes liable to capital gains tax whereas a share exchange does not.

The rules

There is nothing to prevent an individual or institution from buying up shares in the normal way in the market place, and this sort of activity usually precedes a take-over bid. Once a shareholder owns 30% of a company's voting shares, they must abide by the City Code on Take-overs and Mergers and make a *mandatory bid* for the rest of the shares, as, in formal terms, they now have control of the company. In reality, a controlling stake could be much less than 30%. A shareholder holding between 30% and 50% of a company's (voting) shares is obliged to bid for the rest of the company's shares if it increases its holding by 1% or more in a twelve-month period. Once the 50% threshold has been reached, there is no requirement to make a general offer if the shareholding is increased, as all remaining shareholders hold minority stakes. To ensure that a fair price is paid, the offer to acquire shares must be for cash, at not less than the highest price paid in the preceding twelve months.

Merger jargon often refers to offers becoming 'unconditional'. Bidders will usually make their offers conditional on receiving a minimum number of acceptances and on the offer not being referred to the Monopolies and Mergers Commission. Some shareholders agree to sell their stake in a company if and when control changes hands. The City Code recommends that shareholders should not be obliged to sell unless the bidder has received acceptances which amount to at least 50% of the voting rights.

The City Code Timetable allows enough time for advice and information to be obtained and considered but sets limits to prevent uncertainty in the market:

Day -27	The offer is announced.
Day 1	The offer document is posted.
Day 14	Deadline for target's board to recommend action to shareholders.
Day 21	First possible closing date.
Day 39	Last possible day for material announcements by the target company.
Day 42	(*or 21 days after first closing date if later*) Last chance for shareholders who have provisionally accepted the offer to withdraw if offer has not become unconditional.
Day 46	Last date for revised bid.
Day 60	Last possible closing date – offers which have become unconditional must remain open for acceptance for at least 14 more days.

Only the Take-over Panel can grant an extension to this timetable, which it may do if a competing offer is announced.

When an offer has not become unconditional and has therefore been withdrawn or allowed to lapse, the bidder cannot make another offer for a twelve-month period, or acquire any shares which would put it in a position to make a mandatory offer. This allows the target company a breathing space before the bidder can launch another assault.

Although some bidders may be content to acquire just sufficient shares to gain control of a company, usually they would prefer to own 100%. Majority holders therefore have the opportunity to buy out compulsorily minority shareholders at a fair price when 90% of shareholders have accepted the offer. Compulsory acquisition can only take place if the original offer was for 100% of the shares. All shareholders of a particular class must be treated identically, so even where a bidder has purchased shares three months prior to the bid, they must offer the same terms to shareholders holding that class of shares.

Once a take-over bid has been made, it cannot be withdrawn without the consent of the Take-over Panel. This rule is designed to prevent opportunistic bidders from making bids based on prevailing conditions in the market. The Take-over Panel will not usually consent to a bid's withdrawal simply because market conditions have changed and the offer is now at an unrealistically high price. Minority shareholders can, in turn, insist on being bought out.

Monopoly policy

The Monopolies and Mergers Commission has been criticised by firms engaged in merger on the grounds that it holds mergers up while it investigates and this often kills them. Of course in a contested merger this is exactly what the acquiree may want. UK merger policy has often been criticised for lack of direction. The 'ad hoc' approach to merger policy is enshrined in the Office of Fair Trading guide to the Fair Trading Act 1973 – 'Each case falling within the scope of the Act is looked at on its own particular merits and not in accordance with any fixed rules and assumptions . . .' (Office of Fair Trading, 1978). There has never been the same settled view in the UK as in the US about whether mergers are a 'good thing' or a 'bad thing'. On the one hand mergers have been seen as yielding firms of the size and efficiency needed to compete in the world economy, at the other extreme there is a 'small is beautiful' lobby which sees evils in the all-powerful conglomerate corporation. For a long while the former view predominated and there was a presumption in merger policy that mergers were beneficial. However the 1978 Green Paper, influenced by evidence that mergers were unprofitable, recommended that the official presumption be downgraded to one of neutrality. Mr Nott, the Conservative trade minister, subsequently rejected this proposal, though he did suggest that conglomerate mergers should get a more critical look in future, since firms which were 'shopping around when flush with funds might lead to a diminution of competition and no evident efficiency gain' (quoted in the Financial Times, 23 November 1981). In 1988 mergers policy was reviewed.[2] The overall conclusion was that recent work supports the broader conclusions of earlier studies:

> Mergers are often found to be unprofitable by those carrying them out and little in the way of efficiency gains seemed to be realised.

Since 1984 the emphasis on mergers policy has shifted further towards competition (and further away from 'public interest' concerns). To quote the 1988 Department of Trade and Industry report:

> The Secretary of State Mr Tebbit . . . said that references would be made 'primarily', though not exclusively, 'on competition grounds' . . . making it clear that reference on grounds other than competition would be less likely than before.

2 Department of Trade and Industry (1988).

Tactics

Often mergers are agreed by both parties from the outset – the acquiree directors agree the terms and recommend them to their shareholders. But sometimes the acquiree directors recommend rejection. There are two good reasons why they would do this. For one thing, the acquiree directors may be the first people to go after a merger and are thus likely to resist it at any price. But anyhow early resistance makes sense in a price bargaining situation. A key question in merger is how the potential gains are divided between acquirer and acquiree shareholders. To some extent this depends on the tactical skill of the respective managements in the bargaining process. As we will see later on, the evidence is that on the whole, it is the acquiree shareholders who capture most of the gains in mergers.

The tactics of the acquirer will often be to appeal directly to the acquiree shareholders by painting as attractive a picture as possible of the new firm, while perhaps reducing the resolve of the acquiree directors through offering them some sort of role after the merger. If there are single shareholders with significant holdings, such as institutions, pressure may be brought to bear on them directly. The acquiree directors, on the other hand, may set out to attack the claims and credibility of the acquirer, and will often publish revised profit forecasts for the firm under existing management. They often encourage a third firm to make a rival bid in order to introduce some auction-like competitiveness into the bidding. This preferred bidder who gallops to the rescue is commonly known as a 'white knight'.

III HOYLAKE/BAT INDUSTRIES: THE STORY OF A HOSTILE BID

In this section we describe the chronology of a hostile take-over bid. In July 1989, Hoylake, a consortium led by Sir James Goldsmith, was set up to buy BAT Industries. The £13.5 billion leveraged bid was the largest ever take-over bid in the UK. This bid was, in the end, unsuccessful but gives an excellent insight into the bid process and into the logic of value creation. In this case the bidders sought to add value simply by 'unbundling' BAT. They were frustrated by, amongst other things, the existence of what was effectively a 'poison pill' in the form of Farmers Inc, an insurance subsidiary regulated in the US.

Background

BAT Industries had been known as British American Tobacco until the early 1970s. As the anti-tobacco lobby strengthened, BAT changed its name, and diversified into retailing, paper and financial services. However, by the 1980s, the basic logic of corporate diversification was under attack. Increasingly it seemed that the most dynamic businesses were those that stuck with what they did best and minimised the influence of the centre. The prevailing strategic culture was now to be 'focused' and stick to your 'core' business. Take-overs were now commonly followed by the divestment of non-core activities. By this criterion BAT appeared over-diversified. Moreover over the five years previous to the Hoylake bid, BAT's earnings per share growth of 67% had been poor in comparison to some other large conglomerates. Lonhro had managed 173%, and Hanson Trust 354%.

BAT's share of total profits from its core business, tobacco, had fallen from 74% in 1978 to 46% in 1989. Its share of the world cigarette market had declined since 1982. In the US its market share was down from 13.3% to 11%. The capital expenditure of £722 million which the company had undertaken since 1982 was not producing the hoped-for results. Profits, compounded annually, had risen by 4%. Phillip Morris, a rival tobacco company, had spent only £483 million in the same period and had achieved a 12.7% profit rise and a larger market share. However tobacco still contributed around 40% of turnover and 50% of company profits. Brown and Williamson was the world's third largest cigarette producer, but Western taste was moving towards American style tobacco blends and BAT was having trouble competing with the sophisticated marketing of US brands such as Marlboro. The company was responsible for a large proportion of BAT's cash flow and in 1988 provided 48% of BAT's £756 million tobacco profits. B & W had recently successfully entered the Japanese and Chinese markets. Souza Cruz was a vast Brazilian tobacco company in which BAT had a 75% stake. Brazil is one of the world's largest cigarette markets and Souza Cruz held 80% of this market compared with its closest rival R J Reynolds' 9%.

BAT's retailing interests were the weakest elements of the conglomerate's operations and had managed only a 2% growth in profits since 1983. A notable exception was the Argos chain of catalogue retailers. The importance of Argos, which only accounted for 25% of the retail division's turnover, was reflected in the figures presented in the Hoylake offer document. When the Argos contribution was excluded profits for the rest of the retail division had fallen by 28%. Only the paper subsidiaries were doing well, with 13.2% annual growth over five years, but even they were losing market share in the US.

Financial services had been contributing an increasing share of turnover and profits. Since 1984 the proportion of turnover accounted for by this division of the conglomerate had grown from 7% to 22% (8% to 27% as a proportion of profits). In the UK, BAT owned Eagle Star and Allied Dunbar. After a bitterly contested take-over battle, BAT had bought Farmers Inc, one of the largest US insurance companies, operating in twenty-six states with a well developed distribution network. BAT had high expectations of its financial services division – Allied Dunbar was doing well and Eagle Star was the smallest of the UK's top six insurance companies. BAT had bought the company in 1984 but, five years later, its planned reconstruction was still incomplete. It was to be the flagship for BAT's expansion into European financial services: a number of European acquisitions were planned.

The bid

At the time of the offer BAT had a market capitalisation of £10 billion. Goldsmith's offer of £13.5 billion suggested that, unbundled, the companies would be worth far more. The implication was either that the capital market was not valuing BAT correctly, perhaps applying a low-growth tobacco P/E to earnings which were of intrinsically higher quality, or that the BAT companies were earning less than they would have done as independents. Hoylake pointed out that despite the company's attempts to diversify out of tobacco (to the point where tobacco contributed only 50% of total profits) its P/E had not risen accordingly. Hoylake planned to 'unbundle' BAT and 'liberate the parts to benefit shareholders'. Behind the plan was the accusation that BAT had expanded in order 'to use its cash flow instead of returning this to shareholders'. Finally, Goldsmith criticised BAT's accounting policy for its recently acquired subsidiaries in the financial services sector.

The Hoylake finance package was a complicated paper offer which included three types of securities:

1 **Hoylake senior secured loan notes** secured on cash raised from the disposal of certain BAT assets.
2 **Hoylake subordinated notes.**
3 **Loan-stock convertible into shares in Anglo**, a quoted company which ran a leasing business but was recreated as a holding company and vehicle for take-overs by Goldsmith and Rothschild.

With full acceptances BAT shareholders would own 92% of Anglo, in turn holding 75% of Hoylake leaving them with a 69% interest of BAT's tobacco business once the non-tobacco businesses had been sold off. If the offer became unconditional 25% of Hoylake would remain in the hands of Goldsmith and the initial backers in return for their subscribing £868 million in cash for Hoylake shares. Existing shareholders of Anglo and the original Hoylake subscribers also benefited from an 'override scheme' which entitled them to 8% of Hoylake's distributions of BAT disposal proceeds. The deal also offered substantial protection for Anglo's minority shareholders if the bid went through.

There were doubts as to the marketability of the Hoylake paper despite Hoylake's claim that Banker's Trust would provide a market for it. As the bid continued, there were increasing demands for a cash alternative. At this time a market for 'junk bonds' had not developed in the UK and the notes would have to be placed in the US. The Financial Times expressed its concern that the success of the Hoylake bid would constitute 'a leap in the dark for UK corporate finance'. In an unprecedented (in the UK) move towards the US practice of allowing bids to go ahead on the basis of a 'letter of confidence' BAT shareholders were being offered paper that had not been underwritten.

Chronology

June 1989 Hoylake starts to purchase shares. Goldsmith, Rothschild and Packer (the main members of the Hoylake consortium) reveal plans to bid around £13 billion in a leveraged buy-out of BAT. BAT shares jump from 206p to 400p. Goldsmith expresses criticisms of BAT and reveals plans for divestment. Hoylake attracts more stakeholders including GEC and Agnelli.

July There are rumours of a rival bid. At the same time, the State of Arizona orders a regulatory hearing concerning the take-over of Farmers Inc. Hoylake fails to persuade the US Insurance Departments that the question of who owns Farmers Inc is outside their jurisdiction.

August The bid goes to the UK Take-over Panel for scrutiny. They ask Hoylake to stop buying BAT shares until the value of the bid is established. BAT shares fall below 850p for the first time since the bid was launched. The Panel is concerned about unavailability of some of the Hoylake paper which makes up the financing of the bid.

Hoylake formally launch a bid of £13.5 billion accompanied by a scathing attack on BAT's record.

The battle increasingly centres on Farmers Inc, which offers BAT a chance to defend itself by wasting time so that the Hoylake bid can lapse or BAT can put an alternative plan to its shareholders. Hoylake tries to appease the US State Insurance Commission by naming three trustees to supervise the Farmers Group temporarily. Hoylake is also bringing federal legal action against the Idaho Insurance Commissioner. 200 US Senators and Congressmen denounce the Hoylake bid in an open letter to Secretary of State James Baker. There are calls for involvement of the Securities Exchange Commission to protect US securities holders.

BAT's defence document is presented by Patrick Sheehy. James Goldsmith suggests talks with Sheehy and is rebuffed. It emerges that Hoylake does not have the total support of BAT's institutional shareholders. They want to see a cash alternative before they will consider the Hoylake bid. Hoylake is unable or unwilling to provide a cash offer.

BAT release their interim results. Pre-tax profits are up 20%. Earnings per share are up 20% to 32.07p and dividends up by 22% to 9.3p per share.

Bryan Gould MP calls for the Hoylake bid to be referred to the Monopolies and Mergers Commission in order to clarify the government's policy on highly leveraged bids.

Hoylake is still trying to make the bid acceptable in the US. A firm buyer has been found for Farmers Inc if the bid goes through. The French based insurance company Axa-Midi has agreed to buy the company for £2.44 billion, which is no more than BAT paid for it. Hoylake applies to the Take-over Panel for an extension to the sixty-day take-over timetable. The Federal Court in Texas denies Hoylake's appeal against local insurance regulators. Three days later Goldsmith and his friends are derided in Congress, called harmful to BAT's business, employees and shareholders. Hoylake is accused of trying to construct the deal so as to skirt US regulations.

31 August Hoylake owns 2.3% of BAT; only 0.03% is through acceptances.

September The Take-over Panel rejects Hoylake's claims that BAT is frustrating the bid in the US courts. A second US Federal Court rejects Goldsmith's appeal to avoid having the bid reviewed by US insurance regulators. However, in the UK the Take-over Panel takes into account the regulatory problems in the US and allows an unprecedented extension to the UK take-over timetable. It rules that if and when the US regulatory problems are resolved in its favour, Hoylake will be allowed to make a new offer. The current offer must be allowed to lapse (unless Hoylake appeals) and Hoylake cannot purchase any more shares in BAT between now and a new offer being made. BAT is given leave to appeal against the ruling and intends to do so. BAT's share price jumps again by 18p to 814p.

Nicholas Ridley, the Trade Secretary decides not to refer the bid to the Monopolies and Mergers Commission.

BAT announces its counter proposal to the Hoylake bid – a five-stage corporate reorganisation. BAT shares climb 2p to 818p despite a general decline in the market.

29 September Hoylake offer lapses.

BAT's defence

BAT produced a five-stage survival plan:

1 The reshaped group would concentrate on tobacco and financial services.
2 Shareholders were to receive equity in two new quoted companies: Argos and a paper company consisting of the two paper businesses Wiggins Teape and Appleton.
3 Poorly performing subsidiaries were to be sold off, including the retailing operations in the US.
4 Approval would be sought for a buy-back of 10% of BAT shares with the intention of improving earnings per share.
5 The reshaped group would have reduced dividend cover in the range of 2 to 2.5. The board would recommend a further dividend of 20.7p per share in 1989, giving an increase for the full year of 49% over 1988.

November 1989–May 1990 The proposal for BAT's corporate reorganisation are approved. BAT agrees to accept £186 million for its 69% share stake in VG instruments from Fisons plc. BAT announces the terms for the Argos demerger. BAT shareholders are to receive one Argos share for every five BAT shares owned.

On 21 March 1990 BAT releases results for year to 31 December 1989. Trading profits are up by 27% and the businesses due for demerger continue to perform well.

Plans for disposal in the US continue. Bids have been received for the US retail businesses Saks, Marshall Fields, Ivey and Breuner. Profits from these businesses are up

10% There are also discussions underway concerning bids for the two West German businesses Horten and Eurotec. BATUS Inc, BAT's US subsidiary agreed to sell John Breuner's furniture retailing business to the Prism Capital Corporation for the sum of $92.5 million. Breuner also own forty-four rental locations which will be sold off to Brook Furniture Rental Inc for $15 million.

On 10 April 1991 the California Department of Insurance decides to deny the applications of Hoylake and Axa-Midi to acquire control of Farmers Group Inc. The Appleton paper subsidiary is hived off to BAT Investments plc which will be the holding company for the two paper companies. BATUS sells Marshall Fields to Dayton Hudson Corporation for $1.1 billion.

As the Hoylake bid relied chiefly on the intention to create value for shareholders by selling off unprofitable subsidiaries BAT had successfully pre-empted a renewal of the Hoylake bid by setting disposals in train immediately. The BAT restructuring offered shareholders the benefits of unbundling without the necessity of complex finance packages, and without the possibility that a substantial part of the value created would go to members of the Hoylake consortium. The disposals continued.

April–May 1990 BATUS arranges to sell Saks Fifth Avenue for $1.5 billion to Investcorp, an international investment firm. The US retail operations of J B Ivey and Co are sold for $110 million. The terms of the Wiggins Teape and Appleton demerger are announced. BAT shareholders will get one Wiggins Teape Appleton share for every three BAT shares they own. The demerger is approved on 31 May 1990.

Hoylake announces the bid will not be renewed on 23 April 1990.

IV THE ECONOMIC RATIONALE FOR MERGER

To discover whether a merger is worthwhile we need to ask *two* questions (1) Does the merger create value gains? (2) Who gets them?

Suppose firm A with a current market value of £100 million buys firm B, value £50 million. The new firm A* has a market value of £175 million – together the two firms are worth £25 million more than they were separately. Clearly economic benefits have flowed from bringing A and B together, so was the merger a 'good thing' from the point of view of A's shareholders? Not necessarily. It depends what they paid for B. We define the *cost of control* of a merger as the premium the acquirer must pay over the existing market value of the acquiree. If they paid £50 million they have done well, they paid no premium.

Value gain on A*	25m
Cost of control	–
NET GAIN	25m

In practice it never happens that you can buy a firm at its existing market capitalisation. There are two reasons for this. The first is that when we talk about the market capitalisation of a firm we are talking about the current price at which its shares are traded, multiplied by the shares in issue. However, we can never expect to buy *all* the shares in a company at the price at which the marginal share is trading, and would expect to pay a premium to dislodge inframarginal shareholders. This is sometimes called the 'premium for control'. But also shareholders in B will spot the potential value gain to the merger and hold out for a share of it. So A might easily finish up paying £70 million for B. In this case the position of A's shareholders is as follows:

Value gain on A*	25m
Cost of control	20m
NET GAIN	5m

To sum up, value gains are not enough to justify merger from the point of view of an acquirer's shareholders. The value gains must exceed the cost of control, in other words the merger must leave some of the value gains in the hands of acquirers.

Why might the value of a merged firm be greater than the value of the two firms independently?

In the rest of this section we will examine some of the common arguments for merger.

The effect of merger on earnings

Merger can improve earnings by increasing revenues, reducing costs, or both. It can do this by improving the prices which the firm pays for inputs and receives for its outputs, and by improving the efficiency with which it converts inputs to outputs.

By buying up competitors a firm may increase its market power in output markets and this may enable it to charge a higher price for its product. What it also does is give the firm more control over the market so that it can soften the impact of economic fluctuations by passing their effects on to others. The *market power* argument applies to input markets too. By increasing its purchases of input the firm may be able to enforce a keener price on suppliers. A good example of this is food retailing, where a large supermarket chain can account for a significant quantity proportion of the sales of certain branded items and can enforce significant quantity discounts from suppliers. These arguments only seem to favour horizontal mergers, since only these are likely to increase market power in a given input or output market. *Vertical* merger is an alternative way of securing control over inputs and outputs. In this case the relationship with the supplier or customer is *internalised* rather than being left to a market transaction.

In the market power argument firms improve profit by improving the prices of their outputs and inputs. The *operating efficiency* arguments suggest ways in which merger can improve the efficiency with which inputs are converted into outputs. This is usually a question of exploiting *individualism* in inputs by building a larger firm – in other words of achieving *economies of scale*. Though the economies of scale argument springs readily to mind when we think about large firms, it is an argument which often does not bear close inspection. The scope for scale economies depends on the extent to which the merging firms share common inputs, and on the minimum efficient scale for deploying those inputs.

Manufacturing economies of scale It is well established that the technology of certain processes indicates a large plant and the cost savings associated with such plants give their owners a competitive advantage. But significant technical economies of scale only exist in certain industries. In Table III we reproduce some of the data from a fascinating list of research findings on optimum plant size in various industries collected in the Merger Green Paper (1978). While the minimum efficient scale in, say, automobiles, aluminium and calculators is high; in bricks and paint it is small. Anyhow, on the face of it, merger does not always look like the best way to achieve technical economies of scale. By merging the acquirer is getting two plants when what he really wants is one big one – he is buying some capacity he will probably have to close down. More likely the merger will be a permissive factor designed to create the market needed to sustain the larger plant. Either way, the manufacturing economies of scale argument can relate only to *horizontal* mergers.

Table III Some engineering-type estimates of minimum efficient plant size (MEPS)

Product	*MEPS*	*MEPS as % of UK produced sales*	
Potato crisps	30–35,000 tons per annum	10	
Cigarettes	36 billion per annum	21	
Paint	10 million US galls pa	7	
Steel	2–3 million tons pa	8–12	different studies
	4–9 million tons pa	17–37	
	4 million tons pa	17	
Aluminium semi-manufacturers	200,000 tons pa		
Electronic calculators	3–4 million	>100	
Automobiles	½–1 million pa	29–57	
Bricks	25 million pa	.4	different studies
	50–62.5 million pa	.7–.9	

Source: Merger Green Paper (1978)

Administrative economies of scale There can be economies to be made in the deployment of other inputs too – doubling the size of the firm may not mean a doubling in the size of the marketing, advertising, finance and administration needed to service the bigger firm.

The cost savings got by exploiting indivisibilities may occur outside the firm instead of inside, and sometimes it is this that accounts for the lower price larger firms pay for their inputs, rather than the exercise of market power. For example, in the case of a raw material such as steel rods there may be some indivisibilities in transport if it costs as much to send a half full lorry of rods as it does a full lorry, and there may be fixed costs in the accounting department of the stockist that make it relatively cheaper to process a larger order. Thus when a big firm pays a lower price for its steel this may reflect its market power *or* cost savings of the supplier.

In a competitive market such as the capital market we do not expect any participant to be able to influence the price, i e market power cannot be relevant. If big firms are paying a lower price for their finance we must attribute it to indivisibilities in supply – for example financing costs which are partly invariant to the amount of finance raised. In the case of an input such as advertising bought in from an agency we might expect the price to reflect cost savings and market power. There are fixed costs associated with preparing a campaign which make large campaigns relatively cheaper, but whether the agency passes these costs savings on to the customer depends on the customer's market power.

We have been talking about what we can call administrative economies of scale. Since inputs such as marketing, advertising, finance and administration tend to be less specific to particular products than is plant, it is feasible that cost savings of this sort could arise in *concentric* and even *conglomerate* mergers too. However size does not always yield administrative cost savings. Large firms may become slow, inflexible and maintain large bureaucracies. These effects can follow a merger either because of a reluctance to dispose of surplus personnel post-merger, or because of a perceived need to add additional levels of authority in the bigger firm.

Management skills

Merger usually involves a change in management, and mergers are often promoted for just this reason. The argument is that the new team will be able to release value from the existing human and physical capital. When mergers are argued in terms of the acquiree being undervalued, or having assets that could be better used or could be profitably sold off, this is essentially a *management skills* argument. As we saw in Chapter 2 the threat of a change in the management team is often reckoned to be the main sanction shareholders have against inefficient management.

The problem with the management skills argument is that it is rather hard to quantify beforehand and to prove afterwards. In the build up to a merger it is very easy for the acquirer to assert that it will run things better. Ex post, an attempt to judge the performance of the new management team is beset by the problems of measuring the performance and efficiency of firms. Management can argue that the merger has paid off, but for the outsider it becomes difficult to disentangle the relevant performance data from the aggregate results of the new group, and to eliminate the influence of other factors from those results.

Since management skills are often appealed to as a justification for merger we need to ask just how important these are, and what sort of mergers they appear to favour. The question is how *specific* are management skills? We can easily conceive that the transfer of management skills can be beneficial in a horizontal and perhaps a concentric merger, but can it justify vertical and especially conglomerate merger? In other words can a good manager manage anything? Examples are legion of powerful chief executives who impose a tight economic discipline on diverse groups. There is also a legion of successful enterprises who have got into difficulties through diversifying into areas whose culture they did not properly understand.

Views about the omnipotent manager seem to differ internationally. It is noteworthy that in Germany the expectation is that managers are best at those things they know about, and this may explain the historically low level of diversification of German firms compared to those in the UK and US.

The management skills argument is rather akin to other economy-of-scale arguments. The acquirer's management team is seen as a specially valuable asset which can be exploited more fully by using it in other firms. But human assets have features physical assets do not have. It is rather hard to enforce property rights over humans – they are inclined to get up and walk away. The ability to do this, allied to their ability to perceive their own worth, means that managers will constantly seek to capture a larger share of the value gains they generate, by defecting to other firms, setting up their own firms, or using the threat of these as a lever on their present firms. So acquirers cannot be certain about the continued ownership of superior management skills. Nor can they rely on the acquiree management remaining in place post-merger. Often the inevitable disruption surrounding a merger is increased by the loss of key staff.

Financial arguments for merger

If merger brings down the cost of capital it will yield value gains. We saw that the cost of capital of a firm will reflect the amount it raises, the period for which it raises the finance and the risk involved. It is hard to see how merger will systematically affect the term or duration of firms' financing. But it may affect the amounts in which the firm raises funds, and the risk involved.

If the firm diversifies by indulging in conglomerate merger the variance of 'riskiness' of its earnings stream should fall. Will this reduce the cost of capital? In other words, is corporate diversification a thing of value to shareholders?

Diversification

In a perfect capital market diversification by the firm is of no value to shareholders – they can achieve this for themselves by building a portfolio of shares in individual firms. In reality shareholders may not be indifferent between diversification by the firm and doing it themselves, though it is not entirely clear which they will prefer. The loss of *limited liability* will lead them to prefer homemade diversification; the existence of bankruptcy costs will make them prefer the firm to do it. We examined the question of diversification and limited liability in Chapters 2 and 8. We discuss bankruptcy costs in the next chapter.

Internal capital market

Merger is sometimes promoted on the grounds that larger firms can exploit capital market imperfections and get funds cheaper than smaller firms, or even get funds smaller firms could not get at all. The 'group' operates as a mini-capital market for its subsidiaries.

There are fixed costs in raising new finance on the capital market which make it relatively expensive for small firms so the group may be able to raise funds more cheaply on behalf of its subsidiaries. But if the group contains some firms which are net investors and some which are net savers – i e have spare retained earnings, it can avoid the capital market and its costs altogether. This is the *spare cash* argument for merger. The retained earnings of one part of the group can be deployed in another part without cost whereas if the two firms were independent the finance would need to be passed through the capital market – paid out as divided and raised as new capital. Apart from the transactions costs involved there is a lack of speed and flexibility in this process.

Another financial argument for merging is to exploit the *unused debt capacity* of a firm which could be borrowing more than it is. The firm with the ability to raise further low cost debt seems to be in a similar position to the firm with spare cash or excess retained earnings. It possesses an asset that can be better exploited by joining up with a firm with an excess of investment projects. What is really implied here, again, is imperfections in the capital market. In a perfect capital market, as we saw in Chapter 16 the amount of 'cheap' debt a firm employs has no effect on its overall cost of capital. But in practice the existence of tax benefits to debt might make unused debt capacity a positive argument for merger.

The enhanced supply of capital can be used as a justification for any merger and indeed it provides the only argument for the sort of loose confederacy we described as a *financial conglomerate* since finance is the only input those firms share.

Final comments on the arguments for merger

The arguments for merger essentially provide reasons why bigger firms might be better.

Certain things are clear. The first is that it is impossible to generalise about the virtues of size. The arguments for technical economies of scale, managerial skills, financial benefits etc are highly specific to the context of the merger: they depend on the nature of the particular market and industry, the personalities of the management involved and so forth. These are questions the acquirer must study very carefully before going ahead with the merger. The benefits to merger must be robust enough – large enough and certain enough – to cover the costs – the premium paid to the acquirer and the transactions costs, professional fees etc, of the merger.

Managerial objectives

So far we have assumed the acquirer's managers are value-maximisers, but they may not be. Once we admit that managers might be pursuing goals such as *growth* with scant regard for value, our examination of the economic rationale for merger becomes rather redundant – merger is likely to be justified simply because it offers speedy growth. Another managerial objective is *personal risk reduction*. The costs to the manager of bankruptcy can be a loss of income, status, and security, and the damage to his reputation of being associated with failure. The growth objective can be served by any type of merger, but it is clear that diversification mergers may be particularly attractive to this sort of manager since they will yield quick growth and risk reduction. Some writers have developed the notion of merger as a managerial response to uncertainty. In these theories mergers and merger waves tend to be triggered by events in the external environment that increase the uncertainty felt by managers – mergers by other firms, macroeconomic changes and so forth.

The importance of clout

It is often said that in the modern world firms need to be big in order to have *clout*. Hence in the 1960s European governments actively encouraged the formation of firms that could match US competitors in scale. A key requirement for competing effectively in an era of rapid technological change is the ability to *innovate* successfully. Are big firms good at innovation? Innovation involves the generation of new product ideas, their development and subsequent implementation. Small firms are sometimes said to be good at idea generation, although there is no real evidence that the culture of the small firm is more conducive to creative thought. However it is the case that the development stage – bringing the idea to the market – can be very expensive and very risky. The advantages the large firm has in innovation are several. For one thing its size will help it to survive the failure of a particular innovative thrust or a heavy research programme which proves fruitless. This is the diversification argument again.

A second virtue of size is that the large firm can deploy the necessary financial and human resources very quickly and flexibly, transferring them from other operations as needed, without resort to the market place. We have already seen how this argument works in the case of finance. The same argument applies to labour. A small firm could hire the necessary labour, but the large firm has certain advantages – it avoids all the costs of recruitment and selection, and it avoids the risks of joining a new and untried firm from the point of view of the employees.

Finally, the uncertainty surrounding some innovatory projects might make them hard to finance in the normal way – the large firm with adequate internal resources is not constrained in this way. The implication is that there is capital market failure in this area.

Alternatives

When reviewing what are often plausible arguments for merger it is useful to bear in mind that there are other ways of achieving the same thing. An alternative to merger is *organic* growth – the construction of projects within the firm rather than the purchase of ready-made projects. But both merger and organic growth represent 'hierarchical' or 'organisational' methods of achieving a particular economic goal. In both cases the activity in question takes place inside one firm using inputs belonging to the firm. An alternative method of capturing the benefits of size is to make *contracts* in the market place with other independent firms to capture some benefit or other. Arrangements of this sort include joint-ventures, franchises, sub-contracts, service contracts and the like. A merger must prove clear superiority over these contractual approaches if it is to be justified.

An excellent example concerns the tax benefits to merger. Tax benefits are a rather specific earnings-type argument which is sometimes used to justify merger. The potential for this was reviewed in Chapter 3. Essentially, there will be tax benefits whenever a firm which is paying corporation tax can pool its earnings with a firm which has more tax deductions – losses or capital allowances – than it has earnings to set them off against. The benefits are in the form of interest savings through the postponement of tax payments, at the expense of the Revenue. However, leasing apparently provides a much more efficient and less costly method of obtaining the same advantages.

The key advantage of merger over organic growth as methods of growing is speed, and the reduced uncertainty associated with acquiring projects that are already up and running. The choice of hierarchical over market approaches to economic activity reflect the costs of writing contracts.[3]

Another good example is found in the modern automobile industry. The costs of research and development in this highly competitive industry are now very high and can only be borne if the subsequent market is seen in global terms. However car manufacturers have not necessarily responded to this indivisibility by creating monolithic worldwide corporations but by a series of joint-ventures in which R & D costs are shared, and in some cases one partner manufactures a component for both parties so as to capture manufacturing economies of scale as well.

V HOW MERGERS PERFORM – THE EVIDENCE

There have been a great many studies of the success or otherwise of mergers.[4] On the whole research seems to show that mergers generate value gains which are mostly captured by the acquiree. Paradoxically it seems that mergers do not lead to increased profitability. Less surprisingly, perhaps, we find that conglomerate mergers are less likely to succeed than vertical and horizontal mergers.

Value creation

The key test is whether mergers lead to value gains. If firm A and firm B merge to form A*, we want to check that the value of A* is greater than the values of A and B *would have been*. The problem for the investigator is figuring out what the values of A and B would have been. The most comprehensive UK study is that by Franks and Harris (1986) who studied 1900 UK mergers in the period 1955–85 and found evidence that target shareholders gain substantially in mergers while bidders 'gain or do not lose'. Acquiree bid premiums were higher in revised or contested bids, and when the acquirer had a pre-merger holding ('toe-hold').

In the US, Jensen and Ruback (1983) reviewed seven studies of returns to bidding firms post-merger and found an average abnormal return of −5.5%. These results are inconsistent with market efficiency and suggest that changes in stock price during take-overs overestimate the future gains from merger. A later study by Franks, Harris and Mayer (1988) studied post-merger performance of UK and US firms. Though they found negative post-merger performance on average, there were two striking results. First, equity bids displayed much worse post-merger performance than cash bids. Most strikingly they showed that the average post-merger loss of 18.4% sustained two years post-bid using a market model parameterised pre-merger, fell to 1.8% using post-merger parameters.

3 See Chapter 2 for a more detailed discussion of this.

4 A survey of recent work covering both market and profitability based studies of post-merger performance can be found in Caves (1989).

Profitability

The key test of success in a merger is its effect on value, but it is hard to avoid regarding profitability as the major determinant of value. A number of studies have investigated whether improved profitability occurs following a merger. Meeks (1977) examined a sample of 233 UK mergers representing over a third of all mergers between quoted companies from 1964 to 1972. Using historic-cost return on capital employed (adjusted for accounting bias and economic and industry distortions) he found that on average the firms in his sample experienced a decline in profitability relative to pre-merger levels in all seven years after merger. In the US, Ravenscraft and Scherer (1987) used the earnings performance as a measure of post-merger performance and concluded that merged firms performed poorly compared to both their own pre-merger records and a no-merger control group.

Healy, Palepu and Ruback (1992) study post-merger profitability of fifty of the largest US public industrial take-overs between 1979 and 1983. They measure profitability in terms of operating cash flow on the market value of assets and find improved performance (which is consistent with stock returns in the announcement period). They favour this measure because of the problems which arise when acquisition ('purchase') accounting is used as opposed to merger ('pooling') accounting. Three factors potentially distort return on capital for acquisitions: In the year of take-over returns will only include post-acquisition profit of the target; while the balance-sheet will record assets in full; the recognition of goodwill increases assets, while the subsequent amortisation of goodwill deflates earnings; writing-up the acquired assets from historic cost to fair value causes on upward shift in recorded net assets in the balance-sheet and increases the charge for consuming those assets.

Other studies

Some researchers have preferred a case-study approach to surveying mergers, to get a richer insight into their effects. Cowling et al (1977) looked at some horizontal mergers in the UK and found that in these cases efficiency gains were not a significant outcome, but that substantial increases in market power were. Weston (1970) studied, like Meeks in the UK, the performance of mergers in terms of measures of return on investment. He examined mergers in the US from 1937–58, and found conglomerate performance 'average', but with very high variability in the performance of particular conglomerates. However concentric mergers had a very high probability of success.

Porter (1987) observed thirty-three companies over the period 1980–86 and found that many of them disposed of more acquisitions than they kept. The more unrelated the acquired company, the more likely it was to be sold off. Firms were acquired for arbitrary reasons. Simple indicators such as rapid growth or a bargain price served as proxies for the target industry's suitability, or the target firm's long-term profit potential. Porter agreed with Meeks that pressure to grow, and to maintain some level of growth was to blame for the tendency to acquire and diversify to the point where it was inefficient to do so. Once unit performance shows signs of worsening, the firm concerned should recognise its mistake and dispose of unsuccessful subsidiaries. However if, as Meeks and Porter suggest, size, rather the profitability is the maximand, companies will try to avoid doing so for as long as possible.

Mueller (1985) compared the market shares of unacquired companies with the market shares of companies which had experienced changes in control. Both bidders and targets were chosen from the top 1,000 companies in 1950. The 123 acquirers also appeared in the top 1,000 in 1972. The study found that an unacquired business retained an average of

88% of its 1950 market share in 1972, an acquired one just 18%. Although some loss of market share is to be expected with a horizontal acquisition, both horizontal and diversified acquisitions lost out.

VI LEVERAGED BUY-OUTS AND MANAGEMENT BUY-OUTS

In the mid- and late 1980s there was a spate of acquisitions (see Table IV below), often by the company's own management, involving a substantial amount of debt. This wave of acquisitions had its own highly-charged vocabulary (see the glossary in Table V below). A LBO is a highly-geared acquisition; a MBO is an acquisition by management. MBOs tended to be LBOs since high borrowing was often necessary to permit a small group of individuals to acquire a substantial stake in the equity of a sizeable firm. In the UK most buy-outs have been purchased by the company's own managers or directors (MBOs). Massive US-style buy-outs by groups of outside investors have, so far, proved unpopular.

When a leveraged buy-out takes place a substituted part of the target company's purchase price is borrowed using its assets as collateral. In most cases some of these assets are sold off as quickly as possible in order to pay off part of the debt incurred in the purchase. The restructured company may eventually be taken public again and the remaining debt re-financed or retired. In order for the buy-out team to reap a profit the new-look company must be perceived as being worth substantially more than they paid for it. Hence there is an underlying belief that the burden of heavy indebtedness disciplines owners and managers; the restructured company will probably have sold off all but the most productive assets and will be run in the most cost-effective way possible.

Advocates of high gearing have argued that the acceptability, and increased availability of gearing makes sense on a number of levels. It provides opportunities to re-deploy under-used assets, to break up over-diversified companies, and to restructure companies in dying industries whilst providing managers with incentives to increase shareholder value. Employee Share Ownership Plans (ESOPs) have been used to reconcile the interests of shareholders, managers and workers. Debt is also tax efficient. Critics have argued that high levels of gearing destabilise the company sector, particularly if short-term, floating rate debt is used. It has been argued that the necessity of re-paying debt generates actions which aim to reduce indebtedness in the short-term but do not take into account the company's long-term prospects. Critics cite the sale of valuable and necessary assets, lay-offs and cuts in R & D budgets. It has been claimed that management benefit from ESOPs at the expense of employees.

Table IV Management buy-outs and buy-ins

	Number	*£m*
1986	366	1,491
1987	434	3,521
1988	489	4,931
1989	523	7,506
1990	597	3,107
1991	567	2,838
1992	586	3,261
1993	480	2,854

Source: The Centre for MBO Research, University of Nottingham

The number of MBOs fell in 1990 and figures for the first two quarters of 1991 were below those for the equivalent period in 1990. This probably occurred for a number of reasons. The economic downturn in the UK made banks cautious. Even in the boom period UK banks had been less able to accept the idea of heavy indebtedness than the US firms which had moved into the UK in the hope of cashing in on the MBO boom. The latter part of the 1980s saw some of the US banks which had moved into the UK in the wake of financial deregulation pulling out of LBOs. Simultaneously interest rate spreads broadened and banks required tighter covenant requirements.

Table V Glossary

Leveraged buy-out	A company purchase financed substantially by debt.
Management buy-out	An acquisition where the company is bought by its management
Management buy-in	An acquisition where a management team from outside buy the company.
Securitisation	The re-packing of debt, allowing it to be traded on securities markets.
Junk bonds	High-risk securitised debt.
Mezzanine finance	Subordinated debt which becomes between other debt, and equity in the claims hierarchy. As the risk approaches that associated with equity, investors demand interest payments which converge on the rate required by equity owners.
ESOP	Employee Share Ownership Plan

In the US, there was a LBO boom in the post-1984 period. There was increased involvement on the part of investment bankers, whose role in arranging LBO deals was crucial, both in obtaining finance and in supplying it (as contributors to LBO funds). Along with investment bankers, insurance companies and pension funds became involved as participants in LBO funds. The LBO boom took off when the awareness grew of the huge profits which were being made. Shareholders who were being bought out received premiums of up to 40%, advisers could charge large fees for arranging complex finance packages, while the biggest returns of all were achieved by LBO fund-holders who refloated or sold on their companies.

In the UK the numbers of MBOs and MBIs increased over the period 1981–89, reaching record levels in 1988–89 (see Table IV). However at no point did they reach the levels of the LBO boom in the US, and the tendency in the UK has been for management buy-outs rather than leveraged buy-outs by consortia of investing institutions.

VII SOME ISSUES IN EVALUATING TARGETS

A merger will be worthwhile for an acquiror if it leaves shareholders better off. As we have seen this will depend on two things: (1) the BENEFIT – the *value gains* arising from the merger, (2) the COST OF CONTROL – how much of the value gain is transferred to the acquiree shareholders in the merger negotiation. This is the *premium* paid over the market value of the acquiree's shares. A merger should be evaluated in two stages, first estimating the value gains, then the premium the acquirer will have to pay.

Valuing the new firm

If firms A and B merge to form firm A*, the value gained or created is the difference between the value of the new firm and the two original firms, ie

$$\text{Value gain} = V_{A*} - (V_A + V_B)$$

This is what the managers of A must try to predict. The first problem they will face is in knowing if the values V_A and V_B are 'correct'. A characteristic of an efficient stock market is that it anticipates events such as mergers and starts to embody expected value gains into share prices well before the event. So when managers sit down to evaluate a proposed merger they may be working with share prices which already reflect to some extent the market's expectations about the proposed merger and they will need to try and estimate what the true share price of the independent A and B would be.

But the real problem facing management is to estimate V_A* to quantify the value of the new firm. To do this they must estimate the extra cash flows that will be generated by the merger. This may well be difficult, probably much more so than a normal project appraisal. The benefits may reflect factors such as market power and improved management skills that are hard to quantify. But if management cannot put a value on the benefits, they should not be contemplating the merger.

The P/E illusion

Analysts commonly use a price earnings ratio or P/E in valuing the firm. They multiply the firm's earnings by an 'appropriate' P/E to find its value.

Xac plc

Xac is contemplating a merger with either Yog or Zog. The details of these firms are as follows:

	X	*Y*	*Z*
Market value of firm	£20m	£5m	£2.5m
Earnings	£2m	£1m	£1m
P/E	10	5	2½

Assume for convenience that Xac can buy both Yog and Zog at their current market value, ie no premium will be involved. Which should it buy? If the market capitalises the earnings of the new firms at a P/E of 10 then we can assess the two alternatives as follows:

Buy Yog

Earnings of new firm =	2m + 1m =	£3m
P/E		×10
Value of new firm		£30m
Values of old firms 20m + 5m	=	£25m
	VALUE GAIN	£5m

Buy Zog

Earnings of new firm =	2m + 1m =	3m
P/E		×10
Value of new firm		£30m
Values of old firms 20m + 2.5m	=	£22.5m
	VALUE GAIN	£7.5m

Since the premium or cost of control is the same in each case, ie NIL by assumption, buying Zog emerges as the better strategy.

P/E is usually taken as a measure of the quality of a firm – *given* the firm's earnings we expect a firm to have a higher P/E the better its growth prospects and the lower its riskiness. The message of the previous example seems to be that the firm should find the *worst* acquirees it can. This is because each £1 of earnings bought adds £10 to the value of Xog irrespective of where it came from. So Xog ought to buy up earnings as cheaply as it can. In fact it should be clear that the purchase of *any* firm with a P/E less than that of Xog will increase the value of Xog, and yield what has come to be known as an *instant merger profit.* This all hangs on the use of the acquirer's P/E for valuing the new earnings. What economic rationale could we provide for doing this? Clearly there is none. The null hypothesis must be that the earnings will continue to have the value they had before – as measured by the *acquiree's* P/E. If there are value gains to merger they need to be explicitly identified and measured. The best we could say for a procedure of valuing new earnings at the acquirer's P/E is that it is a convenient way of expressing confidence in the ability of the acquirer management to achieve a certain level of growth and risk in any context. It is hard to conceive that such confidence could ever be justified.

The cost of control

The cost of control depends on whether the offer is in shares or cash, but either way it is the *premium* the acquirer pays over the existing market price, V_B, of the acquiree. As before, to estimate the premium we need a figure for V_B which excludes any anticipated merger gains. Hence the price of B immediately prior to the merger, say on the day before, will not do.

Suppose we have the following two firms:

Abba and Baba

	Abba	Baba
Share price	£7.50	£1.50
No of shares in issue	100m	60m
Market value of firm	£750m	£90m

Abba is planning to buy Baba. It anticipates value gains of £60m and is contemplating either a cash offer of £2 per share, or an exchange of one Abba share for every three in Baba.

<u>Cash</u>

In the case of the cash offer the total cost of Baba is £60m × £2 = £120m giving a premium of £30m. Hence the net gain to Abba shareholders from the merger is £60m – £30m = £30m.

<u>Shares</u>

The calculation of the cost of control is less direct in a share-for-share merger since the 'cost' is a portion of the value of the new firm. In this case Abba estimates the value of the new firm will be £750m + £90m + £60m = £900m. If the market is efficient it will correctly perceive the value gains and capitalise them in addition to the value of the independent firms. The Baba shareholders are being given the proportion of this value represented by their shares as a proportion of the total shares in issue in Abba post-merger. Since they are now being given 20m (= ⅓ × 60m) shares this proportion is 20m/(100m + 20m) = 1/6.

Hence their shares are worth 1/6 × £900m = £150m. The premium on issue is £150m − £90m = £60m, and the net gain to Abba's existing shareholders is £60m − £60m = NIL.

VIII SUMMARY

Merger is a popular method of growing. Like other investment decisions the key question in appraising a merger is its effect on the value of the firm. In this chapter we reviewed the economic rationale for merger, the reasons why mergers might lead to value gains. We saw that the potential for gains depends very much on the type of merger, and that merger has to demonstrate its superiority over other ways of achieving the same outcome. From the point of view of the acquiring firm, though, an overall value gain is not enough. There is a cost to merger in the form of the premium it must pay the acquiree shareholders, and the merger will only be worthwhile if the value gain exceeds this premium. Research has shown that on average mergers do seem to lead to value gains but that most of these gains go to the acquiree shareholders. In other words, acquiree shareholders are able to enforce a premium that captures most or all of the gains to merger.

REFERENCES AND BIBLIOGRAPHY

Auerbach, A J (ed) Corporate Take-overs: Causes and Consequences (1988) NBER (Chicago).

Bradley, M, Desai, A and Kim E 'Synergistic Gains from Corporate Acquisition and their Division between the Stockholders of Target and Acquiring Firms', Journal of Financial Economics 21, 1988, pp 3–40.

Caves, R E 'Mergers, Take-overs and Economic Efficiency: Foresight v Hingsight', Journal of Industrial Organisations, 1989, pp 151–174.

Cowling, K, Stoneham, P, Cubbin, J, Cable, J, Hall, G, Dornberger, S, and Dutton, P 'Mergers and Economic Performance', Research Study for the Office of Fair Trading, 1977.

Department of Trade and Industry *Mergers Policy* (1988) HMSO.

Fairburn, J A, and Kay, J A *Mergers and Merger Policy* (1989) Oxford: Oxford University Press.

Farrar, J H, Furey, N, Hannigan, B, and Wylie, O P *Farrar's Company Law* (3rd edn, 1991), Butterworths.

Franks, J R, and Harris, R S 'Shareholder Wealth Effects of Corporate Take-overs: the UK Experience 1955–85', Journal of Financial Economics, 1989, pp 225–249.

Healy, P M, Palepu, K G, and Ruback, R S 'Does Corporate Performance Improve after Mergers?', Journal of Financial Economics, 1992, pp 135–175.

Jensen, M C, and Ruback, R S — 'The Market for Corporate Control: the Scientific Evidence', Journal of Financial Economics, 1983, pp 5–50.

Jensen, M C — 'Agency Costs of Free Cash Flow, Corporate Finance and Take-overs', American Economic Review, 1986, pp 323–329.

Jensen, M C — 'The Take-over Controversy – Analysis and Evidence', Midland Corporate Finance Journal, Winter 1986, pp 6–32.

Littlechild, S — 'Myths and Merger Policy' in *Mergers and Merger Policy*, eds Fairburn, J A, and Kay, J A (1989) Oxford University Press.

Meeks, G — *Disappointing Marriage: A Study of the Gains from Merger* (1977) Cambridge University Press.

Merger Green Paper — A Review of Monopolies and Mergers Policy (Cmnd 7198).

Morck, R, Shleifer, A, and Vishny, R V — 'Characteristics of Hostile and Friendly Take-overs' in Auerbach (1988).

Mueller, D C — *The Determinants and Effects of Mergers* (1985) Oegelschlanger, Gunn and Hain, Cambridge, Ma.

Office of Fair Trading — 'Mergers' HMSO, London, 1978.

Palepu, K G — Predicting Take-over Targets: A Methodological and Empirical Analysis', Journal of Accounting and Economics, 1986, pp 3–37.

Porter, M E — 'From Competitive Advantage to Corporate Strategy', Harvard Business Review, 1987, pp 43–59.

Ravenscraft, D J, and Scherer, F M — Mergers, Sell-offs and Economic Efficiency (1987) The Brookings Institution, Washington DC.

Singh, A — *Take-overs* (1971) Cambridge University Press, London.

Singh, A — 'Take-overs, Economic Natural Selection, and the Theory of the Firm: Evidence from the Postwar United Kingdom Experience', Economic Journal, Sept 1975, pp 497–515.

QUESTIONS

1 Distinguish the different classes of merger and the costs and benefits likely to accrue to each.

2 Is there an economic rationale for conglomerate mergers?

3 In terms of profitability, mergers seem to have been on average unsuccessful, but in terms of value gains, successful. Can we explain this paradox?

4 Why would mergers come in waves?

5 Large is thinking of taking over Helpless. Large presently has 10 million shares in issue, with a market price of £4. Helpless has 4 million shares selling at £2.50. Large believes that, together, the two firms could be worth £55 million and Large is considering financing the merger either through a cash offer of £3.50 per Helpless share or by a one for one share exchange. Find the gains to the merger, and the cost under each of the financing alternatives. What factors would affect the choice of cash versus shares for financing a merger in practice?

6 The Heavy Speaker Company has made an offer to acquire all the ordinary shares of Red Rectangle Turntables. The offer document states that the merger should create gains for the combined group due to the complementary nature of the products. The offer document provides the following information:

	Heavy	*Red Rectangle*
Shares in issue	5 million	7 million
Earnings per share	160p	110p
Price-earnings ratio (P/E)	9	6

The profits forecast indicates an earnings per share of £2.20 for the combined group. Stockbrokers to the group expect the P/E of the combined group to be one point above the weighted average on the basis of pre-merger market values of the firm.

Heavy has offered one new share in exchange for two Red Rectangle shares. The cash alternative is £6.50 for one Red Rectangle share.

Assuming the prevailing P/E for the new group is:

(a) Heavy's
(b) Red Rectangle's
(c) a weighted average of the two

calculate the gain from the merger and the cost to Heavy under the cash and share alternatives. Also calculate the bid-premiums.

CHAPTER 23

Failure and disinvestment

When we study investment decision making we tend to emphasise the positive and talk about techniques for choosing the best projects and making the best merger decisions. But it is important that disinvestment decisions are well made too. On occasion economic activities will 'fail' – projects, parts of firms and even whole firms will cease to have a positive economic value. However the people involved in failure tend not to be so philosophical about it. In the case of a single project, failure can seriously damage the reputation of those managers who sponsored and implemented the project. Larger scale failure can mean a significant financial loss to owners and creditors but also, if it means redundancy, a loss to employees of income, status, and the social relationships of the workplace. Not surprisingly people are reluctant to recognise failure and this means that disinvestment decisions are often forced from outside.

There has been much less research into failure than, say, merger, We do not have a rich body of evidence on why firms fail, or any evidence on whether the right firms are failing.[1] Hence our approach in this chapter is rather different from the last. We examine the legal and institutional circumstances surrounding failure and see if they are likely to be conducive to efficient disinvestment.

In Section I we examine the prevalence of failure and the legal and institutional background. In Section II we consider whether the factor process is likely to be efficient in practice, and present a case-study of the failure of Stone-Platt Ltd – in which we can see the process at work. In Section II we look at the related question of bankruptcy costs. Section IV examines how disinvestment decisions should be made from the point of view of society as a whole. We see that accounting losses may be an unreliable signal for closure. The main empirical research effort in the field of company failure has gone into the development of statistical models of failure prediction, and Section V examines the use of such models.

I THE BACKGROUND TO FAILURE

Insolvency and liquidation

We cannot talk about company failure without sorting out the slightly confusing terminology. In the UK when a company ceases to exist in law we say it is *wound up* or goes into *liquidation*. *Bankruptcy* is something that, strictly speaking, happens only to individuals or partnerships who cannot meet their debts. However in the US they apply the word bankruptcy to companies as well and the same tends to happen in the UK in everyday parlance.

Many companies are wound up each year for reasons which have nothing to do with

1 This is partly because of lack of information – we can trace the records of firms before they fail, but then they disappear – and also perhaps because of lack of interest in the past when company failure was less prevalent.

failure, they may simply have outlived their usefulness and their owners see no further point in continuing the registration. However, our main concern is with companies which are liquidated through *insolvency*. Insolvency is the economic event that gives rise to the legal event of liquidation, but other outcomes are possible. Creditors may be persuaded to hold off while the company's fortunes are revived. Sometimes it is possible to undertake a legal *reconstruction* of the firm. The old firm is liquidated and all parties agree to accept reduced claims on a new legal entity constructed round a viable part of the former business.

Insolvency

The traditional test of solvency is whether a company is able to pay its debts as they fall due. This does not require the company's prospective liabilities to be taken into account before they fall due. The Insolvency Act 1986 provides another test known as a 'balance sheet' test which states that 'A company is also deemed unable to pay its debts if . . . the value of the company's assets is less than the amount of its liabilities, *taking into account its contingent and prospective liabilities*.' The emphasis is usually on when and whether these liabilities will fall due and how the company intends to deal with the situation if they do. Factors such as cash flow forecasts and the availability of financial support would be taken into consideration. The tests of 'failure to pay' are outlined in Table I.

Table I Tests of insolvency	
1	A creditor has served on the company a signed demand for payment of the sum due and the company has not either paid, secured or compounded for the sum to the creditor's satisfaction within three weeks.
	Execution issued on a judgement in favour of a creditor is returned unsatisfied.
2	It is proved to the satisfaction of the court that the company is unable to pay its debts, taking into account its contingent and prospective liabilities.

Liquidation

If the company fails on one of these counts the court can be *petitioned* for an order for *compulsory winding up*. The company or a shareholder can present such a petition, but it is more likely to be an unsecured creditor. There will be a hearing at which the petition will either be dismissed, adjourned or a winding-up order passed. At the same time the petitioner can ask for a provisional liquidator, probably the *official receiver*, to be put in to safeguard the assets of the company, and if the court eventually decides to wind up the firm, he becomes the *liquidator*. Alternatively, and more usually, a company can be wound up without going to the court. The company can initiate a members' or creditors' *voluntary winding up* by passing an extraordinary resolution to that effect, and calling a meeting of creditors. The winding up then proceeds in a similar fashion to a compulsory winding up. Sometimes creditors will ask for the supervision of the court to give added protection in a voluntary winding up.

The job of a liquidator is to wind up the affairs of the firm and realise its assets as quickly as possible. A receiver's task is to manage the business as a continuing entity and on occasion, if he is more successful than the previous management, he can nurse the business back to life. If a debt contract gives the lender a charge over the company's assets then the trust deed will empower him to appoint a receiver to safeguard his assets if the company breaks one of the specified covenants in the deed. Hence receivers are often appointed by banks or debenture-holders ahead of the legal winding-up process.

Table II shows the *order* in which the assets of a company are distributed to people with claims on them in a winding up. Apart from its interest to the people involved, the existence of a pecking order amongst creditors is of some interest from the point of view of the efficiency of the liquidation process. It is sometimes suggested that the existence of preferential creditors who can install a receiver to protect their interests may lead to firms being liquidated which would otherwise not need to be, and assets being sold below their economic value. We return to this question when we discuss bankruptcy costs.

Table II Order of distribution in a winding up

- Creditors having a fixed charge over a particular asset, to the extent of the proceeds of sale of that asset after payment of the realisation expenses of the receiver or liquidator. This includes the fixed charge over book debts, which has become more common in recent years.
- Costs of receivership in relation to a floating charge, and costs of liquidation where a receiver has not been appointed.
- Preferential creditors including, subject to various limitations, claims for local rates, income and corporation taxes, VAT, wages and salaries, social security contributions and superannuation contributions. The wages preference is for a maximum of four months wages with an overall limit of £800 per employee.
- Liabilities for tax arising from the activities of the receiver.
- Debenture holders, to the extent that their claims are covered by a floating charge over the company.
- Costs of the liquidator, where the company has first been placed in receivership.
- Unsecured creditors.
- Shareholders.

Source: Bank of England Quarterly Bulletin, Vol 20, No 4, December 1980, page 433

The prevalence of liquidation

Table III shows the number of companies entering compulsory or creditors' voluntary liquidation in England and Wales in the years 1975–92.

Table III Liquidations in England and Wales

	Total		*Total*
1975	5,938	1985	14,898
1976	5,939	1986	14,405
1977	5,831	1987	11,439
1978	5,086	1988	9,427
1979	4,537	1989	10,456
1980	6,891	1990	15,051
1981	8,596	1991	21,827
1982	12,067	1992	24,425
1983	13,406	1993	20,823
1984	13,721		

Source: Department of Trade and Industry

It is notable that the mid-80s peak in insolvency was in 1985, two years after the end of the recession of the early 1980s. This suggests that for many firms failure was triggered by difficulties in financing recovery, rather than the ravages of the recession itself.

Administration

Legislation in the area of business failure varies from country to country. The differences hinge on how the law regards the debtor, and on whether the aim should be the recovery of creditors' money or the rehabilitation and survival of the company. In the UK the emphasis is on reimbursing creditors. For centuries, British bankrupts were sent to debtor prisons. The 'UK model' traditionally prevails in Canada, Australia and most other western European countries. In the US, bankruptcy is more likely to be accepted as a risk of entrepreneurship. A priority of US legislation is to rehabilitate failing companies wherever possible so that they continue to trade. An ailing US company has two options: it can go into liquidation under Chapter 7 of the Bankruptcy Code, or it can file under Chapter 11, to seek protection from its creditors. Once a firm is in Chapter 11, its management has to produce a reorganisation plan. The company's creditors are arranged into committees to vote on the plan. Since there is no hierarchy to govern the order of reimbursements, the quality of creditors' legal representation is often the factor which determines their seniority.

Chapter 11 gives a company which is failing as a result of a disastrous but isolated event the chance to recover. Manville, the asbestos company, is an example.

Manville Corporation

In 1982 when the Manville Corporation filed for bankruptcy – the biggest US bankruptcy since the 1930s. On the face of it Manville was a very healthy company, with assets of $2.2 billion against liabilities of $1 billion. But Manville was an asbestos manufacturer, and was facing 52,000 asbestos-health lawsuits whose combined damages could run to $2 billion. Mr John McKinney, Manville's chairman, did not intend to wind up the company – quite the reverse. The filing for bankruptcy was a device 'to preserve the company's continuing operations, protect its assets, and achieve even-handed treatment of asbestos-health lawsuits and the claims of lending institutions and trade creditors'.

But some argue that it favours the same managers who brought the company to the brink of bankruptcy. The absence of a hierarchical system to reimburse creditors is also a concern. Small trade creditors may lose out, lawyers can have a vested interest in prolonging and complicating the proceedings, and shareholders, who are the last to be paid in a liquidation,

Table IV Bankruptcy laws

Country	*Liquidation*	*Rehabilitation*
USA	Chapter 7	Chapter 11
Britain	Receivership/liquidation	Administration
Germany	Konkurs	Vergleich
Japan	Bankruptcy law	Corporate reorganisation law
France	Liquidation	Reglement amiable/ Redressement judiciare
Canada	Receivership/liquidation	Companies' creditors administration
Italy	Liquidation	Supervised administration

Source: © The Economist, February 1990

gain at the expense of debt-holders. Finally, the competitors of companies which are trading from the shelter of Chapter 11 argue that it gives them an unfair competitive advantage.

The majority of western European countries now have their own version of Chapter 11, as Table IV above shows.

Administration in the UK

The Insolvency Act 1986 aimed to simplify the liquidation procedure and to offer the possibility of rehabilitation.

Before the 1986 Act, a company in financial difficulties had no means of preventing creditors from enforcing claims while it was trying to negotiate its way out of trouble. Even if a broad agreement had been reached with the majority of creditors, there was no means of binding dissenting creditors to it without going through the courts, which was costly and time-consuming.

The 1986 legislation introduced the role of *administrator*. An administrator is appointed by the court at the request of a company, its directors, or a creditor. The administrator must, within three months, present a survival plan for the company or for part of it, or a plan for a more advantageous realisation of the company's assets than would be the case if the company were wound up. Only one meeting of creditors is necessary to then vote on the administrator's proposal, and a simple majority puts the order into effect.

> *Consumer and Industrial Press Ltd (1988)*
>
> Consumer and Industrial Press Ltd had published a magazine since 1949, but in 1988, they reached the point where net liabilities were judged by accountants to be too great to trade out of trouble. The Inland Revenue successfully petitioned for an administration order. Administrators were appointed to manage the company so that at least one more issue of the magazine could be published, on the grounds that even if the company were not saved by an arrangement with the creditors, the title would fetch a better price if publication continued than if it were sold in a liquidation.

Although administration is often compared to the American Chapter 11, there are differences. The most obvious difference is that in the UK it is the administrator who runs the company and not the company's management. Also in Britain, proceeds from any sales are distributed strictly according to the 'creditors' hierarchy' ie as they would be in a liquidation. There are no creditors' committees to vote on this as there are in the US. Another difference is that in the UK creditors *can* persuade the courts that the company should go into liquidation if no acceptable rescue package has been found, or if attempts to keep the company alive appear to be useless. (In the US, companies have stayed under the protection of Chapter 11 for a number of years.)

II THE ECONOMICS OF DISINVESTMENT

It is rational to *invest* when the expected value of the income from an activity, its economic value (EV), exceeds the opportunity cost of the assets. The opportunity cost of the assets employed will generally be their *replacement* cost (RC). So an activity has a positive NPV when EV > RC. By the same token there should be *disinvestment* when NPV is negative – when the value of the assets in their present use is below their opportunity cost. The only difference is that now the opportunity cost will be the *realisable value* (RV) of the assets in place. So it is rational to abandon a project of firm once its NPV becomes negative, and for an existing activity this occurs when the EV < RV, when the value of the remaining income from the activity falls below the value of assets in their best alternative use. The RV will be the economic value of some other activity within the firm, or the economic value that third parties can achieve with the assets embodied in the price they are willing to pay for them.

Assets which are highly specific may have a very 'thin' market with realisable values well below replacement cost. This divergence between RC and RV can create a 'trap' in which projects or firms, that with the benefit of hindsight would not have been worth creating, are worth preserving simply because of the low value of their assets in other uses. Abandonment is not always caused by failure. An increase in RV can have the same effect when new and more lucrative uses come along for the project's assets.

Is the disinvestment process efficient?

Projects should be abandoned as soon as the value of maintaining them becomes negative. To check this the firm should regularly revalue existing projects in order to compare the present value of the remaining cash flows with the value of the project's assets in their next best use. In the unrealistic world of 'certainty' this problem never arises because the point at which the project will cease to be worthwhile is fully anticipated and defines the project life. In reality, though, project lives are uncertain. The decision-maker makes his best guess and some allowance for the riskiness of the forecast, but if the actual outcome is at the lower end of his or her expectations the project may need to be terminated early.

The risk is that the firm will not spot failing projects promptly. We saw that many firms do not even use DCF for initial project appraisal. But even less firms have a formal DCF system for subsequent monitoring or auditing of projects. More commonly firms rely on signals from the cost accounting system or the perceptions of the marketing department to trigger doubts about the project, projects will only be abandoned at the right time if these signals are reliable indicators of value.

The occasional failure and abandonment of individual projects is an inevitable side-effect of the uncertainty of economic life. In most firms it is a sustainable event – some reputations may suffer but the loss is borne by other projects and the human and physical capital is transferred elsewhere. Sometimes, though, the failure engulfs the whole firm and the loss can be severe, financially to investors and creditors, and for employees in terms of unemployment with its attendant costs. Hence the failure and liquidation of the firm is an event that tends to be resisted by all concerned.

The firm should be liquidated when it has a negative NPV, that is EV < RV. In practice, though, liquidation does not seem to be about *value* so much as about *cash* – companies will be insolvent and face liquidation if they cannot meet their debts as and when they fall due. The link is that *in a perfect capital market a firm should never be insolvent if it has a positive NPV*. Such a firm can always borrow against future cash inflows to meet temporary cash deficits and be confident of being able to pay the necessary interest on borrowing – this ability is precisely what present values measure.

How does liquidation work in practice? The best way to see this is by looking at the case of a failing company.

Stone-Platt

Stone-Platt was a UK manufacturer with long traditions, producing textile and other engineering machinery. In the early and mid-1970s it was exporting two-thirds of its UK output and earning a return on capital of over 20%. However its fortunes started to change dramatically because of changes in the economic environment and Stone-Platt's failure to respond. Stone-Platt's heavy export emphasis had partly reflected the decline in the domestic textile industry, but the world market for textile machinery was undergong significant changes too. Stone-Platt found that the world textile industry was losing its buoyancy, competitors were eroding its technical lead, sterling was rising, and perhaps most significantly the market for the 'big deal' – the supply and implementation of complete textile plants – which Stone-Platt had dominated, dwindled. Now they were forced increasingly to compete in more conventional product markets for individual items of capital equipment.

In 1976 Stone-Platt achieved a profit of £15.8 million. By 1979 this had turned into a pre-tax loss of £2.9 million. Fairly rapidly the following sequence of events took place.

— In 1979 the big Oldham plant was closed and £17.5 million was written-off against reserves. However a covenant in one of Stone-Platt's loan contracts required the maintenance of a certain level of equity. This clause was triggered by the write-off and in turn breached cross-default clauses in other loan agreements. Hence a significant part of Stone-Platt's debt finance became repayable on demand and Stone-Platt's bankers were now in a position to decide its future.
— The Bank of England intervened and appointed a former Governor, Sir Jasper Hallam, to chair a process of renegotiation and settlement with creditors. The creditors led by the Midland Bank agreed to hold off whilst Stone-Platt, which was perceived to contain some viable sections, reorganised. Under the new arrangements the firm was given loans and overdraft facilities until January 1982.
— Certain divisions of Stone-Platt remained viable and it was possible to sell these off. In November 1980 the pumps division was sold for £11 million and in February 1981 the marine propeller division. These sales reduced borrowings by £16 million. Unfortunately these sales of profitable divisions which had been subsidising other activities, depressed the returns on the 'rump' even further. The 1981 loss was £5.7 million pre-tax. There were further write-offs of £15 million in 1981.
— It had been clear all along that a long-term settlement with creditors would only be possible if the equity base could be increased. This required investors who would be prepared to subscribe equity to Stone-Platt. On 12 March 1981 this was achieved and a settlement was made. Forty million new shares were issued raising £10 million. Two city institutions, Equity Capital for Industry and Finance Corporation for Industry, were to take up 12 million with the rest being offered to existing shareholders and underwritten by Hill Samuel, Stone-Platt's financial advisers, and ECI and FCI. In return four clearing banks provided £40 million of borrowing facilities, of which £25 million was a five-year loan and standby credit. This settlement gave Stone-Platt a healthy balance-sheet – £50 million of equity to £30 million of debt – and time for further reorganisation.

The Stone-Platt case shows up an important feature of the failure process. In principle the capital market should extend cash to firms with positive value. In practice, lack of information about the future prospects of the firm and about available alternative uses for its assets make a spot decision impossible. Instead time is needed. If the firm's position can be held the future may unfold and a *search* can be undertaken to find the most valuable method of deploying the firm's assets. The search involves a thorough study by the firm and its advisers of possible internal reorganisations, and an assessment of external possibilities through attempts to sell off parts of the firm. In a world of imperfect information this may be a good way of appraising 'value'. In the case of Stone-Platt the process seemed to work well – the activities of the firm came under close scrutiny from inside and outside. Valuable activities were identified and in some cases floated off, and management changes and policy changes were made in order to salvage perceived problem areas. New finance was provided when investors convinced themselves they had enough information from which to forecast an adequate return to debt and equity finance.

Coda The settlement of 12 March 1981 did not stem the Stone-Platt losses; the ailing textile division was still at the heart of Stone-Platt's problem. Losses mounted during the ensuing year so that by March 1982 the directors were proposing another capital reconstruction. Reckoning that at the present rate shareholders' funds would soon fall to £15 million the Midland Bank led the clearing banks in putting a receiver in. The company was dismantled in a series of sales and management buy-outs which raised £40 million. This was not even sufficient to pay the outstanding debt and preferential creditors. At the beginning of June 1982 shareholders, including FCI and ECI, received letters telling them they could not hope to receive anything from the dismantling of Stone-Platt.

The decision of Midland Bank to 'blow the whistle' on Stone-Platt was criticised in several quarters. Mr Geoffrey Robinson, Labour MP for Coventry NW, felt it marked 'the nadir of the failure of the banks to understand and cater for manufacturing industry'.

The need for time

In theory the firm should be liquidated when EV < RC. In practice there is imperfect information about the value of the firm's assets in different uses: it takes time to search out possibilities for selling off profitable divisions or salvaging and reconstructing part of the firm. In the case of Stone-Platt the search was largely made possible by the status of the company and by the willingness of the Bank of England and Sir Jasper Hallam to be involved. Holding off while a search takes place is an act of faith by investors, and they run the risk that new money is being thrown after bad. This turned out to be the case at Stone-Platt. In practice it seems likely that the decision to hold off will be influenced by factors such as size, status and reputation, and by public policy considerations acting through the influence of agencies such as the Bank of England. Unless factors such as these are reliable signals of value, we cannot rely on the process being efficient. There are clear examples of large companies being rescued by government on public policy grounds. Furthermore we know that small firms are more likely to fail than large. There may be good reasons for this – small firms are more vulnerable to economic fluctuations and less likely to be diversified. We have no evidence on whether the right firms fail, and we never get to know what would have happened if they had not.

The effect of the pecking order

There is a pecking order amongst creditors when a company is liquidated. Secured lenders come first and very often, as in the Stone-Platt case, liquidation is triggered by their decision to appoint a receiver to protect their interests. Does the existence of a pecking order affect the efficiency of the process?

'Equity' often accuse debt-holders of withdrawing too early. This argument looks attractive – since the secured assets are usually vital to the survival of the company, the ability to withdraw them means that the company's survival is effectively dependent on the welfare of one group of investors. On the other hand equity usually have very little to lose by shouting 'foul' when debt-holders send in a receiver. In the case of Stone-Platt, equity shareholders were reported to be disgruntled by the Midland Bank's action. But since the equity interest turned out to be worth nothing at that time, it was in their interests to use any ploy to lengthen Stone-Platt's life – even if the chances of a turnaround were infinitesimally small.

Again, since the receiver's prime task is to recover debt-holders' funds he may not bother to realise the firm's assets for their full value. Searching out the best price will involve him in additional costs at no gain to debt-holders. Similarly the receiver may well find it 'easier' to sell off a firm's assets than to seek to return the firm to sound health even though this might yield a higher value. In extreme cases the aggrieved residue of creditors are able to sue the receiver for negligence. The argument may have some force – it is another issue in company failure on which we have no hard evidence.

Diversification and efficient disinvestment

Large firms are less likely to fail than small, and research shows that the returns of large firms are less 'risky', less variable, than those of small firms. This is partly explained by the greater diversification of large firms. But it is wrong to jump to the conclusion that diversification is an attractive cure to company failure. Economic failure is not avoided by diversification – the difference is that rather than leading to company failure the loss is borne inside the firm. We know that managers, employees and even investors may be reluctant to recognise company failure so that firms may continue to trade after their net present value becomes negative. But is failure more quickly recognised and loss-making activities more speedily terminated inside a diversified firm? This is a moot point. It should be – the firm is both the investor and the manager and has the best information on net present value; the firm may be able to transfer resources smoothly to other uses; some of the 'costs of bankruptcy' – which we discuss in the next section – will be avoided. In practice, without the sanction of the market place firms may continue loss-making activities, *cross-subsidised* by profitable ones, for lengthy periods of time. This may be because of optimism, a reluctance of the project's sponsors to besmirch their reputations, or a failure in the accounting system to allocate costs properly. In this case the shareholder bears costs he might avoid under limited liability and this may well exceed any benefit from avoiding bankruptcy costs.

Bankruptcy costs

When we are building theories in finance we like, at least as a starting point, to assume a perfect capital market in which there are no obstacles to the free operation of market forces. One potential set of obstacles is costs of liquidation or 'bankruptcy costs' and these have assumed great importance in finance. For example, in a 'pure' capital asset pricing model world it is shareholders who build diversified portfolios, and diversification by the firm is not a thing of value to them. But if there are bankruptcy costs diversification by the firm may be in the interests of shareholders. Similarly if there are bankruptcy costs and borrowing increases the risk of bankruptcy, the value of the firm may be maximised by restricting the amount of debt the firm uses, whereas in a pure Modigliani and Miller world capital structure is irrelevant to the value of the firm.

How significant are bankruptcy costs? The answer is that we have little hard evidence, but people often behave as though bankruptcy is something to be avoided if at all possible – in other words they behave as though there are severe costs to bankruptcy. In a perfect capital market bankruptcy is painless – it is the event of a smooth and costless transfer of assets to their next best use, outside the firm. Bankruptcy costs are leakages – losses of value – that occur when the firm is liquidated.

The most tangible costs to bankruptcy are the transactions costs associated with winding up the firm – the expenses of liquidation and particularly the costs of the receiver and liquidator, Warner (1977) examined these costs associated with railroad bankruptcies in the US. On average he found that the costs were 5.3% of the market values of the firms involved, in terms of their values just before liquidation. In terms of the value of these firms a few years prior to liquidation these costs emerged as quite small, and the expected cost was even lower.

If the assets of a bankrupt firm were sold off at less than their true value this would be another cost to bankruptcy. People often claim that this happens – liquidators may go for a quick 'fire' sale or, being the creditors' representatives, may have little incentive to achieve a price beyond what is needed to pay off the creditors. The implication is that asset markets are inefficient around bankruptcy. This idea is attractive, but we have no hard evidence on it. There is no doubt that asset values often *seem* very low in liquidation, but this may be an illusion. People are often reluctant to recognise the decline in value of a failing firm, and its liquidation value comes as a shock. The temptation to cry 'we've been done!' is irresistible.

The third component of bankruptcy cost is also hard to measure. It is the effects of restrictions and limitations put on failing firms by their creditors. Creditors routinely impose certain constraints on the freedom of management – these are embodied in the restrictive covenants written into debt agreements and in the normal course of events these restrictions are not too onerous. But if these covenants are breached as the firm fails, creditors are likely to impose much tighter limits and closer monitoring. The creditors' aim now is to give managers just enough leeway to exploit any possibilities for salvaging the firm whilst avoiding the risk of further losses. We saw this happening in the Stone-Platt case study. In practice this does limit management's ability to pursue new projects, and involves them in a good deal of time, negotiating and being monitored by bankers and creditors.

A final cost of bankruptcy is the damage to managers' reputations from association with failure and the loss of income while they are looking for new jobs. This appears to be a cost to managers rather than shareholders, but managers will seek to transfer it to shareholders by asking higher rewards for managing risky firms.

III SOCIAL DISINVESTMENT DECISIONS

Governments have it in their power to support or subsidise firms which would otherwise fail. Some governments do this, while others decline to, preferring to 'let the market decide', pursuing the very reasonable and generally-held view that profitable operations in the economy should be expanded and loss-making ones closed. We now consider why, even if capital markets are operating properly, it may sometimes be appropriate for government to take a different view.

Burton and Williams

Burton and Williams Ltd owns a steelworks in South Wales. The steelworks has made a heavy loss this year and Burton and Williams has asked the government for financial support.

BURTON & WILLIAMS: INCOME STATEMENT

			(£m)
Sales			180
Materials	90		
Purchased fuels	20		
Employment costs	65		
Other charges	20		
Depreciation	10		(205)
			(25)
Interest charges by government			(14)
		LOSS	(39)

Should the government support a loss-making firm? If it does not, the steelworks will close, so the financial decision is effectively a disinvestment decision. It is worth recalling some principles of decision making from this and earlier chapters. First, only the incremental costs and benefits of a decision should be taken into account, and the appropriate measure of costs and benefits is opportunity cost. Second, investment and disinvestment decisions will have effects in several future time-periods. The surplus of benefits over costs is termed 'contribution' on an annual basis, and 'net present value' is the value of the contribution through time. Is the current loss of Burton and Williams a correct measure of its contribution? And what happens in other years? The accounting loss of Burton and Williams will only measure its contribution relative to this decision if the accounting costs are correct measures of the opportunity cost to society of the resources used by the firm and if the accounting revenue correctly measures the social benefits. A whole branch of economics has evolved around this issue. 'Social cost-benefit analysis' examines under what conditions we can expect a divergence between public ('social' or 'government') costs and benefits, and private ones, and it has developed techniques for estimating these public costs and benefits.[2] In this section we sketch some of the arguments. Clearly if there is a divergence, the use of private costs and benefits will not necessarily yield correct social investment decisions. It is common to refer to the set of prices that would yield an optimal decision as 'shadow prices'. The problem is thus to find the appropriate set of shadow prices underlying the actual prices we observe.

To get the flavour of the adjustments that would be necessary to convert a historic cost profit or loss figure into a measure of social contribution, we will look at just three of Burton and Williams' inputs, and assume for simplicity that the rest can stand as they are.

Labour

The opportunity cost of an idle resource is zero. B & W estimate that if they are made redundant 80% of the workers will not find other employment. The private cost of employing these workers, the cost to the firm, is measured by their wages. But viewed from a social point of view the problem is one of an internal transfer of resources from one use to another within the decision-unit, the economy. If some workers will be otherwise unemployed the cost of using these workers at Burton and Williams is zero.[3] So, if we can assume that the remaining 20% will find work elsewhere which enables them to earn a contribution equivalent to their current salary, the opportunity cost measure of the labour expense is £65m × 20% = £13m.

Depreciation

Depreciation attempts to measure the cost of using fixed assets. It is an allocation of part of the initial cost to a particular time-period. But for decision making what is needed is a measure of the opportunity cost of using the fixed assets. It appears that no offers have been received for the plant and equipment of the steelworks, and that if the steelworks closes they will be idle resources. In this case the opportunity cost of using them is zero. Zero is presumably the private opportunity cost as well, since depreciation does not represent a cash flow of the firm, the associated cash has been spent and is now a 'sunk cost'.

2 A good introduction to this topic is Pearce and Nash (1981).

3 What about unemployment pay, 'dole', which appears to put an extra cost on government when workers are unemployed? Does this make the opportunity cost actually negative? No, dole is irrelevant since it is merely a *transfer* of income from one group in society to another. It does not involve the generation of contribution.

Raw materials

To demonstrate another problem in the transition from private to public costs, consider the opportunity cost of resources acquired from other firms. The private cost of using such resources is in 'normal' conditions of regular purchase, what is paid for them. But what is the public opportunity cost? What is the relationship between the price of the resources and their opportunity cost? Basic microeconomics shows this to be a function of the degree of monopoly of the supplier. Consider Figure I which shows the conventional prediction of theory about the pricing behaviour of rational monopolists.

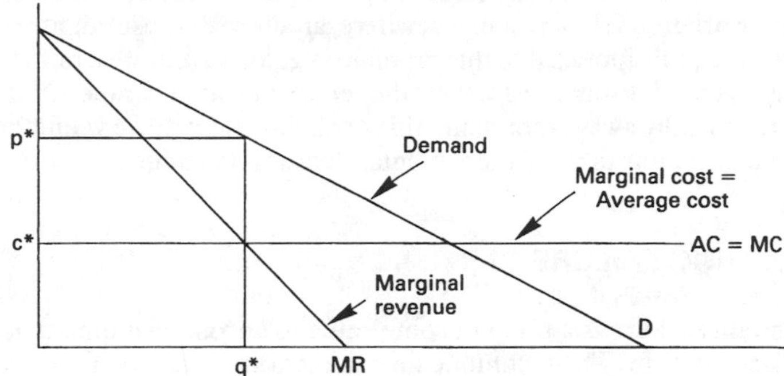

Figure I Pricing by a monopolist

The rational monopolist produces up to the point where marginal cost equals marginal revenue, up to q* with a corresponding marginal cost of c*. But because of the divergence of the demand and marginal cost curves he is able to charge a price of p* at this output level. We assume here that AC = MC. The key perception is that part of the price of the monopolist's output, p*−c*, will be 'monopoly profit', and this will constitute a divergence between the price of inputs provided by a monopolist, and the real cost of the resources being supplied. It has been estimated that 20% of the price of the raw materials bought by the steelworks is 'monopoly profit' of the supplier. So to find the public opportunity cost it is necessary to reduce the private cost proportionately,

£90m × 80% = £72m.

Making these three adjustments will convert the measure of private profit or loss into a measure of social contribution as follows:

		(£m)
Sales		180
Materials 90 × 80%	72	
Purchased fuels	20	
Employment costs 65 × 20%	13	
Other charges	20	
Depreciation 10 × 0%	0	
		(125)
		55
Interest charges by government		(14)
		41

On this basis it appears that the steelworks is currently making a positive contribution.

Though it is hard to fault the logic of this, some readers might argue with the conclusion. It seems that by a sleight of hand we have made a case for subsidising inefficiency. Clearly, governments do not wish to appear to do this. But so far we have only looked at one time-period. Before a proper decision can be made about closure, future periods must be examined too. The plant should only be closed if the present value of all the future contributions it will make is negative. It is possible that in the future, even using social measures of cost, the steelworks will indeed generate a negative contribution. This might happen if for instance there were a general return to full employment in the economy. In this case increased demand from other activities will drive up the opportunity cost of the recources used by the steelworks – the workers might find jobs elsewhere, an alternative use might even emerge for the steelworks.[4] So a full appraisal of this problem is going to require a rather complex and conjectural analysis of future events in the economy as a whole. Not surprisingly governments tend to shy away from doing this explicitly, though we would hope they take these factors into account in their judgemental decision making.

IV FORECASTING FAILURE

An ability to predict failure is a thing of some value to anyone planning to lend or supply goods or services to a firm. The technique for calculating a 'Z-score' for a firm to measure its failure risk was largely developed in the US by Altman. Z-scores are now widely available for UK firms, and in this section we review their use.

Traditionally financial analysts studied the accounts of firms whose credit worthiness they were trying to assess. They concentrated particularly on measures of solvency, such as the *current ratio* which is the ratio of the firm's current assets to its current liabilities, and on measures of financial strength such as 'gearing', and compared these with industry norms or rules of thumb. The problem with this sort of approach is that in a world of complex industrial types it may be hard to define a 'norm'. Moreover ratios share the limitations of the accounting data from which they are prepared. In particular, the data is historic, it describes what has already happened, whereas the analyst actually wants to know what is going to happen, and as far in advance as possible.

The approach of researchers into failure prediction has been to use statistical analysis to make the best use possible of historical data. Various approaches have been used but most recent work uses a technique called *multiple discriminant analysis* (MDA). The MDA approach works by finding the model, in this case a function containing financial ratios, that best discriminates between certain pre-specified groups of objects, in this case the set of failed and the set of non-failed firms.

Note that in this section we are using the word 'failure' rather than 'liquidation'. As we saw, liquidation is a legal event that *usually* follows the economic event of insolvency. But since it is at least possible that the capital market is inefficient with respect to liquidation we could get a situation where, out of two identical insolvent firms, one was liquidated and one survived – the difference being institutional or 'human' factors reflecting such things as the optimism of the creditors and the status of the firm. Because of the potential difficulty of modelling these non-economic factors researchers have restricted themselves to predicting 'failure', rather than liquidation.

We will look at two studies by Altman.

4 Though in this economy there will probably be increased demand for steel too which might raise the opportunity cost of closing the steelworks.

Altman

Altman (1968) took thirty-three US manufacturers that filed for bankruptcy between 1946 and 1965. He paired each of these with a firm of similar *size* and *industry* that did not go bankrupt. Twenty-two ratios falling into five categories – liquidity, profitability, leverage, solvency, and activity ratios – were calculated, chosen on the basis of their apparent relevance and popularity with users. MDA was used to find the five ratios, one from each category, X_1–X_5, and the linear weighting of those ratios, that yielded the best discriminant statistic, Z. The process is essentially an 'iterative search' by computer; repeated combinations of variables are tried until one that 'works best' emerges. Unlike economic model building, there is no theoretical basis to the choice of variables and weights and for this reason the MDA approach to failure prediction has been called 'brute empiricism'.[5]

Altman found the following model worked best:

	Weight	*Ratio*		*Contribution to discrimination*
Z =	.012 .	working capital to total assets	X_1	3.29
+	.014 .	retained earnings to total assets	X_2	6.04
+	.033 .	earnings before interest and taxes to total assets	X_3	9.89
+	.006 .	market value of equity to book value of total debt	X_4	7.42
+	.010 .	sales to total assets	X_5	8.41

Though the performance of the variables in a discriminant function is interdependent, the relative contribution of the variables in MDA can be measured by 'scaled-vectors'[6] and we can see that on this basis X_3, EBIT/total assets, is the main contributor.

There are two types of possible error in failure prediction. We call forecasting as non-failed a firm that subsequently fails a 'type-I error' and forecasting as a failure a firm that does not fail a 'type-II error'. Will the user of Z-scores be indifferent between these two types of error? This is unlikely. Suppose he is a bank or finance house receiving loan applicants. The cost to him of a type-II error, if it leads him to reject a loan applicant who subsequently does not go bankrupt, is the loss of profit on the loan, and if he is lending under capital rationing this cost may approximate zero. Type-I errors are likely to have a much higher cost. Accepting a client who subsequently fails can mean interest and all or part of the principal may be jeopardised. Moreover, considerable administrative costs will be incurred in the process. A 1977 study (see below) estimated the cost of a type-I error at thirty-five times the cost of a type-II.

Altman found that using data for one year prior to bankruptcy on the sample of firms on which the model was estimated, the model accurately classified 95% overall, but within this there were 6% of type-I errors, and 3% of type-II. Using data two years prior to bankruptcy, overall 83% were classified accurately within which there were 28% type-I errors and 6% type-II errors. The success rate of the model fell off dramatically beyond two years' prediction, overall accuracy for three years prior data was 48%, four years – 29%, 5 years – 36%.

In 1977 Altman, Haldeman and Naraianan produced an improved model for failure predictions. Their 1977 sample of failures had a larger average size and included some

5 See Foster (1986), Chapter 14 for this, and for an excellent summary and critique of approaches to failure prediction.

6 Calculated by multiplying corresponding elements by the square roots of the diagonal elements of the variance-covariance matrix.

non-bankrupt failures – firms whom the government had had to support, had been forced to merge, or had been taken over by the banks. They used an augmented list of variables and a refined discriminant technique. This time the best predictor was a seven-variable model comprising the following variables: return on assets, stability of earnings, interest cover, cumulative profitability, liquidity (= current ratio), equity/total capital, size (= total assets). The relative performance of the 1977 and 1968 models is shown in Table V.

Table V Classification accuracy of the 1968 and 1977 models compared

Year prior to bankruptcy	*1977 model*		*1968 model*	
	Bankrupt	*Non-bankrupt*	*Bankrupt*	*Non-bankrupt*
1	96.2	89.7	93.9	97.0
2	84.9	93.1	71.9	93.9
3	74.5	91.4	48.3	na
4	68.1	89.5	28.6	na
5	69.8	82.1	36.0	na

Source: Altman *et al* (1977)

Noting that the 'bankrupt' column reflects the all important type-I error, the 1977 model is clearly more accurate in later years and in year 1, though it performs less well in type-II errors in year 1.

Using Z-scores

The output of the MDA is a Z-score and Z-scores are now available for larger firms from data sources such as Datastream, and can be calculated for smaller firms by specialist agencies. How should Z-scores be interpreted? The critical threshold score between failure and survival can be any value, but once it is found, it can be deducted from the Z-formula so that zero becomes the cut-off – the model predicts failure for companies with a negative Z-score.

The decision whether to use Z-scores in credit and loan analysis depends, as always, on the relative costs and benefits. The benefits can be hard to know. We know that we are likely to be particularly interested in type-I errors. It will only be worth using Z-scores if they yield less type-I errors than the credit or loan analyst would on his own, using traditional ratio analysis, but supplemented by experience and intuition. The benefit would be the number of errors avoided times the cost of an error. We have little information on the performance of Z-scores relative to the performance of the skilled analyst. However, since Z-scores are now relatively cheaply available for larger firms, the çost of incorporating them in the credit and loan analysis may be small.

V SUMMARY

Disinvestment and failure is a less glamorous topic than investment and growth but it is important nonetheless. We need to know just when a firm should abandon a project, and when the whole firm should be liquidated. In this chapter we reviewed the theory of disinvestment, and considered whether the process seems efficient in practice. But we have little hard evidence on whether the right firms are failing. One area in which researchers have made a contribution, however, is in developing statistical models for predicting failure.

REFERENCES AND BIBLIOGRAPHY

Altman, E I — 'Financial Ratios, Discriminant Analysis and the Prediction of Corporate Bankruptcy', Journal of Finance, Sept 1968, pp 589–609.

Altman, E I — *Corporate Financial Distress: A Complete Guide to Predicting, Avoiding and Dealing With Bankruptcy* (1983) John Wiley and Sons, New York.

Altman, E I, Haldeman, R G, and Naraianan, P — 'Zeta Analysis: A New Model to Identify Bankruptcy Risk of Corporations', Journal of Banking and Finance, 1977, pp 29–54.

Farrar, J H, Furey, N, Hanningan, B, and Wylie, O P — *Farrar's Company Law* (3rd edn, 1991) Butterworths.

Foster, G — *Financial Statement Analysis* (1986) Prentice-Hall, Englewood-Cliffs, New Jersey.

Frydman, H, Altman, E I, and Kao, D — 'Introducing Recursive Partitioning for Financial Classifications: The Case of Financial Distress', Journal of Finance, March 1985, pp 269–291.

Hamer, M — 'Failure Prediction: Sensitivity of Classification Accuracy to Alternative Statistical Methods and Variable Sets', Journal of Accounting and Public Policy, 1983, pp 289–307.

Ohlson, J A — 'Financial Ratios and the Probabilistic Prediction of Bankruptcy', Journal of Accounting Research, Spring 1980.

Pearce, D W, and Nash, C A — *The Social Appraisal of Projects* (1981) Macmillan, London.

Waite, M — 'The Corporate Bankruptcy Decision', Journal of Economic Perspectives 3, Spring 1989, pp 129–152.

Warner, J B — 'Bankruptcy Costs: Some Evidence', Journal of Finance, 1977, pp 337–348.

Wruck, K — 'What Really Went Wrong at Revco', Journal of Applied Corporate Finance, Summer 1991, pp 79–92.

QUESTIONS

1 Define a decision-rule for liquidating projects and whole firms. Are there barriers to the efficient liquidation of projects and firms in practice?

2 In a perfect capital market there are no costs to bankruptcy. In reality, bankruptcy is an outcome everyone seeks to avoid. What are the costs?

3 You have been asked by a bank how they can most efficiently predict which of their customers are bad credit risks. Explain how this might be done.

4 You are the chairman of Lameduck Ltd, a Midlands manufacturing company. Lameduck's most recent P & L was as follows:

		(£m)
Sales – Home		10
– Overseas		5
		15
Expenses –		
Materials	6	
Labour	6	
Depreciation	3	
Interest	1	
Other	3	
		(19)
LOSS		(4)

Lameduck's creditors are threatening liquidation. You decide to write to the government to ask for a subsidy to cover your losses.

(a) List the arguments you might use in your appeal and explain why they should influence a government which was maximising social welfare.

(b) Say how you would reply if you were the government, and what extra information you might require.

CHAPTER 24

Investment in working capital

When we talk about working capital we are particularly concerned with three types of asset: cash, stocks and debtors. Why single out these assets from the general approach to investment decision making we developed in the previous chapters? We do this because of the special features its *short-term* nature gives to working capital. Though firms tend to have a permanent need for balances of cash, stocks and debtors, the internal composition of these balances is constantly changing. On the one hand this reduces the risk associated with working capital investment decisions – they are relatively easy to change. But on the other hand it makes the task of managing working capital a continuous one that consumes a lot of managerial time.

The chapter starts by considering the special characteristics of the working capital investment decision. It then examines in turn how the optimal balance can be determined for stocks (Section II), debtors (Section III), and cash (Section IV).

I THE NATURE OF WORKING CAPITAL

We use the term 'working capital' to describe three types of asset:

1 STOCKS – balances of raw materials, partly completed work ('work-in-progress'), and finished goods.
2 DEBTORS less CREDITORS – amounts owned by customers and to suppliers.
3 CASH and SHORT-TERM INVESTMENTS.

The significance of these assets in the asset structure of firms can be gauged from Table I which shows the aggregate balance sheets of UK companies in 1988 and 1990. UK companies had 50% of their gross assets as current[1] assets.

Table I Summary balance sheets of UK manufacturing companies 1988 and 1990 (£m)

	1988	*1990*	*1990 %*
Net fixed assets	123,824	179,286	49.6
Current assets			
Stock and work-in-progress	55,221	57,570	15.9
Debtors and prepayments	73,511	83,575	23.1
Investments	6,769	8,497	2.3
Cash	25,446	32,875	9.1
GROSS ASSETS	284,771	361,803	100.0

1 Accountants usually define as 'current', any asset or liability which is liable to be liquidated within twelve months.

	1988	1990	1990 %
Current liabilities			
Bank loans and overdrafts	19,102	26,680	7.4
Short-term loans	2,755	4,234	1.2
Creditors and amounts payable	71,063	80,611	22.3
Dividends	4,276	5,212	1.4
Taxation	14,364	13,041	3.6
Sundry	1		
	111,561	129,778	35.9
NET ASSETS	173,210	232,025	

Source: Business Monitor, CSO, 23rd edn
Last figures available for 1990 corresponding to the last edition of MA3

The 'cash cycle' and the need for working capital

To see how working capital fits into the scheme of things we will consider the so-called 'cash cycle' of the firm. The starting point and finishing point of economic activity is *cash*. We are leaving aside the cash the firm raises from outside financing, or spends on acquiring fixed assets, and concentrating on the process of paying for raw materials, converting them into the finished product and finally recovering cash by selling the product. Figure I depicts this process and shows how the firm's need for working capital depends on the balance between its production period and payment lags.

In Figure I a firm acquires £X worth of raw materials at time t_1. These spend some time in raw materials stock, in work-in-progress, and finally in the finished goods stock, before

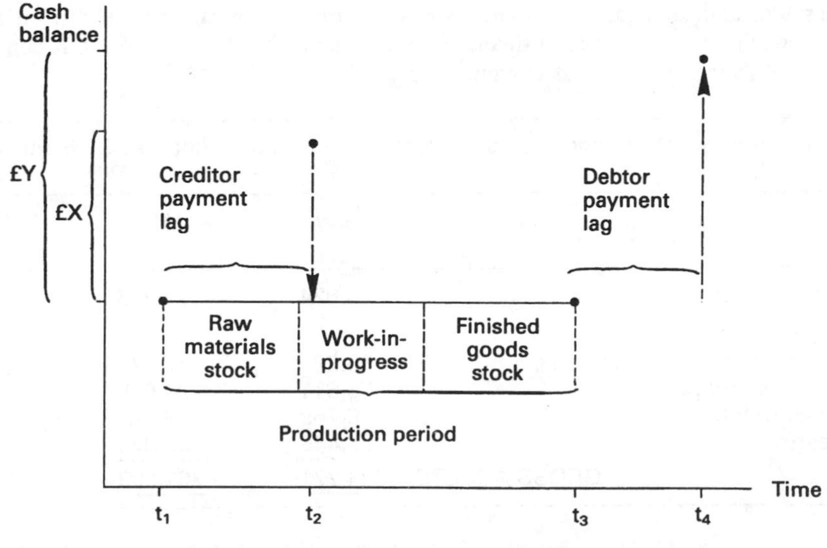

Figure I The cash cycle of the firm

being sold for £Y at t_3. However, there was a lag before the firm had to pay for its inputs, at t_2, but a corresponding lag before its own customers paid, at t_4. So, in this case, the firm had to finance working capital to the tune of £X for the period $t_2 \rightarrow t_3$, and £Y for the period $t_3 \rightarrow t_4$. Hopefully, if the enterprise is profitable, Y is sufficiently larger than X to cover the cost of financing this investment and the other fixed costs of the firm.

Clearly, the working-capital requirement is a function of the payment lags and production period. The task of the firm is to get the working-capital requirement down to its optimum level by efficient management. But this optimum level will vary from firm to firm – the production period depending on technology, the payment lags on market conditions in input and output markets.

To take two extreme examples, think of a supermarket and a whisky distillery. In Figure II we depict an imaginary cash cycle for each of these. The supermarket sales are preponderantly for cash. They have no payment lag on outputs, but they are able to extract two months' credit from their suppliers. Because shelf-life, which is the production period in the case of a supermarket, is on average three days, the supermarket has a negative working-capital requirement – indeed it is able to use its negative net balance on these items to finance other assets. The whisky distillery on the other hand has payment lags on inputs and outputs of two months, but keeps its finished product in stock for ten years.

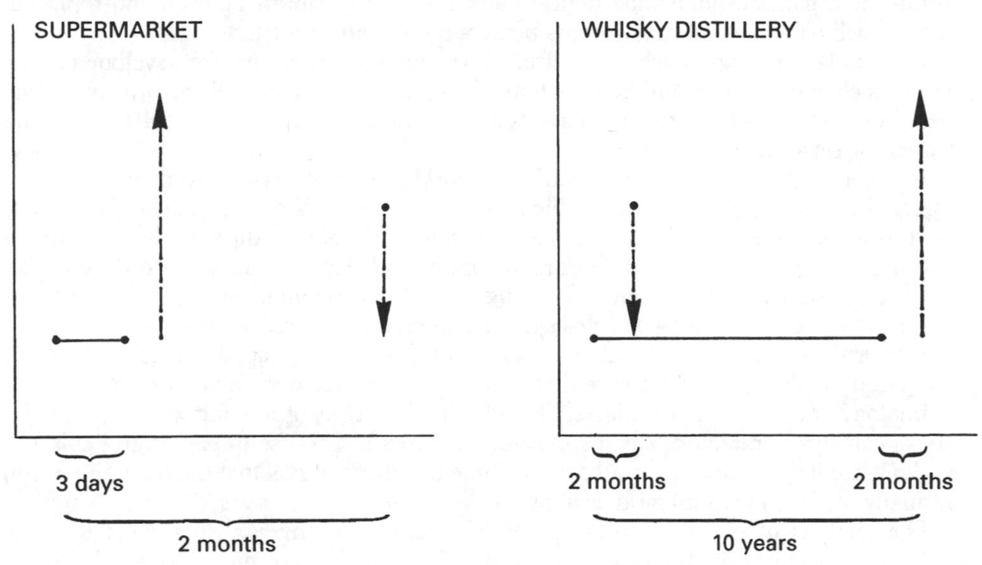

Figure II Some cash cycles

A note on working-capital ratios

When they are examining the firm's working-capital position, analysts commonly use accounting ratios of two sorts; turnover ratios and liquidity ratios. Examples of turnover ratio are *debtor turnover* $= \frac{\text{debtors}}{\text{sales}}$, and *stock turnover* $= \frac{\text{stocks}}{\text{sales}}$. They relate the firm's investment in working capital to sales, and can signal the efficiency with which the firm is investing in debtors and stocks. The two common liquidity ratios are:

$$\textit{current ratio} = \frac{\text{current assets}}{\text{current liabilities}}$$

$$\textit{quick ratio} = \frac{\text{cash and liquid assets}}{\text{current liabilities}}$$

These ratios tend to be used to signal liquidity problems that could lead to insolvency, though as we saw in Chapter 23 the prediction of failure is not so simple.

Making due allowance for the care needed in using accounting data, these ratios can tell us about trends in working capital efficiency and, applied to truly comparable firms, about relative performance. But as we saw the efficient levels of working capital depend very much on the particular firm's lag structure. There are no 'correct' values. The idea sometimes proposed that 2 : 1 is the right current ratio and 1 : 1 the right quick ratio has no foundation.

The cost-benefit analysis of working capital

The characteristic of working capital which distinguishes it from other assets and liabilities of the firm is its short-term nature. The continued need for stocks, debtors and creditors, and cash means that the firm will permanently hold balances of these items, but within these balances individual items of stock will fairly rapidly be used and replaced, debtors will pay cash and new debtors be generated, and so forth.

The fundamental approach to the firm's investment decision that we developed in the previous chapters concerned the valuation of projects. Projects usually involve an investment in working capital and in other assets too – plant, R & D etc. So why pull out working capital for separate attention?

The constantly changing composition of working capital makes the maintenance of optimal balances a continuous task which consumes a lot of labour in many organisations, and this work is often done by the finance department. Because of the short-term nature of working capital the approach to finding the optimum balance looks rather different than for other assets. Like all investment, working-capital investment involves holding balances of assets through time. But working-capital balances are relatively easy to reverse – to run down or run up. The costs of moving to a new level of working capital are generally small compared to the cost of finding that, say, your new factory embodies an outdated technology or is in the wrong place. Though there are risks of holding working capital – stocks can deteriorate and become obsolete, debtors can refuse to pay or go bankrupt, working-capital decisions do not have the same problems of risk that the time dimension normally brings to investment decisions.

The analysis of optimum working-capital balances is an *input* to project decision making, a prior activity. Before a project's cash flows can be determined we need to know what stock levels will be required by the project, and what payment lags will be embodied in the debtors and creditors generated by the project. In this respect the data on working-capital requirements is no different from other technical data the project appraiser will collect from appropriate specialists when she is assembling the cash flows of a project. But though project appraisal is a vital activity, in most firms it consumes much less finance department time than the continuing task of managing the working-capital investment generated by the firm's existing activities. It is this investment task we are looking at in this chapter.[2]

2 The reader who wishes to go into working-capital management in more depth can consult various texts, for example Mehta (1974).

It is useful to distinguish two aspects of working-capital investment, the *investment* decision – the task of calculating the optimal balance of working capital, and the *control* task – the task of ensuring that actual balances are kept at optimal levels. In subsequent sections we review the decision making and control of the three main types of working capital in turn. In each case the optimal investment is found where the marginal cost of holding another unit just equals the marginal benefit.

The *costs* of holding working capital are fairly straightforward to estimate: they are the financing and storage costs. The financing cost is the opportunity cost of the funds invested in working-capital balances. The 'storage' costs include accounting costs, and in the case of stocks, physical storage costs such as warehousing and insurance.

In the main the firm's demand for working capital is a derived demand: stocks, debtors, and cash are all necessary to service the economic activity of the firm. If the firm did not carry balances of these items it would either have to secure the supply of the corresponding service some other way, incurring the cost of the alternative source of supply, or would have to curtail its economic activity, incurring the cost of the loss of contribution from the lost output. The firm would choose the least costly of these alternatives as an alternative to holding working-capital balances. Hence the *benefit* to holding working-capital balances, which is the cost saved, is the lower of these two.

In the case of stocks, running lower stock levels means incurring the increased transactions costs of ordering more frequently. But lower stocks may also bring an attendant risk of running out of the input altogether, in which case the benefit of stock-holding is the avoided loss of contribution from curtailed sales. In the case of cash, lower cash balances will mean the firm must buy and sell securities more frequently. The costs of running out of cash altogether are hard to predict. They range from perhaps a slight loss of face with creditors, and the attendant cost of resorting to quick sources of finance, to the costs of complete liquidation of the firm at the other.

The provision of credit is tantamount to the payment of a subsidy to the customer, so the alternatives to this service are, say, price reductions and discounts. If the firm curtails credit without offering any alternative incentive the cost will be, again, the loss of contribution from curtailed sales.

Sometimes the firm will find holding stocks a worthwhile project in itself. This will occur when, independent of the other activity of the firm, the act of holding yields a return which exceeds the carrying cost. In the case of stocks, this will happen if the firm expects input prices to rise sufficiently to justify early purchase.

Since Keynes[3] it is common to call the balances that firms hold to service their economic activity *transactions balances* for anticipated needs, and *precautionary balances* for balances held to cover unanticipated needs. Balances held to profit from price changes are known as *speculative*.

Though it is analytically useful to distinguish decision making and control tasks, the two are often combined. The process of monitoring levels tends also to be the occasion for judgemental decision making about what they should be. In the case of debtors, the firm may have a standard collection policy, say '30 days net' which might have been calculated in some optimising process or simply be convention. The implementation of this policy

3 Keynes suggested three motives for liquidity preference amongst investors:
'The three divisions of liquidity preference . . . may be defined as depending on (i) the transactions motive, i e the need of cash for the current transaction of personal and business exchanges; (ii) the precautionary motive, i e the desire for security as to a future cash equivalent of a certain proportion of total resources; and (iii) the speculative motive, i e the object of securing profit from knowing better than the market what the future will bring forth.' (Keynes (1936) Chapter 13).

may differ from customer to customer depending on a fairly subtle judgement by the credit controller as to the costs and benefits of extending credit in each case, considering relative market power, the contribution generated by the sale, the value of the customer's goodwill now and in the future, and so forth.

II STOCKS

Stock management is essentially the production manager's concern. The finance manager's interest is simply that the stock balance which results is an investment that needs financing. In other words the finance manager should expect to be handed an optimal stock figure by production. So in this section we will only be looking at the simplest of stock-control models in order to get a view of the factors that influence the optimal investment in stocks. Another motive for looking at a simple stock-management model here is that it provides a useful comparison when we come to analyse the optimisation of cash and debtor balances – tasks which do tend to land on the finance manager's desk.

The transactions balance

Firms hold balances of raw materials, work-in-progress and finished goods, but we will restrict our analysis to raw materials stocks. The first question to ask is – why do firms hold stocks of raw materials at all? After all we can conceive of running a business without stocks of raw materials. You find this behaviour in everyday life – for example in the jobbing builder who comes to work in your house, sizes up the day's work each morning then spends the next two hours touring round buying the necessary pound of nails or half bag of cement. This behaviour may seem rather eccentric but presumably indicates that he puts a lower valuation on the cost of acquiring supplies than he does on the cost of carrying stocks.

We can develop the logic of this trade-off between the costs of *acquiring* and the costs of *holding* in a simple model.

The EOQ model

Assume the following:

1 A firm has a steady and known demand of S units each period for a particular input.
2 The firm consumes the input at a uniform rate.
3 The costs of carrying stocks are a constant amount, C, per unit per period.
4 The costs of ordering more inputs are a fixed amount, O, per order. Orders are delivered instantly.

If the firm replenishes its stocks periodically by placing an order for Q units when stocks are exhausted, its stock-holding through time will follow the 'sawtooth' pattern in Figure III.

Clearly the average balance is $\frac{Q}{2}$, so we can find the optimal balance in terms of the reorder quantity Q. Hence this model is sometimes known as the *economic order quantity*, 'EOQ', model.

The total stock-carrying cost for this firm per period is $\frac{CQ}{2}$, the average stock times the cost per unit. The total ordering costs are $\frac{OS}{Q}$, the cost per order, O, times the number of orders in the period, $\frac{S}{Q}$. So we can define total period stock costs, T, as:

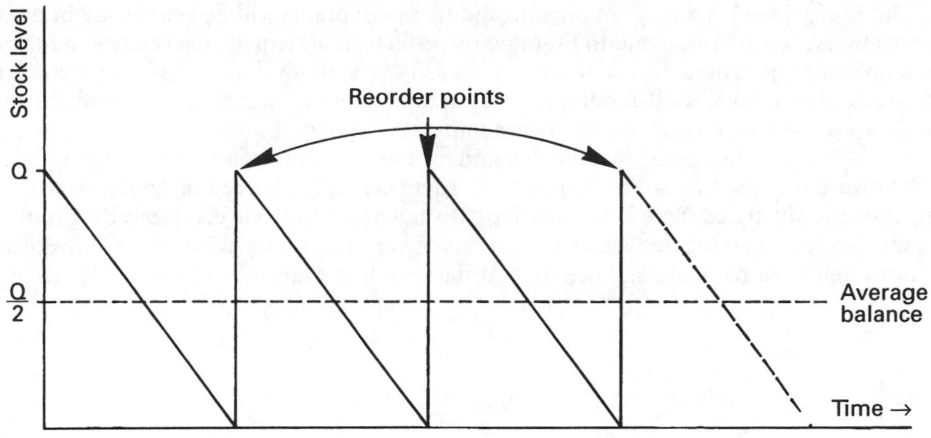

Figure III The pattern of stock usage

$$T = \frac{CQ}{2} + \frac{OS}{Q}$$

From this the order quantity, Q, which minimises stock costs, T, emerges[4] as:

$$Q = \sqrt{\frac{2S0}{C}}$$

To show how we might use this formula, consider a firm which uses 10,000 electric motors per annum in making washing machines. The motors cost £20 each. The accounting costs associated with placing an order with the supplier come to £40 per order. The carrying costs of holding stocks of motors have several components. Space is no problem, but insurance is 2% of the value of stocks, and the firm's cost of capital is 10%.

Hence S = 100,000
O = 40
C = 12%

$$Q = \sqrt{\frac{2 \times 100{,}000 \times 40}{.12}} = 8{,}165$$

So the optimal balance of stock, $\frac{Q}{2} = 4083$ units.

4 PROOF: Differentiating T with respect to Q and setting to zero,

$$\frac{\delta T}{\delta Q} = \frac{C}{2} - \frac{OS}{Q^2} = 0$$

rearranging, $Q^2 = \frac{2SO}{C}$, $Q = \sqrt{\frac{2SO}{C}}$

Testing for a minimum:

$\frac{\delta^2 T}{\delta\delta Q^2} = +\frac{2OS}{Q^3}$, which is +ve for +ve O, S, Q.

The EOQ model is a very simple one and its assumptions will be unrealistic in many applications. We are not going to examine the effects of systematically relaxing all these assumptions. Operations research has gone a long way in developing optimising models for stock which work well in complex real applications. However, it is useful for our purposes to develop one or two of the assumptions further.

The EOQ model assumed that the demand for the input was steady and known and that orders were delivered instantly. In practice orders are not delivered instantly, so we will assume in addition that there is a known lag between order and delivery. Now, the problem is merely one of working out what stock level is observed for the period of the delivery lag prior to being out of stock, and ordering at that level, as Figure IV shows.

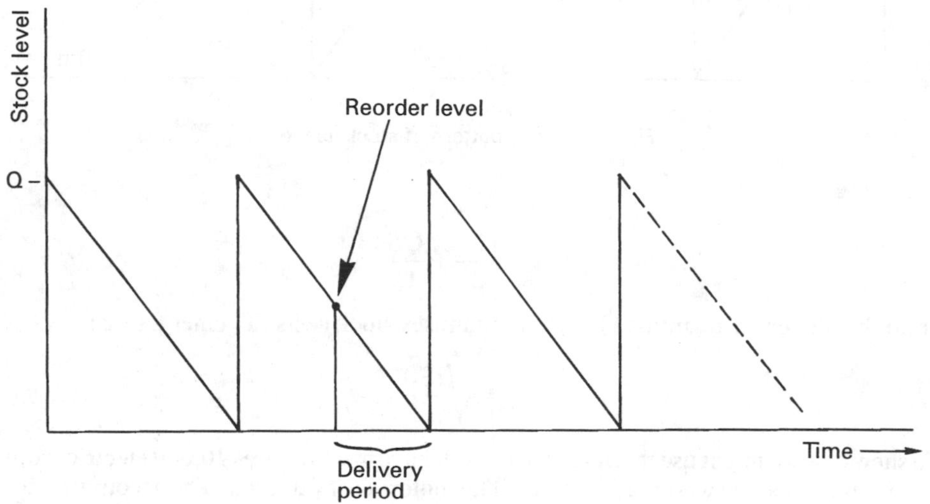

Figure IV Reorder policy in a certain world

Storemen, shopkeepers and the like often put a marker on appropriate numbers of items from the bottom of the bin, or from the back of the shelf, to signal reorder. The reorder slip in a cheque book serves the same purpose.

The precautionary balance

We are still assuming that the moment before the economic order quantity is delivered the firm entirely exhausts its previous stock. But in practice, the firm is likely to hold a precautionary balance as well.

The firm may hold a precautionary balance of stock if it is uncertain about future demand and supply conditions – it may want to keep some raw material in reserve in case of an unexpected order, and it may be uncertain about supply of the raw material itself and seek to cover unexpected hold-ups in supply. Neither of these problems would arise if there was instantaneous delivery so that inputs could be got as and when they were needed.

Suppose the smooth consumption and replenishment pattern of Figure IV represented the firm's expectation, but that it also holds a safety stock, X, against contingencies. Figure V depicts this, and also shows two unexpected events which would otherwise have led the firm to be out of stock. At A the supplier delivered his usual quantity, Q, but a week late. At

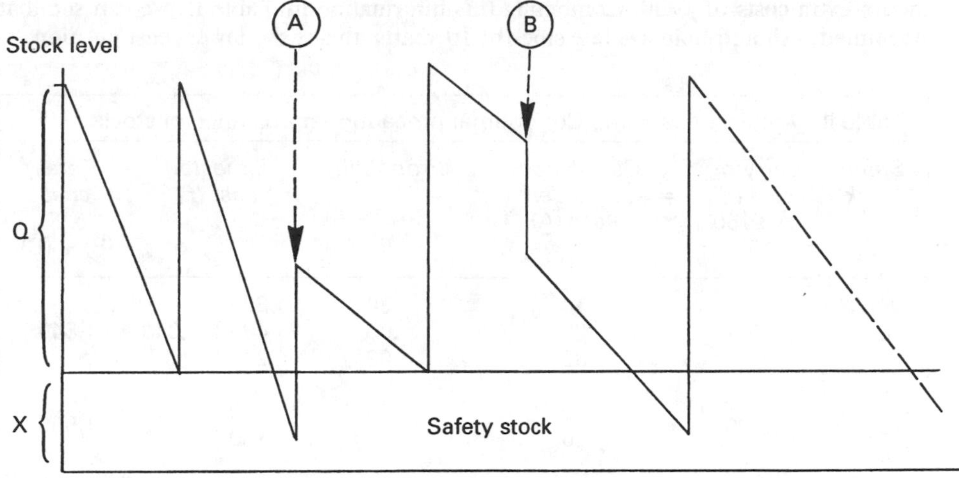

Figure V The need for safety stocks

B an unexpected demand for the input depleted stocks and they had to be replenished in the next order.

In Figure V the safety stock comfortably accommodates these contingencies, but safety stocks are expensive to hold and the optimal safety stock will be one which still permits the firm to go out of stock on occasion. How is the optimal safety stock determined? The firm must balance the carrying cost with the benefits of holding a safety stock, which are avoided costs of going out of stock. So the firm should increase its safety stock until at the margin the carrying costs of another unit of stock equal the expected 'stock-out' costs avoided. Alternatively we can say: The optimal safety stock minimises the sum of safety stock carrying costs and expected out-of-stock costs.

Archimedes Pump Co

In Table II we show some of the relevant data for calculating the optimal precautionary balance of screw shafts the Archimedes Pump Co should keep. For each level of safety stock under review we calculate the carrying cost and the expected out-of-stock cost. The carrying cost is the firm's cost of capital, 10%, plus 2% which is the estimated storage and insurance cost, times the value of the extra stock. Screw shafts cost £1,000 each so the carrying cost is £1,000 × 12% = £120 per unit per annum. The costs of being out of stock are by definition uncertain. They consist of the combined probabilities of being out of stock by various amounts times the costs associated with those levels of 'stock out'. Archimedes estimates that without any safety stock at all it will run out of stock with the following frequencies:

Extent of stock out (units)	*Probability of occurrence*
10	.30
20	.05
30	.02

These are the occasions when demand for a screw shaft will exceed the transactions balance the firm holds. Each time Archimedes finds itself short of a shaft it estimates it incurs extra costs of £400. Combining this information in Table II, we can see that Archimedes should hold a safety stock of 10 shafts: this is the lowest cost position.

Table II Archimedes Pump Co: optimal precautionary balance of stock

Safety stock Ⓐ	*Carrying cost (£)* @ £150 Ⓑ	*Out of stock = excess demand* less Ⓐ	*Probability*	*Expected cost (£)* Ⓒ		*Total cost* Ⓑ + Ⓒ
		10	.30	1,200		
0	0	20	.05	400	1,840	1,840
		30	.02	240		
10	1,200	10	.05	200	360	1,560
		20	.02	160		
20	2,400	10	.02	80		2,480
30	3,600	0	0	0		3,600

In practice the decision as to what size of precautionary balance to hold will often be made judgementally. The calculation of the carrying costs should be relatively straightforward, but the 'out-of-stock' costs may be more difficult to assess. The likelihood of going out of stock depends on the variability of demand for the output, and the reliability of the input supplier and the competitive structure of the input market which will determine the possibilities for alternative suppliers. Similarly the cost of going out of stock depends on the loss associated with non-production. This may be slight if the firm faces easy delivery dates on the job and can reschedule other jobs to use the idle resources in the interim. But if delivery dates are tight and the output market is competitive the customer may be lost permanently, so the cost will be contribution from present and future lost sales.

The speculative balance

In some cases the firm will find it worthwhile to hold speculative balances of stocks in order to take advantage of expected price increases. If prices are expected to rise it will be worthwhile buying stocks early so long as the expected rise in input prices is higher than the cost of holding the additional stock.

At first glance we might expect this to occur approximately half of the time. After all, the major component in holding costs is the cost of capital, and the major component of nominal interest rates is the expected general inflation rate – yet this rate is a composite of specific rates which will lie equally above and below the average. In reality though the odds are more heavily loaded against speculative balances. In general we expect interest rates to contain a positive real component over and above the expected general rise in prices, and on top of that the firm will have to pay a positive risk-premium to finance a project such as speculative investment in stocks. Further, the cost of carrying stocks contains items such as storage and insurance. Figure VI is a pictorial representation of all this. In it we assume (arbitrarily) that the specific inflation rates for commodities in the economy are normally distributed. We can see that only if the expected inflation rate on a commodity is in the shaded area, A, will it be worthwhile holding speculative balances of stock.

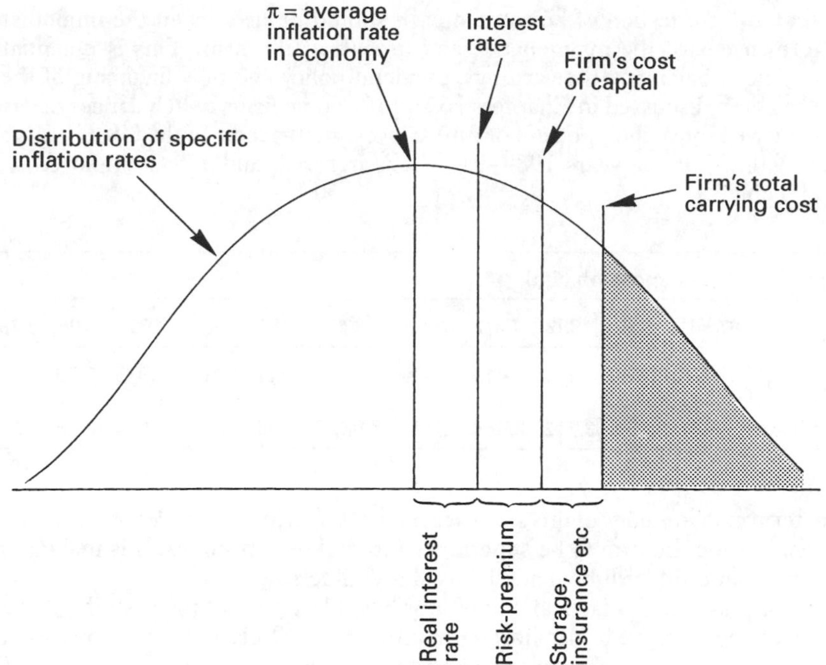

Figure VI The cost-benefit of speculative balances

Moreover, in an efficient market the market process will work to eliminate the potential for speculative gains. If the market shares the firm's expectations about inflation the current price of the input will be bid up until no potential exists for speculative gains – that is, until no firm has a total carrying cost less than the expected rate of future inflation. In such a world there will only be speculative behaviour when a firm feels it can 'outguess' the market.

We have talked about advance purchase as speculative behaviour. But there is no reason why the firm should restrict its speculative purchases to its production needs or indeed to the commodities it happens to use. This brings us into the area of 'futures' trading. In practice firms do engage in futures trading though usually restricted to commodities they know well.

III CASH AND SHORT-TERM INVESTMENTS

Firms need to have cash available to meet their liabilities – payments to suppliers, wages, taxation etc – when they fall due and to pay for the replacement and expansion of the assets of the firm. Some of these payments will be anticipated and some unanticipated. Receipts of cash – from trading, from selling assets, from raising new finance – will be in part unpredictable too. The firm will want to hold transactions balances and precautionary balances of cash. However, the key feature of cash as a working capital item is the existence of a whole range of ways of storing cash as *short-term investments*, which offer a positive return and can be converted into cash with varying degrees of speed. So there are two levels to the cash management problem.

The first is the question of how much cash should be held given the immediate and longer term needs of the maintenance and growth of the firm. This is essentially the strategic issue of balancing the earnings, dividend policy and new financing of the firm, and this has been discussed in Chapters 16 and 17. Some firms hold balances of cash that appear to be well above their present or future investment needs. In the UK GEC is a good example of this. For the years 1984–94 GEC's net cash and assets employed were as shown in Table III.

Table III GEC's cash position (£m)

	1994	*1993*	*1992*	*1991*	*1990*	*1989*	*1988*	*1987*	*1986*	*1985*	*1984*
Net cash	1,352	1,223	811	411	440	1,035	1,241	1,562	1,335	1,228	1,350
Assets employed	3,328	3,101	2,712	2,484	2,328	2,987	2,715	2,895	2,614	2,389	2,409

Long-term cash holdings of this size suggest that GEC judges the returns to short-term investment outside the firm to be superior to internal opportunities. It is making investments that could quite well be made by its shareholders.

The second issue is the tactical one of how best to dispose of the cash that *is* retained inside the firm between cash and short-term investments. This is the question we consider in this section. As a preliminary we will consider how the firm can ensure it is collecting its cash as quickly as possible, how inflows and outflows of cash can be forecast, and examine in more detail the short-term investment alternatives that are available to the firm.

Reducing slack in the system

Before the firm considers how best to deploy its cash it should ensure it is collecting cash as effectively as possible. Of course, all the firm's activities are directed towards the generation of cash, but we are thinking particularly of the final stage in the process, between the issue of a cheque by the debtor and its crediting to the firm's bank account. By this stage all the problems of producing and supplying a satisfactory product and getting the customer to pay for it are over, and it is in the firm's interests to get hold of the cash as quickly as possible. There are three stages in the process:

1 the cheque is in the post
2 the cheque is received but waiting to be paid into the bank
3 the bank is 'clearing' the cheque.

2 and 3 are commonly known as the 'float' stage. There is not much the firm can do about the time it takes banks to clear cheques – this is an institutional fact about banks. But the firm may be able to speed the other two stages. In the US many firms attack 1 and 2 by operating a *lock-box* system. In a lock-box system customers mail cheques to a regional collection box in a bank branch. The box is opened each day by the bank and the account credited. This way postal delays are reduced by regional mailing, and 'paying in' delays are eliminated because the cheques are already in the bank. In the UK though, perhaps because of the smaller distances involved, lock-boxes do not seem to have become popular.

The most useful thing a firm can do is to tighten up stage 2 of the process, and make sure that cash is paid into the bank as soon as possible. The firm should consider daily banking, and if the receipt of cash is decentralised – if cash is collected by local offices or salesmen for example – arrangements should be made for cash to be paid in to local banks each day. There are costs associated with increasing the frequency of banking, largely the costs of clerical time, and the firm should calculate if the interest saving merits these costs. The best solution is to encourage customers to pay direct into your bank by making a bank giro transfer, thus avoiding stages 1 and 2 entirely. This might appeal to customers since it is a much more economical method of payment in terms of clerical effort if there is some volume of transactions, though the increased speed of clearance brings an interest cost to the customer.

In terms of strict logical symmetry we should be recommending the firm to do all it can to *increase* the slack on the payments side just as it seeks to reduce it for receipts. By increasing its creditors' float it will save interest charges. Of course, firms can stoop to all sorts of chicanery, particularly when they are in financial difficulties, to slow down payments to creditors. But as a general rule, though firms will take as much credit as they can from creditors, once they have decided to pay they do so promptly.

A necessary preliminary to cash management is a careful forecast of receipts and payments of cash. The more confident the firm can be about future cash balances the less it will need to invest in costly precautionary balances. Interest rates tend to be positively associated with the 'term' of the investment so the further ahead the firm can anticipate its cash balance the more cash it can store in higher yielding investments.

The cash forecast is a task for the accountant. Some accounting numbers, notably profits, are remarkably difficult to forecast and research has shown that the time series properties of profit approximates a 'random walk'. This problem may be less severe in cash forecasting. Cash forecasts are usually relatively short-term and hence are more likely to embody cash flows about which the firm can be fairly confidence and which may reflect contractual commitments that already exist or are expected to be made fairly soon. How far ahead should cash be forecast? Management will need to judge the trade-off between the usefulness and the increasing unreliability of longer forecasts.

Ways of storing cash

Instead of holding cash in a current account offering zero return, there is a variety of alternative investments available to the firm offering different returns and different degrees of *liquidity*. By liquidity we refer to the speed with which an asset can be converted into cash, and our general expectation is that the more illiquid an investment the higher its return. It is important to note that the liquidity of a security is not the same as its 'term'. So long as a market exists for a security, it represents a highly liquid investment whatever its term. Hence 'Treasury 13¼%, 1997' bonds can be sold tomorrow on the Stock Exchange and cash received at the end of the account a few days later. However, marketability also introduces uncertainty into the outcome. If you hold a bond until redemption the cash you will receive is known with certainty from the outset but the intermediate market price of the bond will fluctuate as interest rates change. If the short-term investment is a company share, which is effectively an irredeemable investment, the firm can have no certainty as to the cash that will be realised when it is sold. These are some of the common short-term investments for firms:

Bank deposits

A popular destination for spare cash is a deposit account at a bank. This can be the firm's own clearing bank which offers the advantage of quick and economical transfer of funds from and to current account, or some other banking institution such as a merchant bank, overseas bank, acceptance or finance house. All of these will take short-term deposits from firms, though we can expect the rate they pay to be slightly less than on less liquid investments.

Certificates of deposit

Certificates of deposit are written acknowledgements of deposits issued by banks. They are associated with longer-term deposits which tend to be between three months and five years, but they offer an accordingly higher return, and are negotiable.

Public sector securities

Public sector securities are government or local authority bonds. Local authority bonds tend to have a term of up to five years, government bonds are available in any term up to irredeemable. More relevant than their term, though, is their marketability. Government bonds are saleable on the stock market, but the market for local authority bonds may be much smaller.

Company securities

Company securities are shares and debentures in other companies. If these securities are quoted there will be a ready market for them.

Model-building approaches to cash management

The EOQ model

Suppose (1) a firm's consumption of cash follows the 'sawtooth' pattern, ie cash is consumed at a constant rate and is replenished occasionally by the injection of a fixed amount of cash from deposit or the sale of securities, (2) we can calculate a percentage 'carrying cost' per period for cash, and (3) there is a fixed cost of replenishing cash. In this case we can use the EOQ stock-control model to find the optimum balance.

If, S = total requirement for cash in the period
O = fixed transactions cost associated with liquidating deposits or selling securities to raise cash
C = holding cost of cash, ie the interest foregone on deposits or marketable securities
Q = optimal quantity of cash to raise at a time
then we know that

$$Q = \sqrt{\frac{2SO}{C}}$$

If a firm expects to disburse £800,000 of cash in the year, sales of securities cost £50 to effect, and the return on securities is 15%, then

S = 800,000
O = 50
r = .15

$$Q = \sqrt{\frac{2 \times 50 \times 800{,}000}{.15}} \simeq £23{,}100$$

Hence the firm should sell securities in lots of £23,100. This implies an average cash balance of $\frac{£23{,}100}{2}$ = £11,550, and suggests that cash will be replenished

$$\frac{800{,}000}{23{,}100} = 35 \text{ times per year.}$$

In reality the cost of replenishing cash has a fixed component – the managerial effort involved and any fixed charge by the bank or broker – but if securities are sold there will also be a variable cost of brokerage which will be a decreasing proportion of the quantity transferred. But the real limitation of the EOQ model is its assumption of certainty and constancy in future cash flows. The EOQ model best describes a situation like the one facing the student who pays his grant into the building society at the beginning of the term, then has to decide how often to go and draw it to pay his weekly rent, food and spending money. His carrying cost is the interest he loses, and he can minimise this by increasing the frequency of his trips to the building society. But the transactions cost for him is the effort of going there.

The Miller-Orr model

Miller and Orr[5] developed a cash management model for use in the situation where the firm's inflows and outflows of cash are unpredictable. They derive a formula to calculate upper and lower 'control limits' for cash. These limits indicate the optimal cash levels at which to buy and sell securities, to reduce and replenish cash respectively. Figure VII shows the operation of control limits.

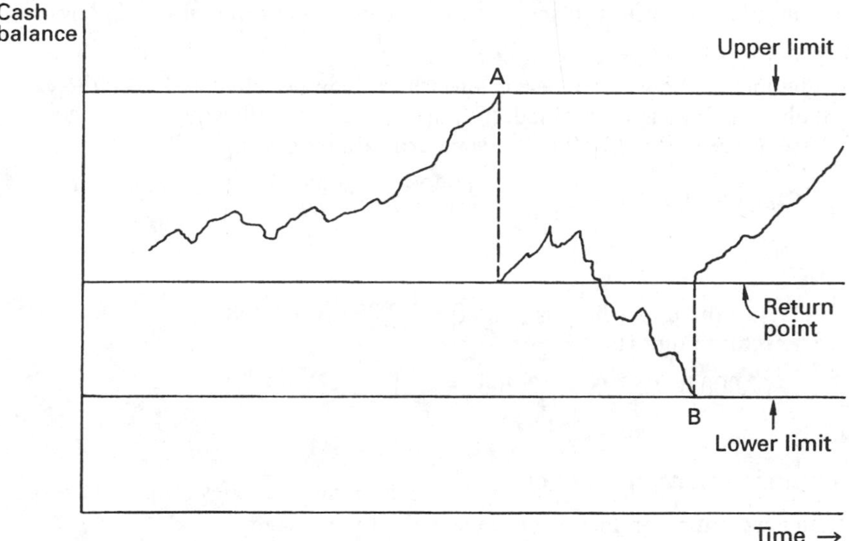

Figure VII Operation of control limits

A sustained inflow of cash brings the firm to A (see Figure VII), which is the level of cash at which it is appropriate to buy securities and reduce the cash balance. At B, on the other hand, the firm sells securities to replenish cash.

5 The initial model is presented in Miller and Orr (1966). Miller and Orr (1968) extend the model to handle long-term and short-term securities.

To implement the Miller-Orr model in practice we take the following steps:

1 Choose the lower limit, which is the precautionary balance – the minimum cash balance the firm can accept.
2 Find the upper limit. Miller and Orr provide a formula for the interval between the limits:

$$\text{interval} = 3\left(\tfrac{3}{4}\,\frac{\text{transaction cost} \times \text{variance of daily cash flows}}{\text{interest rate per day}}\right)^{1/3}$$

The interval is an increasing function of the transactions cost, and a decreasing function of the interest rate. The wider the interval the less frequent are security transactions and the higher the average balance of cash. Hence, the Miller-Orr model is consistent with the EOQ model in this respect. However, Miller and Orr also show that the interval is an increasing function of the variance of the cash flows of the firm, which implicitly measures the likelihood of cash flows restoring themselves without the need for costly security transactions.
3 Find the 'return point' which is one-third the way up from the lower limit:

$$\text{Return point} = \text{lower limit} + \frac{\text{interval}}{3}$$

Thomas & Co

Thomas & Co can buy or sell securities at a fixed cost of £30, and gets a daily return of .05% on those securities. It sets out to estimate its control limits as follows:

1 The firm chooses a lower limit of £2,000.
2 The interval between upper or lower limits can be calculated once the variance of daily cash flows is ascertained. A sample of daily cash flows is analysed and found to have a variance of £1,000,000 (standard deviation of £1,000).

$$\text{So interval} = 3\left(\tfrac{3}{4}\,\frac{30 \times 1{,}000{,}000}{.05}\right)^{1/3}$$

$$= £2{,}298$$

Hence the upper limit is £2,000 + £2,298 = £4,298
3 The return point is:

$$£2{,}000 + \frac{£2{,}298}{3} = £2{,}766.$$

Cash management in practice

In practice we can recommend certain steps to the manager:

1 Eliminate any slack or inefficiency in the collections system. In other words reduce the 'float' to a minimum.
2 Ensure the accounting section is producing regular cash forecasts and assess their reliability by comparing past forecasts to outcome.
3 Generate a 'list' of the alternative short-term investments that are available to the firm, in terms of return and liquidity.
4 Minimise the 'precautionary' balance. Other things being equal the more confidence you have in your cash forecast, the lower the precautionary balance you need, and similarly a store of cash in short-term investments that are highly liquid will reduce the importance of holding idle cash.

5 Make full use of the deposit account at the bank. In both the EOQ and the Miller-Orr models the average balance is an increasing function of transactions costs. The transactions costs associated with transferring from and to deposit accounts are usually negligible and both models correctly predict that in this case the rational firm will run very small transactions balances. In practice many firms respond in just this way – investing their surplus each evening on 'overnight' deposit. By doing this the firm can retain a high level of liquidity at a positive return, and the task of cash management is then to seek securities that offer a higher return and trade this off against the sacrifice of liquidity.

We have talked so far as though firms all have positive cash balances. In reality a great many firms run on overdraft either through choice or necessity, and others, often multidivisional firms, run overdrafts in some divisions and surpluses in others. If the bank is prepared to provide overdraft finance it becomes a matter of relative costs whether the firm decides to hold a cash balance which is always positive, always negative or somewhere in between. The point to note is that even with negative cash balances much of what we have said about cash management carries through. Now, the firm's transactions and precautionary balances measure the leeway it will seek to keep above its overdraft limit.

IV DEBTORS AND CREDITORS

Debtor balances are amounts owed by customers who have received delivery but have yet to pay. Whether or not sales are made on credit depends on the nature of the business – for example retail stores may sell predominantly for cash, whereas a manufacturer of intermediate goods such as vehicle components might have no cash sales. In some businesses the product is largely paid for before it is delivered: in industries such as construction the product is specially ordered and takes some time to manufacture. In this case the customer defrays some of the manufacturer's stock-carrying cost by making payments on-account.

Similarly the period of credit varies from one trade to another – the period of credit allowed tends to be conventional and an individual firm's ability to offer terms other than the ones that are customary in the trade is dependent on the structure of the market in which it is selling.

The debtor balance is determined by the number of customers the firm allows credit to, and the length of credit it allows. In principle the credit decision is the same as any other working-capital decision: the firm should extend credit just so far as the marginal benefit exceeds the marginal cost.

The cost of extending credit has two components. There is a carrying cost – the cost of capital plus the administrative costs associated with credit decision making and with controlling outstanding debtors. There is also a cost associated with the risk of default – a certain proportion of debtors will never pay, and will become 'bad debts'. The benefit of extending credit – the cost of not extending it – is the additional contribution that results from increased sales.

The benefits of credit

Firms offer longer credit to customers in the hope of attracting more business. The benefit is the contribution from that increased turnover. But forecasting the outcome of a given change in credit policy is no easy matter since it is rather hard to know how existing and potential customers will react. This very much depends on the structure of the market in which the firm is selling.

Though it often falls the lot of the finance section to make the credit decision, credit is as much a marketing decision and should be taken in full consultation with the marketing department. If the product is highly differentiated and competition is weak the firm can offer less credit than when the market is highly competitive. On the other hand if the market is competitive any credit concession will fairly quickly be matched by competitors, and the benefit annulled. The ability of the firm to enforce the credit policy it has chosen on its customers depends very much on the same factors – it will depend on relative market power.

Much the same calculus applies to the decision on when to pay suppliers. Hence we tend to find that the larger manufacturer extracts lengthy credit from its suppliers, particularly those which depend on it for a significant proportion of their sales, yet will be 'firm' with its own customers particularly smaller ones.

The individual consumer is in the same position. If we are unfortunate enough to get a tax demand and the telephone bill on the same day, there is a good chance we will pay the telephone first. Both suppliers are monopolists in their market, but the telephone company can and will curtail supplies very quickly if the bill is not paid, while the Inland Revenue is not in the same position and must resort to enforcing its claim through the courts, which is a lengthy and expensive remedy.

Davis and Yeomans (1974) studied the effects of firm size on credit terms. They found that when money was 'tight' in the economy and interest rates rose, there was a shift in the balance of credit terms with larger firms exacting more credit from smaller firms. This is consistent with our analysis. As the cost of borrowing rises, all firms will seek to reduce their debtor balances and increase their credit balances, other things being equal. But the costs of doing this are likely to be higher for the small firm, their relatively weaker market power means that they are more likely to lose customers and suppliers than the larger firm. In short, the effects of a credit policy change depend on market conditions and the responses of competitors. A major drawback of credit policy as an instrument for increasing sales is that the more generous credit terms may have to be extended to existing customers, incurring extra costs for no gain.

Alternative marketing strategies

The credit period is an aspect of price since, if the customer has a positive cost of capital, extending her credit is tantamount to giving her a price discount. The overall package of attributes a product possesses which determine its market appeal is often called the 'marketing mix'. The marketing mix includes aspects of the product such as its price, quality, packaging, advertising, distribution system and so forth. Therefore, a change in credit policy should only be made if it is more profitable than any of the alternative marketing policies the firm could adopt – increased advertising, a change in the product or the package, a price reduction etc.

One alternative which is sometimes offered to customers instead of extended credit is a discount for early payment. Hence the terms of sale might be '3/10 net 30' – if the customer pays in ten days he can deduct 3%, otherwise the normal credit interval of thirty days applies. It is important to know the implicit cost of making an offer like this. If the offer has induced customers to pay in ten instead of thirty days the supplier gets twenty days' usage of cash for an extra 3%. This is equivalent to an annual cost of capital of $3\% \times \frac{365}{20} = 55\%$! However, what matters is when customers *would have* paid. If customers were in the habit of taking sixty days' credit rather than the theoretical thirty then the cost is $3\% \times \frac{365}{50} = 21\%$. If the discount is viewed merely as a payment-hastening device then rates like this, assuming they are higher than the firm's cost of capital, will be prohibitive. By contrast if the rate is lower than the cost of capital it is likely no-one will respond. But if the offer of a discount is seen as an alternative marketing policy which might yield extra sales the cost may be worthwhile.

There are other problems associated with using discounts for early payment. One is that many customers with computerised payments systems on a monthly cycle are not geared to taking advantage of them without using a more costly alternative payments procedure. Another is the problem of what to do with the customer who takes the discount then pays at his usual time. It may be unjustifiably expensive to pursue the balance of the cash.

The cost of credit

The carrying cost of extending credit is relatively straightforward – it is the financing cost and the administrative cost associated with the increase in debtor balance. The financing cost is the firm's cost of capital, the accounting and clerical costs are the *incremental* accounting and clerical costs associated with running increased debtors.[6]

> *Aristotle Manufacturing Co*
>
> Aristotle Manufacturing Co is trying to calculate the cost of a policy which would increase debtors by £1 million. Aristotle's cost of capital is 12% and its extra annual administrative cost tends to be 3% of any additional debtor balance. Hence the CARRYING COST of the new policy is £1 million × 15% = £150,000 per annum.

The risks of credit

Wherever sales are made on credit there is a risk that the goods or services will be delivered but the customer will not pay. Customers fail to pay for various reasons, some good, some bad. Sometimes there is a valid dispute about the quality of the product which would have perhaps led to a refund even if the goods had been bought for cash. In other cases, though, the customer either cynically refuses to pay, or goes into liquidation. There are remedies in law for a cynical refusal to pay, but these are expensive and time consuming.

The risk of non-payment is relevant in two ways to the credit decision. First, the firm should expect that a percentage of its new debtors will fail to pay. The prevalence of non-payment will depend very much on the nature of the business, and the firm should estimate the non-payment rate from its previous experience. Second, though, if the change in credit policy is to generate increased sales it is likely to involve new credit customers with the attendant danger that these will be more risky than the existent customers. Indeed the firm may consciously decide to extend credit to higher risk customers in order to generate sales.

This raises the question of how the credit risk of a customer can be assessed. Firms may use a variety of sources of information to help form expectations about the default risk of a customer. They ask for bank and credit references to see if the customer has managed to achieve a successful trading relationship with its bank and with other suppliers. They try to gauge the reputation of the customer by enquiries in the trade. They make enquiries of one of the credit rating agencies who specialise in the collection and analysis of data on the

6 Not the departmental costs allocated on what accountants call a 'full-cost basis' – i e total departmental costs times the proportion of new debtors to total debtors – since this may be significantly misleading if departmental costs are part-fixed, part-variable.

credit-worthiness of firms. They may insist that earlier sales are paid cash-before-delivery or on-delivery, before a credit relationship is established.

The problem is that enquiries about a customer's past performance as a debtor will assist in judging the 'moral hazard' and will help eliminate the unscrupulous or fly-by-night customer, but they will not tell you much about the risk of the customer going into liquidation in the future. Our inability to know what will happen in the future is the central problem in finance and it poses a problem in making the credit decision. Traditionally people have tried to assess the risk of liquidation by combining the sort of enquiries we mentioned above with a ratio analysis of the customer's accounts. However there is no clear link between this sort of analysis of the past and the probability of future liquidation – expecially if liquidation is to be anticipated sufficiently far in advance usefully to warn the potential supplier. Increasingly, the credit analyst has access to statistical techniques such as multiple discriminant analysis to assemble and analyse the predictive evidence. We examined the prediction of liquidation and the interpretation of the so-called 'Z-scores' generated by multiple discriminant analysis in some detail in Chapter 23.

Separation of decision making and control

In theory the decision making and control aspects of debtors can be separated – the company's credit policy can be determined centrally and applied to the individual debtor accounts by clerks in the credit control department. In practice though the separation is not usually so easy. Though the firm will have a standard credit policy, it may well apply it with different degrees of flexibility to different customers. This is almost inevitable since we saw that the benefits of credit may vary according to the market conditions. So, for example, the firm may decide to allow more credit to larger customers, or customers for products with easily available alternative sources of supply. These decisions tend to be made customer by customer on the basis of the credit controller's experience and judgement, preferably in discussion with the marketing department.

Creditors

The firm's position vis-à-vis its creditors is a mirror image of its debtor position. In the case of creditors the firm's interest is to postpone payment until the marginal benefit in terms of interest saved is just matched by the marginal cost in terms of loss of goodwill of its suppliers. Again, the extent to which the firm can do this will depend on market structure and relative market power.

V SUMMARY

Both in terms of the sums involved, and the amount of finance function time consumed in managing these assets, the working-capital investment decision is important in most firms. Though operations researchers have had some success in developing mathematical techniques for optimising stock balances, in the main firms tend to make judgemental investment decisions for cash and debtors. In either case the fundamental principle is the same – the firm should hold working capital balances up to the point where the marginal benefit of an extra unit is equalled by the marginal cost. Put another way, the firm should minimise the sum of the costs associated with holding and not holding working capital balances. The holding costs are essentially the cost of capital and 'storage' costs – administrative and accounting costs and, in the case of stocks, physical storage costs too. The benefits to holding working-capital balances, which are the costs of not holding them, are associated with the derived nature of the demand for these assets. Working capital is needed to support the economic activity of the firm. If the firm reduces its balances of cash, stocks and debtors too far it will have to acquire the service they provide in some other way, or sacrifice contribution from reduced economic activity. Additionally, in the case of stocks there is an increased cost associated with more frequent replacement.

REFERENCES AND BIBLIOGRAPHY

Cavinato, J L — *Purchasing and Materials Management: Integrative Strategies* (1984) West, St Paul, Minnesota.

Davis, E W, and Yeomans, K A — 'Company Finance and the Capital Market', Cambridge University Press, Occasional Paper No 39, 1974.

Gallinger, G W, and Healey, P B — *Liquidity Analysis and Management* (1987) Addison Wesley Publishing Company Inc, Reading, Mass.

Hill, T — *Production/Operations Management: Text and Cases* (2nd edn, 1991) Prentice Hall, London.

Kaleberg, J G, and Parkinson, K — *Current Asset Management: Cash, Credit and Inventory* (1984) John Wiley and Sons, New York.

Keynes, J M — *The General Theory of Employment Interest and Money* (1936) Macmillan, London.

Miller, M H, and Orr, D — 'A Model of the Demand for Money by Firms', Quarterly Journal of Economics, August 1966, pp 413–455. 'The Demand for Money by Firms: Extension of Analytic Results', Journal of Finance, December 1968, pp 735–759.

Pogue, G A, and Bussard, R N — 'A Linear Programming Model for Short-Term Financial Planning Under Uncertainty', Sloan Management Review 13, Spring 1972, pp 66–99.

Smith, K V — *Readings on the Management of Working Capital* (2nd edn, 1980) West Publishing Company, New York.

Van der Weide, J H, and Maier, S F — *Managing Corporate Liquidity – An Introduction to Working Capital Management* (1985) John Wiley and Sons Inc, New York.

QUESTIONS

1 What is the difference between working-capital investment decisions, and project investment decisions?

2 The Pidgeon Corporation manufactures pooms, using one raw material, the drimp. For each poom manufactured, twelve drimps are needed. Assume that the company manufactures 450,000 pooms per year, that it costs £600 to order drimps, and that carrying costs are £24 per drimp per year. Determine the economic order quantity of drimps and how many times per year inventory would be ordered.

What are total inventory costs for Pidgeon?

Describe the effect on the economic order quantity of (i) an increase in demand (ii) a decrease in carrying costs (iii) an increase in ordering costs.

3 Why do people need to hold cash?

4 State the assumptions of the EOQ model for the transactions demand for cash, and derive the model. How does the model change if the cost of transferring funds has a variable as well as a fixed component?

The Tropicana Company expects to have £120,000 each week in cash outlays next year. It plans to obtain such cash by equal transfers from its portfolio of marketable securities which it expects to earn 10% per year interest. The company predicts that it will incur a fixed charge of £3,000 each time it makes a transfer. How often should cash be transferred?

5 Explain how Miller and Orr developed the EOQ model, and assess the usefulness of cash management models in practice.

6 Squeezem Ltd sells on credit, allowing customers one month to pay. The sales manager is having great difficulty in expanding sales, as competitors are offering more generous credit terms. He has prepared estimates of the effect of increasing the credit period to two or three months. These show a rise in sales revenue from the present level of £600,000 a year to £750,000 with two months' credit, or to £810,000 with three months' credit. However, bad debts, which at present average 1% of credit sales, may be expected to rise to 2.5% with two months' credit, or to 5% with three months' credit. Variable costs are two-thirds of selling price. Squeezem's required rate of return is 25%.

Advise Squeezem on the optimal credit policy, and suggest if any other factors should be taken into account.

7 The Aggro Collection Company employs agents who collect hire purchase instalments and other outstanding accounts on a door-to-door basis from Monday to Friday. The agents bank the cash collected to be remitted to head office once per week at the end of the week. The budget for next year shows that the total collections will be of the order of £5,200,000 and that the estimated bank overdraft rate is 9%. The collection manager has suggested that a daily remitting system should be introduced for collectors.

Advise him, pointing out any other factors he should be taking into account.

Appendix
Present values and annuities

DISCOUNT FACTORS: present value of one Pound received at the end of n years, at different discount rates

n	*1%*	*2%*	*3%*	*4%*	*5%*	*6%*	*7%*	*8%*	*9%*	*10%*
1	.99010	.98039	.97007	.96154	.95238	.94340	.93458	.92593	.91743	.90909
2	.98030	.96117	.94260	.92456	.90703	.89000	.87344	.85734	.84168	.82645
3	.97059	.94232	.91514	.88900	.86384	.83962	.81630	.79383	.77218	.75131
4	.96098	.92385	.88849	.85480	.83370	.79209	.76390	.74503	.70843	.68301
5	.95147	.90573	.86261	.82193	.78353	.74726	.71299	.68058	.64993	.62092
6	.94204	.88797	.83748	.79031	.74622	.70496	.66634	.63017	.59627	.56447
7	.93272	.87056	.81309	.75992	.71068	.66506	.62275	.58349	.54703	.51316
8	.92348	.85349	.78941	.73069	.67684	.62741	.58201	.54027	.50187	.46651
9	.91434	.83675	.76642	.70259	.64461	.59190	.54393	.50025	.46043	.42410
10	.90529	.82035	.74409	.67556	.61391	.55839	.50835	.46319	.42241	.38554
11	.89632	.80426	.72242	.64958	.58468	.52679	.47509	.42888	.38753	.35049
12	.88745	.78849	.70138	.62460	.55684	.49697	.44401	.39711	.35553	.31863
13	.87866	.77303	.68095	.60057	.53032	.46884	.41496	.36770	.32618	.28966
14	.86996	.75787	.66112	.57747	.50507	.44230	.38782	.34046	.29925	.26333
15	.86135	.74301	.64186	.55526	.48102	.41726	.36245	.31524	.27454	.23939
16	.85282	.72845	.62317	.53391	.45811	.39365	.33873	.29189	.25187	.21763
17	.84438	.71416	.60502	.51337	.43630	.37136	.31657	.27027	.23107	.19784
18	.83602	.70016	.58739	.49363	.41552	.35034	.29586	.25025	.21199	.17986
19	.82774	.68643	.57029	.47464	.39573	.33051	.27651	.23171	.19449	.16351
20	.81954	.67297	.55367	.45639	.37689	.31180	.25842	.21455	.17843	.14864
21	.81143	.65978	.53755	.43883	.35894	.29415	.24151	.19866	.16370	.13513
22	.80340	.64684	.52189	.42195	.34185	.27750	.22571	.18394	.15018	.12285
23	.79544	.63416	.50669	.40573	.32557	.26180	.21095	.17031	.13778	.11168
24	.78757	.62172	.49193	.39012	.31007	.24698	.19715	.15770	.12640	.10153
25	.77977	.60953	.47760	.37512	.29530	.23300	.18425	.14602	.11597	.09230

DISCOUNT FACTORS: present value of one Pound received at the end of n years, at different discount rates (*cont*)

n	*11%*	*12%*	*13%*	*14%*	*15%*	*16%*	*17%*	*18%*	*19%*	*20%*
1	.90090	.89286	.88486	.87719	.86957	.86207	.85470	.84746	.84034	.83333
2	.81162	.79719	.78315	.76947	.75614	.74316	.73051	.71818	.70616	.69444
3	.73119	.71178	.69305	.67497	.65752	.64066	.62437	.60863	.59342	.57870
4	.65873	.63552	.61332	.59208	.57175	.55229	.53365	.51579	.49867	.48225
5	.59345	.56743	.54276	.51937	.49718	.47611	.45611	.43711	.41905	.40188
6	.53464	.50663	.48032	.45559	.43233	.41044	.38984	.37043	.35214	.33490
7	.48166	.45235	.42506	.39964	.37594	.35383	.33320	.31392	.29592	.27908
8	.43393	.40388	.37616	.35056	.32690	.30503	.28478	.26604	.24867	.23257
9	.39092	.36061	.33288	.30751	.28426	.26295	.24340	.22546	.20897	.19381
10	.35218	.32197	.29459	.26974	.24718	.22668	.20804	.19106	.17560	.16151
11	.31728	.28748	.26070	.23662	.21494	.19542	.17781	.16192	.14756	.13459
12	.28584	.25667	.23071	.20756	.18691	.16846	.15197	.13722	.12400	.11216
13	.25751	.22917	.20416	.18207	.16253	.14523	.12989	.11629	.10420	.09346
14	.23199	.20462	.18068	.15971	.14133	.12520	.11102	.09855	.08757	.07789
15	.20900	.18270	.15989	.14010	.12289	.10793	.09489	.08352	.07359	.06491
16	.18829	.16312	.14150	.12289	.10686	.09304	.08110	.07078	.06184	.05409
17	.16963	.14564	.12522	.10780	.09293	.08021	.06932	.05998	.05196	.04507
18	.15282	.13004	.11081	.09456	.08080	.06914	.05925	.05083	.04367	.03756
19	.13768	.11611	.09806	.08295	.07026	.05961	.05064	.04308	.03669	.03130
20	.12403	.10367	.08678	.07276	.06110	.05139	.04328	.03651	.03084	.02608
21	.11174	.09256	.07680	.06383	.05313	.04430	.03699	.03094	.02591	.02174
22	.10067	.08264	.06796	.05599	.04620	.03819	.03162	.02622	.02178	.01811
23	.09069	.07379	.06014	.04911	.04017	.03292	.02702	.02222	.01830	.01509
24	.08170	.06588	.05322	.04308	.03493	.02838	.02310	.01883	.01538	.01258
25	.07361	.05882	.04710	.03779	.03038	.02447	.01974	.01596	.01292	.01048

DISCOUNT FACTORS: present value of one Pound received at the end of n years, at different discount rates (*cont*)

n	*21%*	*22%*	*23%*	*24%*	*25%*	*26%*	*27%*	*28%*	*29%*	*30%*
1	.82645	.81967	.81301	.80645	.80000	.79365	.78740	.78125	.77519	.76923
2	.68301	.67186	.66098	.65036	.64000	.62988	.62000	.61035	.60093	.59172
3	.56447	.55071	.53738	.52449	.51200	.49991	.48819	.47684	.46583	.45517
4	.46651	.45140	.43690	.42297	.40960	.39675	.38440	.37253	.36111	.35013
5	.38554	.37000	.35520	.34111	.32768	.31488	.30268	.29104	.27993	.26933
6	.31863	.30328	.28878	.27509	.26214	.24991	.23833	.22737	.21700	.20718
7	.26333	.24859	.23478	.22184	.20972	.19834	.18766	.17764	.16822	.15937
8	.21763	.20376	.19088	.17891	.16777	.15741	.14776	.13878	.13040	.12259
9	.17986	.16702	.15519	.14428	.13422	.12493	.11635	.10842	.10109	.09430
10	.14864	.13690	.12617	.11635	.10737	.09915	.09161	.08470	.07836	.07254
11	.12285	.11221	.10258	.09383	.08590	.07869	.07214	.06617	.06075	.05580
12	.10153	.09198	.08339	.07567	.06872	.06245	.05680	.05170	.04709	.04292
13	.08391	.07539	.06780	.06103	.05498	.04957	.04472	.04039	.06350	.03302
14	.06934	.06180	.05512	.04921	.04398	.03934	.03522	.03155	.02830	.02540
15	.05731	.05065	.04481	.03969	.03518	.03122	.02773	.02465	.02194	.01954
16	.04736	.04152	.03643	.03201	.02815	.02478	.02183	.01926	.01700	.01503
17	.03914	.03403	.02962	.02581	.02252	.01967	.01719	.01505	.01318	.01156
18	.03235	.02789	.02408	.02082	.01801	.01561	.01354	.01175	.01022	.00889
19	.02673	.02286	.01958	.01679	.01441	.01239	.01066	.00918	.00792	.00684
20	.02209	.01874	.01592	.01354	.01153	.00983	.00839	.00717	.00614	.00526
21	.01826	.01536	.01294	.01092	.00922	.00780	.00661	.00561	.00476	.00405
22	.01509	.01259	.01052	.00880	.00738	.00619	.00520	.00438	.00369	.00311
23	.01247	.01032	.00855	.00710	.00590	.00491	.00410	.00342	.00286	.00239
24	.01031	.00846	.00695	.00573	.00472	.00390	.00323	.00267	.00222	.00184
25	.00852	.00693	.00565	.00462	.00378	.00310	.00254	.00209	.00172	.00142

ANNUITY FACTORS: present value of one Pound received per year for n years, at different discount rates

n	*1%*	*2%*	*3%*	*4%*	*5%*	*6%*	*7%*	*8%*	*9%*	*10%*
1	0.9901	0.9804	0.9709	0.9615	0.9524	0.9434	0.9346	0.9259	0.9174	0.9091
2	1.9704	1.9416	1.9135	1.8861	1.8594	1.8334	1.8080	1.7833	1.7591	1.7355
3	2.9410	2.8839	2.8286	2.7751	2.7232	2.6730	2.6243	2.5771	2.5313	2.4868
4	3.9020	3.8077	3.7171	3.6299	3.5459	3.4651	3.3872	3.3121	3.2397	3.1699
5	4.8535	4.7134	4.5797	4.4518	4.3295	4.2123	4.1002	3.9927	3.8896	3.7908
6	5.7955	5.6014	5.4172	5.2421	5.0757	4.9173	4.7665	4.6229	4.4859	4.3553
7	6.7282	6.4720	6.2302	6.0020	5.7863	5.5824	5.3893	5.2064	5.0329	4.8684
8	7.6517	7.3254	7.0196	6.7327	6.4632	6.2098	5.9713	5.7466	5.5348	5.3349
9	8.5661	8.1622	7.7861	7.4353	7.1078	6.8017	6.5152	6.2469	5.9852	5.7590
10	9.4714	8.9825	8.5302	8.1109	7.7217	7.3601	7.0236	6.7101	6.4176	6.1446
11	10.3677	9.7868	9.2526	8.7604	8.3064	7.8868	7.4987	7.1389	6.8052	6.4951
12	11.2552	10.5753	9.9539	9.3850	8.8632	8.3838	7.9427	7.5361	7.1607	6.8137
13	12.1338	11.3483	10.6349	9.9856	9.3935	8.8527	8.3576	7.9038	7.4869	7.1034
14	13.0038	12.1062	11.2960	10.5631	9.8986	9.2950	8.7454	8.2442	7.7861	7.3667
15	13.8651	12.8492	11.9379	11.1183	10.3796	9.7122	9.1079	8.5595	8.0607	7.6060
16	14.7180	13.5777	12.5610	11.6522	10.8377	10.1059	9.4466	8.8514	8.3125	7.8237
17	15.5624	14.2918	13.1660	12.1656	11.2740	10.4772	9.7632	9.1216	8.5436	8.0215
18	16.3984	14.9920	13.7534	12.6592	11.6895	10.8276	10.0591	9.3719	8.7556	8.2014
19	17.2261	15.6784	14.3237	13.1339	12.0853	11.1581	10.3356	9.6036	8.9501	8.3649
20	18.0457	16.3514	14.8774	13.5903	12.4622	11.4699	10.5940	9.8181	9.1285	8.5136
21	18.8571	17.0111	15.4149	14.0291	12.8211	11.7640	10.8355	10.0168	9.2922	8.4687
22	19.6605	17.6580	15.9368	14.4511	13.1630	12.0416	11.0612	12.2007	9.4424	8.7715
23	20.4559	18.2921	16.4435	14.8568	13.4885	12.3033	11.2722	10.3710	9.5802	8.8832
24	21.2435	18.9139	16.9355	15.2469	13.7986	12.5503	11.4693	10.5287	9.7066	8.9847
25	22.0233	19.5234	17.4131	15.6220	14.0939	12.7833	11.6536	10.6748	9.8226	9.0770

ANNUITY FACTORS: present value of one Pound received per year for n years, at different discount rates (*cont*)

n	*11%*	*12%*	*13%*	*14%*	*15%*	*16%*	*17%*	*18%*	*19%*	*20%*
1	0.9009	0.8929	0.8850	0.8772	0.8696	0.8621	0.8547	0.8475	0.8403	0.8333
2	1.7125	1.6901	1.6681	1.6467	1.6257	1.6052	1.5852	1.5656	1.5465	1.5278
3	2.4437	2.4018	2.3612	2.3216	2.2832	2.2459	2.2096	2.1743	2.1399	2.1065
4	3.1024	3.0373	2.9745	2.9137	2.8550	2.7982	2.7432	2.6901	2.6386	2.5887
5	3.6959	3.6048	3.5172	3.4331	3.3522	3.2743	3.1993	3.1272	3.0576	2.9906
6	4.2305	4.1114	3.9976	3.8887	3.7845	3.6847	3.5892	3.4976	3.4098	3.3255
7	4.7122	4.5638	4.4226	4.2883	4.1604	4.0386	3.9224	3.8115	3.7057	3.6046
8	5.1461	4.9676	4.7988	4.6389	4.4873	4.3436	4.2072	4.0776	3.9544	3.8372
9	5.5370	5.3282	5.1317	4.9464	4.7716	4.6065	4.4506	4.3030	4.1633	4.0310
10	5.8892	5.6502	5.4262	5.2161	5.0188	4.8332	4.6586	4.4941	4.3389	4.1925
11	6.2065	5.9377	5.6869	5.4527	5.2337	5.0268	4.8364	4.6560	4.4865	4.3271
12	6.4924	6.1944	5.9176	5.6603	5.4206	5.1971	4.9884	4.7932	4.6105	4.4392
13	6.7499	6.4235	6.1218	5.8424	5.5831	5.3423	5.1183	4.9095	4.7147	4.5327
14	6.9819	6.6282	6.3025	6.0021	5.7245	5.4675	5.2293	5.0081	4.8023	4.6106
15	7.1909	6.8109	6.4624	6.1422	5.8474	5.5755	5.3242	5.0916	4.8759	4.6755
16	7.3792	6.9740	6.6039	6.2651	5.9542	5.6685	5.4053	5.1624	4.9377	4.7296
17	7.5488	7.1196	6.7291	6.3729	6.0472	5.7487	5.4746	5.2223	4.9897	4.7746
18	7.7016	7.2497	6.8399	6.4674	6.1280	5.8178	5.5339	5.2732	5.0333	4.8122
19	7.8393	7.3658	6.9380	6.5504	6.1982	5.8775	5.5845	5.3162	5.0700	4.8435
20	7.9633	7.4694	7.0248	6.6231	6.2593	5.9288	5.6278	5.3527	5.1009	4.8696
21	8.0751	7.5620	7.1016	6.6870	6.3125	5.9731	5.6648	5.3837	5.1268	4.8913
22	8.1757	7.6446	7.1695	6.7429	6.3587	6.0113	5.6964	5.4099	5.1486	4.9094
23	8.2664	7.7184	7.2297	6.7921	6.3988	6.0442	5.7234	5.4321	5.1668	4.9245
24	8.3481	7.7843	7.2829	6.8351	6.4338	6.0726	5.7465	5.4509	5.1822	4.9371
25	8.4217	7.8431	7.3300	6.8729	6.4641	6.0971	5.7662	5.4669	5.1951	4.9476

ANNUITY FACTORS: present value of one Pound received per year for n years, at different discount rates (*cont*)

n	*21%*	*22%*	*23%*	*24%*	*25%*	*26%*	*27%*	*28%*	*29%*	*30%*
1	0.8264	0.8197	0.8130	0.8065	0.8000	0.7937	0.7874	0.7813	0.7752	0.7692
2	1.5095	1.4915	1.4740	1.4568	1.4400	1.4235	1.4074	1.3916	1.3761	1.3609
3	2.0739	2.0422	2.0114	1.9813	1.9520	1.9234	1.8956	1.8684	1.8420	1.8161
4	2.5404	2.4936	2.4483	2.4043	2.3616	2.3202	2.2800	2.2410	2.2031	2.1662
5	2.9260	2.8636	2.8035	2.7454	2.6893	2.6351	2.5827	2.5320	2.4830	2.4356
6	3.2446	3.1669	3.0923	3.0205	2.9514	2.8850	2.8210	2.7594	2.7000	2.6427
7	3.5079	3.4155	3.3270	3.2423	3.1611	3.0833	3.0087	2.9370	2.8682	2.8021
8	3.7256	3.6193	3.5179	3.4212	3.3289	3.2407	3.1564	3.0758	2.9986	2.9247
9	3.9054	3.7863	3.6731	3.5655	3.4631	3.3657	3.2728	3.1842	3.0997	3.0190
10	4.0541	3.9232	3.7993	3.6819	3.5705	3.4648	3.3644	3.2689	3.1781	3.0915
11	4.1769	4.0354	3.9018	3.7757	3.6564	3.5435	3.4365	3.3351	3.2388	3.1473
12	4.2785	4.1274	3.9852	3.8514	3.7251	3.6060	3.4933	3.3868	3.2859	3.1903
13	4.3624	4.2028	4.0530	3.9124	3.7801	3.6555	3.6381	3.4272	3.3224	3.2233
14	4.4317	4.2646	4.1082	3.9616	3.8241	3.6949	3.5733	3.4587	3.3507	3.2487
15	4.4890	4.3152	4.1530	4.0013	3.8593	3.7261	3.6010	3.4834	3.3726	3.2682
16	4.5364	4.3567	4.1894	4.0333	3.8874	3.7509	3.6228	3.5026	3.3896	3.2832
17	4.5755	4.3908	4.2190	4.0591	3.9099	3.7705	3.6400	3.5177	3.4028	3.2948
18	4.6079	4.4187	4.2431	4.0799	3.9279	3.7861	3.6536	3.5294	3.4130	3.3037
19	4.6346	4.4415	4.2627	4.0967	3.9424	3.7985	3.6642	3.5386	3.4210	3.3105
20	4.6567	4.4603	4.2786	4.1103	3.9539	3.8083	3.6726	3.5458	3.4271	3.3158
21	4.6750	4.4756	4.2916	4.1212	3.9631	3.8161	3.6792	3.5514	3.4319	3.3198
22	4.6900	4.4882	4.3021	4.1300	3.9705	3.8223	3.6844	3.5558	3.4356	3.3230
23	4.7025	4.4985	4.3016	4.1371	3.9764	3.8273	3.6885	3.5592	3.4384	3.3254
24	4.7128	4.5070	4.3176	4.1428	3.9811	3.8312	3.6918	3.5619	3.4406	3.3272
25	4.7213	4.5139	4.3232	4.1474	3.9849	3.8342	3.6943	3.5640	3.4423	3.3286

Index